PANDORA'S BOX

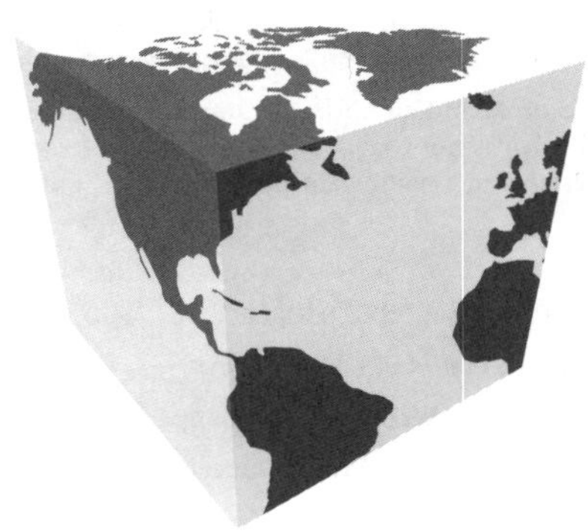

SOCIAL AND PROFESSIONAL ISSUES OF THE INFORMATION AGE

ANDREW A. ADAMS AND RACHEL J. McCRINDLE
University of Reading

John Wiley & Sons, Ltd

Telephone (+44) 1243 779777

Email (for orders and customer service enquiries): cs-books@wiley.co.uk
Visit our Home Page on www.wileyeurope.com or www.wiley.com

Other Wiley Editorial Offices

John Wiley & Sons Inc., 111 River Street, Hoboken, NJ 07030, USA

Jossey-Bass, 989 Market Street, San Francisco, CA 94103-1741, USA

Wiley-VCH Verlag GmbH, Boschstr. 12, D-69469 Weinheim, Germany

John Wiley & Sons Australia Ltd, 42 McDougall Street, Milton, Queensland 4064, Australia

John Wiley & Sons (Asia) Pte Ltd, 2 Clementi Loop #02-01, Jin Xing Distripark, Singapore 129809

John Wiley & Sons Canada Ltd, 6045 Freemont Blvd, Mississauga, Ontario, L5R 4J3, Canada

Wiley also publishes its books in a variety of electronic formats. Some content that appears in print may not be available in electronic books.

Library of Congress Cataloging-in-Publication Data

Adams, Andrew, 1969-
Pandora's box : social and professional issues of the information age /
Andrew Adams and Rachel McCrindle.
p. cm.
Includes bibliographical references and index.
ISBN 978-0-470-06553-2 (pbk.)
1. Technology–Social aspects. 2. Technology–Moral and ethical aspects. I. McCrindle, Rachel. II. Title.
T14.5.A5155 2007
303.48′33—dc22

2007022435

British Library Cataloguing in Publication Data

A catalogue record for this book is available from the British Library

ISBN 978-0-470-06553-2 (PB)

Typeset in 11/16 Sabon by Laserwords Private Limited, Chennai, India
Printed and bound in Great Britain by Bell & Bain, Glasgow
This book is printed on acid-free paper responsibly manufactured from sustainable forestry in which at least two trees are planted for each one used for paper production.

PANDORA'S
BOX

In Memory of Albert Victor Adams, 1919–2006
Always a man ahead of his time.

—*Andrew A. Adams*

To Fred, David, Margaret, J and all my family

—*Rachel J. McCrindle*

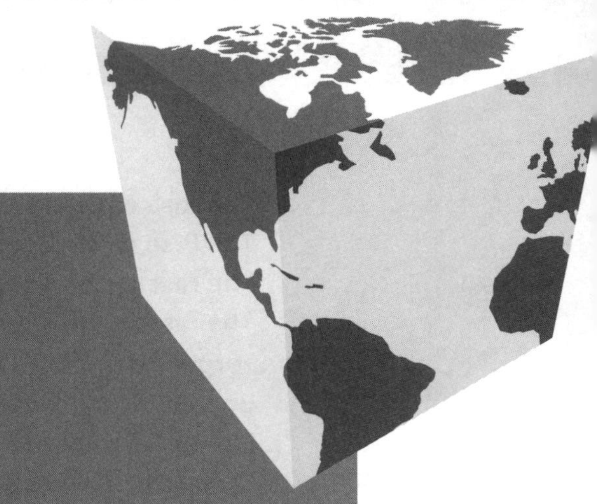

CONTENTS

Foreword **xxi**

Preface **xxv**

1 Introduction **1**

Lessig's Four Modalities Analysis 6
Prophet and Loss: Failing to Foresee the Future 7
Information System Partition 8
The Law is an Ass 10
Globalization 12
The Digital Divide 13
Servant or Master: Computers Making Decisions 15
Discussion Topics 17
Can Laws Be Immoral? 17
Genetically Modified Food, Technologically Modified Humans 17
The Haves and the Have-nots 18
Related Reading 19

2 Emergence and Convergence of Technologies **21**

Introduction 21
Emergence 23
The Rise of Print Media 23
The Rise of the Telegraph and the Telephone 24

The Rise of Broadcast Media 28
The Rise of the Computing Industry 31
The Rise of the Content Industry 33
The Rise of the Internet 35
Convergence 39
Content Producers and Distributors 39
Platform Producers and Content Producers or Publishers 41
Corporate Production vs Individual Creativity 43
Market Sector Integration 44
Digitization 48
The Big Challenges Ahead 55
Discussion Topics 56
Fit for Purpose? 56
E-Tax 56
Competing with Free Beer 58
Related Reading 60

3 Digital Entertainment 61

Introduction 61
The Effects of Digital Entertainment Technology 64
Digital Entertainment — Friend or Foe? 64
The Toy Town Divide 64
Boys and Girls Come out to Play: Stereotyping 66
Health-Related Issues 69
Curse of the Couch-Potato Children 69
Physical Problems 71
Digital Equipment — Part of the Modern Family 72
Does Television Cause Adverse Social Behaviour? 74
Creating Monsters — Do Computer Games Make People Violent? 76
Do Computer Games Fuel Addiction and Gambling? 80
Power to the Player — Benefits of Computer Games 84
Harnessing the Power of the Brain 84
Education and Learning 86

The Silver Gamers 88
Game Development Grows up — the Hidden Agenda 88
Discussion Points 91
Should Computer Games Be Regulated? Rated? Censored? 91
Couch-Potato Syndrome 92
Online Gambling: Menace or Natural Progression? 93
Related Reading 95

4 Censorship and Freedom of Speech 97

Introduction 97
Reasons for Censorship 100
Censorship by States 101
Censorship of Speakers by Governments 107
Censorship of Listeners by Governments 109
Censorship by Private Actors 111
Censorship of Speakers by Private Actors 111
Censorship of Listeners by Private Actors 113
Technology for Expression 114
Technological Developments with Expressive Power 114
Censoring Internet Content 115
Client–Server and Peer-to-Peer Architectures 124
Conclusion 125
Discussion Topics 126
Yahoo! France Nazi Memorabilia 126
ISP Liability for Content 127
BT and the IWF 129
Related Reading 130

5 Sex and Technology 131

Introduction 131
The Nature of Sexual Material 132
One Man's Art. . . 132
The Medium and the Message 133

Use of Technology to (Re)Produce Sexual Material 133
Techno-Sex 134
Anonymity: Reality and Illusion 144
Anon Servers 146
Online Sex and Real Relationships 147
The Future of Online Sex: TeleDildonics? 148
Regulating Sex in Cyberspace 149
Not in Front of the Children: Protecting Children from Sex Online 152
Restricting Access to Broadcast Media 153
Surfing to a Naked Beach 154
'Satisfy Her in Bed': Sex Spam to Minors 157
Online Friendships 159
Child Pornography 161
Types of Material 162
Prohibition, Harm, Possession and Distribution 166
Jurisdictional Anomalies and Conflicts 168
Discovery, Defence and Mitigation 169
Discussion Topics 171
Freedom of Speech vs Censorship of Sexual Material 171
The Toby Studabaker Case 172
Related Reading 173

6 Governance of the Internet 175

Introduction 175
The Internet Protocols 176
The Origins of the Internet 178
Early Arguments 181
The Root of All Evil 185
Commercialization 185
Internet Corporation for Assigned Names and Numbers 186
ccTLDs 188
Alternative Root Servers 188

Commercialization, Ownership and Corporate Identity 189
Trade Marks 189
Trade Marks in Domain Names 191
The Uniform Dispute Resolution Process 196
The Nominet Dispute Resolution Process 198
Criticisms of Dispute Resolution 199
Do Trade Marks Matter in Domain Names or in URLs? 203
The Future of Internet Governance 204
ICANN, DoC, EU and ccTLDs 204
Wiring the World: Who Really Owns 'The Internet'? 205
Discussion Topics 206
Should Trade Marks Be Valid in Domain Names? 206
What Governance Should ICANN Have? 207
How Many Top-Level Domains Should There Be? 208

7 Privacy and Surveillance 211

Introduction 211
Cryptography and Steganography 212
Definition of Privacy 214
Communication Technology and Eavesdropping 215
Ways to Eavesdrop 215
Identity of Eavesdropper 217
Legality of Eavesdropping 218
The Whole Is Greater than the Sum of its Parts 220
Data Protection 222
Data Protection Issues in EU Law 223
Data Protection Issues in US Regulation 227
International Movement of Data 229
Data Protection, not an Impediment to Life 230
Big Brother is Watching You: Automated CCTV Processing 231
Privacy After 9/11 234
Technological Privacy and Surveillance 235

Discussion Topics 237
Leaving Little Trace: Anonymity in the Digital World? 237
Availability of Cryptography and Steganography 238
Data Retention by ISPs 239
Related Reading 241

8 Information Age Warfare 243

Introduction 243
History of Warfare 245
The Technology of War 248
War News 249
Cyber-Wars 250
Satellites — the View from Space 253
Star Wars Technology 254
Network-centric Warfare 255
The Battlefield 258
Robo-Soldier 258
Man or Machine? 259
The Unseen Enemy 260
Mobile Phones as Weapons 261
War Games 261
Information Dominance 263
Intelligence Gathering and Surveillance 265
Discussion Topics 267
Working for Arms Manufacturers 267
Cyberterrorism: Real Threat or Virtual Bogeyman? 268
Overall Benefit or Drain on Resources? 269

9 Technology and The Human Body 273

Introduction 273
Health Information Systems 275
Treatment 276
Electronic Patient Records 276

E-booking 278
E-prescribing 279
Intranets, the Internet and Call Centres 280
Factors for Success 281
Power to the Patient 283
The Internet and CDs 284
Television Programmes 286
Digital Television 287
Self-Diagnosis Kits 288
Online Pharmacies 290
Online Body Trafficking 291
Techno-Medicine 292
Telemedicine 293
Training and Supporting Nurses and Doctors 294
Virtual Therapy 297
Robots in Hospitals 298
Smart Monitoring 301
Computer Modelling 305
Assistive Technology and Rehabilitation 308
New Medical Technologies 309
Implants for Diagnosis and Healing 310
Implants and Prosthetics for Replacement and Reconstruction 311
Digital Flesh and Cyborgs 315
Discussion Topics 318
The Longevity and Social Justice Debate 318
Suggested Positions 319
Owning the Code of Life 319
What Is a Human? 320
Related Reading 321

10 Professionalism In IT 323

Introduction 323
Conduct 327

Practice 333
Whistleblowing 334
Vulnerability of E-mail 335
'Illegal' espionage 337
Consequences of 'Whistleblowing' 337
Due Diligence 338
Personal Responsibility 340
Discussion Topics 340
Self-Incrimination 340
Responsibility for DDoS Attacks 341
Whistleblowing Insecurity 343

11 Online Crime and Real Punishment 345

Introduction 345
A Brief History of Crime and Computers 347
Computer Fraud 348
Malware 351
A Taxonomy of Malware 351
Problems Caused by Malware 352
Malware Authors: Who, How and Why? 359
Hoaxes and Life Imitating Art 362
Computer Security: Cops and Robbers, Poachers and Gamekeepers 363
Historical Roots of Cracking 364
Who are the Crackers? 366
Vulnerability, Risk and Threat 370
Closed vs Open Security 373
Walking the Tightrope: Social Pressures on Security 379
How Much Security Is Necessary? 382
Poachers and Gamekeepers 386
Laws Against Computer Misuse 387
UK Computer Misuse Act 388
US Sequence of Laws 391

Council of Europe Convention on Cybercrime 393
The Growing Problem of Computer Crime 395
Discussion Topics 396
Grey Hat Cracking Should Be Legalized 396
Web Scrapers and Robot Denial Files 397
An Immune System for the Internet 399
Related Reading 400

12 Patents and Copyright 401

Introduction 401
Intellectual Property? 402
Trade mark 402
Patent 403
Copyright 404
The Philosophical Basis of Patents and Copyright 404
Patents 406
A Brief History of Patents 406
Modern Patent Systems 407
Business Methods and Software Patents 411
General Criticisms of Patents 414
Patent-Licensing Companies 417
Copyright 419
Origins and Development of Copyright 420
The Main Provisions of Modern Copyright Statutes 424
US Case Law for Copyright 428
The Current State of Play 434
The Music Industry and Higher Education 435
The Originator's Rights 436
Software Copyright 437
Copyright and the Architecture of Cyberspace 449
Free Culture 449
Discussion Topics 450

Is Copyright the Correct Way to Reward Artists? Does It Promote Artistic Activity? 450
Lack of Legitimate Downloads Caused the Rise of Peer-to-Peer File-Sharing 452
A New Basis for Copyright Law Is Required 453
Control and the Copyright Bargain 454
Related Reading 455

13 Unwanted Electronic Attentions 457

Introduction 457
Types of Unsolicited Communication 459
Static Visual Communication 459
Audio Communication 460
Types of Communication Media 461
Public Displays 461
Broadcast Non-Interactive Media 461
Broadcast Interactive Media 462
Telephonic Services 463
Internet Services 465
The Economics of Unsolicited Contacts 470
Sender Economics 470
Junk mail 471
Cold calling 472
Receiver Economics 474
Referral Economics 477
Social, Legal and Technological Discouragement 481
Malicious Unwanted Attentions 494
Online and Telephone Fraud 495
Electronic Stalking 496
Online Grooming 499
Discussion Topics 500
Tackling Spam at the Transport Layer 500

Opt-In, Opt-Out, Shake It All About 501
Freedom of Speech or Online Stalking 502
Related Reading 503

14 Education and Online Learning 505

Introduction 505
From the Chalkboard to the Virtual Classroom 507
Technology through the Years 507
Visual Aids to Learning 508
Audio Aids to Learning 510
Audio–Visual Aids to Learning 511
Developing E-Learning Environments 513
ICT and e-Learning in Further Education Colleges in England 515
e-Portfolio 516
Videoconferencing 517
Online Encyclopedia 518
Mobile Education (PDAs and Mobile Devices) 519
Electronic Books 521
Electronic Whiteboards 521
Online Marketing 522
Electronic Application and Admission Systems 523
Digital Library 523
Second Life 524
Web 2.0 525
Developing and Embracing e-Learning Resources 526
The Learner Perspective 527
The Teacher Perspective 529
Accessibility of Education in a Wired World 533
Cheating the System 535
Bogus Degrees 538
Discussion Topics 539
One Person's Plagiarism Is Another's Research 539

Overseas Education vs Distance Education 540
The Net of a Million Lies 542
Related Reading 543

15 Living and Working in a Wired World 545

Introduction 545
The Digital Lifestyle 547
Work, Skills and Roles 547
Teleworking 548
The Mobile Office: the 'Non-Office' Office Job 551
The New Role of the Office 552
Smarter Travel 552
Smarter Homes 555
Shopping 556
Buying Entertainment 561
The Sporting Life 562
Technology and the Individual 563
Education 563
Health 563
Crime 564
Religion 564
Communication 565
The Changing Face of Communication 565
The Global Village 573
The Digital Divide 574
The Digital Divide in the Industrialized World 577
E-Government 578
The Digital Divide Between the Nations 579
Discussion Topics 580
The Language of the Digital Age 580
Digital Relationships 581

Digital Divides 581
Related Reading 582

Appendix — Ethical Analysis 583

Introduction 583
Traditional Western Moral Philosophy 584
Rationalism 584
Locke vs Hobbes 585
Hume and Human Passion 587
Kant and the Categorical Imperative 587
Legality and Morality 587
Modern Ethical Theory 589
Utilitarian Ethics 589
Relativistic vs Universal Utiliarianism 590
New Utilitarianism: Singer 591
Computer Ethics 591
Metaphysical Foundations for Computer Ethics 593
Informed Consent Theory in Information Technology 594
Ethical Decisions: Using the Back of the Envelope 594
Information Ethics: ICT Professional Responsibility in the Information Environment 595
The Good Computer Professional Does not Cheat at Cards 596
Conclusion 596
Discussion Topics 597
General: The Death Penalty 597
ICT: Artificial Sentience Rights and Wrongs 598
General: Is Religion an Excuse for Discrimination? 599
ICT: Search Ethics 600
General: Lying to Tell the Truth? 601
ICT: Gender Presentation Online 601
General: Fair Fines 602

ICT: Should Internet Access be a Human Right? 603
General: Prediction of Harm 604
ICT: Programmer Responsibility 605
Related Reading 607

Index **609**

FOREWORD

Technological change catches us unprepared because in the main we are not adequately prepared for the way in which innovation is often a $1 + 1 = 3$ event (the result is more than the sum of the parts, as in: kerosene + antiseptic spray = carburettor).

However we are more often wrong-footed by the way in which the ripple-effects of innovation occur in areas unrelated to the original innovative act.

Around 1450 Gutenberg thought he'd make a fortune by printing thousands of standard liturgical texts and strengthen the position of the Catholic Church throughout Europe. A hundred years later, it only took two weeks for Luther's 95 theses to appear in print all over Germany and ensure that Protestantism undermined everything Rome stood for. At the same time printed vernacular Bibles, printed laws, and print-driven capitalism triggered the birth of the nation state and the end of Christendom. Printed texts negated the hegemony of old age, gave knowledge to the young, and questioned authority. Perhaps the greatest unintended effect came from the print shops, at the time when editors of Biblical appendices on Holy Land geography, coinage, botany, languages, etc., turned their textual-analysis skills to the production of collated, definitive versions of knowledge, and helped give birth to modern scientific method. Thanks to such ripples effects, within three generations of Gutenberg a new, literate mercantile class was living and thinking in ways that would have seen them burned for heresy in their grandparents' time.

Technological change creates new social environments with new values, ethics, morals and aspirations. In most cases the transition to the new way is difficult.

Sometimes it is dangerous. In 1643 the investigation of Toricelli's newly-discovered vacuum could only be pursued in Northern Europe, away from the Pope. But even in London Boyle and others were circumspect, because they knew that a vacuum might represent a 'nothingness' where God's universal presence might not be manifest. If they were to confirm the existence of the vacuum, then the authority of God's Vicar in England (the monarch) might be called into question. They did. It was. And set the stage for constitutional kingship.

Feedback complicates the situation. The use of the new microscope to identify newly-discovered bacteria placed medicine beyond the understanding of the average patient (who had previously enjoyed a master-servant relationship with his physician), conferred unquestioned authority on doctors, and ultimately extended the concept of 'cure' to anti-social tendencies. This in turn gave rise to the pseudo-science of phrenology. Bumps on the head identified personal characteristics which, if socially-undesirable, might be amenable to 'treatment'. This possibility triggered Golgi's interest in the nature of the brain beneath the bumps. The result: neurophysiology and a new view of behaviour.

Second-guessing the effects of innovation can often be difficult when the originating event is arcane. In 1912 Von Laue bounced the newly-discovered X-rays off a crystal lattice, using the diffraction of the X-rays to measure their wavelength. It was then discovered that the diffracted rays produced a visible pattern on exposed photographic paper set behind the crystal. In 1952 this technique showed Rosalind Franklin the helical shape of what turned out to DNA. The contentious questions raised by subsequent developments in the field of genetics are too many to list.

Today we live at the end of a long, historical sequence of such ripple-effect events. Since the beginning of that sequence our behavior, values, ethics, morals, aspirations, and the institutions and social constructs they engendered, have changed beyond all recognition. For instance, present-day issues relating to single-parent families, sexual freedom, feminism, and AIDS, all emerged to some extent from the appearance of the contraceptive pill. The typewriter played an earlier role in this process when it freed women from the kitchen, introduced them to work and financial independence, and boosted the divorce rate.

Thanks to advances in information and communications technology over the last two decades, the innovative process now happens much more frequently. And because the world is a more interactive place, ripple-effects spread rapidly and trigger change faster than ever before. As the authors of this lucid and comprehensive book show, we are now living through a period of considerable social turbulence as we experience rates of innovation which threaten to outstrip our ability to adapt to them. In the main, our institutions and institutional processes fare badly, relics of history established in the past, with the technology of the past, to solve the problems of the past.

So, as the culture of scarcity ends and the era of information abundance begins, we now face long-term questions unlike any we have had to face before. If information technology replaces representative systems with direct online participatory democracy mediated by personal electronic agents acting on the individual's behalf, how will we handle the roller-coaster political ride? When everyone gets to express their talents, what will happen to rarity value? When avatars provide every student with an individually-tailored education, what will replace the old one-size-fits-all tests which assured standards and conformity? If software makes even small communities economically-viable, will we see the end of the nation state? If the media fracture into a thousand channels, what will replace the old public forum of shared opinions and common experience? If the promise of nanotechnology is fulfilled and we are able to manufacture anything from constituent atoms, will we resolve the problem of resource scarcity, and if so, what will this do to international relations? In a world of universal access, what will happen to privacy? In the long run, when data-mining and knowledge-mapping and semi-intelligent software manage every aspect of innovation, production and distribution, will there be any purpose in knowing (i.e. remembering) anything?

These and many more questions are raised by the issues addressed in this book. We have perhaps two decades to find the answers. Andrew Adams and Rachel McCrindle have provided a valuable guide to help get us from here to there.

James Burke

PREFACE

FOR ALL READERS

Although we hope this book is of interest to the professional already working in the computer industry, and to students in fields such as law, sociology or economics, the primary intended audience is undergraduate students studying for a degree in the broad discipline of computing. At the time of writing, the Association for Computing Machinery (ACM) defines four types of degree: software engineering; information systems; computer science; and information technology. As discussed in Chapters 1 and 10, accrediting bodies, such as the ACM, the British Computer Society (BCS) and others in related fields, require that students are taught a suitable level of professional ethics. Exactly what this entails is itself still under discussion amongst those teaching (and researching) this topic.

This book does not purport to teach ethics to the reader. Instead it leads the reader into consideration of the issues raised by the spread of computer and communication technologies into all aspects of life. Some of these issues require professional ethical consideration whereas others require more personal thought. Not everything is an 'ethical dilemma'. The goal of the book is to help readers become aware of the impact of computer and communication technology and become active citizens, within their professional body, within civil society, and within the global community now accessible to many individuals instead of only the rich, powerful and famous.

FOR THE GENERAL READER

Politicians have been talking about 'the (global) information society' since the late 1980s. Sociologists have been discussing 'the information age' for longer. What is clear is that we are in the midst of a social upheaval brought about not by any single invention but by multiple inventions with intertwining effects, and by the speed of their development. Every aspect of life in the industrialized world, from work to home to education to healthcare to warfare, is affected by computer and communication technology. Many of these changes have a positive effect for those who access them, however the 'digital divide' means that there can be a negative effect on society if access to these benefits is restricted to a few. In some cases, there is debate about the impact; for example, computer games have been shown to have both positive and negative effects on children. In other cases, there is a moral issue to be addressed, such as in access to sexual material or dangerous information (for example, information on how to make explosive compounds). There are those who will misuse beneficial new technology, causing harm to society and sometimes destroying the benefits of the technology for all.

Society responds to the challenges raised by these issues in numerous ways. For example, economies have been profoundly changed by e-commerce and digital downloading of entertainment. Laws have required updating in response to those causing harm using the new technology. The digital divide between rich and poor nations, and between rich and poor people has produced a new dynamic of social class. The technology itself changes in response to economics, law and social pressure.

This book is not about answers to the challenges. It is not even an attempt to restrict the questions. It is an information source about what is happening and how the issues might be addressed. This book is written for everyone who is interested in how their lives are directly or indirectly influenced by the technology around us.

The book is deliberately divided into self-contained chapters. There are inter-connections between all of the topics covered, however only where these are exceptionally important have specific cross-references been included. While we believe that the order of presentation is a logical and reasonable one, reading specific chapters or interesting topics in your preferred order can be equally valuable. It has been enjoyable to write. We hope you find it enjoyable to read.

FOR STUDENTS

Many readers of this book will be taking a course entitled 'Computer Ethics' or 'Professional Issues in Computing' as part of a computer science or engineering degree or related academic programme. The immense impact of computer and communications technology in the world cannot be ignored by those who develop them. Not only for the good of society, but also to achieve your own professional goals, the social, legal and ethical aspects of your work must be part of your thinking. Too few technologists engage in public debate about the positive and negative effects of modern technology. As a result, all too often small negative effects are blown out of proportion while ignoring the positive effects. Too many commentators, politicians and judges lack understanding of the differences between technologies such as 'the net', 'the Web', '3G' and 'multichannel multi-platform broadcasting'. It is time that the technologists came out of the computer lab and engaged with the rest of the world so that they not only influence the direction of the technology but also observe and experience its impact. Unlike many textbooks, this one does not contain the answers to specific questions but instead raises some of the issues that you should be thinking about, giving highly relevant case studies and understandable guidance on how to analyse these issues and how to develop your own conclusions about how to act, personally and professionally, as a key member of the information society. We have assumed no deep prior knowledge of ethics or social science and only a basic knowledge of specific technologies. What is assumed is a general background in using modern computer and communications technology.

FOR INSTRUCTORS

Teaching the social, legal and ethical aspects of computing and communication technology requires a unique mix of technological expertise and social science knowledge. This book straddles the two viewpoints to produce a text suitable for both technology lecturers and social science lecturers teaching such a course from their respective positions. The authors of this book have substantial experience in teaching the issues covered in this book to a wide range of students. Our approach is to raise issues which are relevant to the personal and professional lives of students. Our course is based on problems that students may well have come across in their daily lives or to which they can relate as potential issues in their future careers. We teach by encouraging the students to take part in class discussions, both in person and online and have found that students readily engage with this approach to the subject.

Should lecturers wish to base their courses on a more traditional approach to moral philosophy and formal ethical reasoning, this book can also support this approach by providing the necessary background of the 'real world' issues which the students need. It does not attempt to present a particular ethical theory with which to analyse those issues. The choice of such a theory is left to the lecturer, as is the choice of material (general texts about ethical theory, such as Thompson's *Ethical Theory*, or texts specific to computer ethics, such as Bynum and Rogerson's *Computer Ethics and Professional Responsibility*) used to support it. The Appendix gives an overview of ethical theories as a starting point for individual study or for lecturers seeking a suitable ethical approach to use; it is not itself recommended as a basis for teaching students, as it does not cover any one approach in enough detail, but it provides an overview of the variety of schools of thought.

Some of the topics we cover are controversial (sex and war, particularly) and by covering them we hope to provide material which students can relate to on their own terms. Some lecturers may wish to simply recommend students read these chapters and discuss the issues raised privately. Others may wish to tackle them head on. Either way, the impartial and straightforward approach should defuse tensions which might otherwise be apparent. The material can be covered in almost any order. The order presented is in line with our current lecture programme, however we ourselves mix and match the order each year in line with international events and developments. The chapters have been written to be accessed in any order with strong cross-links identified, but no prior knowledge of other chapters assumed.

The specific examples of the benefits and problems of modern technologies are drawn from as broad a range of countries as possible, although our own limited linguistic abilities means that examples are most often from English-speaking nations.

The book is supported by a web site maintained by the publishers and containing visual aids related to chapters, podcasts, and pointers to new issues in the press and online. The Case Studies and Discussion Topics in each chapter have been written to support instructors in developing the analysis, discussion and debating skills of students.

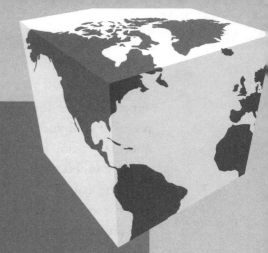

1

INTRODUCTION

There are two primary reasons why people become computing professionals: interest and money. The lucky ones get paid large amounts of money to do things that they are interested in. What they are interested in, and what they get paid for, is solving problems by writing computer programs or developing hardware devices. When computers were rare and expensive, they had little impact on most people's lives; where they did have an impact (such as in code making and breaking by governments), it was hidden and indirect. From the 1960s to the present, however, computers have followed consistent patterns of becoming exponentially more powerful and linearly cheaper in most terms: processing power, memory storage capacity, network bandwidth and so on. Because of this, and their general versatility, computers have become nearly ubiquitous in the industrialized world. The average household unwittingly contains in excess of ten 'computers' – everything from simple microprocessors performing a very limited range of functions, such as ensuring that the freezer does not defrost and the toaster does not burst into flames, to an Internet-connected PC which may also receive satellite television signals and control household systems, such as heating and cooling. Even embedded computers are becoming more powerful and the next wave of development is

expected to be the wireless interconnection of many of these devices with other pieces of equipment inside and outside the home. This is already happening with the ability to remotely program satellite and cable television recorders over the Internet or via a mobile phone (`www.sky.com/portal/site/skycom/remoterecord/`).

The combination of dependence on the correct functioning of these devices and the potential for abuse and misuse by both their owners and third parties (governments, criminals, pranksters or commercial interests) creates the biggest risks that industrial societies have ever faced. It is suggested that we are now in the midst of a social revolution every bit as far-reaching as the industrial revolution: the 'information revolution' moving us from the industrial age to the information age. It used to be reasonable for computer geeks to ignore the potential real-world effects of their work and leave such concerns to others. However, the ubiquity of computer technology means that computing professionals must now consider their work in the same light as the chemist and the nuclear physicist in terms of its potential impact on individuals and society. This is not just in the interests of society, but in the interests of computing professionals themselves. From supporting and promoting professional attitudes to taking part in political debate, the abdication of responsibility by computer nerds needs to stop. The alternative is abuse and misuse of power by large corporations and governments.

This is not to say that a professional attitude and attention to the social and legal ramifications of computing development is entirely altruistic. Despite the huge growth in computer usage and Internet access seen in the last 10 years, to the point where a majority of the population in industrialized countries will use a computer and access the Internet at least weekly, computers and the Internet remain a mystery to most of those users. Where such mystery holds sway, there is always the potential for social reactions (economic, legal and individual) to produce adverse effects on the lives of computing professionals. An extreme example of public reaction to advancing technology can be seen in the area of genetic modification. This might seem a long way from the world of the computer geek but consider that genome sequencing would not be possible on the scale currently undertaken without the processing capabilities of large computers. Without large-scale genome sequencing, genetic modification would be almost impossible to target efficiently.

The public reaction to genetically modified foodstuffs in Europe is, in the opinion of most scientists, completely uninformed and so biased against the technology that even developments which would solve known problems with pesticide and fertilizer use with apparently minimal other risks are blocked under the reaction to 'frankenfood'. Closer to home, for most computing professionals, is the constant discussion over the availability of sexual material online. Despite being utterly discredited (Time, 24 July 1995), an incredibly flawed study from over 10 years ago (Time, 3 July 1995) which claimed that 83.5% of Internet traffic consisted of pornography is still being quoted as a legitimate source by news organizations and lobby groups. In particular such 'statistics' are bandied about by those who advocate severe censorship and control of Internet access and computer usage, even to the point of suggesting that encryption which does not have a 'back door' for law enforcement should be banned, or that truly general-purpose computers be replaced by consumer electronic devices that limit access to information.

Most university engineering courses now include some element of study into social, legal and ethical aspects of the subject. Unlike much of the curriculum in engineering, however, this topic is not one in which a method of solving problems is transmitted from teacher to student. The aim of such a course is, or at least in our opinion should be, to provide a starting point for students to question the effects of their and their colleagues' work. In this book, we aim to raise many questions and provide information about the known and predicted effects of new technology on society. Where possible, parallels are drawn to previous technological developments, sometimes going back centuries, sometimes only a few years. Sometimes opinions are offered on the desirability or otherwise of these effects. It should be noted that such opinions are not always actually held by the authors but are presented to stimulate debate and deeper thought. In particular, each chapter includes some individual case studies and discussion topics. These discussion topics may be structured as a question for debate with starting points on each side put forward or may offer a completely one-sided presentation of the benefits or detriments of a particular aspect of new technology. Such one-sided arguments often form the core of lobbying or public relations exercises by powerful groups and the ability to tell the argument from the polemic and to pick apart a biased view is important.

All of the topics covered in this book could have (and most have had) one or more books written on them. We recommend some of the best (in our opinion) at the end of each chapter. Identifying the ideal order to present these topics was a difficult task and it was obvious to us that there are many equally valid orders. We have therefore made each chapter as self-contained as possible. This means that there are as many references forward to later chapters as references backwards to previous ones. It also means that some material is repeated where important background issues overlap. Readers should feel free to study the material presented in any order they feel appropriate, possibly skipping some chapters entirely. However, the order makes sense to us and we feel there is a reasonable logical progression from issue to issue and chapter to chapter which allows the book to be read as a whole in the order presented.

Before delving into each of the topics in detail, in this chapter we cover some of the major themes which will emerge again and again under the various headings.

The Canadian Cyborg

Steve Mann is a professor of engineering at the University of Toronto. He styles himself a 'cyborg' and has been using wearable computers for over twenty years, recording and broadcasting what he sees, accessing computer files and the Internet constantly to 'augment his memory'. Professor Mann is a world-famous researcher in wearable computing. In 2002, he followed his usual routine when flying to St John in New Brunswick, Canada, informing the airline and airport of his equipment and requesting permission not to have his equipment put through the X-ray machine because it is more sensitive than normal machines to their effects. On his way to St John on 16 February, he was allowed to pass through security with the usual scrutiny. On the way back, however, airport security insisted he turn his equipment on and off for them and put it through the scanners. He was then strip searched and claimed that electrodes he wears to monitor his vital signs were 'ripped from him' during the process. His psychological adjustment to the technology led to him feeling disoriented and requiring a wheelchair for boarding the plane. He also claimed that some of his equipment was significantly damaged and since he did not have funds to immediately replace it, he was feeling significant psychological distress from the 'withdrawal'.

Internet addiction disorder (IAD) is recognized by some psychologists as a psychological condition (though, as with many new conditions, there are significant numbers of psychologists who do not believe in the concept) and there is evidence that regular users may suffer psychological changes when denied access to their mobile (cell) phones. As the number of people constantly used to being in touch with the virtual world increases, the real world is going to have to make adjustments for people with psychological dependencies on their technology. More details on the airport incident can be found at `news.zdnet.com/2100-9584_22-5068619.html` and more general information about Steve Mann at `www.eecg.toronto.edu/~mann` and at `wearcam.org`.

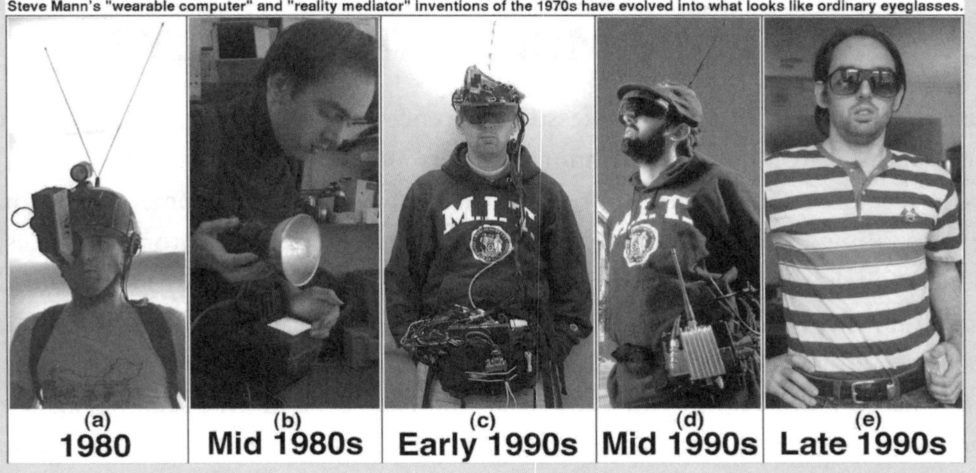

LESSIG'S FOUR MODALITIES ANALYSIS

In his seminal 1999 book, Professor Lawrence Lessig described a means of considering how technology and human society interact. In various chapters in our book, this 'four modalities' approach to analysis will be used (sometimes formally, by describing the element of each mode, and sometimes more informally). Lessig's concept is that there are four interconnected influences on human behaviour: law, social norms, markets and architecture. In the physical world, architecture means physics and geography but online architecture is simply computer code. Markets are the economic realities and how they influence behaviour. Social norms are the pressures put on us by people we know and law is the expressed and enforced power of the state. Each of these interacts with the others and puts pressure on the individual. Each is also acted on by society as a whole. None are completely fixed or completely understood and the interactions are sometimes subtle and sometimes gross.

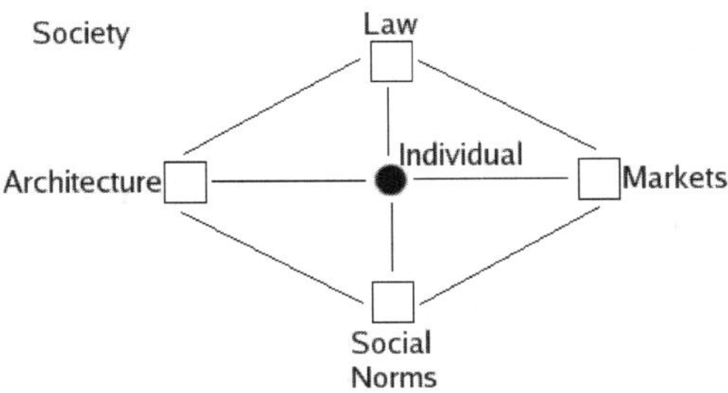

PROPHET AND LOSS: FAILING TO FORESEE THE FUTURE

Intelligent, well-educated experts in science and technology have been making far-reaching pronouncements about the future for centuries. Some of the biggest howlers of failed predictions include:

> *'The abdomen, the chest and the brain will forever be shut from the intrusion of the wise and humane surgeon' – Sir John Eric Ericksen, British surgeon to Queen Victoria, 1873*
>
> *'This telephone has too many shortcomings to be considered as a means of communication. The device is inherently of no value to us' – Western Union internal memo, 1876*
>
> *'Radio has no future. Heavier-than-air flying machines are impossible. X-rays will prove to be a hoax' – Lord Kelvin, physicist and inventor, 1899*
>
> *'The problem with television is that the people must sit and keep their eyes glued on a screen; the average American family hasn't time for it' – New York Times, 1949*

'Man will never reach the moon, regardless of all future scientific advances' – *Lee De Forest, radio pioneer, 1957*

'There is no reason anyone would want a computer in their home' – *Ken Olson, president, chairman and founder of DEC, 1977*

'640 kB ought to be enough for anybody' – *Bill Gates, 1981*

'I predict the Internet will go spectacularly supernova and in 1996 catastrophically collapse' – *Bob Metcalf, 3Com Founder, 1995*

The closest to reality any of these came is Bob Metcalf whose prediction of catastrophic failure applied, but only to the 'dot com' investment bubble, not to the technology or the spread of its usage to almost every home and workplace and even to public toilets! So, when considering the future it is often 'better to keep silent and be thought a fool than speak and confirm the opinion'. Which technologies will become widespread and last and which will die as they are born or flash like a nova is difficult to predict. What is becoming ever more certain is that technology will continue to evolve although we may be reaching the limits of society to adapt to new technology quickly enough for it to be economically viable. Already it can be seen that sufficient technology with wide acceptance can become highly entrenched and outlast several generations of possible replacement purely by commercial inertia (consider the humble audio compact disc, now beginning to show its age but remaining a significant medium for purchase of music 20 years after its introduction, and the audio cassette tape still with its niche markets more than 40 years on). Entirely new technologies are not the only force at work. At least as strong is the combination of new technologies with old (see Chapter 2 for more on this), such as telephony over an Internet connection (voice over Internet protocol) or video on demand delivered to third-generation mobile phones.

INFORMATION SYSTEM PARTITION

In what is now regarded as a classic exposition of the influence of technology on society Meyrowitz (1985) in No Sense of Place argues that television produced seismic upheaval in the social order by giving people access to hitherto restricted information systems: children access to the adult information world, women access to the male information world, ethnic minorities access to the majority's information world and the poor access to the information world of the rich. There are those who have regarded this with horror, such as campaigners insisting that all television broadcast be suitable for young children (i.e. no sex, no violence, no swearing, no moral shades of grey, etc.). There are also those who have objected to the broadcasting of the truth about them or their organizations.

The debate about censorship of information available on the Internet is simply an expansion and intensification of this earlier debate, made more complex by the open and many-to-many nature of Internet protocols. Broadcast television is becoming easier to regulate and more regulated in some ways (e.g. subchannel 'ratings' information allows parents to restrict what their children have access to on the family satellite or cable receivers) and yet less regulated and less easy to regulate in others (hundreds of channels, many of them sourced directly from other countries, and much more extreme adult material being broadcast which was before only allowed distribution in the physical form of videocassettes and DVDs). At the same time, more and more material, including full video feeds, is becoming available over the Internet with much less possibility for restriction by either regulators or parents (see Chapter 4 for more details).

Consider the difference in reporting of the First World War (strong censorship, 'patriotic movies', newsreel cinema footage months old) and the Iraq War (reporters embedded with the attacking troops and in a hotel inside the capital), or the famous sequence of BBC reporter John Simpson 'liberating' Kabul ahead of US and UK troops. The failed coup against Mikhail Gorbachev which brought down the Soviet Union followed the standard pattern of previous power shifts in the Kremlin. Unfortunately for the plotters, Gorbachev's reforms had already lost them control of the information system inhabited by the ordinary people of Moscow. During previous coups, the control of information allowed the assumption of power by plotters before anyone who had the possibility to oppose them could rally support. This time, access to the dissemination of information nationally and internationally allowed Boris Yeltsin to rally support for resistance. It is no coincidence that the most physically and politically oppressive regimes in the world also tend to have some of the most restrictive information systems in place. It is often said that 'you don't miss what you've never had' but it is even more true that 'you don't miss what you don't know exists'.

THE LAW IS AN ASS

When first encountering law, it often seems bewildering with its own strange nomenclature and ways of using five words where it appears that one would do. As it is studied, however, it begins to make sense and a scientist will begin to see the logic involved. This is the most dangerous stage because as one studies in more depth one realizes that law is not truly logical, and that to assume it is can produce grave errors in interpretation. Each piece of law, whether it is a statute, a judicial precedent or an international treaty, is developed somewhat in isolation from other elements of the law. While attempts are always made to ensure that laws do not contradict each other, the existing body of law is too large to avoid such problems. Legislation is the result of individual opinions of existing law, the ideal state of society and the pragmatic view of what might work.

Increasingly, law is both affected by and affects technology, and computer technology particularly. While engineers should not be expected to be lawyers, they do need a basic understanding of the law as it affects them for two reasons: firstly, to know when they (or their organization) need the advice of expensive lawyers; secondly, in order to engage in the political debates that develop the law. The first of these is fairly obvious – why pay for expensive legal advice when the situation is clear cut even to a layman? On the other hand, many computing professionals would question why they should bother with the illogical and messy business of political debate. After all they are interested in the clean joys of hacking elegant code rather than the messy world of the politician. When computers were confined to hobbyists and large corporations' internal data processing, that may have been possible. Now, however, with laws that allow patenting of software ideas (in the United States and maybe soon the European Union), laws that restrict the distribution of computer code (anything from encryption algorithms to device drivers) and laws that decide who has the rights to use particular words in a URL (so far only in second- and third-level domain names but possibly soon referring to the whole of the URL), the everyday interests of the computer literate are subject to more and more regulation. If that regulation was sane, reasonable, unbiased and developed in such a way as to not unduly hamper the development of new technology, it could be left to the politicians and judges to get on with. Unfortunately this is not the case. Far too few politicians and judges have more than a very basic understanding of the strengths and limitations of science in general, much less information and computation theories and practicalities. Such misunderstandings can be seen in the issued statements of both judges and politicians, for example the necessity of describing the Internet as 'not something you just dump something on. It's not a truck. It's a series of tubes' (`www.pcmag.com/article2/0,1895,1985071,00.asp`).

Politicians do not seem to understand that the immense economic potential of the Internet and the Web rests primarily upon its open, end-to-end nature. When judges in France decide that it is the responsibility of US companies to prevent French citizens from accessing the data on their US servers in order to comply with French censorship laws on Nazi issues, they are demonstrating an utter lack of understanding of the international nature of the Web and the Internet. Since politicians and judges do not understand the nature of the technology, they listen to vocal demands for a variety of restrictions on technological development and they pass laws which may or may not have the desired effect but which often place terrible burdens on both the work and personal computer usage of computing professionals. In order to prevent unreasonable burdens, those who understand the technology must become sufficiently politically involved to at least reduce, if not eliminate, the negative impact on their lives. In order to suitably influence the political and judicial arenas, however, one needs a basic understanding of the existing legal situation, and particularly of the law relating to technology.

While all the topics in this book have some relevant legal content there are some which are almost entirely legal in nature, such as copyrights and patents, privacy and surveillance, and censorship and freedom of speech. The law is complex and the law is an ass, but so long as that is kept in mind it can be understood to the extent needed.

Tati vs Kitetoa

A French journalist, Antoine Champagne, ran a website called `kitetoa.com`. On this website, Champagne and some friends publicized their 'White Hat cracking' exercises. Generally, they did this some time after having contacted companies with holes in their systems and, in many cases, having helped the companies plug those holes. When they posted data retrieved from the companies' intranets, they sanitized it to avoid data protection violations, trade secret disclosures and similar issues.

Lawyers for Tati (a French clothiers) alleged that Champagne 'cracked' their computer network and fraudulently accessed Microsoft Access databases on their system between 1999 and 2001. Champagne states that he merely used open proxies on their system to access documents freely available on the system.

As proof of no harm, Champagne produced e-mail exchanges with Tati.fr's systems administrators thanking him for notifying them and for his help in plugging their security holes. The prosecutor in France slapped Champagne with a €1000 fine suspended pending 5 years free of conviction for similar offences under France's computer misuse laws.

Champagne has been threatened by French police with confiscation of his computers if he runs foul of such laws again. `www.kitetoa.com` is still up and running at the time of writing and all the details are available there (in French) but details of new vulnerabilities are no longer posted.

GLOBALIZATION

One of the significant impacts of modern computer and communication technology is that the barriers between societies are being reduced. Sometimes that reduces tensions and produces a lessening of suffering: it is more difficult to ignore starving people in a famine thousands of miles away when their faces and pleas for help appear on television screens in our living rooms. At other times it can increase tensions and even lead to armed conflict: nations separated by thousands of miles may have no conflict despite fundamental ideological divisions, but when the borderless flow of information spreads (sometimes misunderstood) ideas from one place to another it can lead to conflict. One example of this was the violent protests in 2006 in nations as far away as Indonesia against publication in 2005 in a Danish newspaper of cartoons satirizing the prophet Muhammad.

The Internet in particular is accelerating this globalization of information. The many-to-many nature of Internet communication prevents governments from keeping any significant control of information arriving from elsewhere in the world. From radical sermons by religious fanatics to Western ideas of democracy and freedom of speech and thought, each individual can now follow an information path they choose, away from the control of national and local leaders. The problems of jurisdiction and the increased clash of cultures created by global communications systems are a recurring theme in many of our chapters.

THE DIGITAL DIVIDE

The world has long been divided into rich and poor, educated and ignorant, free and controlled. There are equivalent divides on national and international levels. The spread of computer and communication technology has changed the nature of these divides in unexpected ways. In many cases, of course, it has simply widened the divide: the children of the rich have access to the latest top-quality equipment and sources of information, allowing them to maintain their position relative to the uninformed poor. This has always been the case to some extent, in that children from poor homes could not afford encyclopedias and other textbooks or the fees of top-quality private schools. As the cost of computers and Internet access has reduced, access to an equivalent level of information has penetrated lower and lower on the economic scale, but there remains a significant underclass in industrialized society without access to, or knowledge of how to use, such trappings of modern life.

The double-edged nature of the information revolution is also noticeable on a global scale, with the development of outsourcing of computer programming, drug manufacture (and even research and development) and information-centric jobs such as enquiry call centres to countries such as India. Of course, this is leading to the rapid development of a digital divide in those countries even worse than that seen in the industrialized world. The instantaneous communications offered by world-wide telephone and computer networks have merged the stock markets and money markets into a nearly continuously traded global whole. No longer does the market stop when the trader leaves the office: it continues trading around the world and, by the time they start work again the following morning, seismic shifts in fortunes may have occurred. Computer-based trading has allowed the development of automated trading systems which track the stock market as a whole or individual stock prices and perform trades dependent on conditions set by a broker. In some cases, the combination of unusual events (such as major security alerts, major industrial accidents or currency value collapses) and automated trading can lead to a spiralling or oscillating sequence of market trades. Deliberate delays in processing trades or decision making have had to be introduced to avoid too much volatility in the markets.

Individual Stock Market Trading: Pump and Dump Scams

Individual access to computer and telephone communications can also have a significant impact on stocks and shares, the basis of the capitalist economic system. Pump-and-dump scams have been around as long as the stock market: the price of a stock is 'pumped up' by spreading rumours that there is some reason it is about to jump (a new contract, a new product distribution approval or a takeover bid). Once enough people have bought in, driving the price up (the pump), the original holders of the stock sell at a vastly inflated price (the dump), leaving those who fell for the rumour to take the losses as the stock adjusts

> back to its natural price. This shows all the classic aspects of traditional confidence tricks: rely on people's greed, have them do something slightly suspect or even downright illegal (trading on 'inside information' is illegal on most stock markets) and then sting them for their money. The slightly illegal nature of the victims' own activities reduce the chances of complaints to law enforcement agencies. New variations on the pump-and-dump scam involve using usenet, email or other online communications tools to spread the pump information. In another recent variation, voicemail messages are left on mobile phones as though to a wrong number (quite plausible since many mobile-phone voicemail services do not include a personalized message, even where the facility is present). The US Security and Exchange Commission (SEC) prosecuted Michael O'Grady of Georgia in May 2005 (O'Grady pleaded guilty: `www.usatoday.com/money/industries/telecom/2005-05-03-voicemail_x.htm`) and has previously prosecuted email and usenet pump-and-dump scammers. As both information and trading move faster and faster, wild surges in stock market prices are becoming more and more common, which can destabilize the entire world economy.

Developing nations are attempting to leapfrog into the information age without passing through an industrial age, just as Japan leapfrogged the early industrial technologies into the electronics era after the Second World War. Whether they will succeed is impossible to judge but outsourcing of everything from call centres to accounting shows the potential.

SERVANT OR MASTER: COMPUTERS MAKING DECISIONS

Some of the most difficult issues in computing today arise when computer software and hardware is responsible for making decisions which affect people's lives.

We have briefly covered above the problems that may be caused by automated stock-market-trading systems. When these activities cause problems they can result in significant financial loss and possibly even have macro-economic effects in fragile situations. However, even more serious are those circumstances in which lives, not money, are at stake.

From computer control systems in cars, planes and boats to automated dosing machines in hospitals, computers are constantly involved in potentially life-threatening activities in the modern world. Where the decision made by a computer program leads to financial loss or to injury or death, who should be held responsible?

There is a significant level of response to negative incidents in which people 'blame the computer'. When the negative incident is that one's tax bill is out by a few pounds or dollars, this may be an acceptable and humorous way of defusing a sensitive topic or it may enrage the subject of the error. When the result of a computer error is to release dangerous (even fatal) dosages of radiation during radiotherapy for cancer, as happened in 1986 in Georgia (New York Times, via `tinyurl.com/3dkj5c`) the question of who, if anyone, is to blame becomes much more serious. When a medical practitioner makes a mistake and gives a patient a damaging dose of a treatment, an investigation will be carried out by the appropriate regulatory body to determine whether that practitioner is allowed to continue practicing and out of court settlements, or court cases, assign damages usually paid by insurance companies. When computer software is found to have failed, who is responsible?

Software engineering is a difficult task and errors may occur due to any number of causes: requirements may have been incorrectly transmitted to the software team by the customer; errors in the hardware may cause errors in operation; errors in software libraries or compilers may cause errors in the final object code; errors in programming, testing or installation may cause faults; carelessness or negligence may be the root cause, or the problem may be the result of previously unknown interactions within the complex computer system. Assigning blame, preventing future occurrences and developing better software are all necessary steps when someone has been injured or killed (or where such injury or death was avoided only by luck or human intervention). Computer systems are so complex, however, that it is often claimed that perfect software is impossible to produce. How much liability do individuals in software houses have for the results of their work? If their work is then used to produce safety critical software when they did not originally expect it to be so used, do they still remain liable for the consequences?

As more artificial intelligence software is developed and the possibility of self-awareness of computer software becomes apparent, what are the limits of responsibility of the programmers for the actions of their work? If the programmers are not liable then who, if anyone, is?

DISCUSSION TOPICS

Can Laws Be Immoral?

The apparatus of the state decides what is legal and not legal. In the industrialized world, it is claimed that the rights of minorities are protected but within living memory it was illegal to be a homosexual in the United Kingdom. Under the Nazi regime, it was not only legal, it was required, that Jews, gypsies and others were put into concentration camps to be killed or allowed to die. In the People's Republic of China, it is illegal to post discussions of freedom of speech or free and fair elections onto the Internet. In many states in the United States, it is legal to have sex with someone aged 16 but not to take nude pictures of them. In the democracies of the industrialized world, it is generally not illegal to campaign for a change in the law to decriminalize something (e.g. various narcotics and other recreational pharmaceuticals). Other countries regard things differently. Sometimes only those in the legislature have freedom to discuss changes in the law. If one believes a law is immoral, is it moral to break that law? It is sometimes said that 'the only crime is getting caught'.

Genetically Modified Food, Technologically Modified Humans

The idea of a soul-less humanoid machine has been around since biblical times (Psalms 139:15–16). Science fiction has been dealing with the concept since Mary

Shelley's Frankenstein. We have Professor Steve Mann constantly connected to his computers and the Internet; we have people with implanted technology keeping them alive (pacemakers and even completely artificial hearts); and we have almost humanoid robots.

The public furore over genetically modified food (so-called 'frankenfoods') shows how poorly the public sometimes understand scientific advances and risks. Debates over choosing the sex of which embryos produced in vitro are implanted have raged amid speculation about 'designer babies' selected for hair and eye colour, intelligence or sporting ability, while selecting out certain serious genetic defects has become almost routine. Terry Schiavo became known throughout the United States and the world after (arguably) entering a persistent vegetative state; she was the centre of a political and judicial struggle still being played out long after she was allowed to die.

People have been attacked by mobs simply for being thought to be carrying one of the 'new plagues' (AIDS, for instance). Will we see persecution of those with pacemakers or artificial hearts or those whose gestation was decided by genetic selection, for being 'different', not human? Those who differ from the ordinary person can feel isolated and shut out of normal life because they look different. Will people have to hide their augmentations or will society accept technologically modified humans more easily than genetically modified food?

The Haves and the Have-nots

Large parts of Africa, Asia and South America still have not emerged properly into the industrial revolution. Agrarian societies subject to drought and famine when the harvest fails are a world away from the epidemic of obesity in the industrialized societies. The industrialized world is now undergoing an information revolution. Just as large parts of the world have already been left behind, portions of the population in the industrialized world are being left behind in the information revolution. Illiteracy often dooms people to low-paid work and exclusion from many aspects of social interaction. Computer literacy is becoming a similar skill.

Governments and commercial entities are moving as much of their interactions with individuals as they can onto computer systems, supposedly to achieve cost savings (though these are not always evident). Once it becomes uneconomic to support both physical and virtual shop fronts, many retailers may move solely to electronic transactions. Choice for those outside the Internet loop may significantly diminish. Just as those without cars are disadvantaged by the change to edge-of-town supermarkets whose cheaper prices through economies of scale are more than outweighed by the cost of bus or taxi fares to those without personal transport, so those without Internet access may be forced to pay higher prices or do without certain goods altogether. Public libraries may continue to provide free access to information in both paper and electronic forms but, as the Internet becomes 'the world's library', those without the skills to make use of it may find themselves increasingly out of touch.

Various solutions to these problems have been suggested, from the $200 computer for the developing world to limited Web access via a (television) set top box. Whether a digital underclass will emerge is yet to be seen, but it is already a political issue in many countries where the availability of broadband Internet for all is becoming a government policy even when half their population have yet to make use of even narrowband Internet access.

REFERENCES

Meyrowitz, J. (1985) *No Sense of Place*, Oxford University Press, Oxford. ISBN 0-19-504231-X.

RELATED READING

Akdeniz, Y. (1999) *Sex on the Net*, South Street Press, Reading. ISBN 1-902932-00-5.

Furnell, S. (2002) *Cybercrime: Vandalizing the Information Society*, Addison Wesley, Harlow. ISBN 0-201-72159-7.

Goodman, D. (2004) *Spam Wars: Our Last Best Chance to Defeat Spammers, Scammers and Hackers*, Select Books, New York. ISBN 1-59-079063-4.

Hafner, K. and **Lyon, M.** (1996) *Where Wizards Stay Up Late*, Free Press, London. ISBN 0-7434-6837-6.

Lessig, L. (1999) *Code and Other Laws of Cyberspace*, Basic Books, New York. ISBN 0-465-03913-8.

Lessig, L. (2001) *The Future of Ideas*, Random House, New York. ISBN 0-375-50578-4.

Lessig, L. (2004) *Free Culture*, Penguin, London. ISBN 1-594-20006-8.

Levy, S. (1994) *Hackers: Heroes of the computer revolution*, Penguin, London. ISBN 0-14-100051-1.

Levy, S. (2000) *Crypto: Secrecy and Privacy in the New Code War*, Penguin, London. ISBN 0-140-244-328.

Mueller, M.L. (2002) *Ruling the Root*, MIT Press, Cambridge, MA. ISBN 0-262-13412-8.

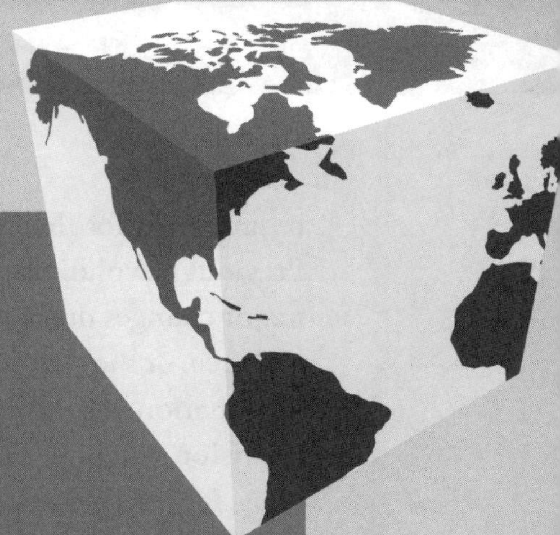

2

EMERGENCE AND CONVERGENCE OF TECHNOLOGIES

INTRODUCTION

The industrial revolution, which was a revolution in the way people lived and worked caused by a change in the available technology, took place over a number of generations. Many scholars now believe we are in the midst of the next phase change in human society: the 'information revolution'. This time, however, the revolution is happening much faster. From the emergence of the first programmable digital computers in the late 1940s via the emergence of the personal computer in the 1970s to the emergence of the Internet into mainstream society in the 1990s, the scale and pace of change has far outstripped that of the industrial revolution. Generations in the industrialized world are also much longer now: life spans are considerably longer and couples are first having children at greater ages. This all leads to a constant

requirement for the individual to cope with a great many changes during a lifetime. Previous revolutions required most individuals to cope with only one or two major changes during their lifetimes – moving from a rural to an urban lifestyle, for instance, or moving from hand-driven machinery to steam-driven machinery. In the information revolution, the people who lived through the change to multichannel television are now living through the change to on-demand services. Those who struggled to deal with videocassette recorders are now dealing with digital video recorders, DVD players and recorders, and PC-based entertainment systems.

In this chapter, we present the emergence of some of the most important technologies and the societal and psychological changes they produced and then we concentrate on the growing convergence of established technologies into synergistic forms which radically alter those effects once more. We draw comparisons between the uptake of recent new technologies and the speed of uptake of previous technologies, and also the failure rates of new concepts and technologies.

Beginning with regular postal services and continuing with telegraph, telephone, e-mail, mobile phone, text message, chat room and instant messaging, the cost, time and difficulty of communicating with other people have all reduced. This has had an enormous effect on society, from the local to the national to the international. Some of these effects are obviously beneficial and others obviously detrimental, but in many cases they are both beneficial and detrimental, or different people make different judgements. However, the genie of data processing and

communication is not only out of the bottle, but continuing to grow and change all the time. The challenge is for people to take advantage of these new technologies rather than allowing small groups of people to take advantage of the majority. Many of the obviously negative effects of modern communication technologies such as spam, cold calling and online harassment are presented in Chapter 13.

EMERGENCE

The Rise of Print Media

The social changes produced by the mass production of copies of written work should not be underestimated. When books had to be laboriously copied by hand and each copy included new and different errors, controlling the dissemination of information within a society was much easier. Ideas were transmitted from person to person with the interpretation of each changing the idea so that eventually something completely different might emerge. Cheap and quick reproduction of texts, everything from full books, such as bibles, histories, political treatises and fiction, to individual flyers and posters allowed anyone with sufficient money to disseminate their ideas unfiltered by intermediate minds. The reader still makes their own interpretation of the writer's words, but there is no doubt as to what the text says whereas with oral accounts what is reported to have been said can always be disputed. Mass sales of printed matter required mass literacy. This brought the publishing business into social policy conflict with the employers of unskilled and semi-skilled labour: literate workers are far more likely to organize on a wide scale, be aware of concepts of trade, economics, the value of labour and other ideas dangerous to the profits of factory owners. This is, of course, a simple view but it sets the pattern for various social changes due to technology. Where a technology requires significant investment which can only be recouped by a social change that may be detrimental to other vested interests, there is a battle between entrenched and new interests. This battle may take many forms: economic competition, lobbying for legal changes favourable to one side or another, or social attacks on the new technology as too dangerous or immoral.

Following the increase in literacy rates, other social changes were wrought by the rise of print media. Various groups which had exerted control over others had that control undermined by access to printed matter. One example of this was the control of the church over the populace. When bibles were hand-copied in Latin, at a time when most people did not read any language and did not understand Latin, the local priest occupied a unique position as the interpreter of the bible and therefore of the will of God. The availability of mass-produced bibles translated into local languages allowed ordinary members of the congregation to read the bible themselves and contest the interpretation of the priest. It is no wonder that the Catholic Church (unsuccessfully) resisted such moves. This demonstrates a theme which will occur in a number of other chapters, whereby control of which information people may access comprises a large part of controlling those people.

Another major change that derived from the growth in print media was the beginning of development of a globalized society. Cheap and easy printing allows for mass production of books, which allows for people in geographically distant places to achieve a similarity of experience which is otherwise unattainable. In addition, newspaper printing allows for the reporting of major events from distant places. This convergence of information has been heightened and expanded by other technological advances. The ability for many people to read the same reports of events none of them witnessed is the beginning of a move away from geographic isolation. Although writing itself was the first step in this direction, it was the rise of the printing press that brought this change to the mass of the population rather than to the privileged few.

The Rise of the Telegraph and the Telephone

The first significant method of near-instantaneous communication over great distances was the telegraph. This required expert operators to encode and decode the messages. While this is not necessarily a skill beyond most people, it made economic sense to restrict access to the communication network to those skilled operators. Laying the wires required significant investment which needed to be recouped quickly. The overall cost of a network was therefore reduced if only skilled, and therefore fast and accurate, operators used the system. The telegraph had a number of features that distinguished it from other communication methods:

- Near-synchronicity: the telegraph was almost instantaneous over the long distance but then relied on local postal services or personal collection for the 'last mile' connection.
- Privacy: If one trusts the postal and telephone services then communication can be assumed to be private. However, at least two operators (more if the message is relayed) have to know the contents of a telegraph message for its transmission.

It is not surprising that the success of the telegraph was most marked in the United States. The combination of a low-density population clustered around existing lines of physical communication (the railroad) in a country where even the fastest previous method of communication (the Pony Express) took days provided the perfect opportunity for the telegraph to succeed. Compare this with the United Kingdom where postal services only took one or two days to go between the extreme ends of the country. Telegraph services were far less used since the benefits were proportionally lower. It should be noted that the telegraph is a digital form of communication: each letter is sent individually using a discrete coding system rather than relying on analogue variations. The main social effect of the telegraph in the United Kingdom was on commerce, rather than individual communications, although the ability to 'wire' money from person to person instantly did have a significant impact.

The telephone offers completely different benefits but also has some disadvantages – for decades, a person had to be at the physical location of a telephone in order to receive the communication, whether the intended recipient or not. Even with the advent of answering machines and now exchange- or switchboard-based voicemail services, the interactivity benefit of the telephone over the telegram or a letter are lost. People are, in general, quite poor at leaving messages on answering machines. The ability to concisely include all the necessary information without hesitation, repetition, deviation or omission is something few people have. Part of this is due to the 'surprise' factor of getting a machine instead of the person. The main one, however, is that missing information can neither be prompted for nor noticed on re-reading. Only very recently have voicemail systems begun to allow replaying of messages before ringing off and, even without the 'surprise factor', people may keep omitting or garbling important elements of a complicated message.

When it first emerged, the telephone system was almost as labour-intensive as the telegraph, requiring operators at each exchange to make the appropriate connections. Automated electrical switching replaced a large number of low-paid exchange operators with a smaller number of higher-paid engineers. Until the development of cell-based mobile phone services, telephone technology barely changed, with the main social impact being the near ubiquity of telephones in homes and businesses and the reducing costs of calls and fixed-rate charges making telephone use more of a constant and less of a necessity-only method.

The biggest change in telephone usage, of course, was produced by cell-based mobile devices. Beginning with radio pagers which only had a single message (they would buzz or beep) that usually meant 'ring the office', numeric services then followed whereby a number to call could be sent to the device. Even with the prevalence of multi-tone push-button phones over older loop-disconnect dial services, these systems typically used human operators to take the number and, later, a short text message to send, with at times understandable but hilarious mistakes in transcription and at others cryptic errors rendering the message meaningless. The text messaging capabilities of pagers is an important concept to recall because it was this which inspired mobile phone operating companies towards an accidental 'killer application'. As mobile phone operators moved to the second generation of services, digital rather than analogue transmission, they initially included a short messaging service (SMS) as a free add-on. In Europe, this quickly became a more commonly used variant of the service than voice calls. Of course, the companies then swiftly moved to generate a revenue stream from such a popular service, but their pricing structure made each individual message cheap enough that it never seemed worth considering the cost.

> Killer app: an application that many people want to use and which ensures the success of the hardware or software platform on which it is based; examples include the spreadsheet for personal computers and text messaging for mobile phones
>
> Short Messaging Service (SMS): a short piece of text passed between digital mobile phones
>
> Multimedia Messaging Service (MMS): pictures or short video sequences passed between 2.5G or 3G mobile phones

A whole new aspect of youth, particularly teenage, culture has grown up in Europe around the use of text messaging. This subculture has its own variants of written language. Because of the very limited number of characters it was originally possible to send in individual messages and because of the inefficient nature of entering text on a numeric keypad, a whole vocabulary of abbreviations for use in text messaging has grown up, further reinforcing the feeling of involvement in a separate cultural zone from ordinary life. Various scare stories about potential health risks from prolonged and regular use of mobile phones have circulated but none have so far been clearly demonstrated. However, one recent study (`bmj.bmjjournals.com/cgi/content/full/bmj;327/7415/582-c`) did show an alarming problem with teenagers' and children's use of mobile phones in that they often do not switch them off before going to sleep and a majority of young people reported regular disturbance of their sleep due to incoming calls or messages – most often messages.

Mobile phones (both voice calls and text messaging) have become an indispensable part of many people's lives, although they can often be a problem to others, when phones are left switched on (and with audible alarms) in places such as cinemas, theatres, classrooms and lecture halls. While more often an oversight than a deliberate act for most, still there are those who believe that they absolutely must be contactable at all times and that any inconvenience to others around them is someone else's problem. Whether inadvertent or deliberate, the distraction to others caused by a phone alert seems highly anti-social.

The Rise of Broadcast Media

The difference between printed media and broadcast media is similar to the difference between a letter and a telephone call. The comparison is not perfect, however, because radio and television broadcasts are not interactive between the listener or viewer and the presenters. In addition, although the presentation itself contains spoken (and, for television, visual) aspects much television and radio is presented according to a prepared script, even when not recorded and edited. There are also significant social differences in people's perceptions of material depending on the medium. One of the best known examples of this is the 1960 presidential election debates in the United States (see `www.museum.tv/archives/etv/K/htmlK/kennedy-nixon/kennedy-nixon.htm` for an in-depth analysis). For the first time, four debates between the two candidates were broadcast on television while the sound was broadcast simultaneously on radio. Polling data differed considerably between those who watched the debate compared to those who only listened to it. Those who watched were far more likely both to believe that Kennedy had performed better and to decide to vote for him, whereas those who listened found Nixon more compelling. In many ways, instant and widespread news reporting has changed the way politics works: it is now far more important to avoid being seen to make mistakes than it is to actually perform well overall. The insatiable appetite of the 24-hour news channels, in particular, means that any negative story is carried multiple times before any 'fix' can be produced.

Broadcast media were originally very heavily regulated in most countries. Part of the reason for this was purely technical: analogue transmission requires a broad band of 'clear space' around it to prevent cross-channel interference. Although radio transmission and reception has improved over the more than a century since its introduction, such advances have been very small incremental changes: the basic technology remains pretty much the same. Only very recently has broadcast digital radio become a reality and there has been a slow take up of both digital audio broadcast (DAB) reception equipment and broadcast provision. Even in the United Kingdom, where the BBC's unique position as a well-funded public service broadcaster often leads to early provision of new broadcast technology, more people listen to digital radio channels via satellite television equipment or over the Internet than use dedicated DAB equipment. Part of the reason for this is the cost of DAB receivers; there was until recently very little available in the way of cheap low-end equipment. The main reason, however, is the durability of existing radio reception equipment, which lasts for many years since it is now a very mature technology.

Despite the capabilities of digital broadcasting to allow for almost unlimited numbers of stations in fairly small sections of bandwidth, many governments (usually through 'independent' agencies such as the Office of Communications (OFCOM) in the United Kingdom and the Federal Communications Commission (FCC) in the United States) are still heavily regulating broadcast technologies and artificially maintaining a scarcity of licenses by restricting the bandwidth available for such services. There are a growing number of people lobbying for a much more open approach to radio frequency bandwidth allocation but, as is common, a number of existing players are lobbying to maintain the current system in which they have privileged incumbent positions.

The Office of Communications (OFCOM): successor to OFTEL and the Broadcasting Standards Authority, with power to regulate the communications industries in the United Kingdom

The Federal Communications Commission (FCC): similar powers in the United States

The Failure of On Digital

The United Kingdom has seen the swiftest move to digital television of any major industrialized nation (`news.bbc.co.uk/2/hi/entertainment/4816832.stm`). Spurred on by the dual engines of the publicly-funded BBC (able to invest in new broadcast technologies without worrying about short term investor returns) and an early analogue satellite system which invested quickly in digital broadcasts as well, the UK government is planning to switch off all analogue television transmissions by about 2010. The first pilot area had their analogue system turned off in March 2005. This was deemed a great success although the only reason it was possible was the provision of set-top boxes and technical support funded by the UK government.

The set-top boxes provided were those for 'Freeview', a BBC enterprise which provides only free-to-air channels. This uses the same technology (and is compatible with) the previous terrestrial digital system originally called 'On Digital' then rebadged to 'ITV Digital'. This offered a smaller scale version of the digital satellite and cable services already available to much (though not all) of the UK population. On Digital offered a combination of free-to-air services and subscription channels, together with subsidized reception equipment. Subscription channels included movies, sports and 'adult' content (late at night, usually channel sharing with more innocuous material, such as teleshopping, during daytime hours).

ITV Digital failed in April 2002 to be replaced by Freeview. The reasons for the failure have been covered in great detail by the press and have even been the subject of a statement in the UK Parliament by the culture secretary. Basically, ITV Digital signed an incredibly expensive deal with the Nationwide Football League to show live football matches from the lower divisions of English soccer. This contract assumed large revenues from subscriptions to the sports channels which would show these matches. The drop in other advertising revenues (following the dot com crash and subsequent global economic downturn) and the non-appearance of high subscription rates for these sports channels led to the contract being uneconomic for the parent companies of ITV Digital. If the parent companies had been liable for the cost, then ITV Digital would probably have survived. As it was, the parent companies managed to claim that the liability only applied to the subsidiary and they let it fail rather than pay out large sums for unprofitable rights.

Subsequently a very small subscription service was launched using the same technology as ITV Digital. The problem is that the decryption equipment needed to ensure that only those who pay for it can receive the subscription channels is expensive to include in the set-top box (this was one of ITV Digital's major costs). The new Freeview boxes do not generally include such equipment, simply that needed for free-to-air subscriptions. Only those who buy new (more expensive) decryption-enabled set-top boxes or those who own ITV Digital boxes can use top-up-TV services. This lack of scale of potential audience is hampering their competition with cable and satellite reception options (which also have the opportunity to amortize fixed costs over a much larger number of channels).

The failure of ITV Digital should not be seen as an example of a badly thought out technology or even of a market that was not there; it was simply the result of a single highly risky decision: to pay relatively huge amounts of money for second-rate sport on the assumption that it would be as lucrative a market as the top flight – in other words, plain old bad management. Further information can be found at `news.bbc.co.uk/1/hi/1897316.stm`.

The Rise of the Computing Industry

There is a famous (though possibly spurious) comment attributed to Thomas J. Watson, the founder and chairman of IBM: 'I think there is a world market for about five computers'. Of course the meaning of this statement depends on what you mean by a 'computer'. If it is defined as any digital electronic device capable of performing automatic computation then there are now more computers in the world than people (consider that most people in the industrialized world own more than 20).

At the time, computers were envisaged as machines for tabulating large amounts of statistical information or a small number of other specialized tasks such as cryptography. In fact, the demand even for these purposes quickly outstripped this supposed blunder. Pharmaceutical companies employed computers to calculate efficient chemical supply logistics, for instance. The first big killer application of computing in business was one which was reinvented for the home Internet boom: airline ticket sales. Before this industry was computerized it took days to book an airline ticket. With computerized seat booking systems, it became possible for travel agents to get a confirmation number over the phone and issue a ticket for a customer within half an hour. In many ways, this was the first true e-commerce system and it set the pattern for a move to computerization of business information, particularly business information where multiple people needed read access to some or all of it at the same time or where multiple people needed instant feedback on an ability to change information (seat availability for instance). When business computing started out, it comprised a 'priesthood' of staff who ran the programs, submitted on punched cards, through the mainframe computer. The minicomputer industry moved things on such that interactive computing could be developed, with multiple terminals timesharing access to the power of a single machine. The wheel turned again in the late 1970s with the introduction of the personal computer and the emergence of the first home computers. This gave individuals the full power of a machine at their own disposal, with removable data storage for transfer between machines. It was the introduction of the personal computer that led to the modern office with a PC on almost every desk.

The social impact of computers was felt first in the job market. Those with a talent for programming, or even just operating the complex machinery of the early computers, were few and far between. As computers have become ubiquitous, most people in white-collar employment have been more or less forced to develop at least basic computer skills. This has also led to a huge new industry in personal and business computer training. Good programmers are also still in demand, which will be music to the ears of most computer science students, no doubt. However, the difficulties of modern computing are often more about identifying the problem to which computer power can be applied, than in getting the computer to perform an understood task. Without the computer revolution, various other social changes would not, of course, have been possible.

The Rise of the Content Industry

Since the Stationer's Guild was granted a monopoly on the printing of books in the United Kingdom (see Chapter 12), there has been a significant commercial sector whose primary purpose is to act as the middle man between the producers and consumers of information. There have been many revolutions in the content industry. Sometimes companies use their existing market strength to move into new markets and sometimes they miss the boat and are superseded. It is interesting to consider the differences in producer and consumer relationships to different forms of content, particularly since there is a growing convergence in both content itself and the companies providing different forms of content.

The social effects of various technologies are often as much to do with the amount, variety and accessibility of various forms of content. While telegram, telephone and e-mail systems all allow many-to-many communications, the content industries rely on the interest of a large number of people in communication from a small number of people. The requirements of one-to-many distribution systems are very different from those of many-to-many systems, although the Internet is providing convergence on some of these aspects.

Consider the production of books. The effort it takes to produce a book written out in long hand with few mistakes in grammar, punctuation and flow of information is immense. To distribute that book to a large number of people each one has to be hand copied, which introduces further mistakes. It is far easier to have a typeset edition which is copy-edited and proofread by people other than the author and significant errors corrected (it is easier to spot the logical, spelling and grammatical errors in someone else's writing than in one's own – when reading one's own, work one reads what was meant rather than what was written, whereas another reader does not have the memory of the intended text). Films require even more people with different skills to produce a finished product which many people will wish to see: story writers, script writers, directors, editors, actors, developers, special effects producers, and so on. In order to supply the demand of the general public for information and entertainment at an affordable level, various compromises are made, sometimes enforced by law and sometimes necessitated by market forces. Copyright is one of those compromises (see Chapter 12 for a much deeper discussion of this issue); another is the acceptance of advertising during television programmes.

Advertising is a particularly interesting aspect of content industries. There are two basic methods of funding television broadcasts: subscriptions and advertising revenue. It should be noted that the television licence fee in the United Kingdom is simply an enforced variant of a subscription system. Advertising was the dominant form of payment for about 50 years, to the extent that the placement of advertising slots even dictates the story format for television shows. One of the distinct differences between made-for-television movies and made-for-cinema movies is the obedience to advertising slots by providing mini-climaxes or cliffhangers to keep the viewer watching the programme through the advert break.

A perennial debate amongst arts critics is the translation of stories between media. Is it really possible to produce a good movie from a novel or to produce a good computer game based on a movie? These days, brand recognition among a wide population is the starting point for many projects, leading to some convoluted genealogies: from Spider-Man comics to the Spider-Man cartoon television show, Spider-Man novels, Spider-Man radio plays, Spider-Man movies, Spider-Man computer games and back to novel and comic-book adaptations of the movies. The outcome of this cycle sometimes becomes heavily ironic. There have been many interpretations of Bram Stoker's classic vampire novel *Dracula* in a variety of formats including film, television, radio and even re-interpretations in written form, such as Fred Saberhagen's Book *The Dracula Tape*. When Francis Ford Coppola titled his version *Bram Stoker's Dracula*, despite being a radical re-interpretation (from such a title one might be expecting a more faithful version), it becomes highly ironic that Fred Saberhagen and James V. Hart were commissioned to produce a novelization of the film. So, when searching for 'Dracula' and 'Bram Stoker' in book catalogues, there is *Dracula* by Bram Stoker and *Bram Stoker's Dracula* by Saberhagen and Hart.

The Rise of the Internet

Although it has been in existence for over 30 years now, the Internet only really emerged into the consciousness of the general public in the late 1990s, primarily due to the development of the Web, which allowed inexpert users to access readable and nicely formatted documents through a simple and intuitive interface. While there had been commercial Internet (and other online) service providers around before that, it was the Web which paved the way for ordinary companies to make significant use of the Internet for communication with their customers. Until the advent of the Web, Internet information provision by companies for customers was usually limited to software companies providing updates. Once the Web came on the scene, however, a feeding frenzy gathered pace, with everyone scrambling to 'be online', to do e-everything. The normal rules and expectations of business plans, identified revenue streams, accountability and sustainability were abandoned. Some businesses survived, often more by luck than judgement, but most were gone as soon as the tolerance of the venture capitalists and banks dried up. The results of the dot com bubble and the aftermath of its bursting included instability in stock markets, ridiculous swings in the technology job market and an overcautious attitude even to well-planned sensible ideas for online business. The upside of this was that there were some less obvious successes and failures of what looked like sure things, all dealt with in a very compressed time frame. Even now, sexual material aside, web sites which make money purely by charging for access to information are relatively few in number. What has succeeded best is access to traditional goods or services which are individually identical and mass-produced, which can easily be delivered or required delivery anyway. In general, things which require individual fitting have been less successful in online sales.

The most successful dot com company to date is Amazon. Starting out as a US online book seller, it has been franchised out to various other countries, including `amazon.co.uk` in the United Kingdom, `amazon.de` in Germany and `amazon.co.jp` in Japan, and has branched out into providing various other types of goods, with a different mix for each country. The first move was into music and movies, a fairly obvious expansion as there are distinct parallels with books: the homogeneity of stock, the small size allowing for ordinary postal delivery, the existing advertising by the publisher for the individual items. It would be easy to think that Amazon is simply an online storefront operating in exactly the same way as an ordinary store, but this is not the case. There are substantial differences. When a customer comes to Amazon's site, if they identify themselves then they may be provided with a personalized 'store' – impossible to do for everyone in a physical shop. In a real location the advertising displays are the same for everyone whereas in Amazon's virtual location there can be as many displays as there are books in the store. One significant way in which the personalization of the online store can be produced is to compare an individual customer's prior purchases, and even searches and browsing, with other customers' activities, and with both publisher and user categorizations of items. Physical stores have long tried to identify appropriate items to display next to each other. Ideally, suitable potential 'impulse buys' are displayed next to probable 'deliberate purchases'. This is done with great success using relatively naive algorithms that mine the activity of Amazon customers. Their highly successful recommendation system even admits feedback from individual customers: as well as not recommending for further purchase books they have already bought from Amazon, the recommendations list allows users to differentiate between items that they are not interested in purchasing either because they are not interested in that book at all or because they already own a copy.

While Amazon has arguably been the most successful online-only business, and online book sales in general are quite successful, another general area which has seen a significant shift to online purchasing is the travel business, particularly airline tickets. In an interesting parallel to the early days of business computer usage, individual purchase of airline tickets was one of the early adopters of Internet selling and has been instrumental in some major changes in the industry as a result. So-called 'bucket shops' or aggregators have been around in the travel industry for quite some time, but the necessity for shop premises, or huge advertising budgets to run a mail order business kept their number limited. Seat pricing on air tickets is an incredibly complex business and it has been suggested that seat availability changes so quickly that it is impossible to ensure that the absolutely best price for a particular trip is being found because by the time it is identified and a decision made to purchase it, one or more aspects of the price may have gone up or down. The introduction of the Web was an incredible opportunity for seat consolidation agents to bring their product to a much larger market. Sending airline tickets through the post generally costs next to nothing compared to the other transaction costs and so is lost in the financial 'noise' of the business; the recent introduction of e-tickets (boarding cards are provided on production of suitable ID and a reference number matching the booking), allow purchasing of flights to be completed wholly online.

The package holiday market is a related industry that is making great use of new technology developments, combining television presentations on cheap satellite and cable broadcasting and even booking via interactive digital television, together with Web-based booking services. Since the purchase of a holiday is done entirely remotely anyway, the advantages for many of doing their own price (and other aspect) comparisons online often outweigh the cost of commission at a high street travel agents. Finally, the explosion of no-frills, low-cost airlines in the last few years depends heavily on direct booking over the Internet. One of the main reasons such airlines can offer ridiculously low prices for travel is the lower cost of selling tickets provided by direct booking only (no agents' or sellers' fees and no contracts preventing airlines from undercutting their resellers) and the ability to advertise constantly changing prices. These airlines are effectively offering a strange type of auction for a limited resource which disappears for the seller if not sold.

> e-ticket: an airline ticket which is not physically held by the passenger but is held in the airline's computer system and accessed by showing suitable ID

This brings us on to our final area of study for the rise of the commercial Internet, which is online auctions. One of the potential strengths of the Internet over previous forms of communication technology is its many-to-many nature: telegraph and telephone are one-to-one communication media; print and broadcast media are essentially one to many; the Internet raises this to a many-to-many model, which can radically alter the economies associated with it. This is nowhere better illustrated than by eBay, the most successful of the online auction sites. Online auctions, where ordinary individual offer the goods for sale as well as buying them, make use of the fact that, while the move from one-to-one communication to one-to-many communication provides an economic efficiency level that has essentially linear growth with respect to the number of people using it, a many-to-many system enjoys efficiency levels dependent on the square of the number of people using it. So, four people using a one-to-many system is twice as efficient as two people using it. But four people using a many-to-many system can produce efficiency gains of up to eight times as much as two. There is a great deal of economic theory about the way auctions run. There are a great deal of variables: how rare an item is, how many people are interested in buying it, what value they place on it and so on.

The obvious benefit of online auction systems for individuals and small businesses is that they provide an infrastructure for bidding and paying, as one might expect, but the biggest thing they provide is a system of trust. By providing a feedback mechanism for both buyers and sellers, eBay provides a mechanism for trusting other sellers without paying for expensive escrow payment and delivery systems (i.e. the cash-on-delivery service offered by parcel carriers, such as UPS). Such escrow systems tend to have a minimum fee which militates against their usage for low-value items: the financial benefit to both seller and purchaser would be lost in the escrow fees. While it is possible to abuse the eBay reputation system by building up a good reputation and then committing fraud, this is still usually an illegal act and will generate police investigation if done on a sufficient scale. eBay's control mechanisms, dependent on identification via physical address, bank and credit card accounts, are sufficient to prevent all but the most dedicated serial fraudster, and such people have more lucrative options available such as advance fee fraud. The fact that the majority of people are naturally quite honest, particularly when there's a visible (though not necessarily enforced) honour system in place, is demonstrated by the success of eBay and other online auction systems. eBay has not only created a market based on the 'one man's junk is another man's treasure' principle but it has also allowed for the sale of virtual items from online computer games (see Chapter 3), thus creating completely new markets. A substantial number of people have entered the trading market, particularly in specialist goods, through eBay and other online auction sites, many of them now entirely self-employed at such work. The online auction house has removed entry barriers for such trading and in fact the lower overheads of small traders can now compete with the economies of scale of large traders, leading to a more efficient market.

CONVERGENCE

In economics and business studies, analysts talk of two forms of integration: horizontal integration, which reduces the number of players in a marketplace or merges two related marketplaces, and vertical integration, which reduces the number of steps in the chain from raw material to eventual consumer. In this section on the convergence of commercial entities involved in new technologies, we present issues involving both types of integration, sometimes at the same time.

Content Producers and Distributors

One simple way to avoid transaction costs is to merge with a supplier. This is particularly effective where the supplying and consuming businesses deal solely or primarily with each other and do not 'play the field'. There may be other reasons, such as quality control, for consumers to wish to merge with suppliers. The biggest internal problems such mergers produce tend to be management difficulties in combining businesses which had completely different goals up to that point. In particular, companies which excel in business-to-business supply of material may find it difficult to cope with contact from individual consumers. Similarly the consumer-facing organization may not appreciate the difficulties faced by the supplying organization. This often leads to a 'local optimization' problem where existing structures (particularly the two formerly separate organizations) still try to maximize their separate benefits instead of global optimization for the company.

In the television business, there have been cycles of joint and separate production and distribution, differing between countries. International sales of television programmes have also added to the confusing mix. As television technology advances towards more channels, often more specialized in their content, and Internet connections become faster, video on demand becomes a more and more compelling idea for the future of television. In expectation of this, content production and distribution companies have been jockeying for position. The biggest merger of this kind, and one of the largest corporate mergers ever to take place, was the AOL and Time Warner merger in 2001 (see 'The Biggest Media Merger in History' feature).

Government regulators are particularly concerned about such mergers because of the dangers of monopoly activity in production and distribution acting against the interest of the public which wants high-quality material sold at the lowest possible price. Vertical integration between large producers and distributors may give rise to market abuse and potential monopoly abuses. In other fields, some producers may be trying to bypass distribution companies, in whole or in part, by offering their products directly to the public through online sites. While this may seem an attractive option, it does have some difficulties: distributors tend to be unhappy at being undercut, or even competed with, by producers and may threaten to withdraw their custom, which can undermine the viability of the company in the short term; customers may expect lower prices when buying direct from the producer, particularly where retail prices have been justified in terms of distribution costs, such as in the music-publishing business.

The Biggest Media Merger in History

In January 2001, the largest US online service provider AOL bought media giant Time Warner in one of the largest mergers ever seen, paying over $103 billion (see 'AOL, Time Warner Merger Announced' at `www.pbs.org/newshour/bb/business/aol_time_index.html`). Poised at the beginning of the home broadband Internet boom, the merger of a content-production and old-media distribution company (Time Warner) with the new breed of virtual distribution company (AOL) seemed a match made in heaven. Two years later, the stock price of the new AOL Time Warner company had fallen by 90% and eventually, in late 2003, the company dropped AOL from its top-level name and reverted to Time Warner, although retaining the AOL subsidiary.

Was the move ill-fated from the start, was it ill-timed or did poor management doom a potentially revolutionary move in the media market? The collapse of the dot com bubble months before the actual merger should have rung alarm bells in the boardrooms of both companies. Founded upon a belief that new distribution methods for old and new content were on the horizon, the merger proved an expensive flop and dragged the new company's stock price well below even the spectacular falls in the high-technology stock market. There are startling similarities in the exuberant expectations of those involved in AOL Time Warner and those of the dot com bubble itself: unrealistic expectations of the ability of an economic market to change overnight. After four years of dismal results and heavy debt, the signs of the real digital delivery revolution in entertainment are just beginning to emerge: digital downloads of music have just begun to outstrip physical CD sales; Sony have announced a plan to make 500 of their back catalogue of movies available in digital download form and broadband access from home is finally reaching a significant minority of European homes at a price they can afford and are willing to pay. So, AOL Time Warner may have been on the right track but their expectations overestimated the capacity of the market to change.

Platform Producers and Content Producers or Publishers

The home video game console market is highly unusual in its structure. The dominant platform is currently the Sony PlayStation, despite only entering what was already a mature and very competitive market in 1994 (in Japan, 1995 in the United

States and Europe). Key to success in this market (which is analyzed in more detail in Chapter 3) is the games, since it is the games that both provide the revenue stream (the consoles themselves are subsidized by the manufacturer) and create demand for a particular console because of the games available only on that platform. However, games production is very costly and quite a risky business – as risky as making movies. Console manufacturers therefore allow, indeed encourage, third-party publishers and developers to create games for their consoles although, in order to maintain the revenue stream from games, they require publishers to submit their games through quality assurance tests run by the manufacturer and to pay a licensing fee in order to get appropriate encryption codes which allow their games to be loaded onto the consoles. There are some remaining tensions, however, since the manufacturers are also developers and publishers of their own games and there are consistent rumours of the quality-control process, in particular, being used to gain an advantage in the games market, particularly where similar games are due to be released by both the manufacturer and a third-party developer around the same time.

There have been (sometimes successful) attempts in other markets to use similar business models. The problem with such models is that they tend to be fragile: a shift in the available technology or a new competitor can swiftly completely undermine market position and leave a company in very poor financial shape. An example is in the photographic-film market. While Fuji and Kodak dominated the market for ordinary film for decades by competing on price and quality against other manufacturers, Polaroid retained a strong position in the instant-camera market. Unfortunately for Polaroid, the rapid rise of digital cameras with display screens undercut their business model which was based on providing very-high-profit-margin, instant-developing film, protected by a number of patents.

Another example is in the computer printer market where some strange interpretations of the Digital Millennium Copyright Act (DMCA) have been presented in court in attempts to prevent third-party suppliers refilling, or creating alternative, cartridges for printers (`www.theregister.co.uk/2003/01/10/lexmark_unleashes_dmca_on_toner/`). The legal arguments have claimed that the chips in their printer cartridges that talk to the drivers via an encrypted communication protocol are a 'technological protection measure', bypassing of which is illegal under the DMCA.

In Europe, such arguments have been rejected at least partly due to environmental concerns regarding the huge amount of landfill material being produced by printer cartridges, typically produced in non-recyclable plastics.

Corporate Production vs Individual Creativity

The early days of many technologies are very often a time of great opportunity. Those who come into the market with the right ideas can become major players very quickly. This was true in the music publishing industry, where some of today's biggest players can be traced back to player-piano-roll makers. It was also true in the movie-making industry where MGM, Paramount and United Artists are still well known names, although now part of larger conglomerates. All of these generally still required fairly large investments of capital at the beginning in order to succeed. An interesting area which did not require such capitalization was the computer-games industry. As recounted in Steven Levy's Hackers, the early computer game market was full of people who had developed a business in their spare time and some of those companies are still big names in the market (Ultima started as a text-only adventure game and is now one of the best known massively multiplayer online role-playing games (MMORPGs)). Individuals in both the United Kingdom and United States continued to make big splashes on various home computer platforms throughout the 1980s and into the 1990s with such major hits as Manic Miner (for the Sinclair Spectrum) and Lemmings (for various home computer platforms) and even Tomb Raider. In the modern mature games market, however, breaking in with a major title is almost impossible. Part of the reason for this is the demands of gamers: they expect top quality in all aspects of the games, from story to interaction to graphics (both artistically and technically). In addition, the marketing of computer games is now on a similar scale to that of movies. In fact, the computer games industry now grosses more than cinema takings, although associated revenues for movies including tie-in game rights maintain a market lead for the movie industry overall. New delivery mechanisms such as downloading games rather than buying them from a store, would seem unlikely to break the hold of the big games publishers. However, other games sectors than the console and home computer are showing signs of small scale development re-emerging. Games for mobile phones currently enjoy a similar level of graphics to the early consoles and computers, as do set-top boxes for digital cable and satellite television. In fact, many early console or home computer games are being re-released in these new formats, bringing old names, such as Atari, back into circulation and providing a resurgence of individual creativity in game production. Since handheld technology is becoming more and more powerful, and we are seeing convergence between television, home computer and other entertainment systems, this is likely to be a short-lived resurgence. However, the new distribution channels may lead to an advantage for smaller development-oriented firms providing new content for existing software platforms, such as 3-D game engines like Quake, Doom and Tomb Raider. A new business model similar to the console hardware–software market might even develop based on an engine–content split. Some small-scale versions of this already exist, with editors for various games being released in ‘update’ game packs allowing fans of a game to release their own extra levels.

> Massively multiplayer online role-playing game (MMORPG): an online game in which a large number of players interact with one another in a virtual world

Market Sector Integration

As their existing markets mature, companies frequently seek to expand their profits by moving into other areas. Usually they concentrate on related fields. A prime example of this in the technology arena is Microsoft’s recent move into the video game console market with the Xbox. Following Sony’s lead of the mid-1990s, coming from nowhere to market leader within a few years, Microsoft have sunk hundreds of millions of dollars into their new venture. On occasion, the very success of their marketing has threatened the venture, with higher demand than anticipated for the consoles (which lose money in the short term) at times driving that division of the company back to the central coffers for further funding. As the installed base of the console matures, Microsoft will expect to begin to see a return on their investment. However, the high basic cost of the Xbox hardware combined with the fact that Microsoft did not own the manufacturing facilities (unlike Sony who were already a major player in the general consumer electronics market) has led Xbox to be far less profitable than PlayStation for an equivalent installed base. The timing of the launch was not ideal, either, coming during a worldwide downturn in the economy which leads to a lower spend on luxury items, such as games consoles and games for them. Xbox has not made an operating profit for the parent company, even at the point where the successor platform (Xbox 360) was launched to keep up with Sony and their PlayStation 3 release. Microsoft, one of the world's biggest companies, has also dipped its toes into a number of other spheres, some more obvious than others: these include the mobile-phone-cum-PDA world, where they are competing with Symbian (the offspring of Psion), Palm and various companies pushing Linux-based machines. Since this is basically a market for small-machine operating systems, this is a fairly obvious move. Slightly less obvious is an attempt to move into the home entertainment electronics market, until one realizes that what Microsoft are trying to do is put a standard PC, running Microsoft software of course, at the heart of an integrated TV–DVD–audio entertainment system.

Many of the large manufacturing concerns of the Far East are already conglomerates in a variety of both technology and large-scale manufacturing or engineering markets. So, whereas Hyundai may be best known for cars in the West, in their home country of Korea they are known for everything from shipbuilding to machine tools, dominating the Korean manufacturing economy. This is due to the rapid development of an industrial base in such countries where there were no existing major local competitors for business and thus the largest corporations could easily move into other markets, but could frequently successfully export in only some of their areas of production. In some cases, it can be more difficult for a large organization rooted in one field to move into a new field than for an entirely new enterprise to enter that same market. This is due to organizational inertia and mistaken expectations within the original company. A new organization does not bring such baggage along.

Of course, there are also companies, or more commonly group brands, which specialize in moving into well-established markets and breaking the mould. The British entrepreneur Richard Branson, with his Virgin brand name, is one such example. This approach is typified by identifying a market in which the existing companies all operate in a cosy low-competition field and where few are willing to take risks. Consider the Virgin Mobile brand for instance. At a time when the major UK mobile phone operators were saddled with huge debts from 'buying' spectrum-broadcasting rights for 3G services from the UK government, Virgin bought up 'spare' bandwidth at wholesale prices from another operator and sold this on to customers at a very competitive rate. Their flamboyant advertising and cut-to-the-bone pricing has made them a significant player in the UK mobile phone market even without their own network of masts. The Virgin Mobile brand was later sold to the dominant cable television provider NTL along with the right to use the Virgin brand in Internet, cable television and landline and mobile phone services. This 'quadruple play' service provision is fast becoming a necessity for providers in the United Kingdom. Satellite television company British Sky Broadcasting bought a small ISP to add an Internet service to its existing telephone and television services, while links with Vodaphone may provide both the fourth element and a 'TV to mobile' service. Elsewhere, 'content' providers, such as Google and Earthlink, are also emerging into the access provision field with their municipal WiFi contract with the city of San Francisco, CA, United States (`news.bbc.co.uk/1/hi/technology/4896104.stm`).

Third-Generation Phones, First-Order Mistake?

When the so-called third generation (3G) of mobile phone services were defined, it was clear that the radio spectrum bandwidth used by existing digital, mobile-telephony services could not be reused and so new regions of spectrum would be needed. In what was regarded as something of a stroke of taxation genius at the time, a number of governments set up an auction for licenses to the new spectrum. In some countries, such as the United Kingdom, Germany and Canada, the existing lucrative digital mobile-telephony market, combined with the late effects of the dot com bubble led to highly inflated bids, on the order of hundreds of millions of dollars (significant revenue even for a G8 nation). The perceived problem of being 'left out' or 'left behind' led to a bubble of investment in spectrum allocation. In economic and business terms, an auction should have been the correct method of determining the economic value of the licenses to use spectrum for 3G. Unfortunately, conducting an auction during an economic bubble is a recipe for an economically inefficient outcome. In a highly competitive market, this would not have caused significant problems but certain elements of the mobile phone market mean that it led to significant negative effects.

The worst aspect of it is the investment in infrastructure which was required for the development of widespread 3G access. When combined with the up-front nature of licensing fees, due well ahead of the associated revenue stream, the auction significantly delayed the rollout of 3G services. Having paid large amounts of money for the licenses, no telecommunications company with one of the new licenses had the immediate financial resources to make the appropriate level of investment, nor any incentive to sublicense the investment to competitors – there were, anyway, very few competitors who did not have a license (and the associated cashflow problems). As 3G phones have finally rolled out in the United Kingdom, these effects may have run their course but the overall economic competitiveness of the UK technology industries may have been crippled for a significant period of time (for instance, BT scaled down its global ambitions largely because of the debts incurred by the 3G license auction then mostly withdrew from the mobile phone market by selling off its mobile arm as O_2: `news.bbc.co.uk/1/hi/business/1323096.stm`).

Did the UK government put short-term revenue generation ahead of long-term economic success and general public benefit from an up-to-date mobile telecommunications infrastructure and should lessons be learned for future similar situations, or was this simply another element of the dot com bubble which will recur in future bubbles but which the government could not (or should not try to) avoid? More information can be found at `news.bbc.co.uk/1/hi/technology/2198401.stm`.

If it is deemed too much of a risk to enter a mature market, one option is to buy an existing player in the market and it is in this fashion that multimedia content production and distribution empires have tended to grow. Whereas book, magazine, newspaper, radio and television all used to be run by specialized organizations focussing on one or two of these areas, we now have groups that include multiple areas, such as Vivendi Universal (which includes European television company Canal+, Universal Music and Movie Studio, Universal Games and French telecoms) and News Corporation (which includes Fox and Sky television and movies, newspapers and book publishing). In previous decades, many Western countries have had strong regulation covering ownership of multiple channels of information dissemination but this has recently been relaxed, though not without opposition from people concerned with the concentration of power allowed by ownership of multiple 'trusted' channels of information.

Digitization

Particularly in the content-publishing industries, but also in the consumer-electronic industries, there has been a rush to 'digitization' as though moving from analogue to digital concepts is always an improvement. However, ask any hi-fi music buff and they will tell you that the best amplifiers available are still analogue ones. The main reason for this is that sound produced in speakers and heard by our ears is an analogue signal. There are sometimes benefits to 'digital' technology over analogue technology but, as shown by the (digital) telegraph and the (analogue, now finally going digital) telephone there are waves and cycles between analogue and digital methods of information transmission. In the last two decades of the twentieth century there were a number of high profile moves across to digital technology, replacing widespread analogue technology. Each of these had well-publicized advantages, but there were also some negatives which were often ignored, and which must be considered as technology and society moves forward again.

Mobile phones

The move from analogue to digital mobile phones was the shift from first to second generation. The move to third-generation phones (high-speed data transmission) is now underway.

Advantages

Digital mobile phones require much less power to broadcast and receive their signals. Thus the handsets for digital mobile phone services were able to be smaller and lighter and also had much longer standby and connection times for the same battery size and weight. Digital signals can contain error-correction elements, allowing for fewer problems with interference from other radio sources. Smaller aerials also allowed the phone to become smaller and not to need a 'pull-out' aerial.

Digital signals can be encrypted much more easily than analogue signals, using public-key encryption protocols. Analogue mobile (and home-based cordless) phones were notoriously easy to eavesdrop on with readily available scanning equipment. While eavesdropping on digital mobile phone conversations is still possible, it is much more awkward and requires more expensive and bulkier equipment.

The lower power requirements for digital mobile signals also allowed for fewer phone masts to cover wider areas or for a larger number of masts to cover smaller areas which has the other benefit of increasing the density of maximum number of connections possible within the same geographical area – very important for high-density business areas, such as the City of London.

Disadvantages

Mobile phone infrastructure is very expensive to install: a mobile phone which is only usable within a small geographic area is not as attractive a product to the consumer. In moving from analogue to digital services, mobile phone operating companies had to maintain their analogue service for existing customers at the same time as developing their digital service for the new customers. This created an entry possibility for new firms who could compete in the new digital segment of the market without the drag of maintaining an analogue service. This is often the case where major investment in infrastructure is required: there is a window of opportunity for new entrants into a market which normally has very high entry barriers.

In addition to the cost to operating companies of the new investment in transceiver stations, customers faced a cost in upgrading their handsets. In order to encourage take-up of the new digital technology, operating companies offered new digital handsets at subsidized prices (sometimes even 'free') providing customers signed up for a long-term contract with the company. This remains a standard practice within the industry but has become something of an albatross around their necks: no company has found it profitable to break ranks as it is deemed too risky a strategy. This has added to the financial burden of upgrading to a digital service, leading to operating companies building up large debts based on estimates of income. When these income streams failed to materialize at the levels expected, the operating companies (sometimes existing landline network operators) were crippled by the debts. The frequency of free or cheap handset upgrades is now a competition element between providers, but this almost certainly encourages more frequent upgrading of handsets than if the customer had to bear the cost directly (all customers bear these costs through higher call and standing charges). Replaced but working mobile phones are a significant source of waste electrical products in many countries now, although recycling of working handsets to developing nations is becoming more common.

Television

While only a minority of the population of the industrialized world had an analogue mobile telephone when digital services became available, analogue television reception was near universal. There are three main methods of broadcasting a television signal, each of which has both a digital and an analogue version: terrestrial broadcast, cable delivery and satellite broadcast. Each television market has different proportions of the population using each type, due to market, geographic and regulatory factors. Moves towards digital provision of signal have moved at a much slower pace than the shift in mobile phone services.

Advantages

Digital television broadcasting shares the advantages of digital mobile telephone services in that error correction allows for higher quality transmission at lower power. The result of this, however, is much more noticeable in television than in telephony. In particular, the ability of a single mobile phone station to maintain more simultaneous connections is not of much interest to the average user, who can only make one call or message at a time (although the new data transmission ability in 3G does now have an impact). While the same is true of television (most people will only watch one channel at a time), the range of options is more important in a one-to-many broadcast system such as television, compared to a one-to-one communication medium such as telephone (conference calls still count fundamentally as one-to-one communication). The potential for encryption of digital broadcasts has also caused a significant shift in the potential of television broadcasts: multiple channel availability and subscription-based services have created a wide variety of services, as covered in other chapters, such as Chapter 3.

Disadvantages

As with digital mobile telephones, digital broadcast of television required a significant investment in new transmission and reception technologies. As with mobile telephones, operating companies have invested heavily in subsidized new equipment for consumers, which takes capitalization away from the production or purchase of content. The number of new channels allows for a much more specialized targeting of content but also spreads the resources of production companies much more widely. Advertising income from targeted channels may be higher (due to their targeted nature) but is more often lower due to the reduced number of total viewers. In such a difficult market, commercial players are increasingly unhappy with subsidized state television services, such as the BBC and PBS, taking viewer share.

Television-based access to the Internet through set-top boxes was expected to become a major avenue of interaction but has so far turned out to be rather a limited proposition: the resolution of television screens is not sufficient for much of the Web content, and those used to using the Internet through computer have not changed their usage whereas those not used to use of the Internet have not found the limited television Internet experience to be any easier to follow.

Digital television services are still undergoing major changes although it will still be many years before any nation is completely digital. Some countries are pushing such services forward centrally. In the United Kingdom, the government plans to switch off analogue terrestrial broadcasting by 2010 (there are also moves to switch off analogue radio broadcasting). Judging by the experience of satellite broadcaster Sky, this date may be brought forward: Sky switched off its analogue satellite broadcast earlier than expected after the vast majority of its customers switched to their digital service quite quickly once the end was nigh for the old service.

Global Media, Local Regulation

Are there any truly global media players or are there simply national broadcasters who reach a global audience? A large proportion of the world's population may have heard of one or more of CNN, the BBC and Al-Jazeera, but a smaller number have viewed them and an even smaller number view them regularly. Multichannel television's market penetration is growing in both the industrialized and the developing world and so access to such services is growing, and indeed access to CNN, BBC and Al-Jazeera is often quoted as a driver for rollout of multichannel television. The introduction of English-language Al-Jazeera and the launch of the US Fox News channel in the United Kingdom have led to a debate about the validity of national regulation of foreign services (particularly news) broadcasting substantially unchanged from another jurisdiction.

In the United Kingdom, specific standards of decency, lack of political bias, and public service broadcasting have been in place since the early days of radio broadcasting. As with many other areas, however, such as the Yahoo Nazi memorabilia case (see Chapter 4), the difficulties of applying national standards to the international communications arena have begun to impinge on television regulation. The UK approach has been to withdraw from many of its previous regulatory requirements for foreign broadcasters (though they still apply to national broadcasters) such as the public service and political balance requirements, but to retain other regulations such as decency and the limited censorship (mostly post hoc and aimed at issues such as incitement to violence). While television broadcasting flows through recognized and centralized channels such as cable and satellite, this is a sustainable approach, but as television broadcasting moves towards video-on-demand (whether satisfied instantaneously or after a delay and delivered via the Internet), this will become more problematic.

Music publishing

One of the early moves to digital publishing was the adoption of the compact disc digital audio standard for music, which replaced the decades-old, vinyl 45 rpm and 33 rpm record formats for the bulk of music publishing. Specialist productions are still available on vinyl distribution but it is a tiny proportion of the music market. The move to digital music was extremely successful – generating new revenues for publishers as consumers replaced their old vinyl with the new digital medium.

Advantages

Compact discs sound better to most people in most circumstances than vinyl records. It would probably surprise most to know, therefore, that on good-quality equipment (high-end home systems, not even professional-level equipment) vinyl records actually have higher quality output than compact discs. The benefits to the consumer are not simply the move to a digital format, although newer digital formats such as super audio compact discs (SACD) and DVD-audio have raised the standard. The benefits include smaller size and less fragility (CDs are smaller and less easily damaged than vinyl records) as well as better value for the majority of consumers – cheap CD players do produce better quality output than cheap vinyl record players, due to the usual issues of error correction and digital rather than analogue reproduction of sound. In addition, a CD can contain significantly more music than a standard long-play vinyl record and no loss of quality is experienced, compared to the difference between a 45 rpm and a 33 rpm vinyl record.

Disadvantages

The primary disadvantage for the consumer has already been mentioned for the other technologies: replacement cost of both the medium and the player. A certain amount of collectible merchandizing was also lost with the move to CDs: every CD can be a 'picture disc' but they must be a standard size and shape (well, almost, since there are non-circular CDs but they are very rare).

For the music publishing industry, the main disadvantage of the CD did not appear for many years, until the format was well established as the primary medium: that of perfect digital copying and transmission. Making a vinyl record is a relatively expensive business. There have always been professional unauthorized copying organizations, but the individual was restricted to making an audio cassette copy which was lower quality and which degraded at each 'generation' of copying. With compact discs, once recordable discs using the same format as standard audio discs became cheap and writers became commonplace, then everyone could copy their CDs and pass them around as perfect copies to their friends. Copies of copies were no longer any worse than the original. This was, of course, nothing compared to the introduction of the MP3 format, which compressed compact disc tracks to such a small size that they were downloadable even at dial-up connection speeds over the Internet. The music industry is now rather regretting its adoption of technology which it does not control and has been trying desperately in recent years to regain control of the technology by various means (see Chapter 3).

THE BIG CHALLENGES AHEAD

Technological changes almost always prompt social and economic changes as well. The introduction of the telegraph put the Pony Express out of business (increasing the speed and reducing the cost of transmission of letters but increasing the time and cost of sending small parcels quickly). Player pianos and sound recording and playback technology led to a significant decrease in musical training and sales of instruments and sheet music. Televised election coverage led to the election of actors to major political posts. The Internet is allowing small local businesses to compete with multinational companies on a more level playing field. It is not only each technology on its own that causes these changes but the synergy of multiple technologies feeding off each other creates the biggest changes. The world is simultaneously getting bigger and smaller: everyone now knows when a bomb goes off halfway around the world, within hours or even minutes of the explosion. The information one has about the daily lives of people in far away places makes each individual's world a bigger place: each person must come to terms with the knowledge of greater suffering elsewhere while continuing their own struggles in life. Yet the world is becoming smaller as well: contact with individuals anywhere on the globe is now possible: a solar-powered satellite phone can connect to the global information network from anywhere on the surface of the world, without any need for infrastructure development. The speed of technological change is still increasing. Economic decisions influenced by major technological developments are becoming more and more risky. Social pressures due to technology are becoming the subject of major policy debates and public lobbying, from privacy to content control to copyright. Whether technology will allow the few to control the many more fully than at any other time in history or whether the same technologies will lead to increased freedom, respect and democracy is the big question.

DISCUSSION TOPICS

Fit for Purpose?

The proliferation of communication technologies in their modern world have led to various non-technical people using inappropriate modes of communication. Far too few people actually think about their mode of communication but use whatever is to hand. Each mode of communication has its own benefits and limitations. It is not hard to think of examples of people sending an e-mail where a quick phone call (or even a visit down the hall to a colleague's office) would have been more appropriate. As the choices both diverge and converge (in form and transfer technology), this trend is likely to continue unless communication literacy begins to be taught. Which are the most and least appropriate methods of communication for the following circumstances?

- Sending a reminder for a small overdue payment (such as a library fine).
- Inviting someone to an informal party.
- Asking someone out on a first date.
- Arranging a date with a long-term partner.
- Thanking a colleague based in the same building for their presentation in a recent meeting.
- Asking a senior manager to act as a personal referee in a job application.
- Sending a formal request for more information in response to a job advert.
- Asking for warranty service on a piece of equipment.
- Reporting a burglary to the police on return from holiday.
- Reporting a burglary to the insurance company on returning from holiday.

E-Tax

Industrialized nations tax various things to fund government expenditure. Almost all of them tax individual income and company profits. However, they also tax transactions of various sorts, including retail transactions. Whether it is called

Value Added Tax (VAT), General Sales Tax (GST) or just Sales Tax, it all amounts to the same thing: taxing people when they spend money in certain ways. The rate of taxation can vary substantially depending on where the item is bought and what it is. Some jurisdictions exempt certain things from this taxation (in the United Kingdom, for instance, books are free of such taxes) or have different percentages on different items. In the United States, sales taxes can include different taxation levels due to different levels of government: state, county and city taxation. Where most transactions are carried out in physical locations with both seller and buyer present it is clear which jurisdiction's rules apply at the point of sale, but difficulties can arise when goods are bought in one jurisdiction and 'imported' into another. In the United States for instance, some states have significantly lower sales tax than neighbouring ones (generally replacing sales tax revenue with property taxes). This leads to people within a reasonable travelling distance of the border shifting jurisdictions for their shopping. The customs-union element of the US constitution pretty much prevents state governments from imposing import taxes on goods brought back into the state this way.

The growth of e-commerce over the Internet has brought this same problem into the international arena in a big way. Of course, mail order firms have always been able to ship catalogues to people in other countries and then send goods, but it is only really with the rise of near-universal holding of credit (and now debit) cards and charging that this has become a sufficient problem for governments to consider. The small amount of sales tax avoidance from international mail order companies was not worth governments' efforts in chasing the lost taxation. However, with many things now bought and sold over the Internet, it is as easy for a buyer to purchase goods from overseas as it is to buy from a local supplier. Improvements in international parcel shipping efficiency has also led to the cost of shipping coming within the margins of price differentials between jurisdictions and quite often below the level of sales tax which can be avoided. Worldwide shipping on light goods (such as DVDs) is now cheap enough that web sites routinely offer all prices as inclusive of shipping to anywhere in the world.

Many jurisdictions already had laws imposing import duties and local sales taxes on goods purchased by mail order, but the problem is that these rules, and their enforcement, are quite inefficient. In the United Kingdom, for instance, purchases of CDs and DVDs from Amazon.com now routinely attract import duty and sales taxes imposed by HM Revenue & Customs and collected via the postal services. Orders from smaller retailers in the United States, Canada and Australia do not (particularly if the boxes in which they ship their goods are not plastered with their logo). Books from Amazon.com, of course, attract no duties as they are currently exempt in the United Kingdom.

There are significant debates in many jurisdictions about how to prevent a significant drop in sales tax revenue due to overseas sourcing of goods via the Internet. One suggestion would be to impose local duties on sellers of goods, but this would suffer from the same problem as in the United States: states that impose low or no sales tax would gain disproportionate benefit of web sales over those imposing significant tax levels. Imposition of taxes and duties at the borders is much more expensive than mandating collection (generally under threat of imprisonment for falsification of transactions) by the seller. For instance in the United Kingdom, the ‘collection fee’ of the Royal Mail for duties and VAT often exceeds the cost of the duty and VAT itself, which is annoying since there appears to be no way of arranging to pay the duty directly and avoid such costs.

Will increased international use of web-based stores destroy the utility of sales tax systems? Tax systems, like all other aspects of government, are simply seen as an acceptable (to the population) and efficient (for the government) way of raising money. If they become too difficult to implement governments will have to find new ways of raising their revenues.

Competing with Free Beer

The collapse of the dot com bubble showed that the inflated value placed on simply getting hits on a web site did not automatically translate into revenue. One of the biggest problems of the bubble was the willingness of investors to put money into schemes that measured their success by the number of visitors to an information site without having a method of translating those visits into income. One of the attractions of the Internet to most users is its similarity to a public library: huge amounts of information available without a gatekeeper charging a toll for access to it. This attitude to the Internet as the world's largest public library has made users reluctant to pay a subscription to access a site. The collapse of the bubble has made this situation worse: many good ideas for web sites now find it impossible to attract sufficient funding to develop their infrastructure while keeping subscription rates sufficiently low to be attractive to individuals. The high minimum charges on traditional payment systems such as credit cards also discourage micro-payment systems (where pennies or even fractions of pennies are paid for each download).

The revenue model most enamoured by early web information providers was that of broadcast entertainment systems on television and radio, where free-to-air broadcasts were funded by advertising revenue. However, as we discuss in Chapter 3, this model is now beginning to break down as the number of channels increases and the number of viewers therefore decreases for each channel. Each viewer only has a set amount of disposable income, which in the end is what funds advertising as part of their purchases. Reductions in broadcasting and production costs have so far kept commercial broadcasting ahead of the game, although subscription income for television channels is now a significant revenue stream as well. On the Internet the expectation (and indeed the fact) of availability of much information for free has kept subscription systems to a small portion of the market, mostly purchased by institutions such as universities and, funnily enough, public libraries. The ease with which individual citizens can publish information undermines many standard business models, such as that of the traditional encyclopedia. The growth of community-sourced, information-provision efforts, such as Wikipedia or subject-specific blogs and discussion areas, show that monetary gain is not the only reason people give of their expertise. Just as the free and open source software movements showed that software infrastructure can be developed communally and without a standard model of ownership, so communal efforts at information provision show that a single expert editorial organization is not the only way to provide useful and correct information, although counter-intuitive facts are in danger of being lost in such a world: controversial subjects such as the history of the

Israeli–Palestine conflict are subject to constant revision by extremists and there is a much greater proportion of poor information than in traditional sources (see www.theregister.co.uk/2005/10/18/wikipedia_quality_problem/ for an admission of this by one of the founders of Wikipedia).

Are the Encyclopedia Britannica, the Oxford English Dictionary and Webster's Dictionary doomed to die, replaced by freely provided online resources, or will new business models emerge that give us once again a small number of expert gatekeepers to wisdom, who are well paid for their efforts? See www.theregister.co.uk/2005/12/19/sanger_onlinepedia_with_experts/ for a possible taste of the future in this area.

RELATED READING

Hafner, K. and **Lyon, M.** (1996) *Where Wizards Stay Up Late*, Free Press, London. ISBN 0-7434-6837-6.

Joinson, A.N. (2003) *Understanding the Psychology of Internet Behaviour*, Palgrave, Basingstoke. ISBN 0-333-98468-4.

Levy, S. (1994) *Hackers: Heroes of the computer revolution*, Penguin, London. ISBN 0-14-100051-1.

Meyrowitz, J. (1985) *No Sense of Place*, Oxford University Press, Oxford. ISBN 0-19-504231-X.

Reeves, B. and **Nash, S.** (2002) *The Media Equation*, CSLI Publications, Stanford, CA. ISBN 1-57586-053-8.

Rheingold, H. (2003) *Smart Mobs*, Perseus Publishing, Cambridge, MA. ISBN 0-7382-0608-3.

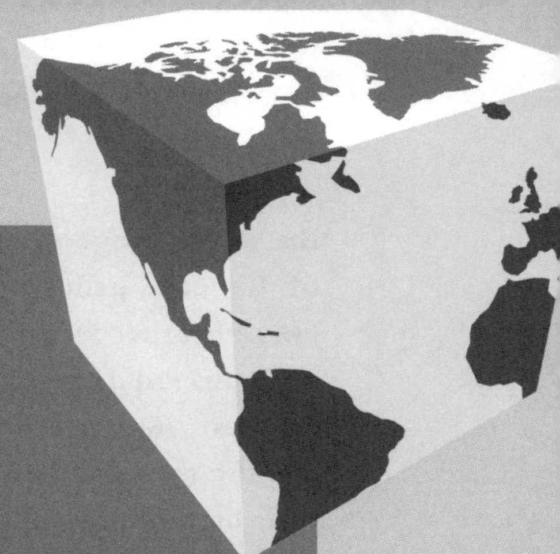

3

DIGITAL ENTERTAINMENT

INTRODUCTION

This chapter considers the impact of different types of digital entertainment on today's society. The entertainment timeline spans from the culture of the ancient Greeks through the centuries to the virtual gaming worlds of today, with each development necessarily impacting on the fabric of society. To put this in perspective, a recent study has shown that children spend so many hours watching television, playing video games and listening to music that their 'media use' could qualify as a full-time job (`foxnews.webmd.com/content/article/101/106496.htm`). The typical American child spends more than 38 hours per week as a 'media consumer' in media-rich homes comprising multiple televisions, CD and DVD players, radios, MP3 players, games consoles and PCs. Indeed, US children are less likely these days to live in a home with a single television than they are to live in one with five or more TVs. Children, however, are not the only consumers of digital entertainment technology: perhaps somewhat surprisingly,

the average age of computer and video game players is 33, the average age of frequent game purchasers is 40 and over 25% are over the age of 50 (www.theesa.com/archives/files/Essential%20Facts%202006.pdf). **Additionally, the older adult population, those over 65, are making increasing use of virtual arcades** (www.usatoday.com/tech/news/2004-05-12-gamer-demographics_x.htm) **and, by the time they reach 75, they will have spent the equivalent of 12 years of their life watching television** (news.scotsman.com/index.cfm?id=265852007).

Today's society embraces and uses many digital and online entertainment products in a multitrillion-pound industry. The global software games industry alone was estimated to be £11 billion ($17 billion) in 2001, with the United States (£4.6 billion), Europe (£4.3 billion) and Japan (£2.5 billion) being the key players. By 2005, this figure had risen to £21.2 billion ($32.6 billion) worldwide with expectations that revenues will increase further to £42.8 billion ($65.9 billion) by 2011 (biz.gamedaily.com/industry/feature/?id=11879). In the United Kingdom, 65.1 million games were sold in 2006 with a cumulative value of £1.36 billion, an increase of over 1% on 2005's record figures (www.elspa.com/?i=5894). As well as increases in retail sales of games, new distribution channels such as mobile and online games are increasing and by 2008 will account for 20% of the total Western world market (www.elspa.com/?i=3429). The film, Internet, mobile device and interactive television markets are also all fuelling the increased growth of the entertainment industry and its global penetration. Additionally, many of today's more general software and digital technology advancements can be attributed to the commercial forces of the entertainment industry and its globalization thereby further increasing the impact of this area of technology.

In today's consumer society, the electronic entertainment business plays a major role in national and global economies. The industry impacts directly on the key stakeholders of its core value chain and those associated directly or indirectly with it. All creative and software industries, such as video or computer games, film, television, music, computer software and books, may be said to share a similar structure based around the creation, publication and distribution of copyrighted material. Each of these products in their own right asserts powerful influences over the consumer and on those developing, publishing, distributing and retailing them as well as, in some cases, console and peripheral manufacturers and middleware and services companies. The video games industry in particular has exhibited rapid growth – video game titles are now bringing in more revenue than films released in the cinema (www.economist.com/displaystory.cfm?story_id=3387239). This has a knock-on effect on the rest of the entertainment industry; for example, music associated with games is getting more 'air play' to listeners than new music artists are achieving on the radio or MTV. As a result, some artists are releasing their songs on video games prior to full CD release, with tracks available to purchase through download sites such as iTunes (www.fantasymusicleague.com/artist.php?id=12218). Fierce competition is also arising between music stars and professional athletes to be featured on the cover of the video game boxes.

In this chapter, we examine some of the latest applications and trends in the entertainment industry and relate them to some of the social implications facing the information society. In particular, we concentrate on the effect of the industry on the consumer and whether increased uptake of the products of this industry is to the benefit or detriment of the consumer.

THE EFFECTS OF DIGITAL ENTERTAINMENT TECHNOLOGY

Digital Entertainment – Friend or Foe?

This section is primarily concerned with the ways in which people act and interact as a result of using digital entertainment. Depending on the study undertaken, computer entertainment has been shown to have advantageous or deleterious effects to the social welfare or health of the user population. Some of these issues are discussed in more detail in the following sections, particularly in relation to television viewing and games usage as these tend to be the most influencing and controversial of the entertainment types and consequently tend to be the focus of the majority of the studies undertaken. It should be mentioned however that there are some recognized problems in identifying trends and impacts of digital entertainment on the population. These are due in some measure to the lack of long-term, large-sample studies, which may account for some of the variances appearing in the statistics which often appear to directly contradict each other. For example, it is easy to see the short-term effects of games usage, but much harder to monitor the longer-term effects that may be caused by repeated game playing. There may also be problems of cultural specificity and of the choice of games selected for the trials. Consequently, this area presents ideal opportunities for further discussion. There are many ways in which we might have described the social implications of entertainment, however the approach taken is to outline a number of key themes and discuss associated social and ethical issues.

The Toy Town Divide

Video and computer games are an expensive commodity, as are many other entertainment devices and toy products that have been transferred from a purely physical medium into their electronic counterparts. The cost of electronic toys carries a premium and, perhaps more importantly, like other electronic items, electronic toys tend to have a relatively short consumer life which creates tensions and pressures for the 'user' to have the latest updated version with more processing power (www.dailymail.co.uk/pages/live/articles/news/news.html?in_article_id=431183). This in turn creates pressures on parents to buy these relatively expensive toys and, if they cannot be afforded, may well contribute to family unrest and a potential 'playground digital divide' with possible social exclusion from peer groups.

There may be further consequences related to the consumer demand from young adults and children for digital items and products which may encourage software piracy, unauthorized downloading of music files, and so on. There is also considerable evidence indicating that the visual impact of digital toys, mobile phones and electronic music devices such as iPods has increased the potential for theft and mugging (www.direct.gov.uk/en/YoungPeople/CrimeAndJustice/TypesOfCrime/DG_10027666; www.timesonline.co.uk/tol/news/uk/article717351.ece). These matters are further complicated by the close relationship between the technology employed and the visual fashion statements made by the equipment. For example, although owners of iPods have been warned that the machine's conspicuous white headphones have become a beacon to thieves and despite being given advice that wearing differently coloured headphones may make them a less attractive target for muggers, users have continued to wear the white headphones as a fashion and lifestyle statement. It appears that many users place a higher value on the 'coolness factor' of being seen wearing an iPod than they do on their personal safety (www.theregister.co.uk/2004/03/30/ipod_this_seasons_musthave).

It may be argued that the introduction and growth of digital entertainment and technologies has not created any new social issues in terms of those who can or cannot afford luxuries related to entertainment. However, there are clearly issues regarding the explosion in digital and visual communication such that there is an expectation that every household should have a range of broadcast and digital technologies available for use by the family. The online and virtual nature of this environment in itself creates the potential for a range of social divisions within a single household. Today's generation has been exposed to commercial pressures and freedom of information hitherto unheard of. It may be argued that games and games technology have provided a pleasurable pathway for the consumer to engage and participate in global environments which as yet have untested long-term social implications.

Boys and Girls Come out to Play: Stereotyping

Over the last 5 years there has been a substantial increase in the amount of computer gaming and the development of virtual environments across the world to support this craze. One of the major issues of debate in this arena is the question – who is the typical computer gamer?

Computer gaming has traditionally been regarded as a predominantly male activity. However, recent statistics indicate that this may no longer the case. A recent report by the Entertainment Software Association in the United States cites that women over 18 constitute 30% of the gaming market, outnumbering the teenage boys who are traditionally seen as the typical demographic. Statistics also show that 38% of computer and video game players are women, rising to 42% when considering online players. Of gamers who play for more than 10 hours a week, 30% are female. These trends are echoed in the United Kingdom where a study by the Entertainment and Leisure Software Publishers Association (ELSPA) revealed that while women do not play as many games as men, they continue to buy and play them as they get older, while male interest in this area declines over time.

Two interesting questions we should consider are: is there gender stereotyping within the gaming community and do females prefer the same types of games as males? Evidence has shown that women prefer different game elements to men. Although there are a number of games aimed exclusively at young females in the 6–11 age group, such as Princess Fashion Boutique which held the number one position in the children's PC game chart from May 2004 until July 2006, and a pink Sony PS2 was launched in December 2006, research has shown that adult women who participate in computer and video gaming do not want stereotypical games related to traditional gender-related issues such as cooking, sewing and baking (news.bbc.co.uk/1/hi/technology/5407490.stm). Research has shown that women tend to prefer games that are goal driven with an underlying narrative to indicate that they are doing something worthwhile ('Chicks and Joysticks', ELSPA white paper: www.elspa.com/assets/files/c/chicksandjoysticksanexplorationofwomenandgaming_176.pdf). For example, within a particular gaming scenario the primary aim of women players may be to 'save the scientist' with 'killing the enemy' being a necessary part of this. Conversely, in the same scenario, evidence indicates that males would tend to be more focused on 'killing the enemy' with the goal of 'saving the scientist' being of secondary importance. These differences and approaches may well be linked to the fact that women are not encouraged to express aggression in public and are less likely to feel comfortable with games involving combat or war. Women also like to take time to analyze facts and form a perfect solution while males want to complete the task quickly and move onto the next stage.

Two of the most popular games favoured by both men and women are The Sims and Sim City, both developed by Maxis Studios. The popularity of Sim City lies in the fact that both men and women like to build new structures; however, women tend to focus more on developing and enjoying the social context that surrounds the new environment. Other games that have been found to have appeal to women are Dancing Stage Megamix (PlayStation 2), because of the active nature of the game, and EverQuest: New Dawn, a fantasy and adventure game, which manages to combine its thriving social community with a continually updated game scenario.

As mentioned earlier, women in particular are attracted to the social element of gaming – both in terms of content and the participatory nature of interactive online environments. Another feature demonstrated by women in the gaming environment is their particular interest in competing as a team member and participating in competitive tournaments. Evidence shows that massively multiplayer online role-playing games MMORPGs are proving to be particularly popular with women as they can develop characters, solve puzzles and engage in social interaction. Within the organizational structure of these online gaming communities women are now playing an ever-increasing role in positions of authority. Evidence also indicates that a substantial number of mothers at home with young children have been entering the online entertainment and gaming environment. Although they may simply be accessing these games for their entertainment value, evidence also suggests that it is a way of alleviating their feeling of isolation from the outside world and a mechanism for sharing parenting experiences with others in similar circumstances.

It may well be that the future development of games and gaming technology will be predicated on cross-gender appeal. Other factors that need to be taken into consideration are the marketing of games so that they appeal to women and the fact that the technical game development arena is still very much dominated by men. This situation may well change over time as more women are attracted, through their increased participation in playing games, to follow a career in the technical aspects of games technology (www.igda.org/women/archives/2006/05/ucla_hosts_even.html).

Research results indicate that the key factors which would encourage increased participation of women in computer games are: interaction with a world beyond that which they can normally enter; better female characters and more of them; more realistic portrayals of women as game avatars; more gender-neutral content and a reduction in sexist game content; and acknowledgement that female gamers exist in terms of marketing and advertising. It is interesting to consider that women's magazines rarely if ever incorporate reviews of games as part of their editorial, while such reviews seem to be an almost compulsory part of magazines aimed at men.

Another area of gaming that is growing in popularity is the 'mobile' games market, which ranges from simple mobile phone games to those of the Nintendo DS and PlayStation Portable. The growth in the use of mobile phones is therefore playing a major role in introducing gaming to women who might not have bothered to explore it previously. Games publishers will need to consider the changing demographics of their client base as they can no longer rely on the traditional market of 19–30-year-old males and young children.

HEALTH-RELATED ISSUES

Curse of the Couch-Potato Children

As the population becomes more involved in the use of computer games, there is the possibility for this activity to become their main focus and hobby. If this is the case then growing numbers of individuals will displace active physical pursuits such as sport and recreation in order to find space and time to continue their gaming activities. The lack of opportunity for cardiovascular development and large muscle movement may well be a contributing factor leading to growing obesity and ill health in the general population. More particularly, this may have a serious effect on very young children and young adults who are being increasingly exposed to this expanding marketplace.

Lifestyle changes in the form of more sedentary jobs, changes in public attitude to sport at school and a general increase in office jobs over manual labour have contributed to the major concerns regarding the health of the population. These trends, combined with changes in diet have led to a serious rise in the level of obesity not only in adults but more alarmingly in young children. It may well be argued that the exponential growth in the use of information technology and its translation into digital media products and the electronic gaming world adds a further dimension to these health issues. Increasing numbers of the population are now playing games, communicating online, watching interactive television, participating in activities such as online shopping and gambling and generally spending more and more time in relatively static positions.

Recent research highlights this alarming trend in the levels of obesity. In 1980, 8% of women and 6% of men were classed as obese; by 2002, these figures had risen to 23.5% of women and 21% of men (`www.iotf.org/oonet/uk.htm`). The 2002 statistics also show that, in addition to obesity, a further 46% of men and 33% of women are overweight (some 24 million people in the United Kingdom alone). In the United States, the figures are even worse with a third of the adult population being classed as obese (`win.niddk.nih.gov/statistics/`). In terms of child obesity, this currently affects one in ten 6-year-olds and one in five 15-year-olds with almost a third of 10-year-olds worrying about their weight.

Research (www.food.gov.uk/multimedia/pdfs/foodpromotiontochildren1.pdf) indicates that while children are watching television, their eating habits are being influenced by their exposure to an advertising regime which generally promotes an unhealthy eating lifestyle. In recent studies, scientists at Liverpool University have confirmed that television food commercials have a direct effect on what children eat. Their research indicated that commercials, particularly those for high-fat snacks, encouraged children to raid the fridge and select snacks high in sugar and fat. The research also found that obese and overweight children were those particularly vulnerable to being influenced by these commercials.

Obesity is reported to reduce the lifespan of an individual by nine years (www.nwph.net/nwpho/Publications/nwh_v2_4.pdf) and increase risks of cancer, diabetes, heart attacks and strokes. For example, weight-related diabetes, a disease more common in overweight, middle-aged men and women, is now being found in children as young as 13 (www.timesonline.co.uk/tol/life_and_style/health/healthy_eating/article491478.ece). The obesity epidemic in children is further exacerbated by almost 20% of them not participating in any organized sporting activity at school and a similar percentage not exercising in their own time. In addition to the health issues the cost to the state is continually rising.

To help address the issues of obesity and unhealthy lifestyles, governments are now advocating the banning of advertisements which promote junk food to children (news.bbc.co.uk/1/hi/health/6154600.stm). Government officials are also in talks with the broadcast media to encourage them to promote healthy pursuits and healthy lifestyles through popular entertainment and children's programmes. One example of this, aimed at children aged four to seven, is the programme LazyTown and its superhero Sportacus who battles Robbie Rotten, a junk-food-eating villain (www.timesonline.co.uk/tol/newspapers/sunday_times/britain/article1290332.ece). Recently, the launch of the Nintendo Wii games console, with its innovative controllers and range of sports-related games, also encourages players to become part of the action by swinging a golf club or throwing a ball rather than relying solely on button presses to drive the game (wii.nintendo.co.uk/9.html).

Such developments are important because, if the sedentary lifestyle of children persists, experts are predicting that we will soon create a generation of children who will die before their parents.

Physical Problems

Adults and children who spend prolonged periods of time playing computer games or watching television increase their risk of suffering from deep-vein thrombosis (DVT). This life-threatening condition has also previously been associated with restricted movement and lack of leg room among air travellers, and predominantly affects the elderly, the overweight and those taking certain medication. Recent research (news.bbc.co.uk/1/hi/health/3441237.stm) has shown an increasing number of occurrences of DVT in younger persons. Although DVT can occur in people who have apparently normal healthy lifestyles there is cause for concern that computer gaming and excessive time spent watching television may well be contributing to the increasing occurrences of DVT, particularly in young people (www.tcd.ie/tsmj/2004/Nintendoisation.pdf).

It has also been suggested that children who watch excessive amounts of television may develop sleep problems as they grow older. In a recent study, scientists monitored 759 people at the ages of 14, 16 and 22. Although none of the 14-year-olds exhibited problems sleeping, it was found that those who had watched three hours of television a day were more likely to experience problems falling asleep or waking during the night when they reached 16 or 22. One possible explanation for this is that watching television leaves them in a state of heightened alertness and physiological stimulation thereby preventing them from falling asleep with ease. The bright light of the television may also disturb their sleep–wake cycle. Children who watch television late into the night may also not be receiving the full recommended amount of sleep per night, increasing the risk of problems with their metabolic and immune systems as well as causing fatigue and depression (pediatrics.aappublications.org/cgi/content/full/104/3/e27).

Endless playing of computer games has been blamed for a range of other health-related problems. For example, increasing numbers of children are suffering from 'nintendonitis' – a repetitive strain injury (RSI) brought about by excessive gaming. One of the first recorded cases of computer-related RSI seen in a child occurred in 1999; the young gamer was treated in a local hospital after having played computer games continuously throughout the Christmas holidays! This condition, also know as tendiopathy, has become increasingly common in recent years amongst children who use high-tech gadgets such as PlayStations or mobile phones (news.bbc.co.uk/1/hi/health/5063364.stm).

It is widely accepted that headaches can be caused by playing computer games for long periods of time in badly lit rooms with poor posture and being too close to the computer screen. Rather more controversially, video games incorporating flashing lights, special figure patterns, scene changes and screen flicker have at times been blamed for triggering epileptic seizures, with children between the ages of seven and 19 being most susceptible and up to 150 individuals being affected each year (Graf et al. 1994). Conversely, a number of other studies have reported that, although some people may discover they have epilepsy through playing computer games, there is no evidence to support the view that computer gaming is the cause of the epilepsy, however it may well be that it is the trigger for an episode (www.epilepsy.org.au/photosensitivity.asp).

Although rare, there have been a number of cases where computer games may have contributed to the death of a player. For example, the playing of computer games was attributed as the cause of death for a South Korean man who died after playing computer games continuously for 50 hours without stopping for food or sleep (www.netaddiction.com/seminars/main_index.htm). In another reported incident, a mother from Louisiana unsuccessfully sued the games manufacturer, Nintendo, after her son died during a marathon games-playing session where he hit his head on a table after suffering a seizure while playing with the console (www.metro.co.uk/news/article.html?in_article_id=39315).

Digital Equipment – Part of the Modern Family

A survey in 2003 by the National Opinion Poll for the Early Learning Centre found that a third of under-threes had a television in their bedroom and that four out of every five children aged under six watched up to 6 hours of television per day. Indeed by the age of six, the average child has already watched television for more than one full year of their lives. Children aged 11 to 15 spend 55% of their waking lives watching television and using computers. This amounts to 53 hours a week, 7.5 hours a day, and represents a 40% increase in a decade (Sigman 2007).

The Government's education watchdog has issued a warning that using television as a virtual 'baby-sitter' is helping create a generation of children whose speech and behaviour is at an all-time low. There are reports that some young children are having difficulty integrating and relating to the basic activities required to start their formal education at nursery and primary school. Some of these young children exhibit behaviour indicating highly undeveloped social skills such as the inability to fasten buttons, use a knife and fork or eat and drink at a table. Research indicates that some children who have long periods of exposure to television may develop speech and communication difficulties (media.guardian.co.uk/site/story/0,14173,1265792,00.html). For example, some children entering nursery struggle to develop their vocabulary, have difficulty speaking clearly and have difficulty understanding instructions.

Young children are in some cases being mesmerized by the television screen and its constantly changing images. However, there are conflicting views with regard to the effects this has on the development of the child. Some experts believe that children's television viewed by very young children can damage their language development, while others believe that in similar circumstances exposure to these programmes can only be of benefit in the language learning experience. Specialist speech therapy advice suggests that adults should limit the amount of time children spend watching television and that the remainder of the time should be replaced by adults spending more time talking and reading to children, helping them to develop their verbal and communication skills.

Evidence suggests that as a society we are becoming addicted to electronic equipment such as television and computers and that this addiction is being passed on to our children. One of the perceived dangers of this is that we are now seeing a generation of children who in many instances are forming closer relationships with their computers than they are with other humans. This is evidenced by a recent survey in which almost one in five youngsters said that the time they spent at the keyboard made them happier than when they were with family and friends. This trend clearly threatens the continuance of the traditional family unit. Evidence also indicates that some children tend to treat their computers more like a family member than a piece of electronic equipment. Many youngsters call their PC a 'trusted friend', are 'extremely fond' of it, talk to it, pine for it when they have to switch it off and are jealous if they find their PC being used by someone else. Some even come to believe that the machine has a personality of its own. A separate survey conducted with 2500 people found that 37% of children and 34% of adults surveyed thought that by 2020 computers would be as important as family and friends (technology.guardian.co.uk/online/news/0,12597,1154989,00.html). Evidence reported in The Media Equation reflects that, subconsciously, adults tend to attribute human characteristics to computers, although they are reluctant to admit this even to themselves.

The effects of prolonged exposure to television and television programmes requires more long-term studies to understand the effects this social experience has on young children. Modern lifestyles now include working parents with young children coping and living in environments which are media rich and available 24 hours per day. It may be argued that young children left to their own devices will develop a range of social and technical skills related to their own personal requirements to interact with television. Conversely, the same rich media used properly within the household may form an integral part of the education process, encouraging study skills and widening the horizon of the young individual (see Chapter 15). The National Literacy Trust provides a good series of links to studies related to the impact of television on children (www.literacytrust.org.uk/talktoyourbaby/TVnews.html).

Does Television Cause Adverse Social Behaviour?

There is a belief by many researchers that children's attitudes to relationships and events are strongly influenced by their exposure to television programmes. Research indicates that violent behaviour occurs in a large number of television programmes and to such an extent that, by the time they reach 18, children in the United States will have had the opportunity to observe more than 16 000 simulated murders and over 200 000 acts of violence (judiciary.senate.gov/oldsite/mediavio.htm). Another study undertaken in the United States reviewed 10 000 hours of broadcast programming between 1995 and 1997 and found that 61% of the programmes contained violent scenes, many of which portrayed this violence in a glamorous context.

Since 1960 there have been over 3500 research studies undertaken to examine the relationship between media violence and its association with actual violent behaviour. In all but 18 of these studies, relationships have been identified between children's behaviour when exposed to violence on television and the likelihood of them displaying aggressive behaviour immediately after viewing the programme. A smaller number of studies have also shown that these changes in behaviour may have long-term effects. Effects of media violence have been variously described as causing above average aggressive behaviour, desensitization to violence, anxiety, depression, sleep loss and nightmares. There is also a possibility that when children are viewing 'unbelievable' violence in superhero films they develop implausible notions about the body's ability to withstand injury (www.telegraph.co.uk/news/main.jhtml?xml=/news/2005/09/16/nhang16.xml).

An example of how children's attitudes are influenced by viewing television programmes is highlighted in the BBC television programme Child of Our Time. The children in this study were shown elements of a television programme where an actor is seen to cuddle a life-sized doll. After watching this, the children were led into the room and were observed to mimic the actor by caressing and stroking the doll. Later, the children were shown another scene where the same actor was striking the doll with a large wooden hammer; this time, when the children were led back into the room they were observed to furiously attack the doll and one normally shy and timid child was observed to completely lose control (www.open2.net/childofourtime/2006/morality1.html).

More recently, the focus of these studies has switched to examining the effects of indirect aggression (gossiping, etc.) within television programmes. An analysis of over 250 hours of soap operas and situation comedies showed that indirect aggression was present in 92% of the programmes and that 60% of this indirect aggression was committed by popular female characters with whom the audience could identify. A second study, involving 11–14-year-olds, demonstrated that watching television soap operas, situation comedies and dramas encouraged them to exhibit antisocial behaviour such as gossiping, spreading rumours, splitting up other people's relationships and verbal bullying (Coyne and Archer 2005). UK soap operas, such as Emmerdale, Eastenders and Coronation Street, were found to have an average of 14 indirect aggression incidents per hour. It has also been observed that many television programmes focus considerable amounts of viewing time on scenes related to drinking alcohol and frequenting public bars and clubs. These scenes are considered strong influencing factors such that young adults believe that this is a social norm and expected behaviour. The Big Brother-style of programmes with contestants and environments designed to provoke reaction have also been the subject of recent controversy (`news.independent.co.uk/media/article2193628.ece`). Another major point of contention is that young children can be seriously affected by the confrontational and sexual content of daytime television where they can observe stressful life scenarios showing adults arguing and behaving irrationally.

Television is a powerful medium and it may be argued that children are particularly vulnerable to the messages it portrays. While it may be accepted that stylized violence can be entertaining and often humorous in comedy and animation, in its more serious representations, for example, in children's drama, direct and indirect violence should always be editorially justified. It is vital that editors consider the consequences of violent programmes and the possible effects this may have on the viewing audience, particularly young children.

Creating Monsters – Do Computer Games Make People Violent?

One of the most emotive and hotly debated issues with regard to entertainment is whether or not the violence in some computer games has an impact on children. There is an argument that computer games are even more influential than television, due to their participatory and interactive nature as opposed to the more generally passive viewing experience of television programmes (news.bbc.co.uk/1/hi/health/720707.stm). A number of studies have investigated these issues but the findings are mixed and some of them are reported here to promote discussion. We have tended in this section to use the terms 'computer games' and 'video games' interchangeably except where explicitly stated.

It is reported that one of the reasons for including violence as a major theme in computer games is that there is considerable commercial demand from existing and potential users of the game; essentially, the consumer demands the violence and is willing to pay for it. Although violence has always been associated with computer games, the technological advancements of recent years have led to it becoming increasingly realistic (news.bbc.co.uk/1/hi/technology/6376479.stm). 'Blocky' white aliens being killed by 'blocky' white bullets have been replaced by pixel-perfect, real-world weapons which appear to kill real-world adversaries. For example, the defining characteristic of the Soldier of Fortune games is the extreme attention to detail of the weapons and the effects they have on the human body, to the extent that much of the game is centred around killing and the mutilation of bodies, rather than completing the game objectives. As the computer gaming experience becomes more immersive and the characters become more realistic in their movements, they become more influential in the minds of the gamers. A consequence of these developments is that some game users have great difficulty in distinguishing between the virtual world in which they have been immersed and reality.

Further technological developments will create even closer relationships between reality and the gaming environment. Currently, the interaction with most game environments is still through keyboard, mouse and joystick. The latest games are starting to incorporate immersive virtual reality environments, where the game user actually feels as if they are an integral part of the game world. With the removal of the traditional input devices, the game user now interacts with the environment through increasingly realistic controls which are modelled on reality (news.bbc.co.uk/1/hi/technology/6418779.stm).

In order to make modern games attractive to the marketplace, the realism concept is also modified: timelines are compressed in such a way that the less attractive and mundane aspects of life are hidden from the user. For example, users who are inserted into the cockpit of a high-speed jet would not want to spend hundreds of hours training before they could fly their first mission. In order to create sensationalism and excitement for the user, weapons of destruction are often digitally enhanced and lead to more mayhem than is possible with their real life counterparts. An example of this enhancement and distortion can be observed in the game Max Payne 2 (`www.rockstargames.com/maxpayne2`), a violent, film noir love story between a cop and a femme fatale murder suspect. The game's production involved a motion-picture stunt crew, professional talent for voice acting and graphic novels, motion capture and authentic digital source material from New York City. The game combines photorealistic city settings and realistic scenarios with cinematic styling features which enables the player to slow down their environment and avoid (in slow motion, similar to The Matrix) the bullets fired at them, an action that is obviously not possible in real life. Another unrealistic feature in many games, particularly at the easy levels of a game, is the ability of players to withstand repeated attacks and injuries which scarcely register on the characters' health meter within the game – again providing a distorted view of the consequences of human injury.

There is evidence from some studies that young children exhibit increased levels of aggressive behaviour as a consequence of playing computer games, at least in the short term. In tests, it has been observed that higher blood pressure and heart rates have been recorded during game play. However, other studies disagree with these findings with some even suggesting that violent computer games act as an outlet for aggression and could possibly have a calming effect on the player. References to some of these studies are found at the end of this chapter.

With regard to suitability of game content, the UK Video Standards Council reports that less than 1% of games are classified as suitable only for over-18s, while 90% are suitable for children under 15. Games which give particular cause for concern are those that promote areas such as gun culture and violence to particular members of society (e.g. 'ethnic cleansing' and racist games) and those that are based around real events such as the Columbine shootings and the 9/11 atrocity.

In general, it is thought that violence in computer and video games is not a problem for the vast majority of the population. However it may represent a cause for concern in the very young and in those who are psychologically unbalanced and who cannot distinguish video game violence from the real thing. To evidence this claim, studies have found that the older a player is the safer they are with regard to playing games. This is because they have a higher level of cognitive maturation and a more rounded and well-formed view of life and, hence, are less affected by the virtual scenarios presented in the game.

Grand Theft Auto: Murder Training?

Few computer games have caused as much controversy as the Grand Theft Auto (GTA) series. A combination of role-playing and action, the goal of GTA is to become a wealthy and respected criminal, through involvement in profitable criminal activity including, but not limited to, stealing cars. The various incarnations of the game to date have included elements of drug dealing, murder and prostitution as well as the eponymous stealing of cars. These games are among the few which dare to buck the trend and feature real anti-heroes as the main viewpoint characters in the game.

Although the games are pretty unrealistic and despite the availability of movies which glorify violence and criminal activity far more than GTA, few entertainment products have caused as much furore, including a number of lawsuits over the effect of playing the game on those who have gone on to perform similar criminal acts. Two recent (though not unique) cases involve teenage boys who have claimed that they were inspired in random armed violence by one or more of the games.

In 2003 in Tennessee, William Buckner (aged 16) and his step-brother Joshua (aged 13) took guns from their home and fired at passing vehicles on a nearby highway. They killed one man and injured his wife and later claimed to have been 'inspired' to enact scenes from GTA. A Miami attorney, Jack Thomson, has brought a lawsuit against the perpetrators, their parents, the Wal-Mart store who sold the game, and the Scottish production company who created the game (see `news.bbc.co.uk/1/hi/scotland/3680481.stm` for more information).

Also in 2003, Devin Moore of Alabama was charged with the murder of three law enforcement officials. He allegedly killed them when stopped on suspicion of driving a stolen car. He is alleged to have been an 'obsessive player' of GTA. Families of the victims are bringing a case against the retailers (Wal-Mart and Gamestop) which sold Moore GTA III and GTA: Vice City, the publisher (Take Two) and the manufacturer (Sony) of the console on which Moore played the games (see `www.theregister.co.uk/2005/02/17/taketwo_gta_lawsuit`).

The inclusion of the console manufacturer might seem the oddest aspect of this, but it must be remembered that games console manufacturers receive a significant portion of the sales income on all games for their consoles, and therefore are equally liable with the publisher and retailer. Similar civil court cases have been brought before for games including earlier versions of GTA. So far, none have been upheld.

Do Computer Games Fuel Addiction and Gambling?

Gambling is generally acknowledged as being addictive. Similarly, we all know how addictive it is to play computer games and how we play for increasingly longer periods of time in order to increase our scores, reach the next level, and so on. For most of us this amounts to little more than a recreational pastime. However for some individuals this becomes a more serious issue and can become an addiction. It has been noted that some children can exhibit addictive behaviour towards playing computer games and that this may manifest itself as compulsive behaviour, lack of interest in other activities, association mainly with other addicts and the experiencing of physical and mental symptoms, such as shaking, when attempting to stop the behaviour. Occasionally, addiction may also lead to truancy or crime to fuel the addiction.

The world's first summer camp for children addicted to playing games or surfing the Internet opened in Germany in August 2003, intending to show children that other activities can be just as rewarding as sitting in front of a computer screen. The new term associated with this problem is internet addiction disorder (IAD), although it is not yet recognized formally as a chronic psychological problem. The scheme, run by German social services and health departments, limited the children to 30 minutes of computer access each day and filled the remainder of the day with a range of outdoor events and activities. The addicts who, prior to the camp, had been accessing the Internet or playing games for more than 9 hours per day were also provided with daily counselling sessions and further advice regarding health, diet and lifestyle. Other camps have since been opened (`www.cbsnews.com/stories/2006/07/03/health/webmd/main1773956.shtml`).

EverQuest and Lineage

In Western society, the EverQuest MMORPG now regularly attracts as many players as the audience for major television programmes. In Korea and Japan, Lineage (and Lineage II) often attract more. Such games have even been cited in divorce cases as the cause of a breakdown in a relationship when one partner becomes obsessive about playing the game. Is there something inherently 'addictive' about such games, or are they simply the latest craze, soon to be replaced? Earlier crazes, such as skateboarding or the Rubik's cube, have affected primarily teenagers. MMORPGs are somewhat different to previous crazes, however, in that they provide an alternative virtual social setting. Both the complexity of the game worlds and the interactivity with other players provide an alternative 'life of the mind' which can be very appealing to those who do not feel fulfilled by their 'real life'. In a small number of cases such games even become the primary employment of players, selling the results of their endeavours for real-world financial gain (www.wired.com/news/culture/0,70153-0.html).

Is the popularity of these games, and the extreme nature of the involvement of a small number of players, something which should concern society? There are many ways in which self-destructive behaviours can manifest themselves. Some are very old (alcohol abuse) and others are new (obsessive online gaming). In themselves, and pursued in moderation, these activities are generally not seen as problematic. It is when they are abused that problems occur. There are two schools of thought about this. One is that people are vulnerable to different forms of obsession and that the more varied forms of behaviour available in the modern world 'push these buttons' on a wider variety of people. The other is that people who obsess over something are suffering from general life problems and that there are simply more and different expressions of this in the modern world. On balance, it seems that there is little evidence that such games are harmful overall although, as with everything in life, they can be abused, so family and friends of those in trouble should be aware of the signs of trouble. The issues raised here are covered further in (Swickert et al. 2002).

Children, however, are not the only ones to become addicted to computers. Many adults are falling into the gambling trap through the numerous gambling sites on the Web and, more recently, on interactive digital television. With the advent of digital gambling, it is no longer necessary for individuals to enter high-street betting shops. They can gamble from the comfort of their home without even getting up from the couch. Digital television services now offer live betting on major sporting events via the interactive television facilities and with dedicated betting commentary and updated betting odds.

Online gambling, interactive television gambling and, most recently, mobile phone gambling, gives access to gambling 24 hours per day and 365 days per year. This massive exposure will inevitably encourage more individuals to access the product and provide opportunities for those already engaged to become excessive users (www.thisismoney.co.uk/credit-and-loans/debt-news/article.html?in_article_id=409959). There is evidence to suggest that the perception of the value of money decreases when paying with virtual cash (credit card). There is also a lack of human contact to question and advise gamblers on the implications of their actions. For example, gamblers may not fully understand the financial implications of complex areas such as spread betting where the amounts of money to be lost or won are not easy to determine but can be substantial.

Online gambling is being blamed for a rise in the number of women gambling addicts as it presents a non-threatening environment in which women can bet (www.timesonline.co.uk/tol/life_and_style/health/features/article662256.ece). Another group at risk from these developments is senior citizens, many of them experiencing mobility issues (www.aoa.gov/prof/notes/Docs/Gambling_Older_Adults.doc). This particular group of individuals may be attracted to enter digital gambling sites and virtual casinos, initially for the novelty value, bearing in mind their lack of mobility, may then be enticed to bet more seriously as they spend more of their available time on the sites. A further risk that can be experienced by senior citizens is that, if they become online compulsive gamblers and lose, they have little chance of rebuilding their lives and replacing their assets. Already statistics indicate that senior citizens account for 2.6% of compulsive gamblers therefore there is clearly potential for this marketplace to grow. Research also indicates that 90% of people who walk into a casino walk out losers – and there is nothing to suggest otherwise for an online casino. It is not difficult to imagine that if this marketplace grows then many software developers and suppliers of online gambling products will modify their interfaces to allow individuals in this age range quick and easy access to the software. Indeed this is already the case in conventional casinos, where pull handles have been replaced by easy to use and highly visible buttons. Responsible developers of online gambling and gaming web sites should follow the model already adopted and used by established casinos and gambling organizations of having a social responsibility partner (e.g. Gamecare) on their site. However, it must always be remembered that making money is not easy – but losing money is!

POWER TO THE PLAYER – BENEFITS OF COMPUTER GAMES

As well as the numerous concerns raised about playing computer and video games, there is also evidence to show that there is a wide range of positive aspects that can result from the application and playing of computer games.

Harnessing the Power of the Brain

One of the most successful applications of computer games has been their use with biofeedback to treat children who are hyperactive or have attention deficit disorder (ADD). Originally developed by NASA scientists, computer games have been used to help these children train their brains to concentrate and focus their attention. Essentially, the brainwaves of the children playing the games are monitored and linked to the controls of the games so that when they produce the correct brainwave patterns, the performance of the joystick or game pad being used to play the game becomes more responsive. Importantly, it has been found that the lengthening of the attention span and calming effect of playing the game persist for a significant period after the game has finished. Similar techniques are now being used to help highly-stressed individuals to remain calm in stressful situations. NASA are also considering using these techniques as a method of training jet pilots to cope with the stress of combat while remaining in control of their highly complex aircraft (news.bbc.co.uk/1/hi/sci/tech/894673.stm).

Building upon this, work is under way to develop computer game products to help children combat ADD and provide a non-chemical alternative to the drug treatments currently prescribed (www.smartbraingames.com/view_products.asp). These games require the child to wear a modified cycling helmet which measures changes in electrical activity in sections of the brain and reports them back via a PC. The company has produced a series of video games based on table tennis, cycling and racing activities, each of which responds to the data generated by the brain and rewards high attention states and discourages the more distracted states; for example, if the child disengages with the task then the cyclist slows down but it wins the race if the child remains focused on the task.

Similar neuro-feedback techniques are also being developed by a US company, to help business professionals, golfers and other athletes achieve peak performance. The Peak Achievement Trainer is a software and hardware device that analyzes brain activity (www.peakachievement.com). In one study, they analyzed the brain patterns of dozens of golfers as they putted and it was found that there was a direct correlation between certain brainwave patterns and successful putting. It was found that golfers were most effective when they 'found the zone' achieved by getting their mind 'out of the game' and letting muscle memory do the work unimpeded. This is thought to be successful as it blocks out the anxiety in the shots.

Another game, the Journey to Wild Divine, recently released in the United States, is using heart-beat regulation as a means of controlling a game situation and, in doing so, promoting relaxation and calmness (www.wilddivine.com/Affiliate2). The game uses a mix of mysticism, high-tech graphics and biofeedback. This game has no violent scenes, but instead promotes a sense of calm with snow-capped mountains, domed temples and lush gardens. With no mouse, keyboard or joy-stick, interaction is via impulses from three fingers of the left hand encased in purple plastic clips attached to the computer. The player controls the actions of the game by changing their heart-beat rate. Levels of relaxation can be tracked by how well tasks such as keeping balls in the air are performed. Developers claim that the game helps individuals find inner peace by teaching them meditative skills that can then be used in everyday life. Such games are not predicted to replace violent computer games, however they may reach a new target audience or be used at different times by the same gamers.

Evidence has also shown that computer and video games can be used very successfully in reducing nausea in paediatric cancer patients receiving chemotherapy and in reducing their perceived levels of pain. A handheld video game has also been successfully used to help treat compulsive self-harming behaviour in young children (Gershon et al. 2003).

Education and Learning

There is evidence that children who have been avid game players for at least five years are often intelligent, motivated and high-achieving individuals who tend to be generally successful educationally, go on to college and obtain better than average jobs (www.guardian.co.uk/uk_news/story/0,3604,462243,00.html). Some studies have shown that students can significantly improve their arithmetic ability and motivation for the subject through game-play scenarios, while others have shown that there can be increased reading comprehension scores through game-playing training programs as an alternative to, or in conjunction with, more conventional teacher-based methods (education.guardian.co.uk/schools/story/0,5500,1336802,00.html). Other benefits include individuals developing high levels of hand–eye coordination, good reaction times, better social interaction, better pattern and rule generation and hypothesis testing and generalization, better spatial visualization and a developed sense of achievement.

Another recent study has shown that a simple computer program, Phonomena, can teach children to distinguish between sounds, dramatically boosting their listening skills by up to 2.4 years in just a matter of weeks (www.newscientist.com/article.ns?id=mg17924101.000). According to the UK Medical Research Council's Institute of Hearing Research, up to a fifth of all children have some problems hearing the difference between some sounds. A program such as this may afford them some significant progress. Independent tests to further establish the validity of these claims are currently being carried out.

While Phonomena has been specially designed to hone the listening skills of children, even normal computer games have been shown to improve visual skills (www.physorg.com/news93192187.html). Another advantage of using computer games is that they can be tailored to each child's individual need. Games have been used extensively in motor and cognitive rehabilitation after strokes and in helping students with learning difficulties to interact with everyday scenarios and assist with the development of their social skills. Games are also being used in virtual-reality therapy situations to cure phobias and trauma and to develop life skills (seriousgamessource.com/features/feature_053006_ptsd.php). Further discussion regarding such games is contained in Chapters 9 and 15.

Various forms of visual and audio entertainment have been shown to enhance study skills. For example, music when combined with exercise has been shown to stimulate the brain. Studies show that men and women perform slightly better on verbal fluency after exercise alone but significantly better if exercise is combined with listening to music. In a separate study, it has been shown that a short period of time spent relaxing watching daytime television can raise IQ by as much as five points with a further two points if a cup of coffee is consumed at the same time.

Another example of using games and visual media for educational purposes is in order to teach numeracy and literacy skills. One such multimedia product is the DVD of the film Spellbound, which enacts the story of a spelling competition. Not only does the film generate an interest in academic achievement, it also incorporates a range of special features designed to encourage and improve spelling, for example by including spelling games. This approach may help promote spelling in an age when text messaging seems intent on changing the traditional literary values. Further information on the impact of computer games on children's aggressive behaviour and learning abilities can be found at www.unitec.ac.nz/?1A61532B-FED5-4C57-85C3-60163A08462F, on the risks to children of using electronic games at www.ime.usp.br/~vwsetzer/video-g-risks.html

and on the benefits of computer games at www.bris.ac.uk/Depts/Info-Office/news/archive/mcfarlane.htm.

The Silver Gamers

Various studies with elderly adults have also shown a range of advantageous effects after playing video games for a period of time. These benefits may variously be evident as faster reaction times, improved self-esteem, improved perceptual motor skills, better concentration and focus of attention, improved coordination, better driving habits and fewer accidents in the home. One study has even found that games may be used to soothe the pain of arthritis.

Indeed, experts predict that computer games could eventually challenge bingo and bowling as the preferred pastimes of Britain's pensioners. The advantage of computer gaming is that elderly individuals do not necessarily need to leave their homes in order to pursue their pastime. To combat the potential isolating effect of pursuing their hobbies at home, online gaming may well present an alternative which will allow them to develop virtual communities.

In a recent study of 350 elderly people, 67% said they owned a computer, of which 50% said they played games. When 40 volunteers, aged 59–84 were given games consoles, including Nintendo's Gamecube, Sony's PlayStation 2 and Sega's Dreamcast, to gauge their interest almost all of them became engrossed in the activity. Given these figures, older people obviously represent a huge untapped marketplace for games companies (news.bbc.co.uk/1/hi/technology/3287891.stm).

Game Development Grows up – the Hidden Agenda

Games are intrinsically designed to be fun, however they may also be used in a more subtle manner to promote other agendas. This section briefly introduces a number of interesting applications where games technology is being used in this way.

One application area has been in army recruitment. In July 2002 a 'shoot-em-up' game was created and launched by the US army as a recruitment tool (www.

wired.com/news/technology/0,72156-0.html). The game was designed to show the nearly limitless career paths a soldier can follow in the army. The game was developed at the Naval Postgraduate School in conjunction with private game companies and was based on the Unreal game engine. This joint approach resulted in the scenarios looking realistic while still being able to be identified with commercial products such as Half-Life and Counter Strike, which was seen as critical to its success. This multimillion dollar investment in designing and maintaining the game for online play represented less than 0.5% of the army's recruitment budget and will be deemed cost effective if only an additional 300–400 enlist as a result of it. Feedback from some recruits indicated that the game portrayed only the action side of the job, with the more mundane yet frequent tasks being ignored. This has prompted the army to improve the game by including a more balanced and authentic feel to the scenarios. Further developments include adopting a more proactive approach to using the game, where online game users attaining high scores may be invited along to a recruitment and selection panel.

Games technology has been used in a range of training simulators including those developed for the military, racing industry and commercial airlines. An example of this has been developed by a major UK rail operator, Thames Trains, which introduced a new £1 million aircraft-style training simulator for train journeys. Using this simulator, staff can be trained and tested with the most unexpected challenges and environments. The system models all aspects of the journey including signals, curvature of the track, noise levels and weather conditions.

One of the most recent applications of educational computer games is a game developed especially to curb speeding by motorists. This game shows the speeding driver exactly how they may die if they continue to speed. People who are caught speeding on German autobahns are to be forced to watch on a laptop what might happen to them if they were involved in an accident. The projected accidents range from a minor shunt to a multiple car pile-up, with vehicles bursting into flames or ending up a mass of twisted metal. The pictures are accompanied by surround-sound and sometimes words flashing on the screen, 'Sorry, sir, you're dead'. Drivers can also push buttons to see what would happen when they apply the brakes at high speed. Police believe that forcing speeders to witness their own virtual accidental deaths will make them think twice before driving so fast again. The program works like a computer game, taking information from speed cameras along the route already travelled and using this to predict what would happen next. This program was introduced in Germany in March 2004. Initial trials have shown that although drivers were angry when they were stopped for speeding, they were found to calm down quickly when shown the game and the possible terminal effects of their actions. Further developments of this initiative include more research and its introduction to young adults in school.

Another more controversial application of computer games is the proposed introduction of PlayStation-style roadside tests (an 'impairment meter') to determine the level of alcohol impairment of a driver. If validated, this system could replace the traditional breathalyzer. In this system, drivers will have to complete tasks on a handheld computer to prove that their reaction times and concentration are up acceptable levels. The tests will determine if the driver is over-tired as well as identifying those who are incapable of driving through the use of alcohol. Drivers will be required to track an object moving across the screen with a pen-like device; periodically an object will pop up in the corner requiring the driver to press a button as they carry on following the line. The second test involves drivers responding to a number of signs flashing up on the screen. This new system is currently being evaluated by the UK's Police Scientific Development Branch in St Albans, Hertfordshire. Recent tests on 170 volunteers at two music festivals have been extremely encouraging.

Games technology is fuelling its own new economies. For example, one of the latest commercial developments in the gaming environment has been the growth of professional players, who build up stockpiles of in-game money, artefacts, even characters, and then sell them online (usually using auction systems such as eBay) to others in the gaming community with less talent or perhaps less time to play (`www.newscientist.com/article.ns?id=dn6601`). This trading in virtual objects draws a parallel with other trading operations such as stocks and shares or other virtual trading commodities. An industry is growing where participants in online games are paying for someone else's expertise to assist them to be successful in games such as Ultima Online. Taking this a stage further, there is now an economic and advertising crossover starting to emerge – a market offering virtual Nike trainers and Levi jeans with which to clothe your virtual avatars for a real-life price (uk.gamespot.com/pc/rpg/there/news_6077346.html). Some of the companies responsible for these games are attempting to stop sales of virtual artefacts in the real world, even to the point of taking legal action in an attempt to prevent online auction sites allowing them as legitimate trading objects. Sony have embraced this concept however, setting up the first auction site entirely devoted to auctioning the objects and in-game 'money' of online-gaming characters (www.newscientist.com/article.ns?id=mg18624973.600). They claim that their new system is being developed primarily to combat fraud by linking the objects on offer to the record of their existence on the gaming servers.

DISCUSSION POINTS

Should Computer Games Be Regulated? Rated? Censored?

In the United Kingdom and much (though not all) of the EU, computer games are subject to ratings similar to those applied to movies (whether at the cinema or home video). These ratings are legally enforceable and prosecution is possible, although relatively rare. In the United States, while there is a scheme (run by the Entertainment Software Ratings Board, ESRB) to classify games as 'suitable for adults only' or 'suitable for teenagers and adults only', it is entirely voluntary. In fact, efforts by some states (Washington, for example) to legally restrict such sales have been overturned by the US federal courts as infringement of free speech.

There are many arguments for and against legally enforceable or 'advisory' ratings on video games. Some of these arguments are common to ratings on all types of material (videos, books and magazines) and some are specific to computer games. We present here some of these arguments to stimulate discussion:

- Video games are unrealistic and so should not be subject to restrictions.

- Video games are interactive and therefore should be more heavily restricted than movies.
- If violence in entertainment is a problem then most children's cartoons would be banned.
- Ratings should be 'educational' not 'prescriptive' – it should be up to parents what their children have, not imposed by the state.
- If parents are happy for their children to have 'adult' material then they are entitled to buy it on their behalf; without legally enforced regulation, all children can buy material and hide it from their parents.
- Children are exposed to material in each others' homes and therefore will get hold of restricted material anyway.
- Trying to prevent children from accessing something is a sure-fire way to make them want to see or play it.
- Extremely violent video games are bad for everyone and should be banned from sale, not just sale to children.
- As we move from physical purchase to downloading or online play, regulation will be impossible anyway, so why bother trying?

Couch-Potato Syndrome

Much of the industrialized world, with the United States leading the way, is reported to be suffering from an epidemic of obesity. The most worrying statistics are those for obesity in childhood. One of the things which is sometimes held up as a cause of this is the amount of time children now spend watching television and playing video games compared to doing more physical activities. Are audio–visual entertainment opportunities causing children to get into a habit of inactivity or is their social environment encouraging them to inactivity anyway, with audio–visual entertainment simply their way of coping with the ensuing boredom?

Society is, in general, less tolerant of risk, particularly when those at risk are children. Laws in various industrialized countries now make it illegal to allow children under 10 or 12 to be unsupervised for significant periods of time. With an increase in the prevalence of both parents in a household working and the greater mobility of people reducing the availability of extended family, there are also fewer people available for supervising children's activities outside the home. The high profile of child-abduction cases in the media exaggerate the risks of children being the victim of such crimes. All these things tend to make parents want to keep their children within closer geographic boundaries than in previous years.

On the other side of the argument, we have the entertainment industries and the advertisers bombarding children with messages aimed to instil a sense that they're missing something if they're not watching all the television shows and playing all the games. Do games featuring skateboarding and cycling encourage children to see these games as substitutes for the real world activity? Is the ease with which skill in these games can be attained a disincentive for children to gain the whole-body motor control necessary for achieving the real-world equivalent and do the 'forgiving physics' of game worlds make physical activity seem less exciting than the virtual world?

Online Gambling: Menace or Natural Progression?

Gambling is a purely economic and virtual activity, except where regulated to be constrained to a physical location. In the United States, there have long been attempts to restrict gambling to certain physical locations. This has led to the creation of gambling centres such as Las Vegas and Reno in Nevada and Atlantic City in New Jersey, together with opportunities for gambling on horse racing supposedly limited to the arenas. Of course, these laws have not been completely successful in restricting activity. So, for instance, many bookmakers in the United States have long operated by phone. The combination of the trust required to take bets by phone and the illegality of the operations have kept such bookmakers outside the regulation of the law. In the United Kingdom, licensing of bookmakers has allowed a legitimate physical business to operate and hence the scope of 'illegal' gambling operations is much less. Taxation on gambling is kept to a limited level in order to prevent the incentive for members of the public to avoid the taxation by using unlicensed operators. The strategy of both the US and UK governments, of keeping gambling under tight (though different) regulatory regimes, is now under severe threat from the rise of online gambling sites.

The virtual nature of gambling combined with its huge profit potential combine to make it one of the most obvious candidates for transfer to an e-commerce model. Worried both by the potential loss of revenue from taxation and the potential harm that unrestricted gambling can cause players, governments are now struggling to regulate the online gambling world. Nowhere is the borderless world of the Internet more apparent than in the potential for online gambling. Since money is now as much bits and bytes as nickels and dimes, the transfer of gambling stakes and winnings is as easy as paying for books, CDs or a subscription to an Internet site. The international banking sector (and, in particular, the major online payment services provided by credit-card companies such as Visa and MasterCard and pure online services such as PayPal) has been pressured by governments into restricting use of their services for gambling. Jurisdictions where 'offshore' gambling sites are based (both in legal terms and the physical servers) are also being brought under great pressure to restrict access by citizens of countries where gambling is strictly regulated.

The same level of trust must be built up by online gambling institutions as for other online traders, and this can be undermined by the lack of protection offered by credit-card companies against gambling outfits. Whereas most credit-card companies offer guarantees on non-delivery of goods (they refund the money and, if too many purchases are not forthcoming, they close the merchant's credit-card account), few if any will make the same guarantees for gambling stakes, if they allow them in the first place. Some of the established European bookmakers have cashed in on the trust their high-street outlets have built up and are among the most successful legitimate online gambling sites. They are in strong competition with newer entries to the marketplace which often team up with the new cheap television channels or are run jointly by the same company. The low entry level of physical infrastructure required by online betting sites means that they can go from small start-ups to major sporting sponsors in a very short space of time. Once their sponsorship appears on mass-market television, they can compete with the long established players very well.

REFERENCES

Archer, J. and **Coyne, S.M.** (2005) An Integrated Review of Indirect, Relational, and Social Aggression, *Personality and Social Psychology Review*, **9** (3): 212–230.

Gershon, J., **Zimand, E.**, **Lemos, R.**, **Rothbaum, B.O.** and **Hodges, L.** (2003) Use of virtual reality as a distractor for painful procedures in a patient with pediatric cancer: a case study, *Cyberpsychol Behav*, **6** (6): 657–61.

Graf, W.D., **Chatrian, G.E.**, **Glass, S.T.** and **Knauss, T.A.** (1994) Video game-related seizures: A report on ten patients and a review of the literature, *Pediatrics*, 93: 551–6.

Sigman, A. (2007) Visual voodoo: the biological impact of watching TV, *Biologist*, **54** (1).

Swickert, R.J., **Hittner, J.B.**, **Harris, J.L.** and **Herring, J.A.** (2002) Relationships among Internet use, personality and social support, *Computers in Human Behaviour*, 18: 437–51.

RELATED READING

Kent, S.L. (2001) *The Ultimate History of Video Games*, Prima Life, London. ISBN 0-76-153643-4.

Levy, S. (1994) “Game Hackers”, *Hackers*, Penguin, London. ISBN 0-14-100051-1.

Meyrowitz, J. (1985) *No Sense of Place*, Oxford University Press, Oxford. ISBN 0-19-504231-X.

Reeves, B. and **Nash, S.** (2002) *The Media Equation*, CSLI Publications, Stanford, CA. ISBN 1-57586-053-8.

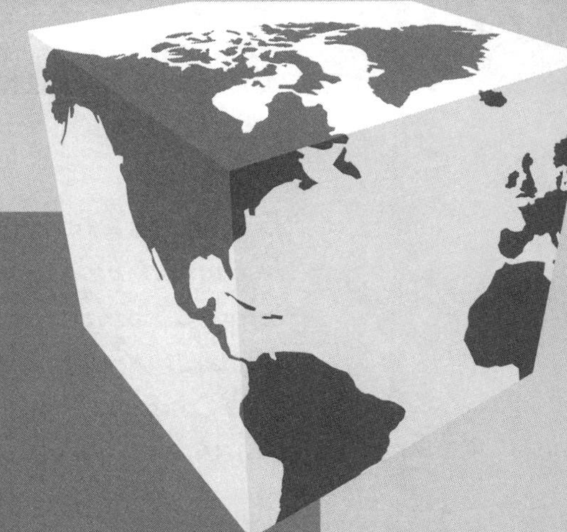

4

CENSORSHIP AND FREEDOM OF SPEECH

INTRODUCTION

There are two main issues about censorship online: freedom of expression and sex. This chapter deals with issues of freedom of expression and censorship, in the names of security, government supremacy, safety and defamation but not on the grounds of decency. Chapter 5 covers issues about attempted censorship of material due to its sexual content. Chapter 7 also covers the related topic of use of networking facilities in the workplace, such as for personal e-mail and browsing.

The human desire (one might even say 'need') to communicate seems to come only just behind our needs for air, food and drink. In societies where physical punishment is banned (or highly restricted), solitary confinement is often the ultimate punishment meted out to offenders who have already been sentenced to loss of freedom of movement and general action. Freedom of expression thus enjoys a high ranking in categorizations of human rights in many sources:

> *Everyone has the right to freedom of opinion and expression; this right includes freedom to hold opinions without interference and to seek, receive and impart information and ideas through any media and regardless of frontiers. Universal Declaration of Human Rights, Article 19 (United Nations)*
>
> *Congress shall make no law...abridging the freedom of speech US Constitution, Amendment I via the Bill of Rights*
>
> *Everyone has the right to freedom of expression. This right shall include freedom to hold opinions and to receive and impart information and ideas without interference by public authority and regardless of frontiers. European Convention on Human Rights, Article 10, Part 1*

It is interesting to note that only the European Convention on Human Rights explicitly qualifies this overall right with the often-assumed responsibilities and caveats to prevent abuse of such rights:

> *The exercise of these freedoms, since it carries with it duties and responsibilities, may be subject to such formalities, conditions, restrictions or penalties as are prescribed by law and are necessary in a democratic society, in the interests of national security, territorial integrity or public safety, for the prevention of disorder or crime, for the protection of health or morals, for the protection of the reputation or the rights of others, for preventing the disclosure of information received in confidence, or for maintaining the authority and impartiality of the judiciary. European Convention on Human Rights, Article 10, Part 2*

The right to freedom of expression, as with almost all rights, is not, can not and should not be regarded as paramount. Even the most ardent of libertarians generally regard some expressions to conflict with one or more rights of others. One person's freedom of expression does not require that others must actually listen to them, so that following a person everywhere expressing an idea constantly and incessantly would be regarded as an infringement on the right of the person followed to be left to enjoy their life without constantly having to listen (sometimes phrased as 'the right to be let alone'). Such 'conflicts of rights' lie at the heart of some of the trickiest aspects of legal and ethical judgements regarding freedom of expression.

> Libertarianism: a political viewpoint demanding the greatest possible individual freedom from state control

The opposite of freedom of expression is censorship. This conjures up various images, from the British Board of Film Censors (who changed their name to the British Board of Film Classification in an attempt to shed the stigma of being a censor) to the People's Army driving tanks into Tiananmen Square. For both of these censors, of course, the origin of their power lies with the state and it is important to realize that censorship can originate with sources other than governments: commercial organizations and individuals can act as censors, with or without the state-based power of courts to back them up. It is also important to note the two aspects of censorship: preventing a speaker from expressing their ideas and preventing a listener from hearing those ideas. So, we can classify censorship into four distinct types:

- Censorship of a speaker by a state.
- Censorship of a listener by a state.
- Censorship of a speaker by a 'private actor'.
- Censorship of a listener by a 'private actor'.

We deal with each of these categories in turn, presenting the main distinct issues involved, before turning our attention to the impact and ramifications of technology for censorship and freedom of speech, and the technological arms race going on between censors on the one hand and speakers and listeners on the other.

In the end, all but the most crazed of despots who takes pleasure in seeing power explicitly abused desire self-censorship by both speakers and listeners, as the most efficient outcome. Self-censorship occurs when people, either through habit or fear (justified or not) of some form of reprisal (even if that is simply the disapproval of their peers) decide to not say something or to not do something. The lack of understanding of computer and communications technology by non-experts can be a powerful tool in promoting self-censorship, leading them to believe that they can be detected or blocked in their activities (publishing or accessing material). Of course, where forces are arrayed in support of censorship orders, the consequences of ignorance can lead to terrible consequences, as can misjudging the tolerance of authorities.

Although the terms used in this debate are frequently 'speaker' and 'listener' and sometimes 'freedom of speech' rather than 'freedom of expression', it is important to remember that these are historical terms or shorthand for the right to produce information and make it available to others and the right to access information made available by others. That information can take many forms: from political speeches and essays through artistic work in all media to the right to 'put on an ugly plaid jacket and a loud polka-dot tie and walk down Main Street' (President Bartlett in 'The Short List' episode of The West Wing).

Before we delve into the details of what censorship is happening, how and by whom, we must consider the reasons for censorship and the reasons it is opposed, without which the rest of the information becomes meaningless.

Reasons for Censorship

Although the precise reasons for censoring, or attempting to censor, someone else's freedom of expression are as many and varied as those attempting the suppression, it is generally because they see some benefit in it. There is nothing so powerful as ideas. But to realize their power, ideas must be expressed in some form. The idea of a steam engine is a powerful one which changed the world, being one of the primary drivers of the industrial revolution. However, the idea of a steam engine had to be expressed in drawings and then in machines before it could change the world. Not all ideas need physical expression to be powerful: the concepts of human rights, democracy and religion have all had profound effects on human history, even where written expressions were not possible. When one desires to control people, the surest way is to control their thoughts. Direct mind control is not currently possible and so control of the input and output is all that can be achieved. Whether the aim is power or profit, control of expression is a vital ingredient in the control of people.

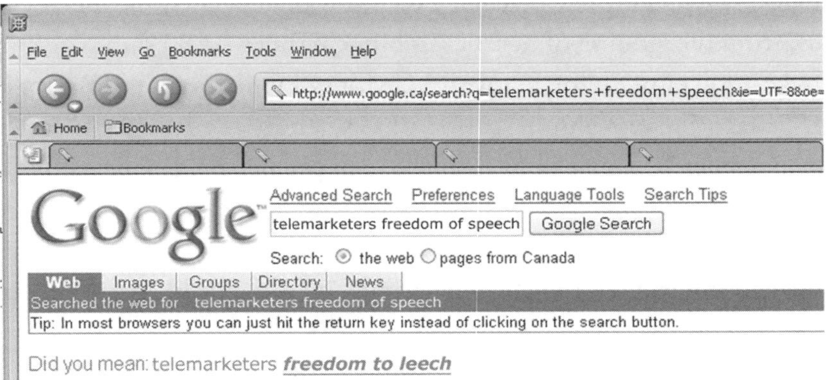

CENSORSHIP BY STATES

A number of national and international organizations are involved in the debate on freedom of expression and many of them concentrate on state censorship. One well-known champion of freedom of expression in the United States is the American Civil Liberties Union (ACLU, `www.aclu.org`). A relatively new organization with a growing impact in this area is Privacy International (`www.privacyinternational.org`), which was formed in 1990 as 'a watchdog on surveillance by governments and corporations'. The work of Privacy International is (as the name would suggest) primarily concerned with privacy issues (see Chapter 7) but their work on censorship is also of high quality. It should also be noted that Amnesty International (`www.amnesty.org`), best known for their unflagging pursuit of the rights of prisoners of conscience, has campaigned for many years on behalf of those silenced by repressive states by any means, rather than just those silenced by incarceration with or without trial.

Censorship, whether by removing access to modes of communication or by direct action (incarceration, threats, execution or murder), has been going on for centuries, from the stoning of heretics in biblical times ('All I said was "that piece of halibut was good enough for Jehovah".', Monty Python's Life of Brian, Handmade Films, 1979), to the excommunication of Galileo by the Roman Catholic Church, to the court-order banning publication of Spycatcher by Chapman Pincher in the United Kingdom and the attempts by Saudi Arabia, the People's Republic of China (PRC) and other countries to control which external web sites their citizens may access on the Internet. As with most topics in this book, this is far too large a topic to cover fully in one chapter and anyway we are primarily concerned with the effects of modern computer and communication technology, thus it is on this last concept that we concentrate.

In September 2003, Privacy International (in collaboration with the GreenNet Educational Trust, `www.greeneteducationaltrust.org.uk`, and supported by a grant from the Open Society Institute, `www.soros.org`) published an important and wide-ranging report into concerted state efforts to censor access to information on the Internet. This report presents an amazing picture of strengthening and widening attempts by states to control what their citizens can see and say. Details of the report make worrying reading for anyone concerned with the openness of the Internet as an applications platform as well as those concerned with human rights and the fundamental concept of freedom of expression. Rather than attempt to reduce a report of more than 50 pages to a few paragraphs, we reproduce here the executive summary and direct readers to `www.privacyinternational.org` for the full report.

> *Silenced is an independent research initiative managed jointly by Privacy International and the GreenNet Educational Trust. The twelve-month project was undertaken through a collaboration of more than fifty experts and advocates throughout the world. The work was made possible by a grant from the Open Society Institute.*

The Internet has evolved to become an increasingly important platform not just for economic development, but also as a support for advocates who wish to express their opinion freely and to work toward the development of democracy. The medium has provided opportunities for citizens to participate in forums, and to discuss and debate issues that concern them. Unlike other media where the information flow is unidirectional – from the government to the masses – the Internet allowed a multi-way communication process giving the chance for anybody to air their opinions and views on issues affecting them. The development of the Internet has led to more horizontal and less vertical communication. Control and censorship has a substantial effect on the Internet because it undermines confidence and trust in the medium and inhibits crucial flows of data.

This study has found that censorship of the Internet is commonplace in most regions of the world. It is clear that in most countries over the past two years there has been an acceleration of efforts to either close down or inhibit the Internet. In some countries, for example in China and Burma, the level of control is such that the Internet has relatively little value as a medium for organised free speech, and its use could well create additional dangers at a personal level for activists.

The September 11, 2001 attacks have given numerous governments the opportunity to promulgate restrictive policies that their citizens had previously opposed. There has been an acceleration of legal authority for additional snooping of all kinds, particularly involving the Internet, from increased email monitoring to the retention of Web logs and communications data. Simultaneously, governments have become more secretive about their own activities, reducing information that was previously available and refusing to adhere to policies on freedom of information.

Governments of developing nations rely on Western countries to supply them with the necessary technologies of surveillance and control, such as digital wiretapping equipment, deciphering equipment, scanners, bugs, tracking equipment and computer intercept systems. The transfer of surveillance technology from first to third world is now a lucrative sideline for the arms industry. Without the aid of this technology transfer, it is unlikely that non-democratic regimes could impose the current levels of control over Internet activity.

One of the most important trends in recent years is the growth of multinational corporate censors whose agendas are very different from those of governments. It is arguable that in the first decade of the 21st century, corporations will rival governments in threatening Internet freedoms. Some American cable companies seek to turn the Internet into a controlled distribution medium like TV and radio, and are putting in place the necessary technological changes to the Internet's infrastructure to do so. Aggressive protection of corporate intellectual property has result in substantial legal action against users, and a corresponding deterioration in trust across the Internet.

A wide variety of methods are used to restrict and/or regulate Internet access. These include: applying laws and licenses, content filtering, tapping and surveillance, pricing and taxation policies, telecommunication markets manipulation, hardware and software manipulation and self censorship.

There are some positive developments within this survey. Countries have established protections, countries have enshrined protections, companies have fought for the rights of privacy of individuals, technologies have sustained the ability of dissident groups to speak freely and access content privately, differences in laws in countries has sheltered the speech of the oppressed. Technological developments are being implemented to protect a free Internet, but the knowledge gap between radical innovators and restrictive institutions appears to be closing.

The Great Firewall of China

Although now emerging from a horrific period of cultural and economic oppression, the People's Republic of China remains a highly repressive regime. As part of the effort to raise the standard of living of China's billion citizens there has been widespread take up of new technologies, primarily in the large cities but slowly extending to smaller towns and even villages. Mobile phones are now quite commonplace and from about 1999 onwards there was an explosion of Internet cafés. China also has a country code top-level domain (cn). See Chapter 6 for details on the repressive nature of the Chinese domain-name system and its effects on freedom of speech.

There are two main forms of censorship affecting Internet communication in China. The first is the arrest and imprisonment of those who use the Internet to criticize the PRC government (`english.aljazeera.net/NR/exeres/40B82C5D-3726-49EF-A319-D59C418FD00C.htm`). It may be that China is simply too big for secrets to be kept, but it would seem from the reports that there are more people imprisoned in China for expressing political views online than anywhere else in the world. The chilling effect of such obvious state action must be horrendous for the average citizen. So, the government of the PRC is involved in large-scale censorship of speakers by both direct (arrest and punishment) and indirect (bans on use of the Internet) means.

The second form of censorship by the PRC government is sometimes called the 'Great Firewall of China'. All primary Internet connections in China are provided by the state and are run via a firewall which blocks access to any site, URL, domain name or IP address deemed 'inappropriate' by the government. This, of course, is a constant battle between the censors and information providers and technologists inside and outside China. It is quite easy (and apparently has been done) for the firewall to block access to the web sites of international news organizations that carry stories critical of the Chinese government. But large numbers of individuals copy all or parts of many stories from various sources on the web every day. A Google search for 'Tiananmen' (the square in which the People's Army crushed a student pro-democracy demonstration in 1989) returns hundreds of thousands of hits. Since this is a tourist attraction in Beijing as well as the site of a major human rights abuse by the PRC government, the firewall cannot easily be set to automatically block every site mentioning the word, although the first page of hits are all obviously about the massacre. In blackly ironic moves, the Chinese government has jailed dissidents for criticism of the censorship regime: even meta-level discussion of censorship in China is not allowed, it would seem (news.bbc.co.uk/1/hi/world/asia-pacific/3250834.stm).

In 2003, China instituted a crackdown on Internet cafés. Following a fire in which a number of users died at a café, the Chinese authorities used safety as an excuse to crack down on the burgeoning Internet café trade, requiring registration by the owners and adherence to strict identification of users and logging of all activity. In addition, they introduced a ban on people under 18 entering Internet cafés, in some cases leading to violent retaliation by gangs of youths denied access. The geeks of East and West have not been defeated by the Great Firewall, as shown by the elgooG web site in September 2002 which was a gateway to Google that reversed all input and output data. A little more awkward, perhaps, but it defeated the Great Firewall's blocking of the world's most popular search engine.

In 2006, Google signed a highly controversial deal with the government of the PRC to run google.cn as a censored search engine focussing on Chinese language sites (NY Times, via www.shorl.com/betamypryfrilo). Google, whose corporate motto includes 'do no evil', has been heavily criticized for the move but has defended the action by claiming that access to Google's expertise in information indexing under censorship is better for the Chinese people than patchy access outside the PRC's legal regime. A simple way to check the censorship of google.cn compared with google.com is to enter 'Tiananmen' into both sites and compare the tourist information from google.cn with the information about the massacre of students on google.com.

Censorship of Speakers by Governments

Governments are limited by geographic jurisdictions in most instances. The most obvious exceptions being war, where one government extends the geographical reach of its power through its armed forces, and international law where governments may agree (bilaterally or multilaterally) to enforce each other's rules, sometimes even where those rules might ordinarily conflict with their own rules. It all depends on the relative positions of the governments. African nations dependent on US aid, for instance, may well agree to enforce US copyrights and patent rights within their countries, even where it is not in their interest to do so otherwise.

In most cases, governments are only able to censor speakers located in their jurisdictions. Direct censorship can involve simple measures, such as issuing legal proceedings (injunctions) which threaten action if a speaker persists in disseminating material of a particular nature, or can be as extreme as incarceration, torture and even execution. The government of the People's Republic of China, even with its modern post-communist economic approach, remains highly repressive in many ways and particularly in the matter of criticism of the government or suggestions that free elections ('democracy on the Western model') should be held. In a self-referential mode, criticism of the government for its censorious nature may itself be subject to censorship. From the direct action of sending tanks in to destroy the pro-democracy student protests in Tiananmen Square to the imprisonment of Yan Jun in December 2003 for two years (`www.rsf.org/article.php3?id_article = 8752`) for posting essays calling for political change, the PRC continues to apply direct censorship.

There was an interesting twist on whether access to computers and the Internet is a fundamental aspect of the human rights to freedom of expression and freedom of access to information. Jerome Heckenkamp was accused in 2002 of having hacked Qualcomm in 1999 and subsequent offences including defacement of the eBay online auction site. Heckenkamp was involved in a bizarre set of pre-trial hearings in 2002 at which he represented himself, following which he was remanded in custody. Afterwards, having followed more standard practice for defendants in a serious criminal trial, Heckenkamp was released on bail under fairly strenuous conditions. It is these conditions which were the subject of an appeal. Unlike cases of, for instance, convicted child pornography traffickers, whose bans on the use of computer equipment and Internet connections have been upheld (albeit with dissenting voices) by federal judges, at least while they are on supervised release (parole, etc.), Heckenkamp had yet to be convicted of any crime. He maintained his innocence, claiming that while his computer was used to commit the crimes, it had been compromised and was simply a link in the chain for other hackers. This defence is not without potential, as two defendants in the United Kingdom (one for computer misuse and one for possession of child pornography) have been released on similar grounds. The US Bail Reform Act requires that pre-trial conditions of release must be the least restrictive necessary to ensure appearance at trial and avoid endangerment of the community. Heckenkamp's lawyer argued that the ongoing ban on Heckenkamp's use of computers violated his First Amendment rights well beyond what is necessary given the circumstances. The complex and difficult nature of investigations in such cases caused continual slippage of the trial date making the censorship an unreasonable burden on the defendant, argued his lawyer. Sympathy for Heckenkamp was undermined when he eventually pleaded guilty in 2004 (`www.landfield.com/isn/mail-archive/2004/Feb/0016.html`).

> First Amendment: the first section of the Bill of Rights which constitutes the first ten amendments to the US Constitution; the First Amendment includes the right to freedom of speech

Thefreeworld.net

The long-running battle over the classification of encryption algorithms and implementations as military weapons (Levy 2000) is not the only example of the commitment to freedom of speech of the United States being rather thin. In particular, the Digital Millennium Copyright Act (see Chapter 12 for more details) has been used not only to shut down web sites supposedly containing unauthorized copies of copyrighted material or code which can decrypt poorly encrypted information (such as the DeCSS DVD decoder) but also to prevent sites based in the United States from linking to sites outside the United States carrying such information (`www.eff.org/IP/DMCA/20031111_321_studios_pr.php`). In response to such measures, free software enthusiasts in the Netherlands came up with the idea of `thefreeworld.net` with the aim of setting up an archive accessible to anyone with an IP number assigned to a network outside the United States, just to make sure that no one responsible for the archive can possibly be arrested for breaking US law even when all their information is stored outside the United States.

DeCSS: a library designed to decrypt the contents of DVDs or video discs encrypted using the weak encryption of the content scrambling system (CSS)

Censorship of Listeners by Governments

Where censorship of speakers is impossible or very difficult, for instance where the speakers are located in other countries, governments may attempt to censor the access of listeners. They may do so, either by direct action (prohibiting or regulating access to certain equipment) or by indirect action (bringing court action against intermediaries). Before the Internet, it was relatively easy for governments to control the wide distribution of imported expression in many cases, although radio broadcasts can be difficult to block while preserving their usage otherwise. For instance, in the Second World War both the Allied and Axis powers broadcast propaganda by radio: Lord Haw attempted to undermine British morale and the Japanese made similar broadcasts in the Pacific using captured Western women (with the name Tokyo Rose coined by US servicemen in the region to describe them); the Allied forces similarly broadcast in local languages into occupied territories, exhorting partisans to support their efforts with sabotage and to assist escaped POWs or downed airmen. While jamming of signals may be possible, it is difficult to do that while retaining usage of the airwaves for permitted broadcasters. The development of the Internet with its open end-to-end architecture has made censorship of listeners particularly difficult. For instance in the 1991 coup attempt against Gorbachev in the USSR, one of the precautions taken by the plotters (following what might be thought of as standard practice in such circumstances) was to monitor international phone lines out of Moscow, cutting off any which appeared to be carrying reports of the coup or resistance against it. Those involved in such monitoring, however, did not understand the whistling and scratching on certain phone lines, allowing fax and computer data to flow unrestricted out of and back into Moscow and between activists. This information flow strengthened the hand of Yeltsin, then the mayor of Moscow, in standing up to the plotters and refusing to recognize their authority. Knowledge of the situation inside Moscow by the outside world and retransmission of arrangements for public demonstrations certainly helped, and may have made the critical difference in numbers.

That, of course, was before the Web and the realization by many governments that here was a new technology that they could not afford to ignore. Today, the Internet is as important (sometimes more important) a means of information dissemination as the printing presses of newspapers and the broadcasting studios of radio and television stations. While telephones have always allowed one-to-one communication, this is inefficient at getting a message across to a large number of recipients (although with massive collusion it would be possible to cascade a single message verbally through the telephone network). The 'traditional' one-to-many newspaper, radio and television industries are vulnerable to censorship applied at source. The many-to-many architecture of the Internet is more of a challenge for censors.

CENSORSHIP BY PRIVATE ACTORS

Although censorship is usually thought of as action by a government, it is also possible, and common, for censorship to be applied by private actors. This is sometimes as overt as censorship by government and can be applied in much the same way, using the apparatus of the state (courts, bailiffs and police) by court rulings. More insidious, however, is the invisible censorship that is sometimes exerted by private actors.

Censorship of Speakers by Private Actors

The most obvious censorship of speakers by private actors is where a law suit is brought against an individual or a publisher either to prevent initial publication of something (prior restraint) or to gain a retraction or apology. In the United States, prior restraint is very difficult. After publication has happened it is possible to sue for damages including public retraction or correction. Other jurisdictions have fewer difficulties with prior restraint. However, it should be noted that modern communications have significantly changed the utility of prior-restraint orders, even when aimed at traditional publications such as newspapers.

In a recent case in the United Kingdom, the Royal Family took out an injunction against daily and Sunday newspapers preventing publications of a sexual allegation about Prince Charles. Since the London court's jurisdiction in such matters does not cover Scotland (which has a separate court system) the main Scottish newspapers carried not only the allegation but the facts about the censorship order. In England, the newspapers (and other media such as television news) were restrained from even discussing the details of the injunction, leading to much hilarity on topical satire shows, of course. A telephone poll at the time indicated that as many people in England thought they knew what the allegations were, mostly through Internet reporting such as the online edition of the Scottish papers, as would have known the details through original publication. It was suggested in court that the fact of the injunction raised the profile of the story such that even more people sought out information about it online than would have read the original report. Without adequate censorship of listeners, such censorship of speakers by governments or by private actors in the face of modern international communications can be very difficult. Of course, such cases are relatively rare. This does not mean that censorship by private actors is rare, however.

One of the most common aspects of censorship is that undertaken by employers. Particularly during economically hard times, employees have a great tendency to self-censor in response to the explicit or implicit demands of their employer. Even where the law supposedly protects individuals against loss of a job for exerting one's freedom of expression, the potential difficulties of losing a job can be so great as to lead to self-censorship. Where general public safety or similar concerns are at issue, many jurisdictions have explicit laws on public disclosure which are rather stronger than the general rights to freedom of expression (see Chapter 10, especially the section on 'Public Disclosure Regulations'). One of the most common types of expression that companies wish to censor is criticism of their policies. In Western Europe and the United States, the issue of outsourcing of 'remote service' types of jobs to the Far East became a major news story.

In the United Kingdom, there was reported public disquiet about the telephone enquiry service for train times being moved partially to India. Reports that the service from India was not only cheaper but actually better (even while saving money, they could get a more highly educated and motivated workforce in India) despite issues of geographical knowledge. Another UK company that was criticized was British Telecom (BT). In January 2004, a worker at one of their retail call centres in Newcastle was suspended for placing an advert on eBay for 'your very own call centre advisor because they're going fast and won't be here much longer'. Although the employee was re-instated after an internal disciplinary hearing, the suspension itself had what is sometimes called a chilling effect. The suspension has had major news coverage and even though the employee was cleared of any wrongdoing by the company, other employees might still think twice about making similar protests (www.theregister.co.uk/2004/01/30/bt_call_centre_worker_suspended).

The news reporting did not say whether the employee had used company resources to create the auction (for which he received no bids). Given the cheap cost and ease of use of home Internet connections these days, it would be strange if he had used work computers. It is interesting to consider whether simply employing someone should give a company the right to take any action against an employee for such an exertion of their right to freedom of expression. BT has ample opportunity to avail itself of its freedom of expression by defending its policies in the news media and, if it is to be believed, no negative outcomes for their current British workforce will result. Is a single, rather humorous, protest grounds for disciplinary action?

Where direct action is not possible, either via the courts or through employment situations, there are some other methods by which censorship by private actors can occur. For an individual, receiving a legally worded request threatening legal action may be enough. Any large corporation makes a cost–benefit analysis before taking such steps, of course, and it is up to individuals to do something similar before making their views known through whatever media. However, a court case can be significantly disadvantageous to an individual even if they eventually win the case. Unless there is absolutely no decent grounds for a case, winning it will not gain back the time and energy spent on court appearances, even though their legal costs may be awarded. Costs may mount during the case in such a way that their resources run dry, forcing them to capitulate, and the prospect of costs being awarded against them (with legal fees for large corporations often running very high as they can afford the best legal advice even if they may not win) also weighs heavily. So, while justice may not be 'for sale' directly in most of the developed world, there are still issues of imbalance in justice to be considered.

Censorship of Listeners by Private Actors

Censorship of listeners by private actors is generally very difficult to achieve, without the collusion of government. Despite this, however, there are steps private actors can take which at least reduce the spread of information even where they don't stop it entirely. The opportunities for such censorship of listeners is very dependent on who the private actor is and any privileged position they hold with respect to modern technology that allows them, either directly or through collusion with other private actors, to indirectly censor listeners.

TECHNOLOGY FOR EXPRESSION

What constitutes technology used for expression and how does the nature of that technology affect the possibilities for censorship? In this section, we attempt to answer these questions at least briefly.

Technological Developments with Expressive Power

From chalk to paint, graffiti on walls has been a method of self-expression for over 2000 years. The anonymity of scrawling 'Romans Go Home!' on a wall in Jerusalem (again, Monty Python's The Life of Brian) is assured providing one is careful. Of course anyone else can come along and efface or change such work. So although it is relatively anonymous, it is static, solitary and easily and quickly censored unless one spends a great deal of time doing it, when the chances of getting caught also increase.

Before the inventions of the printing press and moveable type, portable written documents were expensive and time-consuming to produce, but it could be done. Woodcuts could be used to produce a simple block for printing and leaflets, posters and fliers could be distributed. Even where printing presses are supposedly monopolized there are ways to produce multiple copies of a document on a relatively small scale (in the hundreds, say). The hectograph and other low-technology means of producing hundreds of fliers, leaflets and the like were the standard means of avoiding repressive censors by political agitation groups across Europe even under Soviet repression.

> Hectograph: a block of gelatin onto which is placed a sheet of paper heavily imprinted with ink; the gelatin absorbs the ink and reprints it onto fresh sheets pressed onto the block

In the early days of the Internet, e-mail and usenet became the standard means for the few online to discuss any topic they liked. Parallel developments of bulletin boards for home computers started in the 1970s, sometimes with links across to the Internet. Few people, in the days before the explosion of the Internet into home use and the development of the Web, foresaw that those early days would set the battleground for one of the great battles to come in the 21st century. In those days, almost anything was allowed online except censorship. Of course if one's views were unpopular, one might be flamed and occasional denial of service attacks would happen (setting a script to send multiple messages can overflow the allowed size of a user's inbox or even the disk space of their mail server while the originator's machine simply sends a single copy regularly). Many online then saw the Internet as borderless and beyond the jurisdiction of national governments. So long as it remained a minority channel, it was indeed mostly ignored by governments, although those living under oppressive regimes had to be careful just as they did in other activities. The explosion of home Internet access as more people who had become used to access as students wanted to continue with access, combined with the development of the Web and the subsequent commercialization of the Internet, led governments to pay more attention to the content of all kinds of Internet traffic.

Censoring Internet Content

Although the primary protocol of the Internet is that of a peer-to-peer network, the information architecture of the system both changes over time and differs between applications. There are also other factors that influence how information is expressed and what information can be expressed. Lessig's analysis is a useful model in which to consider such matters. Lessig's model (see Chapter 1 for the details) shows that the activity of people on the Internet is governed by architecture, law, markets and social norms, each of which also influences the other three.

Architecture

Although the main protocols of the Internet are peer-to-peer, the bandwidth available is also a constraint. Linking to the Internet via a dial-up line using a low-speed modem changes a user's behaviour in terms of both sending and receiving information.

Law

We have already considered the main legal effects, both direct (injunctions and punishments) and indirect (letters threatening legal action, known as 'nastygrams'). ISPs are regulated by specific government codes, as are the telecommunications companies that provide the backbone international connections, many of which are still either state-owned monopolies or have significant operational control exerted by the state.

> Nastygram: a letter from a law firm threatening a lawsuit unless certain conditions are met that typically points out the worst-case scenario following from failure to comply and losing the lawsuit

Markets

All individual users are dependent on one (very occasionally more) 'upstream provider' through whose network their Internet traffic flows. These providers both charge for that service and impose conditions on usage. This is a significant factor in censorship issues in all countries not just those, such as the PRC, where ISPs and Internet usage are heavily regulated by law.

Social norms

This is probably the most complex and least understood of the influences on freedom of expression. Particularly in the area of self-censorship, there are significant difficulties in measuring the effect of social norms on freedom of expression.

Examples of censorship by private actors

Before going into some very detailed case studies, we look at a few cases in less detail to demonstrate the effects of some of the above generalities. There have been numerous reports in the press of ISPs being overly cautious in removing material from their servers or removing access to their services by users in response to 'nastygrams'. This is a combination of law, architecture and market forces combining to block freedom of expression without full legal proceedings.

The legal threats may originate with governmental bodies, such as in the case of 'Think of the Children' or a commercial organization in the case of Martin Gallwey and the Bank of Ireland (BoI). In order to transfer money between countries, one needs an international bank account number (IBAN). IBANs are generated via a publicly described algorithm on the web site of the European Committee for Banking Standards (ECBS). Using this information, Gallwey produced a program to generate IBANs and posted it on his web site hosted by the University of Limerick's servers, along with a factual description of the poor level of service (in Gallwey's opinion) he had received from the BoI and which prompted him to find out the method for himself and produce the program. The BoI complained to the University of Limerick that Gallwey's service was against the banking code of the ECBS. The university duly pulled Gallwey's site off their servers, including the description of his difficulties. Legal analysis suggests that the BoI's claims were weak and that an offer by Gallwey to include a warning about the potential hazards of using wrongly generated IBANs was ignored by the BoI. Indeed, since the site had been pulled from the Internet, it would seem that they had no reason to respond positively, since by then the University of Limerick were acting as their agents in censoring Gallwey's freedom of speech. Of course, there are now other options for Gallwey to publish his material and universities are often ill-placed to fight large corporations such as the BoI over material which does not really fall under their remit of academic freedom (Gallwey's reports were not part of official University research or teaching, but personal pages). As we will see, however, commercial ISPs are often no more willing to stand up for their users' rights than are non-commercial 'sideline' providers such as universities.

www.thinkofthechildren.co.uk

This is an interesting case combining social norms and police power with ISP legal ignorance and cowardice. Only due to the strength of character of the creator has the principle of freedom of expression been upheld and a strong precedent (not set in a court of law but in the minds of police, ISPs and users) has been set in favour of the individual.

In 2002, the writer and journalist Paul Carr, in keeping with his general satirical approach to news reporting, created a web site which he called Think of the Children at `www.thinkofthechildren.co.uk` (that URL no longer contains the site but see `www.buzzle.com/editorials/10-2-2002-27424.asp` for a description). It was hosted by a commercial ISP called WebFusion, part of Host Europe. The site contained a satirical take on the over-reaction by some of the media, and some parents, over the admittedly horrific crimes of child abduction, rape and murder. Ignoring the fact that most child abuse is carried out by family members or close family friends, there were national newspaper editorials calling for changes in the law to help protect children from 'sexual predators' and a number of scenes of mob violence aimed against those suspected of being 'paedophiles'. Carr's satirical response was a site that took the worst aspects of the over-reaction and bundled them together. The main home page of the site read:

Welcome to Thinkofthechildren.co.uk

Who are we?

We are concerned parents, many of whom have children of our own and who want the law changed to protect them. Every day in Britain happy, popular children who do well at school are being murdered by evil paedophile scum. Well enough's enough! Its time the law got tough on child murderers.

What do we want?

We want the law changed to make it illegal to murder children and bury them in woodland. We want it to be made illegal for adults to work with children. We want an end to the ridiculous process of 'criminal trials' for suspected child killers.

When do we want it?

Now.

How can I help?

Simple! You can show your support by joining an organized mob, starting your own mob or by signing our petition for change – and don't forget to buy a t-shirt from our shop.

The navigation bar for the site included directions to pages on 'starting your own mob' and 'joining a mob'. One of the most cutting aspects of the site is the aforementioned t-shirts which include one with 'Not Happy or Popular' on the front and 'Don't Kill Me' on the rear.

Such satire has a long and distinguished history in the United Kingdom, including such famous examples as Jonathan Swift's Modest Proposal. Carr was aiming to promote discussion about violence against children. His methods are lawful, though they do skate close to the line on incitement to violence. In fact, it is the extremity of the suggestions on the site that should make it obviously satire. If the satire was buried in small parts of a more temperate presentation then a reasonable person could regard them as incitement to violence. In September 2003, the Metropolitan Police received a complaint about the site from a member of the public. They contacted the Internet Watch Foundation, a non-profit organization whose goal is to identify illegal Internet activity and provide information to ISPs and law enforcement agencies in order to stop it. They confirmed to the police that they too had received a complaint and had viewed the site but believed it to be within the law. Despite this advice, on 23 September 2002, the Metropolitan police sent a fax to Host Europe:

> *This office has received a complaint from a member of the public, in relation to the URL:* `www.thinkofthechildren.co.uk`. *I have viewed the web site and found it to contain articles that could be interpreted as inciting violence.*
>
> *In these circumstances I request that the site be removed from the public domain.*
>
> *If I can assist further or more information is required please contact me on the above telephone number.*
>
> *Regards Jim Pearce.*

Host Europe immediately removed the site from accessibility, claiming that not to do so would put them in jeopardy of being found accomplices in a breach of the Obscene Publications Act. It turned out that the branch of the Metropolitan Police that had issued the take-down notice was the Obscene Publications Unit (OPU). Prior to the implementation of the Human Rights Act 1998 in the United Kingdom, provisions of the Obscene Publications Act did indeed give the police the right to request prevention of distribution of material under investigation. However, the Human Rights Act removed this power from the remit of the OPU directly, requiring them to apply for an injunction to hold material undistributed pending a trial.

The act requires that the judge be satisfied that the outcome of any trial is likely to go against the defendant. In addition, there are very specific provisions regarding journalistic, artistic or literary material which militate against prior restraint. After protests from Carr, Host Europe reinstated his account but asked him not to reinstate the contents of the site which caused the OPU's complaint. As a journalist, Carr decided that this was not reasonable and informed both Host Europe and the OPU that he had reinstated the disputed content, challenging the OPU to charge him with the criminal offence of incitement to violence and to apply for an injunction if they wished to have the site taken down again. Pointing to the large number of supportive e-mails he had received after online reporting of the situation, he also pointed out to Host Europe that their actions could be construed as both breach of contract (nothing on his site violated their terms and conditions of use unless it was proved illegal) and a violation of his right to freedom of expression by collusion with the police to unlawfully remove access to his material. After some discussions with the Host Europe Customer Services manager, Carr finally received confirmation from them that his site would not be removed for its current content, although any requests by the police to remove it for illegal content would be honoured should the content change in a way that violated the law. Carr took this to mean that they would require proof of legal backing for any removal request in future.

As Carr has commented, it would be nice to think that Host Europe and other ISPs would have a legal team that proactively checked their position and required law-enforcement agencies to furnish adequate legal backing before violating the freedom of expression rights of their customers.

Another example of architectural censorship was the interesting case of a recent upgrade to Adobe's graphical manipulation software, Photoshop Creative Suite. It offered very good support for many graphic designers and significant upgrading of capabilities over previous versions but was widely reported (`www.theregister.co.uk/2004/01/15/adobe_anticounterfeiting_code_trips_up/` and `www.eweek.com/article2/0,1895,1440683,00.asp`) to also contain anti-counterfeiting code which would not allow the loading of images of banknotes from certain issuers, including the US Treasury and the Bank of England. This raises an interesting question of how far control of technology should go in attempting to prevent counterfeiting. The Adobe action seemed to go beyond what even some of the banks regarded as reasonable. As reported in The Register, Plexus Digital

Solutions in the United Kingdom has permission from the Bank of England to use scans of banknotes for purposes such as advertising artwork. However, this company was prevented from using Adobe's software (which was pretty much an industry standard with a very large share of the market for such applications) for this purpose. Adobe advised that the company approach the Bank of England for scannable sample notes which do not contain the trigger information. However, the Bank of England, unlike the US Treasury, does not produce such notes. While Plexus had the option of using other software, one can envisage applications (such as the proposed Trusted Computing Platforms) which include such restrictions at a lower level and which reverse the assumption of the right to freedom of expression, requiring explicit permission to scan images of banknotes rather than making it illegal to use scanned images to produce counterfeited notes.

As we see in the discussion topic on Yahoo! France, the issue of what is acceptable (indeed constitutionally protected) 'speech' in some countries crosses the line into what other countries regard as 'hate speech'. CNN reported a case in 2002 of Italian authorities using access passwords found on an Italian citizen's computer to remove images on a US server which were deemed 'blasphemous' in Italy. Such cases highlight the difficulty of the international nature of the Internet and the easy dissemination of information as soon as Internet access is allowed. Whether anyone actually reads what a user puts up of course, also depends on them being able to find it.

Despite the furore over the appearance of trademarks in second-level (or third-level) domains, the majority of web site access is performed using portals and search engines rather than by direct typing of a URL into a location bar. The most popular search engines (currently Google, previously AltaVista) have enormous power in censoring listeners, either by deliberate action or via unintended ramifications of their design. An example of this inadvertent censorship (called 'Googlewashing' by Andrew Orlowski of The Register) happened in 2003 with respect to 'the second superpower', a term initially coined to describe the anti-globalization demonstrators who were coordinating their plans via the Internet (and other social communication means). The term caught on so fast that, within a short time, the UN Secretary General Kofi Annan was heard to use it. A weblogger then wrote a piece in which he used the same term to describe his vision of techno-utopians banding together to create change in the real world via their online discussions (a related idea but one with significant differences). This weblog piece was heavily linked to and commented upon by other webloggers. Because of the way Google's page ranking worked, the original use of the term was not only pushed off the first few pages (studies show that few people go more than a few pages down a Google search) but removed entirely into the 'other links not shown because they're deemed to be irrelevant' portion of Google's listings. This has now been fixed but not before there were allegations that the definition of 'googlewashing' had itself been googlewashed (`www.theregister.co.uk/2003/04/10/google_washes_whiter/`).

Freenet

While avoiding the Great Firewall of China may be child's play, the great majority of all access is still logged (automatically stored) and may be monitored (the log may actually be viewed by someone). In an effort to avoid even the logging of what information is accessed (although some trace of the activity is probably still recorded, though not the content), the Freenet project (`freenet.sourceforge.net`) was developed. Although similar in some ways to some of the other post-Napster, peer-to-peer systems, the primary aim of Freenet is anonymity of both provision and receipt of information. The basic concept of the system is that users provide a portion of their hard drive to hold encrypted information. Direct access to the information held on the hard drive is supposedly impossible without a brute-force cracking approach. Each machine only holds a portion of any document published. Unlike other encrypted peer-to-peer systems, which simply encrypt the connection between the two systems, Freenet encrypts everything it does and does not distinguish between the machine which has a fragment of a requested document and one which is simply passing it along from somewhere else. The entire system is designed for anonymity and to 'route around' any attempt at censorship. Neither what is accessed nor where it is held is supposed to be identifiable, although the fact of accessing Freenet may be possible to monitor.

In an interesting twist, on 17 May 2004 the most popular online payment system, PayPal (owned by eBay) cancelled the Freenet project account (club.cdfreaks.com/showthread.php?t=95940 and www.boingboing.net/2004/05/18/paypal_disgraces_its.html). Freenet is a project supported by donations and the bulk of their funding was coming in through PayPal's 'subscription' regular payments system. The reasons given by PayPal for cancelling the account was for accessing the site via 'an anonymous proxy'. The operator of the Freenet account denies that he has ever used such a thing to access the PayPal account. A quick check of the PayPal 'Terms of Use' pages reveals no such prohibition nor is there any such prohibition in the Acceptable Use policy of items which may be paid for via PayPal (forbidden items include sexual material, gambling and a variety of others but accepting payment for the development of anonymous information service programs is not prohibited). Should banking services (innovative ones like PayPal or traditional banks) place limitations on who may use their services, other than preventing illegal usage?

Client–Server and Peer-to-Peer Architectures

The original peer-to-peer architecture of Internet applications (e-mail and usenet) was rather overshadowed by the more client–server architecture of the Web. Commercial ISPs, partly in an effort to control bandwidth usage, partly to placate governments concerned about identifying middlemen through whom they could exert control, and partly because the ISPs want control, often have very stringent terms on the usage of their services. It remains to be seen whether they are allowed to claim or imply in advertising that their service provides unlimited access and then attempt to limit users' usage.

Another aspect of ISPs' standard terms and conditions which seems less justifiable in economic or technical terms is the restriction against running servers (particularly web servers) on so-called 'always-on' connections. These restrictions seem primarily concerned with limiting users' freedom to self-publish rather than for any technical purpose. It may be that such conditions are not proactively applied but are used by ISPs as catch-alls to allow an ISP to cooperate with any external requests by pointing to an absolute restriction against such services. Most users, of course, use the ISP's servers to run their web sites, but this places them in a more difficult subordinate position regarding external requests. Consider the request made against an academic who had recorded some of his presentations and offered them on his web site as MP3 files (`news.com.com/2100-1025_3-1001095.html`). He happened to share a surname with a well-known singer whose record label sent a take-down request to his university charging violation of copyright, showing that large organizations are prone to request action first and investigate afterwards. Had that professor's web site been on a commercial ISP, it is entirely possible that his site would have been taken down rather than a response pointing out the error being sent back to the record company.

Relying on requesters to have properly investigated before threatening legal action does not work in the current environment, nor does relying on an ISP to stand up for your rights (unless you happen to be an academic whose university generally guarantees academic freedom). Despite the huge strides forward that the Internet has brought in allowing more people the ability to express their opinions, it is by no means a perfect world in this respect and freedom of expression for the individual rather than simply en masse, ignoring specific violations, requires a rebalancing of the scales.

CONCLUSION

Freedom of speech comes with responsibilities. The priorities of government, and in particular their need to provide security for their citizens, sometimes places limits on their ability to tolerate freedom of speech. Different social circumstances dictate different levels of acceptable speech. Some speech offends others. When is that offence sufficient to justify preventing the speech? When is it sufficient to justify allowing the speech but taking action other than speaking out in response and refutation?

Does the stability of a government, or a governmental system, justify banning criticism of the government or governmental system? Does banning certain forms of speech really work in the modern interconnected world or does it simply give it extra credibility? Do governments (or citizens) have the right to require that companies obey moral duties to uphold freedom of speech, even in their operations in countries where such freedoms are heavily constrained?

The correct limits to freedom of speech are difficult to gauge and the impact of communication technology forms a constantly shifting surface on which to base these judgements.

DISCUSSION TOPICS

Yahoo! France Nazi Memorabilia

In one of the most publicized and studied cases of freedom of speech, censorship and international jurisdiction so far regarding the Internet, in 2000 a French judge issued an injunction against US Internet search and directory service Yahoo! ordering them to prevent French Internet users from accessing Nazi memorabilia on sale via auctions on Yahoo!'s US-based site. The French subsidiary (`fr.yahoo.com`) already had in place terms and conditions banning sale of such items, which is illegal under French laws against promotion of racism including glorification of the Nazi regime. An attempt by the French government to have the French court's judgement against Yahoo! applied in a Californian court failed, with a judge ruling that it is up to France to police its own citizens' access to the net rather than try to force US companies to do it for them when the online activity was legal in the United States. Having stood up for its rights, however, Yahoo! has exercised its commercial rights to apply restrictions on usage of its service and the current terms and conditions for Yahoo! auctions state

> *There are some things that you may not list or sell under any circumstances. These include:...*
>
> *Any item that promotes, glorifies, or is directly associated with groups or individuals known principally for hateful or violent positions or acts, such as Nazis or the Ku Klux Klan. Official government-issue stamps and coins are not prohibited under this policy. Expressive media, such as books and films, may be subject to more permissive standards as determined by Yahoo! in its sole discretion.*

As is often the case, rights to freedom of speech are curtailed not by government but by commercial organizations concerned about negative publicity they may receive by standing up for such rights. Should general-purpose sites be allowed to ban the sale of items that are legally allowed to be advertised for sale? If they do impose such conditions should they be subject to stricter 'editorial accountability' than sites with no such restrictions?

ISP Liability for Content

ISPs are commercial organizations: they exist primarily to make a profit. The role of the ISP in the modern world is similar to that of the postal service and the telephone operator in the past: it is only a carrier of relatively anonymous information. Is a telephone operator responsible for the use of their system to plan a kidnapping or to make obscene phone calls? Not generally. Is a postal service responsible for the injury and damage caused by a parcel bomb or the contents of an obscene magazine sent through the post? Not generally. The position of ISPs is not yet as clear cut.

The analogy breaks down, mostly because of the nature of digital information: downloading a copy does not destroy the original, nor does it cost the originator of information on a per-download basis when that information is accessed. By posting information on a server on the Internet it is possible for a large number of people to continually access that information. If society deems that information undesirable (i.e. illegal, such as abusive images of children, racist text advocating violence, untrue allegations of misconduct or unauthorized copies of copyright works), then by the time a court case has concluded that information may have been downloaded thousands of times or more. ISPs have been sued alongside the 'originator' of content alleged to be illegal (e.g. the science fiction author Harlan Ellison sued a number of ISPs as well as the poster when one of his stories appeared on a usenet newsgroup (harlanellison.com/KICK/kick_rls.htm and www.locusmag.com/2002/Reviews/ShropshireOnEllison.html)). In response to the lack of what is sometimes called a common carrier status (i.e. being regarded as solely a conduit and not responsible for what is carried unless it is patently obviously dangerous or illegal), ISPs have naturally become cautious about imposing conditions on their customers. As in the case of thinkofthechildren.co.uk, a small number of complaints can lead to the denial of service for an originator who is acting within the law. ISPs are not qualified to act as judges.

Many ISPs currently operate a 'no server' policy for Internet access: that is, the terms and conditions of service state that the computer attached to the connection (and in these days of cable modems and similar technology, more and more home machines are permanently connected to the Internet rather than only attached intermittently on a dial-up connection) may not be running as a general information-service provider. What this means is that one is not allowed to run a web server (or any other type of server) from a home connection. There are various reasons why ISPs do this: some technical and some financial. The technical ones are to do with the fact that if each customer was running their own web server then the bandwidth available on the shared local loop between home and exchange would be subject to more traffic. If everyone keeps their web sites on the backbone-connected ISP servers then the amount of traffic on the local loop is kept down, which benefits the customers (better connection speeds) and the ISP (cheaper hardware requirements). The financial arguments include the fact that home service is typically much cheaper than business service and business services do not have such restrictions, so ISPs want customers that need to run servers to pay for an appropriate level of service. However, this prohibition has a significant consequence for censorship of speakers: the ISP controls what appears on its servers and can immediately take it off their site following any form of complaint. It is more expensive and more awkward to remove information held on a home server connected to their system, although it is technically feasible. However, this does provide ISPs with the motive and the means to enforce censorship of speakers on the Internet.

Should ISPs be forced to allow servers on home connections but allowed to place a bandwidth limit on both incoming and outgoing service (which they already do in many cases for incoming downloads)?

BT and the IWF

The Internet Watch Foundation (IWF) was established in the United Kingdom in 1996 as a non-governmental body to provide support to ISPs to help them avoid the hosting of illegal content on their sites. Their primary target is images of sexual abuse of children, although they consider their remit in terms of the United Kingdom's obscene publications and anti-racism legislation. Their prime original purpose was to provide a central partnership between ISPs and public bodies (the police, social services, etc.) for the identification of material which it is criminal to distribute and which is held on UK ISP servers by their customers (or occasionally by their employees).

In June 2004, one of the United Kingdom's largest ISPs – the former public monopoly telephone provider BT – announced that it was to begin blocking sites from around the world that 'the IWF has ruled contain images in contravention of the 1978 Children Act' (the Protection of Children Act 1978 provides the primary legislation against possession, distribution and production of child abuse images in the United Kingdom).

The IWF is not a statutory body (it has not been empowered by the UK government in legislation although it does enjoy government support) and there are no apparent procedures for appeal to have a banned site removed from the blacklist. The question this raises is whether this is the thin end of the wedge of a technological censorship regime in the United Kingdom. Until recently, the content the IWF entered on this blacklist was supposed to be only child abuse images (hosted anywhere in the world). More recently they have added incitement to racial hatred and obscenity, if hosted in the United Kingdom (`www.theregister.co.uk/2006/12/29/iwf_feature`). There are campaigns currently running in the United Kingdom to ban 'images of violence against women' and various religious (and other) groups vociferously campaign against material available on the Web. Should an unelected non-statutory body be allowed to decide which bits of the Web are visible to UK surfers? Are the ISPs moving to censor listeners without legal oversight?

REFERENCES

Levy, S. (2000) *Crypto: Secrecy and Privacy in the New Code War*, Penguin, London. ISBN 0-140-244-328.

RELATED READING

Lessig, L. (1999) *Code and Other Laws of Cyberspace*, Basic Books, New York. ISBN 0-465-03913-8.

Shapiro, A. (1999) *The Control Revolution*, Perseus Books, New York. ISBN 1-891620-86-X.

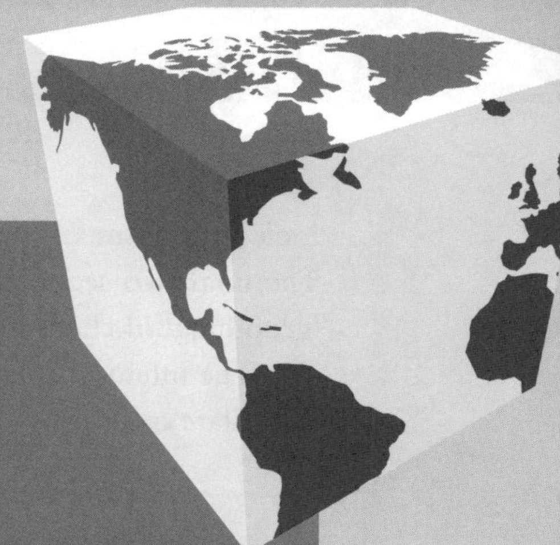

5

SEX AND TECHNOLOGY

INTRODUCTION

This is a difficult topic to cover in a book such as this, because of the sensitivities of some readers. However, sex is a part of human life, and technological developments and sex have a long combined history. The chapters in this book are written to be mostly self-contained, and this one in particular can be missed out should a reader or course organizer feel that the material is not necessary. In addition, due to the sensitive nature of some of the topics in this chapter, it is written as self-contained sections, allowing parts to be skipped over. The ubiquity of references to online matters involving sex requires that the topic be covered in a book such as this.

We begin with a discussion of the nature of what we term 'sexual material'. Even this definition itself is not clear cut. A brief overview of the nature of sexual material in different cultures and different times in history is presented, followed by some details on legislation in various Western countries, and international agreements regarding availability of sexual material. Next we look at the issue of controlling access to material, by topic type and by viewer type. The final two sections cover the separate issues of child pornography and online 'grooming' of children by molesters.

The intent of this chapter is to inform and provide a basis for discussion, not to titillate or to provide a road map for finding sexual material online.

THE NATURE OF SEXUAL MATERIAL

One Man's Art. . .

Nudity or being only partially clothed is variously acceptable or unacceptable in different cultures. Depictions of nudity or partial nudity in art (two-dimensional art, such as a painting, or three-dimensional art, such as a sculpture) may follow cultural norms for 'real bodies' or may deviate from them. The acceptability of various depictions may even vary within a society, being restricted to particular classes or castes. Often, though not always, there are differences in restrictions for the genders. In this book, we are concerned primarily with the impact of technology, and particularly computer and networking technology, on cultural attitudes and laws. Dependent on culture, background, age and attitude, one person's 'art' is another's 'erotica' and a third's 'obscenity'. Through the rest of this chapter we consider, where useful, this categorization of material: art is generally accepted and is usually held to be suitable for universal viewing, although sometimes restricted by age or class; erotica is acceptable, but viewed as definitely sexual in nature and is usually restricted; obscenity is not generally acceptable and is often suppressed in some fashion. There are, of course, boundary areas and differences of viewpoint within cultures and times as there are differences between cultures and over time. Some people may be under the impression that there is a simple shift over time, with less and less being considered obscene, but this is not the case. These boundaries ebb and shift and flow and, even within a single person's lifetime, the boundary can shift either way.

Erotica: socially acceptable sexual material
Pornography: socially unacceptable sexual material

The Medium and the Message

When the term 'online pornography' is mentioned, the category 'nude images of females' is probably what is evoked for most. However, this is not the sum total of what we are considering in this chapter. Material of a sexual nature can be in a variety of forms: textual material: written depictions of romance, love, sex and 'sexually stimulating topics'; sound files; images; video (with or without audio). Sometimes the mode of transmission is also relevant: is the material available whole; is it encrypted; is it for sale or for free; can it be downloaded and kept or is it 'streamed'; is it a 'live transmission' or a recorded piece; is it 'interactive' or a 'set piece'; is it a single sequence or an edited piece?

Use of Technology to (Re)Produce Sexual Material

From fresco painters in classical Rome via the printing press, the telephone and the computer bulletin board to the Internet, technological means of communication have always been used (some might say abused) to produce and disseminate sexual material. The debate about the influence of easily available sexual material has a history just as long. There were schools of philosophy (the ascetics, for instance) in classical times that eschewed pleasure, including material which might inflame sexual desire. The Marquis de Sade's literary efforts were initially suppressed (though not entirely successfully). Work now regarded as 'classic' has been restricted in distribution; Lady Chatterly's Lover was deemed obscene in some countries, as much for the depictions of sex between a noble lady and a servant as for the actual language and explicit nature of the text. Some, such as Tierney (1994), even see desire for easily accessed sexual material as a primary driving force behind technological innovation. The adoption of new technology by the 'sex industry' is seen as a perversion of the initial 'Garden of Eden' purity by others, such as the United Kingdom's Viewers and Listeners Association whose founder Mary Whitehouse became synonymous in the United Kingdom with complaints about sex, violence and swearing on television and radio. Sensational reporting of the prevalence of sexual material on the Internet and usenet in particular (Elmer-Dewitt 1995, based on the work of Rimm of Carnegie Mellon University) is still quoted by pundits and politicians alike in their support of censorship of the online world, despite both the methods and data having been shown to be completely spurious.

Techno-Sex

In this section, we consider how computer and communication technologies have been adapted to use with sexual material.

Telephones

Voice calls

A 'call-girl' was originally a prostitute with whom arrangements were made by telephone. Particularly for business men, it made sense to make arrangements by phone rather than wander into a red-light district.

Premium-rate voice calls

The development of 'premium rate' telephone services (i.e. services where the cost of the call is much higher than the normal 'connection charge') has led to a variety of telephone 'information services' providing sports scores and so on (see Chapter 2). These types of services were also quickly adopted by the sex industry for both interactive and broadcast types of service. Most consumers know, of course, that the provided service is pure fantasy. The broadcast 'sounds of sex' are often no more real sex than that in soft-porn videos (or in many feature films). The self-described 'tall skinny blonde with large breasts' talking dirty down the phone line is as likely to be an overweight lady with grey hair as to be the woman of one's dreams. However, the 'fantasy' is what this is all about. As the providers in the sex industry know well, sex happens as much in the brain as the body.

Premium-rate SMS

While fixed-line telephones have been around and ubiquitous for most of a century with few technical developments directly affecting users, the mobile, or cell, phone continues to see developments. Originally seen as a gimmick, short messaging service (SMS) has become a big hit and the source of much of the service's revenues. An even more recent development has been premium-rate SMS. Subscribing to receive information, such as sports scores, or 'semi-interactive' services, such as requesting new ring tones, were seen as the ways premium-rate SMS might be used.

However, when combined with cheap television broadcast by cable or satellite, premium-rate SMS has led to an interesting recent development. There are a number of channels in the United Kingdom which make their income from a combination of premium-rate SMS and telephone calls, as well as by selling advertising. The channels consist of a number of scantily clad women on picture-in-picture segments of a screen. There are constantly-running adverts for phone-sex lines running in another small part of the screen. The bulk of the screen is taken up by premium-rate text messages making comments on the activities of the women on-screen. Requests to reveal further pieces of anatomy, or to show feet or shoes or for interaction between the women (tickling or kissing) are sent in and some of these are acted upon. The women on-screen encourage multiple messages (whether from one individual or from multiple viewers doesn't matter since each message costs any sender the same and makes the station their profit). In many ways this can be seen as the television/telephone equivalent of a table-dancing club. The attraction for the viewer is the privacy of watching from one's home (see the discussion in the next section on the illusion of privacy afforded by technological access to material). Such premium rate telephone services in the United Kingdom are self-regulated by The Independent Committee for the Supervision of Standards of Telephone Information Services (ICSTIS), which is more likely to receive complaints about 'spam' text messages rather than sex-related services like this.

MMS and camera phones

The development of digital photography has led to an increase in the invasion of privacy with 'voyeur' pictures of people in gym or swimming-pool changing rooms, or 'angle shots' showing semi-nudity in public, such as a shot taken on a staircase looking up a woman's skirt. However, even with very small digital cameras, it is still the case that the photographer is fairly obviously doing something wrong. There is an even bigger problem with camera-enabled mobile phones in that the user appears to be simply using the phone to send a text message or look up a piece of information held in the phone's memory when in reality they may be taking a picture and even sending it out immediately as a multimedia message. This has become a serious enough problem that some gyms and even schools have banned the use of mobile phones in changing rooms, or even the entire premises. There are proposals to criminalize such invasions of privacy in the United States through the draft Video Voyeurism Prevention Act.

> Short Messaging Service (SMS): a short piece of text passed between digital mobile phones
> Multimedia Messaging Service (MMS): pictures passed between 2.5G or 3G mobile phones

Internet 're-diallers'

When many users connected to the Internet via a standard modem, by making a voice telephone call to an ISP, malicious programs (see Chapter 11) could change the phone number to a premium-rate number, even an international premium-rate number. This was particularly a problem with sex sites informing users that they were being 're-directed to our pay server', while changing the default access number, not just the access number for that session. Users receiving quarterly bills for phone services could be hit with enormous bills (tens or hundreds of times their usual bill) after such incidents. This was a particular problem in Australia, with online newsletter Australian IT (`australianit.news.com.au`) regularly reporting on it: on 21 August 2003, it reported that the Australian Telecommunications Industry Ombudsman received 921 complaints about such Internet re-dialling systems in the first quarter of 2003, rising to 1039 complaints in the second quarter. The move of many users to broadband connections has reduced the problem but not removed it. Regulators are still struggling with the problem.

> Re-dialler: a program which surreptitiously changes the number used to dial up an ISP, usually to a premium-rate phone number

2.5G, 3G mobile phone services

In internal discussions, and sometimes openly, mobile phone operators are expecting provision of sexual material to become one of their big money-spinners. However, they are also wary of the possible costs that may come with 'moral outrage' and hence are rather shy about discussing these ideas in public. As with Internet-based material, it is the 'illusion of privacy' that they are hoping will encourage use of these technologies.

BBS

Before the explosion of the Internet beyond universities and the military, home computer users were already using modems to pass information back and forth (see Chapter 2). Sexual material has been available via these Bulletin Board System (BBS) since their inception.

Early home computers, such as the Apple II, had sufficiently good graphics and the technophile owners of such machines were capable of buying or putting together image scanners before they became a common peripheral. This led to the scanning of both professional sex-magazine images and 'amateur' polaroid material and its posting on BBS. However, the slow rates of early modems kept this activity highly restricted to specialist BBS on the whole. Since a good quality (in purely technical terms) image would take up as much space as hundreds of long text files, the owners or operators of many BBS would not carry such material, not through any moral dislike of it, but simply to discourage hogging of the limited connections to their machines. Those BBS that carried usenet newsgroups would also often restrict themselves to non-binary groups for the same reason. BBS dedicated to various sex-related topics emerged, sometimes 'advertised' via the relevant no-binaries newsgroups.

The development of lossy compression formats such as JPEG, which is particularly good for digital photographs, and the benefits and limitations of graphics formats would require a whole chapter by themselves (see Chapter 3 for some information). Users have obviously been forgiving of the limitations of the technology in their quest for sexual material online.

> Bulletin Board System (BBS): an early intermittent networking system allowing owners of home computers to dial in to local servers or each other's computers and pass files around

Mailing lists

Unlike the semi-public activity on usenet, mailing lists can be much more private. Participants can be vetted and to some extent controlled, by the administrator of the list. Participants therefore may well be more open on such lists. However, the private nature of controlled-subscription mailing lists (as opposed to open-subscription ones such as the 'sf-lovers mailing list', the forerunner of one of the highest volume usenet newsgroups) mean that little is known of the details of mailing lists with sexual content, except to note that their existence is apparent from public references on usenet and web pages.

Usenet news

Although the infamous Rimm survey (Elmer-Dewitt 1995) was wrong in its estimation of what proportion of usenet usage is devoted to sex, there is quite a lot of sexual material available on usenet. Usenet was, and continues to be, a huge arena. The fact that only a very small percentage of that traffic is sexual material still allows for huge amounts of material to be available. Before the Web, usenet was the medium of choice for distributing a great deal of material. Of course, system administrators with either moral or commercial grounds for not carrying all of usenet have often deliberately not carried the obviously sexual newsgroups, and the binaries groups have simply too much traffic for many sites, even today.

FTP

To avoid the restrictions on binaries newsgroups, early sexual material in binary form was often placed on FTP sites and the location posted to suitable newsgroups. Sites allowing 'anonymous' uploading (i.e. uploading of material without a specific username on that machine) did exist and some sites which did not intend to allow this did so inadvertently, thus becoming temporary havens for sexual material, the existence of which might be publicized through private or public email lists or via usenet.

Sexual spam

With the growth of personal Internet use and the profitability of paid-for sexual material on the Web, spam has become a means of advertising sex as much as it has for hydraulic materials, medication and computer software. There are two reasons why sexual spam is a specific problem. The first is that while adverts for 'gearboxes for 4X4 vehicles' are annoying, they are not usually offensive for their content, simply for their unsolicited presence in one's inbox. Adverts with subject lines such as 'Teens being rammed' (and that's a relatively tame one compared with some subject lines that appear in the authors' inboxes) can be highly upsetting for some people. There is evidence that some people are being put off using email and the Internet simply because of the sexual spam that comes their way when they first go online. There is a particular problem with children and such spam, which is discussed in the section on protecting children from online sexual material. As with spam in general, so long as some people respond, spammers will keep wanting to send it out. The reluctance of some users to search directly for the material is also likely to mean that sexual spam retains its popularity with the advertisers longer than other spam content. The second reason why sexual spam is a particular problem is that it may reinforce the view that the Internet is awash with sexual material. This can lead to a puritan backlash, such as that following the Rimm report, which can lead to unsuitable attempts at regulation.

The Web

The biggest boon to online sex, of course, was the twin development of the Web and personal Internet access from home. As with all other areas of e-commerce, these were the drivers for an explosion in commercial sites offering sexual material. As with other areas of digital download e-commerce, though, the availability of free material (originally only through usenet then through the free archives of such older material) produced difficulties for those wishing to cash in on sex on the Web. Some commentators have posited that sex is one of the driving forces behind the development and availability of web technology. While it is almost certainly the case that some people have gained much wealth from providing sexual material over the Web, it is also true that it is not a universally easy way to make money. Initial interest by existing print publishers of sexual material (such as Playboy) has not been continued with much enthusiasm. Like the record companies, they see the Web and Internet access as much as a threat as an opportunity. Particularly as many see the Web as a place to find free material, they may be right in that it may undercut their business, particularly as the illusion of privacy is even more secure for downloading than for having material physically delivered. However, the existing organizations may well have a head start on their competitors for delivering more 'technologically advanced' forms of sexual material such as video and live multimedia.

Blue movies

The video recorder, outside the television broadcast industry, was originally a corporate and military tool for training purposes, replacing the more awkward cine-projection. The 'Umatic' format was particularly prevalent in military circles and, as with cine-projection before it, a circle of unofficial 'blue movie' distribution took advantage of the accessibility of the technology and the demand for the material. Many commentators attribute the success of home video recorders to blue-movie sales and rentals. This ignores the fact that it was video recorders, rather than players, that succeeded in the marketplace. Since there was little use for the recording feature for sexual material (before cheap video camera availability) this seems a dubious premise. While the availability of blue movies is undoubtedly a factor in the success of 'home video', it is only one factor among many and probably not the deciding factor.

Satellite and cable broadcasts, first analogue and now digital transmission, with their wide range of channel availability, have led to some interesting issues. Again, some of these involve protecting children from unsuitable material, dealt with later in this chapter. The development of encrypted channels and the protection of 'copyrighted sexual material' owes as much to the sex industry as to Hollywood blockbusters. As with home video, it is probably overstating things to say that sex is the prime reason for success in subscription and pay-per-view services, but it is undoubtedly a factor.

DVD has replaced video tape as the medium of choice for 'physically shipped' home entertainment these days. Despite the possibilities of multiple soundtracks offered by digital broadcasting, this has not really caught on. Nor is it much of an issue in blue-movie DVDs: few consumers are that bothered if the soundtrack is in

Swedish: the plots are so thin that not understanding the words doesn't matter much to most viewers. One aspect of mass-market DVD players, however, does seem to be primarily for the sex market and that is the 'multiple angle' viewpoint. There seem to be three possible uses for this: martial arts films where, particularly in the Far East, there is interest in seeing special stunts from multiple angles; sports material where multiple angles again allow a choice of viewing; and blue movies. Few, if any, martial arts or sports DVDs seem yet to take advantage of this feature, yet it is on almost all mass-market DVD players and the authors therefore assume that it is seen as a necessity for truly professional blue-movie production for DVD distribution.

Computer games

Since the early days of interactive computing (Spacewar on the PDP-1 at MIT), games have always been available (see Chapter 3). What wasn't mentioned in that chapter though, is that sexual elements have been present in some games from quite early on. OnLine Systems published an adventure game called Softporn. In adventure games such as this, the usual 'goal' of the game is to collect various objects and combine or use them in specific locations to complete set tasks. In fantasy settings, this might take the form of finding armour and a weapon and killing a monster. In Softporn, the goal was to find two women and persuade them to have sex with you (in one case, this involved finding a way to obtain a condom as a subsidiary goal). While OnLine Systems made their name from flashy (for the time) use of graphics, Softporn was a text-only adventure, but that didn't stop it from selling well and receiving top marks in reviews. These reviews can still be found online, although care is needed when searching for Softporn on the Web: system administrators may not believe your explanation.

Such adult entertainment has been a constant section of computer games for home use ever since, including such well-known titles as Leisure Suit Larry (also from OnLine Systems), which was released in 1987 and, despite qualms by some computer-store owners about displaying it on their shelves, this graphical sex adventure was named Best Adventure/Fantasy Role-Playing Game of the Year by the Software Publishers Association and spawned six direct sequels and at least one 'upgraded' version of the original with higher-resolution graphics. Improving graphics on PCs and home machines such as the Commodore Amiga and the Atari ST led to more graphically oriented games such as strip poker with various opponents available. In more modern times, there are still sexual computer games, although the availability of more material online seems to have diminished their presence in the marketplace. However, the spirit of the original Softporn and Leisure Suit Larry hackers is still alive, particularly in the world of gaming pinup Lara Croft. Despite a variety of rumours and April Fool jokes, there are no built in 'cheat codes' to turn Lara Croft nude in the Tomb Raider games. However, graphical adventure games such as Tomb Raider consist of two main elements for their graphics: the shapes and the 'skins' and it is possible to download a patch for the game which substitutes topless and nude skins as overlays for various Tomb Raider games, as well as a patch for the end of one of the games for a full-motion video (FMV) of Lara in the shower. Eidos and Core Design have not made particular efforts to suppress the availability of these patches, although they refuse to endorse them, of course.

Peer-to-peer technologies

As mentioned in other chapters, the development of a variety of peer-to-peer technologies has taken the Internet back much closer to its roots than the web culture of servers and clients. ISPs offering 'always on' service but not allowing the running of web servers have been bypassed by peer-to-peer systems. The most high-profile use of peer-to-peer networking has been the sharing of music, but sexual material of all forms (graphics, sounds and text) is also available on peer-to-peer systems, usually as a parallel distribution channel for material available elsewhere. Companies interested in providing paid for material via peer-to-peer systems regard sexual material in the same way those trying to make money from the Internet in other ways do: unless they have a particular legal or cultural normative problem, the marketplace demand dictates that they try to supply it. As we see in the sections on attempts to control the content of the Internet, whether that be to keep sexual material unavailable or to prevent distribution of music and movies, the architecture of the Internet is now a constant battleground of control against freedom and peer-to-peer distribution of sexual material is just one front line.

Anonymity: Reality and Illusion

In the English-speaking countries of the developed world (the United States, Canada, the United Kingdom, the Republic of Ireland, Australia and New Zealand), there is a certain amount of sexual prudishness extant in society that differs from the legal situation. Although the law allows for a variety of sexual material to be legitimately available, the societal norms still restrict how comfortable many feel in publicly purchasing such material. The promises of sex magazines and subscription-only sex channels on television to 'deliver discreetly' and that 'our name will not appear on your credit card bill' show how important some level of anonymity is to at least some of the 'consumers' of such material. This 'anonymity' is obviously limited: in particular, a consumer's access to such material is anonymous with respect to friends, neighbours, and possibly family or partner. It is anonymity to a similar extent that gives Internet users a sense of security when accessing pornographic content online in these countries. However, this sense of anonymity can be misleading. In other European countries, the purchase and utilization of sexual material is both lawful and less often subject to societal censure. In other parts of the world, however, access to material regarded in Europe as non-sexual (or completely harmless though very mildly sexual) may be unlawful or strongly disapproved of by society. In countries such as Iran, with strong puritanical Islamic legal codes, even pictures of women with their hair on display may be regarded as obscene. Thus pictures available in places such as the Internet Movie Database (`www.imdb.com`), drawn from publicity stills or 'celebrity photos' of film stars in revealing dresses, swimwear or similar, are at least socially forbidden and sometimes illegal.

We consider in Chapter 4 the technical status of the user with respect to their ISP and law-enforcement agencies, so we will not reiterate the discussion of the legal aspects of anonymity here. Instead we consider the 'social' aspects of access to online material, and consider whether online access to sexual material has increased the amount 'consumed' or the number of individuals 'consuming' it.

The consumer of sexual material who wishes to hide that consumption, but has no access to computer-based material, must find a way to source that material.

Where the material is legal, there will be legitimate outlets for it, but the consumer must physically visit such outlets, at least in an initial instance although following a first visit it is possible that all further transactions might be carried out by mail and phone, having obtained sufficient information on contact details. Delivery of materials by mail entails the physical presence of a magazine, video tape or DVD. Discovery therefore remains a possibility, the likelihood dependent on who the consumer is trying to hide the consumption from: inadvertent exposure to neighbours or occasional visitors is unlikely, but the chance of exposure to those sharing accommodation must be quite high. Compare this with the chances of exposure from online surfing. The evidence is still there, of course, in caches, proxy records or ISP traces. However, the inadvertent discovery of these is less likely and some straightforward precautions such as clearing browser cache and history before exiting conceals activity from a casual inspection.

Thus we might posit that there will be a segment of society who will be deterred from buying magazines with sexual content, or visiting sex shops, simply on the basis of embarrassment from the possibility of being seen by a known acquaintance, or even simply from the necessity of interacting with the shopkeeper. For those thus deterred, sexual material online could make the difference between consumption and non-consumption. It is a matter of debate whether access to such material has any effect on the consumer, and whether such effects are universally positive or negative, or varied. We simply note here that it is likely that the 'apparent anonymity' of access to material online is likely to increase the number of consumers, possibly only marginally.

Accessing Sexual Material at Work

Viewing sex web sites or receiving sexual material by email at work has become one of the commonest reasons given for dismissal of employees. A survey for the human resources magazine Personnel Today in 2002 reported that 69% of all dismissals in the previous year had been for surfing sex sites on the Web.

> Being the boss is no protection either, as Michael Soden found out in 2004. He was the CEO of the Bank of Ireland. Two of his earliest acts as CEO had been to update the company's computer usage policy, including tightening up the rules on personal use of company computers and Internet connections, and to outsource the IT department to HP. When his work PC was subject to regular maintenance work by the IT department they discovered sexual content on it that contravened the company's acceptable usage policy. Soden swiftly resigned. The case was not over, however, as the Bank of Ireland and HP then argued over Soden's severance package. This might seem strange since Soden had breached company policy but it seems there is one rule for low-level staff, who are frequently dismissed with a worrying lack of due process, and another for executives. The Bank of Ireland claimed that it was not the fact of his breach of company policy that forced Soden's resignation but the fact that it became public knowledge and that was down to the now HP-employed IT staff. Hence the severance package and the Bank's claim that it was HP who should pay it. Full details can be found at `www.theregister.co.uk/2004/11/22/hp_porn_row/`.

Anon Servers

With home computers and commercial ISPs, one can be assured of relative anonymity for online activities. Who is to know that `fluffybunnydemon@flubundem.net` is in fact a highly respected professor of English literature at an Ivy League university. (Note that `flubundem.net` is not registered at time of writing and the authors know of no one who meets this description; it is simply an invented example.) In the 1980s and early 1990s, however, when access to the Internet was mostly restricted to universities, the military and some workplaces, posts to usenet were pretty much directly identifiable. In that case, a highly respected university professor posting to soc.support.transsexual, for instance, to discuss issues relating to gender confusion, was not something that such a person might see as conducive to their career or stability in their personal and professional lives. Thus were born the 'anon servers'. These servers were primarily used to allow e-mail and usenet anonymity. The two were rather intertwined given the existence of various mail-to-news gateways for those with email access but no (or restricted) usenet service. In addition to providing remailer anonymizing services, various sites also acted as unrestricted usenet servers. In order to get around restrictions placed on university or company servers (which frequently did not carry the recreational or alternate (rec and alt) hierarchies, or did not carry the sex-related groups in those hierarchies), users simply had to point their news programs at the remote servers instead of their local one. The end-to-end architecture of the Internet allowed such redirection with little interference before the introduction of strong firewalling operations in response to the explosion of the number of Internet sites and the prevalence of viruses and other attacks. Today, of course, commercial ISPs carry all the newsgroups with legal content and few in Western democracies rely solely on their work or university for access, removing much of the widespread desire for the anonymizing services simply to access sexual material online. Anonymizing services still exist, however (see Chapter 4).

Online Sex and Real Relationships

A recent report by Divorce Online (`www.divorce-online.co.uk`), an online information service about divorce matters in the United Kingdom, indicated that online activities formed a significant part of the petition for a divorce in at least half of cases. The primary activities cited were infidelity with someone the partner had met online or excessive use of pornography downloaded from the Internet. Other possibilities include 'addicted' levels of use of online chat rooms or games. The interesting aspect to note here is not that online activities are causing the breakdown of marriages, but that online activity has become so integral to daily life that it is being cited as the route to activities leading to divorce. As with much else, it is likely that much (or even all) of this activity would take place without Internet access, but Internet access is now the primary route. As mentioned above, however, the 'apparent anonymity' of Internet pornography use and the ease of finding people with similar interests online might be leading to people 'escaping' marital problems with online activities rather than attempting to work them out. Thus, some might see Internet access as responsible for the breakdown of social order in some way. Others see it as an empowering technology 'saving' people from continuing with failed relationships they have no means of escaping. Whether as a user or a provider of these services, it is for individuals to decide their own viewpoint in the light of their morals. Further developments in this area are likely and society will continue to develop mechanisms for dealing with the effects.

The Future of Online Sex: TeleDildonics?

In his 1991 book Virtual Reality, Howard Rheingold considered the way forward. Virtual reality is still mostly a dream more than a decade later and the haptic (physical sensation) interface is still quite rare and primitive. His book is still regarded as a seminal work, however, and his term 'teledildonics' is still an interesting concept.

While we do not subscribe to the view that technological and networking development is primarily driven by sex, it is undoubtedly a factor. Demand for broadband access is being driven by the desire for video on demand, and some of that demand is for 'anonymous' access to a variety of blue material. When suitable haptic devices become available, will we see the online chat rooms and live videocams of the sex industry move across into 'virtual touch'? How will governments react to this development? Will it be regarded as a way to discourage physical prostitution and thus be gently encouraged, or will more puritanical views hold sway, and the practice of virtual prostitution be outlawed alongside its real-world counterpart in some countries? It is difficult to say, but it is certain that whatever developments do emerge, some people will see a way to use them for sexual gratification, and others will try to use that as a means to make money.

It is already the case that many people are engaging in what is called 'cybersex' by some, which involves (mostly textual, sometimes webcam-based) interactions describing actions and feelings, usually accompanied by masturbation on one or both ends of the connection. This is little different to similar activities involving telephones except that (as usual with the Internet) there are a wider range of both professional and ordinary people available to engage with.

> Teledildonics: the use of virtual reality and haptic interfaces to enable remote sexual contact

REGULATING SEX IN CYBERSPACE

In this section, we consider the general question of regulating sexual content on the Internet at all, not how and whether to distinguish between types of user. In particular, there is the separate question of children using the Internet (see the next section). In the offline world, the debate about sexual material has been raging for centuries, possibly even millennia. A combination of social normative pressure and legal restrictions on publishing formed the background to an ebb and flow of availability and censorship of material. Few attempts are being made in the Western democracies to restrict access to online pornographic material. For instance, despite restricting the commercial import and distribution of so-called 'hardcore' material (including the US version of Playboy, for instance), for many years the UK government has made no serious attempt to block such material from being downloaded into the United Kingdom. Modern efforts at censorship of material are still primarily aimed at broadcast providers, where the UK government has straightforward regulatory control, rather than attempting to control the international and widespread providers of material previously banned. The United Kingdom has an interesting status in that the possession of the material itself is not illegal, rather it is the distribution which is banned. Thus while the United Kingdom may not play host to sites serving hardcore material, the surfers who download this material are breaking no law and the social anonymity they enjoy avoids any normative backlash either. The architecture of the Internet and the worldwide credit-card system allow access to a worldwide market.

Censoring the Internet, even for text material, is quite difficult (see Chapter 4). The relatively strong encryption built into modern web browsers to encourage confidence in online commerce, means that it may not be possible for governments to monitor the content of downloaded material. There have been attempts by various ISPs to restrict the language used in textual transmissions, although this can be rather hit-and-miss. For instance, when Genie tried to ban some words from their email and discussion areas they found that their large community of Vietnamese-speaking users were unduly hit since the two-letter encoding system that had been developed to represent Vietnamese characters included the pairs 'it' and 'sh', often juxtaposed. Automated systems for scanning textual communications are possible, but the sheer amount of transmission is likely to overwhelm even the best funded of these.

Automated scanning of binary material is even more difficult, even if actual material being transmitted is not encrypted. The monitoring system must be able to identify the format of a binary transmission (a gif, a jpeg, a tiff, a gzipped tarball or a zipped archive) and then it must be able to quickly and automatically 'scan' the file to see if it is sexual material which violates local law, currently an almost impossible proposition. Just as China is attempting to block access to 'subversive' textual information, so Saudi Arabia is attempting to block access to sexual material. The tools for 'The Great Firewall of China' and the access restrictions in Saudi Arabia are being developed both in-house and elsewhere. It is rather ironic that some of the same people who decried the US government for their attempts to block exportation of encryption code in the 1990s are now protesting against the export of monitoring and blocking software to repressive regimes. While the Internet retains its dual nature of an end-to-end architecture running on concentrated expensive physical international and national backbones, it is difficult to predict which way the see-saw will tilt. However, most governments have realized that they cannot control everything on the Internet and they are placing their monitoring and restricting resources where they believe they are most needed. In the Western world, this is seen to be protecting children, whereas elsewhere it may be preventing anyone from accessing sexual material or 'dangerous' concepts such as democratic freedoms.

Ethics vs Professionalism

There are a significant number of web sites which offer sexual material online. Many of these are substantial companies with large sites including significant security measures to ensure that only paying customers get access to the databases of still images and digital movies. This means that such sites require system administration services, either by employing people directly or by buying in services from professional administration companies. Neither the British Computer Society (BCS) nor the Association for Computing Machinery (ACM) codes of conduct and practice (see Chapter 10) give any advice on whether working directly for a sex site or for a company that supports their activities is consistent with professional conduct. Provided the material is legal in the jurisdiction from which it is offered, the codes would suggest there is no problem. Are there other concerns that should come into play, however? Some would suggest there are.

- It is often alleged that all sexual material is degrading and that involvement in its production, publication or distribution degrades the integrity of the people involved.
- There are risks involved since it is possible some of the material hosted may be illegal.
- Material sourced from other countries may be being produced under duress.
- There are persistent rumours that many online sex sites are used for money-laundering purposes due to the high volume of transactions and the worldwide nature of the business.
- What is legal in the jurisdiction in which one works may be illegal elsewhere and allowing downloads by customers in those countries may be a crime there.
- It is argued that free availability of sexual material is healthy and reduces sexual crime.

- It is a lucrative business and therefore may pay very well.
- Would you be happy explaining to your parents what the company you work for does?

Similar concerns are raised in a number of other areas of business (the weapons industry, for instance) and should be kept in mind when considering jobs.

NOT IN FRONT OF THE CHILDREN: PROTECTING CHILDREN FROM SEX ONLINE

So far, this chapter has focused on the activities of consenting adults, both as the receivers and the subjects of sexual material available technologically. In these last two sections, we consider the problem of children's involvement, either as receivers or as subjects. In this section, we focus on the question of children with Internet access. The final section deals with the even more sensitive issue of child pornography.

The Internet is seen by many parents and educators as a wonderful tool to expand their children's minds. Against the violence and mindless activity offered by computer games (as some people see it), the availability of so much information and interactive possibilities seemed a blessing. However, not all material available online is necessarily suitable for children or so most parents believe. There are a few who argue that nothing should be kept away from children and that 'if they're old enough to ask the question and understand the answer' then they should be able to access the information. However, most people in the West, apparently including most politicians, believe that it is appropriate not to expose children to concepts they are not ready for, to avoid confusing them. We do not attempt to enter into this argument here, we merely consider this majority view that validates attempts to restrict access and see where these attempts lead us.

Restricting Access to Broadcast Media

Films, television and (to a lesser extent) radio all have to deal with the issue of material deemed unsuitable for some age ranges. For films, this led to a rating system which differed between countries in its considerations but was fairly uniform in its method of policing: since cinemas are, generally, ordinary commercial premises, often needing a license of some sort from a local jurisdiction to operate as an entertainment provider, the requirement to police access to films based on their rating was passed on to the film theatre. This form of self-regulation is interesting, since the commercial operation would tend to militate against imposing audience access restrictions which lower profits (a market force). However, the forces of social norms, law and architecture push cinemas in the other direction, since allowing too many minors into adult movies may lead to public opprobrium, including boycotts particularly by parents, to a withdrawal of the license to operate, or to distributors not providing films due to public pressure to keep the rating system working. Thus the film-rating system, a combination of law and self-regulation, has mostly worked for decades. It has kept up with public attitudes to a great extent, and although there have been times when the ratings offices have been out of step with public opinion, the system has had sufficient flexibility to allow it to cope.

The issue of television and radio was more difficult. As with Internet access, viewing of television and listening to the radio mostly took place within private homes. A different compromise was reached with television in the United Kingdom, with the concept of a watershed, sometimes coupled with audio-visual warnings. Anything shown before 9pm is expected to be suitable for children; after 9pm, it is not quite 'anything goes' immediately, but a sliding scale of more 'adult' material being shown much later was adopted. Again, this system is far from perfect but, given the constraints of society wishing to allow adult-oriented entertainment but allowing children freedom to watch and listen, led to a suitable compromise. The implementation of this system has been primarily by a complex of legal and social pressures, with some market influence. Attempts to introduce architectural restrictions have been very limited, primarily to two attempts. The first was the

V-chip technology which was supposed to implant television sets with a sub-channel identifier which would prevent viewing of programs with adult content unless a PIN was entered. The extra cost imposed on both purchasers and broadcasters seems to have killed this idea, showing that without legal mandate the market often overrules architectural restrictions. The second is a similar method based on the set-top box for digital satellite broadcasts in the United Kingdom, which include some PIN entry to allow parents to restrict viewing access based on broadcast information about classification. Without the legal requirements imposed on cinemas, this is limited to social demand and only followed by the larger broadcasters such as BSkyB and the re-broadcast terrestrial channels. The fact that the capabilities of the set-top boxes generally are sufficient for this to be a very low cost addition, seems to make the difference from the V-chip's failure.

> V-chip: an embedded part of new televisions and other broadcast reception equipment allowing age restrictions as to what may be watched, depending on the classification of the broadcaster

Surfing to a Naked Beach

We now turn to access to sexual material online and address the separate issues of inadvertent and deliberate access by children to unsuitable material. There have been some efforts by parts of the online sex industry to self-regulate against both types of access.

Following (Elmer-Dewitt 1995), the first of a series of laws was passed in the United States attempting to force architectural changes to the Internet in an effort to protect children from either inadvertently or deliberately accessing sexual material. The Communications Decency Act (CDA) was struck down in 1997 following the Supreme Court's decision in ACLU (American Civil Liberties Union) vs Reno. The court ruled that attempting to censor online material that is lawful conflicts with the First Amendment to the US Constitution which grants freedom of speech.

In 1996, a portion of the online sex industry did attempt to self-regulate, partly in response to the threat of action under the CDA, but also to protect themselves against further legal restrictions on their activities. The method they chose was to require a valid credit card number from a consumer, even in cases where there was no charge for the service being offered. The principle was that the credit-card system was the only suitable identification system in place which could be used in this way. However, there are two problems with this attempt at self-regulation. First, not all providers of online sexual material took part and indeed, since many of the purveyors were not based in the United States, there was little reason for them to do so. Secondly, even for those taking part, the system itself was far from perfect in two ways: children may well have access to their parents' details and there was no further authentication in the system, particularly where no payment was taken; and many legitimate adult users either did not have a credit card or did not wish to give that information out, in case charges were made which they would then have to query. This lack of trust in the system completely undermined it and given the lack of universality it was later dropped by most as an authentication mechanism, though it remains the most common payment method. However, self-regulation is not completely dead and there are two other self-regulatory systems we must consider: pre-loading warning messages and ratings systems. First, however, we follow the succession of legal wranglings in the United States following the overturn of the CDA.

In 1998, the US Congress passed the Child Online Protection Act (COPA) in an attempt to impose similar restrictions to the CDA but taking into account the court ruling in 1997 on the unconstitutionality of the CDA. Once again the ACLU – together with two similar organizations dedicated to online issues: Electronic Privacy information Centre (EPIC) and the Electronic Frontier Foundation (EFF) – challenged the new law and succeeded in having it overturned. This was followed by yet another attempt with Children's Internet Protection Act (CIPA, also referred to as CHIPA) and by other tacks such as restricting federal funding of libraries to those where restrictions are 'voluntarily' placed on Internet access to prevent access to sexual material.

In addition to the 'adult free speech' issue, the courts have also considered the fallibility of filtering and other censorship mechanisms. Studies have shown that filtering mechanisms suffer substantially from both false positives and false negatives. False positives, where non-sexual material is blocked, most commonly occur when dealing with health issues. False negatives are where sexual material is passed though without detection. While the imperfect nature of censorship methods such as film ratings have been accepted by the courts, the evidence of false positives blocking important health information combine with the high level of false negatives allowing substantial amounts of material through, has mostly led to the discrediting of such schemes in the current architectural setting of the Internet. Separately to the constantly overturned laws such as CDA and COPA, the federal funding of libraries is still a live issue and nowhere near as clear-cut, particular with the softening of the system to allow authenticated adults to request the removal of filters. A recent new twist, however, has led to some library workers complaining of the effect of constantly being subjected to patrons' use of library Internet access to view sexual material.

Now we return to the self-regulation schemes used by some of the online sexual material providers. First, we consider the 'warning page' approach. This has a number of possible technical implementations but the basic premise is that before entering a site containing sexual material deemed unsuitable for minors a page is displayed which contains no such material, but only a warning that the site contains such material. A positive step, often displayed as an 'I am over 18 and my viewing of such material is legal in my physical location' link to select, is required of the user. Sometimes a separate link for 'I am under 18' is displayed which redirects the user to an innocuous site such as a children's television channel or a search engine.

The other main avenue for self-regulation is the Platform for Internet Content Selections (PICS). The concept is quite simple and is technically feasible to implement. However, there remain problems. The biggest problems are that of differing perspectives as to what should be filtered and where to perform the filtration. For instance, lesbian and gay support and political lobbying groups feel that information on sexuality should be freely available to teens, with frank discussions. More conservative elements of society view this as 'promoting deviance' and wish to suppress it. In the United Kingdom, for instance a law banning 'promotion' of 'alternative sexuality' in schools has long been a contentious issue. In Malaysia, images of women in health pamphlets promoting breast-feeding as a way to improve infant health were unacceptable. If a filtering system is available, should upstream providers filter things out entirely from certain portions of the Internet (educational establishments, for instance)? In writing this book (and particularly this chapter) for example, the authors have of necessity had to access material of a sexual nature online, in order to verify the information provided. Since the authors are based at a UK University, their Internet access at work is provided via the joint academic network (JANET), the UK educational Internet service. Personal viewing of sexual material via JANET is prohibited under the terms and conditions. Academic freedom, however, requires that researchers' legitimate access not be denied. With an architecture that identifies material as sexual in nature, some might feel that JANET should entirely block access. Such are the difficulties involved even in this simple idea of self-identification and self-regulation.

Platform for Internet Content Selection (PICS): a voluntary ratings system for web sites used by ISPs and computer-based restriction on the availability of material to certain users

'Satisfy Her in Bed': Sex Spam to Minors

As has been mentioned in previous chapters, children's access to the Internet has increased markedly in recent years. Whereas few children had access initially, there were strong moves to provide many UK schools with access in the late 1990s. Libraries were also encouraged to provide access to the Web as a way of supplementing their printed matter, and home Internet access became not only more common, but children were more likely to have their own computer (separate from a parental machine) and to have Internet access on it. As with all other aspects of raising children, the line between allowing them to grow and develop while keeping them safe raises questions about how (or whether) to supervise their Internet activity. The apparent freedom of online activity can be both a benefit and a danger. In the preceding section, we considered the active pursuit of information and the difficulties that presents in restricting children's access to material which is suitable for their developmental stage. In this section, we consider the passive receipt of unsuitable material.

The problem of spam is beginning to seriously undermine the utility of email as a communication medium for all (see Chapter 13). In terms of children, a recent study by Symantec (`www.symantec.com/press/2003/n030609a.html`) showed that a significant proportion of children were put off the use of email by the bombardment of sexual material. In some cases, this constant stream can harm their development and it is likely to cause an undue association of the Internet with sex. Particularly for adolescents, this association could well have the unfortunate consequence of deterring them from appropriate use of the Internet. Parental monitoring of children's communications is a difficult subject. While some parents do not feel it is unreasonable to open their children's letters or occasionally listen to their phone calls (with or without the child's knowledge), others feel it is a violation of the child's rights. In terms of email, children's groups generally recommend a 'light touch' monitoring of their online activities. Such a light touch in phone usage might be checking the phone bill for premium-rate service usage, number and frequency of calls to specific numbers and so on.

In terms of Internet use, this can be a little more problematic. Frequently, parents have less understanding of the working of the technology than the children themselves do. In addition, the end-to-end nature of the Internet can make monitoring highly difficult, as has been mentioned before. Attempting to ban use of certain technologies is often pointless since there are often other means to the same end. Close communication between parents and children is coming to be seen as the primary way of protecting children online, together with suitable use of 'protective technology' such as spam filters designed to keep inappropriate material out of their inboxes.

Online Friendships

One of the interesting things about the Internet is best summed up by the New Yorker cartoon with the caption 'On the Internet no one knows you're a dog'. The text-oriented nature of much of the Internet allows one to hide one's gender, age or disability. This is seen by many as one of the 'great levellers' of the age, particularly in regard to disabilities or physical variances (being overweight, very short or of a particular ethnic group). In addition to the question of lack of social and physical context to textual material, however, there is also the difficulty that some will abuse this apparent anonymity. This is particularly distressing when considering contacts between children and adults pretending to be children.

There have been a number of cases where child molesters have befriended children online, frequently in web-based chat rooms. Often they pretend to be much younger than they are, frequently very close in age to the group they wish to prey upon, though that is not always the case. There have been enough documented cases where a molester has lured a child to a meeting to lead to public concern over the issue. In a number of cases, the child has avoided molestation either because they realized the problem as soon as the meeting occurred or a parent accompanied the child to an initial meeting and realized the problem. In these cases, however, it was difficult to press charges since no actual crime had taken place. This has led to attempts to introduce, in the United Kingdom, a new offence of 'online grooming'. This was included in the Sexual Offences Act 2003, which came into force on 1 May 2004. The new offence will have to be tested in court, and may well fall at the hurdle of 'reasonable doubt' since it rests on proving the intent of the adult to commit an offence. Where the online discussions include mentions of sexual activity this can probably be proved, but otherwise it might be difficult to show to the standard required in court.

The use of the Internet to perform this 'grooming' has received much attention in the press and has led (at least in part) to the formation in the United Kingdom of the Child Exploitation and Online Protection Centre (CEOP, www.ceop.gov.uk) and the National High Tech Crime Unit (www.nhtcu.org), which supports the national crime and criminal information services and is now part of the Serious and Organised Crime Agency (SOCA). Similar groups exist in many other countries, including the Crimes Against Children section of the FBI.

These law-enforcement agencies' operations include officers pretending to be children or offering to arrange sex with children, in online communications in order to attract so-called 'predatory paedophiles'. A high-profile case in the United Kingdom saw Luke Sadowski convicted under existing laws of trying to procure a child under 16 years old for sex. On his arrest, he was found to be carrying a teddy bear, a pair of handcuffs and a replica handgun. Under the existing laws, however, Sadowski was given only an 18-month sentence and was not placed on the Sex Offenders' Register. The Sadowski case derived from cooperation between US and UK law enforcement officials engaged in attracting paedophiles to 'honey trap' web sites.

The public outrage over 'online grooming' masks the fact that these are only a small percentage of child abuse cases. In most cases, the victims of child abuse know the perpetrator well and online contact is, at most, a minor medium of communication in the crime, if present at all. Since online communications are still very new, society must of course monitor such abuse, but high-profile witch hunts against online activity may well be masking the real social problems already in existence, allowing society to feel as though it is tackling a problem while really it is only attacking a very small part of it. It is also possible that this focus on online grooming is masking the failure of authorities to tackle the much more widespread problem of the distribution of child pornography (see next section). The apparent anonymity of the Internet can also lead to difficulties in the reverse situation, of course, where an adult is fooled into thinking that their underage conversation partner is actually an adult. We consider this issue in the discussion topic on the Toby Studabaker case.

In September 2003, Microsoft made a surprise announcement that they were closing down the 'chatrooms' on their MSN online service. They claimed in press releases and interviews that this was because of concerns over children's vulnerability in these forums. The previously free service has been replaced by a subscription service, allowing Microsoft to identify participants. The problem, of course, is that most children did not subscribe to MSN's new services but moved across to other, still-free services. Many commentators have ascribed Microsoft's move solely or primarily to the fact that MSN continues to lose money for its parent corporation, a decade after it was launched. The fact that MSN Israel, which outsources the chatroom operations at no cost, maintains a free service lends some credence to this view.

CHILD PORNOGRAPHY

As with the attempt to define 'pornography' earlier, what at first appears to be a simple exercise becomes fraught with difficulty when the details are considered. Freedom of speech (as exercised in the Western world, this includes all forms of communication, not just spoken or written words) conflicts with other values: the protection of children, the revulsion of the majority against sexual depictions of children, strict views on nudity and so on.

It might seem simple to define child pornography legally and to enforce it. After all, most cultures regard sexual activity involving children as abnormal and highly damaging to the child. Cultural norms see child abuse, particularly sexual abuse, as one of the worst crimes possible. Thus we have laws against the sexual abuse of children in most countries. Most of the Western world has long had a concept of 'age of consent' and sex with someone under that age is regarded as a serious crime. However, there are difficulties involved. Teenagers frequently indulge in sexual activity where both participants are below the age of consent. Some countries have different ages for males and females or for heterosexual or homosexual activity, such laws sometimes conflicting with other laws on equality of the genders and of those of various sexual persuasions. Other countries do not have an 'age of consent'; for instance, until 1999 there was no such concept in Japanese law. Since then Japanese law specifies 13 as the age at which consent to sexual activity may be regarded as possible. This differs considerably from the 'age of majority' in Japan (20) which itself differs from the age at which one is considered no longer a child (18). Countries not including an 'age of consent' rely on the general laws about rape, which includes any form of duress, including the purely psychological. The younger the person involved the more likely it is that sexual activity is regarded as having been performed under duress. Of course, the age difference is also taken into account in such cases, and laws concerning sexual activity between minors differ vastly as well. Laws differ between states in the United States as to age of consent and also differ depending on marital status, as do laws in Middle Eastern or Indian sub-continent countries. This is all to show that even the concept of 'sexual abuse of children' is not universal in the details of its application.

Types of Material

Just as there is a variety of general sexual material available online, so there is a variety of material which some people would consider child pornography. Various countries draw the line between legality and illegality of such material at different points. We first give a list of the material to be considered in this section including some analysis of the openness with which such material is available and then consider the arguments regarding where the line should be drawn and where it is drawn in various places.

Text descriptions

These are freely available on web sites and usenet newsgroups. The sub-culture involved commonly cloaks itself under the term 'incest' and although mixed with textual descriptions of incestual relations between consenting adults, much of the material is about sexual activity between adults and children or between children and children, sometime but not always incestual. A whole nomenclature of categorizations has been developed for usenet articles on the groups dedicated to this topic, to allow readers to search for their particularly desired material. In much of the Western world, at least, such material is not only legal, but protected by law as free speech, despite its textual depiction of acts otherwise deemed illegal and the distaste with which such material is regarded by much of the population. In certain jurisdictions, however, such as the Republic of Ireland and Australia, such textual depictions are illegal.

Created images

These are images created from scratch but which apparently involve children in sexual activity or 'sexually provocative' positions. The status of using underage models to produce such material is a different discussion which is not covered here. As computer-graphics platforms become ever more sophisticated, it becomes more and more difficult to distinguish between 'created art', 'photographed reality' and 'altered photography'.

Altered images

Just as modern graphics programs allow for the creation of apparent child pornography so they also allow for the manipulation of pictures of a sexual nature to make it appear as if children are involved. Even more so than with created imagery, the source of such material can be difficult to judge. A recent attempt to amend US law to classify such images as illegal failed with the judgement that the justification for outlawing sexual images of children was that only the original act of abuse necessary to produce the pictures renders them unprotected speech under the constitution. Since no act of abuse is necessary to produce an altered or created image, there is no constitutional justification for outlawing them. However, in the United Kingdom, such images are deemed child pornography. In a case reported in The Times in August 2006 (`technology.timesonline.co.uk/article/0,,20411-2306067,00.html`), computer software was used to alter images of adult pornography so that the models appeared under age.

Non-sexual images

Just as 'pornography' might be regarded as 'in the eye of the beholder', so might child pornography in some cases. A court in the United States (US v Knox 1993) convicted a man of maintaining a collection of child pornography simply for having photographs of children in public places in bathing suits, and so on. The judge ruled that the 'emphasis on the pubic regions' and various other aspects of the collection meant that the intent of the photographer was sexual in nature despite the photographs being of public activity.

Nude pictures of infants are quite common in family albums and even shown on television and billboard adverts, yet usually these are not seen as child pornography, although a photography student at a UK college was arrested when having a photographic development laboratory develop a series of shots of her four-year-old son naked for a college project. Various 'art books' showing photos of naked children are freely available, although sometimes these can lead to controversy, such as the cases of Sally Mann and Tierney Gearon. Sally Mann is an art photographer whose work includes nude depictions of children, both her own and other models. Her work has consistently raised controversy, including issues of artistic freedom and freedom of speech. It should be noted that her work was not published in book form until the children were all adults and they were consulted about (and gave permission for) publication. In March 2001, the UK police raided a Saatchi gallery exhibition which included pictures of Gearon's children (aged six and four) photographed playing naked. The BBC coverage of the exhibition included small online versions of some of the photographs, including one of the two photographs alleged to be illegal. Other less celebrated cases of photography students using their own children for nude studies have also raised controversy.

Finally on this topic, there is the issue of naturism: the practice of going about daily activities naked. Although a minority pursuit, this is a family activity and is legal in many jurisdictions in the Western world, albeit usually restricted to specific places. Since it is regarded (literally) as natural by the practitioners, taking pictures during activities is also regarded as natural, even where child naturists are involved. Such 'naturist' pictures are the source of some images distributed across the Internet and may even be protected speech in the United States on the same grounds as 'altered images', although the Knox decision indicates that a collection of pictures focussing on children would be regarded as illegal. Magazines showing such child-naturist pictures are sold openly in some European countries such as Germany and the Netherlands.

Sexual images

Images of children in positions where the sexual intent of the photograph is undeniable or where the pictures are of children involved in sexual activity are the most extreme case. They are illegal in almost all jurisdictions, although the level of enforcement is highly variable. In some places, the laws have been passed simply to appease powerful foreign entities such as the United States and Europe, but then local enforcement is sketchy at best and non-existent at worst. Local law enforcement may be under-funded, may regard child pornography as secondary to the abuse of children, on which they focus their resources, or they may resent the interference of foreign countries in local affairs and social norms.

Such images may also be sub-categorized as to the severity of actions depicted as in the five-point scale adopted by the UK Court of Appeal for considering sentencing issues for those convicted of possessing child pornography images.

Operation Ore

While there have been a number of high-profile, online, child-pornography distribution cases since the early 1990s, the most widely reported one in the United Kingdom is 'Operation Ore' (`news.bbc.co.uk/1/hi/uk/2652465.stm`) in 2003. Operation Ore started with an earlier case, Operation Avalanche (`news.bbc.co.uk/1/hi/uk/2445065.stm`), in the United States. Landslide Promotions was the name of a gateway site which provided separate authentication operations to allow charging for access to servers offering child pornography. The operators of Landslide, Thomas and Janice Reedy, also maintained some of the sites accessible via the gateway, using servers situated in countries as widely spread as Russia and Indonesia. In addition to building a case against Thomas Reedy (sentenced to 1335 years for distributing child pornography, among other related offences), Operation Avalanche led to the credit card details of some 250 000 subscribers to the gateway service being recovered from Reedy's computers and financial records. The follow-up operation by UK police into those who had paid for access via the Landslide Gateway was named Operation Ore. Over 7000 individuals were on the list. Police reported that they were overwhelmed with trying to deal with the investigation. Other countries whose police have reported difficulty in coping with the huge number of reports deriving from Operation Avalanche include Canada and Australia.

The presence of a credit-card charge made by the company is not necessarily proof that the credit-card holder had signed up for access through Landslide Promotions. Credit-card fraud is another potential explanation. Although the investigations by UK police have led to arrests and prosecutions of some for possession of child pornography, many others have been found to have no illicit material on their computers. The pressure of even being accused of such a crime has led to the suicide of a number of suspects (`www.theregister.co.uk/2004/12/21/child_porn_suicide_shame`).

Prohibition, Harm, Possession and Distribution

The debate about pornography in general centred for much of the 20th century on the effect on the consumer. The debate raged about whether viewing pornographic material (and associated sexual activity, whether auto-erotic or not), particularly 'violent' or 'degrading' material, led the consumer to be more likely to commit illegal acts themselves and on whether legal sanction for pornographic material was in itself degrading to the subjects (usually women). The final conclusion of many social scientists was that any negative effect was likely to be immeasurable for most, whereas in others the purging of violent fantasies was a healthy safety valve. Of course, these conclusions are not shared by all, particularly those who object to the material in and of itself and seek to justify its suppression by quoting any study showing negative effects.

It is interesting to note, however, that the issue of child pornography does not usually centre on this debate, although the issue of altered or created images is beginning to bring it to the fore. It is generally expected that adult images are of consenting (and usually paid) adults. Ignoring the possibilities of economic necessity or 'social duress', this means that the material is produced 'ethically' and so long as no substantial harm derives from the viewing, then modern law has no basis on which to ban the material. In the case of child pornography, however, the opposite assumption is made about the circumstances of its production. Indeed, even the very fact of further distribution is a source of continued distress to the victims whose images circulate.

However, reports of how consumers and distributors of child pornography operate, such as those in (Jenkins 2001), do lead to a very difficult ethical dilemma. Since possession of child pornography is in itself a very serious crime, there is a 'prohibition economy' around its circulation. Such prohibition economies are well-studied in the areas of ordinary pornography, alcohol prohibition in the United States in the 1930s and 'recreational narcotic' usage from the 1950s onwards. In addition to the marked increase in the price that can be gained for illicit materials (thus providing an incentive for those with a criminal bent to focus on such lucrative possibilities), the online distribution of child pornography demonstrates a probably unexpected and wholly dismaying aspect. Those with existing large collections or those engaged in active production of new material will make material available, frequently through a number of levels of mis-direction and anonymity safeguards – see (Jenkins 2001) for details of the mechanisms though, fortunately, not the specific channels. However, the amount each distributes is very limited. Pure consumers on the discussion channels 'accompanying' the distribution channels who ask for further material are often encouraged to contribute something themselves. Thus, the prohibition, which leads to the difficulty of obtaining material, may itself be a mechanism for encouraging the abuse of children. This does not in any way excuse the consumer or producer, nor do the authors mean to imply that consumption of child pornography should be seen as a 'victimless crime' in itself, as many in the pro-drug-legalization community regard narcotic abuse. As has been mentioned, the continuing psychological effect of further distribution on those depicted in child pornography must be counted a crime. In the current social circumstances, however, it would appear that no debate is possible on the approach to child pornography, given the extreme reaction of the mass of the public to the whole subject.

Jurisdictional Anomalies and Conflicts

As mentioned above, child pornography is illegal in most jurisdictions today, although the definitions vary. As with other aspects of the law, there are times when internal contradictions are also apparent. For instance, despite the various ages of consent for sexual activity in different US states, the 1984 Child Protection Act defines a 'child' as any person under the age of 18 for these purposes. Thus, while in most places sex is legal from the age of 16 (and younger in various places under a variety of circumstances such as the age of the partner or the marital status of the couple), pictures of the sexual activity or even nude pictures of a sexually active person are still classed as pornographic. One example case (Jenkins 2001, page 36) is of a 24-year-old male convicted of possession of child pornography for having nude photographs of his 17-year-old girlfriend, with whom he had legally been having sexual relations. The high age of the definition of 'child' in this case strongly conflicts with the law in other jurisdictions. In the United Kingdom, for instance, one of the daily newspapers has contained photographs of topless models for decades. Following UK law, these models had to be at least 16 years old. The United Kingdom's Sexual Offences Act 2003 redefined this age limit and made the change retroactive such that possessing older copies of the newspaper could now be regarded as possession of child pornography. One wonders how the United Kingdom's copyright-deposit libraries have dealt with this issue and, indeed, the publishers who (it is assumed) retain an archive of the papers and probably the original submitted photographs. Under US law, the UK newspaper was creating and distributing child pornography from 1984. It is no surprise that this newspaper is not distributed by airlines flying to the United States. There does not, however, appear to have been any attempt by the online version of the newspaper to restrict their models to over-18s, nor was there a warning about the age of some of the models. Thus a US citizen could easily unwittingly be guilty of downloading material illegal in the United States from an apparently legitimate source. Such are the difficulties posed by the poor semantic labelling on the Internet combined with cross-border access and variable jurisdictional statutes.

Discovery, Defence and Mitigation

Despite the public horror at the crime of possession of child pornography, the law is not always an ass in these circumstances, even when an accused acts in a way that most would find incomprehensibly naive at best. There are some recent cases in the United Kingdom that deserve mention. Firstly, we have the case of a teenager (under 18) in the North East of England who was identified by police as having downloaded large amounts of child pornography. The case was proven quite easily but in sentencing the judge took account of the age of the offender and his plea that his sexual curiosity had led him to the illegal material through obvious links rather than through deliberate and sustained searching. In keeping with this the judge refrained from incarceration, insisting on therapeutic intervention and placing the boy's name on the Sex Offenders' Register for a substantial period, meaning that any further sexual offences would lead to a harsher sentence and to loss of certain other liberties including some travel restrictions and barring him from certain jobs and voluntary work involving children.

Next we have a couple of high-profile cases involving pop stars. Gary Glitter was convicted of possession of child pornography after submitting his computer to a repair shop. During their work they discovered the material on his hard drive. Pete Townsend was arrested as part of Operation Ore. He claimed to have been researching the topic for a book on the subject and was not convicted of possession.

Finally, we have the case of the 'trojan' storing child pornography of which the computer owner was unaware. Since many computers owners are unaware of the presence of remotely controlled programs on their machines, such programs often being used for distributed denial of service (DDOS) attacks (see Chapter 11), the judge in this case found that the owner was obviously not guilty of possessing or distributing child pornography. The publicity surrounding this case and the large number of virus attacks recently may make it more difficult for computer owners thus infected to claim complete innocence in the future. For a computer expert who might be able to fake the requisite hard-drive configuration, this defence might also be unbelievable to a court.

Many jurisdictions distinguish between possessing child pornography and distributing it (as with drug laws). However, there are differences. The Paedophile Unit of the United Kingdom's National High Tech Crime Unit issued the following advice to the public, still available on numerous local police force web sites (e.g. `www.herts.police.uk/main/faqs.htm`), about unwanted receipt of obscene material online:

> *I have opened my email and it appears to be an indecent image of a child. What should I do?*
>
> *The possession of indecent images of children is defined under Section 7 of the Protection of Children Act 1978 (as amended by Section 84 of the Criminal Justice and Public Order Act 1994). It is also an offence to manufacture, distribute or cause to be distributed such images and these include pseudo-images. These are all serious offences, which are subject of custodial sentences. In cases like this notify your local police or the Paedophile Unit who will advise you accordingly.*
>
> *Can I just email you the image for you to look at?*
>
> *No. This constitutes an offence of distribution to which there is no defence in law.*
>
> *What should I do with the image then?*
>
> *The image is obviously evidence of an offence and will be treated as such. Do not delete it but inform your local police. They will speak with you and take a written statement from you, which will produce this image as an exhibit. The image will be copied onto a disk, CD-ROM or made into a hard-copy print. It can then be deleted.*
>
> *You should then contact your ISP and inform them about this and consider 'blocking' the sender's e-mail address using the facilities on your email account.*
>
> *I don't get images but I get web site addresses which take me to sites involving children. What should I do?*

In cases like this it is acceptable to send us the web addresses. Do this by copying the addresses and forwarding an email to your police force's Paedophile Unit. The unit will then work with various organizations to try to close down these sites and arrest the offenders.

DISCUSSION TOPICS

Freedom of Speech vs Censorship of Sexual Material

The one-to-many nature of most communications media before the Internet allowed the identification of suitable gatekeepers who could be depended upon to prevent, or at least highly restrict, access to undesirable material by the majority of people. For example, it is known that there were sources of extreme sexual material in both printed and movie formats available for much of the 20th century, but these sources were limited in nature, difficult to find and subject to legal sanctions when discovered. The ability to enforce society's desire to restrict access to certain material is far more limited now that Internet access is common than it was when information required a physical embodiment, particularly when that physical embodiment was expensive to produce and copying involved significant generational degradation. The Internet has changed things in two ways: digital information can be copied without degradation and it can be transmitted in ways that make it indistinguishable from other material. The many-to-many nature of Internet communication facilities also undermine the idea of regulating gatekeepers to material (the local book or video store were required by law not to sell adult material to minors and not to stock material deemed too explicit for society). The very many-to-many and digital nature of the Internet preclude significant censorship. Therefore attempting to restrict the type of material that is available online by regulating intermediaries is a strategy that is unlikely to succeed. Societies will have to rely on detecting and punishing the producers and consumers of such material or change the underlying nature of the Internet and computers. As can be seen in other chapters, some would like to do just that – large copyright middlemen, for instance, who also dislike the democratizing nature of many-to-many communications.

The Toby Studabaker Case

In July 2003, UK television and newspapers featured an apparent 'child abduction' case which appeared at first to be a case of online grooming leading to a possibly tragic end. Shevaun Pennington, a 12-year-old girl from Wigan in the North East of England had gone missing from home. Her movements were tracked and it was found that she had travelled to Manchester airport where she had met up with a US man, Toby Studabaker. Further investigations revealed video footage of them together at London and Paris airports.

Interviews with Shevaun's parents revealed that the girl had been using Internet communications tools for what many would feel was an excessive period of time every day. Her parents had attempted to curtail this by restricting her to only five hours a day (previously she had been spending up to 11 hours a day online). Her use of the computer was in a family room, not her own bedroom or other 'sequestered spot'. Forensic examination of the data held on her computer confirmed that she had been in contact with Studabaker for some time. Interviews with Shevaun's friends indicated that she had referred to her 'American boyfriend'.

This might seem a familiar sort of tale to many, with the minor added twist of an international element. After a couple of days, however, an unusual twist emerged when Studabaker contacted his relatives back in the United States from Stuttgart in Germany and talked to the FBI who, of course, were camped out with his family. Studabaker claimed that in his online conversations with Shevaun she had claimed to be a 19-year-old student at college. When he made the arrangements to meet her, he claimed he had no idea that he might be on his way to becoming a child abductor. Shevaun returned under her own steam to her family and Studabaker was arrested in Germany on a charge of child abduction.

Once the case came to court in the United Kingdom, following Studabaker's extradition, and he was convicted, various facts were revealed which throw Studabaker's claims of lack of knowledge into question. In particular in the sentencing phase of his trial, it was revealed that he had been accused of seeking inappropriate contact with underage girls on a number of previous occasions, although never convicted of an offence. Ignoring Studabaker's guilt (now proved in a court of law), the original claims raise interesting questions. There are many young people whose age is indeterminate (in both directions) between their early teens and mid 20s. Online activity, as we have discussed, frequently hides identity. How should adults act to avoid impropriety and how can parents be sure that their child's online activities do not include masquerading as older than they are, leading them into 'reverse grooming' as it might be called? A bright 12-year-old might well be the intellectual equal or superior of an average 30-year-old, particularly in the text-only milieu of the Internet, so blaming the adult for being deceived might be seen as extremely harsh.

REFERENCES

Elmer-Dewitt, P. (1995) On a Screen Near You: Cyberporn, *Time Magazine*, 3 July 1995.

Jenkins, P. (2001) *Beyond Tolerance: Child Pornography on the Internet*, New York University Press, New York. ISBN: 0-8147-4262-9.

Tierney, J. (1994) Porn, the Low-Slung Engine of Progress, *New York Times*, 9 January 1994.

RELATED READING

Akdeniz, Y. (1999) *Sex on the Net*, South Street Press, Reading. ISBN 1-902932-00-5.

Akdeniz, Y., **Walker, C.** and **Wall, D. S.** (eds) (2000) *The Internet, Law and Society* (Chapters 9 and 10), Longman, Harlow. ISBN 0-582-35656-3.

Edwards, L. and **Waelde, C.** (2000) *Law and the Internet* (Chapter 12), Hart, Portland, OR. ISBN 1-84113-141-5.

Rheingold, H. (1991) *Virtual Reality*, Secker and Warburg, London. ISBN 0-671-69363-8.

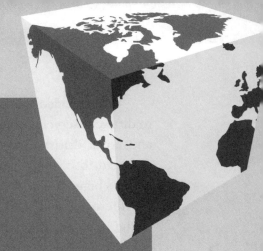

6

GOVERNANCE OF THE INTERNET

INTRODUCTION

Could anything sound more tedious and boring than the governance of the Internet? In a world where geeks and nerds are accused of social inadequacy and monomania, surely those interested in the minutiae of who controls the technical functions of the domain name system, Internet Protocol (IP) address block allocation and new variants of the protocol itself, are the saddest of the lot? This is one of those topics that appears to be even more irrelevant to most computer professionals than the vagaries of copyright or the details of data protection legislation. As with these other topics, however, this is only a boring subject until one realizes the immense power exerted behind the scenes and exactly how that power affects people's day-to-day interactions with the Internet. We're not talking here about how fast the IP stack can be implemented, but of who controls access to the entire infrastructure of the Internet and, most relevantly, who controls access to the Web via URLs.

Who decided that `Amazon.co.uk` and `Amazon.com` could both exist and point to different servers? Who decides that `scoobydoo.co.uk` belongs to Hanna-Barbera and not a British fan of the cartoon? How does a system which was originally designed to connect a few thousand academic and military computers allow the world's biggest information distribution scheme to run? Can the US president order the Internet shut down? These questions and others are not irrelevant to the future of the Internet. They are the fundamental questions of who has control and who oversees the exercise of that control.

USER FRIENDLY by Illiad

The Internet Protocols

At its core, the Internet runs two very simple protocols: the Internet protocol (IP), which constrains how data packets are formed to encode information, and the transfer control protocol (TCP), which determines where packets go. In fact, it is the very simplicity of these protocols that has allowed the Internet to develop so quickly. Because they are simply a way of ensuring that information being passed between two computers can successfully find a reasonable path without having a significant overhead of control, without requiring a specific route plan to get from one computer to another, and by ignoring the actual content of the packets of data, TCP/IP is an immensely flexible tool.

The original designers of the protocols did not, indeed could not, have foreseen where their invention would lead. They had a specific goal in mind: to ensure that communication was robust and reasonably fast. However, they did realize that they needed to design for a system orders of magnitude larger and more complex then the original. Because of the flexibility of the system they created, a plethora of services has been able to grow and spread throughout the world without needing a central controller 'picking winners' from among competing architectures.

The basic principle behind the Internet is that intelligence happens at the two ends of a connection and the transport layer is only as smart as it absolutely needs to be to allow the intelligent systems to communicate with each other. This is based on the concept of packet switching rather than line switching, which is the fundamental difference between the telephone network and the Internet: telephones were originally line switched, consisting of a dedicated piece of copper that could be traced between any two connected telephones. Originally by manual plugging in of connectors by operators, then by electrical automatic switching and finally by electronic switching, the telephone network places its intelligence in the network, with dumb terminals performing highly limited tasks: indicating the desired destination and encoding the transmission. These days, the telephone network is mostly a packet-switching system emulating a line-switched system but the principle of operation remains the same. Of course telephone lines have played (and still play) a part in the development of the Internet and the Internet is now being used to replace the dedicated phone-line networks, with Voice over IP (VoIP) systems becoming common. But the telephone line is and was used simply as a way to connect to the edge of the Internet while the fundamental flexibility of the IP still allows innovation and decentralized control, far more than the phone system which it will likely eventually replace.

> Voice over Internet Protocol (VoIP): a system to allow an Internet connection to be used in the same way as an ordinary phone, sometimes interconnecting with the existing phone system for incoming and outgoing calls

The Origins of the Internet

The development of the Internet is chronicled in detail and with insight in (Hafner and Lyon 1996) and the organic growth of control of the Internet is detailed in that book and in (Mueller 2002). Between them they give highly detailed accounts of the history, current state and current difficulties of running the Internet on both the political and technical levels. The more recent (Goldsmith and Wu 2006) expands the analysis to consider the connections between infrastructure and services with governance and governments.

In the 1960s, at the height of Cold War paranoia, the Pentagon wanted a communications system which could survive a 'limited nuclear exchange'. The line-switched telephone system was incredibly vulnerable to being partitioned into many smaller networks. Therefore the Advanced Research Project Agency (ARPA) funded the first wide-area-network project, which developed a system called ARPANET. It was during this project that the request for comments (RFC) system was developed: three postgraduate students (Steve Crocker, Vint Cerf and Jon Postel) were trying to set the technical specifications for the communication protocol. In order to avoid politics and ego getting in the way of their efforts they presented draft specifications under the title 'Request For Comments'. The name (and to some extent the agreement and compromise-oriented process it suggests and in some senses actually embodies) remains the primary tool for Internet protocol specifications even now.

By the 1970s, ARPANET was not the only wide area network in operation and incompatible systems were in operation elsewhere. Between 1973 and 1981, various efforts to define a truly interoperable networking protocol were undertaken, leading to the TCP/IP proposed standard in RFC0791. Released the same day, RFC0790 detailed the name and number assignments for the first hosts to be connected to the Internet. By 1982, there were 25 networks joined via the Internet protocol (most in the United States but with a couple in Europe) comprising around 250 hosts. At this point, Jon Postel was personally responsible for assigning new blocks of addresses and for updating the `hosts.txt` file which contained the mapping from names to numbers. The original `hosts.txt` file was held on a computer operated by the Network Information Center of the Defense Data Network, hosted at SRI International in California. Each machine connected to the Internet would download a copy of the `hosts.txt` file on a regular basis and new machines would not be visible to all until every machine had copied this file. Some of those involved in developing the Internet protocols realized early on that this was an unsustainable approach and various RFCs of the time (e.g. 799 and 814) talked about hierarchical solutions to the name–address issue. As an initial step, the (supposedly temporary) first top-level of the domain name system was defined as .arpa in late 1983 on an e-mail discussion list.

Various other networking systems around the world were in operation by this time, many of them based on the X.25 LAN system of the International Telecommunications Union (ITU). The United Kingdom's Joint Academic Network (JANET) is one example, dating from 1984. Now, of course, almost all of these systems are either connected directly to the Internet or use the TCP/IP protocol internally. Some wide area networks, such as the US military network, use variants of the TCP/IP protocols which may be slower but are designed to include more security features.

> Domain name server (DNS): a computer that maps domain names to IP addresses

But, back to our main concern: the development of the DNS. Discussions went on about what the top-level domains (TLDs) should be and who should administer them. Jon Postel's original proposals to split by 'type' of organization (.edu for education, .gov for government and .mil for military) had various complaints raised against it. Many of those involved in the discussion believed that geographical location should be the top-level domain marker and this was put into practice when the .uk domain was assigned to Andrew McDowell of University College London for administration. By October 1984, this led to the ISO-3166 list of country abbreviations being adopted as a set of top-level domains (now called the ccTLDs). It should be noted that the ISO-3166 country code for the United Kingdom is GB not UK, but the '.uk' domain is now (and was then) too well established to change. In addition to the ccTLDs the list also included the generic TLDs now so familiar: '.com', '.org', etc. There were complaints that this might lead to confusion about which domain would contain some organizations, the classic example being the non-profit research organization where Postel himself worked, SRI, which is not an educational institute, a non-profit organization or a commercial company, but which contains aspects of all three. Postel's response was 'This is a naming system, not a general directory assistance system'.

Top-level domain (TLD): the rightmost part of a domain name, either a generic such as '.com' or a country code such as '.uk' or '.de')

Of course, domain names are now seen very much as a form of directory assistance and the delegation of authority envisaged by Postel has to some extent been forced back by the arguments over trade marks in the second and third levels of domain names.

Chinese State Control over the .cn ccTLD

The Chinese government exerts stronger control over Internet access than almost any other in the world (see Chapter 4). Control over the services and sites accessible to Chinese Internet users is not the only control the PRC government exerts: it also controls the ccTLD for China ('.cn'), which includes some quite interesting differences to many other countries. The delegated authority for the .cn domain is China Internet Network Information Centre (CNNIC, `www.cnnic.net.cn`). A sample of the rules included in China's name registration system is:

> *Article 11. Restrictions for the naming of domains at and below the third level*

> *(1) Without official approval from the relevant state authorities, domain names including words such as CHINA, CHINESE, CN, NATIONAL, etc. may not be used;*
>
> *(4) Classifications of industries or generic names of goods may not be used;*
>
> *(6) Names that are harmful to the interests of the state, society or the public may not be used.*
>
> *Article 28. Servers located in China and connected to China's Internet, whose registered top-level domain names are not CN, must report and file a record with the CNNIC.*

Early Arguments

The US National Science Foundation (NSF) funded much of the expansion of the Internet in the 1980s and early 1990s, providing the NSFNet backbone system to improve connection speed and reliability. However, there were some early problems with this, particularly in connection with the expanding European networks. It was in everyone's interest to have a single interconnected network, and yet some of the European involvement was with commercial firms. The European Community also backed the ITU's Open Systems Interconnection (OSI) standards development rather than IP. Another problem the European public bodies had was that the US government has always retained a level of control over the governance of the main Internet name and number allocation system. The European government agencies much preferred to follow the less popular but more internationally governed system of the ITU, an independent international body dating back to the mid-nineteenth century whose raison d'etre is to promote interoperability between national telecommunications systems. The United States has always resisted efforts to bring the Internet within the scope of ITU control.

Having taken over from the Department of Defense as the main funding body for non-military Internet issues, the NSF enforced its prohibition against commercial use of its subsidized backbone by control over the domain name and IP number allocations held at SRI. This was overcome by delegation of control over part of the number space to Reseaux IP Europeans (RIPE) in 1992. In the same year, the Internet Society (ISOC) was formed, mostly through the efforts of those who had been working on the Internet since its early stages, including Crocker, Cerf and Postel. The goal of ISOC was to formalize the governance of the Internet and avoid it degenerating into chaos. ISOC attempted to bring together the various relevant formal and informal entities already in existence, under a single new formal structure. Unfortunately the vision of a formal organization bringing together interested parties and committed to finding working solutions (rather than to producing unrealized paper-based definitions of systems, which is how ISOC members described the workings of the ITU's OSI) failed to materialize.

Before we jump forward to the problems with a commercial Internet and the apparent abuse of power by the current domain name controllers, we must differentiate between the different roles played by various organizations in running the infrastructure of the Internet: IANA, IETF and the DNS root are some of the most powerful influences on the Internet today.

Internet Assigned Numbers Authority

The first mention of the Internet Assigned Numbers Authority (IANA) was in RFC1083, granting that authority to Jon Postel. He had the de facto authority under a contract with the Defense Advanced Research Projects Agency (DARPA, the successor to ARPA). The RFC, however, made no mention of this contract, but presumed upon the authority of the Internet Activities Board (IAB), which later formed the ruling body of ISOC. The operating function was delegated by Postel under this authority to the DDN-NIC. The job of the IANA is to allocate IP address blocks to organizations to ensure uniqueness. Only such an allocation by IANA allows for an entry in the DNS root for those numbers.

> Internet Assigned Numbers Authority (IANA): the body which assigns blocks of IP addresses to networks

> Internet Engineering Task Force (IETF): a body which approves changes to the main protocols of the Internet

DNS root

When a computer requests the IP address for a domain name, it asks a domain name server (DNS) which has a known IP address. Part of the process of setting up a machine with an IP address and Internet connection is to identify the domain name server of which it should ask such questions. But the server does not contain the full database for the whole Internet. That would be unsustainable. Instead, a local server contains only its own block of addresses and possibly some cached names: it is highly likely that almost every server in the world caches the IP address of `www.google.com`, for instance. For all other names, the server asks another server further up the chain of domains for information but it does not request the address: that would simply move the requirement for holding the whole database one level up the chain. Instead, the server asks for the Internet address of the server which contains the answer. This is recursively followed up the tree until the root server (well, one of the small number of mirrors of the root server) is queried, if necessary.

Let us consider an example: the user on machine phx.rdg.ac.uk types the address `info.swimming.org` into their web browser. First, phx.rdg.ac.uk checks its own cache of name and IP address links. Many machines have a small number of hosts for which they keep the addresses: typically these are machines that they access very often (such as their upstream mail server) and whose addresses do not generally change. It may also run its own name caching of recently requested addresses. Let us assume that the address of `info.swimming.org` is not available, however. So, phx.rdg.ac.uk asks its name server (the one for the rdg.ac.uk domain, e.g. dns.rdg.ac.uk) for the answer. The dns.rdg.ac.uk server holds two sets of information: its own addresses (the rdg.ac.uk domain), for which it will provide the answer for any query sent to it, and the address of the ac.uk domain server, say dns.ac.uk. This server does not hold all the ac.uk domain IP addresses but it does hold the addresses of the DNS servers for all other ac.uk domains and the DNS server for the uk domain, say dns.uk. The uk domain server holds the addresses for the dns servers for all subdomains in the uk (org.uk, co.uk, ac.uk, gov.uk, etc.) and the address for the root servers (currently A–M, A being the master). The dns.uk server requests from a root server the Internet address of the name server for the org domain (say `dns.org`) and passes this information back down to dns.ac.uk which passes it back to dns.rdg.ac.uk, which then queries `dns.org` for the address of `info.swimming.org`. The `dns.org` server does not hold all the addresses for the org domain but does know which machine holds those addresses, in this case `dns.swimming.org`, and passes this information back to dns.rdg.ac.uk, which then asks `dns.swimming.org` for the Internet address of `info.swimming.org`. The `dns.swimming.org` server knows the address of `info.swimming.org` and passes it to dns.rdg.ac.uk, which finally gives that information back to phx.rdg.ac.uk.

> DNS root: a server which points to the authoritative server for a particular TLD

Of course this does not happen every time there is a query because the various levels in the hierarchy cache the results of various requests for a certain length of time and often 'forward cache' expected queries. For example, the dns.ac.uk server would probably have the `dns.org` address in its cache and might maintain it whenever the copy in the cache is timed out. This provides quicker service and a robust response to failure of links in the chain, although it does introduce some delays in 'propagation' of some types of change, such as the Internet address of a major DNS. There are technical ways around this which are not the subject of this chapter. The real meat of this chapter is the power that is granted to the root server: whoever controls the root servers (in fact, whoever controls the primary root server, since all the rest are bound by contract to slave their database to its database) also controls which top-level domains are visible. While this might not seem a great deal to control, it is actually a major issue. It is also a lever to control other aspects of the domain name system, particularly when a new contract is signed for a top-level domain (see the next section, on ICANN and the ccTLDs).

Cache: a local copy of a piece of memory usually held externally; standard, backward caching involves storing frequently or recently accessed information

Forward cache: a local copy of information regularly updated in the expectation that it will be wanted at some point soon; access to a cache is quicker than access to the external source and so forward caching may reduce response times if the correct choices are made regarding which information to store

THE ROOT OF ALL EVIL

In this section, we discuss who controls the root servers that 'ground' the domain name server system and why that gives them power. We also look at how country code domains are run and the interaction between country code authorities and the root authority.

Commercialization

The attempt to create a non-profit organization independent of the US government (ISOC) failed quite spectacularly to successfully exert authority; the supposedly subordinate IETF, which was in reality a separate and powerful group, maintained significant control. ISOC never truly recovered from its initial problems in 1992. In the meantime, a company called Network Solutions Incorporated (NSI) had been granted a contract by the US government in 1991 to perform the IANA function for the military networks and in 1992 signed a contract with the NSF to perform the same function for the non-military networks. However, NSI still subcontracted the running of the system to Jon Postel.

During the early 1990s, the Internet was opened up to commercial traffic and commercial internet service providers (ISPs) emerged. The NSFNet backbone was officially decommissioned in 1995 as the primary backbone but by that point it was mostly irrelevant anyway as the new commercial ISPs had already transferred much of their traffic to commercial backbones operated primarily by telephone companies. By then the transformation of the Internet was already well underway. NSI's agreement with the NSF allowed it to charge the NSF a fee for registration of subdomains and NSI controlled the top-level domains that existed. A few months after the NSF–NSI contract was signed, Tim Berners-Lee released the Web onto an unsuspecting Internet.

Within a few years (by late 1994), the NSF was paying for thousands of commercial registrations per month. This was obviously an untenable situation as the numbers of requests was increasingly exponentially. In 1995 therefore an amendment to the NSF–NSI contract allowed NSI to charge for commercial (.com, .net and .org) registrations while NSF continued to pay for .edu registrations and (as an interim measure) .gov registrations, pending other government funding being identified. Even in these early days the question of who was allowed to register a trade mark name in the second level was at issue. Below we follow the sequence of events related to this. Although how these issues were (and are) dealt with is dependent upon who controls the root, the struggle for control of the root forms the backdrop to the foreground struggle for individual domains.

Internet Corporation for Assigned Names and Numbers

By the late 1990s, the NSF was clearly the wrong government department to be overseeing the development of the Internet, now a clearly commercial domain with growing economic impact, particularly in the United States. We were in the early days of the dot com bubble and there were three major players in the struggle for control of the root at this point: the US Department of Commerce, ISOC and the international Council of Registrars (CORE), and Network Solutions Inc. What emerged was the Internet Corporation for Assigned Names and Numbers

(ICANN), which was to incorporate the IANA function due to expire from NSI's contract in late 1998.

Although containing the apparent trappings of international influence and grass-roots support demanded by groups such as ISOC, there were considerable misgivings about the makeup of the initial board of ICANN and its accountability to the Internet community at large. Over the next few years, ICANN did indeed perform some much needed housecleaning on the management of the generic top-level domain system, removing NSI's monopoly over registrations and curbing its wholesale prices, bringing competition into what had been a licence to print money. However, most of the rest of ICANN's operations have attracted more and more criticism as time has gone on. In particular, the 'artificial scarcity' of generic top-level domains (gTLDs) has been a source of considerable annoyance to some. There were still only five gTLDs as late as 2000 and then only a small number were added, some of them quite bizarre: .info was reasonable but .museum and .aero seemed rather strange additions. See the Alternative Root Servers section for the problems raised by the .biz top-level domain.

> Internet Corporation for Assigned Names and Numbers (ICANN): a non-profit organization set up to perform IANA operations

ICANN's operation, accountability and even its authority remain controversial matters in the Internet world. The US Department of Commerce (DoC), originally supposed to officially renounce any legal claim to control over the root server two years after the creation of ICANN, still retains it but seems unwilling to use it to leverage any change in ICANN policy. The continued unwillingness of the US DoC to either use or renounce its authority is a continued source of irritation to those interested in Internet governance. In 2006, the US DoC renewed its contract with ICANN to run the IANA function, many years after it was supposed to cede the authority to control who deals with this vital function. The contract runs until 2011 (see `www.icann.org/general/iana-contract-14aug06.pdf`).

ccTLDs

So far we have concentrated on the situation with regard to the generic top-level domains. Indeed it is the generic top-level domains that see the most registrations and the most Internet traffic. But the ccTLDs are not without importance. Firstly, there are the ccTLDs which are sometimes referred to as pseudo-generic. Remember that the ccTLD list is based on the ISO list of two-letter abbreviations. Thus Tonga in the South Pacific, with ISO country code TO, has made significant amounts of money by licensing international use of its country code to groups playing on the ignorance of a large number of web users with descriptive names such as `send.browser.to`. Another small Pacific nation, that of Tuvalu (a former British colony which gained independence in 1978), has also seen a bonanza due to its fortuitous country code of TV.

ICANN inherited country code delegations to individuals, non-profit organizations and sometimes commercial companies. There has been a significant pressure by ICANN to force ccTLD delegated authorities to move to new contracts which officially recognize ICANN's superior authority in various matters, including following ICANN policy on trade marks and similar issues. Two of the oldest and biggest ccTLDs, however, have refused to play ball with ICANN and this is rapidly becoming a matter of international policy and politics. These major refuseniks are operators of the British (uk) and German (de) ccTLDs: Nominet and DENIC, respectively.

Alternative Root Servers

All of the above has assumed that there is one and only one root server (albeit with many mirrors). This is not actually the case. There is nothing legal or technical to prevent breakaway alternative roots which offer alternative namespaces. While the assignment of blocks of IP addresses does require a consistent approach, the mapping of names to those numbers can be done by anyone. It is only inertia and a belief that a single authority is the way to go that has preserved ICANN's near-monopoly position so far. It is this technical fact that alternative roots not only could exist, but do exist, that has prevented ICANN from acting in certain circumstances. The current alternative roots generally operate under a much more cooperative regime, trying not to step on each other's toes and recognizing each other's hierarchies. In deciding which would be the seven new gTLDs, ICANN showed a rather strange sensibility: denying requests for the obvious TLD of .web (possibly due to its existing alternative root implementation) but allowing the new .biz domain which also had an alternative root structure.

> Alternative root: a server which supplements or supplants the 'official' root DNS

COMMERCIALIZATION, OWNERSHIP AND CORPORATE IDENTITY

Having described how the convoluted and contentious history of ownership of the root and the power to decide policy has shifted and changed over the last 30 years, we can now focus on what is the most visible, though not necessarily the most important, aspect of domain names. This is the 'ownership' of, and right to use certain words and phrases in, domain names. In particular, the right to use an unadorned and recognized name (possibly a trade mark) in the com hierarchy has been a source of legal and policy problems since the emergence of the Web, which transported the Internet from an arcane source of information for dedicated command-line enthusiasts into the world's most used computer application.

Trade Marks

A trade mark is a graphical sign (an icon, if you will) or, more recently, a word under which a particular person or organization is well known for their goods or services (see Chapter 12). Different organizations may use the same word or mark in different arenas provided there is no possibility of confusion between their products and services. Thus Apple Corp., the recording company (publisher of much of the work of the Beatles), and Apple Inc., the computer company, co-exist except when Apple Inc. trades in music. The major (though not the only) issue involving trade marks and computer technology is that of trade-marked terms in domain names.

Apple Corp. vs Apple Inc.

Apple Computer Inc. (Apple Inc.) was allegedly named by Steve Jobs after the Beatles' record label, Apple Corporation Ltd. (Apple Corp.), because of his love of music and the Beatles in particular. In 1981, Apple Inc. made an agreement (after a court judgement ruled they were infringing) with Apple Corp. not to enter the music market to avoid causing trade mark confusion. Unfortunately by the mid 1980s, Apple Inc. had conveniently forgotten this and starting selling music-related software. This led to a 1991 judgement against Apple Inc. which cost over $26 million for breach of a trade mark agreement. This was not the end of the story however, as Apple Inc. returned to the music business again, first launching the Apple iPod personal music player and then starting a music download system called Apple iTunes Music Store. Advertising for the iPod has even called it a device from 'AppleMusic'. In September 2003, therefore Apple Corp. instigated yet another trade mark agreement violation suit (`news.bbc.co.uk/1/hi/entertainment/music/3685988.stm`). The judge in the case, heard in London, United Kingdom, admitted to owning an iPod but ruled that this would not bias his hearing of the case. At the time of writing, the case has been decided in favour of Apple Inc. (`www.bbc.co.uk/6music/news/20060329_apple.shtml`), allowing it to continue to use its trade mark in selling both standalone music devices (the Apple iPod and variants) and contents (the Apple iTunes Music Store). Apple Corp. are lodging an appeal.

Trade Marks in Domain Names

The principal problem, so far, with trade marks and the domain names system has always been as second-level identifiers in gTLDs and second- or third-level identifiers in ccTLDs (third level in the United Kingdom, which uses generic second-level classifications such as co.uk and org.uk, but second level in others such as Germany (.de) which have no such classifications). The issues are primarily the same, although the means of dealing with it have differed between countries.

Many trade mark holders were quite slow off the mark in seeing the potential benefits of owning their mark as a second-level domain in (principally) the .com gTLD. One of the many reasons for the importance of the .com domain was that early web browsers, in an attempt to reach out to the uninitiated, defaulted to allowing a single word (such as 'foo') to be entered into the address field by automatically translating it with 'www.' at the beginning, '.com' on the end and a default protocol of http (turning it into `http://www.foo.com/`). It was this, more than anything else, which transformed the DNS in exactly the way from which Postel had demurred: from 'a naming system' to 'a general directory assistance system'.

A decade later there is more variation (as well as more possible browsers: Microsoft's dominance in terms of the number of installations aside, there are more up-to-date, decent browsers available than ever before). Some browsers still try `www.foo.com` whereas others simply report an error and others submit any unrecognized domain to a web search engine. Still the damage was done in the mid 1990s when there was a scramble by large organizations to catch up with the growing potential of the Internet and, rightly or wrongly, to own all the second-level (or third-level) domains of their recognized brand names. General Motors for instance wanted `buick.com` and vauxhall.co.uk instead of being happy with `gm.com/buick` and `gm.co.uk/vauxhall`.

Unfortunately, being late to the party, quite a few large organizations found that their names (trade marked or not) had already been registered. Many had been registered for legitimate purposes (such as the man who registered `ty.com` to display photos and other information about his son named Ty for the rest of the family to access). Ty Inc., manufacturer of the Beanie Baby line of toys, was not happy with this. Others, such as harrods.co.uk, were registered in a deliberate attempt by a visionary to settle prime virtual real estate and make a killing by selling it to interested parties afterwards. Some organizations made do with alternative versions of the domain names, others paid (sometimes exorbitant sums) to the registrants, but others decided to go to court. In a few early cases, the domain registration organizations were named as co-defendants in trade mark violation suits.

(Reverse) Domain Name Hijacking

Registration of well known names for the purposes of selling them on, or to redirect traffic looking for other organizations to one's own site, is known as domain-name hijacking. However, attempts to use legal or para-legal processes (see the 'Dispute Resolution Processes' section) to grab a legitimate name that an organization simply wished it had the foresight to register first has become known as reverse domain-name hijacking and is arguably as big a problem as domain-name hijacking.

Typosquatting

In addition to registering actual trading names many of those simply looking for extra traffic (and sometimes those with a grievance) have taken to registering domains which are misspellings or naive variants of names. So, for example, `www.goohle.com` used to redirect the user to `www.uniairlines.com`, an online holiday site.

VeriSign's Site Finder: All Your Typos Are Belong to Us

VeriSign is the company that currently owns Network Solutions Inc. (NSI), which operates the .com and .net TLDs. In late 2003, VeriSign unilaterally amended the operation of the domain name server for .com and .net such that instead of returning an 'unknown address' response when given an unregistered domain name to resolve, it returned the IP address of its Site Finder service. Site Finder is a search engine which takes the words from the unsuccessful domain name query and returns a list of (potentially) appropriate sites. There was a major outcry from a variety of sources:

- organizations involved in the development of technical DNS operations, such as the Internet Software Consortium (the non-profit organization that develops BIND, the most widely used name server software);
- ISPs such as AOL who operated similar services for their clients based on the 'no such address' response to the DNS query;
- open standards advocates who argued that such a unilateral move was an abuse of power: much of the success of the Internet comes from common standards and people being able to develop new systems which rely on adherence to those standards by the majority of Internet systems, particularly the core systems such as DNS;
- trade mark holders who viewed this system as a massive example of 'typosquatting'.

After a few days, ICANN stepped in and requested VeriSign to 'voluntarily suspend the service until the various reviews now underway are completed'. It also instituted reviews by the Security and Stability Advisory Committee of the IAB. However, VeriSign refused to voluntarily withdraw the 'service'. ICANN therefore followed up two weeks later with a legal demand that VeriSign discontinue the service, citing that it violated their contract with ICANN. VeriSign reluctantly suspended the service denying that there had been any substantial impact on Internet usage. In the meanwhile, the Internet Software Consortium released an update of BIND which replaced a Site Finder response automatically with a 'not found' error: an inelegant solution but a usable one, at least until VeriSign might decide to shift the Site Finder location. But this was not the end of the story as VeriSign then took ICANN to court claiming antitrust violations. In May 2004, a federal judge dismissed the request for a trial, following a failure by VeriSign to provide sufficient grounds to show an antitrust violation. VeriSign did not appeal this within the time limit but maintain their right to reintroduce the system and periodically threaten to do so.

'Sucks' Domains

It is popular for those with a grievance against an organization to register the organization's trading name with 'sucks' appended. Although most would agree that this is a rather childish protest surely it could not be argued that such a registration could be mistaken for an official site of the company? As we shall see, though, there have been reverse domain-name hijacking attempts made on such registrations.

Generic Domains

Of course the main winners in the 'domain name as directory service' game are those who had the foresight to register completely generic words in domain names. Incompetence at the highest levels of the system, however, have made even some of them controversial, such as the long running battle over `sex.com`.

`Sex.com`

Sex sells, and absolute sex sells absolutely, to coin a variation on a well-known quotation. The Internet is used as much to transmit sex-related information as any other type of information (see Chapter 5). Online sex sites have been some of the most successful in generating income solely from the provision of digital downloads.

One early entrepreneur in the use of the Web to deliver sexual material realized that a generic name, such as `sex.com`, would be a great asset to such a business and duly registered it. This went well for some time but then a rather unethical businessman decided that he would like the domain name sex.com. Since it was taken (and in use for a very profitable business), it was unlikely that it would be sold to him. He therefore sent a forged transfer of domain notice to NSI, who changed the record in terms of both the IP number to which the name resolved and the name of the registrant. When his site stopped being pointed to by sex.com, the original owner realized something was wrong and contacted the domain name registration service. He was baffled when they claimed that they had received a valid transfer request and processed it. Even when he demonstrated to them that the notice did not have a signature matching the original registration, NSI refused to admit that they had done anything incorrect and would not transfer the registration back. It took a long-running (years long) court action (www.eff.org/Spam_cybersquatting_abuse/Cybersquatting/Kremen_v_NSI/20030725_opinion.php) to force NSI to return the registration to its original owner, during which he estimates that he lost many thousands of dollars in revenue (based on prior usage and the growth of usage of sex sites on the Web during this time). In addition to the return of the registration, a separate case against the perpetrator of the fraudulent transfer was successful, although the victim has yet to see any benefit from the result since the perpetrator fled the United States to avoid the consequences; he was arrested almost six years later in October 2005 (www.theregister.co.uk/2005/10/28/sexdotcom_cohen_arrested/).

A company such as NSI receives thousands of registration changes per day and it is unreasonable to expect them to perform significant checks on their validity, since this would raise the costs of registration much higher for very little gain. However, their refusal to acknowledge their mistake was a significant problem. Unfortunately, domain name registrations are not regarded as 'owned' by the registering person or organization. Registration is simply a service offered by the registration company. This changes the legal relationship between the registrant and the registration company and makes it much harder for registrants to seek redress following erroneous action by the registrar.

The Uniform Dispute Resolution Process

In response partly to a growing number of lawsuits, which cost a great deal of time and money for the participants, and also in response to suits naming domain registration companies as co-defendants, the gTLD registrar NSI issued a 'Domain Dispute Resolution Policy statement' in which it pointed out that it did not have the resources to investigate all requests for domain registration ahead of time for possible infringement. As part of the new contract for registering a domain it required registrants to sign a contract avowing their intent and right to use the domain and gave NSI the right to remove or reallocate the domain registration when presented with a court order or an arbitration judgement against the registrant. The most controversial part of the policy was the privileging of trade mark holders over all other possible users of trade marked terms in domain names.

> Dispute resolution policy (DRP): the method a domain registration organization uses to decide disputes that arise over 'ownership' of a domain

It must be noted that this goes far beyond normal practice. For most trade marks there is nothing to stop use of the mark in other fields. Only where trade marks have reached a particular level of notoriety (such as Rolls-Royce) are they sufficiently important to prevent use by anyone other than authorized operators in any sphere. Most trade mark laws confine restrictions to a specific vertical market in a specific geographic location. The point of trade marks used to be protection of the public from 'passing off' rather than protection of the good name of the organization, although this seems to have been mostly forgotten in the modern world of corporate arrogance. The right to set up shop in a different field with a similar (or even identical) name is simply the real world equivalent of a domain name, surely?

The original dispute resolution policy did not really achieve any of its goals except to reduce (but not extinguish) the number of court cases naming NSI: however, quite a few lawsuits were subsequently brought by those subjected to reverse domain-name hijacking rather than by the trade mark holders. Some of the most egregious examples of Internet land grabs include the attempted reverse hijacking of 'clue', 'perfection' and 'roadrunner'. In 1995, there was an attempt to take `pokey.org` from a 12-year-old boy (see the various documents referenced under '`POKEY.ORG`' on `www.domainhandbook.com/dd2.html`).

Once ICANN entered the frame it also entered the trade mark dispute and it commissioned the World Intellectual Property Organization (WIPO) to produce a proposal to solve the issue. This would have been perfectly reasonable if WIPO were a democratic organization with the remit to ensure a fair and commonly applicable intellectual property regime. As can be seen from other WIPO treaties, however, WIPO is principally a tool of intellectual property owners to expand and enforce their ideas about what should be protected and how; it is not a democratic representative body dedicated to the benefit of the people at large. This is confirmed by WIPO's own medium-term plan and vision document from 2003:

> *The main objectives of the Medium-term Plan, as expressed in the past remain constant: maintenance and further development of the respect for intellectual property throughout the world. This means that any erosion of the existing protection should be prevented, and that both the acquisition of the protection and, once acquired, its enforcement, should be simpler, cheaper and more secure.*

Accordingly WIPO's plan was for it to be the (only) first-line arbiter of disputes and that its decision should be enforced until overturned by a court of law. WIPO even went so far as to expand its remit to 'right of personality' (i.e. the names of the 'famous', however that is defined) and copyright violation, suggesting that all domain registration should be subject to its arbitration should there be complaint of violation of any type of intellectual property.

This overreaching caused a backlash and even the rather unrepresentative ICANN would not stomach its claims. The final WIPO report restricted the scope of the new Uniform Dispute Resolution Procedure (UDRP) to the trade mark issue in second-level domains. ICANN has been attempting to push ccTLDs organizers into signing up to the UDRP since it was put into force for the gTLDs and has been refusing to honour requested transfers of ccTLD delegation without the new delegatee signing up to UDRP, among other ICANN- and US-centric procedures.

It must always be remembered that each country has its own trade mark regime (lack of a regime counts for such purposes as a regime: simply an empty one). If one accepts the basic premise that trade marks in domain names should be subject to some procedure other than a court action (which is by no means a given, see the 'Criticisms of Dispute Resolution' section) then the UDRP as stated is not particularly unreasonable. Anyone who feels their rights have been violated may apply to an (ICANN-accredited) resolution-service provider. They must submit evidence of an 'abusive registration': that the domain name is identical, or confusingly similar, to a trade or service mark in which the complainant has rights; the defendant has no legitimate interests in the domain name; and that the domain name is being used in bad faith. Note that all three are required for proceedings to be brought. The policy also sets forth appropriate definitions of 'bad faith': the acquisition or registration of the domain name is solely to offer it for sale to the rights holder, or their competitors, for greater than the out-of-pocket expenses incurred in the acquisition; there is a pattern of registration to prevent the rights holder from registration of suitable names; the apparent purpose of the registration is to disrupt the business of the rights holder; there has been an attempt to use the domain name to attract users by unfair association with the rights holder's mark. The full policy is available from the ICANN web site (`www.icann.org`). It should be noted that even with this policy as set forth there are disputes as to the meaning and legitimacy of the term 'confusingly similar'.

The Nominet Dispute Resolution Process

Nominet (`www.nominet.org.uk`) is the UK domain name authority administering the .uk ccTLD. Unlike ICANN, which is primarily a self-perpetuating board originally chosen by the US Department of Commerce, Nominet is a membership organization. Any person or organization with an 'interest in the .uk domain system' may become a member and the board are elected by the membership. The

Nominet Dispute Resolution Process (DRP) also privileges trade mark holders over others with possible uses for a domain name. In order to have grounds for action under the Nominet DRP, a complainant must have rights in a name similar to the domain name and grounds for asserting that the domain name is an abusive registration. Grounds for an abusive registration are similar to those of the UDRP, although Nominet also provides example grounds on which legitimacy of the registration may easily be shown:

- use of the domain name in question (or a similar one) to offer legitimate goods or services (before the complaint was made);
- having a well-known association with the name or a similar one;
- the domain name is generic or descriptive and fair use is being made of it.

Even the Nominet DRP is not without its problems: consider the requirement to be making 'fair use' of a 'descriptive or generic name'. In trade mark law, one cannot trade mark a generic or descriptive name anyway, so it is unclear why 'fair use' has to be made of the registration. The Nominet DRP also makes an exception that 'tribute or criticism sites' do not automatically constitute fair use if the name under which they operate is identical to the name in which rights are held.

Criticisms of Dispute Resolution

There are criticisms levelled at the various dispute resolution processes and the related issue of 'sunrise periods' for new gTLDs.

> Sunrise period: a period of time during which registrations to a new gTLD are allowed only by trade mark holders for their trade marks and variants

Philosophical Problems

As mentioned above, the UDRP in particular spreads its reach beyond the full trade mark and service mark systems. It should be noted that the purpose of existing laws is to prevent 'passing off': directly or indirectly seeking to mislead the public into thinking that goods or services are offered by a well-known provider, by misuse of their trade marks. Apart from a very few incredibly well-known brands, it is perfectly permissible to set up in a different arena of business using a name which is trade marked for another business. One could even open a shop called, for instance, McDonald's Hardware, right next to a McDonald's Restaurant. Provided there were no similarities of brand logo (the 'golden arches' of McDonald's is a trade mark in the original sense of the term), the food retailer would have no legal recourse to stop it. There would be problems if the hardware retailer wanted to branch out into food retailing (as seen in the case study Apple Corp. and Apple Inc.). Preventing anyone from registering identical names to a trade mark in a domain name is simply preventing electronic shop windows from using the same names for different purposes, but preventing 'confusingly similar' names seems to be ludicrous. Either a name has sufficient brand recognition that people know how to spell it or they do not. If they do not then there's no benefit to be gained by someone using a similar domain name.

Procedural Problems

The hardest hitting criticisms of the UDRP (in particular) come not from the basic principles, which may be debated on both sides, but from the implementation, both in terms of the letter of the system (which appears to set the scene for corruption) and in the actual process of deciding cases, which is almost certainly unfair. The problem with the procedures as laid down is that ICANN accredits arbitration groups, from which the complainant then gets to select who will be the judge. ICANN originally accredited three arbitration providers: WIPO, the National Arbitration Forum (NAF) and eResolution (a new organization set up for this specific purpose). Given that the complainant is the one who chooses the arbitrator and pays the fee for the arbitration, this seems to be a recipe for corruption, which has been alleged, particularly by (Geist 2001). What Geist calls 'forum shopping' occurred, with complainants favouring the arbitrator with the record of awarding judgement to the complainant. According to Geist's analysis, two years into the operation, judgements were given for the complainant in 82.2% of cases heard by a

WIPO arbitrator, in 82.9% of cases heard by NAF and in only 63.4% of the cases heard by eResolution. Since then eResolution has withdrawn, leaving NAF and WIPO as possible arbitrators. Since arbitration is carried out by accredited 'experts' (in fact the list of potential panel members is now very similar with most accredited by both organizations) how do NAF and WIPO manage to skew the results? Again, Geist's analysis shows the method: panelists who have found in favour of complainants before are more likely to be allocated future cases. Allocation of cases is done by deliberate choice of the WIPO or NAF administration rather than by rotation or random allocation (this is a slight simplification, see (Geist 2001) for more details). In many of the cases brought under UDRP, panelists have chosen to ignore the explicit 'and' of the UDRP rules on how to decide if a registration is abusive and have adopted an 'or' approach: if any of the conditions are met, they decide the registration is abusive and award the case to the complainant. In others, panelists have explicitly ignored the stated rules of the UDRP and awarded the case to the complainant in flagrant violation of both the spirit and the letter of the UDRP (e.g. in the case of Julia Roberts v Russell Boyd, WIPO UDRP Case No D2000-0210). It should be noted that ccTLD dispute resolution processes such as the Nominet DRP do not share many of the procedural flaws of the UDRP.

Freedom of Speech Issues

The right to register a domain name could be considered a fundamental aspect of freedom of expression (see Chapter 4). There are already laws against causing damage by the use of a web site: defamation laws; laws to allow trade mark holders to sue for 'passing off'; even criminal fraud laws in serious cases. This can easily be seen as another way for private actors to attempt to stifle freedom of speech on the Internet. Cases of domains registered as `<name>sucks.com` (where <name> is a big brand) are an example of this. Disgruntled customers have registered such names for various purposes: sometimes just to put their bad experience with a company on the Web, sometimes to report their attempts to gain compensation, sometimes as a focal point for gathering class-action cohorts. Surely no one in their right mind would consider that `<name>sucks.com` could possibly be the official web site of any organization. Nevertheless, in an obvious attempt to prevent freedom of protected speech (if the speech itself was illegal they could have used that route), companies have attempted to get the 'sucks' domain transferred. Some groups have even suggested that such domains be banned from registration.

Abusive Complaints

In addition to suppression of freedom of speech, there are other forms of abusive complaints brought before the DRP panels. One example is that of the Easy Group of companies. Starting with EasyJet, one of the first low-cost airlines in Europe, the founder of the Easy Group has gone on to develop a variety of other businesses (from car rentals to Internet cafés) under the 'Easy' brand name. The 'Easy' name and the distinctive bright orange colouring and font form a recognizable brand. It is true that some other entrepreneurs have attempted to take advantage of this and used the 'Easy' colouring to imply that their business is one of this group. That is quite clearly 'passing off' and has been subject to successful litigation. However, the Easy group has launched several less reasonable cases, apparently in an attempt to 'own' the concept of 'EasySomething' (not to be confused with their actual EasyEverything and EasyAnything brands). They have attempted to get web sites shut down and transferred to them from companies that have traded under that simple (or should that be Easy?) and obvious name since before the founding of EasyJet, never mind the EasyGroup (`www.theregister.co.uk/2002/11/12/easyart_com_to_face_stelios/`).

Sunrise Periods

Many commentators regard the artificial scarcity of gTLDs as a prime cause of the trade mark disputes. Without the .com TLD becoming the default 'directory assistance service' the scramble for second-level domain registrations would not have happened. So, perhaps the way to avoid this is to quickly introduce many more gTLDs aimed at commercial enterprises, possibly with distinctions for different types so that shops can register in .store, manufacturers can register in .mfg and so forth. For the moment, that is not going to happen. As mentioned above, ICANN has been highly reluctant to expand the number of gTLDs and only created the .biz domain for general commercial operators, although the .pro gTLD may also serve.

With these limited new domains, however, the trade mark holders have arranged their pre-emptive 'pound of flesh' in that ICANN has declared that all new gTLDs which are open to commercial registration have a 'sunrise' period in which only registered trade mark holders will be able to register domains. Particularly given that there are multiple traders legitimately using trade marked names in other spheres who have not the need or resources to apply for a trade mark, and for whom the new .biz TLD would have been a welcome addition to their web presence, this seems to destroy a certain amount of the purpose of expanding the number of gTLDs.

Do Trade Marks Matter in Domain Names or in URLs?

As we have seen, trade mark holders now enjoy even more power over the second level of the gTLD system than they do in the ordinary world. This is actually part of the standard WIPO approach, entirely consistent with their other activities: push the boundaries in one sphere and then use it to claim 'analogous' extensions in others. If the trade mark holders have their way, pretty soon we'll all have to be saying 'That's Easy™' whenever presented with a simple task to perform. Of course now that the second level of the gTLDs is stitched up and many of the ccTLDs have been stitched up by ICANN, we can expect WIPO and the trade mark rights holders to attempt to broaden their horizons. After all, they own that word, do they not? It is not just a case of finding a balance between protection for the consumer and benefit to the company of maintaining a positive brand image, WIPO and the trade mark owners talk constantly of ownership and theft. So, the logical extension of this is first to try to prevent the use of a trade-marked term, or any 'confusingly similar' term anywhere in a domain name registration. But that's not all. After all, the full URL appears at the top of the browser and the page title appears in the browser window's title bar. These are highly visible places. Surely only official owners of a name or trade marked term should be allowed to use the term in those places. Then again, more and more people are finding sites via search engines. Surely any search for a trade-marked term should return the official sites first – and maybe only return the official sites. While this may seem like reductio ad absurdam, consider that WIPO's initial proposal wanted to make UDRP cover all allegations of intellectual property violations and to provide a non-court method of removing someone's domain name registration under a non-judicial process of so-called arbitration (the UDRP fails to follow several of the requirements for official definitions of arbitration, it should be noted, such as equal access to appeal procedures). Large corporate concerns generally attempt to grab everything within their grasp (see Chapters 4 and 12). In fact, they are mandated to do so by their legal obligation to maximize shareholder value: there is no mention of ethical behaviour in such laws, so unless shareholders have set specific rules, that is the game. It is up to governments to ensure that grabs for power and resources by corporate entities do not upset the balance of the common good. So far, in arranging the domain name system, it would appear that the politicians have either been bought off or are too incompetent to represent the people on such matters.

THE FUTURE OF INTERNET GOVERNANCE

ICANN, DoC, EU and ccTLDs

Despite constant pressure over the last few years, ICANN continues to survive. NSI, now owned by VeriSign, maintains its operation of the primary root servers and even abuses that from time to time. The US Department of Commerce seems torn between pressure to remove US-centric authority from the global Internet structure and doubt that ICANN can be allowed to go its own way. Its indecision is leading to apparent paralysis, while the arguments go on. The UK and German ccTLDs, holding out on signing away their authority to ICANN, are seen as the last bastions of people power (both Nominet and DENIC are held in higher regard by most interested parties, except WIPO and trade mark holders, than ICANN). The European Commission is beginning to get involved and is putting pressure on ICANN, Nominet and DENIC to come to amicable terms. Whether it will ultimately back the European ccTLDs against ICANN remains to be seen, although if the ccTLD authorities have a strong case then the Commission might have the authority to make the US Department of Commerce finally make a decision and force change upon ICANN. Then again, the Department of Commerce might support ICANN against 'old Europe'. The alternative root servers sit in the wings waiting for cracks to appear in ICANN's monopoly over the DNS root and the ITU has been champing at the bit to take over for years (ever since the TCP/IP system became the dominant internetworking protocol, really). An uneasy kind of peace has been maintained for the last few years but the pressures are growing and, just like a geographic fault line, lack of small adjustments could lead to a seismic shift at some future point.

> Nominet: the UK ccTLD (country code top-level domain) administration organization (`www.nominet.org`)
>
> Deutschland Network Information Center (DENIC): the German ccTLD (country code top-level domain) administration organization (`www.denic.de`)

Wiring the World: Who Really Owns 'the Internet'?

This chapter has focused primarily on the 'big picture' at the mostly abstract level of running the Internet and the domain name and assigned IP number authorities. But there is a physical level below that which could have as much influence as, if not more than the political and software moves. After the NSF moved away from primary funding of the backbone, telecoms providers moved into the business. Users often forget that international (and high-speed national) connections are provided by profit-making companies. In many countries in the world, this remains a single national monopoly provider, although World Trade Organization (WTO) rules are moving towards requiring competition to be introduced. As the industrialized world moves away from dial-up modem connections towards broadband access, there is also a thinning of the field: small local ISPs were once common in every city in the United States and United Kingdom, for instance. These days, it is mostly the big players: the Baby Bells (not so Baby any more as the US sector reconsolidates) and a few other players (cable operators) in the United States; BT, Wanadoo, Deutsche Telecom and a few cable companies in the United Kingdom and much of Europe. It is companies such as BT, PacBell, NTT and Telekom Malaysia (the Malaysian monopoly telecommunications company) that own the still relatively small number of massive international connections. Many of them, partly to keep customers locked in to their service and partly in fear of or in collusion with the 'copyright industries' seek to restrict what one can do with an Internet connection and try to turn the PC into a glorified television, that is a receiver for a one-to-many communications channel, with the electronic equivalent of the phone service bundled in. In all the fighting about root servers, domain names and trade mark holders, it is important to remember these sleeping giants who quietly control so much of the infrastructure.

DISCUSSION TOPICS

Should Trade Marks Be Valid in Domain Names?

Prior to the advent of the Internet (and the Web in particular), trade marks were geographically restricted. For instance, the image of a battery-operated rabbit toy is one of the principal trade marks of Energizer batteries in the United States. In the United Kingdom, however, their major rival in the business, Duracell, used an almost-identical image to promote their product and this was completely legal. So we now have two worldwide companies sharing the international idea space linking rabbit toys to batteries and yet the commercial world has not crumbled around their ears. The reason is that there are already laws in place to prevent companies causing deliberate or inadvertent confusion by customers between brand names. Only where such confusion is a problem are trade marks enforced. For a very few major brands (such as Rolls-Royce), their image is so strong (for quality and reliability) that it crosses the boundaries of any product. Most brands are strongly associated with a product or range of products.

Granting trade mark holders rights in the use of their trade marks in second-level (third-level, for ccTLDs) domains is the thin end of the wedge and already causes problems. How many users actually start their web use these days by typing in a domain name? The majority of users use either portals (such as Yahoo!) or search engines (such as Google) rather than typing domain names. If the site that appears when typing in `www.<trademark>.com` is not the company they are looking for, most people will then try something else. It is only a problem if the site they reach is confusing and existing trade mark laws are sufficient to prevent this. How far will we go in banning the use of trade marks in URLs? Will we reject any appearance of a trade marked term in a URL, even if it is inadvertent (e.g. part of a word)?

Expansion of local trade mark registrations to cover a global naming system is a step too far. It significantly expands on the power held by a trade mark owner and has major consequences in terms of freedom of expression as well (see Chapter 4). We have already gone too far and this poor decision should be reversed. Infringers of trade marks should be taken to court on the basis of strong evidence of confusion, dilution or passing off and courts should penalize trade mark holders for suits with ulterior motives, such as attempts to gag criticism.

What Governance Should ICANN Have?

As mentioned above, ICANN is basically a US organization applying US ideas and concepts to a global system. It is unrepresentative of the wide range of users and is biased against both non-US businesses and ordinary users in favour of large companies and those based in the United States. Even if we accept that their policy decisions have been valid (such as the introduction and contents of the UDRP as stated) then their implementation of these policies leaves much to be desired (continued support of WIPO despite strong evidence of bias and even stated violation of the principles of the UDRP). Unfortunately, the obvious replacement for ICANN, the ITU, has a public relations problem in that its bureaucratic approach stifled networking development in the 1970s and 1980s and doubts persist about its ability to do a better job at protecting the efficiency and openness of the Internet.

Do we actually need an overall authority? In some ways, the Internet is already an anarchy. Anyone can offer any service on any port. Unconnected internal networks run their own namespaces, which use identical IP addresses without central control. However, the total anarchy approach may lead to an uncontrolled monopoly situation arising. Consider the dominance of NSI and its violations of 'good neighbour' behaviour in introducing systems such as Site Finder. Without something like ICANN, NSI would be able to throw its weight around without any check or balance on its antisocial activities. We probably need something like ICANN, but it needs better legitimacy among a wide base of users, both in types of user and nationalities. This is a tricky question that will not be answered overnight. As the Internet becomes more and more an 'invisible' infrastructure, the governance of the infrastructure becomes more important, even if less visible to the majority of people. This will be one of the intellectual battlegrounds of the coming decades.

How Many Top-Level Domains Should There Be?

One of the main accusations against ICANN is that it has restricted the number of top-level domains without adequate reason. When it did 'dip its toes' in the water of expanding the set of TLDs, the new set seemed bizarre. Why was the aerospace industry deemed more worthy of a topic-specific domain (aero) than the car industry? Why was a six-letter word (museum) allocated a TLD rather than a three-letter contraction (mus)? Given the controversy surrounding 'adult' information online, why were the TLDs sex or xxx not included in the system?

There would appear to be two reasonable approaches to TLDs: restrict them to a very small number of gTLDs plus the ccTLDs or allow any 'justifiable' TLD. The decision between these choices requires an examination of the role of the TLD. Currently, the TLDs are mostly a human-oriented aspect of URLs. The original concept was that organizations would choose the appropriate TLD for their type of work: non-profit organizations would use .org, businesses would use .com and educational establishments would use .edu. Only .edu remains a 'pure' domain restricted to those truly involved in education. There are many for-profit companies that have the same registration for .com and .org and there are individuals and non-profit organizations that register .com domains. The .net TLD, originally supposed to indicate a backbone site, was opened up by ISPs keen to ride the wave of 'net' awareness by offering .net TLD e-mail addresses and web sites. So, the genie is already out of the bottle in terms of restricting access to the existing TLDs. Introduction of new TLDs while trade mark issues remain a major problem simply forces trade mark holders to register ever more domains in each new TLD. It would be an interesting project to try to find out how many of the new .biz domains use the same name as a prior .com domain but are being run by a different organization.

REFERENCES

Hafner, K. and **Lyon, M.** (1996) *Where Wizards Stay Up Late*, Free Press, London. ISBN 0-7434-6837-6.

Mueller, M.L. (2002) *Ruling the Root*, MIT Press, Cambridge, MA. ISBN 0-262-13412-8.

Geist, M. (2001) "Fair.com? An examination of the allegations of systematic unfairness in the ICANN UDRP", aix1.uottawa.ca/~geist/geistudrp.pdf.

Goldsmith, J. and **Wu, T.** (2006) *Who Controls the Internet?*, Oxford University Press, Oxford. ISBN 0-19-515266-2.

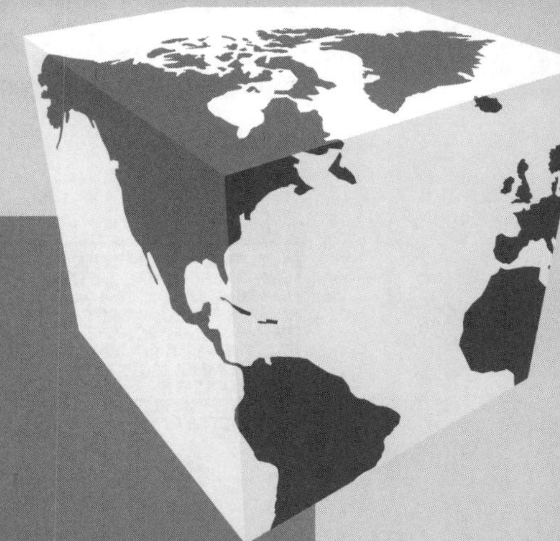

7 PRIVACY AND SURVEILLANCE

INTRODUCTION

One of the biggest issues of the information age is that of privacy. As with most issues, this is not new but simply the latest iteration of an old battle. How much about an individual's actions are the people around them entitled to know? How much is government allowed to know and since a government is made up of people, what restrictions are placed on who in government can access that information, and what controls are in place to avoid abuse of access? Again, as with many of the topics covered in this book, we start with some historical aspects of privacy and the compromises that have been made, and then move on to the problems for privacy presented by modern computer and communication technology.

Cryptography and Steganography

Consider the following scenario: a small group of people are plotting to overthrow a government. They are geographically separated and at least one of them is completely within the power of agents of that government. In order to avoid detection, they must find a way of communicating that is hidden from the government. This is the plot for which Mary, Queen of Scots, was executed in 1587, as reported in Steve Levy's book Crypto. The method used to keep the communication secret was a substitution code, using different symbols for the English letters, rather than the more usual substitution-code method of using each letter to represent another.

This substitution code is one form of cryptography, where the meaning of a message is hidden. The other most common form of secret communication is steganography, where the relevant portions of a message are concealed by being part of a larger message containing innocuous information. A very simple example of such a hidden message is contained in the following two sentences. Take every fourth word, starting with the first one, as the 'hidden' message:

You, Jack and I are going away soon. Being late is very subversive.

The problem with cryptography and related technologies is that everyone would like 'the good guys' to have them and for 'the bad guys' not to have them. As

Levy notes, the Caesar cipher (a simple form of substitution code) was developed to allow army movement and attack orders to be concealed from enemies who might waylay messengers. Code making and breaking is still one of the obsessions of military organizations the world over (see Chapter 8). Thus we see that one of the important concepts of 'privacy' is that of secure communications. But it is not the only one.

Cryptography: literally, 'secret writing' – a way of encoding information such that the meaning is not easily clear without some form of 'key'

Steganography: literally, 'hidden writing' – a way of hiding information within a larger mass of information, so that the information is not accessible without some additional information

Caesar cipher: a substitution code formed by replacing every letter of a message with a letter 'rotated' through the alphabet by some number between 1 and 25.

'The Worst Boyfriend in the World'

A web site, `www.breakthechain.org`, that advises people not to pass on e-mail 'chain letters' features at least two examples of real people who have faced significant problems because of apparent breaches of privacy with respect to e-mails they sent. Although there are many 'urban legends' associated with such breaches (such as the example of two co-workers who get rather friendly while accidentally broadcasting on the company PA), there are two well-documented cases of UK citizens suffering significantly due to e-mail circulars. A search on `www.breakthechain.org` for 'Trevor Luxton' and for 'Claire Swires' gives details of the cases, including examples of the e-mails which circulated.

In both these cases, it is alleged that the e-mail which circulates comes from Trevor or Claire. They were sent to a small group of people at least one of whom then forwarded the message to others. The saucy nature of the content caused a cascade effect of every recipient sending it to more than one other recipient. E-mail circulars can cause all sorts of problems simply because of the scale of the reproduction (see Chapter 13). In this case, however, we are concerned with the breach of privacy which started the whole thing off. Even if we assume that Claire and Trevor sent the original messages (which is difficult to establish without expending significant resources), then whoever first sent these out to further recipients breached a trust. Every person who further sent these lurid tales on then committed a further breach of the privacy of the subject. This is made worse by the fact that once it reached people who did not know the subject then every person further circulating the tale was indulging in the modern equivalent of vicious gossip.

Many companies, including the ones which employed Claire and Trevor at the time the chains started, have acceptable use policies which forbid the circulation of such material. Even where personal use of work e-mail is either allowed or ignored, most companies do not wish to provide facilities for passing around such material, in particular given the potential negative consequences to the lives of the subjects.

Unfortunately, as soon as something is committed to electronic text, it is at risk of being forever circulated around the net. If Claire and Trevor did send the original messages, they have been punished far beyond their transgressions; if they did not, then they have been made infamous and subjected to the worldwide equivalent of being made the class whipping boy (see www.thisislondon.co.uk/news/articles/1462350 for more information).

Definition of Privacy

The definition of privacy we will be taking in this chapter is broadly based and involves information in all its forms. Not just what we say, but to whom we say it, or even simply that we are communicating at all, never mind the contents. Various declarations of human rights have included some aspects of privacy:

> *The right of the people to be secure in their persons, houses, papers, and effects, against unreasonable searches and seizures, shall not be violated, and no Warrants shall issue, but upon probable cause, supported by Oath or affirmation, and particularly describing the place to be searched, and the persons or things to be seized. US Constitution, Amendment IV via the Bill of Rights*
>
> *No one shall be subjected to arbitrary interference with his privacy, family, home or correspondence, nor to attacks upon his honour and reputation. Everyone has the right to the protection of the law against such interference or attacks. Universal Declaration of Human Rights, Article 12 (United Nations)*
>
> *Everyone has the right to respect for his or her private and family life, home and communications. Charter of Fundamental Rights, Article 7 (European Union)*

It should be noted that these successive declarations (from the eighteenth, mid-twentieth and late-twentieth centuries) are each more explicit than the last: it is not just 'papers' and 'correspondence' that is protected from invasion, but 'communications' as well as 'private life'.

COMMUNICATION TECHNOLOGY AND EAVESDROPPING

Ways to Eavesdrop

In this section, we consider the major forms of communication, how to eavesdrop on them and possible ways to foil eavesdropping.

Direct Speech

The simplest form of communication is to speak directly to the person with whom you wish to communicate, while within their hearing. In order to eavesdrop, someone must be physically within hearing range or have a microphone and recorder or transmitter within the range of the voices. Modern transmitters can be exceedingly small yet high bandwidth. Some even transmit on variable frequency ranges with pseudo-random patterns to avoid detection. Modern distance microphones can pick up conversations in the open and even via the vibrations made in window glass by the noise within a room. Specialist scanning equipment can sometimes detect the radio signals of transmitters or even the inadvertent low-level signals put out by recording devices. White-noise generators can mask sounds from microphones without interfering unduly with direct human hearing.

Written Communication

Various techniques exist for encoding or hiding the actual content of a message, including cryptographic and steganographic techniques. The most difficult-to-break cipher is a 'one-time pad' which is virtually unbreakable even with modern computers. Projected developments in quantum computers, however, might make even one-time pads breakable. With steganographic techniques, the task is finding the needle in the haystack first and then deciphering the contents which may also be encrypted.

Telegraph

Since telegraphs were operated by humans, the secrecy level was very low unless cryptographic or steganographic techniques were used.

Telephone

Since telephones are a line-switched technology, the main issue involved is that if a particular line can be accessed at any point along its length it is possible to listen in. Early analogue phones also used human operators to connect calls giving the same privacy problems as with telegraphs. In addition, party lines (lines shared by different households) were an early privacy issue. Governments had machines for encrypting the signal to make it difficult to simply tap the line although these required both ends to be using a similar machine for the system to work.

E-Mail and Other Internet-Based Systems

Since the Internet is packet switched rather than line switched, monitoring Internet-based communications can be quite difficult if end-to-end applications are used rather than server-hop-based systems such as the standard mail protocols. However, the bottleneck of access is usually via an ISP and eavesdroppers, both lawful and unlawful, rely on that. With the advent of public key cryptography, however, the possibility of end-to-end encrypted communication has meant that it is possible to hide the information being transmitted although the initial target is known. Multi-hop-encoded transmission can hide some of this information as well. This is the principle used in peer-to-peer networks, particularly the encrypted formats and ones specifically designed to evade eavesdropping and censorship, such as freenet (see Chapter 4).

Mobile Telephones

Law enforcement officers have been worried by the expansion of mobile telephony and have placed great pressure on operators to ensure compatibility with eavesdropping techniques used by legal bodies. The encryption routines built into modern digital telephones do avoid some of the privacy problems with earlier analogue models, such as easy 'phone cloning' and eavesdropping by standard wireless communications scanners.

> Phone cloning: copying the identification information for a mobile phone to allow diversion of text messages and calls made on that phone's account

Identity of Eavesdropper

There are essentially two types of eavesdropper: governmental and non-governmental. In general, governmental eavesdropping is regulated and legal, although recent allegations about bugging of the telephones and offices at the United

Nations by permanent Security Council members is on less solid ground. In most countries, electronic surveillance by non-governmental operators is highly restricted or completely banned. An exception to this is the monitoring by employers of the use their employees make of Internet communication methods. In the United Kingdom, for instance, employers can monitor their employees' e-mail provided they tell their employees quite clearly that such monitoring is happening (they may not, however, monitor telephone use). Other than that, monitoring is only allowed for the purposes of ensuring system security and operation. Of course, end-to-end encrypted communication systems can make it as difficult for the company system administrator to eavesdrop as for anyone else. Few people, however, consider the potential for their e-mail to be intercepted and so they do not use encryption systems. This can be a significant problem where companies are involved in sending commercially sensitive information over the Internet or even simply over company intranets. We consider these issues more closely when we look at data protection.

Legality of Eavesdropping

The legality of, and uses for, information obtained by wiretapping (originally the term used for tapping into telephone wires but now often used for any form of surveillance of electronic communication) is different in each country. We present the historic and present situation in both the United Kingdom and the United States.

> Wiretapping: interception of electronic communication, originally by routing a telephone connection through an extra device

The legality of law-enforcement agencies listening in to telephone conversations was first confirmed in US law in the Olmstead v United States case in 1928. The ruling in this case gave an open licence to law-enforcement operatives to listen in (without a warrant) to the phone conversations of suspects provided they did not have to perform a physical trespass in order to do so. That is, they could not enter a private residence without a warrant to place a radio bug and capture all conversations but they could attach a listening device to a telephone line at some point outside the property and listen to all the conversations. This ruling was overturned in 1967 in Katz v United States which held that bugging a public phone booth was illegal and, by implication, that listening in on phone conversations without a warrant was generally not allowed. Thus in 1968, the United States passed the Omnibus Crime Control and Safe Streets Act setting out the rules for wiretapping and for warrants to be issued.

In the United Kingdom, there are similar laws governing warrants to listen in to phone conversations, including the Interception of Communications Act 1985 and the EU Telecommunications Data Protection Directive 1997. A striking difference in approach still exists, however: in the United Kingdom, tape recordings of telephone conversations are not allowed as evidence in court, they are merely useful for investigating and may be used as evidence to obtain a warrant for a physical search. In the United States, however, wiretaps have been instrumental in any number of convictions over the last century. This is currently a significant matter of political debate in the United Kingdom.

The advent of computer-mediated communication and, in particular, packet-switched networks (such as Internet protocol networks) rather than line-switched networks (such as the public telephone network) created a problem for law-enforcement agencies seeking to eavesdrop. This has led to extended rights for law-enforcement agencies to monitor packet-switched information at its most vulnerable point, which is the ISP server. Such rights have been enshrined in UK law in the Regulation of Investigatory Powers Act 2000 (also known as the RIP Act). In addition to allowing for investigations with a warrant, the RIP Act simultaneously makes it a criminal offence for anyone else to eavesdrop on communications, except for employers (who inform their employees of monitoring) and system administrators monitoring activity to ensure service (to check for faulty software configuration, for instance). The access used by system administrators must, of course, be proportionate to the potential problems (see Chapter 10 for information on due diligence in such cases). The powers of law-enforcement agencies in a number of countries (and specifically the United Kingdom and United States) have been expanded since 11 September 2001.

The Whole Is Greater than the Sum of its Parts

So far we have concentrated on communication as 'conversation'. But privacy in the modern world is much more than this. Consider the amount of information currently stored in a variety of databases about each individual in the developed world: name; address; contact details; bank account details; credit-card account number, credit limit, current debt level; where you shop; what you buy; which television channels you watch; what web sites you visit; to whom you send e-mail; from whom you receive e-mail; where you go on holiday; who you work for; what they pay you; what films you watch at the cinema; whether you have been accused of any crimes; whether you have been convicted of any crimes; whether you have been subject to disciplinary proceedings at work; what your promotion prospects are; how much electricity and gas you use in each quarter of the year; what household goods you have; how much your possessions are insured for; whether you have any particularly expensive items (such as antiques, jewellery or artwork) that is separately insured; what you eat; with whom you visit the cinema and restaurants; what books you have read (either from the library or bookstores); what movies you like to rent or buy...

The list is almost endless. Commercial organizations would love to be able to compile much of this information in one place and 'mine' the data from it. While they do not particularly have your best interests at heart, most people do not mind too much if they know some things about us. Consider `Amazon.com's` 'Recommendations' service. Many people found that an excellent, useful place to be informed about books they have not otherwise heard of. But what about proposals in the United States that the FBI should be able to review library loans of citizens to try to identify patterns of book borrowing that indicate a nascent plan to commit terrorist acts or to commit serious crimes? Would you like a knock at the door asking about your involvement with Al Qaeda because you happen to have an interest in Islamic militant ideology? How about advertising via your cable or satellite network that is specifically psychologically designed to appeal to you? It could be as harmless (and as useful) as Amazon's service. On the other hand, it could lead you into addictions such as smoking, alcoholism or gambling. Just because it's legal does not mean it is not harmful if taken to excess and targeted advertising may lead you into a temptation you've been trying to avoid. It's all a matter of power and choice.

Individual freedom to associate, read, and move around, without wondering who is tracking your movements, is a fundamental right. It is these sorts of issues that have led to many developed nations passing strict laws protecting personal data against certain types of use. Unfortunately, data protection is one of those subjects where the interesting ramifications and debates depend on a good deal of detailed knowledge in order to be understood. We must therefore present the principles and details of the current legal situation to set the scene for the discussion topics.

Unproved Allegations and Future Crime

In August 2002, two 10-year-old girls went missing in Soham, Cambridgeshire, UK. In December 2003, Ian Huntley, the caretaker (janitor) at their school, was convicted of murdering both of them. Soon after the trial, the Bichard Inquiry (`www.bichardinquiry.org.uk`) was set up by the government to look into the fact that, although he had not been convicted of sexual offences, Huntley had been the subject of various allegations regarding sexual misconduct, often with underage girls. In addition to the in-depth inquiry, which found that standard checks were not properly completed (e.g. personal references were not taken up), there has been a great deal of public discussion about whether the facts of unproven allegations about misconduct should have been enough to deny Huntley a job at a school. The public debate, as usual, has focused on the fact that Huntley was guilty in this case and may have been guilty of the allegations that had been made against him in the past.

The difficulty here is that the protection of one group (children) can mean serious harm to another group (those wrongly accused of abuse). This is a general concern and needs a much more sensible debate that it is getting in the UK press. 'Innocent until proven guilty' has been the foundation stone of British justice for a very long time. Various prior miscarriages of justice regularly coming to light show that this is not a matter on which society can be complacent. Yet, the protection of possible future victims must not be lost in the principle. There is a debate among academics (criminologists, psychologists and related researchers) about the best way to tackle allegations of abuse.

In Huntley's case, the right outcome would have been for one of his earlier victim's allegations to have been proved if it were true. Had that been the case it would be hoped that his presence on the Sex Offenders' Register would have prevented his gaining employment at a school, although of course the Bichard Inquiry shows that the procedures for checking for potential problems need revisiting. On the other hand, blanket storage of the names of the accused in all cases could lead to two possible problems: the overloading of the system of checking and the inclusion of innocent victims of false allegations. The moral panic over paedophiles causes even more severe concern for victims of false accusation: it would be bad enough to be suspected by 'the system' due to a previous false allegation but to allow the hounding by vigilantes on such evidence would itself be a crime. As with many aspects of privacy there are no right answers, simply the best place to draw the line among potential evils, a line which must be constantly kept under review for changes in the situation that require changes in the approach.

DATA PROTECTION

There are two strands of data protection and privacy regulation in the Western world: the US approach (self-regulation and market forces) and the EU approach (government regulation and strict laws). Here, we present the difficulties that arise in international trade following from the interface between the two regimes. In this section, we look generally at the intent of these approaches then focus on the details of the approaches in turn.

Various European countries have long had stringent data protection legislation in force. In some places, such as Scandinavia, the regimes have always been very harsh and given a great deal of rights to the data subject, the person about whom data is held. The principle of this kind of protection is that opt-in explicit permission is required for any use of provided or garnered data. In other European countries, a slightly more free situation developed in which the holders of data were able to use it for a number of purposes but were required to meet certain standards, including accuracy and accountability. A few European countries had very little legal regulation at all and left it to courts to decide cases where harm had resulted from poor practice in processing data. By 1996, however, common European minimum standards were agreed. This was an important step forward in the development of the single market in Europe: once each country implemented the European Union Data Protection Directive (EUDPD) there would be no reason not to allow for the free movement of personal information between countries, since it would be subject to appropriate protection wherever it went. In addition, common standards for allowing the transfer of data to countries outside the European Union were agreed.

The general principles of data protection agreed in Europe were based on the idea of allowing appropriate processing of data about people but with strict controls on permission or necessity, accuracy and accountability.

Data Protection Issues in EU Law

We have been talking so far about 'personal data' in this chapter without really defining exactly what is meant by that. Under the EUDPD, there are two categories of data: personal data and sensitive data. Personal data includes anything which can be linked directly to you (the 'data subject'): your name, address and other contact details but also data linked to codes which identify you, such as government ID codes (national insurance number, passport number, social security number, etc.). Once a connection to an individual is established, all the information specifically connected to it is regarded as personal information, such as what you bought, where you went, your credit history, and so on. Credit information is in a particular class of its own and we return to it later. Sensitive data is quite clearly defined and includes racial or ethnic origins; political opinions (such as party affiliations); religious (or similar) beliefs; membership of officially recognized trade unions; physical or mental health conditions; sex life; criminal activity (allegations, court proceedings, verdicts and sentences).

Data subject: an individual identified by personal information

Now that we have defined what we are talking about in terms of personal data, we can concentrate on the rules governing individuals or organizations who might wish to process such data. Under the EUDPD, all data that is held 'in an accessible format' is covered and not just data held on a computer (as was the case, for instance, in the United Kingdom under the Data Protection Act 1984, which was superseded by the Data Protection Act 1998 implementing the EUDPD). For the purposes of the act, 'in an accessible format' could mean that the data is held in a filing system which allows systematic access.

Personal data: information about a specific data subject, such as name, address and employment details

From here, we focus on the UK Data Protection Act 1998 (DPA98) as it implements the more general requirements of the EUDPD, under which a number of different frameworks would be sufficient. It is easier to present this with an actual implementation than continuing to talk in completely generic terms. Anyone wishing to process personal data in the United Kingdom must, unless covered by one of the exemptions, notify the Information Commissioner of their status as a data controller, with suitable information including contact details, nature of data held and purpose of data processing. The data controller, in a commercial organization of any size, is usually a senior manager, sometimes even a board member such as the Chief Information Officer (CIO). They are not expected to oversee every person working with personal data in their organization. Instead the data controller is responsible for the management of data processing within the organization and is required to ensure that appropriate training is provided to those with access to data, including guidelines laying out their responsibilities under the DPA98. The data controller is also responsible for ensuring that adequate funding is available to implement data protection policies. It is no use having a policy that says everyone with access to data must be trained if there are no resources available for such training (see Chapter 10 for the concept of due diligence). Policies must also be in place to follow the rest of the requirements under the DPA98 including:

- Responding to requests by data subjects for a copy of information the organization holds about them.
- Ensuring that if errors in data are reported they are investigated and corrected in a timely manner (even if someone claims an organization holds incorrect data about them, the organization may choose to retain that data if it can honestly show that there is good reason to believe it to be true following an investigation).
- Ensuring deletion of data once it is no longer required.
- Abiding by requests to stop direct marketing use of data on request by the data subject.
- Abiding by requests to stop all processing of data (where feasible) upon request by a data subject, or justifying continued processing (for example, although it is a requirement to stop processing data if so requested, it is possible to retain data while a debt exists).
- Providing descriptions of automated decision processes used in certain applications that are understandable by the average person (this is limited to certain circumstances such as employers and not to voluntary commercial transactions such as applying for credit).

> Data controller: the named person in an organization responsible for overseeing personal data processing

> Information Commissioner: the UK government appointee responsible for adjudicating and advising on the Data Protection Act and Freedom of Information Act
>
> Sensitive data: information about a data subject such as health information, sexual preferences, religion and trade union membership

There are two categories of data about which there are more stringent rules: sensitive data and credit history records. In order to process sensitive data, there must be an absolute need for such information or the subject must have given explicit permission for such information to be held. In the case of credit history information both individual financial institutions and credit-checking agencies are covered in the United Kingdom and United States (and most other countries) by financial services regulations which impose more stringent controls than ordinary data protection rules (particularly in terms of ensuring accuracy of information). In the United Kingdom, this is overseen by the Financial Services Authority (the FSA, `www.fsa.gov.uk`) and in the United States by a similar body in each state (e.g. the Office of the Consumer Credit Commissioner in Texas, `www.occc.state.tx.us`). However, financial institutions and credit-checking agencies are allowed to continue to process accurate information about bad debts even when requested to stop processing data. In the modern capitalist world, accurate information about prior financial irregularities are deemed necessary and thus override personal desires to have such things expunged. Access to such information is even more strictly controlled than normal, however, to take this into account.

If we take this to its extreme, then even a personal address book or a list of members of an informal social club would require notification to the Information Commissioner and a lot of serious rules meant for large organizations being applied to individuals or small groups. Generally, there are exemptions to this. In the United Kingdom, for example, the Information Commissioner's web site (`www.ico.gov.uk`) includes a self-assessment form to help small organizations to decide if they must notify. Of course, not having to notify does not relieve you of the requirements of following data protection principles, as a woman in Sweden found. Mrs Lindqvist was an active member of her local church congregation. One of her activities involved helping people prepare for their confirmation ceremonies and she ran a small web site to give advice and support. One of the aspects of this web site included contact details for others approaching confirmation and some other bits and pieces of information, such as the fact that one of them had an injured foot and therefore only worked part time. None of the people whose details were on the site had given explicit permission for the data to be so displayed. Mrs Lindqvist was prosecuted under Sweden's implementation of the EUDPD. She was found guilty of violating various provisions and given a fine. She appealed to the European Court of Justice, which upheld the Swedish ruling in case C101/01 (judgement made September 2003, see `www.out-law.com/page-4051`).

Data Protection Issues in US Regulation

The US approach to privacy is quite different to that taken in European states (and all across the European Union after 1996). In keeping with the general market-driven approach in the United States, the Federal Trade Commission (FTC `www.ftc.gov`) has general guidelines about appropriate privacy polices and enforces adherence to published policies. The concept behind this is that if data protection is important to consumers then they will use companies with the more protective regimes and a 'race for the top', as it is called in legal circles, will ensue among commercial organizations to provide suitable protection. This is, of course, balanced against the benefits of using data to its fullest commercial advantage and this is where the regulatory role of the FTC comes into play to prevent corporations from publishing one policy but covertly using a different one in an attempt to gain the best of both worlds. From a European viewpoint, however, this approach has not met with a great deal of respect and there have been difficult negotiations over international movement of data from the European Union to the United States. Credit-checking data in the United States, as in the European Union, is covered by separate quite strict legislation, particularly as regards liability for holding and disseminating incorrect information about bad debts.

Federal Trade Commission (FTC): the US government agency responsible for trade issues, in particular inter-state trade

The FTC has been heavily criticized in the past for ignoring violations of policies, monopoly positions in the marketplace (what is the use of a competition policy if there is only one player in a particular market?), and changes to policies without adequate notification or protection but public pressure has led to a more interventionist attitude in recent years (see the Victoria's Secret case study). However, this has not led to harmonious relations with the European Union over the data of European citizens held in or transferred to the United States.

Victoria's Not-So-Secret Online Shopping Info

In 2003, a customer of Victoria's Secret, the lingerie store, realized that their online system was laughably insecure. The 'customer id' number was transmitted as part of the URL and there appeared to be no other checks on identification of the browser being carried out. He checked this out by entering a random 'customer ID' into his browser URL and found the shopping details of another customer displayed on his screen. This may have been a breach of computer misuse laws by the customer (see the 'Open Proxies' section in Chapter 11). The privacy and surveillance issue is whether the attitude of Victoria's Secret was reasonable or not. Despite having a privacy policy which assured customers of the discreet nature of the online service, the company's response to being told of the insecurity of the 'previous order' information was that 'no credit card details are accessible, so what's the problem'?

Was this a serious ethical (and possibly illegal) breach or was Victoria's Secret right that simply being able to access details of orders via customer number is not a particular problem? After all, one would have to know someone's customer ID before being able to target their details, or would one? The New York Attorney General Eliot Spitzer (well known for his gung-ho attitude to online matters) reached an out of court agreement with the company in which they agreed to pay a $50 000 fine and sort out the technical issue (www.theregister.co.uk/2003/10/21/victorias_secret_to_pay_up/).

In April 2004, the FTC held a workshop on the problem of Spyware, but stated that there appeared to be no need for a specific law on spyware since the majority of it was already illegal under existing laws such as computer misuse legislation.

Spyware: programs surreptitiously or covertly installed on a user's computer that report usage to a third party, frequently without the awareness of the user

International Movement of Data

In addition to ensuring that the European single market would not be impeded by different data protection requirements in various European countries, the EUDPD also contained provisions regarding the export of data to other countries. Personal data can be exported to countries with adequate data protection regimes (as of writing, this is still quite a short list, details of which are available on the European Union's and national data protection officers' web sites); to countries with adequate contractual requirements stated and enforced by the exporting organization; to countries where a 'safe harbour scheme' has been agreed and organizations meet the safe harbour requirements. Under the safe harbour scheme, US companies who are members of trade organizations which have appropriate 'codes of practice' on data protection are deemed to therefore have sufficient safeguards not to need contractual obligations on data protection. The safe harbour scheme is primarily an arrangement to ease the burden of requiring contractual negotiations on use and onward transfer of data by US companies in their dealings with their EU counterparts. There are some questions in the United States as to whether a data protection regime such as that set out in the EUDPD would be constitutional.

The safe harbour scheme has been criticized by consumer rights organizations in Europe as being a cosmetic operation only, given the rather weak position held by the trade organizations and the limited level of enforcement by the FTC of such policies. Recent activism by the FTC and state officials, such as Eliot Spitzer, has somewhat mitigated these criticisms but it has not silenced them completely.

Data Protection, not an Impediment to Life

In all considerations of data protection rules, whether they be statutory or codes of practice, it should be remembered that the rules are not designed to prevent the ordinary processing of data to the benefit of both parties. There have been some high-profile cases in the United Kingdom where data protection has been used as a shield against allegations of ridiculous behaviour, to the detriment of the general public, the data subject or both. So, when considering data protection, although avoiding a paternalistic position, it should always be remembered that ethical behaviour can require an organization to act beyond the simple interpretation of the rules and possibly to seek a way within the data protection legislation in which an appropriate outcome can be found. One important fact to remember is that processing data with the explicit consent of the data subject is always permissible. This includes processing sensitive data, export of data and automated decision making. It also includes processing where it should be obvious that it is necessary for the execution of a contract between the data subject and the processing organization. These issues are central to some of the case studies and discussion topics in this chapter, but we present one such case briefly here as well.

In 2003, a utility company in the United Kingdom cut off its supply to an elderly couple, for non-payment of the bill in late autumn. In a subsequent bout of cold weather, one of the couple died, almost certainly contributed to by lack of the heating previously provided by the utility company. The local social services heavily criticized the utility company for not informing them of the possible hazard to the couple caused by the removal of supply. The utility company claimed that their hands were tied by the DPA98.

In media interviews later, the Information Commissioner made plain his view that the protection of personal information such as unpaid bills could not be seen as overriding the protection of life offered by the social services to such vulnerable people. The Information Commissioner's office prepared new guidance following this case. In particular, it should be noted that even had the utility company believed they could not inform the social services of the situation without permission, they did not seek such permission from the individuals concerned. This is the sort of narrow thinking of which the Information Commissioner is highly dismissive, in respect of organizational considerations of data protection (see news.bbc.co.uk/1/hi/uk/3344495.stm).

BIG BROTHER IS WATCHING YOU: AUTOMATED CCTV PROCESSING

George Orwell's Nineteen Eighty-Four has haunted the world for over half a century with its bleak dystopian outlook. The concept of an all-seeing, all-hearing government, controlling its citizens by manipulation of information, fear and even by changing the very language they speak, remains a powerful metaphor today. Every time we are subjected to further surveillance of our daily lives, the question of whether we are moving towards the world of Nineteen Eighty-Four is raised.

The inspiration for Orwell was the development in the United Kingdom, just after the Second World War, of a paternalistic socialist society. Orwell was really trying to write about 1948, but placed his dystopia in the unimaginable future time of 1984 instead. Although the United Kingdom has demonstrably not become Orwell's dystopia, the fears remain. One of the greatest sources of this worry is the explosion in video surveillance in the United Kingdom in the late 1980s and

1990s. The United Kingdom has more CCTV cameras in operation per resident than any other country in the world. A reasonably conservative estimate in 1999 by Norris and Armstrong was that an average person in London was filmed on more than 300 occasions, by over 200 different cameras, every day. More cameras have been installed since 1999, especially in London. It is now difficult for any UK urban citizen to avoid being captured on camera unless they do not leave their home.

One of the difficulties in envisaging a practical implementation of Orwell's dystopia (he was not attempting to lay out a realizable world, but it can be a useful exercise in avoiding relatively similar circumstances) is that of who actually does the watching. If we assume that one person is capable of closely monitoring five others at a time and working an eight-hour shift every day in this role (a bold assumption given the research showing how poor people are at such work) then to watch every citizen for all 24 hours each day would require three-fifths of the population to be engaged in the surveillance effort. Even now, where potentially hundreds of camera are supposedly monitored by a small number of operators, the cost of operators often outweighs the cost of the technical equipment over time. The answer to the surveillant's dream is, of course, for further technology to take over the task of watching.

Significant applications of automated processing of CCTV images have already been developed and deployed. For example, charging for use of London's inner city streets depends on a system of Automatic Number Plate Recognition (ANPR) which ties daily payment for entry to the zone, attached to the number plate of the vehicle in question, with images taken at all vehicular entry and exit points of the zone and selected spots within it. The system automatically issues a penalty notice if payment is not made for a detected vehicle. The small percentage of number plates not automatically recognized by the system are flagged for human deciphering. Without the automatic processing of over 99% of the vehicles entering the city (particularly those entering and leaving multiple times as well as those of residents within the zone who are exempt from the charge) this system would be impossible to administer. The alternative, to have toll entry and exit points physically controlling the flow, are also unrealistic, being both too costly to run and too disruptive of traffic to help.

The same ANPR technology has been attached to a significant number of existing traffic control cameras (ostensibly installed to check for accidents on major roads and to allow for diversions in the event of major snarls in traffic flow). In a significant piece of positive PR for this system, the 'getaway car' used in a robbery which involved the shooting dead of a police officer was tracked from Bradford in the North of England down to London (`news.bbc.co.uk/1/hi/england/bradford/4455918.stm`). However, the human rights implications of this system have registered with both the public and the United Kingdom's regulatory authority for surveillance matters, the Office of the Surveillance Commissioners (`www.surveillancecommissioners.gov.uk`). The 2005–6 Annual Report of the Chief Surveillance Commissioner of this little known UK regulator raises the question as to whether the systematic attachment of ANPR systems to existing traffic and general CCTV cameras and the routine tracking of most or all vehicle movements is a step too far in surveillance, and in particular whether the data thus collected is being held securely enough.

Various projects funded by UK, US and EU government bodies (respectively, the Engineering and Physical Sciences Research Council; the National Science Foundation; and the EC Framework programmes and their Preparatory Action for Security Research) are aimed at developing more sophisticated automatic analysis of individual activities captured by CCTV cameras (see `www.iscaps.net` for one example of an EU project). The UK and EU funding bodies are beginning to look more closely at the social and legal issues related to these developments, funding both separate projects (e.g. `www.urbaneye.net`) and parts of technology projects (for instance, one of the authors was funded to consider the social and legal acceptability of the technology produced and suggested by the ISCAPS project). The problems caused by the overuse of such systems in democracies and the potential abuse of such systems by authoritarian regimes are considered by human rights organizations and academics studying the development of automated CCTV-processing software.

PRIVACY AFTER 9/11

Few people will deny that the political direction of the so-called 'liberal democracies' of the West was fundamentally altered on 11 September 2001. There has been an undeniable shift in many governments' attitudes to the correct balance between freedom of speech and action, freedom from surveillance and even the principle of 'innocent until proven guilty' following the first ever organizational terrorist acts on the United States mainland. Previous acts of terrorism, such as the Oklahoma City bombing or the Unabomber, were by individuals acting alone rather than by an organization. Thus, as far as the United States was concerned, the world changed radically in late 2001. Instead of concentrating on protecting their assets abroad and helping their allies, the threat came home. The 9/11 perpetrators do not appear to have used advanced communications techniques for any aspect of their planning (in fact, so far as we can tell they used the simple expedient of planning all their activities during in-person meetings, sometimes in remote locations such as Afghanistan and sometimes in Western countries such as Germany). Despite this, the newly created US Department of Homeland Security, together with the agencies it coordinates in tracking terrorist threats, such as the CIA, National Security Agency (NSA) and FBI, have placed a high value on increased power to perform surveillance on electronic communications.

Shortly after 9/11, the United States and United Kingdom (as well as a number of other countries) passed new legislation supposedly to deal with the 'new' terror threat. In keeping with public expectations at such a time, there was little party political opposition to quite radical changes in balance between surveillance in the name of security and the individual freedoms of citizens. If all the measures thus implemented could be shown to be both necessary and effective against terrorist threats, there might have been little further discussion of the PATRIOT Act (the US law) and the Terrorism Crime and Security Act 2001 (the UK law). However, civil rights groups have been quite critical of both acts, viewing them as omnibus bills containing a wish-list of authoritarian powers, many of which have no link to terrorism and no conceivable use in combating terrorism, but useful in other law-enforcement activities. More than five years on, the debate is becoming more normal with scrutiny being made not only of the original acts (with a possible view to reining in those powers which seem unreasonably broad) but also of authoritarian proposals such as those contained in further bills being proposed by members of the US Congress.

> USA-PATRIOT Act: Uniting and Strengthening America by Providing Appropriate Tools Required to Intercept and Obstruct Terrorism Act 2001, passed shortly after the terrorist attacks on 11 September 2001

TECHNOLOGICAL PRIVACY AND SURVEILLANCE

As mentioned in the introduction to this chapter, the 'technology' of privacy of information (including communication) and the technology of surveillance have been in an arms race for millennia (Levy 2000). Certainly the issue of privacy of communication has been at the heart of digital computing since its inception. The early fundamentals of theoretical computer science along with the first digital computers, were developed during the Second World War in the effort to break the Nazi Enigma codes. The Cold War was rife with encryption development and cipher-cracking efforts. Again, as Levy notes, even mathematicians working on the abstract concepts of encryption were under surveillance and covert or even overt pressure to work for the government or not to work on the issue at all. Of course, that changed once the personal computer revolution led to a need for commercial encryption systems.

The advent of the Internet brought another sort of privacy to the fore, that of anonymous speech. In the 1980s and 1990s there were a number of 'anon' servers which would anonymize the origin of an e-mail or a posting to usenet (see Chapter 5). The original servers are now mostly closed, for one or both of two reasons. Firstly, one of the principle reasons for having anonymization services was the lack of cheap and easy home Internet access. Secondly, accusations of being a route for the distribution of child pornography led to those providing such services to drop them as too much of a personal risk even where such allegations were entirely unsubstantiated. See Chapters 4 and 5 for different viewpoints on such services.

> Anon server: a server which receives incoming communications and passes that information on to other Internet servers in such a way as to hide the origin of that information

These days there are two ways to consider privacy: be ultra-cautious and use many hops, each encrypted and anonymizing, to get anywhere; or trust to the fact that there are too many people and not enough 'spooks' to be watching everyone if you take some simple precautions. If government really does believe a specific person to be a major threat there are generally sufficient resources for them to find out what they're doing. Commercial-grade encryption of the content of much communication is sufficient to stop casual snoopers from listening in to the content of messages. If the very fact of accessing certain sites is information that a user wishes to avoid anyone finding out, then services such as freenet or browser anonymization are probably necessary. The downside of such things is that simply using them may be picked up, depending on the sophistication of the surveillance. In the long run, it is almost impossible to communicate without some trace of the fact of it, even if not the content, being available to someone with the right resources.

DISCUSSION TOPICS

Leaving Little Trace: Anonymity in the Digital World?

How possible is it in the modern world to leave little trace of one's existence? In many European countries it is a legal requirement to have an identity card and inform the police of one's address. In the United Kingdom and the United States these ideas have been resisted even after 9/11 (although the idea of a national ID card and the associated database has been pushed through the UK parliament). But beyond that, how possible is it to avoid leaving traces in the modern world?

Most things in the modern world cost money. Banks keep significant records of transactions so, to avoid leaving a trace, cash should be used for as many transactions as possible (and shop loyalty cards should also be avoided). The government tax authorities like to be able to identify all of their citizens in order to assess taxation against them. Health services are difficult to get hold of on a cash payment basis in most countries, although day to day services might possibly be available (dental work and prescriptions are possible but hospital treatment is much more difficult). Internet access is difficult but not currently impossible. Cash may be paid for Internet café access in many countries (although increasingly they are being expected to keep records of the identity of users). Subscription to anonymizer services can be difficult without electronic banking, however, since such subscriptions are usually charged to credit cards. Telephone services vary from country to country. A landline phone service is difficult to get without leaving a significant trace of address. A bank account is needed for most contracted mobile telephone services but pay as you go variants are often available with cash purchase of top-up vouchers possible. Mobile phones leave significant trace information behind, however, including location down to transceiver cell. Future plans include embedded GPS in phones which operates even when the unit is switched off.

Travel by plane usually requires photo ID these days even in countries without government identity cards. Toll roads usually allow for cash payment, but ownership of a car will usually involve significant public (vehicle registration) and private (insurance) records. There are proposals in the United Kingdom to attach number plate recognition systems to many of the large number of CCTV traffic cameras already in place. Initially the claim is that these will be used transiently and records of movements only kept where there are problems such as lack of road tax or insurance. Whether this remains the case once the system is in place depends on how much the law-enforcement authorities are trusted to keep this information safe and use it proportionately.

These are just a sample of the ways in which modern life leaves traces in the system. Most people do not bother about them and expect the incompetence of public and private bodies to protect them from the worst excesses of too much information availability.

Availability of Cryptography and Steganography

For decades, the US government classified cryptography as a military weapon, going to great lengths to try and prevent dissemination of cryptographic algorithms or implementations, particularly 'export' of such information. These efforts are described in great detail in (Levy 2000).

The UK RIP Act 2000 introduced a legal requirement to provide decryption keys to law enforcement officials conducting legitimate investigations. Claims that production of such keys are impossible (through having forgotten them or by deletion or corruption of files containing them) have a reversed standard of proof (you are assumed guilty unless you can prove this inability rather than the prosecutors being required to prove positively that you are deliberately concealing them). The infrastructure of e-commerce is based on convincing the public that encrypted information transfer between their computer and web servers is more-or-less immune to interception.

Encryption of e-mail is available but very few people use it as it is generally proprietary added services for specific mail handlers unlike, for example, the binary attachment MIME standard which is understood by most modern mail-handling software. In many areas of life, the phrase 'if you've nothing to hide then you've nothing to fear' is quoted by authoritarian-leaning politicians, and law-enforcement and security-service personnel. This phrase, though wonderfully simple to understand, fails to capture the difference between privacy and secrecy. It includes the assumption that government is entitled to know everything about everyone and that government can be trusted with this information, both not to misuse it itself and not to allow non-governmental agents access to it (by design or by incompetence).

Should access to strong cryptographic and steganographic software be regarded as a reasonable human right or are governments correct in saying that use of such technology is an indication that the user has something to hide and is therefore immediately a suspicious character? Does the need of the FBI to be able to intercept telephone calls when approved by judicial review take precedence over the right of citizens to be able to conduct personal or business communications without fear of their unlawful interception by private investigators or criminals?

Data Retention by ISPs

At present EU-based ISPs retain records of usage by their customers only so far as they are required for the correct operation of their systems, typically only for a few months at most. There have long been proposals to require ISPs to retain usage (and even copies of all transmission) data for anything up to seven years. ISPs have long fought against this, but only in their own interests since proposals for longer-term storage of data places the costs of such retention on the ISPs rather than with the government authorities. In the United Kingdom, for example, a law initially requesting ISPs to maintain such data was passed in 2003. As expected, the voluntary scheme has attracted little cooperation from ISPs, who are concerned with the potential competitive disadvantage of being one of the few who cooperated when the majority did not (both from the direct financial costs and potential customer backlash). While there was originally an option to extend the legislation to compel ISPs to retain data, it expired in December 2004 but was extended to December 2005. It was not exercised before the second expiry date.

Proposals for a Europe-wide equivalent directive are still being debated by the European Council (the body made up of ministers from the member states). Given the national legislation in place, it is no surprise that these are being pushed hardest by the UK government. They are being resisted by various other European countries, such as Germany and Austria whose citizens are typically very wary of government data collection about citizens. Back in 2002, the proposals for an EU directive on data retention were heavily criticized by the European Data Protection Commissioners, in a joint statement, as being fundamentally incompatible with human rights declarations, including the European Convention on Human Rights. The proposed EU Charter of Fundamental Rights (which is incorporated into the proposed EU constitution) is also held by various analysts to include the 'right to privacy' which is incompatible with such proposals.

There are consistent rumours (consistently denied) that the US authorities will propose similar legislation. However, the NSA has long been suspected of gathering significant amounts of such data, so it is possible that the United States has no need to require ISPs to keep what the NSA are collecting anyway.

REFERENCES

Levy, S. (2000) *Crypto: Secrecy and Privacy in the New Code War*, Penguin, London. ISBN 0-140-244-328.

Norris, C. and **Armstrong, G.** (1999) *The Maximum Surveillance Society: the rise of CCTV*, Berg, Oxford. ISBN 1-85973-226-7.

RELATED READING

Brin, G.D. (1998) *The Transparent Society*, Perseus Books, New York. ISBN 0-7382-0144-8.

Whitaker, R. (1999) *The End of Privacy*, The New Press, New York. ISBN 1-56584-569-2.

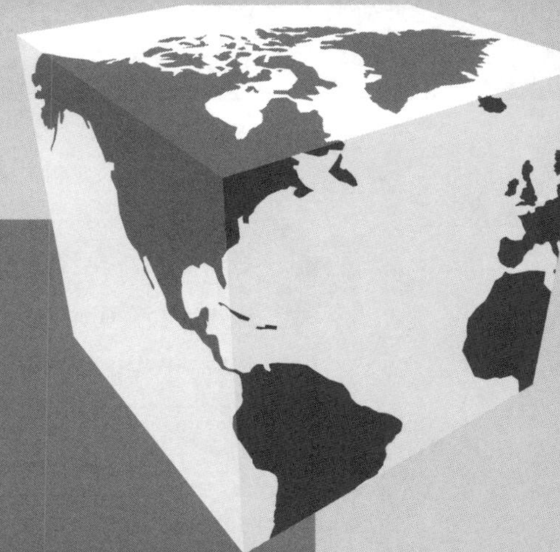

8

INFORMATION AGE WARFARE

INTRODUCTION

This chapter outlines some of the major developments in modern warfare and how they have been influenced by developments in information technology. Until recently, warfare reflected the mechanical or industrial society of the period; today the military arena is dominated by global conflicts within an information age. The traditional battlefield is changing such that military assets and troops are no longer simply protecting their boundaries with conventional military forces. Warfare and conflict now also include political and fundamentalist adversaries who wage war from within the online environment. This is more than cyber-terrorism; it is a new and developing global change in how nation states and individuals are attempting to resolve conflicts or pursue hostile acts in support of their aims and ideals.

> Cyber-terrorism: a terrorist attack on the electronic infrastructure of a country, designed to cause disruption to daily life and possibly to cause significant physical consequence

This chapter also describes how, in a society which places increasing reliance on electronic control systems, there is a huge potential for cyber-attack and a breakdown in a nation's communications infrastructure, by targeting areas such as air-traffic control, public utilities, civil administration and telecommunications.

In today's information age, where it is possible to watch military and terrorist conflicts from our armchairs, media and information control becomes a key weapon. The immediacy of broadcasting from the front line, relayed via news broadcasts, can provide both positive and negative influences in the way people perceive the nature of the conflict and the reasons for it. Issues of information dominance are also discussed here.

Throughout the chapter, examples are given to illustrate key technologies and the possible effect they may have in various scenarios; reference is also made to the translation of these military developments to everyday life, and the potential or actual violation of human rights that can occur.

HISTORY OF WARFARE

The history of warfare can be traced from early times when the deployment of weapons and strategy resulted in the acquisition of land, wealth and the creation of new states. Modern warfare is generally described in terms of countries using their economies and industrial systems to support their military operations.

The First and Second World Wars are good examples of times when huge amounts of human labour were used to produce the armaments to wage and win the war. Throughout and since this time, technological innovation has been translated into military applications or developed from military applications for commercial use. An example of modern warfare which utilized the technological developments of the time was the synchronization of machine guns to fire through aircraft propeller blades, which represented a major breakthrough in aviation dog-fighting in the First World War. Another example was the development of the submarine and the technical advances of operating underwater which provided a substantial advantage in marine warfare. Similarly, in the Second World War, the development of radar systems allowed for the early warning of incoming aircraft, which previously could only be detected by visual sightings.

Throughout history, technical innovation has fuelled the race for military superiority: the development of rocket technology in Germany in 1942 was marked by the launch of the V2 rocket; and the United States dropped atomic bombs on Hiroshima and Nagasaki in 1945. Technology through the wars has also accelerated many peacetime activities, for example the development of Frank Whittle's prototype jet engine from 1937 (`www.ieee-virtual-museum.org`; `edition.cnn.com/SPECIALS/cold.war/experience/technology/`).

The history of information technology starts in the early days of 1822 with the development of the Difference Engine by Charles Babbage, known to some as the 'Father of Computing', and continues to the algorithmic and encryption work of Alan Turing during the Second World War, and onto the development of the Internet in the 1960s and the Web from the late 1980s.

The development of the Internet can be traced back to the arms race with the Soviet Union and the launch of Sputnik 1, the first artificial earth satellite, in 1957. In response to this launch, the US Department of Defense established the Advanced Research Projects Agency (ARPA) and developed the United States' first successful satellite within 18 months. Several years later, ARPA switched its focus to computer networking and communications technology and developed ARPANET, which initially connected four American universities, expanded into academic and military networks and then further developed to what we now know as the Internet.

Advanced research Project Agency Network (ARPANET): the forerunner of the Internet

Following the First and Second World Wars, we moved into the 'Cold War' phase where the race for supremacy in technology was at its highest, with the superpowers seeing domination of the sea, air and, ultimately, outer space as a primary goal. Meanwhile, computer technology was developing at an enormous pace with the move from mainframes to PCs in the early 1980s. In this period, substantial research and development programmes were undertaken by the military agencies of most countries and particularly the US Department of Defense.

Computer cracking was being observed as early as 1985; young people operating from their homes were caught surfing the Internet and entering corporate computer systems. One early group who were caught carrying out this activity were known as the '414' crackers, this being a reference to their telephone area code in Milwaukee, Wisconsin. With the development of new computer chips supporting ever greater processing speeds allied to the massive developments in super computers, military powers and individuals had at their disposal electronic devices with massive computing and problem-solving abilities. These increases in computing power also brought with them greater potential and challenges for the cracker.

Today the explosive growth of computer technology and the Internet has provided the world with a platform and mechanisms to communicate on a scale that Babbage, and even Turing and his colleagues, could only have dreamed of. Today we live in an environment where military devices and international communications can be at the fingertips of almost every individual in any part of the world. It could be argued that the power of this technology in the wrong hands could create havoc and destruction across the world.

Internet 'How to' Guide to Terrorism

A web search for the two words 'explosive' and 'recipe' returns hundreds of thousands of hits. Similar results are available for 'poison' and 'recipe'. The top ten hits for each include pages containing accurate instructions for how to produce explosives and poisons. Even before the development of the Web, there was controversy over the digital distribution (via FTP) of a subversive work called The Anarchist's Cookbook (`www.beyondweird.com/cookbook.html`). Originally written in the late 1960s, and highly controversial even then, the book includes instructions on making explosives from household chemicals, detonation device construction and similar material. The free and simple availability of such works without any method of tracking their distribution was one of the first furores about the open nature of information dissemination over the Internet (see Chapter 4 for more on these issues).

It is just as easy on the Web to find various other information useful to people who wish to commit terrorist acts: how to rig up electronic devices to act as remote triggers; how to hide objects so that they will not be detected during frisking; cryptographic techniques for use with physical as well as electronic messages. There are fears that the free availability of this information makes terrorist attacks more likely, but this is preposterous when you think about it. People do not become terrorists because they see instructions on making bombs on the Internet – they become terrorists because they believe they have to in order to achieve their goals. However such information may make terrorist attacks more likely to succeed.

THE TECHNOLOGY OF WAR

The technologies employed by societies in conflict are closely related to the social and technical developments of the period, moving from the agricultural revolution through the industrial revolution and to the information age. Over time, wars were generally linked to the acquisition of land, property and wealth and then later to industrial and commercial resources. Many of today's conflicts however are also linked to conflicting ideological positions and politics, and to the desire for nations and nation states to control data, knowledge and the consumable resources needed to sustain mankind.

As wars and conflicts have developed many industrial and commercial structures and organizations have been established to underpin, develop and manufacture weapons technology. In today's information age, the race to provide new and developing technologies consumes increasing proportions of national budgets and fuels a massive industry. For example, in today's complex military environments, strategic decisions and military scenarios are generated by computer technology, solutions are analyzed and strategies determined from the data to ensure success and to minimize one's own casualties.

Throughout time, military advantage has relied on 'secure' information being conveyed from command to battlefront by flag, signal, carrier pigeon, smoke signal and so on. Today we rely on high-speed, electronic, encoded communications across and between battlefields which can be local or global. The techniques developed in space exploration and satellite technology have allowed 'superpowers' to communicate, view and carry out military operations anywhere on the planet and 'in space'.

Communications technology, if secure, has transformed battlefield operations, such that enemy targets can be 'acquired' and eliminated with virtually no human intervention. However, although friends and foe can be identified in battlefield scenarios, complex systems are not yet 100% reliable and many examples of 'friendly fire' tragedies have occurred (www.spacewar.com/reports/Humans_Still_A_Factor_In_War_999.html).

The global development of information technology and the exponential expansion of programmers and developers has created a large number of individuals who have both the skills and abilities to operate within this environment. With the development of massive interconnections across the world and an abundance of people who can access the systems, security of data has become paramount. Safeguards are continually being developed to ensure that communication systems and data stores are protected against infiltration and exploitation. Cyber-warfare has now developed not only in terms of breaching or interfering with military systems but, possibly more importantly, entering, altering and controlling worldwide economies and commercial environments such as banking, major corporations, criminal records and so on (www.nato.int/docu/review/2001/0104-04.htm).

The technology of war now includes the media and communications arena, where world events, political scenarios and military conflicts across the world can be viewed in real-time from our homes. Information-age warfare is not restricted to the battlefield; the tools available can be used to influence potential enemies before and after the conflict.

War News

War reporting has been going on ever since there has been an organized press (see www.newseum.org/warstories and www.bl.uk/collections/warfare1.html for some good background). The first officially titled war correspondents appeared during the French revolutionary and Napoleonic wars (1792–1815). By the late nineteenth century, with the US Civil War (1861–65) and the Boer Wars (1880–81 and 1899–1902) modern communications technologies and the development of photography had substantially changed war reporting. The honesty and potential political bias of war reporting have always been controversial. In particular, once swift means of communications were available, the information reporters sent back to their newspapers and, later, newsreel producers was potentially disastrous in pure military terms. The effect on national morale and recruitment efforts became just as, if not more, important than military intelligence issues by the First World War (1914–18) and strict controls were enforced on war correspondents in both World Wars (1914–18 and 1939–45). The photographs and film footage from the liberation of the death camps at the end of the Second World War remain some of the most enduring images of news reporting ever made.

The Vietnam War (exact dates uncertain – it was never officially declared as a war) was the first major conflict of the television age and it is often asserted that it was the immediacy of the television coverage that led to much of the anti-war sentiment in the United States. For the first time the true horrors of a war in a foreign country was being brought into the homes of the citizens of an industrialized nation.

By the Gulf War (1991), television was a dominant force in the information elements and censorship of news coverage was very limited, but even this was eclipsed by the Iraq War (2003) when not only were there 'embedded' reporters living with troops and reporting on their experiences (though not their movements) but television, radio and newspaper reporters remained in a Baghdad hotel throughout the invasion. This hands-on approach however comes at a price. In 2005, 89 journalists were killed while on 'active duty' in conflict zones and a further 61 in accidents or natural disasters (`media.guardian.co.uk/presspublishing/story/0,,1693108,00.html`).

From a different perspective, modern technology is creating a new culture of amateur or 'citizen' reporters. Members of the public use mobile phone photographs, videos and text messages to report an event before official news crews can get anywhere near the scene. A key example of this was the London bombings on 7 July 2005. (`www.guardian.co.uk/attackonlondon/story/0,16132,1525911,00.html`).

Cyber-Wars

With the growing interconnection of computerized systems across the world, cyber-warfare is becoming an ever more menacing threat to world peace and stability. In the Cold War years, it was generally accepted that the electro-magnetic pulse generated by atomic explosions would destroy and render useless many of the electrical and electronic systems controlling public utilities. Today's scenarios have moved this risk to a higher level, as practically all commercial, military and personal systems are computer controlled and many are linked to the Internet, and there are now many more ways in which to sabotage these controlling networks.

One aspect of cyber-warfare is the substantial growth of virus attacks on systems worldwide, where programs are introduced to cause chaos and destroy systems through the use of worms and Trojan horses (see Chapter 11). The military manifestation of this is the logic bomb, designed to disable and create havoc on the targeted infrastructure and military environments. These software devices can implant a worm or virus, which can be activated by a certain event, creating the possibility of widespread chaos. There are many worldwide examples of how breakdowns in computer and communications systems can affect public life whether caused by malicious events or innocent computer failure. Examples include the recent power blackouts in the United States, the temporary closing down of air-traffic-control systems due to computer failure and worldwide viruses closing down banks, web sites and commercial company operations.

Although not perpetrated as a military offensive, a recent example of the havoc that can be caused is demonstrated by the Sasser worm released in May 2004. The originator of this virus was an 18-year-old student living in Germany who targeted a flaw in the Microsoft Windows operating system and infiltrated computer systems across the world, affecting computer operations operated by coastguards, government agencies and hospitals (`edition.cnn.com/2004/TECH/internet/05/03/sasser.worm/index.html`). It is suspected that the author of this virus was also responsible for the Netsky virus, which also plagued Internet users during 2004.

Around the same time, the author of one of the next-generation super-worms was also apprehended in Germany. Government agencies in several countries worked with Microsoft which offered a substantial reward in order to track down the culprit. This latest super-worm was potentially more damaging than Sasser as it allowed its authors to gain control over computers that were then able to send large amounts of spam e-mail messages or flood web sites with data in an attempt to force them offline.

Cyber-warfare often manifests itself as computer programs designed to infiltrate a country's infrastructure possibly disabling its military systems, commercial systems and databases. Countries that are attacked would become paralyzed, as their traffic-control systems would fail, money markets would collapse and defensive weapons systems would malfunction.

As increasing amounts of the world's information is stored on databases then the ability to create worldwide chaos by infiltrating or corrupting this data also increases. Conversely, the same data can potentially be used to track and apprehend others. For example, a little known company called Acxiom is the world's largest processor of consumer data; its customers include nine of the top 10 US credit-card issuers, as well as nearly all the retail banks, insurers and automobile manufacturers. It is reported that after the FBI released the names of some of the hijackers following the 9/11 tragedy in New York, Acxiom ran a computer search and located some of them in its databases. (www.fbi.gov/pressrel/pressrel01/092701hjpic.htm; www.cooperativeresearch.org/context.jsp?item = a0900attawayne; www.city-journal.org/html/14_2_what_we_dont_know.html). This example shows the potential of interconnecting government systems with commercial database information for effective tracking of potential terrorists and lawbreakers. This may be easier to say than carry out, as the releasing of such data to government agencies may be seen by many as a contravention of human rights and an invasion of privacy.

Many argue that cyber-warfare is essentially a non-lethal warfare scenario and that human and material assets are generally unaffected. However, a counter argument may well be that the political instability and fear generated by such an attack on countries which have not developed technologies to defend against cyber-attacks could be catastrophic, possibly encouraging retaliation with the use of chemical and nuclear weapons.

Although cyber-warfare has been very much developed and used by military and government organizations, the technology itself has no frontiers. The inquisitive gamer sitting at home in a bedroom can become part of the cyber-environment and ultimately create havoc and disruption. There are also many examples of programmers, working in isolation or in small groups, whose challenge in life has been to enter secure military and commercial databases in order to demonstrate their own technical capabilities. Terrorists and those wishing to destabilize the world have the opportunity to enter the digital battlefield, attacking vulnerable locations and in some cases leading nations into aggressive pre-emptive actions as they assume they are being attacked by other nation states.

There are already published examples of cyber-warfare, including incidences during the 2000 Arab–Israeli war, which involved Israeli hackers crippling a key web site of the Lebanese group Hezbollah; the site was bombarded with automated e-mail messages, which essentially closed it down. Hezbollah retaliated by carrying out a similar attack on the Israeli government web site. These attacks continued for some time until effective mechanisms and defences were put in place. It is not difficult to image the chaos that could ensue if the same approach was taken in a conflict between major superpowers (www.landfield.com/isn/mail-archive/2000/Nov/0019.html).

Satellites – the View from Space

Satellites are used today for many commercial applications such as television transmissions, global positioning, data communications and Internet traffic. However, they are also used for many military applications including surveillance, espionage, secure communications and the potential delivery of offensive and defensive weapons systems. Satellite-data-driven tools such as Google Earth are also now being used by terrorists to help plan their attacks (www.telegraph.co.uk/news/main.jhtml?xml=/news/2007/01/13/wgoogle13.xml).

The harnessing of commercial satellites in addition to existing military satellites has become common practice due to the ever-increasing demand for data bandwidth. The greater role of communication-based technology is evidenced by 10 times more satellite capacity being used during the Iraq War (2003) than the Gulf War (1991). For example, although many precision-guided weapons use the US-operated global positioning system (GPS) satellite constellation or laser guidance, some weapons (such as unmanned Predator drones) use satellite bandwidth to provide a live video feed to operators who may be many thousands of miles away. Some cruise missiles may also transmit live video footage or receive updated target information via satellite. Commercial imagery is also being used to add to the satellite images of ground contours and so on, available for military purposes. The harnessing of these commercial satellites is made possible by the military using its own encryption technology to secure the communication before passing it through the commercial network.

> Global positioning system (GPS): a network of satellites that allows the precise pinpointing of the position of a receiver by correlating the difference in distance (measured by time) to multiple satellites

Star Wars Technology

There is growing evidence that space will become an increasingly important environment for weapons and systems. It is predicted that the United States may see its investment in this area growing from $10 billion in 2004 to $500 billion by 2024. If this is realized then the fear is that a new arms race may emerge. Evidence suggests that the United States is gradually merging its long-term, military, space command tasks with the civilian space operations at NASA. Russia, in turn, having lost the ability to keep pace with the US military capacity on Earth is showing signs of being able to compete outside the planet's atmosphere. China and India, the world's two most populous countries, are also aggressively pursuing space programmes (`news.bbc.co.uk/1/hi/world/asia-pacific/6276543.stm`). Europe lags behind in this race, although the European Space Agency has announced plans to press ahead with its Galileo satellite-positioning systems, which at least gives some independence from the US GPS.

While the main thrust of the US military space programme is the creation of a missile defence system, effectively a laser defence network designed to shoot down incoming enemy ballistic missiles, there is evidence that future plans may involve developing offensive weapons with the ultimate ambition of achieving 'full-spectrum dominance' in all areas of warfare. The development of such a network would enable real-time predictive information to locate, identify, track and target enemies on any battlefield on Earth.

However, the implementation of these systems by the United States would almost certainly be in contravention of the 1967 Outer Space Treaty which outlaws the use of offensive weapons in orbit. The consequences of pressing ahead with this programme may create tensions between the world's superpowers as they battle for supremacy in space. Tensions already exist as this potential development by the United States would be in addition to their abandonment of the 1972 Anti-Ballistic Missile Treaty, put in place to ban missile defence shields (archives.cnn.com/2001/ALLPOLITICS/12/13/rec.bush.abm).

Network-centric Warfare

In the future it is expected that warfare will experience a shift from being platform-centric, concentrating on its vehicles, to being network-centric, built around a system of shared data and communications. Tomorrow's battlefield soldier will use the latest developments in technology to provide tactical advantage over the enemy. Soldiers will operate within an information domain over a secure network that provides them with maximum information about the enemy while at the same time ensuring that the enemy has little or no appreciation of the forces and tactics being deployed against them.

By operating within secure coordinated networks, the capabilities of the fighting force are exponentially greater than existing methods of deploying troops. In the United States this technology is called future combat systems (FCS, www.army.mil/fcs) and similar programmes such as future infantry soldier technology (FIST, www.army-technology.com/projects/fist/) are also being developed in the United Kingdom.

Advances in network-enabled warfare means that human and machine can work together by utilizing a range of technologies to engage with the enemy and destroy it. For example, the development of smart missiles with radar-link sensors and short-range weapons with similar velocities to tank shells will provide a substantial advantage over the enemy. In ethical terms, it may be argued that the development of scalable lethal weapons, which can stun rather than kill, may also provide opportunities for peace keeping rather than the ultimate destruction of the enemy.

Tomorrow's soldier will be a fearsome beast; all weapons systems will be connected through and around the soldier's body using wireless technologies such as Bluetooth and its successors. With on-board-computer technology feeding back to remote systems, the soldiers will have at their disposal an enormous number of resources including artificial intelligence systems providing them with 'real-time' option scenarios as the battle progresses. In addition to being able to call in remote weapon systems, such as smart mortar bombs and loitering missiles, they will be able to view, through integrated head sets and optical devices, battleground information day or night and in any weather conditions. When this equipment is combined with the latest satellite navigation systems, the soldiers of tomorrow can be deployed in hostile conditions in relatively small numbers and launch multiple weapon systems from safe locations.

Although these modern advances provide for substantial improvements in battlefield efficiency, inevitably the individual will still require a personal weapons platform and the latest developments in body protection in order to survive should they be detected. Considerable work is now being undertaken to immerse the above technologies into machine environments and produce smart robots which would replace humans in the battlefield.

WiFi Landmines

There has been a widespread international campaign to ban the production, sale and deployment of landmines (see `www.icbl.org`) since the early

1990s. The argument is that, although they are very useful during a war, their long term-effects on civilians after conflict has ended put their use squarely over the line into a war crime. The problems with landmines comes from their indiscriminate deployment, with little or no regard for tracking and recovering them after the end of hostilities, and the indiscriminate nature of their long-term capability. Anti-personnel landmines are regarded as the worst culprits since their deployment in an area effectively destroys the potential for any peaceful use of that land afterwards. By December 2003, 141 countries around the world had acceded to the Mine Ban Treaty including almost all EU member states. However, of the five permanent members of the UN Security Council only the United Kingdom and France had signed up. Russia, China and the United States are not currently signatories. The United States has put forward the argument that it uses landmines judiciously and with careful records of their deployment. It points to the border between North and South Korea as an area that could not be adequately defended without the use of landmines. It also points to new technological developments which it says will significantly reduce or even eliminate the long-term consequences of land-mine deployment.

The US Army announced in April 2005 that it planned to deploy 25 batches of the 'Matrix' system of remotely detonating, anti-personnel landmines to Iraq. These landmines do not explode due to a physical trigger, but in response to a wireless LAN signal (`www.theregister.co.uk/2005/04/12/laptop_triggered_landmine`). There are two variants of the landmine, one containing steel balls, intended to be lethal, and another containing rubber balls, intended to be non-lethal and possibly for use in controlling crowds in the same way that 'rubber bullets' or 'baton rounds' are used. Given the susceptibility of computer networks to cracking (see Chapter 11) then whether or not these mines do remove or reduce the long-term civilian casualties, the potential for them to backfire on US personnel seems significant.

THE BATTLEFIELD

It may be argued that remotely operated machines will fight future wars and conflicts. Advances in artificial intelligence have resulted in the development of robots and unmanned aircraft and vehicles, which have the ability to operate in military environments where they can react to situations in an autonomous way.

New electronic warfare technologies are being developed using high-energy electronics in missiles, aircraft and satellites. These new weapons can penetrate and destroy electrical and electronic systems, while ensuring that physical assets, buildings and resources remain intact. This technology is effectively the opposite of nuclear warfare, which results in the total destruction of material and human assets.

Examples of new weapons technologies can be seen in unmanned aerial vehicles (UAVs), such as the Predator drones which can be deployed in military environments to provide intelligence for ground troops or to guide and launch offensive weapons at identified targets (`news.independent.co.uk/europe/article624667.ece`; `www.post-gazette.com/pg/06038/651627.stm`). These technologies were used in recent military campaigns in both Afghanistan and Iraq.

Robo-Soldier

Studies are being undertaken into how modern technology may enhance or improve the individual performance of soldiers. For example, in a $50 million research programme, the US military is developing powered exoskeletons for its soldiers aimed at improving their speed, strength and endurance. The key benefits they hope to achieve through such developments are better protection against enemy and friendly fire and the ability to carry heavier loads, march faster over longer distances, lift heavier objects, use larger weapons and leap greater heights or distances (`news.bbc.co.uk/1/hi/sci/tech/3502194.stm`).

One of the great challenges in these developments is in blending the technology with the human, to the extent that the troops can wear and use the exoskeletons as a natural extension of their body rather than as an additional piece of equipment that they have to operate. To be effective, the exoskeletons also need to operate silently, be fuel-efficient and not interfere with the operator's duties such as being able to shoot through gun sights or crawl through undergrowth and remain camouflaged.

The exoskeletons will also contain a range of other features and sensors to expand the operator's field of vision, incorporate wireless networks to communicate information about battlefield conditions, and interface with GPS, thermal cameras and physiological monitoring systems with the ability to report back to command and control.

Man or Machine?

Another example of how new technology is affecting the modern battlefield are the developments underway in the design of military aircraft cockpits. In a similar way to the battlefield soldier, the traditional gunner in an aircraft who viewed the enemy through a gun sight has now been superseded by twenty-first century technology. High-speed fighter jets now require pilots to be immersed in the technology of the environment; for example, the new UK Eurofighter can only be flown in a computer-controlled fashion and many of the on-board control and weapons are automatically activated. The latest developments will ensure that the pilot of tomorrow will be linked interactively to the flying and weapons platform of the aircraft. The complexity of flying is now so demanding that the human brain cannot operate quickly enough to respond to the multiple tasks involved. In tomorrow's combat environment, life or death decisions may require multiple nanosecond responses in order to survive. With the advances in artificial intelligence and the latest developments in interfacing techniques, we are faced with this moral question – are we controlling the machine or is the machine controlling us?

The Unseen Enemy

In today's military environment the aggressor who can deploy weapons at the earliest opportunity while not being observed has the major tactical advantage. However, the concept of stealth is not new; throughout the ages troops and military equipment have used camouflage techniques to hide their presence. Early developments in radar technologies and underwater detection systems, such as those by Anti-Submarine Detection Investigation Committee (ASDIC, later the technology was renamed as SONAR) have provided a method by which aggressors and their equipment can be detected. These early-detection methods have been continually improved over time and have benefited from the advances in information technology and computing power. The latest systems can mask the identity of military assets such as aircraft, rendering them invisible to electronic defensive systems. The US Department of Defense has been reluctant to discuss the existence of these aircraft but an estimate would indicate that at least since the mid 1980s the United States has invested in substantial research and development in this area of stealth technology.

Stealth technology can now be observed in the F-117 Stealth fighter Nighthawk, probably one of the most sophisticated aircraft ever built, and the B2 Spirit Stealth Bomber which was deployed in operation Desert Storm. The latest developments on quiet and unobservable aircraft are built upon the already highly complex technology environments that are present in most military aircraft. Research is also currently looking into ways of rendering military vessels such as warships and tanks invisible to both the eye and radar by using cloaking materials which 'grab' photons of light (www.timesonline.co.uk/tol/news/uk/article669203.ece).

The majority of military and commercial aircraft are now designed to be flown with the aid of computer systems, navigation and detection systems that replace or supplement the crew of the aircraft in appropriate situations. Military aircraft have complex computer technology which operates their weapons systems, link the systems to target acquisition and ensure appropriate deployment of weapons at the most appropriate ranges. More recent developments of military aircraft involve pilot-less aircraft, which are remotely controlled from safe locations, possibly thousands of miles from the battlefront.

Mobile Phones as Weapons

The Internet and communication systems can also be used to directly trigger aggressive events in locations across the world. Once the user has connected to the system and is interfacing with it, information can then be used to target the individual or the users and in some cases electronically activate explosive devices. A recent example of the use of mobile phones for terrorist activity was in the Madrid rail bombs of March 2004, where a number of bombs were activated by mobile phone signals (`news.bbc.co.uk/1/hi/world/europe/4659547.stm`). During the Afghanistan war, a rebel leader answered his mobile telephone, was targeted on its signal and killed by a missile.

War Games

With the advances in computer technology, software applications and artificial intelligence a range of simulation scenarios are now possible within the military environment. The distinction between games developers and military experts has now become blurred, with full-scale military scenarios enacted on screen and the consequences of the decisions observed. The latest technology also enables virtual battle training, by combining mapping and topographical data with live sequences of military action to provide realistic visual environments. In these war games scenarios, it is also possible to include logistics problems thereby allowing supply chain management to be modelled and appropriate logistics support to be provided to appropriate personnel and equipment for each battlefield scenario. An example of this application is the joint development by the US military and commercial developers of a training simulator called Asymmetric Warfare Environment. This simulator is essentially a multiplayer role-playing game used by military personnel to train troops in urban warfare situations before they are airlifted to the battle zone (www.marcusevans.com/events/CFEventinfo.asp?EventID=10402).

On an even larger scale, each year a Coalition Warrior Demonstration brings together forces from the United Kingdom, the United States, Canada, Australia, New Zealand, NATO and South Korea (www.cwid.org.uk/). Military users, industrial observers and academic researchers demonstrate, evaluate and exploit new and evolving command, control, communications and computers: intelligence, surveillance, target acquisition and reconnaissance (C4/ISTAR) technologies. The Defence Science and Technology Laboratory (DSTL) hosts the event at its purpose-built high-technology battle laboratory near Portsmouth in the United Kingdom and it can simulate a coalition-level operation and scenario within a conventional warfare setting.

Modified commercial computer games are also now becoming a vital part of military training. Examples of these include Doom, Sub Command, Decisive Action, Platoon, and Eurofighter Simulator. However, commercially available simulation programmes can also be used for covert or terrorist activities. For example the sophisticated facilities that have been developed for the training of pilots and flight crew formed part of the planning of the terrorist activities of 9/11, where civilian aircraft were flown by terrorists and used as weapons of destruction. In response to these actions, scientists are developing a computer based 'Assisted Recovery System', capable of preventing terrorists from crashing civilian aircraft into buildings and possibly even allowing them to automatically be landed safely (www.safee.reading.ac.uk; www.dailymail.co.uk/pages/live/articles/news/news.html). The device uses GPS technology to alert pilots if they are on a collision course with a building, overrules the captain's instructions, and diverts the plane safely 30 seconds before impact. There are also claims that it could be adapted to prevent aircraft from entering no-fly zones and other restricted areas. There are indications that if tests go well and it receives regulatory approval it may be in place on all planes in as little as five years. There are some concerns however from pilots that if such a computer system took control at the wrong moment it could lead to lethal consequences.

INFORMATION DOMINANCE

Driven by the advances in information technology, which are increasingly significant in modern day warfare, is the concept of information dominance. This involves the tight integration of propaganda and new media into the overall military command structure. This information then becomes as much part of the weapon arsenal to be deployed against the enemy as conventional weapons.

The 2003 conflict in Iraq was the first theatre where the full effect of this approach was used. During this campaign the allied forces reportedly set up 15 information dominance centres in the United States, Kuwait and Baghdad. The overall objective of achieving information dominance involves both building up and protecting friendly information, and degrading or destroying the information received by the enemy (`www.guardian.co.uk/analysis/story/0,3604,1118096,00.html`). For example during the Iraq conflict 'friendly information' was built up by embedding journalists within Iraq. This is evidenced by the subsequent MoD analysis that showed that 90% of the journalists' reports presented a 'positive or neutral' outlook on the conflict.

The use of psychological warfare is not new. Throughout history, passing on misleading information and demoralizing the enemy has been a legitimate tactic. With the advantages in worldwide communication technology and the ability of news channels to beam information directly from conflicts, the population is now exposed to real-time information on world events. By manipulating media sources and electronically blocking certain media types, powerful nations can influence world opinion. Conversely with the freedom of information and the multiple media sources by which it can be communicated, individuals and interest groups can also influence world opinion.

Misinformation and demoralization of military personnel can now be more easily achieved by using commercial communication technologies. SMS messaging, satellite phones and videophones are all technologies, which allow direct and almost instantaneous communications with friend and foe. Gone are the days that radio broadcasts to the population and leaflet drops were the vital propagation tools, today at the press of a button individualized messages can be sent to electronically connected individuals across the world.

In modern military planning scenarios the control and dominance of the information delivery systems is considered vital. During conflicts, information distribution is generally intended to raise the moral of troops, while disrupting and demoralizing the enemy and its supporters. It has also been shown that information dominance and the targeting of unfriendly information is vital to post-conflict reconstruction. Considerable efforts are taken to ensure that the broadcast information supports the aims and objectives of the occupying or victorious forces, and that information media sources supporting subversive elements are controlled - effectively censored. An example of how unfriendly information is dealt with was evidenced by the pressures placed upon television channels such as al-Jazeera when they reported on various aspects pre and post conflict of the wars in Iraq and Afghanistan.

The Internet and world wide web can also be used as a means of making personal statements, for example through weblogs, whereby an individual relates their personal experiences in order to promote or highlight a particular cause or concern. For example, during the war with Iraq, Salaam Pax, aka the 'Blogger of

Baghdad' became a cyber-celebrity for his blog, which documented everyday life under Saddam Hussein. In this instance the web afforded him the anonymity to write his personal account.

It is reported that since the war in Iraq began more than one thousand web sites have been targeted by anti-war crackers, defacing the sites with a range of anti-war, anti-USA or anti-Iraq slogans. It is believed that these hackers fall into three categories, US-based patriots, Islamic extremists, and peace activists who are against all forms of war. This behaviour demonstrates a move away from traditional cracker motives of gaining kudos by breaking into a web site, to these new groups using cracking methods to exploit the communication medium as a means of spreading their political message. The Ganda e-mail virus was the first example of a virus exploiting the on-going war – being spread through offering satellite pictures of Iraq and screensavers mocking President Bush.

Intelligence Gathering and Surveillance

An integral part of all military operation is the need to observe the opposing forces and to gain secretive information with regard to their capabilities and actions. The information age has provided the platform for the rapid expansion of surveillance devices and operations in the military, commercial and private sectors.

With the end of the Cold War and the need to combat new forms of threats, military analysts now consider that combating cyber-warfare is the number one priority. Current military surveillance techniques include the monitoring of telephony and Internet traffic, observing battlefields and hostile locations by combinations of high flying aircraft and satellites, and locating tracking and monitoring devices in buildings or on individuals. Examples of these systems include the location of information monitoring stations in various worldwide locations. It is reported that Menwith Hill RAF station in North Yorkshire, England, is the largest electronic monitoring station in the world. Run by the National Security Agency (NSA) of the United States, it is one of a global network of Signals Intelligence bases, which monitors the world's communications and relays information to NSA HQ at Fort Meade in Maryland, USA.

National Security Agency (NSA): also known as No Such Agency

Another example is the capabilities of submarines such USS Jimmy Carter, a Seawolf class nuclear vessel, which has a sixty foot section added to its centre allowing the crew to put in place, on the seabed, 'electronic labs' that will enable them to listen into international phone messages being carried through fibre optic cables on the seabed.

It is reported that many of the hundreds of space satellites orbiting the earth have a surveillance capability which allows them to track and monitor individuals almost anywhere on the planet. These devices incorporate high definition cameras, listening devices, infra red sensors and other monitoring devices which ensure that, whatever the weather conditions, monitoring is still possible.

The monitoring and detecting of tomorrow's enemy in the cyber-world will require new forms of detection and decryption. Across the world, police, security intelligence services and government agencies are developing new technologies which give them the ability to intercept, read and share the contents of e-mail traffic. President Bush signed the Uniting and Strengthening America by Providing Appropriate Tools Required to Intercept and Obstruct Terrorism (USA PATRIOT) Act, giving sweeping new surveillance powers to both domestic law enforcement and international intelligence agencies. Many other countries already monitor Internet traffic, for example in Russia, President Vladimir Putin substantially strengthened the rights of the secret services and government agencies, granting them extensive monitoring powers over the media, and direct access to all Internet transactions.

For many years spying, monitoring and surveillance has also operated in the commercial and private sector, using in many cases technologies developed for military applications. Surveillance by CCTV is now commonplace in town centres and employers premises. However recent developments now allow for face recognition and vehicle identity checking. CCTV data can also be networked and transmitted to central databases for analysis and further action.

In order to counteract terrorism a range of measures are being introduced such as voluntary or compulsory photo ID cards, which will eventually incorporate biometric data such as fingerprints, and iris scans. The latest developments in voice print technology are also being used. For example, it has been suggested that this technology was used to track down Khalid Sheikh Mohammed, when after the 9/11 attacks he gave an interview on Al-Jazeera television.

The tracking and monitoring of private individuals is growing. It is now possible in many countries, to monitor telephone conversations, track credit card transactions, monitor access to roads, city centres, and buildings through CCTV cameras, and determine a person's location by analyzing mobile phone signals. This information and the data obtained from these sources can form part of an overall computer profile of the individual, which at a later date can be cross referenced with other database information pertaining to the individual. Once gathered this information has the potential to be shared with other organizations and agencies.

It is argued that many of these devices and systems are intended to be used to prevent crime, protect property and track criminals and dissidents. However, each country faces a human rights and privacy dilemma. Some countries have responded with the introduction of legal guidelines, however the attitude to guidelines and enforcing of laws varies widely across the world. In an information technology rich environment, where for example a child can take your photograph by phone camera and send it around the world in a few seconds, we need to consider the real dichotomy of harnessing the abilities of the information age with the need for privacy. This topic is covered in more detail in Chapter 7.

DISCUSSION TOPICS

Working for Arms Manufacturers

Modern munitions are including more and more information technology components. Cruise missiles are effectively unmanned planes with a warhead. Unmanned vehicles (autonomous and remote controlled) are becoming a larger and larger part of the arsenal of a modern military force. Even such simple things as bullets, grenades and landmines are gaining high tech appendages. All of these require research, development and deployment by hardware and software engineers. What is the moral position in working for companies doing such development? The codes of conduct for professional organizations do not provide advice on such decisions. Provided the work being done is legal, it is up to the individual whether they are prepared to work in such an environment. It is tempting to try and take the moral high ground and say that you will refuse to work for any company involved in the development or production of weapons. However, this will make it quite difficult to find work. Almost all large companies have some involvement in defence areas. it is almost impossible when working for such a company to know when your individual work will later be incorporated in weapons development.

There is also the question of whether that is the moral choice. Development of so-called 'smart bombs' improve the accuracy of such weapons and reduce the collateral damage of civilian casualties. Of course, those deciding on the valid targets even with such bombs can still make decisions which cause unintended consequences (the bombing of the Chinese Embassy in Bosnia and the civilian deaths caused by the failed attempts to take out Saddam Hussein at the beginning of the Iraq War). Since the United States has refused to sign up to a ban on usage of landmines is the development of the Matrix WLAN-enabled mine a reduction in the harm caused by such weapons or a further excuse for the United States to continue using them?

Practical personal considerations must also be taken into account when making such decisions. Small companies may be offered the chance to participate in a military contract and you will suddenly be faced with the dilemma of finding a new job very quickly, becoming unemployed or working on such projects. Considering these issues ahead of time and having plans to follow your own morality, whatever that tells you to do, is the way to avoid finding yourself in a moral dilemma.

Cyberterrorism: Real Threat or Virtual Bogeyman?

The approach of the year 2000, with its concomitant worries about the collapse of diverse systems necessary to modern life raised awareness of just how much we depend on computers, from banking to power systems and from hospitals to radio and television broadcasting. Following the terrorist attacks of September 11th 2001, the prospect of terrorist attacks on the networked computer infrastructure of the industrialized world was considered.

There have been individual attacks ascribed to 'terrorists', mostly the political defacement of web sites belonging to well known organizations such as Al Jazeera television or Israeli political organizations. However, large scale attacks aimed at infrastructure such as electricity grids or stock exchanges have not been successful yet. There are constant calls for further investment in computer security for infrastructure and a greater degree of integration in awareness of the issues.

As with all areas of terrorism, the reluctance of security services to reveal how much they know and how many attacks they thwart (and particularly how they thwart them) means it is difficult to judge exactly how much terrorists are involved in such attacks. Certainly the concept that major areas of infrastructure such as hospital computers or the computers running power plants are actually connected to the Internet is a worrying one given the insecurity generally in evidence. Of course, the problem with networking is that it only takes a computer which is connected to the Internet to also be connected to an internal network and there is potentially a way through to the critical machines.

The general opinion is that the lack of serious problems in 2000 was due to the massive preparation effort. Is such an effort needed to avoid a real terrorist incident on electronic infrastructure, or is this another example of bogeymen in the cupboard being used to increase government powers and budgets? Are terrorists really interested in such targets or are we overestimating the importance of electronic communications?

Overall Benefit or Drain on Resources?

The world's major nations have increasingly developed information technology warfare in the name of maintaining global stability and billions of dollars are being spent annually by the military on Information Technology related research. It may be argued that much of our lifestyle and many life enhancing applications, such as the Internet, have been developed from the enormous sums of money spent on military and space race developments. However these associated perceived benefits should be viewed in relation to the growing high technology arms race, where the world's most able academics are being employed by wealthy nation states to develop weapons systems designed to maintain their military superiority and dominance. Is this morally defensible in today's society?

In addition the constant development of new and ever more expensive weaponry has drained the resources of some of the world's poorest nations, transferring a significant proportion of their meagre wealth back to the industrialized world with its arms manufacturers, whose development work is highly subsidized by government funding. Does military research cause more harm than the world gains from the side benefits?

RELATED READING

Eisenhower Institute, The Future of Space: the Next Strategic Frontier, www.eisenhowerinstitute.org/programs/globalpartnerships/fos/newfrontier/weapons.htm (last accessed 25 July 2007).

Federation of American Scientists, Information Warfare and Information Security on the Web, www.irational.org/APD/cyber/wwwinfo.html (last accessed 25 July 2007).

Goldstein, H. (2006) Modelling Terrorists: New simulators could help intelligence analysts think like the enemy, *IEEE Spectrum*, September 2006, 18–26.

Independent newspaper, Inside the Head of a Super Hacker, news.independent.co.uk/sci_tech/article1173788.ece (last accessed 25 July 2007).

KMI Publications, Military Information Technology Online, www.military-information-technology.com (last accessed 25 July 2007).

Pons, S. and **Romero, F.** (eds) (2004) *Reinterpreting the End of the Cold War*, Frank Cass Publishers, London. ISBN 0-203-00609-7.

US Army, America's Army Game, www.goarmy.com/aarmy (last accessed 25 July 2007).

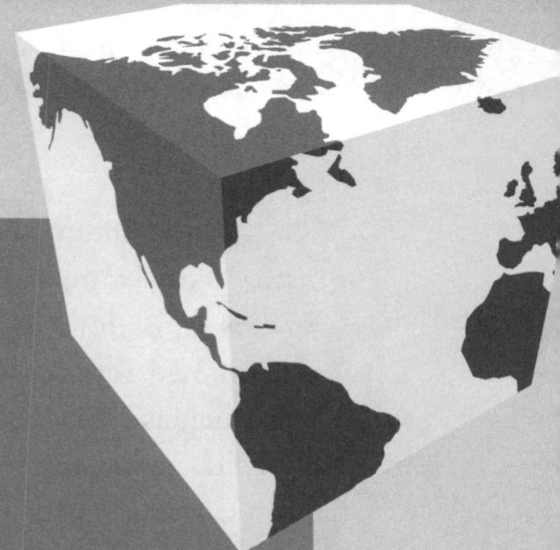

9

TECHNOLOGY AND THE HUMAN BODY

INTRODUCTION

Health care is an extremely important yet complex and costly activity with regard to its infrastructure, the physical resources it requires and the staffing levels that it demands across the profession. These costs are continually increasing as public expectations for health care rise, diseases such as Acquired Immuno-Deficiency Syndrome (AIDS), cancer and mental illness are more prevalent, and demographics shift towards an aging population who require on average more frequent and longer periods of care in hospital. In combination, these factors place ever-increasing demands on a country's health services and the efficient delivery of its health care. Increasingly, the integration of digital information and exploitation of new technologies are having a significant impact on health care delivery, saving lives and improving quality of life while minimizing costs to the service.

Within the medical profession, advances and shifts have occurred in many areas. For example, computers are increasingly being used in the management of hospitals, for the keeping of electronic patient records and the provision of streamlined services such as e-booking and e-prescribing. The Internet and web sites such as NHS Direct (www.nhsdirect.nhs.uk) or the US-based commercial site WebMD (www.wbmd.com) provide exhaustive resources of information for health professionals and the general public. Prevention of illness through education, nutrition guidance and other techniques also becomes possible when linked to information and communication technologies.

> National health service (NHS): the United Kingdom's government-run health system

Techniques such as 3-D imaging and virtual reality have been exploited in areas such as digital diagnosis, training of surgeons and the control of phobias. 3-D prediction and manipulation of protein structures and DNA have been made possible through digital techniques and computationally powerful machines. More powerful computing has also allowed the modelling and prediction of the outbreak and spread of infectious diseases such as Severe Acute Respiratory Syndrome (SARS) and the H5 N1 strain of the bird influenza virus (www.nih.gov/news/pr/nov2004/nigms-15.htm).

There has also been a shift from in-patient care to ambulatory and home-based care brought about through the development of advanced telemetrics and smart homes. A culture has also developed for the use of home-testing kits for conditions ranging from pregnancy and high or low blood pressure to cancer and AIDS. Surgical advances have been made possible through techniques such as digital diagnosis, non-invasive medicine and minimally invasive surgery (using cameras, lasers, magnetic resonance imaging (MRI) scans, robotic surgery, etc.) as well as the application of teleconsultations interfacing with the home, rural hospitals or, in some cases, battlefields.

Information and communication technology has also supported advances in often highly emotive and controversial areas such as transplants, implants, genetics, eugenics, and reconstructive and prosthetic surgery. Whilst many of these advances have beneficial consequences, for example implants inserted within the brain to prevent tremors occurring in patients with Parkinson's disease or within the body to help regain movement and control, there are always discussions and disagreements with regard to how far it is acceptable to go in fusing technology with human life. These arguments extend from enabling and restoring natural life right up to the possible creation of 'super beings' or those adapted for life in inhospitable environments, as science fiction starts to become science fact in terms of what is now technologically feasible.

This chapter sets out to explore a number of issues related to the ways in which technology is influencing health and the human body.

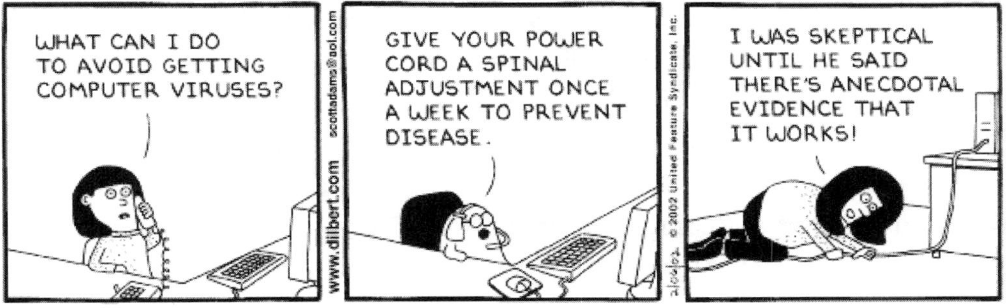

HEALTH INFORMATION SYSTEMS

One of the ways in which communication and information technologies are influencing the health service is in the development of its infrastructure and supporting practices. These advances manifest themselves in many guises ranging from the core IT systems required to run the business, to web sites which promote health services and health call centres, such as the United Kingdom's NHS Direct which provides individual medical advice and guidance, to the development and full implementation of electronic patient records. This section outlines a number of ways where the adoption of ICT is being used to assist health services in operating more efficiently.

Treatment

Computers have played a part within health services for a considerable time. One of the first uses of computing in hospitals some 40 years ago was for the planning of radiotherapy treatment to ensure that correct doses of radiation were applied to the parts of the body being treated. More recently, the use of ICT has been important in the development and use of other techniques such as radioisotope imaging, ultrasound imaging, computerized tomography, X-ray and MRI scanning (www.news-medical.net/?id=7873). Systems have also been developed to enable computer manipulation of these images: to enhance the visibility of selected objects; to aid diagnosis; to allow storage and retrieval of these images from central databases; and to link the images directly to patients' records. Aside from the diagnostic advantages, by having such imaging and document management systems, time spent searching or waiting for the necessary information to arrive can be reduced dramatically.

> (Nuclear) magnetic resonance imaging (MRI): a system which uses the way in which the atoms of various elements react differently to magnetic fields to build internal pictures of the body

Electronic Patient Records

Since the early 1970s, computers have also been used in the general management of hospitals in terms of keeping track of patients and for bed occupancy.

This application has developed extensively to include full details of patient treatments, storing of test results and discharge dates as well as planning of staff rotas and resource management. Such systems may be seen as the forerunner to the implementation and adoption of electronic patient (medical) records that is currently being developed in the United Kingdom and elsewhere. For example, the mission of the Medical Records Institute based in the United States (www.medrecinst.com/about.asp?id=199) is to promote and enhance the development and use of electronic health records and related applications of information technology.

The use of electronic patient records is intended to make the system more ubiquitous and efficient. For example, a universal online system would enable a patient's records to be accessed on demand at any location, the system would also allow the transfer of records between doctors' surgeries to become faster and more efficient. This is important, given that the population now travel much more widely and relocate more often than in previous generations.

These records and 'smart' health information cards carried by individuals would enable vital medical information to be easily accessed, for example, at an accident scene where the person may be unconscious and unresponsive. Having medical information such as allergies or previous medical conditions immediately available may influence diagnosis and assist in more rapid and effective treatment.

One specific example of developments in the electronic patient record area is the linkage of the United Kingdom's NHS hearing screening programme for newborn babies with its baby registration scheme. The Newborn Hearing Screening Project, which began in 2001, enables early identification of hearing problems in babies (www.library.nhs.uk/screening/ViewResource.aspx?resID=57183). The NHS Numbers for Babies Project, launched in October 2003, allows midwives to issue NHS numbers at birth and thus provides a common link between a patient's records across the NHS, both electronic and manual. It is the foundation of the move towards electronic health records (www.connectingforhealth.nhs.uk/nn4b). By linking the two projects, the NHS claims that fewer babies will fall through the hearing screening process and that the amount of data entry required will be reduced. This project also represents the first nationwide Web-based system deployed on NHSnet, the NHS's secure wide area network.

E-booking

Computers are used extensively in doctors' surgeries for keeping records. The first UK instance of this was in 1978 at a surgery in Devon. Doctors also use computer systems to obtain drug information and for authorization and printing of repeat prescriptions without the patient needing to visit the doctor. Reminders for regular screenings can also be highlighted and sent to patients automatically.

> e-booking: allowing patients to book appointments online instead of them being allocated by a hospital

Other methods and systems are being investigated to improve the efficiency and cost effectiveness of the health service including electronic booking systems and e-prescribing. An example of this is EMIS Access, which allows patients to make appointments over the Internet to see their doctor. This system, as well as allowing patients to view doctors' timetables online and book or cancel appointments 24 hours a day, can also allow patients to send confidential queries to their doctor and to update their own contact details. Patients can access the online booking system through their doctor's web site or through a portal such as the Patient UK web site (`www.patient.co.uk`). This system has been successfully used in many practices across the United Kingdom and has been found, unsurprisingly, to appeal to many middle-class professionals who are very computer literate. The benefits are not only for patients who use the system. It has also helped to free up reception staff who can concentrate on developing other areas of their practice's service. It must be remembered however that such systems can only be used by certain groups of patients – many socio-economic groups and age groups do not have access to or training in this technology area. It should therefore be considered as a way of augmenting the facilities available to patients rather than as a replacement for methods of access.

A new multi-million pound system is also under development in the United Kingdom to allow patients to book hospital appointments online. This is supposed to enable patients, at the point of referral to hospital by their GP, to choose the hospital they would like to attend at a date and time to suit them. This system, The National Electronic Booking System, is said to be the first of its kind in the world (www.connectingforhealth.nhs.uk/news/public_accounts_committee.pdf). The project, part of the NHS's £12 billion IT upgrade, is overseen by a government agency called Connecting for Health and is the biggest civil IT scheme in the world. As well as setting up a centralized medical records system for 50 million patients in England, it involves an online booking system, e-prescriptions and fast computer network links between NHS organizations (news.bbc.co.uk/1/hi/health/6354219.stm).

One success story has been the adoption of sending text messages to remind patients to attend their hospital appointments. It is reported that on average 11% of all UK hospital appointments are missed, rising to as many as 20% in London hospitals and wasting some £400 million each year. After successful trials in Cambridge, where missed appointments fell from 8% to 1%, and in Glasgow, where missed appointments dropped from 20% to 5%, the automated process of sending 'Don't forget your appointment' to patients' mobile phones 48 hours before their appointment is to be adopted in all NHS hospitals (www.remindpatients.com; www.healthcare-computing.co.uk/eventinfo/pressreleases/2007/remindpatients.htm).

E-prescribing

A recent survey (www.managedhealthcareexecutive.com/mhe/article/articleDetail.jsp?id=133409) predicted that e-prescribing would be one of the e-health applications most likely to exhibit significant growth in the near future. Indeed, with handheld devices such as personal digital assistants (PDAs) becoming more common, e-prescribing becomes much more of a reality. The use of e-prescribing has the potential to bring significant benefits, such as recalling a patient's history, finding alternative drugs, checking for adverse interactions between drugs, and a substantial reduction in paperwork. However, for it to be successful and for the traditional prescription pad to be replaced, a number of limitations still need to be resolved, including the need for doctors and pharmacists to have the appropriate hardware and software and for interoperability issues between different providers of equipment and software to be resolved (www.hoise.com/vmw/03/articles/vmw/LV-VM-03-03-25.html).

> e-prescribing: using networked computer systems to transmit prescribing information between doctors and pharmacists instead of a physical prescription slip

Intranets, the Internet and Call Centres

Intranets such as NHSnet are emerging as a way of creating nested systems of interactivity offering the opportunity for groups to define working practices and create shared documents, information and working practices. Most groups or services also have an Internet presence to provide general health and contact information for members of the public.

As the infrastructure to support medical systems is being developed in hospitals, it can be further exploited to provide a range of other IT systems related to patient well-being. For example, advances in IT and communications technologies now enable modern facilities such as digital television, radio, telephony, e-mail and the Internet to be provided at patient bedsides. These developments raise a number of issues, such as the level of payment for the services provided, whether or not access to Internet sites is restricted and the need to design the systems so that all patients can use them regardless of age, disability, native language or computer experience.

Another area where IT has had a significant impact is in the provision of web sites and call centres to provide health information and advice. Many such centres, such as NHS Direct, encourage people to call and discuss their problems with online advisors rather than immediately calling out their local doctor. The advisors then classify callers into those who require emergency treatment, those who can be referred to their doctor and those who can be advised to treat themselves. There is, however, a debate about the effectiveness of this approach and whether it reduces demand on other parts of the NHS (www.bmj.com/cgi/content/full/321/7254/150). Casualty departments in hospitals, for example, have reported increases in numbers of patients coming directly to them instead of being referred by their doctor.

Factors for Success

Whilst there are undoubtedly many advantages to be gained by adopting and exploiting ICT within the health service, there are other factors that need to be taken into account if successful widespread adoption is to occur. These include designing funding models to support their development and integration, ensuring that any IT system enhances rather than hinders current working practices, guarantees operational reliability, provides security and protection of confidential information, has appropriate standards to ensure interoperability between systems and provides accessibility of health information to all authorized sectors of society.

Underpinning many of these systems and applications is the requirement to adopt international standards. Information interchange can only take place if standards are developed for the storage, recording, retrieval and delivery of information such as patient records, test results and so on. The other essential area is that of data security and confidentiality, both to protect data from loss through corruption and to prevent access to confidential health information regarding patients. This becomes particularly important as nationwide and international networks (e.g. NHSnet) link all hospitals and health authorities.

Although it has always been important for records to be kept secure, the electronic nature of them means that they can be accessed faster, in larger numbers and through more ways than was previously possible. Without appropriate security, patients could be the victims of blackmailers or the information could be obtained and used by commercial interests in relation to the provision of insurance or mortgages, thereby possibly disadvantaging and discriminating against certain members of society. For example, there are worries that insurance companies and other companies may gain access to brain scans, which can also show whether a person is likely to suffer later in life from conditions such as multiple sclerosis or dementia and consequently refuse to provide life insurance.

There is also some concern as to what data will be held in medical databases. For example, while the NHS Numbers for Babies Project seems to have been readily accepted, much more controversial has been suggestions that DNA samples will be taken from every newborn baby in Britain and held in a national database that would eventually hold everyone's genetic profile. Although doctors would then be able to use this database to predict patients' risk of serious diseases, critics are concerned that exploitation of the system may lead to some people being unable to purchase health insurance or find work if they are considered to be at high risk of cancer, heart disease or other illnesses, effectively creating a genetic underclass and raising questions about privacy and consent. Aside from this, Bristol University already has a project underway, sponsored by the Wellcome Trust and the Medical Research Council, to collect DNA samples from 25 000 children and parents – making it the world's biggest DNA bank from a general population (www.alspac.bris.ac.uk/press/hgc2.shtml).

The United States recently passed legislation preventing companies from obtaining customers' DNA. In Britain, commercial organizations are currently prevented from accessing customers' genetic material. Violation of the US Health Insurance Portability and Accountability Act 1996 (HIPAA) which had deadlines for compliance in 2004, carries fines of up to $250 000 and a jail term of up to 10 years. HIPAA requires the full involvement of every member of the health service professions to keep patient records confidential. This means that any activities that might compromise the security of the system, for example, denial-of-service attacks (worms or viruses), equipment malfunctions (file deletion or data corruption) or a lack of contingency plans (data backup and restoration) may also be considered to violate the HIPAA.

POWER TO THE PATIENT

New technology and the wider availability of health information to the person-on-the-street could be said to have changed the way in which health professions and the public interact. In the old-style economy, information tended to be clinically focused on diagnosis, treatment or identifying targets for health promotion. In the new-style economy, information tends to be much more about individual well-being, life-style and choice.

In the old-style economy, the exchange of health information was generally between health professions and patients with the majority of information being given by the health professional to the patient. In the new-style economy, information exchange is much more of a multilayered process involving patients, consumers, and health care professionals. This is partly brought about by patients being much better informed than they used to be through using technologies such as the Internet to research their condition and symptoms. This means that an individual can now participate much more in the clinical decisions that are made rather than relying purely on the judgement of the health care professional. There are also suggestions underway that e-mail interchanges between patient and doctor might be an effective and efficient way of 'seeing' patients, offsetting the costs incurred by telephone calls, missed appointments and requests for prescriptions. Supporters of this idea suggest that e-mail gives doctors more time to think about conditions and prescribe appropriate solutions while patients have more time to reflect on and grasp the information that is central to their care. It is also suggested that the doctor–patient relationship may become more personal and resultant visits to the surgery more efficient and less stressful. However, it is also noted that while some patients may welcome this approach and be more comfortable with this, others may miss the lack of face-to-face interaction and feel that the relationship is compromised. There is also an issue about the time that a doctor would need to spend reading and responding to e-mails, especially if seen as an addition to, rather than a replacement for, the traditional way of working.

What is not in doubt is the overall impact of the recent changes, which considerably alter the relationships between patients, health professionals and careers. This promotes the suggestion that there should be a joint effort between patients and health care professionals to create and evaluate the new information systems and health portals and establish practice guidelines that define these shared experiences.

The Internet and CDs

Use of the Web to distribute health care material has increased enormously in recent years. Indeed, searching for health information has become one of the most popular online activities. The Internet provides us with medical information on demand – why wait for a doctor's appointment when the Internet gives unmediated access to health information 24 hours per day, 7 days per week? The health care professional is no longer the only gatekeeper to health information. This independent approach to gaining medical information is also partly fuelled by individuals becoming less attached to their doctor either through the developing trend for shared practices or through their own transient behaviour, meaning that a long-lasting professional relationship with their doctor does not get established.

Globally the number of health resources accessible over the Internet is immense. A recent Google search for 'health' returned one billion possible sites in just over one tenth of a second. These include web sites and discussion groups run by private individuals, governments, health foundations, health interest groups and commercial ventures offering services, products and advice to individuals. Information provided on the Web is in some cases highly organized, such as the UK National Institute for Health and Clinical Excellence (www.nice.org.uk) and Health Education Authority, the US Dept of Health and Human Services (www.os.dhhs.gov) and Health Canada (www.hc-sc.gc.ca), while on other sites the information presented is much more informal in its nature, although the degree of organization does not necessarily say anything about the quality of information on the site. For example, individuals running special interest sites maintaining informal linkages of interest to smaller communities may perhaps hold more specific information about a particular disease or condition.

If used well, the Internet can provide a useful source of information. For example, patients now have the opportunity to be more informed about their conditions. This may help them decide if they need to see their doctor and what questions to ask about their specific condition. However, with this greater access to information, comes the issue regarding the quality of the information available, and the potential damage that could occur if an individual accesses an unscrupulous site. Potentially detrimental health issues could arise when either accurate information is used inappropriately or when inaccurate information is taken as correct and used as such.

For minor problems, some self-diagnosis web sites which are constantly updated, such as `www.medicdirect.co.uk` and `www.netdoctor.co.uk`, may provide a useful source of self-diagnosis. Additionally, in some cases information gained by the patient about their symptoms may lead to visiting the doctor and having an illness diagnosed, however in other cases it may lead to unnecessary worry or even 'cyberchondria'. This is a new condition whereby individuals look up their symptoms on the Internet, and then wrongly self-diagnose themselves as having a serious illness. By the time they arrive at the doctor they are expecting the worst and have difficulty in believing that they are not ill.

> cyberchondria: related to hypochondria, a mistaken belief that one has a strange and, often, life-threatening disease, reinforced or brought about by excessive information about diseases available online

Another important role of web sites such as `www.bbc.co.uk/health` is to provide individuals with the opportunity to find support groups and to join in discussions supported by online experts about various health problems. As some medical conditions are extremely rare, these support groups provide a unique opportunity for worldwide discussion forums to be created. Web sites may also offer a source of information for individuals too embarrassed to seek advice from their doctor. If used as a first stage this may be an important device in directing them to see their doctor.

Some web sites offer fitness training planners, either for a cost (e.g. www.bodydoctor.com) or for free (e.g. www.nike.com), which encourage individuals to increase their fitness levels. These sites ask the user to complete a questionnaire and deliver a personalized fitness regime by e-mail or mobile phone. Such sites can serve a very useful purpose particularly given the frequently reported obesity crisis which, as well as causing premature deaths (up to 10 years off life expectancy), is estimated to cost the UK economy £2 billion per year (bmj.bmjjournals.com/cgi/content/full/327/7427/1308-d).

Prevention of illness through education, nutrition guidance and other techniques also becomes possible when linked to other information and communication technologies such as diagnostic and preventative health-awareness CD/DVDs.

Television Programmes

Television programmes addressing health issues are also on the increase. This powerful medium and its programmes have had a significant impact through both its reporting of content and its ability to reach very large numbers of people simultaneously. As well as bringing information about various conditions to the public's attention, programmes can also promote healthy living and exercise. A positive example of this is the recent UK programme Fat Nation: the Big Challenge, which encouraged a community to become involved in exercising and losing weight while simultaneously encouraging the viewers to do the same.

More controversially, there has been a growth of reality television programmes where people compete to win plastic surgery as prizes, which potentially encourage men and women to have plastic surgery on camera. Such shows have been criticized by some as dangerous or trivializing cosmetic surgery and of giving some patients false hope. Another contentious health issue associated with television is the advertising of potato crisps, chocolate and fizzy drinks by sports and media stars. These adverts, targeted at children, are alleged to be contributing to the obesity crisis (archpedi.ama-assn.org/cgi/content/abstract/160/4/436). Discussions are continuing between various governments, television companies and food manufacturers on the correct guidelines for whether, when, how much and in what way 'junk food' should be advertised to children. Under new proposals, from 1 April 2007 in the United Kingdom, junk food adverts are not allowed in or around programmes made for children aged four to nine, with this being extended to children up to 15 from January 2008. (www.telegraph.co.uk/news/main.jhtml?xml=/news/2007/02/23/nads23.xml).

Digital Television

Another recent development that has the potential to substantially impact on health care is digital television. By the very nature of its delivery and the vast choice it offers, digital viewing can create special interest communities focussed on people's health and lifestyles, in addition to the more traditional mass-audience programmes.

The interactive nature of digital television can also be exploited. Popular television programmes, for example, soaps and long-running dramas have long been tackling sensitive issues, offering help-line numbers for viewers to call to discuss the matter further or receive additional information. With digital television this facility is enhanced through the provision of the interactive button which can immediately send more information directly to the viewer's home. There is also an increasing tendency for programmes to have live web chats and interactive sessions after the programme in order to continue the debate.

Digital television is also being considered as a way of offering additional facilities such as electronic booking of appointments with GPs and health care advisors; personal health record-keeping linked to personal fitness and health goals; filling in of repeat prescriptions; ordering health supplements or medicines; online chat rooms for health advice and counselling and services such as NHS Direct.

Self-Diagnosis Kits

One example where access to knowledge and new technology has the potential to be of great benefit, but also carries with it the capability of causing great harm, is in the area of self-testing medical kits. Self-diagnosis has moved on a long way since the early days of the thermometer, and recent advances in technology have enabled a vast range of more high-tech and affordable self-diagnosis tests to be available on the high street and over the Internet. For just a few minutes of a person's time and a few drops of their blood or urine, a whole range of diseases, conditions and risks can be determined and monitored.

Thousands of these tests are now available over the Internet and a smaller number of more closely regulated products from high-street pharmacists. Market research (www.guardian.co.uk/health/story/0,3605,1077039,00.html) undertaken by Mintel in October 2003 revealed a booming market, with over £55 million a year spent on self-diagnosis in the United Kingdom alone. By 2005 this figure had risen to £68 million; a figure that is continuing to rise and is predicted to reach £94 million by 2010 (www.marketresearchworld.net/index.php?option=content&task=view&id=400). The most common kits purchased are pregnancy testing kits (£35 million), blood-pressure monitors (£9 million) and ovulation tests (£5.3 million), however, an increasing variety and number of these tests are becoming available on the market including those for serious conditions and diseases such as prostate cancer, osteoporosis, HIV, Hepatitis C, Anthrax, and colon cancer. Another sign of the increasing popularity of these kits is the fact that many pharmacists are moving home-test kits from behind their counters onto freestanding displays.

Some of these tests are carried out entirely at home in a few minutes using a sample of blood or urine; these tests can be based on a simple indicator such as a colour change. Other tests rely on the person sending a sample to a laboratory for analysis, for example, cheek swabs for genetic tests and nails or hair for allergy testing. Another popular area for testing on the Web is that for mental health. For example, www.netdoctor.co.uk, invites site visitors to determine their state of mind by answering a number of computer-based questions. Its depression test, for example, asks eight questions about mood and encourages the person to see their doctor if they answer yes to more than two. Some sites such as `www.rethink.org` see their value as being not in diagnosis but in raising awareness of mental health, and encouraging people to seek help if needed.

Physical based tests can be divided into four overlapping categories:

- Screening tests to detect if a person is likely to have a disease, for example prostate cancer, osteoporosis, bowel cancer, Alzheimer's and diabetes
- Diagnostic tests to determine if a person has a particular disease or condition, for example pregnancy, food intolerance, Chlamydia, sore throat, cystic fibrosis, or HIV
- Monitoring tests to track the progress of a known condition or response to therapy, for example tests to monitor warfarin levels for blood-clotting disorders, blood-glucose levels for control of diabetes, and blood pressure levels for hypertension
- Predictive tests that use genetic and other material to assess whether a person is at risk of developing conditions such as deep vein thrombosis or heart disease.

There are numerous reasons why people are turning to these kits, ranging from responding to messages from the government urging them to take greater care of their own well-being, to reducing the waiting times to see the doctor, to the convenience of carrying out the test in their own home, to the embarrassment of approaching a doctor, to saving costs by not visiting the doctor in person.

The key question is whether these kits do good or harm. Certainly, such tests enable the individual to monitor their own physical and mental well-being from the comfort of their armchair or bathroom, allowing them to monitor their condition or watch for warning signs that they are developing a particular condition. For example, individuals can measure their cholesterol and triglyceride levels, two types of fats in the blood, to help minimize their risk of cardiovascular disease. Kidney disease is one of the most serious complications of diabetes, but it can be detected by a simple test and is treatable if caught in the early stages. There is some concern that these tests may be doing more harm than good, resulting in serious problems if people rely on them when they should be seeking the immediate expertise of health care professionals. This is particularly true given the recent shift in the home diagnostics market from monitoring chronic illnesses to diagnosing serious or potentially fatal diseases. To minimize risk and maximize the gains from self-diagnosis, there are a number of key issues of which we should be aware including the variable quality of the kits on sale, the degree of accuracy of the results obtained, the appropriateness of the tests and the lack of counselling accompanying the test results.

Online Pharmacies

In the age of e-commerce, Internet pharmacies are gaining a presence. Such sites may provide a convenient service for non-prescription drugs as long as it is noted that some of the natural remedies may cause side effects when taken with other drugs. However, a greater danger is entering our lives, often in the form of Internet spam, offering prescription drugs cheaply and without consultation. Self-medication can have serious consequences and research shows that it is on the increase. For example, a National Audit Office survey suggested that as many as 600 000 people in the United Kingdom had bought prescription medicine over the Internet (www.nao.org.uk/publications/nao_reports/02-03/0203255.pdf). The drugs on offer tend to be from e-pharmacies based outside the United Kingdom, because although the United Kingdom has strict laws regulating the availability of potentially harmful drugs on the Internet, currently the Department of Health can only prosecute UK-based web sites.

Frequently offered drugs such as Ritalin (an amphetamine-like drug), Viagra (a sex enhancer), Prozac (an anti-depressant) and Xenical (a weight-loss drug) should only be taken with medical advice due to possible side effects such as paranoid psychosis, dangerous interactions with other drugs, heart problems and digestive troubles. There is also no guarantee of the quality of products, some of which have been found to contain safe but ineffectual substances and others to be highly reactant and dangerous substances.

ONLINE BODY TRAFFICKING

For a few, the Internet has afforded a new way of making money. One of the most famously reported incidents is that of a kidney for sale on an Internet auction site in September 1999: 'Fully functioning kidney for sale. You can choose either kidney. Buyer pays all transplant and medical costs (`www.cnn.com/TECH/computing/9909/03/ebay.kidney`). Of course, only one for sale, as I need the other one to live. Serious bids only.' Bids reached $5 750 100 before the site was alerted and the kidney advert was removed. Although this instance was probably a prank attracting prank bids, it does highlight a very serious issue, especially given the large number of people awaiting kidney transplants. There have been several other instances. In July 2003, an Austrian man was reported to have received a four-month suspended jail sentence and a €2000 fine from a German court for offering his kidney for sale on the Internet (`news.bbc.co.uk/1/hi/world/europe/3065551.stm`). The 48-year-old factory worker tried to sell his kidney for €66 000 in a final attempt to save his girlfriend's failing business. Under Germany's transplant law, illegal trading in organs can carry a jail term of up to five years.

In another case, a woman who advertised her services as a surrogate mother on an American web site and who subsequently agreed to sell her unborn baby to three childless couples was jailed for two years in May 2004. The sentence was for obtaining property by deception, referring to payments she received while pregnant and for three further offences under the Adoption Act. Subsequent DNA tests revealed that none of the three husbands was the baby's father (`archive.cravenherald.co.uk/2004/5/22/100476.html`).

A third widely reported case was that of a British couple who allegedly bought two baby girls over the Internet from an American woman via a baby broker who, unknown to them, had already sold them to an American couple. Once the couple realized what the broker had done, they fled their home after initiating a fast-track adoption process in the US. Eventually, both US and British courts ruled that the babies should return to the United States. Although not entirely the Internet's fault, this case highlights the role the Internet can play in such practices (`news.bbc.co.uk/1/hi/wales/1221330.stm`).

More recently, an ongoing trade in the trafficking of babies over the Internet from countries such as Kazakhstan, Columbia, Guatemala and Cambodia has been exposed. Many orphanages in these countries advertise their adoption services on the Web targeting them at Western couples desperate to adopt a baby. Under new rules on international adoption it is possible to adopt babies legally from these countries as long as a number of formal procedures are adhered to. For example, the British Government insists that prospective parents living in the United Kingdom are approved for adoption by their local social services department. However, an investigative journalist reported that, by using resources and contacts found from the Web, it was possible to circumvent these rules and for 'unauthorized' adoptions to occur. In this case, the Internet is providing a medium to attract prospective buyers worldwide (news.bbc.co.uk/1/hi/world/europe/4649383.stm).

Web sites (e.g. www.fertility4life.com/mni) are also beginning to appear that advertise sperm or egg donation for sale. Aside from the moral issues associated with this practice, if such ventures are not set up properly, with proper screening of donors, they carry the risk of transmission of diseases such as Hepatitis C and AIDS and the risk of creating babies from donors with unknown physical, social and intellectual characteristics. Other key issues that must be addressed include the health screening of donors and an assurance that a donor does not father multiple children in the same area, producing the risk of half siblings meeting and eventually marrying. There have been a number of examples of web sites operating in the United Kingdom and abroad which have allegedly flouted these rules.

TECHNO-MEDICINE

Medical treatment and training are now carried out using the latest in technological aids. The expert doctor may be half the planet away diagnosing your condition or guiding a less experienced medic in performing an operation. Medical students and trainee nurses practice on simulation dolls before being let loose on real patients and robots are used in physiotherapy and even as nursing assistants.

Telemedicine

Telemedicine is a discipline that has its roots in the early days of National Aeronautics and Space Administration (NASA) when physiological measurements of the astronauts were telemetered from the spacecraft and space suits during space flights (www.elecdesign.com/Articles/Index.cfm?AD=1&ArticleID=12859). Since then the exponential rise in low-cost computing power coupled with other technological developments, such as satellites and the Internet, has enabled telemedicine to advance as a discipline. As technology has matured, so too has the international use of telemedicine with the United States, Canada, the United Kingdom and Scandinavia being among the leaders in this developing field. Telemedicine has now reached a level whereby complex applications such as remote diagnostic analysis and teleconsultation are possible along with the ability to send complex information sets, such as radiographic pictures or computerized axial tomography (CAT) scans, around the world in a real-time regime.

> Telemedicine: the practice of medicine where the practitioner and the patient are in geographically distant locations

Telemedicine has a number of implications for the improvement of the quality of health care. These include access to health care for those who live in remote or isolated areas, the ability to act rapidly in an emergency when local specialist care is not available, and the ability to bring a wider range of services such as radiology, mental health services, and dermatology to underserved communities and individuals. Telematic technology can also achieve access to specialist advice previously only available in a hospital, without the need for a patient to leave the doctor's surgery. It also has an increasing potential for use in the home and enables the merging of primary care, community care and social services (www.jacksonholestartrib.com/articles/2007/03/19/news/wyoming/826ef0a9657454c3872572a200269273.txt).

Studies involving nurse practitioners running minor injury units to avoid unnecessary transfer of patients from rural or community hospitals to large hospitals have shown telemedicine to be both clinically effective and safe. Telenursing is also starting to move into the home. Patients can be equipped with videophones and equipment such as an electric stethoscope and a digital blood pressure monitor thereby allowing them to receive medical check-ups at home. Although the cost of nurses having to travel to patients' houses is reduced, the cost of having to provide individual patients with the necessary equipment may be high and therefore the technique may be better suited to communities such as care homes where the costs can be distributed across a number of people. In situations however where constant monitoring is required then the use of telecommunication equipment either to provide continuous vital sign monitoring or to facilitate patient care at home, rather than relying solely on in-person care may become very valuable, especially given the increasing trends for home health care.

Training and Supporting Nurses and Doctors

In its oldest form, telemedicine encompasses aids to decision-making such as remote expert systems that contribute to patient diagnosis or the use of medical online databases. Indeed, expert systems or clinical-decision-support systems date back to the 1970s when MYcin was developed as a rule-based expert system (`smi-web.stanford.edu/projects/history.html#MYCIN`) designed to diagnose and recommend treatment for certain blood infections. Since then such systems for decision support have gradually become more powerful, reliable and accurate. Today's systems incorporate knowledge from experts and previous experience into expert and decision-support-system frameworks as a way of assisting diagnosis and treatment across all areas of medicine from antibodies and infections to trauma management. There are still ethical issues to consider, however, when relying on a computer to provide diagnosis of symptoms including those of blame should there be mis-diagnosis due to inaccurate or incorrect advice being derived from the system.

There are also issues regarding whether the expert system should be an augmentation to the traditional consulting process or a replacement for it. Notwithstanding medical issues, the use of such a system may mean that there is a change in the social interaction between patient and doctor. Some patients will welcome this change but others will miss the traditional relationship. Individuals are also less able to ask computers a question and receive counselling than they are with a doctor or other specially trained people present. Such systems may be considered as beneficial for extending and enhancing a doctor's knowledge, however equally they could cause problems if doctors start to rely too heavily on them rather than on their own professional judgement.

The Internet may also provide a resource by which doctors can research new diseases and the latest treatments as well as finding a wide range of training material to help guide them through their studies. Of course, as mentioned earlier, it is paramount that this information is correct.

One of the most high-profile and extensive sources of online medical data is the Visible Human Project (www.nlm.nih.gov/research/visible/) which was established in 1989 by the US National Library of Medicine with the remit of building a digital image library of volumetric data representing complete, normal, adult male and female anatomy. The Visible Human project amounts to in excess of 60 GB of information and has been designed to serve as a reference data set for the study of human anatomy, to serve as a set of common public domain data for testing medical imaging algorithms, and to serve as a test bed and model for the construction of network-accessible image libraries. The data sets have been applied under license to a whole range of educational, medical and industrial applications in 48 countries.

Another computer-driven technology, once considered to reside in the games market, that is being put to increasing use in the medical arena is the use of virtual reality. Virtual-reality simulators and virtual patients are also being developed as pre-surgical planning and teaching environments. This approach helps both the novice surgeon and the more experienced surgeon who can continually add new surgical techniques to their own practice. Having virtual environments in which to develop these practices, avoids having to pass the steep learning curve onto the patient. Virtual environments also allow the novice surgeon to navigate around the body and to explore the material in non-linear ways and hence allow a deeper understanding of the body or the procedure to be undertaken. For the more experienced surgeon, a virtual environment and a 3-D representation of a person's anatomy allows them to explore in detail delicate surgical procedures before carrying them out for real.

Based on flight simulation technology, patient simulation systems create a virtual hospital environment using sophisticated software, video graphics and life-sized mannequins. Some of these simulators also include tactile feedback so that trainees can insert needles or other surgical tools into a plastic box, the contents of which give the sensation of cutting flesh or pushing through body parts such as the throat or colon. Technology is now such that these mannequins may be very lifelike having plastic ears and hair, veins into which substances can be injected, eyes that move, a beating heart, lungs that breathe and a pulse. These virtual patients may be programmed to act like any adult or paediatric patient that a doctor or other health professional might encounter. It enables them to perform routine medical procedures as well as training them to respond to rare and complex medical conditions and life-threatening emergencies. Such systems include Stan D. Ardman ('standard man' `society.guardian.co.uk/health/story/0,7890,1532540,00.html`) and Morgan, who automatically produce a simulated response based on a student's actions or interventions, thereby producing distinct and unique experiences for each trainee, depending on their decisions, actions and response time to activities such as intravenous drug delivery, consolidated portfolio reporting, airway management and respiratory therapy. Another simulator, Simantha™, (`www.vnunet.com/vnunet/news/2120592/doctors-touch-feely-simantha`) enables advanced training for intervention procedures, such as using balloon angioplasty and stents to open blocked blood vessels which, left untreated, cause heart attacks and high blood pressure.

Simulators may also be used to teach people to work as a team under stress. For example, the University of Chicago's patient safety centre is developing a regional simulator centre for training doctors, nurses and paramedics to handle biochemical attacks or other mass casualties. Another area where simulator training may produce benefits is in the area of professionalism and humanism, where doctors develop their bedside skills, for example how to deliver bad news about an illness or injury.

Medical school professors say that simulators help their trainees build confidence and make mistakes before treating real patients (www.cbsnews.com/stories/2004/07/19/health/main630454.shtml). Indeed this view is backed up by Fried et al. (2004) and Seymour et al. (2002), which have shown that surgical residents trained on simulators made fewer errors and operated more quickly than those who trained via the traditional 'see one (observe an experienced doctor), do one (carry out a supervised procedure followed by an independent one), teach one (train others to do the procedure)' training approach.

Virtual Therapy

Another area of application for virtual reality is in the treatment of phobias, stress and pain. Virtual reality can simulate situations through modelling what people hear, see, feel and even smell. By combining these senses it is possible to recreate a very realistic but controlled picture of a place or situation in which a person has been in or may find themselves in. By controlling the factors within this environment, various de-sensitizing treatments may be undertaken. Participants wear video goggles and earphones to immerse themselves in a simulated situation or experience; therapists then use biofeedback sensors and heartbeat monitors and other equipment to try to pinpoint the events that raise patient anxiety.

There are a number of different applications to which the use of this technology has been applied. These include the work of Dr Shelly Brundage at George Washington University who has used these techniques for curing people with anxiety disorders and phobias such as fear of flying, heights, spiders, public speaking or interviews. She is now developing the technique to assist patients who have severe stuttering problems.

This form of virtual reality exposure therapy is seen as a more cost-effective and less stressful way to desensitize people traumatized by various situations. For example, virtual reality treatment has shown promise in helping Vietnam veterans and World Trade Centre attack victims suffering from post-traumatic stress disorder, a condition that is often characterized by flashbacks, anger, isolation, and depression that can last for decades. Friedman (2004) found that nearly 17% of all US soldiers who took part in the 2003 invasion of Iraq reported combat-related mental illnesses. One of the latest studies in this area has been established by Professor Albert Rizzo at the University of Southern California. 'Virtual Iraq' is a computer program that recreates front-line experiences, forcing veterans to confront their war-zone memories in a controlled environment (www.guardian.co.uk/science/story/0,,2016913,00.html). This application is being developed as part of a $2.7 million research study at the Naval Medical Centre, San Diego, and Camp Pendleton into how virtual reality therapy compares to traditional therapy to combat post-traumatic stress disorder. If successful, this technique may be used to augment counselling for the disorder at military bases across the United States. One of the key issues here and in other trauma-based applications is not to make the technology so real that it creates further trauma.

Virtual reality therapy is also being used as a distraction technique in painful dental and medical procedures, including chemotherapy and physiotherapy. In these instances, success arises because the patient's attention is no longer focused on the wound or the pain but on the virtual world instead. One example of this is 'Snow World' designed specifically for treating burn victims, whereby patients undergoing treatment can fly through a frozen canyon with an icy river and waterfall and shoot snowballs at snowmen, igloos, robots and penguins standing on narrow ice shelves or floating in a river (www.temple.edu/ispr/examples/ex03_07_23.html).

Robots in Hospitals

Large and small robots are being used in medicine in a variety of ways, from distributing medication in care homes to aiding surgeons with precise internal surgery.

Robotic Surgery

Robotic surgery systems, such as the da Vinci Surgical System, have incorporated advances in both robotic and computer technology and are designed to offer surgeons additional precision and control in complex minimally-invasive procedures (www.intuitivesurgical.com). Minimally-invasive surgery is performed through small rather than large incisions and minimizes trauma to tissue, muscles and vessels. Patient benefits include less blood loss, less scarring, less risk of post-operative infection and faster recovery times.

Robots can directly assist the surgeon by using delicate computerized arms that replicate the movement of the surgeon and monitors that show in magnification the operation in hand. They can allow surgery to occur remotely with the robot operated at a distance. Robotic surgery has enabled more delicate procedures to be carried out – for example, allowing keyhole surgery to be undertaken where previously open-heart surgery was necessary, carrying its greater risks and longer recovery times. More than 25 000 people undergo a coronary artery bypass operation each year, and minimally-invasive procedures performed by robots are becoming increasingly popular.

Robotic Nurse

Although the thought of robotic nurses may appear at first glance to be inappropriate, when faced with a serious shortage of doctors and nurses it may be an acceptable option, particularly as they are shown in some studies to be gaining acceptance by the profession and the patients.

Some robotic nurses such as the TUG, HelpMate and Robocarts (www.usatoday.com/tech/news/techinnovations/2004-07-06-hospitalbot_x.htm) are starting to make inroads into hospital wards. These range from robots designed to deliver bedding, medical supplies, X-rays, food and other materials around the hospital, to motorized tables and drug cabinets. One of the reasons behind the introduction of these robots is to lower costs and free up workers for more critical tasks. In one hospital, two HelpMate robots are used to transport medicine from the pharmacy to nursing stations throughout the six-floor, 352-bed hospital making as many as 30 trips a day (without tiring).

Robots can be programmed to speak a variety of languages, use wireless radios to call elevators or open automatic doors and are polite, asking people to ‘please stand aside’ when they get into a lift, ‘please examine my contents’ when they make a delivery and saying ‘thank you’ after completion of the delivery task. While it may seem ill-advised for a machine – even a smart one – to carry around drugs or medical records unsupervised, the TUG and HelpMate come with cabinets that can be mechanically and electronically locked. The HelpMate includes a fingerprint scanner for extra security.

When another robotic nurse, Pearl, entered service at Pitt's School of Nursing and a retirement community in Oakland, it was found that people loved it, partly because of the sheer novelty but also because it offered very practical help. Indeed, in some ways, it gave better help than that which could be offered by a human counterpart. For example, it did not get impatient with elderly patients walking very slowly and it did not mind repeating an instruction many times for patients suffering from dementia. It is expected that these robot nurses will eventually be able to give further help to the elderly enabling them to stay longer in their own homes, for example by monitoring them to ensure that they have not fallen or giving them bathroom reminders if necessary (www.thematuremarket.com/SeniorStrategic/Robot_nurse_escorts_schmoozesthe_elderly-5260-5.html).

Other robots, called Companions, are being used to give doctors or nurses presence from a distance (www.temple.edu/ispr/examples/ex03_03_06b.html). In this instance, the Companion's operator, usually a doctor or nurse, uses a joystick at a computer station to send the Companion to a patient's room. Once in the room, the Companion's screen, which displays the operator's face in real-time, uses full pan-tilt-zoom capabilities to address multiple people in a room or to zoom in for a close look at an individual patient's wound. Studies have shown that patients follow and respond to the Companion's head as if it were a real person. New robots are being developed with additional devices such as stethoscopes, which allow Companions to gather physical data as well as providing the visual and audio input.

In other care situations, robotic voices are being used as automatic dial facilities to ask patients at regular intervals whether they have taken their medicine. These robotic voices raise the issue of a cost versus contact caring model. Whilst it is generally accepted that a personal visit to a patient by a nurse would be more advantageous, in reality, there is a much greater cost associated with each visit made as well as a limit to the number of visits that can be made by a nurse in a day, particularly if patients are dispersed across a wide geographical area. By foregoing the physical contact, 15 patients per hour can be contacted compared to only five or six patients per day by a traditional nurse's visit. This not only cuts costs but it means that the nurses can concentrate on those patients most in need of a visit.

Robotic Laboratory

Hospital laboratories make use of computer-controlled analyzers for testing samples and report their results to a central hospital computer. Robots are also being introduced into the laboratory in order to handle huge amounts of patient blood and fluid tests and virtually eliminate human error. Some laboratories are allowing networked access to these results. No longer does a technician have to sort through racks of samples looking for the right one. Instead, a patient's blood is stored in a bar-coded test tube. The robot places the tube on a conveyer belt, reads the bar code, and sends it down a track as mechanical arms dip into the blood to perform the test. After each test, the robot reads the bar code again before sending it onto the next test. After completion of the analysis, the sample is stored in a refrigerator which is also tracked on the system's computer.

Smart Monitoring

Aging demographics are becoming important – both from a health point of view to enable more home-based care to occur and from a commercial perspective as development of systems to assist the elderly and disabled are becoming a revenue source for many companies. For example, high-tech systems to monitor the elderly are becoming more commonplace as the elderly population increases. It is widely known that the proportion of older people in the world is growing, with more developed countries leading the process. In the United States alone, the number of people over the age of 65 is expected to double from 35 million in 2000 to

70 million by 2030 with similar increases being exhibited worldwide. In the United Kingdom, there are around 10.8 million older people (men aged over 65 and women aged over 60) and for the first time in history there are now more people aged 60 and over (21%) than there are children under 16 (20%) in the United Kingdom. According to the United Nations Population Division (2004), globally the number of people aged 60 or over will more than triple by 2050. The increase in the number of 'oldest old' (aged 80 or over) is expected to be even more dramatic, being more than fivefold.

The support of this ever-expanding older population has become of increasing concern, as has the need to give greater attention to the design of products and services to older consumers, as well as the preference for keeping them in their home environment rather than a care environment for as long as possible. Although not exclusively the realm of the elderly, much of this support has manifested itself in the development of a range of monitoring devices.

Health care diagnostics and the monitoring of the elderly and individuals at risk from a range of medical conditions is moving increasingly into the home and everyday environment. This monitoring may be of physical symptoms, such as diabetic patients monitoring their own blood glucose levels and adjusting their insulin dosage accordingly, or of a behavioural nature, such as monitoring an elderly person to ensure that they are not neglecting themselves, have not fallen and have remembered to take their medicine.

High-Tech Nursing Home

The number of people aged 65 or older in Japan is set to exceed the 30-million mark, accounting for some 25% of Japan's population. There is therefore an urgent need for Japan to put into place strategies for coping with its elderly population and the strain that this is putting on the economy.

As part of this strategy the world's first high-tech retirement home has been built on the outskirts of Osaka (`news.bbc.co.uk/1/hi/sci/tech/1829021.stm`). The retirement home, called *Sincere Kourien*, is run by Matsushita

Electrics, has 106 beds and a fur-covered robotic assistant teddy bear for each of its elderly residents. Teddy conceals a microcomputer and a local network connection. He regularly asks the residents questions and monitors their response time to these questions. He also records how long the residents spend performing various tasks and alerts staff to any unexpected changes or delays. Initial feedback has been encouraging, with most residents liking and accepting the bear due in part to its voice recognition interface which removes the technological barriers frequently evident with conventional computer systems.

Voice-activation and interactivity remove the need for pushing buttons, frequently a difficult task for the elderly who may have motor control problems caused by diseases such as Alzheimer's or physical disabilities such as crippled hands from arthritis.

Homes are becoming increasingly 'smarter', with everyday household appliances being used to monitor our well-being. For example, the smart toilet can also act as a set of scales and a chemical analyzer, monitoring parameters such as weight and body-fat ratio, heartbeat, blood pressure, and glucose levels, the results of which can be sent automatically via the Internet to a patient's doctor. One of the key issues with these developments, however, is how far can this monitoring be taken before our privacy is compromised beyond an acceptable level. For example, monitoring could be not only for health problems but also for dietary content with analysis linked to the local supermarket: if a person were deemed to be short on roughage, an order of beans or pulses could be sent automatically from the system to the supermarket and delivered that same day.

Other products include scales that can indicate not only how much body fat an individual has but also where in the body this fat is accumulating, for example in vital organs such as the heart and kidneys. A bathroom mirror has also been developed that can take infrared pictures of an individual's hair and skin, recommend beauty treatments to enhance their features, and dispense mineral water with the correct degree of acidity to suit their complexion.

Researchers at Accenture, a technology consultancy company, are developing a number of products including the 'persuasive mirror', which manipulates images of a person in real time depending on what they have been doing during the day (www.accenture.com/NR/exeres/44E3chOAF-D302-472A-A24B-D8221BA8397B,frameless.htm?NRMODE=Published). It could, for example, be used to encourage individuals to live healthier lives by showing them what will happen to their appearance if they take no exercise and do not watch what they eat!

Monitoring is not only restricted to our homes. Mobile technology makes it possible for patients to be connected to their doctors away from the surgery. For example, patients with pacemakers can use systems to transmit electrocardiograph information over telephone lines to the surgery; smart cuffs can be worn to detect changes in blood pressure; and electronic underwear, sensitive to fluctuations in the wearer's heart rate, can call the emergency services if the individual suffers a cardiac arrest. Wearable technology, such as the electronic underwear developed by Philips, possesses ambient intelligence and as such represents a considerable advance over previous techniques that utilize mobile phones, since the user is not required to hold a device in front of their heart for it to work and the device does not intrude on the user's everyday life. Another product with ambient intelligence is an airline seat being development by QinetiQ. Smart sensors within the seat are able to detect when a passenger is at risk from deep vein thrombosis (DVT) by analyzing the way that they have been sitting. The system alerts cabin crew who will encourage the passenger to move around.

Wireless monitoring and sensing systems are also being developed that can monitor the behavioural patterns of elderly individuals in an effort to keep them living independently for as long as possible. For example, radio frequency identification (RFID) tags and magnetic sensors can be attached to everyday objects such as mugs, tea, jars and so on, and switches attached to cupboards. These sensors are activated when an individual interacts with any of the objects. If there is a change in an activity pattern or if there is a long pause while an activity is being undertaken a video clip on a nearby television prompts the person with what to do next. Activity monitoring takes this one stage further whereby a series of cameras are placed around the home to watch what a person does, where they go and how they get there. Software analyzes the recorded movements for features such as facial expressions, posture, gait, focus of attention, and how they interact with the objects in the home. By analyzing an individual's centre of gravity for example, the system can calculate whether they have fallen and if they need assistance. Other research is also underway to analyze behavioural patterns in order to detect early warnings signals of diseases such as Alzheimer's.

Computer Modelling

Population Modelling

The above examples concentrate on monitoring the well-being of individuals, however technology is also being used to monitor and model populations as a whole. By combining satellite-based geographic information system (GIS) information with computer models based on statistical data from repositories of information such as the Centre for Disease Control, the World Health Organization and the Texas Department of Health, it is possible to identify where infectious diseases may occur and to make predictions about how they will spread.

By combining geographic information with other data such as economic indicators, health care policies and practices, population information, social interaction models and common travel patterns it is possible to predict the likely spread of disease. Other influencing factors that can be taken into account in the model are the level of health care available in the region and, in some cases, the proximity of large populations to animals such as pigs and poultry.

In this way, health officials can be alerted to the risk of epidemics and pandemics. By taking this approach, countries can be medically prepared to deal with the onset of an outbreak by preparing resources and stockpiling vaccinations. Governments can also put in place strategies for containing outbreaks by restricting global movement across national boundaries or via airports. In recent years, such approaches have been used to model the airborne spread of foot-and-mouth disease, Severe Acute Respiratory Syndrome (SARS) and Buruli ulcer, a disease caused by skin-eating bacteria prevalent in at least 31 countries in Africa, the Western Pacific, Asia and South America.

Scientists in the United States, as part of the national Models of Infectious Disease Agent Study programme (MIDAS, `www.nigms.nih.gov/Initiatives/MIDAS`), are currently developing computer models to combat the potentially deadly H5 N1 strain of the bird influenza virus should it become spread by person-to-person transmission. By simulating the outbreak of this avian flu in a hypothetical human community, the researchers hope to answer key questions about how best to contain the virus, so that policymakers, public health workers and researchers are able to test the effectiveness of their intervention strategies should such an outbreak occur. In order to simulate the spread of a possible avian flu outbreak, the researchers are developing models of a hypothetical Southeast Asian community of about 500 000 people living in neighbouring small towns. The computer simulations incorporate data on population density and age structure, distribution of schools, locations of hospitals and clinics, travel and the infectiousness of the virus. Computer models are then developed that allow the researcher to predict the impact of decisions such as vaccinating specific groups, using antiviral medication, restricting travel or implementing other public-health measures in a variety of scenarios. The objective of the project is to develop strategies that will reduce the rate of disease transmission between people, enable the spread of disease to be contained locally and quickly reduce the number of people infected to zero, thereby eradicating H5N1 from the community.

Molecular Modelling

Computer modelling is also important at the molecular level where computer systems can be used for database screening, graphical visualization, molecular mechanics and active-site modelling of a few hundred atoms, such as a few base pairs of DNA to larger three-dimensional structures of proteins and their amino acids (`www.pubmedcentral.nih.gov/articlerender.fcgi?artid=306376&tools=bot`). This ability afforded by the performance of modern, grid-computer systems, visualization techniques and molecular mechanics algorithms has led to a much greater understanding of complex structures within the human body and of its genome. The current challenge is to improve modelling accuracy still further and extend biosimulations to higher levels of complexity – for example, to groups of proteins working together to repair damaged DNA and, beyond, to intracellular components, structures and communication paths.

Computer Modelling to Track Tuberculosis

As well as tracking worldwide outbreaks of diseases such as SARS, computer modelling techniques are being used in the United States to study how infectious diseases may spread throughout a building. Tuberculosis (TB) is an airborne disease of the lungs, spread by coughing and sneezing. According to the Center for Disease Control, 5.1 of every 100 000 people in the United States were reported to have TB in 2003 (`www.cdc.gov/tb/surv/surv2003`). An unusually high occurrence of TB was found in a homeless shelter and factory in Texas.

To identify the cause of the infection and to simulate its outbreak, Oppong and Mikler, two researchers at the University of North Texas, used computer analysis to replicate the buildings, the residents of the shelter and the workers in the factory, and the way in which the residents and workers moved around the interior of the buildings. Computer programmers used an agent to represent each individual. The programmers directed the movements of these agents based on actual data and indicated the state of their health with different colours. The agents were programmed to spread the TB bacteria by simulated coughing and sneezing. Other environmental factors were also considered, such as the settling rate of the bacteria, air flow, heating and cooling systems, architectural elements, social interaction and habits like smoking. For individuals in the model known to have TB, information was included about the date they were tested, the stage of their disease, their location within the building and time spent there. Different vaccination and incubation scenarios were also explored.

The research showed, unsurprisingly, that the well-used areas of the building had a high concentration of TB germs, but also that ventilation in the building may have played a role in the spread of TB (www.unt.edu/resource/04mappingfeature.htm).

Assistive Technology and Rehabilitation

New computer technologies are also being used to enable the development of devices to assist individuals with disabilities lead a more normal life. These may include devices developed to control an individual's environment on the basis of speech, voice, acoustics or haptics (touch) and may also include rehabilitation devices or training environments to assist patients recovering from stroke, injury or trauma (www.gentle.rdg.ac.uk).

For example, a new wheelchair that uses gyroscope technology has been developed to enable the wheelchair to stand up and balance on two wheels. This wheelchair, the Ibot, uses three computers to determine the centre of gravity and electric motors to move the chair upright. The Ibot can also climb up and down stairs by tumbling its wheels. In addition to allowing users to navigate stairs, curbs and to go 'off-road', the Ibot also enables wheelchair uses to raise themselves to a more social height to conduct conversations at eye level and to reach items from supermarket shelves (www.ibotnow.com/ibot/index.html).

A joint venture between Japanese industry and Tsukuba University is developing and commercializing a 'robotic suit' that helps aged or physically disabled people walk and move up and down stairs. The powered suit, Hybrid Assistive Limb-5 (HAL5), consists of a computer, a battery backpack and four motors that attach around the knees and hip joints. The motor-powered devices guide movement of the legs as the computer calculates the user's next motion by detecting faint electric signals from the muscle. The suit enables the user to walk smoothly at a speed of 4 km per hour with little physical exertion. There are already 100 advance orders for the suit mainly from people with disabilities. A version for supporting arm movements is also underway with the eventual goal of making a suit thin enough to be worn like underwear which will allow users to run and move their arms freely (www.newscientist.com/article.ns?id=mg18624945.800).

NEW MEDICAL TECHNOLOGIES

Computer technologies are also enabling many advances to be made in modern medicine and the ways in which doctors and surgeons can cure or alleviate their patients' symptoms. These advances may take many forms ranging from enabling global tissue-matching databases to be developed, to assisting medical diagnosis through CAT and MRI scans, to performing surgical procedures, to enabling the human form to be monitored, restored or altered in some way through the fusion of a technological component within the human body.

Computer technology also supports and enables the advancement of many other essentially biological procedures. These may include use in disciplines such as eugenics whereby genetic selection and modification occurs, perhaps to create a 'designer baby' whose umbilical blood could provide stem cells for an older sibling suffering from an incurable disease; or for use in cloning and tissue engineering, with the objective of 'growing' a new organ for a person urgently needing a transplant but for whom there are no available donor organs.

Altering the human form in some way or using the technology to support other medical procedures has frequently led to fierce and emotive debates, not so much over what is medically possible but rather over what is medically, individually, culturally and religiously acceptable. These levels of acceptance range from one extreme to the other depending on an individual's role, beliefs and personal situation. This section highlights a number of advances where technology has been used to interact with an individual to monitor, restore or enhance human capability.

Implants for Diagnosis and Healing

The last few years has seen a growth in the area of nanotechnology and the development of a number of micro devices to assist in the diagnosis and treatment of potentially life-threatening conditions such as cancer and heart disease. These developments include a range of biological micro-electromechanical devices, known as bioMEMS (www.rdmag.com via tinyurl.com/2wnk5a). These devices can be implanted into the body to deliver measured drug doses, to carry new cells to stimulate damaged tissue repair, or to administer drugs to break down the material lining blocked arteries.

One potential application of this technology is for cancer detection and prevention, where a microchip can deliver a cancer vaccine in precise doses to specific parts of the body thereby improving the effectiveness of the drug while limiting the effects of its toxicity. It is also possible that microchips with attached sensors could detect mutated genes or high hormone levels indicating the potential for malignancy.

Various techniques are being developed for sending these microchips around the body including the use of bacteria to propel small drug-delivery structures through the bloodstream; the use of precise robotic surgery techniques to implant the chips; and the use of external magnetic fields as a power source for microscopic motors. A fish-like microbot has also been developed with the potential to 'swim' through a patient's body and perform delicate, non-intrusive microsurgery on blood vessels. This microbot brings to life the 1966 science-fiction film Fantastic Voyage, in which a submarine and its crew are shrunk to microscopic proportions and injected into the bloodstream of a scientist in order to remove a blood clot from his brain.

In another application of nanotechnology, researchers from Cambridge University are working on an electrochemical device described as an 'interface implant'. This device is being used to bridge the scar tissue of a spinal chord injury so that it can connect the healthy nerve fibres above the scar to the fibres below which have lost contact with the brain. Research is being undertaken to combine brain and nerve cells with silicon and polymer circuits in order to create a living computer, that could in the future form the basis of computer-controlled artificial limbs. In

2006, the first real-life example of using a direct implant to control a computer cursor was announced (www.nytimes.com/2006/07/13/science/13brain.html).

Although not on a nanotechnology scale, miniature cameras have been developed that are small enough to be swallowed by a patient. These 'pillcams' are being used for medical diagnostics within the human gastro-intestinal tract. In doing so they are replacing the traditional approach of using an endoscope, a technique that is relatively unpleasant for the patient and limited in its ability to access the central regions of the intestine. The 'pillcam', measuring 27 mm by 11 mm, consists of a single miniature camera, a light-emitting-diode-based flash, a radio frequency transmitter chip and two silver-oxide batteries. The camera takes two colour images per second which are relayed to a data recorder carried in a belt worn by the patient. Around 57 000 images of the entire length of the gut are generated over the seven-hour operating life of the pillcam. At the end of the investigation, the images are downloaded to a workstation, a video of the gastro-intestinal tract is created and diagnosis is undertaken by the consultant.

Implants and Prosthetics for Replacement and Reconstruction

Advances in implant technology and in surgical techniques have enabled many defective body parts to be 'replaced' such that some or all of the functionality lost is returned to the individual. For example, over 50 000 people have had cochlear implants, a small electronic device that stimulates and amplifies aural signals to combat deafness.

Devices for replacing loss of body function have been around for many years; they have included false teeth and crude wooden and metal legs for amputees. However it was not until after the Second World War that a significant advance in prosthetic aids was made and since then a range of increasingly intelligent devices have been developed. Common to all synthetic devices are concerns related to the body's immune systems and fact that it will try to reject the invader object or cover it in some kind of protective coating. It is also important to remember that most of the solutions within a human body are saline in nature and so they can attack and degrade any man-made device operating within the human body. A cardiac pacemaker for example can become covered in protein deposits over time due to the body's immune response. However, because the pacemaker's electrical impulses are powerful the deposits do not disrupt its functioning. These and many other issues need to be considered when designing artificial or 'bionic' body parts several of which are described below. Another important issue that needs to be considered is the aesthetics of the prosthetic, which for some wearers, though certainly not all, is extremely important. This means that not only is functionality of the limb important but other parameters such as its colour and texture.

Artificial Eyes

Artificial retinas are being developed to treat eye disorders such as age-related macular degeneration or retinitis pigmentosa. Essentially the prosthetic retina is a miniature disc with an electrode array that is implanted in the back of the eye. It captures visual signals with a small video camera sited on a pair of glasses and then converts them to electrical impulses, which stimulate the optic nerve. The first prototype contained 16 electrodes and, when implanted in a recipient who had been blind for 50 years, enabled him to differentiate between everyday objects such as a knife and a bowl and to see large letters. Later versions have between 50 and 100 electrodes and research is already underway to develop a next-generation device that will have 1000 electrodes and will allow the wearer to see well-defined images (`news.scotsman.com/health.cfm?id=1013292006`).

Conventional cornea transplants involve cutting the central portion of the damaged cornea and replacing it with a donor cornea which is stitched to the eye. Researchers in Japan however have recently developed a technique whereby it is possible to grow corneas in a laboratory environment from just a few cells taken from a healthy cornea of a donor or the patient. The cells are incubated at body temperature for two weeks until the cornea has grown to about two-thirds of an inch wide. The new cornea is 'peeled off' its growing culture and placed directly onto the defective eye. In about 10 minutes, it fuses with the eye. Aside from the non-invasive nature of the procedure, it also means that because only a few cells are needed a single donor can give sight to hundreds of patients rather than only one or two.

Intelligent Limbs

In recent years, major advances have occurred in prosthetics research and development. One of the most significant milestones in this development has been the electronic arm developed at Edinburgh's Princess Margaret Rose Orthopaedic Hospital and given to Campbell Aird, a Scottish hotelier who had lost his arm several years previously to cancer. This arm allowed him to control movement through micro switches and pressure points and although it was not a complete match for his real arm, it had more functions than had been possible with previous electrically powered devices. It also gave the recipient full use of his arm whereas previously movement in prosthetic limbs had been confined to limited use of the wrist or elbow. To give it a more lifelike and aesthetic appearance a skin-like covering complete with wrinkles and fingerprints was applied.

Another researcher, Professor Peter Kyberd, has developed a lightweight intelligent prosthesis that looks and behaves like a human hand. Its key advance is in using microprocessors to control the functions of the fingers, with each finger having force and slip sensors in the tip. This approach affords a greater degree of control and dexterity. For example, if an object being held by the hand slips, vibrations are generated and detected by slip sensors and the hand automatically tightens its grip until the slipping stops. The microprocessor control of this device is by signals translated from the patient's brain activity (eprints.ecs.soton.ac.uk/12417). Another group of UK scientists at Advanced Control Research in Plymouth are developing a microchip for users of prosthetic limbs, enabling them to move their arms much more freely and allowing users not only to open or close their hand but also to simultaneously move their wrist and elbow. This microchip, combined with a pattern recognition system can read up to four different signals at any one time thereby creating the greater degree of movement. Preliminary trials have shown that the technology is very effective and easy to use.

Implants can also assist stroke patients to walk properly. A UK firm has developed a simple implant that consists of an electrode sewn into leg nerves.

The electrode activates muscles that lift the foot and provides help for individuals suffering with 'Drop Foot', a medical condition often associated with stroke patients, which means that sufferers drag their leg rather than lift it when walking.

Face Transplants

Whilst the fitting of artificial limbs has now become a widely accepted practice, much more controversial is the issue of face transplantation and the debate regarding its acceptability. For individuals who have a substantial disfigurement this may seem like a dream come true. However, even for these individuals, the issue is highly sensitive as a person's identity and personality is frequently linked with their facial features.

The technology is already in place to be able to carry out this surgical procedure but this is a very emotive subject with deep ethical, legal and moral issues as well as psychological consequences for patients of the families of donors and body rejection issues. Although computer modelling suggests that the face would look like neither the donor nor the recipient before injury, this still needs to be established in practice. There are also questions raised over identity and consent. Of course, like other medical areas, there are varying degrees of transplant procedures ranging from skin and fat transplants to that of muscle and bone. The first apparently successful face transplant was carried out in July 2006 in France (`news.bbc.co.uk/1/hi/health/5141266.stm`).

Brain Implants

Procedures are advancing still further to the point where implants are being placed in individual's brains to control illness and to enable those who are paralysed to control their support environment. For example, volunteers who are paralyzed from the neck down have had microchips implanted on the surface of their brain to enable them to perform everyday tasks by thought processes. Such practices raise ethical as well as medical and technical considerations, for example the chip must interpret signals correctly and the person, not the computer, must remain in control. Other potential applications for brain implants are for patients with 'locked-in syndrome' – coma patients who are conscious but who have no muscle control and are incapable of communication.

Other neural implants include the insertion of electrodes deep into the brain in order to control Parkinson's disease tremors (www.wired.com/wired/archive/15.03/brainsurgery.html). By connecting these electrodes to wires that run under the skin to a miniature, battery-operated pulse generator sewn into the chest, the electrodes can be used to permanently stimulate the cells within the brain and control the tremors. This procedure greatly improves the quality of life of the sufferer enabling them to return in many cases to a normal existence. Indeed, this type of implant has been successfully applied 1000s of times since its first adoption in 1991.

Similar techniques of using an electric probe to induce neurones to activate in a more regular pattern have also been used to alleviate stroke pain, cluster headaches and phantom limb pain.

Digital Flesh and Cyborgs

Whilst many individuals recognize the potential of integrating technology with the human body to create a better quality of life, many others are worried about the extent to which this fusion might ultimately take place and in particular, the potential implications related to identification and control of individuals. For example, they are worried that, in the future, implants may be used in humans for the primary purpose of surveillance and control. These fears are, at least technologically, not totally unfounded: millions of animals already have identifying chips the size of a grain of rice and research is underway to investigate whether movements of rats can be directly controlled through implants. It is interesting to note that much of the brain implant work currently being undertaken has military sponsors. For example, the US Defence Advanced Research Projects Agency (DARPA) has funded research at Duke University, North Carolina, and two monkeys, Ivy and Aurora, have been taught to play warlike video games using brain electrodes to choose their targets.

As technology advances so to does the potential to blur the distinction between man and machine. Whilst this situation is clearly acceptable to some individuals, to others it is viewed as developing an unacceptable cyborg culture paralleling the fears created by directors of science-fiction films from the early days of Metropolis in the 1920s to the Terminator, Robocop and Borg films of the 1990s and beyond.

The key question arising is what exactly is and what isn't a cyborg? Cyborgs have been defined as 'a human who has certain physiological processes aided or controlled by mechanical or electronic devices' or 'a person wearing glasses or riding a bicycle' or 'an organism with a machine built into it with consequent modification of function'. So although the term 'cybernetics' was not coined until the 1940s, by Norbert Wiener, and the term 'cyborg' remained undefined until Dr Manfred Clynes in the 1960s, in reality cyborgs could, from the definitions given here, encompass any individual having undergone any of the medical procedures described above. Indeed an individual wearing glasses, a hearing aid or riding a bicycle would also strictly qualify, although very few would agree that these devices made them a cyborg.

Implantation of Direct Neural Interfaces

Matthew Nagle was left paralysed from the neck down after his spinal cord was severed in a vicious knife attack in 2001. He uses a wheelchair, is unable to breathe without a respirator, and has been told by doctors that he has no chance of regaining the use of his limbs. In June 2004, after a three-hour operation at New England Sinai Hospital in Massachusetts, he became the first recipient of a brain implant that allows him to control everyday objects by thought alone.

The implant or 'BrainGate Neural Interface' creates a direct link between his brain and a computer that translates neural activity into actions enabling him to interact with his environment (`edition.cnn.com/2006/TECH/02/22/brain.gate`).

During the operation, 100 hair-thin electrodes on a 4 mm^2 silicon chip were attached to the surface of Mr Nagle's brain. They were positioned just above the sensory motor cortex, where the neural signals for controlling arm and hand movement are produced. When Mr Nagle thinks a particular thought, for example, to move a cursor up and left, this causes his cortical neurons to fire in a distinctive pattern. The resultant signal is transmitted through a metal socket attached to his head to a shoebox-sized amplifier mounted on his wheelchair, where it is converted to optical data and sent via a fibre-optic cable to a computer. BrainGate then learns to associate different patterns of brain activity with particular movements and devices.

The project, led by Professor John Donoghue, a world expert in neurotechnology at Brown University in Rhode Island, has shown encouraging results to date. By using software linked to devices around the room, Mr Nagle has been able to think his television on and off, change channel and alter the volume. In the most recent tests, he has been able to use thought to open and close an artificial prosthetic hand and move a robotic arm to grab sweets from one person's hand and drop them in another. The ultimate aim is for the BrainGate implant to enable paraplegics to regain the use of their limbs, by sending signals to their muscles rather than to devices.

The latest advance made by Prof Donoghue, the scientist working with Mr Nagle, is the control of a computer cursor through direct neural interface (www.nytimes.com/2006/07/13/science/13brain.html).

It could be argued that the key distinction between a human and a cyborg might be that in the case of a human any technological implant such as a heart pacemaker or a hip replacement is viewed as a necessary intrusion and seen as a modification intended to compensate for deficiencies. In contrast, for a cyborg to be created, any implants undertaken would be with the intention of enhancing normal functioning such that the individual could see for a greater distance, hear across wider frequency bands and run faster than is normally possible for a human. This definition might also be related to the purpose of the implant and whether it has been undertaken to replace a loss of control function or to augment control of an individual's environment. As an example of this, in 1998, Professor Kevin Warwick had a silicon-chip transponder surgically implanted in his upper left arm to enable him to control and interact with his environment. He later extended this work in 2002 by connecting the implant to the nervous fibres in his arm. In this experiment, he investigated the possibility of transferring electrical signals responsible for movement from himself to the computer and vice versa.

The cyborg debate is further fuelled by the increasing distinction between early mechanical add-ons and replacement body parts and the more recent implants, which are increasingly electronic in nature enabling a much closer integration between the human flesh and the technology. The extent to which machines themselves can become more intelligent and take on the characteristics of a human are also fierce topics for debate. As research continues into giving machines human characteristics and encouraging them to mimic or adopt human characteristics, it raises many other social, legal and ethical considerations. These relate to the extent to which such adoption of human characteristics by a machine should be encouraged or discouraged; by what measures can we tell if a machine is intelligent and whether machine intelligence is the same as human intelligence. These are all questions for further debate.

DISCUSSION TOPICS

The Longevity and Social Justice Debate

This house believes advances in medicine that significantly extend life should only be allowed where they:

- Are available universally, not only to the rich
- Do not significantly reduce quality of life.

Governments should ban (and rigorously enforce that ban on) life-extending medicines or technologies that cannot meet these requirements.

Suggested Positions

Pro: It is already the case that wealth, on average, buys longer life. This is true both between and within countries. Further developments can only increase this social injustice. Policies to enforce such a ban will ensure that both private and public funding on life-extension science will be focused on means and methods suitable for all and not restricted to a wealthy few. Further increases in life expectancy will only destabilize society and lead to civil unrest and extremes of government, possibly following revolution.

Con: The wealthy already have longer lives than the poor. That is one of the drivers for capitalist economies. As well as money providing a 'nicer' life, it also provides a 'longer' life. Governments should not legislate against things that are positive for some, on the grounds that they are not positive for all. Unless such a life-extension mechanism was found that actually harmed some for the benefit of others then it should not be banned. We already have such technologies: heart pacemakers, kidney dialysis, vitamin pills and organ transplants. Such a proposal would require the banning of some or all of these, or place an incredible extra burden on the state to provide them to everyone who needs and wants them.

Owning the Code of Life

It is already the case that patents may be obtained in some jurisdictions on genes and gene sequences. The strong economic position of the United States combined with its tendency to use this to push through bilateral and multilateral patent agreements which converge other country's laws with its own means that this will probably spread to become near universal. Now that the human genome has been mapped, the issue of whether to allow the patenting of human genes becomes more and more pressing. As related advances in gene therapy and (embryo and adult) stem-cell research progress, it is likely that human genetic information will become ever more important to health on both an individual and societal basis.

Should patents be allowed on human genes and gene sequences? The argument for allowing them is that without some guaranteed way of getting a return on the investment needed to isolate and identify human genes and their operations, a great deal of expensive research will not be done and the consequent benefits will never appear. The argument against is that our genetic information is so fundamental to who we are as individuals that allowing any form of ownership related to it is the same as enslavement. Has the principle of patenting genes already been established and so the patenting of human genetic material is the logical consequence of that, or are there steps beyond which the logic of legal development violates the basis of human dignity?

What Is a Human?

The ability of the medical profession to keep people alive at both ends of life has increased incredibly in the last hundred years. With the availability of incubator units able to keep premature babies alive from early in the third trimester of pregnancy to the ability to keep people alive on life support apparently beyond brain death or while in persistent vegetative states brought on by external trauma or stroke, the question that is being raised more and more often is not 'can we keep someone alive?' but 'should we keep them alive?'. The case of Terry Schiavo in the United States became a national political and legislative issue, almost causing a constitutional crisis (`www.nytimes.com/2005/03/22/national/22schiavo.html`). Sufferers from Parkinson's disease are already being treated by having electrodes implanted in their brains which provide a base level of stimulation to motor centres which mask out the neural 'white noise' that causes the tell-tale tremors of the condition. As mentioned above, there are new potential neural bridging solutions being offered to severe quadriplegics, while permanent artificial hearts are being developed and temporary ones are already in operation. How far can one go in replacing the biological human body and brain with technological, engineered solutions before the result no longer qualifies as human, with all the rights that brings: the right to life, the right to freedom of expression, the right to own property?

REFERENCES

Fried, M.P., Satava, R., Weghorst, S., et al. (2004) The Use of Surgical Simulators to Reduce Errors, in Advances in Patient Safety: From research to implementation Vol 4, Agency for Healthcare Research and Quality (AHRQ) and the Department of Defense (DoD)-Health Affairs, available at www.ahrq.gov/downloads/pub/advances/vol4/Fried.pdf.

Friedman, M.J. (2004), Acknowledging the psychiatric cost of war, *New England Journal of Medicine*, 351: 75–77.

Seymour, N.E., Gallagher, A.G., Roman, S.A., et al. (2002) Virtual Reality Training Improves Operating Room Performance: Results of a randomized, double-blinded study, *Annals of Surgery*, **236**(4): 458–464, available at www.annalsofsurgery.com/pt/re/annos/abstract.00000658-200210000-00008.htm.

RELATED READING

Armoni, A. (2000) *Health-Care Information Systems: Challenges of the New Millennium*, Idea Group Inc (IGI), Hershey, PA. ISBN 1-878289-62-4.

Evans-Pughe, C. (2006) Smarter Prosthetics, *Engineering and Technology*, **1**(3): 32–36.

Hoffman, H. (2004) Virtual-Reality Therapy, *Scientific American*, **291** August: 58–65.

Mizrach, S. Should there be a limit placed on the integration of humans and computers and electronic technology? www.fiu.edu/~mizrachs/cyborg-ethics.html (last accessed 25 July 2007).

Rosen, J. and **Hannaford, B.** (2006) Doc at a Distance, *IEEE Spectrum*, **43**(10): 34–39.

Telemedicine and Advanced Technology Research Centre, US Army, www.tatrc.org (last accessed 25 July 2007).

Telemedicine and E-health Information Service www.teis.nhs.uk (last accessed 25 July 2007).

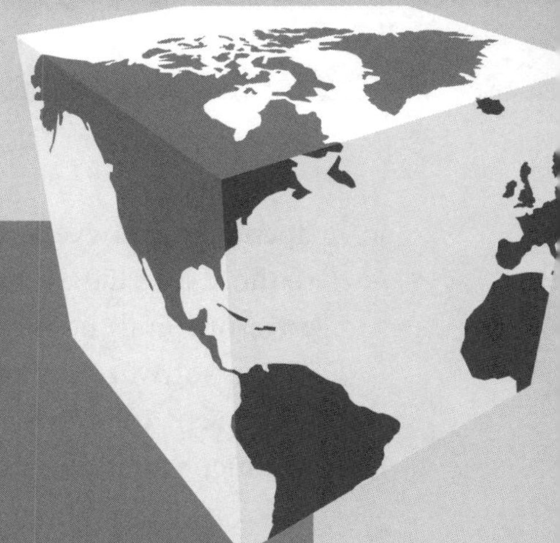

10

PROFESSIONALISM IN IT

INTRODUCTION

What is 'professionalism' and 'professional conduct'? The use in sport of terms such as 'professional foul' might lead to a belief that professional conduct is to do whatever is necessary to get ahead and protest innocence if caught in the act. The use of the term 'professional' as a contrast with 'amateur' can lead to a view that being paid to do something makes one a professional. In terms of a career using the skills developed in a science or engineering degree, however, the term 'professionalism' means acting in a responsible and appropriate manner. That does not just mean doing the job you are paid to do, following instructions and taking a pay cheque. Being a professional is about taking care over the effects of your actions, making appropriate decisions and taking responsibility for the results of your decisions and actions. That is the heart of professionalism: taking personal responsibility.

In some professions and in some places, professionalism is externally judged and enforced as well. The most obvious examples of this are for doctors and lawyers, where practising medicine or giving legal advice are restricted to those who have passed specific exams and have registered with appropriate (often governmental) bodies. To operate as a software engineer or act in other capacities in the software industry, you are not generally required by law, or even by all employers, to be professionally accredited. The level of enforcement of professional conduct varies according to the organization and the employer. Some employers make it a condition of employment to maintain professional membership of a body such as the British Computer Society (United Kingdom) or the Association for Computing Machinery (United States). Other contracts specify that you must have, work towards, or maintain the status of Chartered Engineer, for instance. Such status in the United Kingdom is governed by the Engineering Council and the British Computer Society (BCS) acts as their authorized examining and disciplinary body in software engineering and related fields, so 'personal responsibility' does not mean complete individualism.

Modern society and organizations are a complex web of relationships, dependencies and interacting actions and reactions. Being professional does not require you to take responsibility for things over which you have no control, but it does require you to recognize where you do and do not have control and influence. Professionalism does not mean becoming selfless and abandoning self-interest, but it does mean tempering self-interest and weighing possible personal gain against the effects on others within and outside your immediate circumstances. All this can seem quite daunting to the new graduate starting out on the first steps of their career. There are already enough pressures to succeed, or at least to avoid complete failure, and those pressures will only increase, not decrease, in the modern competitive business world. So why should you try to act professionally? One selfish reason is that you may well be being judged on your professionalism, even where it is not specifically spelled out in your contract. Another is that, as with being a member of any social group, all members of the group (and therefore you as well) are judged by those outside it according to the actions of those within it. By taking responsibility for your own actions, and doing what you can to make sure others take responsibility for theirs, you are enhancing the reputation and standing of your group, and therefore of yourself. Finally, while it may indeed be possible to get ahead in life by being cutthroat, there are substantial financial and legal risks involved with such an approach.

> Professionalism: maintaining an ethical approach to one's job within the structures of an association

So, that tells you why you should strive to be a professional, but the question still remains as to what professional behaviour actually is. One of the simplest answers to this can be found within the codes of appropriate 'professional bodies'. Although in the end, only you can decide what professionalism means to you, and only you can decide what the appropriate course of action is in particular circumstances, the codes of the BCS and the Association for Computing Machinery (ACM) can provide good guidelines on where to start.

In this chapter, we cover some of the basic advice common to such codes and consider the benefits that should derive from following their advice in specific situations. We also cover conduct (how you behave) and practice (what you do), derived from the BCS and ACM codes, 'whistleblowing' (public disclosure) and 'due diligence' (covering your back).

Discovery of Customer Malfeasance

Consider the following scenario: you are a field engineer for a software company that provides bespoke accounting programs. Your job entails visiting a customer when they report a problem that cannot be replicated without the data they use. Many companies are not willing to transfer their financial information to another company so you must visit their site and work through the problem with their employees demonstrating the problem. As a software engineer in this field, you understand a great deal about taxation rules, accounting regulations, and so on. In tracking down the problem, you realize that the reason the customer has a problem is that they are trying to make your program (written with due respect for accounting standards) support their false accounting procedures. You are completely certain that what this company is doing is illegal. Their attitude while you are there makes you believe that this is a wilful act and not a misunderstanding on their part. There are a number of possible actions you can take, with various possible consequences:

- You might tell the customer that what they are doing is illegal and refuse to provide a fix for their software.
- You might tell the customer that you understand the problem but that you must consult with your colleagues before working on a fix.
- You might consult by phone with your management for advice.
- You might fix their software so that it does what they want.

In any of the first three cases, your company may react in a number of different ways:

- They might decide that they should not support illegal accounting practices and refuse to provide a fix.
- They might order you to provide a fix as requested.
- They might arrange for other programmers to provide a fix.

If you are ordered to provide a fix you might or might not be willing to comply with such a request. How far should you be willing to push the (fairly obvious) ethical case that you should not be aiding and abetting tax fraud? Would you personally or your company be criminally liable if you did? What does due diligence require in such a case?

CONDUCT

Conduct is about how you behave. It is a more general concept than 'practice', which is about what you do and is covered in the next section. First and foremost, the concept of 'good conduct' is that of being a good citizen, of being a positive force in the world. This can generally be described as working in 'the public interest' (BCS Code of Conduct) or as following general 'moral principles' (ACM Code of Ethics and Professional Conduct). Acting in this way requires more than just acting in an honest and trustworthy manner. It requires specific thought about the potential effects of your actions. In a professional environment, you generally have a duty to your organization, whether your employer, your university (while a student), or a charity when doing voluntary work. Wherever and whoever you work for, with or under, it is up to you to act always with appropriate consideration for the world at large as well as the legitimate interests of your employer. Specific examples of how this applies to computing professionals can include:

- Advising the appropriate people of threats (possible negative consequences of actions or policies) and risks (chances of threats actually occurring) according to your professional knowledge and training. Where your judgements are overruled, you should seek guidance and advice from suitable experts on whether your judgement was correct (and thus whether you should consider other measures, such as public disclosure) or whether your judgement was flawed (in which case you should try to learn from the mistake).

- Working, and encouraging or requiring others to work, with regard to public health and safety. This includes not only those working within your specific environment on a regular basis, but also visitors and the general public. Environmental concerns, particularly, should form a part of your considerations. For most computing professionals, of course, major environmental issues are concerned with power usage and disposal of equipment. For those working in supporting major industrial control systems, however, the avoidance of a disaster on the scale of Bhopal (`www.bhopal.com`) or Chernobyl (`www.un.org/ha/chernobyl`) should be paramount in their considerations.
- Maintaining suitable regard for the legitimate interests of other businesses and the general public. These will include your company's customers and suppliers as well as competitors. Internally, trust between individuals and departments is a necessary factor in maintaining a healthy business. In general, while short-term gains may be made by cutting corners or lying about defects or threats, in the long term it is rarely in the interests of shareholders or employees to be found having falsified information: consider the situation of cigarette manufacturers and their knowledge of the cancer-causing effects of smoking (`www.ash.org.uk`).
- Not discriminating or allowing others to discriminate against fellow workers, customers or suppliers on unsuitable grounds such as race, gender, religion or sexual orientation. Most legal jurisdictions include laws against such discrimination, which then constitute a threat to an organization in which illegal discrimination occurs, in addition to the moral imperative.

Health and Safety

Health and safety issues are among the most contentious in any workplace. Many employers follow health and safety guidelines slavishly, to the detriment of the general working conditions of their staff; others play fast and loose with the rules and put their staff at serious risk of injury. Many computer professionals must deal with hardware as well as software and this brings all sorts of health and safety issues to the fore. The main thing that should be remembered in dealing with health and safety is that common sense should always be used, particularly when workplace necessities cause some sort of hazard wherever they are stored. Episode 20 of Bastard Operator from Hell (`www.theregister.co.uk/2004/06/24/bofh_2004_episode_20/`) exemplifies what can happen otherwise:

> *What the hell's that?' the PFY asks as he enters Mission Control, narrowly missing a huge pile of paper just inside the door.*
>
> *'That would be the identified hazards in our workplace,' I reply.*
>
> *'What the* **BLOODY HELL** *are they playing at?!' the PFY snaps, echoing my own frustration. 'They've been annoying us for more than a bloody year now!'*
>
> *'They claim that the IT Division's injury rate approaches that of a small civil war so they're paying particular attention to the Division, and our office in particular.'*
>
> *'So that's the office covered then?'*
>
> *'No that pile is just for this room!'*
>
> *'You're joking!'*
>
> *'No, they've really gone overboard,' I reply, grabbing several sheets of paper. 'These bookshelves, >tap< >wobble<>wobble<, are not fixed to the wall and have heavy objects at a height which raises its centre of gravity dangerously.'*
>
> *'But they made us put them there because they said they were too low before and would cause back strain in lifting!'*
>
> *'Uh huh. >flip<And this table>clank<>clank< has a wobbly leg, which could mean that if someone stumbled into it, it would collapse, dropping that machine onto someone's foot.'*
>
> *'It was them who made us turn the table around because they said it blocked an egress path.'*

'Again, yes. >flip< These boxes of tapes are also dodgy, bump into them and they might topple down on top of you...'

'But they said the tape room was too overcrowded for people to access and that we'd have to store some tapes in a different location!'

'Uh-huh. > flip < The table top bulk eraser has no electrical earth.'

'It's double insulated! It's not supposed to have an earth! The only way it'd cause a problem unless you poured water down it! Anyway it's isolated on the deskside UPS.'

'AH HAH!' *I cry ' > flip < Overvoltage warning lamp on deskside UPS unit.'*

'It's done that since we bought it. It's perfectly alright. Anyway, it's only an eraser.'

'You're talking to the wrong man. > flip < That > scuff < carpet tile in the doorway has lifted, causing a trip hazard.'

'THEY BLOODY LIFTED IT WHEN THEY WERE TESTED THEM TO SEE HOW WELL STUCK DOWN THEY WERE.'

'Again, I am not disagreeing with you.'

'So you're just going to fix all these things now so that the solutions will be next inspection's problems?' he asks sarcastically.

'Not at all. I rang the inspector bloke, who, it has to be admitted, has the personality of a tampon vending machine, who told me that once we read the 150-page newly-revised safety-in-the-workplace manual, we'll know all we need to about making the place safe.'

'I don't do manuals,' the PFY snips.

'Yes, that's what I said, but he told me that it's our responsibility to have a safe workplace. He also said that he'll be doing fortnightly inspections to ensure that we comply with the company's new work-safe policy.'

'What new work-safe policy?'

'Buggered if I know. Anyway he said he'd walk us through the main points today so that we could make a start and avoid the non-compliance penalties.'

'Penalties?' the PFY says

'Yeah, in the work-safe policy. It's a carrot and stick idea, with more of the stick than the carrot. Apparently, the company's considering moving to a deferred bonus for staff and contractors, and this could be one of the things that puts the kybosh on your bonus. You know, too many accidents, no bonus.'

'The bastard!'

'No, no, he's just doing his job, keeping us safe. Anyway, he should be here anytime to...'

> Knock Knock <

'Just thought I'd grab the bull by the horns and get down to business as soon as pos..' he starts, tripping on the aforementioned carpet tile, then regaining his balance momentarily by standing on the large stack of H&S violation reports ...

...which slides out from under his foot.

'Whoops!' he says, ploughing into one of the aforementioned bookcases.

> Wobble <

*> **CRASH!***

'Hey, they were right about that bookcase!' the PFY cries, surprised.

> Clank! <

> Crash <

'And that table!'

> Topple <

> Crash < > crash < > crash <

'And the boxes of tapes.'

> KZZZZZEeeerrrrt! <

> ZZzzzzzzzzzap <

> Bang! <

'Maybe that overvoltage light was actually working after all,' he mumbles as the smoke clears. 'Bloody lucky we had a Health and Safety bloke to point it all out to us...'

> slam <

'What the hell is going o...' the Boss starts, crashing into Mission Control to see what all the noise is about.

> trip <

> Wobble <

> CRASH <

> BZZZERRRRRT! <

> Zip < > Zip < > zzzzap <

... one ambulance ride for two later ...

'This place is a ***BLOODY DEATHTRAP!'*** *I gasp, recounting the past half-hour.*

'I'd agree,' the PFY responds. 'We definitely need to be putting some things into place.'

'Warning signs?' I suggest.

'I was thinking more of a video camera. I almost pissed myself when the boss face planted the bulk eraser. A memory like that would have been priceless on tape.'

'Yeah. And we could have made a tidy little sum from those bloopers shows too.'

'Ah well, there's always next time,' the PFY sighs, picking at the corner of a floor tile...

For further references on how not to act professionally, consult `www.theregister.co.uk/odds/bofh` and `bofh.ntk.net/` where the full BOFH archives lurk.

PRACTICE

Just as general rules of conduct should dictate how you behave, the practice of what you do within that conduct is also the subject of professional ideas. In the course of your professional duties, you will be subject to a number of challenges and temptations. For instance, as a system administrator, you will almost certainly have access to most of the data on your systems, from e-mail to financial information. Few organizations protect individual files with encryption, relying instead on general access restrictions to preserve confidentiality. You might, therefore, have access to the chief executive's pay details in the accounting system or to the personnel director's e-mail. Unless you have a need to access such information for legitimate purposes, you should not 'go fishing' for interesting information. In fact, where such information consists of individual personal details (including the chief executive's salary or discussions of promotion prospects, for instance) then it is a violation of 'data protection' principles in many jurisdictions even to access the data and may be a violation of computer misuse laws, even though you have general access to the machines, to view data that you have no professional justification to access. See Chapters 7 and 11 for more details on data protection and computer misuse, respectively.

In addition to being careful in your dealings, and most people would find the above examples quite obviously unprofessional, you must make sure that you are competent to perform your duties. This involves not overstating your experience, whether applying for a post, moving between jobs for one employer or taking on expanded duties. In addition, while your prior education and training may fit you for a particular role at first, the computing industry moves so fast that no one can let their knowledge stand still. Not only should you make efforts to keep up with new developments and new technologies (even going so far as to demand suitable training from your employer) but such learning will be of direct benefit in keeping you employable and flexible, a necessary career advantage in the modern world, where few computer professionals stay in one job for more than five years.

There are some particular areas where you should be very careful about claiming levels of expertise and ensuring that your knowledge is up to date:

these include computer security and procurement activities (for both software and hardware).

The level of enforcement of professionalism varies from organization to organization. Membership of the BCS, upon which is dependent the status of Chartered Engineer for software engineering, requires adherence to the code of conduct and the appropriate codes of practice. Society disciplinary procedures can, following a complaint, lead to disciplinary action requiring responses as diverse as remedial action or further training to retain membership, or, at worst, can involve expulsion from the society for serious and continued breaches of the codes. Similar sanctions may be applied by the ACM, as mentioned in the preamble to their code of ethics and professional conduct:

> *The Code and its supplemented Guidelines are intended to serve as a basis for ethical decision making in the conduct of professional work. Secondarily, they may serve as a basis for judging the merits of a formal complaint pertaining to violation of professional ethical standards.*

WHISTLEBLOWING

One of the ethical dilemmas facing many people in modern democracies is what to do when confronted with unethical, or even illegal, behaviour by others. In the United Kingdom, the problem of balancing one's duty to one's employer with duty to the public was deemed important enough to result in an act of parliament: the Public Interest Disclosure Act 1998. Other jurisdictions have different rules, though many have similar principles even where the minor details might be different. You should note that reporting possible criminal activity to the police or health and safety violations to the appropriate government body is not the same thing as public disclosure. 'Public disclosure' means revealing to members of the general public information to which they would not ordinarily have access and of which you are aware due to your employment. The most common way to perform a public disclosure is by talking to a member of the press, although there are other possibilities, such as posting on one's own or someone else's blog, in chat rooms or on some other form of web site. In order to demonstrate the potential problems, practical and legal as well as ethical, in public disclosure, we present two recent cases, one from the United States and the other from the United Kingdom.

Vulnerability of E-mail

In the United States, Bret McDanel used to work for an ISP that offered, among other services, a so-called secure web e-mail system. During the course of his work he discovered that there was a serious security vulnerability in the e-mail service. He reported this to his employers as a serious issue. McDanel left the ISP's employ shortly after reporting this problem. About six months later, he discovered that the ISP still had not fixed the vulnerability. McDanel decided that the ISP had enough time to fix the problem and so contacted 5500 of the ISP's customers (staggering the e-mail transmission to prevent flooding their servers) with an e-mail telling them there was a problem and directing them to his web site for details. When it found out what was going on, the ISP deleted the unread copies of McDanel's e-mail, without the permission of their customers, and made a criminal complaint against McDanel under computer misuse legislation. The complaint was not aimed at claiming a 'Denial of Service' attack due to the volume of mail, but on the grounds that by revealing the vulnerability, McDanel had 'impaired the integrity' of the ISP's service (`www.securityfocus.com/columnists/179`). See Chapter 11 for details of computer misuse legislation in the United States and the United Kingdom.

McDanel was convicted on this rather tenuous interpretation of the computer misuse legislation (this is the only reported case of revelation of a vulnerability being grounds for such a charge without evidence that the vulnerability was exploited by the person who revealed it or by someone they encouraged to do so). Even though he had served his sentence he decided to appeal the conviction, aided by staff at the Stanford Center for Internet and Society (`cyberlaw.stanford.edu`). During the case the federal prosecutors reversed their position and requested that the Appeals Court overturn the verdict, which they did (`cyberlaw.stanford.edu/about/cases/McDanelOpinion.pdf`).

Safety-Critical Software

Nowhere is the necessity of professional behaviour more relevant than when producing safety-critical software. A great deal of software is mission critical and can cost significant amounts of money if it fails in some way, but when software is involved in control of physical devices, it can also put the health and even lives of people at risk – this includes software which provides information to humans controlling devices such as air-traffic-control computers. They do not directly control the physical devices but they are the primary (much of the time, the only) direct source of information to the humans who work together to control the aircraft (air traffic controllers and pilots). The highest level of professionalism is therefore required when working on safety-critical software development. In most cases this will require strict adherence to a much more stringent design and documentation regime than is usual. In such development it is not simply good enough to do the job well, it is necessary to demonstrate that the job is being done well. This serves a two-fold purpose: first, in the process of demonstrating that the development is being done properly many potential errors can be averted – at least that is the case when the process itself is properly designed; second, fully documented procedures fulfil the due diligence requirements such that if something does go wrong it was unforeseen and hopefully unforeseeable, so the developer is not liable. Of course if the manager and originator of the process did not follow standard practices they too may then be liable. As with all aspects of professional behaviour, however, the documented process for safety-critical software development is not the only requirement of the professional. They must engage their full capacities and be willing to raise issues both of process and content if they believe something is wrong. Once again, this serves the double purpose of trying to get the end product as correct as it is possible for it to be and covering the developer from legal and moral responsibility should something tragic happen. Further information on safety-critical systems can be found at www.bcs.org/server.php?show=conWebDoc.1642 and www.acm.org/serving/se_policy/safety_critical.pdf.

'Illegal' espionage

In the run up to the Iraq War in 2003, a UK government civil servant, Katharine Gun, went to the British press with a story on bugging of UN Security Council member delegations in the UN building. Espionage in the United Nations is illegal under the UN treaty. Ms Gun was a translator working for the UK's Government Communications HQ (GCHQ) in Cheltenham. She was sacked over her revelation to the press and initially charged under the Official Secrets Act, although the case was dropped in early 2004 just as it was about to come to trial (news.bbc.co.uk/1/hi/uk_ politics/3659310.stm).

Consequences of 'Whistleblowing'

In the United Kingdom, the Public Disclosure Act supposedly provides protection for those who reveal illegal activity or activity that is against the public interest. Despite this, Ms Gun lost her job and was for a year under charge for a criminal offence. It should be noted that the Public Disclosure Act was not invoked by Ms Gun in her own defence (either to protest dismissal or to protest against the criminal charges) before the trial, although whether it might have been brought up during a trial is a moot point given the dropping of charges.

In the United States, a perfectly accurate piece of information about an ISP at the very least misleading customers (by claiming their system was secure when they knew for certain that it was not) is supposedly protected by the First Amendment rights to free speech of the US constitution. Nevertheless, Mr McDanel served a sentence in a federal prison for warning the ISP's customers of the vulnerability of their (supposedly secure) communications.

Such cases might lead you to believe that it's never worth blowing the whistle and revealing damaging information about your employer's activities. However, remember that the codes of conduct you should be following as a professional mean that you should consider the public interest alongside your own and your employer's interests. Where you draw the line is up to you. How bad something has to be before it requires public disclosure is a judgement only you, in possession of all the facts, can make. But the tales above should convince you that following all internal procedures before going public is the only sensible way to proceed. As in all other aspects of your work, you must make sure you have acted with due diligence before 'going public'. In the United Kingdom, reading the Public Disclosure Act yourself, or taking legal advice about the possible ramifications both personally and professionally, would be advisable.

DUE DILIGENCE

Whether it is a case of internal disciplinary procedures or a court case against you (whether criminal or civil, against you alone or you as an employee), when something goes wrong, you want to have a defence against sanctions (loss of pay, loss of your job, a fine or a prison sentence) being applied. Your best defence is always 'due diligence'. In its simplest form, the concept of 'due diligence' is that you did everything that could have been expected of you in the circumstances in which you found yourself. Part of due diligence is to be found in following the relevant codes of professional societies and showing (both generally and specifically) that you have a professional attitude to your job and your role. So, what does due diligence mean for a computer professional and what can it protect you against?

Consider a hypothetical situation in which you are one of the system administrators for a bank. An investigation by the banking regulator has found that the remote access system you use to offer out-of-hours support for software problems has been compromised and used to commit a serious fraud. You were responsible for setting up the remote-access system in order to allow you to respond to out-of-hours calls from the comfort of your own study, rather than having to get dressed and drive 30 minutes to the office just to spend five minutes restarting a software communications conduit. Under what circumstances can you claim that you were not to blame for the fraud?

There are various aspects to this situation that you would need to consider to demonstrate due diligence:

- You had appropriate training in network security to set up such a link.
- You had documented the choice of software to use, including a cost–benefit analysis and a threat–risk analysis for various options.
- You had properly installed the system, including following regulatory and internal security procedures for remote access.
- You had not revealed confidential information to unauthorized persons about the system (such as the protocols used, the hardware in use, possibly even the very existence of the remote link).
- You had allocated suitable time to testing the security of the system, possibly even employing a more qualified security analyst or recommending their employment to your management.
- There were appropriate logs of usage and those logs were checked regularly to ensure sequential attacks were identified.

If you have done all of these, and show a general professional attitude to keeping your working knowledge up to date and ensuring that your work is authorized, it is unlikely that you would be held liable by the regulator or even be liable to internal disciplinary proceedings by your employer.

PERSONAL RESPONSIBILITY

To a great extent, this chapter contains the core message of social, legal and ethical aspects of work in computer and communications technology. The technology itself is generally completely neutral in ethical terms: the technology is not good or bad in itself, it is how people use that technology that determines its effect. Provided you maintain awareness of the use and possible misuses of the technology you are responsible for developing and maintaining, and that you take responsibility for your own actions, you are a professional and can take pride in what you do. The modern world would not be the same without computers and communication technology. Only those frightened by the potential of computers want to put the genie back in the bottle. It is up to those of us who understand how they work to do our best to make sure the genie is mankind's servant and not its master. However, in all this talk of personal responsibility, we should not ignore the fact that we are members of a professional community as well. Although you should take personal responsibility for your actions, you do not have to (and indeed should not try to) do it all alone. That's what bodies like the BCS and the ACM are there for: to provide general and specific guidance and advice on situations, technology and dilemmas and to help us develop the mental tools necessary to work professionally.

DISCUSSION TOPICS

Self-Incrimination

Consider the following scenario. Imagine you are the chief technical officer (a board-level appointment) of a company. The IT systems support manager reports to you that the CEO has been making fraudulent expense claims by booking two business-class seats for himself and his partner but claiming one first-class seat for himself. The proof provided is the spreadsheet which is the expense claim form, the original e-mail that arrived in the CEO's inbox from the online travel booking and the amended version of the e-mail that was submitted as a 'receipt' along with the claim form.

This is clearly a breach of the company regulations regarding expenses. However, there is no valid reason why the IT systems support manager should have been viewing the e-mail inbox of the CEO or the finance office expense claim forms. Which of the following actions are appropriate?

- Report the possible financial irregularity to the Chief Financial Officer.
- Start internal disciplinary proceedings against the IT systems support manager for violating the internal policies.
- Sack the IT systems support manager for an obvious violation of confidentiality of the CEO's e-mail.
- Get personal legal advice.
- Get company legal advice.
- Talk informally to the CEO and advise him there may be a problem.
- Talk informally to the IT systems support manager and warn him not to 'go fishing'.

Responsibility for DDoS Attacks

Distributed denial of service attacks are becoming worrying commonplace. Sometimes they are simply nuisance attacks but more commonly they are linked to extortion and there are worries about potential terrorist activity. The majority of distributed denial of service (DDoS) attacks are carried out using zombies (cracked computers under the control of a third party) gathered into bot-nets (groups of zombies controllable as a package rather than requiring individual commands). In the 1990s, most zombies were corporate PCs. With the widespread adoption of always-on broadband for home PC networking, this has now switched to home PCs, as discussed in Chapter 11. It is notoriously difficult to trace the perpetrators of such attacks. The victims would like to be able to hold someone responsible for their losses. Legislators would like to find some way of reducing the potential for such attacks. So, who might be made liable? Computing professionals should be engaged in such debates and even without legal liability should be doing what they can in their roles as programmers or systems managers to reduce the poisoning of the digital environment.

Software producers

There is an argument to be made that the producer of operating system software – principally Microsoft since most of the zombie PCs run Microsoft Windows operating systems – should be made liable for shipping products that are highly insecure and lead to systems being easily infected. Microsoft is a large company with significant assets so making them liable is attractive to those seeking damages after the fact.

PC owners

Individuals are responsible for maintaining their car in good working order and may be held liable if it fails on the highway causing damage to others. Insurance is therefore available, and in most jurisdictions mandatory, to cover potential losses. Keeping a car in good working order is often a requirement of such insurance, leading to fewer road deaths due to preventable mechanical problems. This would severely increase the cost of owning and using a home PC, however, which would not be politically popular. In addition suing a large number of individuals for the use of their machines in an attack would probably be uneconomic.

ISPs

Most zombie programs use non-standard ports for part of their operation, both in infecting other machines (and being infected in the first place) and in carrying out operations such as DDoS attacks. Given that most users make limited use of their machine (web access, e-mail access, some online gaming), it should be possible to restrict most machines access over broadband to the common ports and to throttle (reduce to small numbers of packets) their usage of these ports unless a specific request is made by the PC user. While this might well require an increase in customer services offered by ISPs, it could have the greatest positive effect on reducing the number of DDoS attacks, which incidentally could improve the service to other customers of those ISPs whose shared bandwidth is swamped by such attacks. Alternatively ISPs could offer basic services with most ports blocked and a separate (possibly insured) service with more ports open and unthrottled.

Whistleblowing Insecurity

Imagine that you are working for a large financial institution in their in-house systems department. You come across a security hole in their system which would be difficult and very expensive to deal with and report it to your manager. He decides that the risk is too small to justify the expense, despite the potential problems. You disagree with him about the judgement. Which of the following is the first step you should take, or can you think of other possibilities?

- Look for another job.
- Talk to the press and expose the company's cavalier attitude to vulnerability.
- Report the problem to the financial regulatory authorities (if there are suitable channels).
- Go over your manager's head and report it to the board.
- Write about it in your personal blog.
- Write about it anonymously on, for example, Slashdot.
- Assume your manager knows better than you and do nothing.

What outcome is your goal? If your first reaction does not produce your desired outcome, what should you do then? Are there any of the above which you should never do? What laws might protect you if you reveal the issue to outsiders?

REFERENCES

Association for Computing Machinery, Code of Ethics, `www.acm.org/constitution/code.html` (last accessed 25 July 2007).

British Computer Society, Codes of Conduct and Practice, www.bcs.org/BCS/AboutBCS/codes/conduct/ (last accessed 25 July 2007).

Travaglia, S., Bastard Operator from Hell Official Archive, bofh.ntk.net/Bastard_Indexes.html (last accessed 25 July 2007).

Travaglia, S., Bastard Operator from Hell, The Register, www.theregister.co.uk/odds/bofh/ (last accessed 25 July 2007).

11

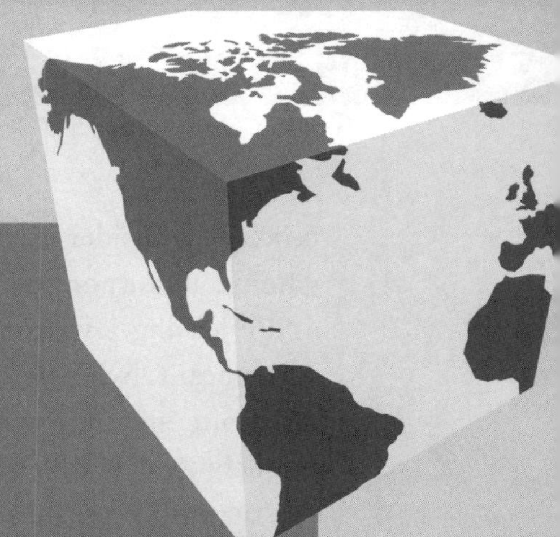

ONLINE CRIME AND REAL PUNISHMENT

INTRODUCTION

Computer misuse (sometimes referred to as computer crime) has been receiving a significant amount of press attention over the last few years. As the breadth and depth of computer usage has spread throughout business and personal space in the industrialized world, the potential for criminal misuse of computers has increased as well. Although many activities are simply old crimes committed in new ways there are also new acts deemed unwelcome by society and for which criminal sanctions are imposed. From the electronic equivalent of graffiti and criminal damage, to electronic theft or fraud, new detection, prosecution and rehabilitation measures are needed in the information age.

We consider two types of criminal activity involving computers. There are many ways of categorizing crimes committed using computers in some form, but the one we will follow here is the distinction between computers as the means to commit a more 'traditional' crime (which we call 'crime using a computer') and computers as the primary target of the crime ('computer crime'). Consider two simple examples which fall easily into these categories: gaining unauthorized access to the computer system of a bank to steal money and releasing a virus on the Internet which randomly deletes data on the affected machines. Obviously there are activities which fall between these two stools such as gaining unauthorized access to a web server and uploading files which are then publicly available. The type of data uploaded and whether it overwrites the prior site or simply uses the connection is the deciding factor in whether this is truly a computer crime or a crime using a computer.

Before going further into the details of the sorts of computer crime and crime using a computer that occur and how others attempt to prevent the offence or punish the offenders, we briefly digress into a discussion on the nature of criminality. It should be remembered that 'crime' is not an abstract concept with a permanent unchanging meaning. What one society (or government) considers a heinous crime, another may consider protected as a human right. This distinction holds for the same society at two different times as well as for two different societies at the same point in time. 'Crime' is a socially defined concept. In this chapter we consider crime from a legalistic point of view: if certain activities are defined by the law of a particular jurisdiction as criminal, then they are called a 'crime' (in that jurisdiction) for our purposes. We reserve the right to criticize those jurisdictions for their definitions, however.

> Crime: a violation of the law subject to state sanction of a fine or loss of liberty

USER FRIENDLY by Illiad

A Brief History of Crime and Computers

When computers were huge room-sized collections of vacuum tubes and mercury memory lines, programmed by soldering or by using crocodile clips or telephone-switchboard-type connectors, there was no such thing as computer crime, one might think. However, by the late 1940s and 1950s, there was already a 'computer' accessible to thousands of people worldwide: the 'public telephone system'. The telephone network and the telegraph network can be seen as the predecessors to the modern Internet.

Some of the social effects of the Internet are modelled on similar effects of the telegraph and telephone. Since charges were made for use of these networks and since they were used for commercial purposes, there were both crimes using the networks (e.g. schemes designed to defraud banks by taking advantage of 'wire transfer' mechanisms for sending money over the telegraph system) and network crimes (e.g. using equipment to tap into the lines and make calls without paying). The United States has successfully evolved the concept of the wire-fraud criminal to cover issues such as fraudulent offerings on electronic auction systems. The playground term of 'phone phreakers' has been applied to people who make calls without paying – the first crackers (the more popular term 'hacker' has too confused a meaning and so the more precise term 'cracker' is used in this chapter). Phone phreakers naturally graduated to the challenge (and the potential profits) to be gained from unauthorized access (whether remote or direct) to computers.

> Wire fraud: fraudulently obtaining funds by altering or counterfeiting the traces of funds transferred over telegraph, telephone or computer networks
>
> Phreaker: an expert in using internal signals to fool the phone network into allowing free calls or access to restricted services

By the 1970s, the development of various computer networks (including the Internet) and of ad hoc bulletin board and dial-in network capabilities, exposed ever more computers to external attacks, which have always commanded strong media interest. It should be noted, however, that even with the spread of Internet access (and other forms of networked information and communications technology), most criminal activity involving computers is committed by 'insiders' rather than external attackers. It may be a different story for acts which are against the law but not criminal (such as much infringement of intellectual property rights, although the copyright industry tries to portray – and would like to change criminal law to make – such things crimes; see Chapter 12). It should also be noted that most external 'cracking' activity relies on the ignorance and innocence of insiders to gain access; internal attacks more often involve misuse of legitimate access rather than finding ways around the security systems.

Computer Fraud

One of the most common, because it can be one of the most lucrative, crimes involving computers is committing fraud by accessing or changing electronic information. In the modern world anything that is, or can be, an abstract concept of business is held as electronic information. For example, a company usually tries to keep sufficient stock in a warehouse to meet all the expected demands of their customers. If a database query reveals that the last widget in a warehouse is never used, an employee might well use their computer access to print out a false collection order and use it to obtain a widget, knowing that it will probably go unnoticed for a significant period. If this period exceeds the length of time that the paper records are kept then there may be no record of the theft for detectives to trace. The computer element of this crime is two-fold: access to the database to check on the susceptibility of the warehouse to the misappropriation of the widget and access to the correct form to carry out a convincing fraudulent collection at the warehouse. The major crime here is theft and the courts would deal with that. The abuse of trust and possible misuse of the computer system would usually be thought of as subsumed into any sentence handed down for the theft. Only in cases where it is obvious that something society frowns upon has occurred, but for which no case can be made or for which there is no crime on the books, are the minor enabling 'computer crime' offences used to prosecute, in a parallel to the prosecution of Al Capone for tax evasion rather than gangster activities.

Phishing: directing a web browser to a clone of a secure site to obtain login details.

Phishing

Phishing is a new variant of an old scam. The old version of the scam involved writing a program that looked like the login system and leaving it running on an open access machine. A new user then types in their username and password which is logged by the program. The first versions of such programs would then terminate with an appropriate 'user/password not recognized' error, making the user think they'd mistyped their password. More advanced versions of the system would log the user in transparently, possibly even continuing to run after that user had logged out. This is one of the standard ways of cracking other users' accounts in places such as universities with general-access computers.

The modern form, 'phishing', started in the mid 1990s and was aimed primarily at customers of America Online, Inc., (AOL). An e-mail, often spoofed to appear as coming from AOL, asked users to reconfirm their details to ensure their account was kept up to date (or some other spurious reason) and gave a uniform resource locator (URL) into which users were asked to enter the information. The URL would often, but not always, be something that the ordinary user might misinterpret as a legitimate AOL-related site, such as A0L.com (with a zero replacing the letter 'O') or AOLsecurity.com, implying that it is a subdivision of AOL. Another method used HTML links such as '< A HREF='www.phisher.org'> AOL.com< /A >' to display 'AOL.com' in the email while linking to 'www.phisher.org'.

Although gaining access to people's AOL account (including their e-mail and various other information) is bad enough, phishing then entered the mainstream of fraud and organized crime. Instead of attempting to get hold of users' Internet access provider (ISP) connection details, phishers moved on to online banking access information. The scam is the same: users are contacted (often through a major spam distribution) with a URL which appears reasonable but which takes users to a fake site that asks for full security details (most legitimate sites only ask for partial verification on each login).

Two variations on this are even more interesting. The first involves using non-standard character encoding to point a user to a different site by substituting in the name non-English letters (such as the Scandinavian 'ø' in place of the English letter 'o') that display as English letters on English-language systems – the ability to use internationalized lettering in domain names is not universal. The second uses a flaw in Microsoft's Internet Explorer web browser (see `news.zdnet.co.uk/0,39020330,39119033,00.htm`) that was later discovered to affect some other browsers at least in part (`www.mozillazine.org/talkback.html?article=4078`). It involved using special characters '%00' and '%01' which made Internet Explorer (IE) show only the characters occurring before them while using the domain name after the characters. So, '`www.bank.com`%01%00 `www.phisher.org`' would display as '`www.bank.com`' in the location bar of the browser window although actually loading pages from '`www.phisher.org`'.

As Internet-based banking services become more common phishing may overtake credit/debit cards as the biggest source of fraud. All the major European and US banks have been hit by phishing scams and the saving grace is that they are now ensuring that their customers are informed about the problem and are explaining how to avoid details being phished: type in the URL of the bank's home page manually or use your own bookmark;

never give all your security details at once; contact your bank if you think your account's security has been compromised. Typing in the URL manually has dangers as well: 'passive' phishers exploit typosquatting with URLs that are misspellings of legitimate bank URLs: for example, `bqnk.com` for `bank.com`. Phishing scams are here to stay and there are undoubtedly more variants to come; hacking of the domain name system (DNS) to point to false sites is now a reality (dubbed 'pharming') as are re-diallers that point to false sites. Who knows what new tricks will be born now that organized crime has got in on the act?

Pharming: using DNS cracks to perform phishing attacks

MALWARE

One of the biggest problems for any computer user or administrator these days is unwanted software 'infecting' the computer.

Malware: malicious programs running unwanted and usually covertly

A Taxonomy of Malware

What most people call 'viruses' are various types of unwanted programs running on machines. Here we give definitions of the four most common types of 'malware'. In the rest of this chapter, we use the phrase 'malware' to cover the whole taxonomy and use the individual terms to distinguish the different characteristics where useful.

Trojan Horse

Trojan horse programs masquerade as something else (a program or data file) but once run or opened do something unexpected. Trojan horses are potentially dangerous. They have effects ranging from printing out an insult (such as 'If this were a malicious Trojan horse it could have deleted all your files') to deleting all the files to which you have access, potentially including the operating system, and, in extreme cases, damaging hardware.

Virus

A virus is a program that is embedded within another program or data file and which can copy itself into other programs. Many modern viruses propagate by sending themselves out by e-mail as a Trojan horse. A virus also typically contains a 'payload' which performs some other operation (usually damaging) as well as propagating itself.

Worm

A worm is a program that copies itself across a network without needing a Trojan horse or virus to gain access to a system. Worms can also propagate between networks by Trojan horse or virus mechanisms but they then infect local networks once one machine has been infected.

Zombie

A zombie is one of the many kinds of payload that viruses, worms and Trojan horses deliver. It allows the infected machine to be accessed or controlled by a third party over the network.

Problems Caused by Malware

We categorize the effects of malware into internal and external effects and primary and secondary effects: that is, what a piece of malware does to the computers it has infected (internal); the effect it has on other computers and the physical world (external); the direct operation of the malware (primary); and the resulting problems experienced (secondary). There are also what we might term tertiary effects which are the issues around trying to avoid being infected by a virus in the first place. These tertiary effects are discussed in the section on Computer Security.

Anyone who has ever had to deal with a computer infected by malware understands at least one of the secondary external problems caused by such attacks, which is the time and effort spent in trying to clean up. Since, in a business setting at least, time is money in a real way as staff must be paid, this translates directly into a monetary cost. This is one of two secondary external effects, the other being any problem or cost associated with the lack of the facility offered by the computer in the first place. Although there are computers which are rarely or never used, most in the workplace are used on a daily if not hourly basis or are in nearly continuous use. Virulent malware can devastate an organization's operation, given how dependent on computing facilities many modern organizations are. The scope of these secondary effects usually depends at least partly on the direct effects the malware has, although the time taken to purge a system depends on the skill of the programmer at hiding the malware among the system's normal operation. In some cases this can lead to malware with more limited direct effects so that it can hide better: a wolf in sheep's clothing is easily spotted when eating another sheep since that is not normal sheep behaviour.

To consider the other primary and secondary direct effects of infection by malware, we present a typical infection scenario and track its consequences. Following this we give a list of standard malware operations.

Zombie Infection by an e-mail Trojan Virus

The most common method of infection at present is by an e-mail attachment. An e-mail comes in and the recipient attempts to access the attached document by selecting it within their e-mail client. This then either runs the malware directly or opens an application and loads the attached document into it and runs the malware embedded in the document. Once the malware is running, it replaces one or more of the operating system's necessary component programs with a new version which, besides performing some or all the ordinary operations of that program, also performs its own malicious plans.

Since malware is distributed by e-mail one of the first malicious actions is usually to access the e-mail program and send a copy of itself to everyone in the address book (sometimes called the 'propagation phase'). For large organizations with global address books as well as personal ones, this can mean that a single infection within their network immediately results in an individual e-mail to every user in the organization. Advanced malware programs use some sophisticated methods to create the e-mails, including embedding their code into a document from the infected user's file space and sending it out attached to a copy of an e-mail already sent by the user.

Having propagated by e-mail, the malware typically moves to a second phase of operation (sometimes called the 'payload delivery' or 'operation' phase). It may become a zombie program on the infected machine, allowing a remote user some level of control over it. Such zombies typically use security vulnerabilities to increase their level of access to the machine (attempting to gain 'Administrator' privileges on Windows machines and attempting to gain 'root' access on Unix machines), sometimes referred to as 'elevating privileges'.

Having gained some measure of control over the system, the malware then broadcasts its existence in some way to the originator of the program, typically by sending some form of coded message to an Internet relay chat (IRC) channel, including information such as its level of access and the Internet Protocol (IP) address of the infected host computer. The originator's computer monitors the IRC channel on the appropriate servers for infected machine details. They do not care if others can see the details since this form of zombie usually requires a password to order it to perform operations, although 'open zombies' have been known. They allow crackers other than the originator to locate zombie machines and use them for their own purposes without having to instigate the infection.

> Propagation phase: the operation of a piece of malware in which it infects other machines
>
> Payload phase: the operation of a piece of malware in which it performs its malicious intent

Now the originator has access to a possibly huge number of machines, until someone notices the infection and cleans it up or, at least, disconnects the machines from the Internet. What can the originator do with this resource? A recent worrying development in malware is an 'unholy alliance' between malware and spam (unwanted e-mail). Accounts sending large amounts of spam e-mails are now routinely shut down by ISPs (see real-time black-hole lists and other approaches in Chapter 13). Spammers have taken to using zombie machines to download spam contents and addresses and send large quantities of spam using the mail account of the infected user (or other users on the infected machine if they have elevated their privileges).

Sometimes malware continues to perform its operations until purged by the machine's owner. In other circumstances, it self-destructs, sometimes taking with it a great deal of the data on the infected system and in extreme cases even managing to damage some of the hardware attached to the system. In our scenario we assume that the zombie continues running until purged.

Primary internal effects

In using the e-mail system to propagate itself, the zombie uses substantial bandwidth which slows down legitimate network usage. While under external control any data held on the machine may be accessible to the zombie controller. If insufficient precautions have been taken to secure machines with personal data on them, this may violate 'due diligence' requirements (see Chapter 10) for avoiding prosecution under data protection laws (see Chapter 7) or may be a cause of action for a private prosecution under privacy policies. Data may be accessed using the zombie or personal information may be revealed in the attachments sent out as part of the propagation effort.

Primary external effects

During large scale infections by a new (or new variation of a) piece of malware, significant proportions of Internet traffic may be comprised of virus-propagation traffic (see `news.bbc.co.uk/1/hi/sci/tech/736208.stm`). The spam being sent is obviously an irritation at best and a significant problem at worst (see Chapter 13).

Secondary internal effects

In infecting a system, a piece of malware which hides itself by overwriting part of the operating system may well use a crippled or incompatible version of the file it replaces. During any use of the zombie to send spam e-mail, the machine may well be so slow at performing other operations, including network access, that it becomes useless for legitimate purposes. In response to both propagating and spam e-mails, bounces from invalid addresses and auto-filters for spam and viruses may overwhelm the user's inbox with automated responses (see Chapter 13 for further discussion of such effects).

Secondary external effects of scenario

Once the infection is noticed, the machine must be disconnected from any networks and may be unusable for hours or even days depending on the difficulty of identifying and removing the infection. At worst the hard drive of the machine may have to be completely wiped clean and the operating system and all data files reinstalled from scratch. If this happens then data may be lost because of lack of backup. In the case of a personal machine, original media may not be available for all the programs which came pre-installed on the machine (it is common for machines to ship with a limited range of original media for pre-installed software these days, or even none at all). If the retail supplier has gone out of business it may even be impossible to regain such software without paying for replacement copies.

Other Common Malware Operations and Their Effects

Denial of service attacks

Infected machines may be used to commit denial of service (DoS) attacks as a primary external effect. Where multiple machines are used this is called a distributed DoS (DDoS). One or more machines is used to send a constant stream of Internet packets to a particular machine.

A single infected machine is unlikely to be able to overwhelm another completely but there are technical tricks that can be applied to attempt this. Even in these circumstances however, a single source attack can be easily solved by blocking all incoming Internet traffic from that machine's IP address. Where a wide range of machines, possibly in many locations around the world, are involved in a DDoS, this can be much more difficult to block.

> Denial of service attack: a way of preventing an Internet-connected machine from pursuing its normal operation by overloading its network connection with spurious traffic
>
> Distributed denial of service attack: a denial of service attack from multiple sources

Where there are many infected machines attempting to propagate their infection, particularly within an organization with a global address book, a secondary external effect can be an inadvertent DDoS on internal or external mail servers receiving the propagation e-mails, simply because of the volume of e-mail messages being passed around the system. E-mail services may be brought to a halt as server disk space is overloaded and an entire network can become completely congested with nothing but propagation e-mail messages. A particularly difficult aspect of this for large organizations is that fixing of software problems is frequently done by network updates but a congested network may prevent this. Physical action is then required, such as switching off most of the machines on a network and only switching them back on a few at a time to allow for remote administration. More advanced malware may also turn off remote administration capabilities rendering this an even more difficult operation. Some potentially devastating malware programs have failed to create the effects their authors hoped for because of propagation efforts preventing newly infected machines from carrying out their payload phase.

Damage to hardware and software on the infected machine

A common payload of malware has the primary internal effect of deleting some or all the data on the hard drive of an infected machine. Sometimes this is a post-payload phase giving a secondary internal effect designed to remove evidence of how the malware infected the machine and precisely what it did while the infection was live. Depending on the security systems in place in the machine and on the level of privilege to which the malware has managed to gain access, this can be anything up to completely wiping the entire hard drive of the machine.

Other primary internal effects may include deleting all data files associated with one or more applications (such as all Microsoft Word files or all Adobe Photoshop files) or even replacing their contents with gibberish but leaving their size unchanged. Sophisticated malware may even be able to do this in a way which leaves any associated time stamps (time and date of last change to the file) unchanged as well. In some circumstances, it may even be possible to damage the hardware of an infected computer as well as the software on the hard drive (see details of the CIH (or Chernobyl) virus at `www.sophos.com/pressoffice/news/articles/2004/04/va_cihfive.html` for the first recorded example of this). Components including the drives and the motherboard of a machine can use re-writable firmware allowing for upgrades of the onboard driver software in case of bugs needing fixing or efficiency improvements becoming available. In other cases, certain sequences of commands sent to a piece of hardware can cause it to perform self-damaging operations. An example of this latter scenario is the possible incompatibility between graphics cards and monitors. Sending an image signal with too high a frequency refresh rate to some monitors can cause their converters to burn out trying to keep up with the signal. In some cases, malware can even embed itself in the firmware on the motherboard of a machine causing re-infection even if the hard drive is wiped or replaced.

> Firmware: the embedded programs in the chips on a circuit board, often capable of being updated as a complete program by a process called 'flashing'

Interference with operation

Some malware has as its primary internal effect an interference with certain operations. For instance, interfering with word-processing programs and causing random errors, crashes and erratic behaviour. Such infections can, at times, be indistinguishable from the normal operation of some unstable application software. Other interference operations cause random fluctuations in the screen settings or screen effects (similar to those used in some screensaver programs) such as the 'screen meltdown' effect where windows droop and 'melt' onto the bottom of the screen. Such operations are sometimes a secondary internal effect used to hide the payload or propagation phase by making the machine unusable, allowing the malware time to complete its operation.

Malware Authors: Who, How and Why?

Who?

Authors of malware have as wide a variety of motivations as crackers generally. There are two main categories into which we might put such people, however, which is 'creative malware programmers' and 'script kiddies'. The creative malware programmer is a highly skilled programmer who knows a great deal about the ways computer systems and networks operate and is simply putting those skills to use in what is usually regarded as an unethical (or even criminal) way. Script kiddies are those without great skills in programming who download malware from the Internet, make some minor alterations and start the distribution and infection process. Some script kiddies learn from the malware they download and watch how it operates and 'graduate' to becoming creative malware programmers but most indicators are that there are a great number of script kiddies who simply use what's available, the way joyriders steal and race other people's cars as opposed to hotrodders building or adapting their own machines (who may then misuse those machines by racing them on public streets). Script kiddies are typically young people (as the name might suggest) who are not yet in the labour market. They are usually from middle- or high-income backgrounds rather than poorer areas, but this is simply because access to computers and the Internet is more common among such groups. As access becomes more widespread it is likely that the backgrounds of script kiddies will broaden out. Creative malware writers come from a variety of backgrounds and may well be successful programmers in their day jobs.

How?

The creative malware programmer will use a variety of information sources and programming environments, including legitimate virus and vulnerability warning web sites and so on. See the Closed vs Open Security Debate section surrounding flaws in operating systems, which are applicable to both cracking and malware programming. To a great extent there is little to choose between the information sources used by creative malware programmers and ordinary programmers since malware is primarily just a way of spotting and misusing an unintentional feature of existing systems.

The operating methods of the script kiddies is a little more interesting, however. In computer science degrees there is a difficult circle to square in that the benefits of code re-use and the necessity of working in a programming team are stressed and yet sharing or copying programs is often regarded as plagiarism. Software engineering courses often bemoan the lack of code re-use and yet this is precisely what script kiddies do. Typically they source code fragments or even complete pieces of malware from the Internet (or individual transfers), make a few minor adjustments such as including their own messages and then 'release them into the wild' (i.e. inflict them on the world at large). Taking this a stage further there have even been programs that provide simple (graphical) interfaces to create and release malware. Such programs have been available since at least the early 1990s and a web search produces hundreds of thousands of hits for 'virus creation tools', of which an early hit links to a database (`vx.netlux.org`) of 127 different systems such as:

Bayros Virus Creation Kit

Author:Bayros

Author's notes: [BVCKIT] – Bayros Virus Construction Kit v1.0 is programmed and compiled in Turbo Pascal 7 with 146 lines .[BVCKIT] – Bayros Virus Creation Kit is being distributed as SHAREWARE. This does not mean it is free! If you use BVCKIT to develop software, you are required to register. Remember if you will not register this program the program itself will expire after 30 days. Thanks

Why?

Most script kiddies are typically young and disaffected. The thrill of doing something illicit can be as great or greater for the originator of a massive virus attack as for vandalizing some piece of public property or painting graffiti on a school wall. Creative malware programmers often have more complex motivations, ranging from boredom in a tedious day job or simply the challenge of writing the 'perfect' self-replicating program. Indeed the first recorded incident of a worm program on 3 November 1988 (`world.std.com/~franl/worm.html`) was a computer science student releasing a program onto his local network to see how it would work, replicating itself onto all the other machines on the local network. He was too 'good' a programmer, however and his creation quickly exceeded his ability to track and control its spread, getting out into other networks and causing a distinct slowdown of the already fairly slow networks in operation at the time, because of an inadvertent denial of service problem.

The concept of the self-replicating virus was put forward in an academic paper by Fred Cohen (a student of Professor Adleman, one of the creators of the RSA encryption algorithm) in 1984. Cohen conceived of a useful tool for building up ad hoc networks of interacting computers, in much the same way as the SETI@Home (`setiathome.berkeley.edu`) and cancer-busting (`www.grid.org/projects/cancer/faq.htm`) systems work voluntarily today, allowing 'spare cycles' of computing power and memory to be allocated to useful projects with little overhead. Even in 1984, however, Cohen recognized the potential dangers of computer viruses and his paper warns of the dangers of misuse.

Since few creators of such programs are ever caught we are reduced to believing what people who claim to be malware programmers say about themselves (mostly anonymously on online forums). Reported motivations range from trying to force users to abandon using Microsoft software by showing up its weaknesses to it being a joke that did not really do anyone any harm. There have been recent signs that organized crime and spam companies have been using malware and paying people to write them to achieve specific primary or secondary effects (see Chapter 13). We return to the subject of the motivations of computer criminals later when considering crackers.

Hoaxes and Life Imitating Art

As we mention in Chapter 13, one example of the 'e-mail circular' problem is virus-warning hoaxes. One of the most famous was the 'Good Times' hoax, first released in 1994 and regularly re-circulated for many years. This hoax claimed that simply opening an e-mail with the subject line 'GOOD TIMES' could perform all sorts of nasty operations on your machine and that you should delete the message unread. In 1994 there was no capability for such a virus to work in this way. The parsing of an e-mail message at that point was simply done by a text reader and there was no known way to use this to access the operating system (running attached binary files was a completely separate operation). People forwarding this hoax to knowledgeable friends were often derided for their credulous simplicity.

By the late 1990s Microsoft had included the rendering engine of the Internet Explorer web browser into their mail tool, Outlook Express. This rendering engine has had many vulnerabilities. There are other vulnerabilities based on embedded documents (for example, a section of a spreadsheet embedded in a word-processing file so that the full power of the spreadsheet can be used within the word processor without needing to open the spreadsheet application). Such vulnerabilities introduce the problem that simply opening the 'message' portion of an e-mail could allow infection by malware. See US-CERT Vulnerability Notification VU#932283 at `www.cert.org` for an example of such a vulnerability.

Besides the irony of a hoax threat becoming realized at a later date, hoaxes (or apparent hoaxes) do demonstrate two aspects which individually are pretty harmless, but which in aggregate cause harm (beyond the avalanche of unwanted e-mail discussed in Chapter 13). In the general case, hoax virus warnings desensitize non-expert users to the problem of malware. Having been bombarded with message after message about the hoax viruses, real warnings are then ignored. In the more specific case a hoax warning about a particular type or name of a virus can be released and then followed later by a real implementation. People receiving legitimate warnings about the actual virus may well ignore them because they've 'already seen the hoax'.

US Computer Emergency Response Team (US-CERT): a group that collates and distributes details of known threats and vulnerabilities in common software

COMPUTER SECURITY: COPS AND ROBBERS, POACHERS AND GAMEKEEPERS

So far we have covered what is primarily an autonomous crime once the malware is released although we briefly covered the use of malware as a form of cracking attack (zombies). Before covering the laws governing criminal misuse of computers we need to cover more human-directed interference. Despite the overlap in terms of zombies or use of other malware to allow cracking, the motivation of the cracker tends to be somewhat different from that of the malware creator. In this section, we cover some of the history of hacking as it relates to cracking, the motivations of crackers, some difficulties with definition and the economic and social consequences of unauthorized access to a machine.

Historical Roots of Cracking

The original hackers, as immortalized in the seminal book by Levy (1994), were primarily so-called because of their abilities to make the minicomputer do what they wanted it to do. The initial use of the term by the Internet and computer community in the 1960s and 1970s was a mark of respect for those with such skills. The use of the term by news organizations to describe those involved in gaining unauthorized access to a system led to the Hollywood film Hackers (which is about as accurate in its portrayal of computers and hackers as A Funny Thing Happened On the Way to the Forum is at depicting Roman daily life: any resemblance to facts living or dead is entirely coincidental).

However, the misuse of the term 'hacker' by the news media to describe cracking is not the whole story. At MIT, hacker was used as a modifier to describe being good at various technical things, including practical jokes (which persist to this day), such as the regular re-branding of the dome at MIT (`hacks.mit.edu`), and having a detestation of or at least contempt for barriers such as locks, 'Do Not Enter' signs and password-protected computer systems. Although modern-day hackers may dislike the use of the term by the media, there is at least an element of truth in it.

The 8.5-Second Crack

In 1999, a small group based in Russia, with helpers elsewhere, ran an 'Internet scanning project' designed to scan most computers connected to the Internet and test for 18 known flaws in their security. Details of the entire project can be found at `www.viacorp.com/auditing.html`. Various targets of their scan took exception to their poking and prying and responded in a number of different ways: a denial of service attack by an unhappy British target took down their small Russian ISP and e-mails from various places accused them of computer crime. The most interesting response, though, is what happened to one of their Japanese collaborator's machines: a Linux box running ssh and Apache only. Such a setup would ordinarily be thought to be fairly secure, since it had limited external access and was running a fair amount of automated cracking-detection software. Some unknown group managed to compromise this box and remove almost all trace of the fact that the system was compromised in just over eight seconds. The full sequence of events took longer than that since initial access to the system was gained through ssh using a legitimate user's account. The unknown attackers had tracked down an employee who connected to the machine from his home Microsoft Windows NT computer using ssh. They cracked his home computer first and monitored his ssh and ISP login details. A few days later the attack on the Linux box happened in the following way: login over ssh by the employee's ordinary ISP; execute a command with a known buffer overflow vulnerability and use that to gain root privileges; run a custom kernel module which masks other activity from the automated security checking software; install a 'backdoor' into the system, safe from the automated checking because of the kernel module, which masquerades commands as other types of network packet; close the original ssh session 8.5 seconds after it opened.

The Japanese group that was attacked were heavily paranoid about their security and it still took them days to realize their machine had been compromised and a great deal longer to track down what had happened. They never figured out where the attack originated since it was being perpetrated by a compromised computer in Australia over an anonymous international phone line for the initial ISP login.

Who are the Crackers?

Internal Threats

Contrary to the image of the hacker as a secretive figure connecting remotely to an organization's servers, most unauthorized access events are perpetrated by someone who works for the organization. The most common type of event is that of using the technical capability of accessing information, but outside the authorized purposes for doing so.

Consider the example of a bank. Almost all banks, for efficiency reasons, require employees to hold an account with them, into which their salary is paid. Even relatively low-level employees need access to account transactions to perform their allocated jobs but to do this they must effectively be given access to all accounts. This includes the accounts of the workforce and so 'window shopping' to check up on the salaries of one's manager's or the senior executives is easily achieved. So long as such employees have been given appropriate training on what their job entails and the fact that accessing account details to satisfy curiosity is not allowed, then they are definitely committing an offence, under UK computer misuse laws, of unauthorized access to information (such access would also be a violation of data protection legislation within the EU and in a number of other countries as well). Whether or not it is possible to track such usage depends on many factors but it is technically against the law.

Even where an employee does not have (or need) access to certain information, there are two other reasons why employee cracking is more common than external attacks. These are trust and access. It is much easier for employees to access information about what systems are running and what security policies are in force and they are well placed to have a significant amount of background information available which makes social engineering attacks easier. In addition, many organizations' computer networks have a much higher level of trust attached to internal machines than to connections coming in from external sources (see the 'Walking the Tightrope' section later in this chapter). Thus an employee is already on a higher step within the 'security pyramid' than an external attacker. In some cases, the security of an organization is so poor that simply being any level of employee potentially allows access to the most sensitive data held by that organization.

External Threats

Although internal attacks are more common, external attacks do represent a significant problem for an organization's systems security. Not all crackers are malevolent, however, though where one draws the line between legal and illegal, ethical and unethical, may vary.

White hat

So-called 'white hat crackers' are experts in intrusion and defence technologies and methods. They are individuals or organizations employed to attack a system using the same means as malevolent or 'black hat crackers' but who are doing so to test and improve the security of the system. Their activities are usually carried out with due regard to avoiding damage to the normal operation of the employing organization, although occasional negative consequences cannot be avoided entirely. Given that the attackers are known quantities and that it is expected that they will be amenable to abandoning the attack or helping to fix any problems, the potential downside of a white hat attack are often thought to be less problematic than leaving the system unchecked for vulnerabilities.

Grey hat

Some people do not regard 'grey hat' as a valid designation, categorizing all crackers as white or black depending on their point of view. Grey hat cracking is similar to white hat, in that the aim is to identify potential vulnerabilities and inform the organization of their weaknesses. The difference from white hat attacks, however, is that grey hat attacks are not requested by the target. Grey hat crackers are enthused by the challenge and do not intend any harm. Many computer scientists go through a grey hat phase at some point in their lives, often limited to their educational establishment's network. Some of the more enlightened system administrators, where it is plain that no damage has been done, will not seek punishment for grey hat attacks, although they do not often welcome such attacks. Some regard such attacks as no different from black hat attacks and have even sought criminal prosecution against grey hat attackers. Although a relatively extreme position, there are reasons for not regarding grey hat attacks as ethical, given that unintended consequences are much more likely than with white hat attacks, since there is no agreement on how and when to halt the attack should disastrous consequences ensue. Committed grey hat crackers maintain that without their subversive activities the level of security in the commercial world would be much poorer and that they perform a service for which the companies they attack should be seeking them out and thanking them, since every loophole closed is one fewer vulnerability to a black hat attack. See the Tati vs Kitetoa case study in Chapter 1 for an example of grey hat cracking.

Black hat

One might think that black hat cracking is an unequivocally immoral action. However, depending on the target, the purpose and the fact that misusing technical abilities is unethical, some might argue that higher moral purposes can sometimes be served by black hat cracking. Such cracking involves gaining unauthorized access and trying to do something with it. In some cases this is done for the sheer joy of breaking in and the activity is simply the cracker's way of putting graffiti where he should not have been able to be. In more sinister cases, however, the hacking is committed in the furtherance of other criminal activity, ranging from accessing information to committing fraud to vandalism by deleting data (to much the same end as the malware creator may take pleasure in the chaos resulting from their activities). In the case of cracking, however, the activity is much more focused and the cracker has a direct link and a greater degree of control over the consequences of their actions (absent unforeseen side effects). So if the actions committed once access is obtained are criminal and the unauthorized access itself is also criminal, then how could any act of black hat cracking be regarded as moral? This comes under the same heading as other technically illegal actions that generally come under the banner of 'direct action'. In real-world terms such actions range from disrupting deliveries by lying down in the vehicle entrance to a site, to breaking and entering to obtain documents showing illegal pollution. We can identify similar levels of action online, from cracking a company's web site to protest their actions by replacing their web site with criticism (this has happened to both the Labour and Conservative political parties in the United Kingdom in recent years) to cracking a company server to obtain documents showing illegal pollution. Such online versions of direct action are sometimes referred to as 'hacktivism'. Since they are carried out with a plain intent to harm the victim (even if some might see the harm as justified) this is definitely black hat cracking, however immoral the actions being protested or the site being defaced. A claim that web defacement hacktivism is simply exercise of freedom of speech ignores the fact that it is easy to put up one's own information on the Web, although there are sometimes difficulties in doing so (see Chapter 4) or in using an appropriate URL (see Chapter 6).

Princeton Cracks Yale Admissions System

In the summer of 2002, a scandal developed when student admissions officers from Princeton revealed to their Yale counterparts that the Yale site for applicants was rather insecure (`www.theregister.co.uk/2002/07/26/princeton_hacks_yale_admissions_site`). The Yale site allowed applicants to 'log in' using their name, date of birth and social security number. All of this information was on every application the students made and so for 11 students who applied to both Yale and Princeton, the admissions officers in Princeton used that information (which after all is only semi-secret) to access records on the Yale system. Once Yale systems administrators were informed they were able to identify 18 different incidents of access from Princeton administrators' computers to the 11 students' records. Stephen LeMeneger, the manager of the Princeton admissions office was suspended during an investigation. He claimed that the accesses were solely designed to check the vulnerability of Yale's system and that there was no malicious intent (such as checking the details of admission offers at Yale or using other confidential information to boost Princeton's chances of attracting the students). Yale reported the incident to the FBI who investigated the matter. Although no criminal charges were brought, LeMeneger lost his job over the scandal. This was one of the most widely reported cases of 2002. Security analysts' online reporting focused as much on the minimal security of the Yale system as on the legal and ethical question of the Princeton employee's actions. The news value of the story, already high because of the involvement of senior officials from an Ivy League University, was also increased by allegations that one of the students whose records were accessed was that of President Bush's niece Lauren.

Vulnerability, Risk and Threat

Technical Vulnerability

In the early days of computing and the Internet, computers were generally open in many ways. Password systems were rare and even where remote access was possible, the number and type of connected systems was highly constrained. Even when individual accounts on real-time systems were introduced, an honour system was far more in evidence than any strong password encryption. Richard Stallman (described by Levy as 'the last great hacker', though this is often disputed by others) led a campaign at MIT to use 'carriage return' (i.e. no password) or one of a small number of known words. Such naïveté and honour could not last, of course and the concepts of e-commerce, online banking and similar modern Internet applications would be complete non-starters without a password system.

When physical access to a mainframe system was needed to run programs and when data was held on cabinets full of punched cards, the most important element of computer systems security was locking the building at night and employing a guard to patrol the building. Once computers became networked and home machines with modems became common, the level of system security needed to be tightened up. As we discuss in the 'Walking the Tightrope' section, however, some aspects of systems security must be weighed against the cost of implementation. This is not a book on computer security and so we do not go into great detail about the types of vulnerability and how to combat them, but we simply consider the sorts of problems that exist and their real-world consequences.

The basic concept of a password is simple: you have a one-way function, give it the correct input and it matches the stored output. Give it any other input and it does not match. Because the function is one way, it is extremely expensive to figure out the correct input for a given output. This system relies on a 'law of large numbers' in that given enough possible combinations of inputs it would take longer than is feasible to try out every single one. If, however, the range of possible inputs is known to be limited, the number of possibilities that need checking can be considerably reduced. One simple reduction is trying dictionary words, rather than all possible combinations of letters and numbers. As we see in the next section, however, the obvious solution to this (banning the small proportion of possible passwords which consist of dictionary words) has social consequences when taken to its logical extreme. Such consequences may not only be undesirable in and of themselves, they may also undermine the supposed gain in security that they are meant to produce and they are based on the problem that people are part of the security of any system and in many cases they are the weakest link in the security chain. Forgetting that people are part of the system is a major flaw in any system design.

The Weakest Link: Social Engineering

The infamous cracker Kevin Mitnick says that he never employed a password-cracking tool in his years of breaking into other people's systems. Besides his undoubted technical abilities to understand how complex systems such as the phone network could be exploited using simple techniques, Mitnick's strongest weapon in attempting to access systems is his ability to get people to tell him what he needs to know. System security is not about an impenetrable wall around a system with complete access on the inside and complete invulnerability on the outside. It is more a series of steps which it is difficult, but not impossible, to surmount. Whether it is escalating privileges or figuring out a password, there is often a series of small steps which, when put together, achieve the goal. Although each small step seems perfectly innocent, or at worst a minor problem, it is the combination of steps that is the vulnerability.

Social engineering is a huge topic, not only of interest to crackers of computer systems but to anyone with a desire for knowledge that is not readily available. The principle is based on the fact that most people really want to help their fellows, provided they trust them and that far too many are easily persuaded into trust. Mitnick and Simon (2002) uses social engineering scenarios to illustrate this, showing how apparently innocuous information provision (sometimes simply confirming information the questioner already has, or appears to have) builds up to a dangerous breach. However, such elaborate pyramid schemes may not always be necessary to obtain the information desired. On two recent occasions, there have been 'public surveys' on computer security issues. Everyone will have seen the 'clipboard in the street' survey asking random strangers for 'a few minutes of their time' for an important survey. In this case, the survey was about computer security and among the 20 or so questions were included the name of the firm the person worked for and enough information to derive their username and password, sometimes explicitly, sometimes by two or three questions. Until it was pointed out at the end of the interview, few seemed aware that they were giving away such vital security information. Under the guise of checking the usage of common words and easily guessed mnemonics as work (or online) passwords, the interviewer would ask questions such as:

'Is your password a common name or word from the dictionary?'
'What word is it?'

If the bold approach did not work, many of those interviewed would still reveal it in the space of a few questions:

'Is your password the name of one of your children?'

...

'What are your children's names?'

In the first survey, respondents were willing to reveal their password simply on the offer of a free pen for taking part in the survey. The later survey involved slightly higher bribery, giving a free chocolate egg, since it was being conducted in the run up to Easter. (See `www.theregister.co.uk/2003/04/18/office_workers_give_away_passwords` and `www.theregister.co.uk/2004/04/20/password_surveys` for details.)

When senior managers are willing to reveal their passwords to a complete stranger at Waterloo rail station, it appears that all the technical security measures in the world will never be enough to provide even halfway decent security in most firms. Ignoring the technical aspects of security, however, is not a particularly sensible option either. Education of the workforce (including those in charge) about the reasons for security policies and the sensitivity of password and access information must go hand in hand with technical measures to ensure proper security.

Closed vs Open Security

Responsible Disclosure

There is a big debate among the computer-security and vulnerability-tracking community about the correct way to treat vulnerability information. When a new exploit is discovered by an ethical person the correct ethical response is obviously to inform the company that produced the software about the problem. The question is whether anyone else should be told about the problem and, if so, then in how much detail. The US-CERT (`www.cert.org`) is one of the best-known computer-security clearing houses. Now part of the US Department of Homeland Security (`www.dhs.gov`), CERT's role is to assess the level of threat (how dangerous is an exploit to systems which are exposed) and risk (how likely is it that a vulnerability will be exploited) and advise interested parties of their analysis. Even the experts at a place like CERT disagree about the best policy on disclosure of vulnerability information. With closed-source software, the users of the software are generally dependent on the originator to produce a security bug fix. If the vulnerable software is vital to a business they have little option but to continue to run it even with the vulnerability, although extra monitoring might reduce the threat this poses. But what should an ethical engineer do if the software producer fails to produce a fix in a reasonable length of time? The vulnerability exists but it is possible they are the only person outside the program production company who knows of its existence. Revealing the vulnerability has two potential benefits: wider publicity might force the program production company to give it a higher priority and makes system administrators aware of the problem. Depending on the type of vulnerability, they have a number of options open to them before a patch is available: if the service affected is not mission-critical they might simply take it offline (or make it available only on request for limited times); if it is mission-critical, then they can set up extra monitoring to check if attacks are being made against the vulnerability and manually deny access where possible. On the other hand, black hat crackers also monitor the Internet for such announcements and publicizing the vulnerability informs them that it is there for the exploitation. Another touchy subject is the release of sample vulnerability exploitation code. People who release such code claim that they are providing a useful service for system administrators to check their own systems for vulnerability, including checking that a so-called patch from the software vendor fixes the bug.

Chapter 10 includes an interesting case study ('Vulnerability of E-mail', on page 335) where a former employee of an ISP publicly revealed a flaw in their so-called secure e-mail service because it had not been fixed within six months. He was charged with offences under the US computer misuse laws since his actions 'impaired the operation of' the company's servers. His conviction was later overturned but this further enflamed the debate about responsible disclosure. All sorts of possible fixes to this problem have been proposed, including 'closed' distribution lists for vulnerability information. However, as we point out in Chapters 12 and 4, it is difficult, if not impossible, to restrict the distribution of digital information.

Security of Open Source and Closed Source Software

A parallel debate goes on about the relative merits of open source (or free) software and closed source (or proprietary) software in terms of its security. Some open source advocates argue that 'to many eyes, all bugs are shallow': where enough people have access to the source code then whenever a bug is found a fix will be found quickly since there are many people looking for a way to fix it (while retaining the correct functionality). Closed source proponents argue that access to the source code can mean that 'to many eyes, all vulnerabilities are shallow' and that crackers with access to the source code are more likely to be able to find vulnerabilities and exploit them to their full potential. Empirical measurement of these two arguments is difficult given the different numbers and types of systems using the two different models. Although it is true that many fewer viruses have been written and released for Linux than for Windows systems, this remains true for other types of Unix which are often closed source. The identification and exploitation of vulnerabilities in Windows is at least as much about the monoculture (of both application and operating system software) as it is about the quality of the system. And given that most cracks and viruses attack known vulnerabilities for which patches have been released, the problem is now more one of automatically patching systems while retaining quality of service for the user (and keeping the cost of system administrator time down) than it is of finding the vulnerability or of finding the fix once the vulnerability is identified.

Monoculture

Microsoft Windows, in its various flavours (95, 98 (inc SE and ME), NT, 2000, Server 2003, XP and Vista) runs on the vast majority of personal computers. More personal computers are permanently connected to the Internet as home 'always-on' broadband connections become the norm rather than the exception. It is this fact, more than any other, which leads to the pre-eminence of Microsoft products in both the number of vulnerabilities identified and the number of exploitations occurring. When faced with a choice of being able to attack (with malware or a cracking attack) 80% or more of the Internet's machines or fewer than 10%, most computer criminals will go for the biggest and easiest target. It is also obvious that where there are more machines vulnerable there are more that will fall to a particular problem (particularly where self-replicating malware is the problem).

Besides the operating system monoculture, Microsoft's success in promoting its applications (Word, Excel, Outlook, Outlook Express, etc.) has created a monoculture of applications as well as a monoculture of operating systems. This provides an easy and obvious path for the criminal to take. In addition, since the software vendor for operating system and applications is the same, there is much more evidence of reuse of highly complex code between the operating system and applications and between different applications. Rather than developing a proper standard for the transfer of data between applications, when you own the desktop and both applications, it is easier for the programming team to provide a messy pass-through of data and cross-calls of subroutines than to define clean application programming interfaces (APIs) and use them. It has even been alleged (in the Department of Justice vs Microsoft antitrust case) that Microsoft deliberately obscured such interfaces to prevent third-party software developers from gaining suitable access to operating system or application calls. Deliberately obscure interfaces are much more likely to contain vulnerabilities than cleanly defined ones.

This is not to say that the open source software community are necessarily Less-Holey-Than Microsoft when it comes to producing clean APIs and not using fast-and-dirty programming tricks to get faster, more efficient or easier to program code. However, the variation and customization of personal systems running Linux and Unix do provide a double protection, particularly against malware. Any exploit is likely to be specific to a small number of the many possible choices of application software and thus, even where a vulnerability exists, both the number of potential targets and the routes for multiplication of exploited systems is much reduced. Particularly in the case of malware, the spread of such problems (and the secondary impact on the Internet generally) is not linearly connected to the number of vulnerable systems on the Internet: it is proportional either to the square of the number of systems or to the factorial of the number of systems (depending on the particular method of exploitation). Slower spread of self-replicating malware also gives a chance for the defences against it (virus signatures and security patches) more time to spread as well.

Given these problems, the sensible person might ask why the monoculture is allowed to flourish? The main reason is efficiency; the secondary one is successful marketing. It is usually more efficient for one company to have a single or small number of systems running on their machines. It also cannot be denied that Microsoft have convinced the world that they are the best choice all around. Although this latter might change with Linux being seen as a significant challenger to Microsoft's desktop dominance (having already cracked the server market to a great extent), if one (or a small number of highly similar) Linux desktop installations are installed around the world and connected to the Internet the same monoculture problem may well rear its ugly head in the open source world. Such a problem can already be seen with the Apache open source web server which is attacked more often and has been subject to just as many vulnerabilities as Microsoft's IIS system. Debates about the relative security of the two systems can be found on almost any system administrator discussion board, featuring many of the arguments from this section and the previous one.

Security by Obscurity

A number of the issues above can be thought of as using the model of 'security through obscurity', from the closed source argument to the non-disclosure argument. In the early days of remote connections to computer systems by telephone lines, many systems did not attempt to put password protection on the dial-up connection: indeed on some of them, such facilities were not available or at least were not standard parts of the system. The method used to keep such systems secure was to keep the phone number secret (or at least obscure). This is such an obvious security loophole that these days it is strange to even think that anyone could believe this was reasonable. The concept of war-dialling was born, whereby a computer with a modem randomly, or following some pre-determined sequential list, dialled telephone numbers, ringing off once connected unless it got a modem response it recognized. In many cases, large firms simply had their dial-up lines connected to the next available socket or number in their internal system which had sequential direct-dial numbers; by starting with their switchboard number and going through the system, war-diallers could eventually connect to an insecure connection giving full access to the computer provided a suitable terminal program was working on the dialling machine.

> War-dialling: the practice of randomly or sequentially dialling phone numbers to see if an unprotected computer is attached to them

Once passwords and similar security measures were instituted, war-dialling became much less useful for crackers. Once many local networks started being attached to the Internet with little in the way of discrimination between internal and external information requests, war-scanning of random or sequential Internet numbers became a more favoured technique. Even now, port-scanning a set of Internet addresses is a popular pastime for crackers looking for vulnerable machines and many properly secured systems will flag up a sequence of apparently innocuous requests as a potential cracking attack. Over-reaction to this can cause problems occasionally, as can be seen in the '8.5-Second Crack' case study above.

The most recent development in this area is war-walking (or, occasionally now, war-driving), to search for wireless network systems without adequate (or, in many cases, any) security restrictions on connection have been installed. Given the well-known war-dialling problem from the early days of remote access it is perhaps surprising that wireless networking was developed and installed in many companies without much in the way of simple, easy-to-configure security available. Companies who thought their networks had a secure firewall protecting them from the Internet have installed wireless network systems to enable employees with laptops to connect from any room in the building (some addicted technophiles even taking their Internet connections with them to the lavatories). Suddenly anyone with a laptop and a wireless connection can happily surf their intranet and the Internet from the café on the street outside their offices.

> War-walking or -driving: the identification of unsecured wireless networking connections by running a computer or dedicated device in potential locations

Not all war-walking is necessarily illegal or even immoral given that some socially-minded (or is that socialist-minded?) technophiles have installed their own deliberately open wireless connections for the use of anyone walking by. In parts of major cities such as London and New York, one can find arcane chalk or paint marks on the pavements and walls indicating the appropriate settings for open-access wireless networking. Of course whether such networks are deliberately open or by oversight can be a source of problems for the innocent Internet-junkie looking for a fix in a strange city.

Walking the Tightrope: Social Pressures on Security

The issues raised about the dangers of computer crime can tend to make one believe that system administrators are just not doing their jobs properly by allowing such dangerous states of affairs to continue. In this section, we look at the reasons why security is not tighter in many companies. Following this we briefly look at a model of security which allows reasonable risk and threat assessment: the pyramid approach.

Usability, Accessibility, Security

The reason computers are everywhere is that they are useful and convenient. Part of this utility is their usability and accessibility. Unfortunately, in some cases usability or accessibility are in direct conflict with security. Consider the simple example of passwords. A password is one of the simplest levels of security possible and probably the easiest to implement. However, it has significant vulnerabilities. Passwords rely on encryption functions (see Chapter 7 for more details on one-way functions and encryption). The longer a single password is in use the more likely that an attacker will be able to break it.

Whole dictionaries of common words and short phrases in use as passwords have already been cracked. This is quite easy: pass the word through the encryption system being used and check to see if the encrypted version is the same (for systems where the encrypted version of the file is available for some reason). Even where the encrypted version of the password file is not available, automated systems can run through a dictionary of thousands of words in minutes if the system attacked is not set up to detect this. So, a system administrator will want to prevent users from using common words in their password.

The best passwords are strings of unconnected letters, numbers and punctuation. However, such passwords are also difficult for humans to remember. If a system administrator enforces a system in which passwords must be difficult to remember, users will write them down. It is amazing how many passwords can be found on self-adhesive notes or scraps of paper stuck to monitors, under keyboards or in desks. Although the password '£%Kd*3gW' may well be relatively secure from a brute force cracking attack using a dictionary encoder, it is so difficult to remember that it is likely to be stuck on the side of the screen for all to see, including a courier delivering a package. Frequent renewal of passwords and a restriction on reuse, although highly desirable from a technical point of view for the reasons mentioned above, are also liable to make passwords difficult to remember and cause people to write them down.

Such problems are also often at the root of issues such as open database proxies, open access wireless networks, and so on. Another problem is the overworked, underpaid, constantly harassed systems administrator. They are not likely to be checking their system for vulnerabilities, keeping up with the CERT list or instituting difficult-to-use security features on the system as all this just increases their workload. Where their performance-related pay involves meeting 'quality of service' targets which require constant availability rather than security, the natural inclination of even the most ethical system administrator is to let things slide and make it easy for the users to get what they want, while praying that the crackers and malware writers never knock on the door (security by obscurity, again).

The Pyramid Approach

Much of the coverage in this chapter so far might make it seem that nothing will ever be secure and therefore there's no point in even trying, so one might as well just sit back and hope for the best. Nothing could be further from the truth. The real way to approach security is to do cost–benefit analyses, have policies which are actually put into practice and be aware of the whole issue. As mentioned above, cracking systems is not usually a means of finding a single crack through which a system is broken wide open at the first attempt. More normally, it is a sequence of steps: gain access to a network through a badly configured firewall; gain access to an ordinary user's account through poor password security; gain power user status through a misconfigured database server; gain access to the web server administration account through an unpatched vulnerability in the web server software; use the administrator privilege on that machine through poor privilege management across the network to gain top-level access to the machine that is the real target. This is sometimes called the 'pyramid cracking approach': each step in the chain gains more access and each by itself might not seem like such a problem. The aim of security is to block as many routes to the top as is feasible while maintaining usability. There are a variety of possible blocks at the bottom, some technological (installing and maintaining proper firewall software) and some social (explaining the necessity of a good password procedure to staff and ensuring that writing down passwords for all to see is a disciplinary offence).

The pyramid approach to security aims to give attention to each of the levels in the pyramid and identify suitable actions in each case. Where the security measures at a particular level place an unacceptable burden on the organization, a trade may be made by spending more effort on 'connected blocks' which have less impact on the overall usability of the system while providing roughly similar levels of protection to an escalating attack.

In all of this, due diligence must be applied to ensuring compliance with suitable standards. For instance focussing on denying write access to a database holding stock information may be worth spending much more effort on than preventing read-only access to the same database in some circumstances. However, for a database containing customer details, data protection legislation or regulations may well dictate that equal attention is given to preventing read access to the information by unauthorized persons (see Chapter 7).

Finally, there is a well-known triad of security access controls: something you know, something you have and something you are. Identification systems frequently use two of these in tandem to provide access: a swipe card (something you have) and a PIN (something you know) to access a building or a bank account; a passport (something you have) with a photograph (something you are). The more secure the system being protected the more levels of protection are put in place. The most secure building and computer systems in the world use multiple variants of all three to gain access: a swipe card with photo, a PIN and an iris scan. This is good for physical access control, but generally remote access over the Internet is controlled solely by a password mechanism, although security 'dongles' which attach to a particular port and contain encrypted challenge–response firmware are not unknown for high security systems to which remote access is required.

How Much Security Is Necessary?

Almost everyone who has remotely logged in to a computer system will have seen a message such as 'This system is for authorized users only. If you are not authorized by Organization X to access this computer, disconnect now'. What purpose does such an announcement play? Surely anyone with a username and password knows that they have legitimate access and that anyone coming in by other means is cracking? In some cases any access to a system produces such a warning. There are two purposes to such announcements: the legal and the social. The social aspect is to make people aware that they might be committing an offence if they are not socially authorized to use the system even if they have technical authorization. Without such a warning someone who has been given (or found) the username and password details to a system might legitimately claim that they believed their access was reasonable. This leads to the legal reasoning for such warnings. If an 'innocent mistake' is possible then courts generally do not convict defendants, since criminal convictions must be 'beyond reasonable doubt' and the possibility of an innocent misunderstanding is often enough to create reasonable doubt. Putting such warnings on the screen every time a system is accessed removes that defence since it is made clear that access to the system is restricted and not open.

Before the spread of significant open-access information servers (usenet, gopher, veronica, archie, anonymous file transfer protocol (FTP) and, finally, the Web), access to a machine required a deliberate act. Once general information services became prevalent, however, the problem of the extent to which information which was 'apparently open' should be regarded as 'truly open' developed and the problem of easy cracking came up: information servers run as root on Unix machines used standard tools such as 'more' to page through information with more lines than the terminal accessing it. Unfortunately (for security) these standard paging mechanisms included commands allowing a user to 'break out' into a normal shell. Such commands have a general-utility purpose when used normally, allowing other things to be done although saving one's place in the file. However, since root had run the paging process the shell obtained gave root access on the host machine. It is difficult to define this legally as cracking a system since the intent and level of knowledge of both the user and the information provider have to be considered in proving that it was reasonable for the user to know that the information provider had not intended such access to be granted and that the user intended to (or did) use the system for something which was illegal.

Two more modern problems mirror this early difficulty: open proxies and deep linking.

Open Proxies

Modern database systems are designed and programmed to be used as servers and allow access to the local database over a network. Unfortunately, in the name of 'ease of use' some of the systems come automatically configured to allow access to any machine on the network. Where a machine is either directly or indirectly connected to the Internet this sometimes means access to the database is open to everyone in the world, by default. Many smaller companies do not employ fully qualified (i.e. expensive), full-time system administrators. Under-qualified personnel running databases the world over are leaving such database settings open to the world. There are more complicated scenarios and technical details to this but since this is not a textbook on database administration we will leave those complexities to one side.

For our purposes, the scenario described here is sufficient to demonstrate the problem: since the Internet is basically an information transfer system with secure protection on valuable or secret information sources is it an offence against computer misuse to find and examine open information sources? The modern Web would not work without the search engines which automatically download, copy and index the massive amounts of information available. So, how can it be an offence to simply read information which is clearly open? How is it the responsibility of the passer-by to avert their eyes from the contents of a room in a house with no curtains on it? To use an analogy from physical property: an open gate (or just a gap) might be taken as implicit permission to pass through a fence into a field at that point; however, an open front door does not present implicit permission to enter the building and start rifling through personal letters. The law in these areas is grey and, as mentioned above, depends on proving intent and knowledge on behalf of the person accessing the information. This is not a case of 'ignorance of the law being no defence' but of 'ignorance of the system administrator's intent' being a reasonable defence. Evidence of activity indicating that the discovery was not inadvertent, such as scanning a set of IP numbers belonging to a particular organization's Internet-connected machines, looking for open proxies, rather than simply identifying one by 'accident' while pursuing legitimate information, is generally the pivotal point in proving criminal intent in such cases. The most sensible route of course, is to 'lock the door before the horse gets into the field', that is, to ensure that open proxy servers are not running on an organization's network and that appropriate fences, signposts, doors and walls are in place such that 'innocent mistake' defences are no longer viable should anyone enter without permission.

> Open proxy: a system connected to the Internet which allows forwarding of connections to an intranet service not generally accessible to machines on the Internet

The Deep-linking Controversy

Although open proxies involve a grey area which seems to many to make deliberate unauthorized reading of information barely lawful, there is a similar issue at stake with large web sites where other sites use the hyperlinking and formatting capabilities of the Web to create sites which link to, or include, parts of other web sites. There are two aspects to this which we shall consider in turn. The interesting thing about the legal controversy here is that it is exactly the things which make the Web work (hyperlinking and variable formatting) that create the so-called problem. The reason the Web took off and created a demand for personal access to the Internet in a way which FTP, e-mail, simple mail transfer protocol (SMTP) and other earlier information protocols did not, was the combination of reasonable formatting independent of local display and the power of hyperlinking.

Simple deep linking

'Deep linking' is alien to the 'pure' concept of the Web. It assumes that a web site is a self-contained database which should only be accessed by the top page and 'drilling down' to individual articles in exactly the way that the designer and administrator of the site intended. It ignores the basic fact that putting information on the Web without restricted access basically puts everything equally 'at the surface' of the server. The thought processes of those complaining about deep linking are locked into a twentieth century mindset of ownership not only of the information but of the way it is presented and viewed.

One organization creates a web site and designs it so that one enters at the top page, performs a search or selects a subject and is guided to the information they want while constantly downloading advertising (which pays the bills) in the process. Another organization has people submitting interesting news stories and uses links on its web site to guide people directly to the web pages containing the relevant stories. Some people (often the majority) go only to the second site and see only the single page from the first site in which they are interested, by using a so-called deep link. There have been court cases brought to prevent such deep linking but in general they have been dismissed, providing that there is no obvious attempt to reformat the remote page or to pass off its content as one's own.

Framing external sources

The framing, or more recently the complete reformatting, of external pages has been more controversial than simply deep linking. In general, the case against deep linking is weak. After all, the viewer is being 'sent' to your site, but directly to where they're interested in going. With framing, this becomes more problematic because individual pages of another site are surrounded by the identifying marks of linking site, possibly a rival. This first came to prominence with the case of the Shetland Times and the Shetland News (see `www.netlitigation.com/netlitigation/cases/shetland.htm`), rival news organizations in the Shetland Islands. The Shetland News included headlines from the Shetland Times as the text of hyperlinks to

Shetland Times articles. The links were 'embedded frame' links such that the article from the Shetland Times could appear to some as a Shetland News article. In particular, the advertising that supported the Shetland Times did not necessarily appear. Unfortunately for lawyers interested in having a court decision in these cases, it was settled out of court and thus a judgement creating precedent was not handed down.

The present and future of the Web and computer crime

Recent developments in web browser standards provide even more difficulties in deciding who owns small pieces of text and who can do what with the formatting and appearance of a deeply linked page. The separation of formatting and content into style sheet and content pages and the embedding of content into more easily reformatted XML content, have all produced further controversy. What is most clear is that the areas of computer crime, intellectual property and business models for information provision are all in a chaotic state of flux and are interrelated subjects.

Poachers and Gamekeepers

The employment of former crackers (sometimes ones with significant criminal records) is an ethical dilemma for many organizations. To protect themselves against attack, one way of proceeding is to hire someone who has both the technical skills and knows the mindset of the crackers trying to get in. However, cracking is (generally) illegal and one wonders if crackers should be rewarded by receiving significant salaries for using their knowledge to ward against people just like they used to be, particularly when it must be considered that a significant part of their experience was gained in illicit activities.

This ethical dilemma is not unique to computer crime. For centuries, the concept of employing a local poacher as the gamekeeper has been the standard way of preventing too much poaching. On the other hand those with significant criminal records are barred from becoming police officers in most of the industrialized world, to reduce corruption within the police force.

However, there are just not enough people with the skills needed, as can be seen by the number of grey hat or (hopefully former) black hat crackers who are employed by companies large and small and even by law enforcement agencies to advise them on computer crime. When you have to get the information from somewhere and the only source is from the criminals then legitimate authorities hold their noses and cooperate with the 'lesser evil'. On a larger scale, the US Witness Protection programme, protects many former gangster who themselves have committed significant amounts of violent crimes, because their testimony can be used to break large gangs and put not only the lower levels in prison but those organizing things as well.

One encouraging note for the future of this is that law enforcement agencies are turning to expert external companies and employing civilian experts of their own more and more these days, for all sorts of specialist work such as forensic examinations and this trend includes aspects of computer crime. The rise in formal training in computer security is also a cause for optimism that fewer former crackers will be turning security guru.

LAWS AGAINST COMPUTER MISUSE

As mentioned in Chapter 1 and other chapters, the laws in many places related to computer and communications issues frequently lag behind the technological development until some major incident forces action. In terms of computer crime, however, we are long past that point and most of the industrialized world has laws against many aspects of computer misuse. These laws are mostly aimed at the primary effects of computer misuse and other laws are used to cover the secondary aspects such as violation of privacy, fraud, and so on, which may result from the misuse. These laws are primarily aimed at the direct cracking effort, although they can be used against malware creators as well in most cases. There are some significant doubts as to how well they are suited to dealing with (D)DoS attacks, although since the perpetrators of such attacks are incredibly difficult to identify, how to prosecute them has so far been less of a problem. As always, it would be impossible to cover all the different laws on this topic in all the jurisdictions of the world, so we present the UK and US laws as well as the fairly recent Council of Europe Convention on Cybercrime, which despite its European origins includes other major industrialized nations (the United States, Canada, Japan and South Africa) among its signatories as well as 32 countries in the Council of Europe. The success of such a treaty shows how seriously the problems of computer crime are being taken by governments.

UK Computer Misuse Act

Before the Computer Misuse Act (CMA) 1990 came into force in the United Kingdom, it was almost impossible to convict someone of computer crime. Crime using a computer was prosecuted under the appropriate offence, such as fraud or theft but, until the CMA, the only methods of prosecution were under analogies to physical property laws such as trespass or convoluted concepts such as theft of electricity. To rectify this situation the CMA defines three types or levels of offence related to unauthorized access to a computer system.

Unauthorized Access to Data

Note that the offence is unauthorized access to data, not unauthorized access to the system. Although this means that simply breaking in to a system and then immediately logging out would not be a crime, it is a crime to view data on a system to which you have access (and possibly even technologically unfettered access to the data) if you are aware you should not be accessing that data. As we said above when discussing computer security generally, misuse by a member of an organization is at least as much, if not more, of a problem as external attacks. The maximum penalty for violation of this clause is six months' imprisonment and a £2000 fine.

It should be noted that even though this law was enacted in 1990, only a single case had gone to a jury trial by 2004. All other cases were either dropped by prosecutors for lack of evidence or the obvious innocence of the accused, or the accused pleaded guilty without a trial (often asking for multiple other cracking offences to be taken into account in sentencing). In the case that went to trial, the jury accepted the defendant's claim that his computer was under the control of other unknown crackers who had installed a zombie on his machine and used it as an intermediate hop point and who caused the zombie to self-delete after the attack but before the accused was arrested. Although this is not an unknown tactic the interesting thing about this case was that the jury believed this defence despite significant expert evidence on the prosecution side indicating a lack of any evidence of such a 'self-deleting zombie' infection or indeed any experience that such things were in circulation at all. (See `www.bcs.org/server.php?show=ConWebDoc.6232` for some discussion of these issues.)

Unauthorized Access with Intent to Commit or Allow Further Offences

The 'further offences' may be either computer crimes or other crimes. Intent to commit other offences in general can be a difficult thing to prove, for instance intent to commit fraud. However, because of the specific inclusion of this more serious offence in the CMA it allows the type of data and reasonable inferences about the uses to which that data might be put to be used to increase the severity of punishment, without requiring proof of conspiracy to commit fraud, for instance. An example might be unauthorized access to a bank's computer records and copying credit card numbers, name and address details from a number of customers. The only believable reason for anyone to copy such data would be with an intent to commit credit card fraud or to sell the information to someone else to commit such fraud. But law-enforcement agencies would not usually wish to allow that information to be distributed or used before arrest and prosecution and so would use this section of the CMA to gain a greater punishment than was available for simply accessing the data. Similarly, accessing information on the security details of a system without appropriate need and authorization to access such information can be seen as intent to commit further offences under the CMA itself and can be prosecuted under this section. Violation of this clause can lead to up to five years' imprisonment and an unlimited fine.

Unauthorized Modification of Data

This does have some limitations. Any access to a computer system will generally generate some form of logging information. Technically unauthorized access causes modification of such logs in ways that would not happen were the unauthorized access not to take place. However, the UK courts have ruled that it is the deliberate or inadvertent act of altering significant data that falls under this act. It is unclear at the moment on which side of this line the deleting of log files in an attempt to hide the unauthorized access (a common practice among crackers and indeed one of the signals that system administrators now use to detect that an attack has succeeded) lies and it would probably depend on exactly how the judge and prosecution viewed the intent of an offender. The penalties for violation of this clause are up to five years' imprisonment and an unlimited fine.

Scope of the CMA

The scope of the CMA includes any target computer or the offender being physically located in the United Kingdom. The target of the attack need not be specifically chosen, so long as the intent to commit an offence exists. This allows for the scanning of random or sequential IP addresses until a vulnerable machine is identified (and which happens to be in the United Kingdom) to be an offence in the United Kingdom. The timing of an offence is also non-specific leaving a fair amount of leeway in terms of the automatic copying of data but not actually viewing it personally, for instance, to still be considered an offence.

Changes Following the Terrorism, Crime and Security Act 2001

As with a number of other subjects (see also Chapter 7), there have been some changes in computer misuse law in the United Kingdom following the 9/11 attacks. The UK bill passed in late 2001, in response to those attacks, included computer misuse activities which might be carried out by terrorists under terrorism legislation. Having used one of the physical communications devices of the modern world (an aeroplane) to commit a horrendous terrorist act, there are serious concerns that digital communication infrastructure might also be under threat. The United Kingdom, the United States and other governments have all (separately and in groups) discussed the potential of a 'digital 9/11' terrorist attack. Thus, where significant infrastructure is concerned (such as the London Stock Exchange, the computers running power supplies or transportation systems) attempts to access these systems in an unauthorized manner may be regarded as a potential terrorist threat and the sanctions (longer interrogation periods, more intrusive surveillance and so on) and penalties applied to terrorist crimes may be applicable for computer misuse crimes.

In 2004, the UK parliament also initiated a major inquiry into whether the computer misuse laws required a major update (including, but not limited to, considering implementation of the Council of Europe Convention on Cybercrime). Most of those presenting evidence have said that a major revision should be considered to cover issues such as open WiFi access points, open proxies, (D)DoS, commercial web sites offering physical goods and digital downloads and a host of other issues which are in a legal grey area of statute law and which many judges do not appear (or in many cases believe themselves to be) qualified to properly adjudicate.

US Sequence of Laws

It must be remembered that the United States is a federal system and that the US government only has jurisdiction over offences with inter-state or international ramifications. Each state in the United States has its own variants on computer misuse laws for offences that are entirely internal to that state. In this section we only consider the federal legislation, which starts out much earlier than that in the United Kingdom with the 1984 Omnibus Crime Control Act making it an offence to 'interfere with the operation of a federal interest computer', defined as 'a computer owned or operated by the US government or a financial institution'; or where computers based in two or more states of the United States (or one within the United States and one within a foreign jurisdiction) were involved in the offence. This was amended in 1994 to include computers used in 'inter-state commerce or communication' again including both inter-state issues within the United States and international issues involving the United States. In 1996 this was emended again to include computers 'exclusively for the use of a financial institution or the

US government, or, in the case of a computer not exclusively for such use, used by or for a financial institution or the US government and the conduct constituting the offence affects that use by or for the financial institution or the Government; or which is used in inter-state or foreign commerce or communication'. Unlike the UK legislation, the US statutes have left it to the courts (and prosecutorial authorities) to decide what level of 'interference' with an operation demands what level of sentence or even whether a particular act requires inclusion within the definition of criminal act at all. The US legislation much more easily copes with the concept of malware, although the UK legislation has been used under the definition of unauthorized modification of data to cover such things.

Changes Following the PATRIOT Act 2001

The United States' legislative response to the 9/11 attacks was the Providing Appropriate Tools Required to Intercept and Obstruct Terrorism (PATRIOT) Act (see also Chapter 7). It had an effect on the US federal law on computer misuse, expanding once again the definition of a system, unauthorized access to which may be considered a federal offence in the United States, to include 'a computer located outside the United States that is used in a manner that affects inter-state or foreign commerce or communication of the United States'.

This final expansion has worried some people elsewhere in that a significant proportion of the world's Internet traffic is routed through the United States and the broad wording of this section of the PATRIOT Act could be construed to include routers in Virginia (through which much international traffic, with neither source nor destination in the United States, ends up travelling) which also process United States commercial and government traffic. As with many areas of law, although current politics may preclude such an interpretation, there is always the risk of abuse at a later date by a more authoritarian government.

Offences and Penalties Under Federal Law

The maximum penalty for 'damaging a protected computer' was extended under the PATRIOT Act from 10 to 20 years' imprisonment. Such penalties require that the total losses be at least $5000 (following the PATRIOT Act such losses can be aggregated from a number of computers rather than requiring at least one individual case above this threshold).

Council of Europe Convention on Cybercrime

As mentioned above, although this is a Council of Europe treaty, a number of non-European countries are also signatories to it. The goal is to ensure at least a minimum level of cooperation and consistent regulation of computer-based or computer-aided criminal activity both in terms of law enforcement cooperation and in terms of criminal sanctions. The Convention on Cybercrime has five divisions of offence:

- Offences against the confidentiality, integrity and availability of computer data and systems – for example, illegal access to systems, illegal interception of computer data transmissions; illegal interference with transmission or system operation and misuse of devices;
- Computer-related offences – for example, computer-related fraud or forgery;
- Content-related offences – primarily relating to child pornography (see Chapter 5);
- Offences related to infringements of copyright and related rights – for example, use of computers to infringe copyright (see Chapter 12);
- Ancillary liabilities and sanctions – for example, aiding and abetting other offences and corporate liabilities.

As can be seen above, the Convention on Cybercrime encompasses a wide range of matters, only some of which are covered in this chapter, others mostly being covered elsewhere. The detailed provisions also include procedural structures such as minimum standards for the gathering of digital evidence (a difficult task, both legally and physically, which we have not covered in this chapter). Finally, the Convention also provides a suitable framework for international cooperation on identifying, arresting, extraditing and trying alleged computer criminals. As is often the case with international criminal cooperation it is this aspect of the treaty that has delayed ratification by all but a small number of the signatories to the treaty (ratification incorporates the treaty provisions into national legislation enabling the provisions to take real effect: before that a treaty is simply an agreement of intent). National governments are always suspicious of other governments' adherence to their own standards of justice and punishment and national politics frequently interfere with the actual implementation of such treaties. As of writing not enough signatories have ratified the treaty and thus even those countries which have ratified it are not bound by its provisions. Other than in respect of the international cooperation aspects, both the UK and US national legal systems substantially follow the appropriate provisions of the convention, although the relevant laws are spread around many acts and not only specific computer crime legislation, such as the copyright provisions embedded in the Digital Millennium Copyright Act in the United States and the 2003 Statutory Instrument on Copyright in the United Kingdom.

Gary McKinnon's Extradition

In November 2002, UK citizen Gary McKinnon was arrested on suspicion of cracking various US military computer networks in 2001. He was arrested at the request of US federal law enforcement officials, who then requested his extradition. This is an interesting case on the issue of jurisdiction, one which may well recur if the Treaty on Cybercrime is ratified by enough signatories. The United Kingdom and the United States have long had wide-ranging extradition treaties, but these are normally only called up in cases where an offender (typically a UK or US citizen) has travelled to the other country, allegedly committed a crime and then returned to his homeland. In the case of McKinnon, however, he is accused of using computers in the United Kingdom to crack US military computers over the Internet, without physically visiting the United States. His extradition to the United States was approved by courts and government in summer 2006 and at the time of writing he has been extradited and awaits trial in the United States. His extradition was controversial because of two issues. The first is that the actions he is accused of perpetrating are illegal under the CMA.

The normal usages of extradition would mean that he should be prosecuted in the United Kingdom, which was his location at the time of the offence. The second controversial aspect is that he has been deported under UK legal provisions enacting a controversial new extradition treaty with the United States, which both countries have signed but which the United States has not yet ratified; the UK government enacted the treaty without a rider stating that it should come into effect only upon mutual ratification. McKinnon has also been extradited under anti-terror rules and UK civil rights campaigners have claimed that he is in significant danger of the United States not abiding by appropriate fair-trial rules. It has even been suggested that the United States could ship McKinnon to Camp Delta at Guantanamo Bay, Cuba. Although this extreme position is unlikely, it is strange that McKinnon was not prosecuted in the United Kingdom, rather than allowing his extradition.

THE GROWING PROBLEM OF COMPUTER CRIME

It is clear that the criminal misuse of computers will be with us for many years to come and probably forever. As computer and communication technology become ever more embedded in ordinary life, vigilance will be needed, the same way good locks are needed on one's home. A balance must be struck between the different aspects of controlling computer misuse (which includes things other than cracking and malware creation and distribution, and which are not always criminal). Use of criminalization must be kept for those things where it is both appropriate and effective and the level and necessity of criminal sanctions should always be kept under review. Other avenues such as technological preventives, education (of both potential victims and potential abusers) and other legal changes (such as allowing civil suits rather than criminal trials) should always be considered by society as potentially more effective means of prevention, deterrence and retribution.

Criminalization only really works when it has a suitable deterrent effect or if the incarceration of those responsible keeps sufficient proportions of potential malefactors away from opportunity. Other forms of crime are also being linked to cybercrime in recent developments. For instance, DDoS attacks are now being launched and stopped, followed by a demand for payment to avoid further attacks. Businesses which operate solely or primarily online are the main targets of such attacks – online casinos for instance. Small e-commerce sites are also often targeted. Such small operations often do not have the necessary technical expertise to understand how to quickly shift their servers and are often reliant on low-cost ISPs (their margins may be small, so low-cost ISPs are necessary parts of their cost base) who may not themselves have the capability to protect the site against DDoS attack.

DISCUSSION TOPICS

Grey Hat Cracking Should Be Legalized

Analogies to homes and businesses abound when discussing the ethics of grey hat cracking. If someone leaves their front door open does that give you the right to enter and rifle through their private belongings? Many small businesses do not have significant security while people are at work, so does that give you the right to walk in and start looking through unlocked filing cabinets? A policeman sees someone walking down a street at night checking every door to see if it is locked. On confronting him, he finds that the man is wearing a striped shirt and carrying a bag marked 'SWAG'. Well, okay, maybe he is carrying a set of tools that would allow him to bypass an alarm system and sundry other breaking-and-entering equipment. In the United Kingdom, he can be arrested and charged for 'going equipped'. There have been proposals to define 'going equipped to crack' as a computer crime, combining the presence of tools used for cracking with the Internet equivalent of trying every door in the street, which is systematic port scanning. The UK CMA incorporates a small aspect of this, in that there is no requirement to demonstrate that a cracker deliberately targeted a particular system, just that they did gain unauthorized access to it, while intending to gain unauthorized access to something. In reaction to the growing problem of computer crime, we might make the laws more draconian. However, this ignores the fact that burglars are a small percentage of society and that an even smaller number of police are sufficient to provide reasonable insurance against them or to capture them after their activities. On the Internet, however, there appear to be too many crackers and not enough policemen (the lack of qualified and employed law enforcement officers is a constant complaint of business but no one wants to pay for enough double-qualified specialists – computer experts who are also trained policemen).

In such circumstances perhaps it is time to allow a certain sort of vigilantism: not the type that goes after the offenders, but those who check up on the security of others as a pastime but intend to do no damage. Perhaps the litmus test for criminality should not be the accessing of information but what is done with that information and how the intruder acted: whether they installed a back door for further access, whether they read large amounts of data or 'sampled' what was there to estimate the value of where they'd penetrated, whether they quickly and efficiently informed the victim of their successful attack and provided information on plugging the hole. As we said in the introduction to this chapter, criminality is defined by society and if the actions of grey hat crackers have positive results, assuming sane and positive attitudes on behalf of the 'victims', surely they are to be applauded and encouraged for identifying security problems that might allow black hat attacks to succeed, rather than being criminalized.

Web Scrapers and Robot Denial Files

In 1993, the first forerunners of Google were being developed. In keeping with the concept of the Web of information, with threads of hyperlinks being the structure, spiders (or web crawlers) were developed. However, many of the sites linked to the Web at that time had limited bandwidth and processing power available to them. In fact a number of the machines running as web servers were simply individuals' desktop machines. This was all very well for the usual amount of web access that went on in those days when there were hardly more people online than were publishing information. There was no Google and, in particular, there was no

Slashdot to generate overwhelming traffic to sites: people found new information by following individual links. Denial of service problems caused by too many people requesting pages from a low-bandwidth site were rare. Into this sphere, the first web crawlers emerged. Instead of requesting a single page from a site, looking through it and maybe requesting one or two more pages within minutes, the simple early spiders would download a document, scan through it for other links and download all those documents as well, indexing the original document as a separate process. If you were running a site with many documents that had internal links between them a single visit by a spider could end up requesting the entire site within a few seconds. Given the low bandwidth and low power of the server this could amount to a denial of service attack by accident. However, the new spiders were the beginnings of a useful communal tool for the Web. Without Google and its predecessors, the Web would not be the immensely useful tool for finding information that it is. Instead of making accusations of criminal behaviour or trying to block requests from spiders completely, a protocol was developed where web servers have a configuration file called 'robots.txt' at the top of their domain (see `www.robotstxt.org` for the current protocol). To act responsibly, the authors of web crawlers programmed their systems to read this file and then follow the limitations it described. Originally this was simply a list of directories not to be crawled – pages under construction, placeholders, and so on. Later, more sophisticated protocols were added such as indicating dynamically created pages that should not be requested, speed of requests to ensure that a low-power server was not overwhelmed and so on.

A more recent variant of the web crawler is the web scraper, which looks for certain kinds of information – prices of particular goods from various online stores for instance – and then aggregates it into new web pages, often using a database. The originators of this information are usually unhappy with such things as they are likely to attract customers away from their sites. As a consumer one might think this is reasonable but the world of e-commerce is not that simple: aggregate deals, special offers, tax, postage and packing charges all differ between sites and can lead to the headline prices produced by web scrapers being unrepresentative of the actual deals on offer. In addition, some web scrapers download almost the entire contents of another site and automatically create a copy (or at least a close equivalent). This is a violation of copyright and can lead to problems such as out-of-date information. Since web scrapers are automated services it should be possible to have the robots.txt protocol indicate in a fair amount of detail what the limitations are for automated access. In fact, the protocol does include at least a coarse-grained version of this. However, the users of web scrapers are often making a profit from their actions and ignore the protocol. Should web scraping which ignores the robots.txt instructions be considered hacking? It is, after all, a violation of the implicit 'terms and conditions of use' of web sites and the argument that this is an automated system that cannot distinguish the terms of use is falsified by the existence of the robots.txt protocol.

An Immune System for the Internet

The number of worms and viruses that exploit known vulnerabilities for which patches have been released but which still cause problems for many users is large and growing. Even if a machine is up-to-date with patches, constant bombardment from infected machines can cause denial of service or at least an annoying slowdown. There have been a number of apparently benevolent worms released in the past few years which attempt to patch vulnerable systems and block the entry of other worms and viruses. Given that so many business and home users seem reluctant to take measures to keep their machines patched and part of the solution rather than part of the problem, it's time for the good guys to fight fire with fire and release well tested and robust worms which carefully fix the problem on any system they infect and then cautiously seek out other vulnerable hosts to fix. There will be some problems caused: patches are not always compatible with other programs; it is the propagation of some worms that causes a denial of service and not a payload action; installing patches often requires a reboot. However, since the machines which are subject to most of the problems are the unpatched yet still networked machines which cause so many problems for others (including the spread of malicious worms), it is the fault of the owner of the machine: if they kept their machine patched and secure they would not be vulnerable.

REFERENCES

Cohen, F. (1984) Computer Viruses: Theory and practice, in *Computers and Security*, **6**(1): 22–35.

Levy, S. (1994) *Hackers: Heroes of the computer revolution*, Penguin, London. ISBN 0-14-100051-1.

Mitnick, K.D. and **Simon, W.L.** (2002) *The Art of Deception*, John Wiley and Sons, Inc., Indianapolis, IA. ISBN 0-471-23712-4.

RELATED READING

Anderson, R. (2001) *Security Engineering*, Wiley, Chichester. ISBN 0-471-38922-6.

Furnell, S. (2002) *Cybercrime: Vandalizing the Information Society*, Addison Wesley, Harlow. ISBN 0-201-72159-7.

Mitnick, K.D. and **Simon, W.L.** (2005) *The Art of Intrusion*, John Wiley and Sons, Inc., Indianapolis, IA. ISBN 0-7645-6959-7.

Shimomura, T. and **Markoff, J.** (1996) *Takedown*, Warner Books Inc., Brentwood, TN. ISBN 0-786-88913-6.

Thomas, D. and **Loader, B.D.** (2000) *Cybercrime: Law Enforcement, Security and Surveillance in the Information Age*, Routledge, London. ISBN 0-415-21326-6.

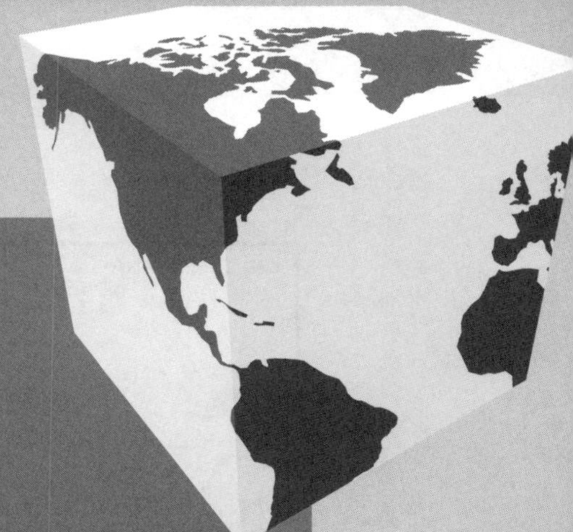

12

PATENTS AND COPYRIGHT

INTRODUCTION

The impact of digital technologies can be seen starkly in the world of copyright. In particular, the move to digital, infinitely copyable and easily distributed forms of information has created a significant difficulty for large industries engaged primarily in the distribution of information. Thus the abstruse legal realm of copyright has become a battleground in deciding how technology will be allowed to develop and how individuals may use the technology at their fingertips.

Similarly the move away from physical goods as the primary things of value in the economy of the industrialized world has led to pressure to allow ownership of ideas – not only how to make certain objects but even such abstractions as pieces of mathematics, programming algorithms and ways of doing business. Thus the even more abstruse legal realm of patents has become another battleground in deciding how technology is developed and how business may be done.

INTELLECTUAL PROPERTY?

Some legal scholars believe that the name 'intellectual property' is a menace. They argue that it imbues those things to which it is ascribed with a whole host of attributes, besides the attributes they share with 'property', that they do not exhibit or mistakenly ascribes the properties of a trade mark to copyright material. In keeping with such an argument, this chapter deals separately with the various concepts that make up 'intellectual property'. We begin by defining the four main concepts often described as 'intellectual property'.

> Intellectual property (IP): a body of law including copyright, patents, trade marks, trade secrets and other intangible rights; an attempt to claim ownership of ideas by describing them as someone's 'property'

Trade Mark

A trade mark is a graphical sign (an icon, if you will) or, more recently, a word under which a particular person or organization is well-known for their goods or services. Different organizations may use the same word or mark in different arenas provided there is no possibility of confusion between their products or services.

Thus Apple Records (publisher of much of the work of the Beatles) and Apple Computers co-exist except when Apple Computers trades in music (see the case study in Chapter 6 for details). The major (though not the only) issue involving trade marks and computer technology is that of trade-marked terms in domain names, which was covered (along with related issues) in Chapter 6.

> Trade mark: a sign or word identifying a particular organization trading in a specific area of commerce protected by law from another company trading in the same area under the same sign or word

Trade Secret

A trade secret is a process or formula which is a closely guarded secret within a company. An example is the exact recipe for Coca-Cola. Although the 'ingredients' are listed on the side of the can, the proportions, the method of mixing and so on are carefully kept secret. Anyone who sees the formula is required to sign a non-disclosure agreement. Trade secrets are similar to patents but require concealment of their details rather than disclosure and have no time limit. However, anyone legitimately discovering (including 'reverse engineering') the details is free to use that knowledge, unlike patents which protect, for a limited time, against anyone else applying the process or formula. Since trade secrets are rare in computing and related fields, we do not cover them further.

> Trade secret: information about a process or product that is kept secret within an organization and forms a basic part of its business, protected by law from dishonest disclosure

Patent

A novel and non-obvious design for a physical or chemical object, or a process to produce physical or chemical objects, may be protected by a patent. In recent years, this concept has also been applied (within some jurisdictions) to processes with more abstract results such as computing algorithms or business methods. In return for publishing details of the process or design, the inventor is granted, for a limited period and in a limited geographic jurisdiction, a monopoly on the use of the design or process or on the sale of the resulting object.

> Patent: a legally enforced monopoly on production of something or a method of producing something

Copyright

Literary and artistic creations are protected from certain forms of duplication for a limited period from their creation. This even extends to the owner of the physical piece for artwork such as paintings or sculpture. The creator of a work has the right to charge for duplication or refuse to grant permissions to various actions involving the work, such as the creation of a 'derivative work', the 'public performance' of a work and sundry similar actions.

> Copyright: a legal restriction on free copying of artistic or literary works, including their transformation into other forms such as adapting a book into a play or film script

THE PHILOSOPHICAL BASIS OF PATENTS AND COPYRIGHT

The concepts defined above may seem obvious and just, simply because they are part and parcel of modern societies. However, the very concept of allowing abstract ideas to be treated as the 'property' of a single person or group of persons is not (and never has been) without its detractors. Even ignoring the collectivist attitude to all property of the Marxist and Maoist traditions, there have been philosophical thinkers in the West who have argued against any protection in law for 'intellectual property'. For instance, in 1813 Thomas Jefferson wrote in a letter to McPherson (about patents):

> *If nature has made any one thing less susceptible than all others of exclusive property, it is the action of the thinking power called an idea, which an individual may exclusively possess as long as he keeps it to himself; but the moment it is divulged, it forces itself into the possession of everyone, and the receiver cannot dispossess himself of it. Its peculiar character, too, is that no one possesses the less, because every other possesses the whole of it. He who receives an idea from me, receives instruction himself without lessening mine; as he who lites his taper at mine, receives light without darkening me. That ideas should freely spread from one to another over the globe, for the moral and mutual instruction of man, and improvement of his condition, seems to have been peculiarly and benevolently designed by nature, when she made them, like fire, expansible over all space, without lessening their density at any point, and like the air in which we breather, move, and have our physical being, incapable of confinement or exclusive appropriation. Inventions then cannot, in nature, be a subject of property.*

Although Jefferson was speaking primarily about patents, his argument can equally well be applied to copyright material. The central point to consider is that ideas can be infinitely duplicated and restrictions on their use, re-use and adaptation are wholly artificial. There is, of course, an opposing view that the sum total of a human's being or existence, in a philosophical sense, is contained within their ideas and that therefore the expression of their ideas is inalienable to them and hence their property. The original US constitution is a useful text to consider in this debate, primarily because it was a specifically created and debated 'fresh start' rather than the evolved and compromise-driven situations that are the norm. Of course, the law of the United States is now itself an evolved and compromise-driven body. The final outcome of the debates over copyright and patents in the constitution of the new United States was itself a compromise, of course. Some argued for strong patent and copyright laws arguing that such laws would accelerate the development of industrial and intellectual endeavours in the new country. Others argued that anything other than strictly time-limited, clearly delimited rights would lead to abuse over time. The final outcome is, like many compromises, still the subject of debate. For instance the 1996 extension to the term of copyright (the Sonny Bono Copyright Term Extension Act) was unsuccessfully challenged in the US Supreme Court (Eldred vs Ashcroft). The actual wording regarding copyright and patents is that the US Congress has the right to 'promote the Progress of Science and the useful Arts by securing for limited Times to Authors and Inventors the exclusive Right to their respective Writings and Discoveries'. This is one of the two general philosophical bases for copyright and patent law and the principle to which at least lip service is paid in most debates today about the content of patent and copyright law.

PATENTS

A Brief History of Patents

The earliest patents granted in the United Kingdom were issued by means of 'letters patent', an open document in which the crown (the monarch) granted a monopoly for the production or sale of goods. Grants of monopoly recognizable as patents were also issued in fifteenth century Venice, but the modern patent system primarily derives from the unbroken evolution of the British legal concept of patent.

Crown commands restricting certain (primarily commercial) activities, such as the monopoly on weaving woollen cloths granted in 1331, were one of the principal means of the exercise of Royal power in the Middle Ages. The first 'patent' recorded in the United Kingdom was made by Henry VI in 1449 and granted a twenty-year monopoly on the manufacture of coloured glass for chapel windows. Monopolies in the production of everyday necessities (such as coal, iron, salt, soap and starch) under the reign of Queen Elizabeth I caused great unrest and led in 1601 to the revocation of many of these monopolies and the introduction of the right of appeal to common law courts against patent grants. This later led to the 1624 Statute of Monopolies, which specifically refers to patents being granted only for 'inventions'. The main thrust of this statute made monopoly illegal except in certain specified circumstances, including a 14-year monopoly for new and inventive practices. The interesting restrictions on patents in this law were the length of 14 years (the time taken to train two apprentices) and the restriction that a patent should not be abused by raising prices to the state nor to the general harm of trade.

Although the arrangements for legal arguments about the validity of a patent in the United Kingdom were rather clumsy, the system remained substantially unchanged through the period of the Industrial Revolution. This was despite criticism from many inventors of the time, including James Watt, one of those credited with inventing the steam engine. Such criticisms of the patent system by well-known inventors continue today (see below for James Dyson's criticisms).

Meanwhile, there had been a revolution in the American colonies and arguments raged among the founders about whether to allow intellectual property law of any kind in their new republic (see Jefferson's letter above). The content of these discussions is covered in the section on copyright below. At this point, we simply note that the original US constitution allowed for a variety of intellectual property rights to be established, including patents, but restricted their grant for the purpose of promoting 'the progress of Science and the Useful Arts'.

Modern Patent Systems

The patent systems in most countries now have similar bases in both justification and operation. The basic principles are that an invention must be both novel (i.e. it has not been thought of before, whether previously patented or not) and non-obvious. In return for lodging a description of an invention with a Patent Office and demonstrating a working prototype, a monopoly is granted on use of that invention for a period. This period is usually around 20 years, although some specific types of invention (such as pharmaceuticals) have different rules. During the period of the patent no one else is allowed to use, make, import or sell, the patented invention, even if they can show that they came up with it independently. Note that there are restrictions, however: one can patent an 'improvement' on an existing patented device even if one is not the holder of the original patent. However, holding an 'improvement' patent does not guarantee the right to use, make, import or sell the improved device without the original patent owner's permission. However, the original patent owner cannot adapt their device with the 'improvement' without the permission of the holder of the 'improvement' patent. Except in special cases (such as pharmaceuticals), the patent holder is not required to grant licences to others at all, even if they are not taking advantage of the patent themselves. The expectation of lawmakers is that if a particular patent is valuable enough then the various parties will be willing to make a deal. The section below on criticisms of the modern patent system describes the various ways this may not be the case and the problems that can arise. Given that particular jurisdictions contain separate patent offices, the question of patenting a device in more than one jurisdiction or honouring patents issued elsewhere is a complicated and difficult one, some aspects of which are addressed below.

Telegraph

The electric telegraph was patented in 1837. Hundreds of patents, many of them by Edison's company, followed over the next century.

Telephone

Alexander Graham Bell patented the telephone in 1876. Thousands of patents on telephone receivers, exchange equipment, transmission lines, and other equipment have been filed, many of them by AT&T (Bell's company, later a state monopoly) and by Edison.

Sound Recording

The original phonograph, invented by Edison, was patented. Alexander Graham Bell and his cousin Chichester Bell, produced an improved variant on the idea called a 'graphophone'. They approached Edison with a request to pool their patents.

Edison would have nothing to do with these 'pirates' whom Edison regarded as having stolen his idea.

> Pirate: a highly emotional term used to describe someone who the user believes is unfairly trading on their creation

Movie Making

In 1908, the major companies holding patents on various film-making and exhibition equipment formed the Motion Picture Patents Company. This followed years of mutual litigation and 'patent wars'. This new group demanded licensing fees from all makers, distributors and exhibitors of motion pictures. A group of independent companies (primarily exhibitors who saw their profits under threat from this monopoly) worked outside this system and, despite constant harassment (legal, commercial and physical), these independents managed to flourish. In 1915, the US courts ruled that the Motion Picture Patent Company (MPPC) was operating 'against the public interest' in pursuit of their monopoly. It should be noted that one of the issues leading to the 'antitrust' finding in 1915 was the agreement with Eastman Kodak to supply only MPPC-licensed companies with film stock.

Spreadsheet Software

In 1979, one of the first 'killer apps' for personal computers was invented: the spreadsheet. It was not patented. As Dan Bricklin, one of the co-inventors, relates (`www.bricklin.com/patenting.htm`):

> *Why didn't we patent the spreadsheet? Were we stupid?*
> *This is a very common question, since, by the late 1990s, software inventions were routinely patented. Today, it seems negligent to ignore patents. However, in 1979, when VisiCalc was shown to the public for the first time, patents for software inventions were infrequently granted. Programs were thought to be mere mathematical algorithms, and mathematical algorithms, as laws of*

nature, were not patentable. The publishers of VisiCalc, Personal Software (their name at the time – later renamed VisiCorp), retained a patent attorney who met with executives from Software Arts and Personal Software. The patent attorney explained to us the difficulty of obtaining a patent on software, and estimated a 10% chance of success, even using various techniques for hiding the fact that it was really software (such as proposing it as a machine). Given such advice, and the costs involved, we decided not to pursue a patent. Copyright and trade mark protection were used, and vigorously pursued. The enormous importance and value of the spreadsheet, and of protections in addition to copyright to keep others from copying our work, did not become apparent for at least two years, too late to file for patent protection.

Killer app: an application that many people want to use and which ensures the success of the hardware or software platform on which it is based; examples include the spreadsheet for personal computers and text messaging for mobile phones

By 1981, the chances of patenting software in the United States improved greatly and today it is commonplace in the United States. In Europe, however, patents on software are highly limited. Basically, in Europe one has to come up with an entirely new concept which happens to be implemented partly in software before being granted a software patent. Simply coming up with an improvement to existing software (a better way of word-wrapping in word processors, for instance) is unlikely to be granted a patent in the European Union. There have been controversial proposals to introduce much wider software patenting into the EU system. Coalitions of software developers on both sides of the argument have lobbied hard for and against these proposals. In particular, the open source and free software communities lobbied hard against patenting of software. Given that such software does not, simply by its existence and use, generate revenue, in the way that proprietary systems do, these groups feel their method of development is under threat. Given that software patents exist, and have existed, in the United States for many years and that open source and free software is successful there, these arguments may seem overblown.

Proposals to include software patents within the European patent regime were defeated by the European Parliament, although at least some of the strength of feeling was against the way the European Council and Commission kept reversing parliamentary amendments to the proposed legislation rather than against the software patent issue. The legislative battle continues however, with different means being pushed which might achieve the same ends. There are claims that the proposed European Patent Litigation Agreement would, if passed, result in software patents being allowed (see the Foundation for a Free Information Infrastructure – an anti-software idea patent lobby group, `www.ffii.org` – for this interpretation).

Business Methods and Software Patents

One of the most controversial areas of patent in the modern world is the types of 'inventions' that can be patented. Although originally 'historic' items and methods, such as leather production, were monopolized under Royal Grant, the justification for allowing patents in a modern world is that they 'encourage innovation' by ensuring reward for useful inventions through allowing a limited monopoly. In different parts of the world, different things can be patented. The two most contentious issues now are those of computer software and 'business methods'. The most significant players in the patent world are the United States and Europe and there are significant differences between them on these issues.

In the United States, a wide scope of patentability is in force, allowing the patenting of computer software and of ways of doing business. In Europe, a small proportion of computer software is patentable and business methods are not patentable. As with copyright, the rise of the Internet has created great strains on business and political relationships between the United States and Europe on patent issues. New software and business method patents related to the Internet are difficult to enforce on a naturally international network and the 'shrinking of the world' in communications terms forces a clash of cultures where before an ocean intervened.

Since more and more companies are operating worldwide there is pressure to harmonize the business environment. Harmonization always has opponents, however, in terms of who harmonizes to whose existing state or whether there is a compromise by which both parties shift to a median position. In terms of patents there is great difficulty in finding a median position since something is either in a category of 'patentable invention' or it is not. There is no individual middle way for classes of inventions. Thus, although politicians might regard allowing patents on X but not on Y as a suitable compromise between two areas one of which allows both and the other of which allows neither, companies involved only in sector X or sector Y would regard it as a betrayal of their interests if the decision might harm their business.

It should be noted that 'business method' patents are not under discussion in the EU having been rejected as a concept by most of those involved. The threat they pose to businesses in Europe is seen as far greater than the opportunity they represent. There have been a number of high-profile business method patents in the United States and we present two examples to illustrate the concept: the patents on Amazon's 1-click shopping and IBM's 'restroom queuing algorithm'.

Amazon's 1-Click Shopping

In the late 1990s, Amazon.com, one of the earliest successful e-commerce businesses, implemented a system for 1-click shopping based on the 'cookies' concept of keeping information held in an indexed file on the user's computer. Instead of choosing items from the online store which the purchaser then confirmed before exiting, one-click shopping automatically processed an order request with a single click on a web button, provided the purchaser had already logged in to the system. They applied for, and were granted, the patent on this method of e-commerce. None of Amazon's managers have ever stated whether this was supposed to be a proactive or a protective patent: that is, whether they wanted to enforce it against other online retailers (requiring a licence payment for its use) or whether they filed it to avoid a costly legal battle in overturning another company's patent in a similar or identical idea. In 2001, Amazon sued rival bookseller Barnes and Noble over their similar single-click, cookie-based shopping technique. The case triggered a shockwave of protest on the Internet not only against such obvious patents being granted by the US Patent and Trade Mark Office (USPTO) but against companies who benefited from the openness of the Internet and then turned to heavy-handed, legal tactics once they became a large company. The issue was eventually settled out of court with a secret deal as to the terms. Whether Amazon caved in because of fear of losing their patent or whether Barnes and Noble paid for the right to continue is unknown. See www.oreilly.com/news/patent_archive.html for links to various discussions of the case.

IBM's Restroom Queuing Algorithm

In 2002, IBM received US Patent number 6 329 919 and attempted to quietly drop the patent some months later. The patent in question describes a method for using a computer to allocate queuing numbers on a first-come first-served basis to passengers on aeroplanes, boats and trains wanting to use the restrooms. Customers then do not have to stand in dangerous queues waiting their turn, but may sit safely in their seats until their number comes up. This concept probably sounds familiar as it has been in use for single-queue facilities at supermarket delicatessen counters (and elsewhere) for years. Unfortunately for IBM and fortunately for comedians and lecturers in IT law everywhere, this piece of nonsense was picked up and plastered over the online news sites. Whether the intention was to meet a target for patent filing, to embarrass the company or to embarrass the Patent Office is unknown. Chris Andrews, IBM spokesman, refused to comment further than, 'We dedicated that patent to the public so that we could continue focusing on our high-quality patent portfolio'. The USPTO declined to comment on whether the patent would have been overturned on further examination by them. See `news.com.com/2100-1017-961803.html` for more details.

General Criticisms of Patents

Separate from the specific arguments about software and business method patents there are discussions about the role and detail of patent law and implementation. Such criticisms are a constant facet of business life, going all the way back to the original 'letters patent', criticized for granting a monopoly on life's necessities (compare this with the patent enforcement arguments surrounding the availability in the developing world of pharmaceuticals to combat AIDS). As we may see from the examples of the Amazon one-click patent and the IBM restroom queuing patent, the USPTO in particular is granting patents almost as unjust as the original letters patent. Some criticize the USPTO on the grounds of incompetence but others defend the institution, which is obviously underfunded in attempting to deal with the rush of patent applications derived from applying old ideas to modern inventions: the telephone, the personal computer, the Internet and so on. The sheer mass of information present in the modern world of science and technology means that something which is 'obvious' to someone working within a field of development is not necessarily 'obvious' to someone from outside it.

There would appear to have been a move away from the original intention in the US Constitution (agreed with by many though not all legislators in other countries) that intellectual property laws exist to promote creative work, to the benefit of the people as a whole, by granting rights to monopolize their creation in some way. Instead, in the modern corporate world the intention seems to be to use every means possible to gain a monopolistic position and to maintain that monopoly for as long as possible. This monopolization by large concerns does not wholly support the current patent policy, however. For instance, consider James Dyson, the British inventor of the 'bagless vacuum cleaner'. He is an outspoken critic of the current Patent System which is, he says, too skewed toward large companies and against private inventors. The cost of filing a patent and the renewal fees charged for retaining it every year are, he says, so large as to force inventors to sell licences for a fraction of their worth to see any return on their investment. He and others, such as Lessig, describe modern corporations as behemoths that may pay lip service to the idea of innovation but are highly risk averse. Only the immediate threat of a rival producing a patent and stealing the market forces change, they claim. The 20-year life span of a patent was designed to allow sufficient time for an inventor to recoup the costs of development and marketing of a new invention. In the modern world of computers and technology, of course, 20 years is an immense period. The Internet has only been in existence for two patent lifetimes and the Web for less than one patent lifetime. Had the concept of a spreadsheet been patented when VisiCalc was produced, the original idea would only have dropped its patent in 1999 and patents on all the enhancements would still have been in force. The fact that most personal computers run a spreadsheet, a word processor and a number of other standard office tools, all of which have been developed and improved without the protection of patents is, some argue, a valid reason to believe that innovation in the computer software field can, and will, happen without patent protection.

Since patent law justifies a monopoly (something generally forbidden in the laws of capitalist countries) some argue that patents have no valid philosophical basis in law and it is only corruption that retains the status quo or extends the scope of patent law. Others argue that the confusing array of incompatible file formats and software interfaces have reduced the benefits from computer developments and that patented inventions would have led more swiftly to stable, usable programs with less money wasted on marketing and gimmicks and more spent on improving the product, therefore arguing for stronger protection for computer programs and business methods in patent. (Computer programs are not without protection, however. Programs are protected as copyright material, as described below.) The lack of international agreements on what can and cannot be patented are also a significant problem in the modern interconnected world. Had Amazon's 1-click patent been supported and fully enforced in the United States, an interesting situation might have arisen. Such a patent is definitely not valid in Europe. Given the nature of the Internet, what is the scope of such a patent? Consider the following scenarios and try to figure out in which of them a court action could be taken (and judgement enforced) to support the 1-click patent.

- A European company with no US subsidiaries sells its products to US consumers using 1-click and ships direct from European sources.
- A European company with a US subsidiary sells its products to US consumers using 1-click and ships direct from European sources.
- A European company with a US subsidiary sells its products to US consumers using 1-click and ships from its US subsidiary.
- A US company with a European subsidiary sells its products to US consumers using 1-click and ships from the European subsidiary.
- A US company without a European subsidiary uses servers provided by a European 'web services' company to sell its products to US consumers using 1-click and ships within the United States.
- A US company maintains a server in Europe to sell goods to European citizens using 1-click and ships direct from the United States.
- A US company uses servers in the United States to provide two interfaces: customers with a delivery address in Europe can access a 1-click service to buy

goods shipped from the United States; customers with a delivery address in the United States cannot access the 1-click service.

All these scenarios (except possibly the final one) describe the basic structure of companies selling goods on the Web. The rise of patent-licensing companies has led to exactly these sorts of issues arising. At least one UK company reported receiving, in 2003, demands for payment of a licensing fee for a US-only patent on a software-implemented business method where they did not have a US subsidiary. (See below for further discussion of patent licensing companies.)

One of the big reasons for criticizing the patent system, particularly in the United States, is the number of patents granted that fail one or both of the 'novelty' and 'non-obviousness' tests. The biggest problem is that once a patent has been granted it takes costly litigation and a high standard of proof to have it overturned (an overwhelming weight, as opposed to the balance, of evidence). These practices were put in place when far fewer patent requests were being submitted and the USPTO had sufficient staff to consider each application properly. With the number of applications per year approaching 300 000 in the United States, even the US Federal Trade Commission (FTC) has recently called for changes, in particular for a non-litigation method of challenging patents combined with a 'balance of probabilities' approach to overturning a patent. The USPTO has started some reforms already, in seeking external advice on the novelty of software patent applications (`www.uspto.gov/web/offices/com/speeches/06-02.htm`). The Electronic Frontier Foundation (EFF) runs a 'patent-busting' project to gather sufficient evidence of prior art to challenge patents (`www.eff.org/patent`).

Patent-Licensing Companies

The rise and financial demise of many technology companies (the dot com bubble); the granting of many patents on software-implemented business methods, many of them on flimsy grounds, it must be admitted; and the increase in the number of small- and medium-sized business in the United States has led to the blossoming of a particular type of company: the patent licensing company. Where previously most people were employed in agriculture and by large business concerns, the last 25 years has seen an immense rise in the number of workers employed by smaller companies, often in high-technology arenas. These smaller companies have neither financial 'deep pockets' nor substantial portfolios of patents and they are therefore vulnerable to claims for patent-licensing fees, even for patents granted on thin grounds. The management of such companies often cannot afford to take risks when receiving letters demanding payment of licensing fees. As long as the patent exists and their business is potentially infringing on the patent they cannot afford large legal bills for advice on the strength of the case against them. If they hold a substantial patent portfolio in related technology, they could possibly work out a cross-licensing deal with the owner of the other patent.

Even patent portfolios, however, provide no defence against 'patent-licensing companies'. These companies buy up large numbers of patents from dead companies, often for small sums since the patents are not on firm grounds nor are they necessarily being enforced against others. Many patents are filed to protect against someone else filing them and claiming licensing fees but are never enforced against anyone else; this model of 'defensive patenting' increases the burden on patent offices, worsening the general situation. The companies buying up the patents employ only lawyers, legal assistants and market researchers. They target small companies who are not able to challenge the patent in court or afford to waste the time of their managers fighting legal battles. If the cost of the licence is not too extreme, many simply cave in and pay the licence fees in search of an easy life. Although some people argue that a patent is a valuable asset and therefore should be tradable in this way, others regard it as an abuse of the system, particularly in light of the negligible sums often paid for a patent or for the entire bankrupt company. The number of such firms appears to be inexorably on the rise in the current climate, although modern communications are also being used as a means of gathering a 'class action' to challenge flimsy patents.

> Patent licensing company: a company which owns several technical patents but does not make use of them directly, instead licensing them to other companies

COPYRIGHT

Copyright law has always been a specialist area and it has become increasingly obscure through much of the twentieth century. The complexity of copyright law is present in all sources: international treaties, an individual country's legislation, and cases setting precedent. Strangely, for what was once an abstruse aspect of law that had little impact on everyday life, copyright law is now one of the most contentious and discussed areas of law, overtaking the death penalty for column inches in newspapers and the source of many flame wars, court cases and lobbying hours. We are generally persuaded by the arguments of, among other, Lessig, Litman and Vaidhyanathan that current copyright law has swung the balance too far toward the interests of distribution companies and certain types of creative talent, to the detriment of the general public and probably against the interests of most authors and artists themselves. Books putting the case for the current state and apparent future direction of copyright law seem few and far between. Perhaps this is inevitable, since only those who rail against current practice see the need to preach their case. As with the rest of this book, the intent is to stimulate thought by and debate among the readers. Thus, presenting the case primarily from the standpoint of the 'unbelievers' in the status quo seems a reasonable tack to take. The specific case of computer code, as opposed to books, music, films and so on, is left to a separate section since it is of particular interest to the expected readership of this book and because the software industry depends so heavily on copyright.

> Flame war: a bad-tempered and often insulting exchange over textual communication

Origins and Development of Copyright

As with patents, the history of copyright starts with the prerogatives of the crown in the United Kingdom. Again, as with patents, the original intention was not anything we would recognize as a valid intellectual justification, which came later. The word 'copyright' itself originally meant exactly what it said: the right to make a copy. The Stationers' Company Charter issued by Queen Mary Tudor in 1557 restricted the right to print books to members of that guild. Until the Statute of Anne in 1710, it was this charter which controlled printing in the United Kingdom (and similar executive orders by British Governors in the American Colonies were in place until the American Revolution). The Statute of Anne is the first Act which recognized the role of the author in the creation of a literary work, this being the first attempt by publishers to maintain their monopoly by appealing to the 'starving artist' image.

Before the invention of movable type in the sixteenth century, making a copy of written material was laborious and time consuming: libraries were mostly hand-written, occasionally printed from laboriously engraved plates. Acknowledgment of authorship was only done as a matter of scholarship and as a claim to authority; it was often missing and occasionally fraudulent (in an attempt to increase the authority of a piece by ascribing a respected name to it as author). With the printing press and the growing literacy of the population in the United Kingdom in the eighteenth century (the rise of a much larger literate middle class was enabled and required by the industrial revolution), the profits to be gained from printing fiction and non-fiction grew ever larger. The profits from intangible 'property' have grown and grown since 1710, to the extent that it is one of the largest parts of modern industrialized economies.

As mentioned in the introduction to this chapter, the new states in North America following the American Revolution passed a variety of new copyright statutes that set them apart from their original colonial power, which Acts formed the basis of the first Federal Copyright Act of 1790. One of the most contentious issues was the international recognition of copyright. As Vaidhyanathan (2001) covers at length, the early United States refused to recognize British copyright. This led to an interesting situation in that the work of US authors such as Samuel Clemens (better known under his nom de plume of Mark Twain) were at a commercial disadvantage to UK-based authors such as Charles Dickens and Arthur Conan Doyle: a US edition of a Dickens or a Doyle could be produced without any payment to the author (the 'Royalty' payment that so eloquently shows the original basis of copyright as a Royal prerogative) whereas an edition of Twain was protected by copyright. Besides the author's royalty, the monopoly a single publisher had on Twain's works allowed the publishers to set prices higher than the unbridled competition in the market for Doyle and Dickens allowed. Interestingly, despite the publisher's protestations that lack of copyright leads to a paucity of material, the most popular books in the United States in the late nineteenth century were 'pirate' editions of UK works, produced in mass quantities and at low cost by the US publishers. As Twain noted, of course, the boot was on the other foot in some ways in the other direction, since UK law did not recognize US copyright either. Twain himself was canny enough to realize that spending a short period in Canada every time he finished a work allowed him to register his copyright there and thereby achieve copyright recognition throughout the British Empire. In 1891, the United States signed a treaty with the British Empire recognizing mutual copyright protection. Besides arguing strongly for mutual recognition of copyright, Twain was one of the strongest proponents of the 'copyright as property' strand of copyright philosophy and argued throughout his life for perpetual copyright. During his lifetime, the copyright time limit was not significantly extended, but in 1976 the United States moved much closer to his dream by passing a law granting copyright to an author for their lifetime plus 50 years.

Only by signing the 1979 Berne Convention, in 1989, did the United States come fully into the international copyright-law framework. This international family of copyright starts with the Berne Convention of 1886 and wends its way around Europe for the next century: Paris 1896, Berlin 1908, Berne (again) 1914,

Rome 1928, Brussels 1948, Stockholm 1967, Paris (again) 1971, Berne (again) 1979 and culminating with the World Intellectual Property Organisation (WIPO) Copyright Treaty in 1996. Vaidhyanathan posits that the US resistance to joining the Berne/WIPO family was because, until the late twentieth century, the United States was a net importer of copyright material and thus the US public was a beneficiary of 'pirating' the works of those in the rest of the world. Once the United States became a net exporter of copyright material, it not only finally joined the world in an international club recognizing and mutually protecting copyright works but became one of the strongest proponents of that protection worldwide and have begun to put international pressure on nations such as China and Malaysia to comply with the same treaties to which the United States only recently joined up.

> World Intellectual Property Organization (WIPO): an international non-profit organization that promotes the interests of holders of intellectual property rights

Following that whirlwind tour of the US development of copyright, what were the differences between the US views and those of the Berne/WIPO family? Other than mutual recognition of copyright, there were two primary differences between the United States and the Berne/WIPO approaches: the term of copyright protection and moral rights of the author.

The term of protection for most places outside the United States has been at least the lifetime of the author plus a set time since the original Berne Convention. The WIPO Copyright Treaty moved the limit from 50 years after the author's death (Berne 1979) to 70 years after the author's death. Note that the WIPO Copyright Treaty is just that, a treaty, and so it is left to individual countries to enact appropriate local laws to follow the treaty. In the United States this has been done with the 1998 Digital Millennium Copyright Act (DMCA) and the 1996 Copyright Term Extension Act. In Europe, the European Union Copyright Directive (EUCD), which has yet to be implemented in many countries, is the mechanism. It should be noted that the 70 years of protection following an author's death was a provision put in place first by Germany to account for the loss of intellectual property during the Nazi regime of 1933–1945 and yet it was pushed through as the new basis for harmonization in the WIPO Copyright Treaty.

The moral right originates in the French approach to copyright law, shared with a number of other mainland European countries. It is a set of rights that are inalienable: not only can an author not be induced to give them up an author cannot choose to give them up. The extent of moral rights in the WIPO Copyright Treaty is highly restricted, primarily to artistic and some musical works, although the treaty does not restrict countries from including stronger moral rights in their local law. The ramifications of the moral right are two-fold: the right not to have a work denigrated and the requirement that the author is always recognized as such. In US and UK terms this means little other than always noting the author's name, whereas in France and Germany income from distribution and public performance must always flow at least partly to the author. Thus, for Hollywood films, which under UK and US law are regarded as the property of the studio that produced them, income from theatrical showings and home-video distribution produces a small but steady stream of income to the 'author of note' that is, the main producer of the film. In France the moral right of an artist can have interesting ramifications for 'commercial commissioned artwork'. In one case, an artist provided a car company with a sculpture for their corporate offices in France. Despite having paid the bill, the company decided that the artwork was too ugly to display in their offices and stored it in the basement. On hearing of this treatment of his work, the artist sued the company (which owns the object but not the copyright and certainly not the moral rights) and won, requiring the display of his work in the company offices. The suit was decided on the grounds that public knowledge of the commission meant that hiding the piece away was a denigration of the artist's work, in violation of his moral rights.

> Moral rights: a set of provisions in certain copyright laws and treaties requiring that a work not be treated in such a way as to malign the creator

The Main Provisions of Modern Copyright Statutes

Having toured around the development of copyright law internationally, we now focus on what copyright law means today and the ramifications for everyday life in a digital and connected world. Despite the lack of full WIPO implementation around the world so far, we concentrate on the provisions of the WIPO Copyright Treaty which is, or will be within in the next few years, implemented in most jurisdictions and the unchanged background from previous treaties.

This list of protected works is not exhaustive:

- Written fiction: novels, short stories, poems, plays;
- Artistic works: paintings, drawings, sculptures, photographs;
- Choreography: in written form and in specific performances;
- Musical compositions: in written form and in specific performances;
- Computer programs: in original source code and compiled object code;
- Databases: only in their method of aggregation not necessarily in their contents;
- Architectural designs: both in terms of blueprints and in terms of the actual building.

Since works are regarded as 'protected' by copyright, there must be some actions against which they are protected:

- Reproduction: making copies;
- Distribution: giving away new copies, for profit, for costs or for free;
- Making a derivative work: writing a sequel to a work of fiction, producing a movie or a play or a song or a written work based on something originally in another form, sampling recordings of music;
- Public performance: reading a book out loud, performing a play, singing a song, playing a recording of audio and or visual material;
- Photographing a piece of art.

A worrying new type of prohibited action has been introduced following the WIPO Copyright Treaty (embodied in both the US DMCA and the EU Copyright Directive) which is the banning of distribution of the means to circumvent 'technological protection measures' (i.e. technology deployed to prevent copying). Such measures have been highly criticized on many grounds, including the fact that exactly what constitutes a 'technological protection measure' has not been defined nor has what constitutes a means of circumvention, the fact that this might prohibit other reasonable activity which simply has as a side effect the ability to circumvent technological protection measures and that it is an unnecessary restriction on the freedom to program computers.

Digital Millennium Copyright Act (DMCA): passed in 1998 by the US Congress

European Union Copyright Directive (EUCD): Directive 2001/29/EC of the European Parliament and Council of 22 May 2001 on the harmonization of certain aspects of copyright and related rights in the information society

The Sklyarov Case

Adobe believed that Digital Rights Management (DRM), the ability to control what users do with digital copies of copyright material, was the solution to the goal of cutting out the physical copy (and its concomitant costs) in the sale of books. To this end they designed a DRM format called 'eBook' and produced an end-user product called eBook Reader. The purpose of the DRM regime was to prevent various electronic activities which are usually taken for granted on a modern computer, including the ability to select part or all of the text and copy it into other applications. Besides preventing someone from easily producing an exact digital copy of the content (as opposed to the formatting information) this led to incompatibilities with the way some users worked. Examples of users who had problems with eBooks included users with screen-reading software that could not access the application through the standard text-interfacing libraries or users who wished to have copies for personal use on platforms where Adobe's official reader was not available.

A company in Russia called Elcomsoft responded to user demand by producing a program called Advanced eBook Processor, which allowed users to translate the contents of an eBook into the more widely usable Portable Document Format (the format produced by Adobe Acrobat and read by Adobe Acrobat Reader). Under Russian law at the time, this was not illegal. Advanced eBook Processor was sold over the Internet including being shipped to downloaders in the United States. Adobe regarded this as a severe threat to their business which was, after all, based on supplying the eBook production tools to publishing houses on the grounds that said publishers could then confidently release their material in digital form without worrying about further redistribution outside their control. The reason Elcomsoft were able to produce Advanced eBook Processor was that the method of 'encryption' used in the eBook format was weak. In July 2001, Elcomsoft employee Dmitry Sklyarov attended Defcon 9 a 'hacker's conference' in Las Vegas, United States. At the end of the conference he was arrested by the FBI on a complaint by Adobe that he, both as a programmer of Advanced eBook Processor and as a representative of Elcomsoft, had violated the 'anti-circumvention' provisions of the DMCA. This was the first time that the criminal provisions of the anti-circumvention clauses had been applied.

There was an outcry among electronic rights' activists, including calls for a boycott of Adobe. Following this negative reaction, Adobe withdrew their original complaint. However, in an interesting twist, the Department of Justice decided that they would continue with the case despite the withdrawal of Adobe's complaint. Sklyarov was held, first in detention and then on bail (but his movements were restricted to California) for five months, after which he was permitted to return to Russia on a binding undertaking that he and the Elcomsoft chairman, Alexander Katalov, would return to California to face trial. In a Kafka-esque twist when Sklyarov and

Katalov applied for US visas to attend hearings on the case in October 2002, they were denied.

During the trial it emerged that Elcomsoft, which the Department of Justice prosecutors had been trying to represent as a group of hackers with no regard for law, had both US federal government agencies and Adobe itself on their client list. Eventually, in December 2002, the jury returned a not-guilty verdict. For more detailed accounts see `freesklyarov.org`, `www.eff.org/IP/DMCA/US_v_Elcomsoft`, `news.bbc.co.uk/1/hi/sci/tech/1514969.stm` and `news.bbc.co.uk/1/hi/technology/2585661.stm`.

This case raises the following issues:

- In domestic violence cases, it is well known that prosecutors will not proceed without a complaint and testimony by the victim, so why, when Adobe publicly withdrew the complaint, did the Department of Justice continue to press the matter?
- The company is located in Russia and did not violate Russian law by producing the software. There was no proof offered in court of specific instances of US-located persons or companies who had used the Advanced eBook Processor to violate US copyright law. Sklyarov and Elcomsoft were prosecuted for violating the DMCA, not for import/export violations. US law does not apply to Russian citizens engaged in business that does not involve the United States (the programming of the Advanced eBook Processor); therefore, surely the offence was in shipping to the United States, which was not an act of Sklyarov personally, but of the company.
- Given the outcome, surely an investigation into the actions of the Department of Justice was warranted. Elcomsoft was brought close to bankruptcy by legal fees and Sklyarov was held in the United States for five months away from his family (both children were under 3 years old at the time of the arrest). Given that Adobe withdrew the original complaint, what is the justification for having held him for so long?

It should be noted that the use of language in describing copyright can itself be contentious. Those in favour of stronger copyright regard non-prohibited actions as 'exemptions' to copyright law, whereas those in favour of weaker copyright regard them as 'rights not explicitly removed' by copyright law. It is a case of whether you regard law as 'what is not specifically allowed is forbidden' or 'what is not explicitly forbidden is allowed' and which viewpoint a judge holds is one of the grounds for deciding case law in copyright. Actions not prohibited by copyright law in most jurisdictions include:

- Copying of a portion of a printed work for personal research or teaching purposes;
- Lending out by official libraries;
- Making archival copies: in some circumstances and by certain agencies, that is, copies which are never distributed;
- Recording audio or video broadcasts for personal purposes, for example, time-shifting or space-shifting;
- Sharing copies of audio recordings with friends (in certain jurisdictions);
- Producing a 'parody' (only in certain jurisdictions);
- Quoting relevant limited portions of a work in the course of a review: including all types of protected work, not just written work;
- News reporting.

US Case Law for Copyright

So, we have covered the statutes and treaties governing copyright law. But copyright law has always been as much about the court's interpretation of statute as about statute itself. In the United States, until the Napster case, the thrust of most court decisions has been that copyright statutes were limited to controlling the technology and business methods in existence at the time the statute was passed. Thus we have the following cases which all allowed a new technology to flourish and develop although a new copyright statute was negotiated and passed. In many cases, companies which had successfully commercialized new technology quickly became powerful enough to demand a seat at the table in negotiating new statute law and themselves became major players in the copyright industries. Such new players have frequently found themselves on the opposite side of the argument in respect of further technological innovation. See (Litman 2001, Chapter 3) for a detailed account of these cases and the renegotiations of copyright statute that went with them.

Player Piano

A 1908 case held that player pianos did not infringe on the copyright of the composer or publisher of the musical score they reproduced. In derivative cases, the early phonographs of Edison and others also did not infringe on copyright. The US statute of 1909 provided for a compulsory licensing scheme for mechanical music reproduction, with an exemption for coin-operated machinery. This exemption was later to provide the safe harbour needed for the swift rise of the jukebox industry following the development of the 45-rpm 'single' in the 1940s.

> Player Piano: an addition to a standard piano or a standalone unit incorporating a piano's musical parts to enable automated playback of music recorded on paper tape; it produced much higher quality music than the recording media of the time

Movie Adaptations

In the most obvious case of the courts coming down on the side of existing players in the copyright industry, there was the 1911 decision that the Kalem Company movie Ben Hur infringed on the copyright of Harper Brothers, publishers for General Lew Wallace's book Ben Hur. Note that it was the publisher and not the author whose copyright was violated by the movie. This decision led to two results: first, the fledgling movie industry (already in turmoil over patents and monopolies) suddenly had to negotiate for the rights to derive a script from a book or play; second, the movie industry, already rich, began to lobby Congress to amend the copyright law to provide them with suitable copyright for their productions, particularly following the collapse of the patent-based MPPC.

Video Recorders

In what is possibly the most celebrated case in copyright law in modern times, Universal City Studios (and Disney Corporation) sued Sony Corporation of America in 1982 for manufacturing and selling Betamax videocassette recorders. At issue was the capability for recording television broadcasts, which Universal Studios claimed infringed on their copyright on the movies shown on television. The court ruled solidly on the side of Sony based on two important principles: first, that copying a television broadcast to either 'time-shift' a broadcast to a later time or to 'space-shift' a broadcast to another person's home was legitimate 'fair use' under which a copy can be made without explicit permission; second, that since the videocassette recorder had substantial usages which did not infringe copyright, the mere fact that it could also be used to infringe copyright was not sufficient to ban the manufacture and sale of the machines. For more details, see the Museum of Broadcast Communications' web site by way of `shorl.com/gifameginony`.

> Betamax: a high-quality, home-video recording standard based on the professional Betacam system which was defeated by better marketing of the lower-quality VHS standard

Personal MP3 Players

When the first solid-state portable music players were released in the late 1990s (using the MP3 encoding system to fit sufficient music onto the machines to make them worthwhile), the recording industry tried to have their manufacture and sale banned on the grounds that they were machines designed solely for infringing copyright. After a number of appeals, they finally lost the case and personal MP3 players are now common, as are video recorders (both the original analogue videocassette version and the more recent digital versions recording onto hard drives and DVDs).

Motion Picture Expert Group Audio Layer 3 (MP3): a highly compressed audio file format which removes 'unheard' or 'fringe' elements of CD-quality audio files

MP3.com

In 2000 in New York, the first of a number of cases which appear to many commentators to run against the previous tide of allowing technology to bypass existing copyright requirements was decided. Universal Media Group (UMG) Recordings (part of the same company involved with Disney in the Betamax case) had `MP3.com` shut down. `MP3.com` offered a service whereby a user could log on to their system and 'register' their 'ownership' of a CD. They did not need to upload a copy of the CD themselves but simply register the fact that they had a copy of the CD at that point. After it had been registered, they would be able to stream or download from their account an MP3-encoded version of any song on that album to wherever they happened to be. `MP3.com` purchased their own copies of the CDs to re-encode into MP3 format. The court ruled that the copies provided to users were infringing copyright and ordered the service shut down. It should be noted that all the users could have performed the service directly themselves, probably perfectly legally under the US Home Recording Act and following the RIAA v Diamond MP3 player decision. It is interesting to note that similar cases were brought regarding early radio broadcasts but decided that radio broadcast was not covered under previous statute law and was therefore legal.

Recording Industry Association of America (RIAA): an industry lobby group representing the large music recording labels in the United States

Peer-to-peer

Following on from the DMCA and the MP3.com decision, the peer-to-peer file sharing service Napster was shut down in 2001 on the grounds that it facilitated illegal sharing of copyright material. Although this appears to overturn the precedent in Universal v Sony, the judge was clear that the problem was Napster's intent, as shown in its advertising and ancillary features. Since the clear intent of the Napster company was to increase people's access to music to which they did not have legitimate rights, the service was found to be infringing copyright. The significant difference with video recorders is that those taping the broadcast already had legitimate access to the material, whereas those downloading music from Napster had no such access.

Napster

A whole book could be, indeed (Merriden 2001) has been, written on the Napster saga. This case study merely covers the main points. A student, Shawn Fanning, dropped out of his college course in the United States because he had a vision for a piece of software that he and his friends could use to easily share the MP3 files they were all making and passing around anyway. His uncle, John Fanning (who already owned a computer games company called NetGames), saw the business opportunity in this and took some legal advice. The contents of that advice is, of course, confidential but interviews have revealed that he was advised that he had a good defence.

Previous cases such as Player Piano and Betamax (Universal v Sony) combined with the existing fair-use right of sharing home recordings could well be seen as legal armour against the claims of the record companies. As can be seen with KaZaA and Morpheus, this might have carried the day had the new Napster company not been so proactive in promoting the use of the service to share copyrighted material.

Napster lost an initial court case in July 2000, but remained online until July 2001 when the courts shut them down until they could prove that they were not allowing the use of the service to share unlicensed copyrighted material. Between the initial and final judgements in the case, however, the immense publicity caused by the case itself (widely reported in both traditional and new media news outlets) led to an incredible surge in the number of users. At its peak, the number of users registered on their system is estimated to have reached 58 million (Merriden 2001). Following the curtain coming down on Napster's file sharing, one of the big five international record companies in the RIAA (Bertelsmann) broke ranks and bought Napster. Napster was relaunched as a pay service at `www.napster.com`, `www.napster.co.uk`, `www.napster.de` and other country-specific URLs. The name and logo have been something of a draw but it had already lost much of the momentum to Apple's iTunes download service.

In something of a reversal of the Napster decision, the RIAA failed in attempts to get the groups behind the KaZaA and Morpheus file-sharing systems shut down. Whereas Napster was a centralized system with a server promoting itself on the back of sharing unauthorized copies of MP3s, the judge in the KaZaA and Morpheus case followed the Universal v Sony decision and decided that both KaZaA and Morpheus had sufficient uses for non-infringing purposes (sharing public domain works or authorized MP3 distribution of material such as Grateful Dead concert recordings and songs released by unsigned bands) and that preventing the distribution of their code or the operation of their systems was not justified.

DeCSS

In 2000, the US magazine 2600 (`www.2600.com`) published details on its web version, and links to sites for downloading, of the DeCSS code for unscrambling the content of DVDs. The Motion Picture Association of America (MPAA) sued 2600 magazine for violating the DMCA by helping to distribute a mechanism for defeating a digital content encryption system. In what many commentators viewed as a bizarre decision, the MPAA's case was upheld despite arguments that the DeCSS code had legitimate uses and that the free speech and freedom of the press rights of 2600 magazine were being violated. In Norway, Jon Johansen (the author of the DeCSS code) was subjected to two criminal trials for copyright violation for producing the code but was acquitted both times and has gone on to sue the Norwegian Economic Crime Unit for his lost economic opportunities during the case (which included having the computer he used to produce the code impounded).

> DeCSS: a library designed to decrypt the contents of DVDs or video discs encrypted using the weak encryption of the content scrambling system (CSS)

The Current State of Play

The critical players in this game of statute and case law pursuing ever tighter controls on how and what the public can view are the content distributors, as represented by industry groupings such as the RIAA (`www.riaa.com`), International Federation of the Phonographic Industry (IFPI, `www.ifpi.org`), British Phonographic Industry (BPI, `www.bpi.co.uk`) and the MPAA (`www.mpaa.org`). There is a growing group of academics and civil rights and consumer associations trying to gain a foothold in lobbying for changes in the law in the United States, the European Union and internationally: see the EFF (`www.eff.org`), the American Civil Liberties Union (ACLU, `www.aclu.org`) and the Open Rights Group (ORG, `www.openrightsgroup.org`) for details. However, these groups do not appear to be making much headway yet. Some movement in the US situation can be seen, such as proposals to amend the DMCA to shift the balance of copyright law back toward individual rights, fair use and technological and business advances. Such moves are counterbalanced by other proposals for further tightening the law in favour of distributors, for example, by forcing entertainment equipment manufacturers to include digital rights management hardware in their machines, and proposals to grant wide-ranging protection to the content broadcast by television companies.

The Music Industry and Higher Education

Ever since Shawn Fanning was inspired to create Napster by his friends swapping their MP3s over the college network, file sharing and universities have been linked. Free access to uncapped, high-bandwidth networks has been a feature of educational institute Internet systems since before the Internet was commercialized. It is not, therefore, surprising that college students are some of the most prolific users of peer-to-peer file-sharing software. The pop music industry has always courted the sales offered by college-age young people, exploring their new freedom from the constant eye of parental supervision and trying to define themselves in terms of their tastes and that of their peer group. Tapping into that market with the latest 'cool' item is always the dream of such marketing. The peer-to-peer networks seemed like a death knell to the recording industry and they lashed out.

Although commercial ISPs have to consider their customers' reaction to any violation of the anonymity of their Internet usage, universities do not provide Internet access for personal purposes. They provide it as part of the educational package. As such, if a university is faced with a legal challenge to their students' usage of the Internet they are more likely to be willing to provide identification and to impose non-legal sanctions on the offenders. Also, unlike commercial ISPs, such sanctions are not simply restricted to cutting off Internet access. Ultimately, universities may deny students their degrees (and consequently change the course of their future careers drastically) in response to violations of terms of use.

Fairly early on in their battle to retain control of distribution of music and to ensure that money changed hands for every copy produced, the music industry (represented by the RIAA in the United States, the IFPI internationally and the BPI in the United Kingdom) realized that some high-profile cases against university students would help to create a chilling effect on users' assumptions that their peer-to-peer activities were anonymous. As such, some of the first legal actions by the RIAA were against universities or university students (`p2pnet.net/story/4522`).

The Originator's Rights

Among all this discussion of distributors and users, we have so far made little mention of the actual producers of copyrighted works: authors, composers and performers. As mentioned above, the early copyright systems made little of the originator's rights, being focused on the monopoly rights of distributors.

Some authors, such as Mark Twain, have publicly argued on behalf of increased rights for authors, though usually at the expense of the consumer rather than against the rights of publishers. Since movies have a complex and almost impossible-to-untangle concept of 'authorship' there is little pressure coming from within that industry. It is within the ranks of the music industry that we see the greatest level of interest from the artists themselves. Some composers and groups, such as Metallica (who sued Napster for infringement of their material) are on the side of the recording-distribution companies in their quest for ever greater control and legal protection. Others, such as Janis Ian and Jon Perry Barlow of the Grateful Dead, regard the distribution companies as hypocrites who themselves are responsible for the impecunious state of many musical artists and regard the new possibilities of the Internet and digital downloads as a way around what they see as a commercial and artistic stranglehold by big business.

Some commentators are drawing parallels between the RIAA and MPAA coalitions and the MPPC, which eventually fell through a combination of direct action (independent companies ignoring their legal claims) and court action (anti-trust suits). Compelling though these parallels may seem, the politics of the day are different and thus the outcomes may differ despite the similarities in operation.

Software Copyright

In the early development of the computer industry, software was regarded by computer manufacturers as something they provided to sell their computers. The cost of the machines themselves was so large that the added cost of developing and maintaining bespoke software was small change in comparison. Gradually, however, as machines became cheaper, programs became larger and more complex and high-level programming languages became available, software began to be seen as a separate entity. Beginning in the 1960s, there was a split in the ideological viewpoint of software. A small group, primarily led by Richard Stallman, then at MIT, believed that software was primarily an infrastructure concept and should be freely shared on both ideological and pragmatic grounds. This concept underlay many of the most popular Unix and Internet utilities, even carrying over to the concept of non-proprietary versions of Unix once that system was 'closed off' by AT&T. Richard Stallman's ideas are the basis, though not necessarily the core, of the two strands of 'non-proprietary' software: free software and open source software.

The proprietary strand of software developed primarily with the release of personal computers, even though the roots of it lay in the days of mainframes and mini computers. Starting with the early personal computer games for machines such as the Apple II and with the early 'productivity applications', such as VisiCalc and WordPerfect on IBM PCs, a strand developed that saw computer programs as 'intellectual property' and expected payment for each individual copy. Given this approach, payment for each 'copy' of the software versus the share-and-share-alike approach of free software (open source is a later variant of similar ideas), the early days of the computer software industry can be seen as similar to the current state of the music industry.

Following some confusion, the status of computer programs as copyrighted in terms of both their source and object code was established. Various court cases, often described as the 'look-and-feel' cases, between companies such as Microsoft and Apple established the limits of what elements of computer programs were protected. The resulting cases decided that the actual program itself was protected, not any of the ideas embodied in it. Copyright is not the sole preserve of the proprietary software companies, however. Copyright also forms the legal basis of the free and open source software approaches. Without copyright in software programs, the General Public License (GPL) and all the myriad other variants of free and open source software licences would be unenforceable.

We do not have the space in this book to rehearse the arguments about proprietary versus open source and open source versus free software. For suitable diatribes on each side, see the web sites of the GNU project (`www.gnu.org`) and the Open Source Initiative (`www.opensource.org`) on the one hand and the Initiative for Software Choice (`www.softwarechoice.org`) on the other. Here, we show examples of three software licence agreements: a version of the GNU GPL; the Berkeley Software Development (BSD) Open Source license and the Microsoft Windows 2000 End User License Agreement (EULA). We then dissect the Microsoft EULA for a particular version of Windows Media Player, which caused a stir of controversy when it was released.

> End User License Agreement (EULA): the terms and conditions which a software publisher tries to impose on its users

The GNU GPL

The Free Software Foundation and GNU Project present and maintain two licences: the GNU General Public License (the GPL) and the GNU Lesser General Public License (LGPL). We only cover the GPL here. See `www.gnu.org/licenses` for more details including advice on which licence to choose and the differences in effect. It should be noted that the GPL relies heavily on two central concepts of copyright law as applied to software: that the original author owns the code; and that derivative works may only be created with the permission of the original author. The GNU GPL is too large to include here in its entirety. Particularly interesting sections are excerpted and reproduced here. Numbering of sections has been left intact to indicate where material has been omitted. The explanatory material (preamble and explanation) has also been omitted.

GNU GENERAL PUBLIC LICENSE
TERMS AND CONDITIONS FOR COPYING, DISTRIBUTION AND MODIFICATION

1. *You may copy and distribute verbatim copies of the Program's source code as you receive it, in any medium, provided that you conspicuously and appropriately publish on each copy an appropriate copyright notice and disclaimer of warranty; keep intact all the notices that refer to this License and to the absence of any warranty; and give any other recipients of the Program a copy of this License along with the Program.*
   You may charge a fee for the physical act of transferring a copy, and you may at your option offer warranty protection in exchange for a fee.
2. *You may modify your copy or copies of the Program or any portion of it, thus forming a work based on the Program, and copy and distribute such modifications or work under the terms of Section 1 above, provided that you also meet all of these conditions:*
   (a) You must cause the modified files to carry prominent notices stating that you changed the files and the date of any change.
   (b) You must cause any work that you distribute or publish, that in whole or in part contains or is derived from the Program or any part thereof, to be licensed as a whole at no charge to all third parties under the terms of this License.
   (c) If the modified program normally reads commands interactively when run, you must cause it, when started running for such interactive use in the most ordinary way, to print or display an announcement including an appropriate copyright notice and a notice that there is no warranty (or else, saying that you provide a warranty) and that users may redistribute the program under

these conditions, and telling the user how to view a copy of this License. (Exception: if the Program itself is interactive but does not normally print such an announcement, your work based on the Program is not required to print an announcement.)

These requirements apply to the modified work as a whole. If identifiable sections of that work are not derived from the Program, and can be reasonably considered independent and separate works in themselves, then this License, and its terms, do not apply to those sections when you distribute them as separate works. But when you distribute the same sections as part of a whole which is a work based on the Program, the distribution of the whole must be on the terms of this License, whose permissions for other licensees extend to the entire whole, and thus to each and every part regardless of who wrote it.

Thus, it is not the intent of this section to claim rights or contest your rights to work written entirely by you; rather, the intent is to exercise the right to control the distribution of derivative or collective works based on the Program.

4. *You may not copy, modify, sublicense, or distribute the Program except as expressly provided under this License. Any attempt otherwise to copy, modify, sublicense or distribute the Program is void, and will automatically terminate your rights under this License. However, parties who have received copies, or rights, from you under this License will not have their licenses terminated so long as such parties remain in full compliance.*
5. *You are not required to accept this License, since you have not signed it. However, nothing else grants you permission to modify or distribute the Program or its derivative works. These actions are prohibited by law if you do not accept this License. Therefore, by modifying or distributing the Program (or any work based on the Program), you indicate your acceptance of this License to do so, and all its terms and conditions for copying, distributing or modifying the Program or works based on it.*

NO WARRANTY

11. BECAUSE THE PROGRAM IS LICENSED FREE OF CHARGE, THERE IS NO WARRANTY FOR THE PROGRAM, TO THE EXTENT PERMITTED BY APPLICABLE LAW. EXCEPT WHEN OTHERWISE STATED IN WRITING THE COPYRIGHT HOLDERS AND/OR OTHER PARTIES PROVIDE THE PROGRAM 'AS IS' WITHOUT WARRANTY OF ANY KIND, EITHER EXPRESSED OR IMPLIED, INCLUDING, BUT NOT LIMITED TO, THE IMPLIED WARRANTIES OF MERCHANTABILITY AND FITNESS FOR A PARTICULAR PURPOSE. THE ENTIRE RISK AS TO THE QUALITY AND PERFORMANCE OF THE PROGRAM IS WITH YOU. SHOULD THE PROGRAM PROVE DEFECTIVE, YOU ASSUME THE COST OF ALL NECESSARY SERVICING, REPAIR OR CORRECTION.

12. IN NO EVENT UNLESS REQUIRED BY APPLICABLE LAW OR AGREED TO IN WRITING WILL ANY COPYRIGHT HOLDER, OR ANY OTHER PARTY WHO MAY MODIFY AND/OR REDISTRIBUTE THE PROGRAM AS PERMITTED ABOVE, BE LIABLE TO YOU FOR DAMAGES, INCLUDING ANY GENERAL, SPECIAL, INCIDENTAL OR CONSEQUENTIAL DAMAGES ARISING OUT OF THE USE OR INABILITY TO USE THE PROGRAM (INCLUDING BUT NOT LIMITED TO LOSS OF DATA OR DATA BEING RENDERED INACCURATE OR LOSSES SUSTAINED BY YOU OR THIRD PARTIES OR A FAILURE OF THE PROGRAM TO OPERATE WITH ANY OTHER PROGRAMS), EVEN IF SUCH HOLDER OR OTHER PARTY HAS BEEN ADVISED OF THE POSSIBILITY OF SUCH DAMAGES.

The intent of the GPL is to allow software developers to release their code 'into the wild' and allow others to improve upon it but without allowing someone else to add improvements and then profit from the joint work by denying others the same rights to the new code. It is possible and does happen, that companies sell code derived from an existing code base subject to the GPL. In such cases, once the fee has been paid and the code is received, the purchaser gains all the rights bestowed by the GPL.

The BSD Open Source Licence

The GPL and the BSD licences form the two most prominent strands of thought in free and open source licensing. The primary difference between them is that the BSD licence places fewer restrictions on what is allowed with respect to derivative works. With the GPL, one is not allowed to distribute the object code of a derivative work without giving access to the source in some meaningful way. With BSD, distribution of the object code of the original or derivative works without accompanying source code is permissible. What follows is a template, available from `www.opensource.org/licenses/bsd-license.php`, to create a BSD-style licence for a new product or project.

> Berkeley Software Development (BSD) license: a software licence originally associated with software issued by the University of California at Berkeley

Copyright (c) <YEAR>, <OWNER>

All rights reserved.

Redistribution and use in source and binary forms, with or without modification, are permitted provided that the following conditions are met:

** Redistributions of source code must retain the above copyright notice, this list of conditions and the following disclaimer.*

** Redistributions in binary form must reproduce the above copyright notice, this list of conditions and the following disclaimer in the documentation and/or other materials provided with the distribution.*

** Neither the name of the <ORGANIZATION> nor the names of its contributors may be used to endorse or promote products derived from this software without specific prior written permission.*

THIS SOFTWARE IS PROVIDED BY THE COPYRIGHT HOLDERS AND CONTRIBUTORS 'AS IS' AND ANY EXPRESS OR IMPLIED WARRANTIES, INCLUDING, BUT NOT LIMITED TO, THE IMPLIED WARRANTIES OF MERCHANTABILITY AND FITNESS FOR A PARTICULAR PURPOSE ARE DISCLAIMED. IN NO EVENT SHALL THE COPYRIGHT OWNER OR CONTRIBUTORS BE LIABLE FOR ANY

DIRECT, INDIRECT, INCIDENTAL, SPECIAL, EXEMPLARY, OR CONSEQUENTIAL DAMAGES (INCLUDING, BUT NOT LIMITED TO, PROCUREMENT OF SUBSTITUTE GOODS OR SERVICES; LOSS OF USE, DATA, OR PROFITS; OR BUSINESS INTERRUPTION) HOWEVER CAUSED AND ON ANY THEORY OF LIABILITY, WHETHER IN CONTRACT, STRICT LIABILITY, OR TORT (INCLUDING NEGLIGENCE OR OTHERWISE) ARISING IN ANY WAY OUT OF THE USE OF THIS SOFTWARE, EVEN IF ADVISED OF THE POSSIBILITY OF SUCH DAMAGE.

The BSD licence is particularly short because it is just about the least restriction it is possible to place on a piece of software and still call it a licence. The intent of the BSD licence is to allow further open source or proprietary derivatives to be created. It is as close as possible to explicitly putting something into the public domain for anyone to use as they wish.

The Microsoft Windows 2000 Professional EULA

Although there are hundreds, possibly thousands, of free or open source software licences, it seems that every piece of proprietary software has its own individual licence. This licence from Microsoft is chosen not because it is a particularly good or bad licence, as such things go, but because it is the licence under which one of the most commonly used systems is available. The complete licence would be too large to reproduce here, so only some of the main terms are reproduced.

Installation and use.

You may install, use, access, display and run one copy of the Product on a single computer, such as a workstation, terminal or other device ('Workstation Computer'). A 'License Pack' allows you to install, use, access, display and run additional copies of the Product up to the number of 'Licensed Copies' specified above. The Product may not be used by more than two (2) processors at any one time on any single Workstation Computer. You may permit a maximum of ten (10) computers or other electronic devices (each a 'Device') to connect to the Workstation Computer to utilize the services of the Product solely for file and print services, internet information services, and remote access (including connection sharing and telephony services). The ten connection maximum includes any indirect connections made through 'multiplexing' or other software or hardware which pools or aggregates connections. You may not use the Product to permit any Device to use, access, display or run other executable software residing on the Workstation Computer, nor may you permit any Device to display the Product's user interface, unless the Device has a separate license for the Product.

Storage/Network Use.

You may also store or install a copy of the Product on a storage device, such as a network server, used only to install or run the Product on your other Workstation Computers over an internal network; however, you must acquire and dedicate an additional license for each separate Workstation Computer on or from which the Product is installed, used, accessed, displayed or run. A license for the Product may not be shared or used concurrently on different Workstation Computers.

TRANSFER - Internal.

You may move the Product to a different Workstation Computer. Transfer to Third Party. The initial user of the Product may make a one-time transfer of the Product to another end user. The transfer has to include all component parts, media, printed materials, this EULA, and if applicable, the Certificate of Authenticity. The transfer may not be an indirect transfer, such as a consignment. Prior to the transfer, the end user receiving the transferred Product must agree to all the EULA terms. No Rental. You may not rent, lease, or lend the Product.

LIMITATION ON REVERSE ENGINEERING, DECOMPILATION, AND DISASSEMBLY.

You may not reverse engineer, decompile, or disassemble the Product, except and only to the extent that it is expressly permitted by applicable law notwithstanding this limitation.

The Product is protected by copyright and other intellectual property laws and treaties. Microsoft or its suppliers own the title, copyright, and other intellectual property rights in the Product. The Product is licensed, not sold.

EXCLUSION OF INCIDENTAL, CONSEQUENTIAL AND CERTAIN OTHER DAMAGES. TO THE MAXIMUM EXTENT PERMITTED BY APPLICABLE LAW, IN NO EVENT SHALL MICROSOFT OR ITS SUPPLIERS BE LIABLE FOR ANY SPECIAL, INCIDENTAL, INDIRECT, OR CONSEQUENTIAL DAMAGES WHATSOEVER (INCLUDING, BUT NOT LIMITED TO, DAMAGES FOR LOSS OF PROFITS OR CONFIDENTIAL OR OTHER INFORMATION, FOR BUSINESS INTERRUPTION, FOR PERSONAL INJURY, FOR LOSS OF PRIVACY, FOR FAILURE TO MEET ANY DUTY INCLUDING OF GOOD FAITH OR OF REASONABLE CARE, FOR NEGLIGENCE, AND FOR ANY OTHER PECUNIARY OR OTHER LOSS WHATSOEVER) ARISING OUT OF OR IN ANY WAY RELATED TO THE USE OF OR INABILITY TO USE THE PRODUCT, THE PROVISION OF OR FAILURE TO PROVIDE SUPPORT SERVICES, OR OTHERWISE UNDER OR IN CONNECTION WITH ANY PROVISION OF THIS EULA, EVEN IN THE EVENT OF THE FAULT, TORT (INCLUDING NEGLIGENCE), STRICT LIABILITY, BREACH OF CONTRACT OR BREACH OF WARRANTY OF MICROSOFT OR ANY SUPPLIER, AND EVEN IF MICROSOFT OR ANY SUPPLIER HAS BEEN ADVISED OF THE POSSIBILITY OF SUCH DAMAGES.

Under the terms of this licence:

- Microsoft is not liable for anything except possibly to return your money if the product is defective, unless local laws specify other liability.
- You have leased the software not bought it and cannot try to figure out what may be wrong with it even if Microsoft cannot or will not fix an apparent problem.
- If using the system as an Internet server you must limit the number of concurrent connections to ten.

Warranty Disclaimers

All three of the licences above include a 'warranty disclaimer' which states that the author and provider of the software take no responsibility for it, except where required to do so by national law. It should be noted that car manufacturers in the United States used to include similar such warranty conditions in the terms of sale for their cars, limiting their liability for defective products to the replacement of the defective part. This was eventually overturned in court and motor car manufacturers became liable for death and injury resulting from defective parts or assembly. The 'No Warranty' clause in off-the-shelf software sales has yet to be seriously challenged in court, although the basis of the car manufacturer liability case, that ownership or use of a car was necessary to the standard way of life at the time, may now be said to hold in terms of computer software, particularly operating system software.

Contentious EULAs

Besides the 'no warranty' clause, various other aspects of EULAs have been issues of contention in the last few years. So-called 'shrinkwrap' and 'clickwrap' licence terms in particular have caused controversy. We concentrate on two instances of this: the 'no reviews' licence term and the 'DRM required' update terms.

> Shrinkwrap licence: a licence for software that is deemed to be 'accepted' by opening the clear plastic wrapping on a box containing media
>
> Clickwrap licence: a licence for software that is deemed accepted by clicking 'I accept' during a download or installation operation

No reviews allowed

Network Associates used to include licence terms for some of its products prohibiting users from publishing benchmark tests or reviews without the company's permission.

Installing this software constitutes acceptance of the terms and conditions of the license agreement in the box. Please read the license agreement before installation. Other rules and regulations of installing the software are:

(a) *The product can not be rented, loaned, or lease – you are the sole owner of this product.*
(b) *The customer shall not disclose the result of any benchmark test to any third party without Network Associates' prior written approval.*
(c) *The customer will not publish reviews of this product without prior consent from Network Associates, Inc.*

In January 2003, a judge in New York City ruled that this was not only unenforceable, but illegal to include, on the grounds that it attempted to violate users' constitutional rights of freedom of speech (`library.findlaw.com/2003/Jul/29/132942.html`). Although it may be possible to sign away one's rights in some circumstances, software licensing was not deemed to be one of those circumstances. The New York Attorney General Eliot Spitzer, who brought the case, said 'Whether the subject is political debate, debate in the arts and sciences, or debate over what software to buy, we must protect free and open speech from intimidation. The public has a right to information about products and technologists have a right to create and innovate, so long as they adhere to the law when doing so' (`www.oag.state.ny.us/press/2003/jan/jan17a_03.html`).

DRM required

Microsoft Windows Media Player (WMP) is a piece of 'middleware' to play music and movies on a computer. Version 7 of WMP was bundled with Microsoft Windows 2000. Unfortunately, this version contained a bug which compromised the security of the operating system. Microsoft therefore released a 'security patch' for WMP, in the form of an updated version, available without charge as an upgrade file to anyone with the previous version. The licence terms of this update and security patch caused a stir when released. The new version was moving toward Digital Rights Management implementation and gave Microsoft the right to check your computer for 'compromised' DRM software and to disable it.

> *Digital Rights Management. Content providers are using the digital rights management technology contained in the applicable OS Product ('DRM') to protect the integrity of their content ('Secure Content') so that their intellectual property, including copyright, in such content is not misappropriated. Portions of the applicable OS Product and third party applications such as media players use DRM to play Secure Content ('DRM Software'). If the DRM Software's security has been compromised, owners of Secure Content ('Secure Content Owners') may request that Microsoft revoke the DRM Software's right to copy, display and/or play Secure Content. Revocation does not alter the DRM Software's ability to play unprotected content. A list of revoked DRM Software is sent to your computer whenever you download a license for Secure Content from the Internet. YOU THEREFORE AGREE THAT MICROSOFT MAY, IN CONJUNCTION WITH SUCH LICENSE, ALSO DOWNLOAD REVOCATION LISTS ONTO YOUR COMPUTER ON BEHALF OF SECURE CONTENT OWNERS. Microsoft will not retrieve any personally identifiable information, or any other information, from your computer by downloading such revocation lists. Secure Content Owners may also require you to upgrade some of the DRM components in the applicable OS Product ('DRM Upgrades') before accessing their content. When you attempt to play such content, Microsoft DRM Software will notify you that a DRM Upgrade is required and then ask for your consent before the DRM Upgrade is downloaded. Third party DRM Software may do the same. If you decline the upgrade, you will not be able to access content that requires the DRM Upgrade; however, you will still be able to access unprotected content and Secure Content that does not require the upgrade.*

Although this is probably no worse than the EULAs of a number of other applications, the objectionable aspect of it is that this version of WMP is the only way to upgrade existing software which was part of a purchased bundle to repair a security problem. There are three options when faced with such an EULA: accept it; leave existing software with security holes on your machine; remove the security-compromised software or at least do not use it. None of these options appear particularly positive if you object to the EULA's terms (www.onlisareinsradar.com/archives/consumer_rights).

COPYRIGHT AND THE ARCHITECTURE OF CYBERSPACE

The Internet is at the same time the biggest opportunity for and the biggest threat to creative works the world has ever seen. As more and more people gain fast access to the Internet, the possibilities for on-demand delivery of all forms of entertainment and information are huge. Existing laws and social norms cannot survive untouched, that is plain. However, the influence of existing vested interests in retaining their current business models have led, at the same time, to the possibilities of unprecedented control of how, when and for how much people will gain that information and the potentially disastrous collapse of existing modes of doing business, including ways of supporting the creators of new work. How long this tension can continue and what the outcome will be is impossible to judge. The only thing that is certain is that we will be living in interesting times for some years to come.

This chapter has not covered all aspects of the copyright and patents debates. We have not touched on the music sampling debate, radio airplay, web broadcasting and re-broadcasting, proposals for 'secure computing bases', or the combination of patent, copyright and trade secret law on which the computer games console industry depends (see Chapter 3 for a brief review of that topic) and we have only briefly mentioned the DRM debate. The realm of copyright, patents and trade marks is so bound up with the development of technology and the legal and social consequences and ethical considerations that therefore arise, that a brief introduction such as this can only scratch the surface.

FREE CULTURE

Inspired by the example of free and open source software, Lessig and others created the idea of the 'Creative Commons' (creativecommons.org). Whereas most copyright-protected work contains the mark © and the phrase 'all rights reserved', the Creative Commons project aims to enable creators to maintain some of their rights but allow others to make use of their work without constantly having to negotiate every detail. (Lessig 2004, p. 282) lays out the rationale for this project. Creative Commons licences allow a creator to specify that others may do some or all of the following:

- copy and redistribute the original
- create derivative works.

There are restrictions that are similar to the restrictions in free or open source software licences:

- Attribution: the original creator must be given credit for their work.
- Non-commercial: redistribution and derivative works may only be used for non-commercial purposes.
- Share-alike: the creator of derivative works must allow similar freedoms to those using their work as they were granted.

These licence terms are very much 'pick-and-mix'. See the Creative Commons web site for an explanation of how to indicate these restrictions and exactly what they mean.

One of the significant services offered by the Creative Commons organization, in collaboration with major search engine providers such as Google and Yahoo!, is that of searching the Web specifically for material which is available under an appropriate Creative Commons licence (`search.creativecommons.org`). A significant number of photographs, for example, are available on the flickr picture-sharing service (`www.flickr.com`) under various Creative Commons licences.

DISCUSSION TOPICS

Is Copyright the Correct Way to Reward Artists? Does It Promote Artistic Activity?

Since the Statute of Anne, publishing companies have claimed that stronger and longer copyright is needed to promote creativity and reward artists for their work.

Yet authors are constantly dropping out of print long before their copyright expires, musicians are denied access to the market and paid a pitifully small portion of the profits until they become behemoths such as Metallica or Madonna. We even have major musicians such as George Michael comparing his Sony contract to slavery and Janis Ian saying she'd rather get $2 each by selling thousands of CDs directly than get five cents per CD on a recording contract with a publisher who also controls every aspect of the CD including how many get produced and where it will play.

Copyright is a monopoly and, in general, monopolies are deemed to be inconsistent with economic efficiency. In the United States, the basis of the copyright monopoly was originally argued as a way of ensuring that the public good was served by encouraging creators and distributors with a clear business model from which they could benefit. In the modern world, many commentators such as Lessig, Litman and John Perry Barlow argue that the concept of 'the public good' has been entirely lost in the current debate. They contend that the situation is now effectively indefinite protection (with constantly extending protection never allowing works to enter the public domain) and complete protection (by banning services such as `MP3.com`, suppressing freedom of speech in the DeCSS cases, and so on). Is it now time to consider sweeping away the old regime and renegotiating the copyright bargain for the modern world?

For years, many countries have levied duties on blank media (audio and videocassette tapes) and paid royalties on aggregation measures to decide who gains how much. Should such levies be considered for bandwidth, with the proceeds being returned to authors, musicians and movie makers? If it was legal and paid for, surely most users would happily allow anonymous monitoring of their downloading from peer-to-peer networks? With the artists being paid directly they would then be in the driving seat in terms of advertising and radio airplay. The existing businesses of the RIAA members would, indeed, be destroyed by such a move, but since they do not create, what is the justification for their continued existence, if it can be seen as contrary to the interests of both ends of the chain: the producer and the consumer? No other industry gains such legal protection to prevent being overtaken by new technology in the modern world, so why are record companies an exception?

Lack of Legitimate Downloads Caused the Rise of Peer-to-Peer File-Sharing

The major music publishing companies have loudly blamed peer-to-peer file-sharing services for a claimed reduction in sales (their claims are hotly disputed both in terms of whether their sales are actually falling and in terms of the reasons for differences). One thing that is clear, however, is that the publishing companies dropped the ball on consumer expectations as the Internet took off. Although Napster, `MP3.com` and others were offering easy to use and free or cheap services to access music online, the recording companies took years to bring any form of legitimate downloads to market.

When such systems have been brought out, they have significant problems: highly restrictive Digital Rights Management regimes which prevent the user from accessing the material they have bought on multiple devices in multiple locations and pricing structures that have been ridiculed. By setting the rate for download per song, with little or no discount for a full album, at equivalent to or higher than the cost per song for the album on CD, the music publishing companies have shown their greed and undermined their own case that the reasons for the price of CDs included significant amounts of per-item costs in distribution and retail. All economists agree that the distribution costs, even for heavily DRM-protected downloads, should be much cheaper than those for physical discs: there are no discs to press, no labels to print, no cases to manufacture and assemble, no truckers to pay and no warehouses to maintain. Given that Amazon can afford to undercut the high street on books, CDs and DVDs in most cases by removing the cost of retail space and associated staffing, surely the economics of downloading dictate that it should be cheaper than other means.

When CDs became the dominant distribution mechanism for recorded music, rapidly displacing vinyl records and reducing the sales of pre-recorded audio cassettes, the recording companies increased the price per item although manufacturing and distributing the discs was cheaper. Over the years they have consistently defended this with a variety of arguments but what it really comes down to is greed and what the market will bear. Music fans have been forced to pay up, do without, or find ways to get the material more cheaply or for free: buying from pirate distribution channels at much lower costs or copying (first onto audio cassette and then onto writable CDs) friends' originals. Once digital downloading became possible and reasonable it was clear to all that it must be cheaper for the recording companies to provide them than it was for them to ship CDs. But still, the cost per song remains at or above the cost per song from the high street. So, the recording publishers were very late in coming to the world of digital downloading of music and provided difficult-to-use systems, so it is their own fault that peer-to-peer services remain far more popular than their legitimate counterparts.

A New Basis for Copyright Law Is Required

Even copyright lawyers agree that copyright law is a minefield. (Litman 2001) argues that any law that cannot be adequately explained to the average high-school child should not be deemed to apply to people in their everyday lives. There are other areas of law so complex as to defy reasonable explanation to high-school children, such as the tax system, but most of these are not something that people have to deal with every day of their lives. Over the course of the twentieth century, the pace of change of information technology (and by this we include all forms of information transfer, distribution and reproduction) accelerated from being a luxury in 1900 to a necessity in 2000 (education experts are saying that children without home access to fast Internet connections may be significantly disadvantaged compared to those that do).

The philosophical basis of copyright law rests on the premise that the most efficient way to reward creators for their work and to provide a financial environment allowing future work is to place restrictions on the making of physical copies of existing works. Although this was a reasonable compromise between attempting to control all reproduction of intellectual ideas (clearly impossible even in the sixteenth century) and lack of any controls leading to a paucity of work being produced and disseminated, it is no longer the case that works must be physically copied. Without the requirement for physical distribution and with no restriction on the number of copies that may be made from a single original nor a generational degradation in copying copies, the concept of making a charge for each individual copy is outdated and unreasonable. Ever-increasing attempts to control digital copying will not work and in the interests of a stable and continued flow of creative works, a new structure for rewarding creativity is needed.

Control and the Copyright Bargain

The law of copyright is often represented as a bargain between the general public, who desire access to old and new creative works, and the creators who have physical and creative needs (raw materials, a place to work, food to eat, disposable income, and so on). To provide for those needs, the public agrees to a limited monopoly on certain forms of reproduction in exchange for which works are widely distributed and the economic basis for future production is guaranteed. Of course, there are problems with this model: unless one can convince a wealthy patron to support the initial work, many do not have the resources to put into creating the first work from the proceeds of which to fund future ones. However, this is seen as a useful quality control: not all supposedly creative work is really worth paying the author to produce. This bargain mostly worked during the industrial revolution. Enough guarantees and competition among middlemen (printers, publishers, retailers) existed that quality control did not often descend into outright censorship of something a large portion of the audience desired (we are ignoring state censorship as a separate issue here).

In the modern world, however, the right to create and share is in danger of being undermined by the desire of a group of middlemen to retain their oligopoly over distribution and the huge profits they have leveraged in this area. Attempts by the music industry to force manufacturers of general-purpose machines (such as personal computers) to limit their range of utility to protect the music industry's business model should be strenuously resisted. In addition, attempts to allow copyright distributors (and it is primarily distributors not creators who are engaged in these efforts) to set far more restrictive terms of access than are set in law must be resisted. Consider the case of Adobe's eBook-reading system which was not compatible with screen-reading software. Should such proprietary software become the norm and restrictions on accessing the content of materials (or even providing the software for others to do so) become illegal, then society becomes dependent on the goodwill of the providers for access which should be a basic human right. The terms of the copyright bargain have already swung too far in favour of creators and distributors (the length of protection being set at a full lifetime beyond the death of the original creator is ridiculously overlong) and should not be allowed to move any further in that direction.

REFERENCES

Lessig, L. (2004) *Free Culture*, Penguin, London. ISBN 1-594-20006-8.

Litman, J. (2001) *Digital Copyright*, Prometheus Books, Amherst, NY. ISBN 1-57392-889-5.

Vaidhyanathan, S. (2001) *Copyrights and Copywrongs*, New York University Press, New York. ISBN 0-8147-8806-8.

RELATED READING

Davenport, N. (1979) *The United Kingdom Patent System: A Brief History*, Mason, Homewell. ISBN 0-8593-73157-3.

Drahos, P. and **Braithwaite, J.** (2002) *Information Fedualism*, Earthscan Books, London. ISBN 1-85383-917-5.

Gregory, D.A., Saber, C.W. and **Grossman, J.D.** (1994) *Introduction to Intellectual Property Law*, BNA Books, Washington, DC. ISBN 0-87179-823-9.

Lessig, L. (1999) *Code and Other Laws of Cyberspace*, Basic Books, New York. ISBN 0-465-03913-8.

Lessig, L. (2001) *The Future of Ideas*, Random House, New York. ISBN 0-375-50578-4.

Lohr, S. (2002) *Software Superheroes from Fortran to the Internet age*, Profile Books, London. ISBN 1-86197-243-1.

Merriden, T. (2001) *Irresistible Forces: The business legacy of Napster and the growth of the underground Internet*, Capstone, Oxford. ISBN 1-84112-171-1.

Samuels, E. (2000) *The Illustrated Story of Copyright*, Thomas Dunne Books, New York. ISBN 1-86197-243-1.

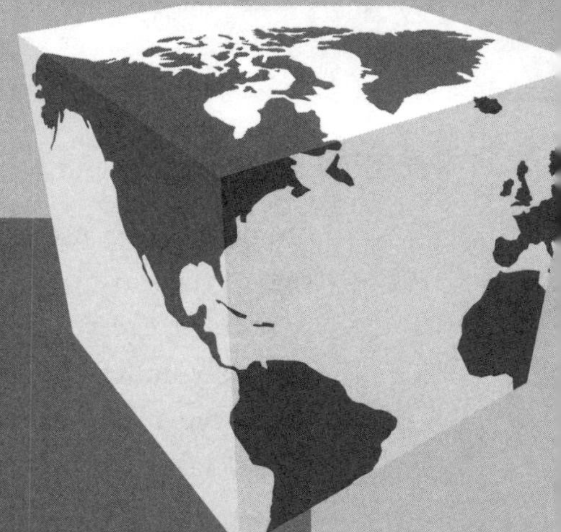

13

UNWANTED ELECTRONIC ATTENTIONS

INTRODUCTION

Besides all the benefits it has brought, the rise of electronic communication media has also led to an unfortunate side effect. The easier it is for more people to communicate with one another, the greater the chance that some communications will be intrusive, unwanted and even constitute harassment. With commercial communication, the primary driver is the economic cost versus the potential economic benefit: where the benefit accrues to one party at the expense of the other there is an imbalance which needs addressing by some form of regulation.

So, there are two major issues in unwanted electronic attention: economically motivated attentions, primarily advertising, the worst examples of which are unsolicited e-mails and instant messages and pop-up or pop-under windows spawned by web pages; and harassment by electronic means such as online stalking, use of chat rooms to groom children for abuse, and so on. These are two of the most obvious and objectionable misuses of modern communications. In particular, everybody loves to hate spam: this and other plagues on the Internet are seriously undermining the utility of the Internet and in some cases have completely destroyed useful elements of online communication. The ways to deal with such antisocial behaviour require a combination of technical, legal and social approaches. Often only a coherent approach combining all such forms of defence can have a significant impact on the problem. Unfortunately such coherent responses are too often slow to develop and the antisocial elements have moved on to a new format by the time the rest of society protects itself. This is not to say that such responses are worthless: without them the earlier forms of unwanted attentions would continue and add to the annoyance of the new form.

Pop-up window: a web browser window containing advertising that appears on top of the current web browser window; pop-up windows often recur when closing the window – it may be necessary to close the browser or even reboot the machine to remove them

Pop-under window: a web browser window that appears under the current browser window; pop-under windows are often not noticed until the original browser windows are closed or minimized, which often makes it difficult to identify the web site that created the new windows

We begin in this chapter with an overview of various means of communication and how they have been used in ways which some people regard as unwanted. We then focus on the different forms of unwanted attentions prevalent in the information age, not all of which use the Internet as their direct medium of operation, but almost all of which depend on computer processing for their efficacy. We move gradually from the commercial to the malicious before finally considering the unholy alliance of malicious and commercial communications that has recently emerged.

TYPES OF UNSOLICITED COMMUNICATION

Every day every person in the industrialized world is subject to any number of unsolicited communications. Many of them are unobtrusive enough that we mostly pay little attention (they do impinge but do not obtain full conscious attention). The psychology of advertising and persuasion is too complicated for us to present here, so as an introduction we simply concentrate on what these messages are and how they are communicated.

Static Visual Communication

Advertising is everywhere, from the sides of houses to the backs of buses. Even private cars often display bumper stickers or window stickers showing where the vehicle was purchased. If one travels around much, it is definitely noticeable that different visuals are used and accepted in different countries. In some European countries, for instance, it is perfectly allowable to display bare-breasted women in advertisements for anything from women's underwear to beer or tobacco. In other countries, such semi-nudity is not allowed in public advertising.

Almost every newspaper and magazine we read contains static advertisements, sometimes difficult to distinguish from the content of the publication itself. In Germany in the mid-twentieth century, fiction regularly included sections where the hero of the tale would sit down to a satisfying bowl of Brand X soup. Close examination would reveal a small marker at the top of the page to indicate this was an advertisement.

Much of the early content on the Web was funded by text or image-based advertisements downloaded along with the desired content. Although this has become less of a viable business model, mostly because companies found that the advertising they were paying for did not translate into sufficient sales to support the advertising budget, the meta-level of this world still exists in the form of major online advertisement aggregation companies such as `doubleclick.com` and their competitors. The static image advertisement which is a link to the advertised product sales site is simply the tip of the iceberg in this respect, however, as we shall see below. Static visual communication also includes text, although text requires much more attention to parse than images.

Audio Communication

Audio communication is an interesting format for advertising. It can be synchronized with still or moving images or be a separate channel of its own. Different communications can form part of a single stream of communication: audio advertisements between records for example. Audio communication can also be an attention-seeking device, such as the beep emitted by a computer to indicate a change of status, an error or some other simple 'alert'.

Moving Visual Communication

Movement attracts attention. There is no simple way to avoid this fact: it is hard-wired into mammalian brains mostly because, in nature, movement can be dangerous and so requires attention to form a judgement on the potential risk. It might just be a tree waving in the wind but it could be a predator ready to jump on you. Advertisers are well aware of this fact and so animated advertisements are a favourite for inclusion in web pages. This idea is also used in television and cinema advertising. Consider the method of making a phone number for a service memorable: computer graphics are used to make the numbers change size, shape or colour in turn as they are pronounced by a narrator. This focuses the viewer's attention on each number in its correct position in the sequence.

TYPES OF COMMUNICATION MEDIA

Public Displays

From billboards to shop fronts and even on the back windows of other people's cars, it is impossible to avoid still image advertising in the developed world. In certain places (Times Square in New York and Piccadilly Circus in London, for example), large-scale, moving images are already in place and, as the cost and fragility of such displays reduces, they are likely to become even more common. Recent developments in both organic light-emitting diodes and 'digital ink' systems are bringing down the cost of creating and operating large-size visual displays.

Broadcast Non-Interactive Media

Advertising has long been one of the mainstays of broadcast television and radio. Intrusive as it is, people have mostly accepted the necessity of television advertising as the prime source of funding for free-to-air broadcasting. As subscription-based services become more common, the percentage of the broadcast time dedicated to advertising on some channels has reduced, in some cases to nothing and in others (such as some movie channels) to between programmes only. As we covered in Chapter 2, the development of video-on-demand services and digital video-recorders are also undermining the basic advertising-driven, free-to-view television broadcasts. This breakdown of the economic basis of the 'standard' business model for non-interactive broadcast media is creating one of the battlegrounds in copyright (see Chapter 12). Broadcasters are requesting control over devices that can be used to record, copy and redistribute television programs. It is already generally possible to download many popular US television shows from the Internet (by way of usenet newsgroups particularly) as soon as they have been shown. Some members of the television industry are reacting in similar ways to the music publishing industry and are trying to stop the progress of technology instead of trying to find new business models. While general-purpose computers remain more profitable (and more economically valuable to business) than closed hardware systems, it is doubtful that such efforts can succeed. However, defence of basic freedoms (in particular the freedom from external control and censorship) must be undertaken by those who understand, otherwise they are in danger of undermining potential future convergence of interest between the content publication industries and the technology manufacturers.

Broadcast Interactive Media

The move to digital television services on terrestrial broadcast, cable provision and satellite broadcasting has brought in the new so-called 'interactive' television services. Much of this is little more than a new combination of old technology (teletext plus extra channels) put together into rolling news segments on headlines, weather, sport and business, for example. The interactivity is relatively limited on most services although on cable (and satellite, when using an addition phone line uplink) there is the slow growth of more advanced interactivity: instant messaging to programme presenters; head-to-head gaming; instant voting systems for reality television shows. Finally, of course, advertisers have caught on to the potential for interaction during advertisements or even during programmes themselves. So instead of just product placement, there is now an option to request more information about everything from cars to soap powders and even the ability to order immediately. Such 'direct' ordering is also available as an interactive service on home-shopping channels, which also make use of interaction for auctions, often in parallel to their original telephone-based systems and increasingly with Internet-based access as well.

Telephonic Services

Fixed-line Telephones

Fixed-line telephones provide direct access to residences. Originally, making a telephone call was a more expensive way of communicating a certain amount of information than sending a printed leaflet or a written letter. New technologies (automated switching and direct dialling, trunk links capable of carrying multiple conversations over a single backbone connection and packet-switching services that completely replace line switching) have gradually brought the cost of carrying the communication down. This has shifted the cost burden from being based primarily on the medium to the human involvement.

Telephone selling (telesales) is the modern equivalent of the door-to-door salesman. It is just as intrusive in many ways to the recipient, but much more efficient for the seller. Until recently, it still required a person to perform each individual call. When it started, it required telesales operators to physically dial each number from a list: marking those who were interested, not interested or not answering, on the paper list. This was improved by a database being used to bring up numbers or call them automatically and on which the caller could record the response. These days, a computer system controls every stage of the process, proactively estimating the time until a caller becomes free, how long it takes to make calls at this time of day (including how many rings until someone picks up) and autodials numbers to reduce the 'down time' of callers. The most advanced versions of this system can even tell the difference between a person answering and an answerphone or automated answering service picking up the call. A recent development has also led to an increase in pre-recorded messages being played to receivers of calls. Where simplistic autodiallers are in use this results in the amusing concept of a recorded message playing to an automated answering service – just two machines talking to each other, which is appropriate considering the unwanted and unnecessary nature of many of these messages. When 'aggressive' settings are used on autodialler services, a substantial number of dead calls which occur.

> Cold call: a sales telephone call from a company with whom the recipient has no prior relationship
>
> Dead call: a telephone call which terminates as soon as the recipient connects, caused by over-eager automated prediction of operator availability

Mobile Telephones

In the United Kingdom, mobile telephones have a separate number base from fixed-line connections and the excess connection charges are usually applied to the caller's bill, not the receiver's. In the United States, mobile phones share the same number range as fixed lines and the excess charges are usually applied to the receiver. This changes the use of mobile numbers for unsolicited contacts in two ways: in most countries there is no inclusion of mobile numbers in telephone directories and the cost of calling them may be both significantly higher than to fixed lines and less susceptible to bulk-call discounts. Therefore unsolicited calls to mobile numbers are less common. However, as call costs come down and more people provide their mobile phone number to a variety of commercial organizations (which may then sell on their customer contact lists), unsolicited calls to mobiles are becoming more frequent.

Text Messaging

As mentioned elsewhere, text messaging was the surprise 'killer app' for mobile-phone market penetration in the United Kingdom and Europe, though much less widely used in the United States. Although originally free, mobile phone operators soon realized they had a money-making opportunity and began to charge for messaging. Charges vary but remain relatively low and bulk discounts are available. Despite the limited number of characters available, using text messaging services to send advertising is on the increase, particularly for services delivered to a mobile phone, such as ringtone downloads.

> Killer app: an application that many people want to use and which ensures the success of the hardware or software platform on which it is based; examples include the spreadsheet for personal computers and text messaging for mobile phones

Multimedia Messaging

Still image and video-clip messaging is still relatively expensive and capable handsets have not reached full penetration of the market yet. However, these systems are beginning to be used for advertising, just as text-messaging services have been.

Fax

Sending advertisements by fax used to be an awkward business because fax machines scanned documents 'live', that is, they scanned them and transmitted the scan information as it was created. As computer memory became cheaper however, it became economical to produce cheap fax machines that had sufficient memory to scan one or more pages and keep them in memory. In addition, personal computers also gained fax capabilities. The spread of the fax machine as a business necessity also encouraged unscrupulous advertisers to send large numbers of unsolicited fax advertisements to large numbers of recipients. As with e-mail spam, junk faxes have threatened to destroy the utility of the technology completely, by overwhelming the medium with costly unwanted communications.

Internet Services

The Origin of the Word Spam

Spam is a trademark of the food company Hormel, for its tinned processed meat (`www.spam.com`). In their comedy sketch show, the Monty Python team had a sketch involving a café which served nothing without spam and in which a bunch of Vikings sang a song consisting mostly of the word Spam with occasional other words ('wonderful Spam, lovely Spam') thrown in. Occasionally this song overrode the conversation about a customer who wanted something to eat which did not contain spam. The overwhelming nature of the product and the song in this sketch inspired use of the term first to describe programs that produced lots of extraneous output (e.g. debugging messages that cannot be turned off) and then later to overwhelming multiple postings on usenet and by email (`catb.org/jargon/html/S/spam.html`).

Usenet

There had long been occurrences of people being stupid or deliberately obtuse and abusing the open nature of usenet by cross-posting messages to many groups, many of them inappropriate for the topic. But in 1994, a pair of Arizona lawyers named Laurence Canter and Martha Siegel started the avalanche (`news.com.com/2008-1082-868483.html`). Every year the United States runs a random 'lottery' to gain a Green Card (permanent residence and work permit). Although legal advice is not needed to enter it, Canter and Siegel were among the law firms who offered pricey services to those who did not know any better. On 13 April 1994, they decided to send out multiple messages to all the usenet newsgroups that their Internet Service Provider (ISP) carried, offering their services in helping to submit an application to the Green Card Lottery. Their postings led to a huge flame war that engulfed almost all of usenet. It was also the first little ripple in a wave of unsolicited inappropriate commercial advertising which disregards all etiquette and attempts at discrimination of subject on usenet. However, worse was to come when the plague spread to direct e-mail.

E-mail

There are many forms of e-mail that are unwanted. In some cases, there is a fuzzy dividing line between what is spam and what is simply unwanted. The most common form is unsolicited commercial e-mail (UCE), sometimes called unsolicited business e-mail (UBE). Other forms of unwanted e-mails include electronic chain letters, pyramid schemes and other financial scams.

UCE spam is simply the spread of advertising from physical mail to telephone to e-mail. It is much more prevalent, however, because of the economics of sending e-mail compared to the other forms of communication. On the whole, individual pieces are not generally offensive (apart from the problem of advertisements for sexual material being sent to children – see Chapter 5). What primarily causes the problem with UCE spam is simply the amount of it. What is a minor annoyance when it consists of one in 100 e-mails becomes a major issue when it reaches 50 in 100. For individuals who receive small amounts of ordinary e-mail it may become even more of a problem since they may receive the same amount of spam as a major user and thus it may be that spam is over 90% of their incoming messages.

Chain letters have been around for a long time. They vary a great deal in content but all use some method of trying to persuade the receiver to pass it on further. Simple ones prey on superstition – false anecdotes about people who 'broke the chain' and suffered disastrous consequences. They can circulate for a long time as it takes only one recipient at each stage of distribution (typically multiple copies are supposed to be sent) to continue the chain. Their effect is limited to those who receive them directly, however.

Two variants of the chain letter or e-mail have different implications. Pyramid scheme communications give a number of names and addresses of people to whom you should send money and then says you should delete the one at the top, add your name at the bottom and send it out. It promises rich rewards for complying and dire warnings that this only works if everyone 'plays the game' and sends the money. Anyone with an ounce of sense would realize that the money has to come from somewhere, eventually the pyramid will be saturated and that sending money 'up the pyramid' has no link with people further down the pyramid sending money back up. Still, such schemes continue to circulate by snail mail and e-mail.

The second type of chain e-mail with significant wider consequences is typified by the 'sick child' plea. The message asks for two things, first, that the recipient send a postcard or get-well card to a sick child in a particular hospital, usually to break some sort of record to form a 'lasting memorial' for a terminally-ill child and, second, that the recipient pass the request on to as many others as they can. The origins of this type of chain e-mail are difficult to track down. Although it is possible that there was once such a campaign, or even that some sick child somewhere is still trying this, the vast majority of them are hoaxes. Beyond the increase in bogus e-mail messages that everyone has to deal with there is a 'real world' consequence of the named hospital or hospice receiving significant amounts of mail, usually for a non-existent patient, which takes vital resources away from their job of dealing with the sick and terminally ill and may even overwhelm their post services to an extent that vital medical communications go astray or are delayed.

Finally, we come to the use of e-mail for fraud, which comes in two primary forms: phishing, which is dealt with in Chapter 11, and 419 scams. Nigerian Criminal Code Section 419 is the section that deals with financial fraud, in particular 'advance fee' scams where (usually illegitimate) transactions require a pre-payment. It is difficult to find someone who has had an e-mail account for more than a few months and who has not received at least one 419 e-mail. They usually begin something like this:

Humble Greetings from Nigeria. Please pardon the personal approach when we have not met but a MUTUAL FRIEND indicated that you might be willing to help in this matter. I am Uliyem Uliyeman and my uncle was previously the Chief Financial Officer of the State Nigerian Oil Company. Following his death late last year we discovered that he maintained foreign accounts in your country which contain in excess of $100,000,000. He set up security requirements with the bank that require a national of your country to provide documentary proof of the identity of anyone trying to withdraw the funds...

The initial contact plays on the recipient's greed (as does any good confidence trick) and offers a proportion of the funds in return for help in obtaining them. Anyone naive enough to respond will be asked to provide sums of money for anything from bribes to taxes to transfer fees to ensure the eventual access to the funds. Once the victim has run out of patience or money or both, all contact addresses go dead. Although there are sources of such frauds in other countries, most of them, whether appearing to involve Nigeria or not, are actually run from Nigeria, although some variants on the scheme have come up in Western Europe and North America. The most common of these European and American variants is the 'international lottery' win requiring pre-payment of tax or similar before the large prize can be released. For those of us not naive enough to be taken in, the individual scams themselves are not particularly bothersome. However, the number of such messages arriving in e-mail inboxes can be a significant proportion of the unwanted e-mail, adding to the general decline in the utility of e-mail as a form of communication. See `www.theregister.co.uk/2004/07/09/419_scam_anatomy/` for a detailed description of the process of a scam. See Chapter 7 for further information on online frauds.

> Nigerian 419 scam: the section of the Nigerian criminal code which criminalizes 'advance fee fraud'

Last, but not least, there are e-mails which would be perfectly acceptable if not for the number of them that we receive. The latest truly funny joke doing the e-mail rounds is fine to receive once, or even maybe twice, but once one has received it from 50 different people in four or five versions, it simply adds to the overload.

The Web

One of the first business models of how to make money from providing 'free' information on the Web was to advertise other web sites or real-world companies. Despite the bursting of the dot com bubble, advertising on web sites, particularly those which provide information freely, is still common. Most users have learned to ignore most advertisements or to scan them quickly and move on to their purpose for visiting the site in the first place. This can be difficult to do when advertising is deliberately designed to obscure the desired content, or where useful aspects of web operation (e.g. referrer logs) are hijacked and their utility destroyed by unscrupulous commercial exploitation. Examples of advertising over-stepping its bounds on the Web include:

- Pop-up windows: one of the features of 'active' web pages is that they can 'spawn' extra windows. Often this is a legitimate part of the operation of the site, creating a new window to display help material, a lookup tool or similar. However, this ability was quickly hijacked by unscrupulous advertisers not only embedding their graphical advertisement in a downloaded web page but spawning a new window with their web site in it.

- Pop-under windows: a variant on pop-up windows where the new window appears 'behind' the main browser window and is not seen until the main window is closed or minimized. See the Referral Economics section below for the reasons these variants are still in use.
- Browser hijacking: a JavaScript or Java program can take control of the browser, disable the main controls and download various pages.
- Overlay graphics: bugs in the HTML-rendering routines of browsers allow advertisers to deliberately push advertisements out of their 'correct' location within the browser window and overlay the main parts of the page. This frequently makes the page unusable for viewing the intended content.

THE ECONOMICS OF UNSOLICITED CONTACTS

Some unwanted electronic communications (the latest joke) are sent innocently and become a problem entirely because of volume and repetition and some are deliberately malicious (fraud, chain letters), much of it is sent with some otherwise legitimate financial motive. In this section, we present the reasons why new technologies and their developing economics are leading to more and more intrusion into our everyday lives. Companies have been using 'direct mail' marketing campaigns for decades and the use of telephone, e-mail, SMS and other technologies is simply an extension of this. The reason it is becoming more and more of a problem, instead of a mild irritation, is a combination of the more intrusive nature of some of the contacts and the economics of the situation meaning more contacts are made, at a higher cost to the recipient.

Sender Economics

The economics of unsolicited direct advertising depend on a number of factors: how much it costs to make the contact, what percentage of those contacted make some form of purchase and how much profit is gained on the transactions thus enabled. The basic arithmetic is that extra business must be generated (above and beyond business that would happen without the direct advertising) at a sufficient level of return to justify the costs of the advertising. It must be remembered, however, that direct advertising can sometimes backfire in that if it is intrusive and annoying enough it may put off customers who would otherwise have considered buying some product from the advertiser. It is not the total cost of an item that makes it worthwhile (or not) to send out unsolicited advertising, therefore, it is the profit margin on each item sold compared to the cost of the advertising and the sales it generates.

Junk Mail

For high-profit-margin items, the benefit gained from some sales may therefore outweigh the costs of sending out many unsolicited contacts by letter. It should be noted, however, the costs for sending junk mail are not in a strictly linear relationship to the number sent out. There is the cost of designing the leaflet or brochure (which is a single one-off cost for each mailing), possibly with an additional linear cost for 'personalization' of all or part of the leaflet. Then there is the cost of printing, which is neither one-off nor linear: it includes a setup cost for the printing and then a per item cost, typically with a smaller setup cost for reprinting further batches, as well as the linear cost per item. There may be step changes dependent on the number to be printed since different methods of printing entail different costs but may only be economic at higher quantities.

Typical 'response levels' for direct mail marketing are between 0.1% and 2% of those mailed. As with all advertising, however, companies would be much happier if they could identify more easily groups of people more likely to respond. As mentioned in Chapter 11, detailed profiles of an individual's habits (do they drink wine, do they buy new or second hand cars and so on) may be worth substantial sums to the right commercial organization. It is primarily these sorts of filtering mechanisms (and reduced design and printing costs) that have allowed computer technologies to influence direct-mail marketing campaigns.

However, blanket campaigns where everyone in a specific geographic area is targeted (either impersonally as 'Dear Householder' or by getting a geographic name and address listing) are still undertaken where suitable profiled lists are unavailable or prohibitively costly.

Cold Calling

Cold calling (unsolicited telesales calls) has a much more linear cost basis, although even so there is some variability. The two primary linear costs are the cost per call and the cost per hour. It costs an hour's wages to employ a telemarketer whether they get 50 responses or none. However, unanswered calls are not usually charged by the telephone company (there is often a fixed-line charge dependent on the number of outgoing calls that can be made simultaneously as well). However, with good planning and enough calls being made it is possible to estimate reasonably well how many calls will be answered at any particular time of day on any particular day of the week. Changes in the labour market have also meant an increase in the number of people willing to work, for relatively low pay, outside normal office hours, which offsets the reduction in the number of people at home during those hours (caused by other changes in the labour market). The economics of telesales have some similarities with direct mail in that there is a desire to contact only those interested in making a purchase. However, the more linear costs associated with telesales means that the products advertised in this way tend to be higher profit (in terms of monetary value and margins) goods and services.

The cost of telephone calls has been dropping considerably in recent years, particularly for bulk-calling organizations, leading to a significant expansion in the types of goods and services it is feasible to market in this fashion. Other technology advances have also improved the cost profiles. In addition, specialist companies offering telesales services have emerged, allowing smaller companies to run campaigns (sometimes associated with other forms of advertising such as television or print media) without having to pay the setup and long-term running costs of such advertising. Information technology support in terms of well-indexed information about the product or service also allows for general telesales staff to make calls which would previously have needed a highly trained salesperson.

The move to Voice over Internet Protocol (VoIP) has brought telephone spam (particularly the pre-recorded message variety) even closer in economic terms to e-mail spam, particularly in terms of lowering the international contact cost. This is moving telephone spam into the same jurisdictional problems of e-mail spam as well as producing more problems with the technological ability to trace the call.

Other Telephonic Advertising

Fax, SMS and automated call advertising all have similar economics. The cost is nearly linear for the sender and, with computer access to all these types of technology, the associated fixed costs can be kept low. However, the non-interactive nature of such contacts can be limiting in terms of the sales possibilities.

Spam

Cold calling and spam are the two most reviled forms of marketing. In the next section on receiver economics we examine why. Here, we consider why spam (and other forms of Internet marketing) continue despite the negative attitude of most people. The main reason there is so much more spam than direct mail and cold calling (most people receive a few pieces of junk mail per day and at most a couple of cold calls per day compared with tens or even hundreds of e-mail spam messages) is that it costs so little per message to send out. Whereas employing a telesales work force or buying in a telemarketing service costs pennies per person contacted, it is possible to pay one hundred dollars to send out millions of e-mail messages. Such services themselves are often advertised by way of spam e-mail, both acting as salt in the wound to most people, but also directly demonstrating their effectiveness to those who go on to use their services. Given the low cost of sending spam e-mail advertising, the response rates need only be tiny to justify, in pure economic terms, the monetary cost.

So, there are two things driving most 'real' commercial spam (see below for a discussion on commercial meta-spam and non-commercial spam problems): the reality that enough people will follow up occasional pieces of spam whether or not they realize they are encouraging it; and the perception that it is a useful piece of marketing. Since much spam these days is sent out indirectly by way of large spam companies it can actually be difficult for the company being advertised to differentiate between ordinary new custom and any generated by spam. Of course a distinct surge in customer numbers following a spam campaign indirectly confirms its efficacy. Thus, even if everyone did stop responding to spam, then it is possible that the amount of spam sent would not significantly diminish for some time, if ever. Of course, the world is full of people who cannot see the consequences of their actions and thus a complete halt of responses to spam is unlikely.

Given these economic conditions, it is therefore also unlikely that commercial organizations will all stop sending spam. A variety of approaches will, therefore, be needed to minimize the amount of spam sent and the effects of it when sent. The methods needed will be a combination of social, legal and technological discouragement.

Receiver Economics

So far we have been considering monetary economic values only. On the receiving end of unsolicited and unwanted commercial contacts, however, it is not only money that is spent, although that does happen, but time is wasted and interference in other activities is caused. In some cases, it even completely destroys the utility of some aspect of modern technology by overwhelming it with noise.

Unless the amount becomes significant, junk mail is easily dealt with, simply by throwing it away after opening, or even in some cases before opening when it is obvious that it is unwanted and unsolicited. The monetary cost of delivery is, on the whole, entirely paid by the sender. Occasionally unsolicited mail will be sent with some charge to be paid by the recipient but this is usually a mistake and rare. The same cannot be said of junk faxes. Although the cost of the phone call is paid by the sender the printing cost of receiving material is paid by the recipient. When faxes were first introduced this was significant and it remains an appreciable cost. Besides the paper and ink or toner cost, there is the 'wear and tear' on the receiving fax machine which is not a problem with small quantities but can significantly reduce the working life of a machine when large amounts are received. In addition, for companies that rely heavily on their fax machine for business, such as incoming orders, the time when the fax machine is engaged on junk fax calls is time that it is unavailable to receive legitimate business. Unlike home telephone and fax lines, businesses can rarely afford to have their contact details removed from public listings, indeed they often go to great lengths to advertise their contact details. Since most fax machines are office-based rather than personal, junk faxes typically offer business-oriented services or supplies, everything from stationery to building material. This makes junk faxes no less antisocial, however.

Unsolicited telesales calls do not cost the recipient money in the same direct way that junk faxes do, but as well as interrupting whatever the recipient is doing, they tie up the phone line against other calls. This is slightly less of a problem with modern digital telephone exchange services including automated answering services and call waiting system, but it is still annoying. Most annoying of all are badly set, automated-calling services which regularly make 'dead calls' (particularly to those who answer quickly) and continually re-enter a called number into the queue until a successful contact is made. Many companies making telesales calls withhold their caller line ID (see below for further discussion); even if they leave a number it connects to an uninformative answering machine, leaving the recipient with no straightforward option to stop the unwanted calls except going to their telephone company and raising a possibly time-consuming, formal complaint.

At present, however, by far the most costly form of unsolicited advertising to the recipient is spam e-mail. It has been estimated that dealing with incoming spam costs businesses a significant proportion of their staff time, besides time and money spent on installing and maintaining anti-spam filters on their e-mail servers (`news.bbc.co.uk/1/hi/business/3068627.stm`). Small businesses may not be able to afford such services directly and may have to do without them or pay external contractors for the service. Anti-spam filters also come with the risk of false positives blocking legitimate e-mail and, of course, false negatives occur regularly leaving at least some spam to be dealt with manually. For home users, the situation can make a significant difference. Few home users of the Internet have the expertise to install and maintain good anti-spam filtering systems, so must rely on commercial ISP filtering. Although there has been a significant take-up of fixed-cost, always-on broadband connections, a significant proportion of home Internet users remain on dial-up, charged per minute connections. On such connections, spam costs the recipient more per message than it costs the sender (who is probably sending enough outgoing traffic that they are using a business rate always-on connection of some form).

Finally, any web page that takes over a user's browser and redirects them to an unwanted web site interferes with the usage of their machine and Internet connection, all for someone else's benefit.

UK MPs Read No Evil

In 2003, the UK parliament installed spam filters on their e-mails. Unfortunately, the settings on the spam filter were rather poorly researched and in an attempt to block out unwanted advertisements for sexual material, the filters were blocking legitimate e-mails from constituents, researchers and even other MPs regarding the Sexual Offences Act which was proceeding through parliament at the time (`www.theregister.co.uk/2003/02/04/mps_barred_from_reading_their`). Luckily the system had been set up to store rather than delete the blocked messages and MPs were able to get them released following a phone call. What really irritated MPs was the fact that the spam filter did not even block spam well so they were faced with far too many false positives (legitimate e-mails blocked as spam) and false negatives (spam e-mails allowed in). MPs from Wales (and particularly those in the Plaid Cymru Welsh nationalist party) were even more incensed when Welsh language or dual-language e-mails were blocked in an attempt to clean up the language in e-mails coming in and going out from MPs e-mail accounts (`www.theregister.co.uk/2003/02/05/plaid_up_in_arms_as`). A common Welsh term was possibly being wrongly identified as an English swear word.

This is always the problem with filtering technology – throwing the baby out with the bath water – by 2003, however, installation of filtering software should not have been as difficult as it appears to have been for the UK House of Commons IT staff.

Referral Economics

As mentioned above, a reasonable proportion of the profit made by web sites comes from advertising other sites. In the real world, advertising rates are set according to some indirect measure of their effect: how many people the Neilsen company (`www.nielsenmedia.com`) say watch a television programme (and their socio-economic status) determines the amount advertisers will pay for a slot during that programme. The reason for this is that it is impossible to measure the direct effect such advertising has in terms of purchasing behaviour. With interactive television systems this may change and such a change has already taken place on the Web.

At first, sites deemed ‘popular’ were simply paid to include graphics and texts advertising products, possibly with links to the advertiser’s web site. This relied on self-reporting of popularity by the maintainer of the advertising site – a recipe for shady dealings if ever there was. The architecture of the Web came to the rescue, however, since the HTML image tag (IMG) allows an image to be sourced from anywhere on the Web – it is not required to be on the same machine as the page itself. This allowed advertisers to host their own images and keep them updated with new information without having to rely on the host to update them. Their own logs showed the number of image downloads, to measure the popularity of a site. However, always having the same advertisement on a popular page that is visited regularly is not the best use of advertising – changes are much more noticeable to readers and so advertising aggregation services were developed allowing a single agency to provide a random selection of advertisements to each visitor to a site. However, these systems are still vulnerable to spoofing of ‘hits’ by an automated program requesting the advertisement. Measures are now generally calculated in terms of the number of different IP addresses which request an advertisement in any one day, mostly avoiding the spoofing issue.

However, seeing is not the only thing web surfers can do. The real measure of success is the number of people who, having seen an advertisement, then select the link and visit the advertised site. Money is paid on the basis of 'click through' fees and this encourages browser hijacking and pop-up windows – unscrupulous click-through hosts produce pop-up windows and so one cannot tell if it is the advertised or initial site that is hijacking one's browser.

Advertisers are not blameless however, as can be seen by their actions in using e-mail spam, meta-tag misrepresentation and referrer-log abuse. Meta tags are a simplistic method of attaching unseen indexing information to web pages. They were an early attempt to fix the semantic grounding problem of the Web: how to differentiate between references to a man called Tailor and a web site about a clothes maker. Meta tags were supposed to include useful terms to help search engines categorize the web site. Unfortunately, since the meta tags are inserted manually, there was again a recipe for abuse: sites interested in a lot of traffic, particularly those paid for advertising on the basis of the number of different IP address downloads, had a significant incentive to spoof the system. They did, in such large quantities that meta tags are now close to useless as a means of improving search engine effectiveness: too many sites lie about their contents for the information to be trusted. This is one of many examples of potentially useful technologies having their utility completely destroyed by abuse.

> Meta tag: an HTML tag that does not produce information in a browser window but is supposed to provide information about the page

Another example of such abuse destroying a useful automated tool is the referrer log scam. Unless a browser is specifically set to deny such information, a web server can request the uniform resource locator (URL) of the 'referring page', that is, the site from which a user clicked through to another site. This has been useful for verifying clicks through, although more sophisticated systems use differentiated URLs which give information about the origin of the access within the URL, but point all visitors to the same target site. However, interactive web sites, such as blogs (web logs) realized one of the potential benefits of referrer logs: if a user finds a site interesting they may well find sites that refer to this one interesting as well. This is particularly true when a significant proportion of visitors to a site have found it by way of a specific link. This is one of the examples of simple but effective automatic identification of human online behaviour to the benefit of users.

Unfortunately, such systems have become useless because unscrupulous site owners abuse the system by running programs that search for blogs with referrer logs. Once they have identified such a site, the blog page is then requested multiple times, reporting the program owner's site as the 'referrer page'; this produces a list of referral pages consisting only of such spammed referrals (very often sex sites).

Spam in Blog Comments, No-Google Meta-tag and Googlebombing

As discussed above, referrer logs for blogs have been spammed into uselessness. Because of the effect that blog comment posts can have on search engine rankings spam in comments has also become a major issue. This is exacerbated by the relatively small number of standard software packages on which blogs tend to run. Once an automated method has been developed for uploading comments to a particular version of a widely used piece of blogging software, the utility of the discussion boards can be destroyed by aiming to raise the search-engine page ranking of the advertised site rather than reaching those reading the discussions. There have been two different responses to this: the 'nofollow' tag in URLs and Googlebombing by bloggers.

Google recognized that the page-ranking system is significantly influenced by blogs. It introduced the '-noblog' search switch to enable searchers to avoid results influenced by blogs, but few users know how to use Google beyond typing words into the search box. Once comment spam became a significant problem, Google effectively surrendered and introduced the 'nofollow' tag. Search-engine programs ignore URLs that contain 'nofollow' for page-ranking purposes. Google requested blog owners to add the tag to URLs in comments on their blogs. Although this would solve some of the problem of spam affecting page rankings, it also removes a significant source of page-ranking information.

Rather than include 'nofollow' in their system, some bloggers have started to 'Googlebomb' to promote 'useful' pages up the page rank instead of the advertised sites. As we write, the most prominent example of this is the Wikipedia page on online poker, now in the top ten of Google's page ranking for the search 'online poker' because of blog googlebombing. Although this may be a good technical tactic, it is fighting fire with fire and burning down the Google forest in the process, so is controversial.

Googlebombing: creating many new links to a site to increase its search-engine ranking

Social, Legal and Technological Discouragement

One of the causes of antisocial behaviour online is the apparent anonymity of online activity. A local trader who flyposted their neighbourhood with advertisements would be held accountable for such actions, at the least having to put up with verbal responses to the activity. In the global village of the Internet, however, spammers (both those whose service is being advertised and those who actually send the messages) are subject to far fewer sanctions. In this section, we discuss the various attempts to discourage the sending of spam and other unsolicited contacts: technological fixes to stop or prevent spam being sent or received, ideas to socially sanction spammers and laws which make spam illegal or, at least, allow some method of opting out of a list.

Caller Line ID

Despite the line-switching nature of traditional telephone networks once automated switching became the norm for telephone calls, it required sophisticated equipment and telephone company cooperation to identify the source of an incoming call. With digital switches, however, the pendulum swung in the other direction again and caller line identification (CLI) became simple to operate. An extra modulation on the 'ring' signal even allows CLI to be provided before a recipient has answered the call, allowing recipients to 'screen' their calls based on the CLI of the caller. Some, however, objected to their number being transmitted in this way and so a means of hiding the originating number was introduced. Of course, the number is only hidden from the recipient: the phone company can still identify the numbers. In some cases, it is entirely sensible not to provide a CLI: consider public phone booths for instance. One of the common uses for CLI is to catch missed calls so that a recipient can try to call back someone who tried unsuccessfully to contact them. If the call came from a public phone booth, this would be pointless, as the chances of calling back and getting hold of the call originator rather than some random passer-by (if indeed anyone answers) are negligible. Large organizations that have their own switchboards may not have direct-dial numbers for the extensions used to phone out and providing the main switchboard number would simply lead to many calls back for whom there is no way of identifying the original caller, wasting the time of both the recipient calling back and the switchboard operators. Those who have been the subject of too many negative calls (phone harassment or cold calling) can automatically block incoming calls from anonymous sources.

Most cold calling companies either withhold their number or provide a number which is directed to a useless automated service (saying 'someone called you and will try again later'). So, although the UK Data Protection Act (see Chapter 4 for details) provides for the right of an individual to 'prevent processing of their personal data for the purposes of direct marketing', this is a somewhat useless right when receiving regular dead calls, since the CLI (or lack thereof) does not provide sufficient information to identify the offending organization.

Data Protection: Privacy Policies and Calling Lists

Of course once a cold-calling organization has someone's details, the avalanche has already started and it is too late for a pebble to vote. This is because it is a time-consuming and sometimes difficult process to find out from whom the calling company received the details. Even then, by the time the originating company had been identified they would almost certainly have sold those details on to a number of other organizations, some of whom may have sold them on further, ad infinitum. There are two possibilities for avoiding overload of unsolicited contacts, whether it is by phone or e-mail, which are sourced from lists provided by organizations which legitimately hold people's contact details: the first is to require organizations not to pass on customer contacts; the second is to regulate the activities of those making contact by maintaining and enforcing non-contact lists.

In the European Union, data protection legislation requires organizations not to pass on customer contacts, but only as an opt out: organizations are required to provide mechanisms for customers to avoid their details being passed on and it is a violation of data protection law to pass such information on without permission. The usual way to implement this is to include a tick box somewhere on a form (whether paper or online) which indicates whether or not customers are willing for their details to be passed on. Unfortunately for customers, there is no standardization of forms and on some forms there is more than one box (internal and external contacts, for instance) and it also varies whether ticking the box gives or withholds permission. The inefficient nature of this legislation has led to schemes, some governmental, some industry-based, to explicitly opt out of unsolicited contact (see below).

In the United States, data protection is run much more on free-market grounds. The principle is that customers can choose whether or not to do business with companies that sell their information to others and that market forces will decide which works better. The role of the government, the Federal Trade Commission (FTC) in particular, is to act as the arbiter when companies say they will act in one way but then proceed to act in another. So the FTC operates by checking companies' published privacy policies against complaints or suspicions. In particular the FTC enforces the Gramm–Leach–Bliley Act which prohibits 'pretexting' – gaining personal information (particularly financial information) under false pretences (`www.ftc.gov/privacy/privacyinitiatives/glbact.html`).

Non-contact lists can be effective in certain circumstances, but not in others. To demonstrate this, we consider two such systems in the United Kingdom: the Telephone Preference Service (TPS, `www.tpsonline.org.uk`) and the Mailing Preference Service (MPS, `www.mpsonline.org.uk`). The Telephone Preference Service was set up in the 1990s and was originally an industry group of companies who believed that contacting people who dislike receiving cold calls was not economically efficient. Because there was no real sanction behind the service it was regarded by many consumers as a public relations fig leaf. However, the Data Protection Act 1998 codified the TPS (and a similar scheme for fax numbers called the Fax Preference Service (FPS), `www.fpsonline.org.uk`) in such a way that it became an offence to make a call (or send a fax) to someone who had opted out. Once it had legal backing, the scheme began to bite and the UK Information Commissioner has the power to fine companies based in the United Kingdom who make contact with those listed in the TPS. The MPS, unfortunately, is still in the situation 'enjoyed' by the TPS when it was first set up. It is a completely voluntary scheme with only a small fraction of companies who send junk mail signed up to it.

Without statutory backing there is no effective sanction against those who violate it. Similar schemes exist in other countries both with and without statutory approval and with and without effective sanction. For example, see www.donotcall.gov for the United States equivalent to the TPS, run by the FTC.

Spam-blocking

Despite attempts by some to remake the Internet into a one-to-many broadcast system such as television and print media, it remains, at base, a peer-to-peer network. To achieve the basic goal of robust, efficient distribution, many of the protocols and services in operation on the Internet remain relatively anonymous. In particular, 'push' technologies such as e-mail (as opposed to 'pull' technologies such as the Web) contain the seeds of misuse in their specification. To allow intermittent connections to the Internet, not just by individual machines but by whole networks, e-mail uses asynchronous transfer of data between servers, neither of which is required to be the originating machine nor the final destination. Some of the most useful aspects of e-mail services (mailing lists and digests; automated vacation messages and forwarding; and mail gateways to usenet, the Web and file transfer protocol sites) rely on the nature of the simple mail transfer protocol (SMTP).

SMTP, although extended many times to add new capabilities, is one of the oldest protocols still running in a form close to its original specification (www.ietf.org/rfc/rfc2821.txt). One of the problems with trying to deal with spam is that SMTP was developed as a 'trusting' protocol which in the main defaults to allowing rather than blocking messages. This was all very well when the Internet consisted of primarily military and academic sites and only a few hundred of them at that. With over half of all e-mail traffic consisting of unwanted commercial or malicious messages, however, this trust has been broken. The problem is that e-mail is now such a vital part of the day-to-day use of the Internet by many people and businesses, that replacing SMTP with an improved, less susceptible protocol, would cause too much disruption in the short- to medium-term, even if it then allowed for a much greater long-term benefit in terms of spam reduction. In addition, Internet engineers are often suspicious of any attempt to shift the balance in Internet protocols away from trust toward distrust. Too often such distrustful protocols are proposed by those with something to gain, usually some form of dominant market benefit.

One of the biggest problems in spam e-mail is that too many mail servers operate 'open relays' that accept e-mail for relaying on to other addresses from any IP address. Despite campaigns to close down such open relays there are still far too many operating in this way. The reason many administrators give is that they have users who wish to send e-mail from a variety of connection points (home dial-up, customer offices, Internet cafés) and it would be too much work to restrict the sources of e-mail. A recent and increasing phenomenon has been the use of PCs, which have been cracked and had remote operation software installed, to send spam e-mail. This would not be solved, although it would be improved, by better authentication mechanisms.

> Open relay: a mail forwarding server which accepts incoming mail from anywhere and passes it on

The most success in stopping the negative effects of spam have been achieved by spam blocking or spam filtering. Spam blocking involves attempting to identify spam messages from their content and their header information and either deleting or bouncing them. Spam filtering uses the same technology but, instead of bouncing or deleting the messages, the spam is filtered into a separate inbox. Users can then check the filtered e-mail for any false positives (if they wish and have the time). Such systems can be effective in reducing the amount of spam each user has to deal with and some of them have flexible rules. All of them , however, require staff time to keep them working in terms of manually identifying false positives and false negatives and so, as is often the case, small businesses and individuals have to spend relatively more resources than large ones. Commercial ISPs offering home Internet services are beginning to compete on the quality of their spam blocking (and e-mail virus filtering).

Web Publishing vs e-mail Distribution

This section has mostly covered commercial spam and the attempts to stop it at source, on distribution or on receipt. As discussed, though, not all unwanted e-mail consists of undesirable communication. Even ignoring e-mail circulars, virus warning hoaxes and the like, every so often there will be a flurry of messages that flood the e-mail system and can cause problems. They typically start with a single user creating, or sending a link to, a humorous article. Examples include the 'George Bush 419' (www.theregister.co.uk/2003/01/27/beware_new_nigerian_bush_spam) and the 'Revocation of the Declaration of Independence' (www.truthorfiction.com/rumors/d/declarationrevocation.htm). The originator sends this joke to 10 or 20 friends who each pass it along to 10 or 20 friends. Someone adds something to it or creates an alternate version or a response and so it goes. All just fun, until the originator has received 25 variants of the original and 50 copies of their own creation from people who do not realize where it came from. This is because there is no way to tell if someone has seen it or not without sending them an e-mail asking them if they've seen it, at which point it's just as easy to send it. Eventually such round robins tend to fade away, particularly if the joke is based on current affairs, but they can come around again and again as new variants are created.

This abuse of e-mail (completely innocent and only a problem because of the volume of duplicates arriving in inboxes) may become less of a problem as more Internet users develop proficiency in the wide variety of other communication tools offered by the Internet, from instant messaging to blogs and chat rooms. For example, if a joke is posted to a chat room or blog that most of one's friends read, there is no point in e-mailing the same joke to all one's friends. Similarly, a quick instant message saying 'have you heard the one...' will provide instant feedback about how well known the joke is already and most people will stop trying to retell it when their IM buddies have all heard it. After all, most people realize that retelling known jokes is not cool.

The Tragedy of the Commons

The reduction and sometimes destruction, of the utility of communication tools is an example of what is termed a 'tragedy of the commons'. In 1968, Garrett Hardin published an article that began with a quote regarding the threat of nuclear war: 'It is our considered professional judgement that this dilemma has no technical solution' (Wiesner and York 1964).

Hardin's article shows the problems that develop where property (in the example case, land) is held 'in common' (i.e. free for all the community to use as they see fit individually) and where there is a resource drawn from that land which has an unknown but finite capacity for regeneration. Overuse of the land beyond the point of regeneration leads to a collapse of the entire commons. The example used by Hardin is of herdsmen grazing cattle on a piece of common land. Since each herdsman owns his own cattle and receives the total amount from sale of the cattle, it is in each herdsman's interest to increase his herd as much as possible. Without other factors keeping the number of cattle down, the total number of cattle grazing on the commons will eventually exceed the ability of the land to support those cattle. An ecosystem such as grazing land will suffer a complete collapse in such circumstances, destroying the livelihoods of all the herdsmen.

There are parallels to the use of electronic communication tools in that there is a point at which the utility of the tools collapses under the weight of abuse, denying both the ordinary user and the abuser the benefits of the technology. As with the classic tragedy of the commons, no one can tell when that point will be passed; in the electronic communications field, it will be different for different users: the tipping point coming when most users give up. The ecosystem may never recover as users move on to other options, which may be less usable in some ways but hopefully either less susceptible to abuse or not yet targeted.

Meta-spam

One of the most annoying features of much spam is the completely false nature of it. Unlike junk mail, door-to-door salesmen and cold-calling telesales, a great deal of the unwanted e-mail received from unknown sources does not even have accurate contents, let alone accurate information about its origin. The message may contain a virus or similar (see Chapter 11). A URL prominently displayed in the body of the message may well point to a page for which the mail originator receives a referral fee. Some relatively sophisticated e-mail messages may cause the automatic loading of a web page in the default web browser simply by the user opening the message in their mail handler.

The most annoying form of spam with inaccurate content for many is what might be called meta-spam: e-mails sent not with the purpose of communicating with the recipient per se, but with the intention of checking the validity of the e-mail address. In its simplest form this involves sending messages to an e-mail address to see if it is bounced by the mail server as non-existent. A few commercial ISPs do not actually bounce incorrectly addressed messages but simply delete them. Their reasons for this vary from keeping down the volume of their outgoing material, to avoiding denial of service (DoS) attacks based on bouncing messages, to not cooperating with meta-spam.

There are more sophisticated variants, as well. Some mail-handling programs include the facility for downloading HTML content from the Web, such as graphics, rather than embedding them in the message itself. With e-mail becoming more about sending a nice-looking document these days, this capability does make sense since it allows for caching (locally or on the Internet) of backgrounds and common elements such as graphical emoticons. However, as with many useful capabilities, this is being abused by spammers who may then include a small (practically invisible) graphic in their messages with a URL which allows them to tell whether a particular e-mail message has been opened in a mail handler. This confirms not only the existence of the targeted mailbox but that there is a person actually reading the box. Large-scale spam organizations can charge higher rates if they can demonstrate the validity of the mailboxes on their lists. Intermediaries who do not send anything other than meta-spam also exist, providing a service to both commercial spam organizations and to anyone wishing to send their own spam out. Such intermediaries sometimes use double-edged meta-spam, which both advertises their wares for sale and confirms the validity of their e-mail lists at the same time.

Another common validation feature of meta-spam is the 'select here to opt out' section common to a great deal of spam. So prevalent is this dodge, where the 'opt out' URL simply confirms the existence of a mailbox and a reader, that the general advice to users these days is not to make any such request (either by sending a reply message or by visiting a URL) as it will, in the vast majority of cases, simply lead to more, not less, spam arriving. Those few companies which legitimately operate 'ethical' direct marketing by way of e-mail and offer a real opt-out service are so few and far between that they are swamped by the meta-spam. This presents an immense problem for any new law which attempts to make opting out the primary legal method for keeping spam out of one's inbox.

CAN-SPAM and other anti-spam laws

The problem of e-mail spam has become such an obvious drain on business resources and personal Internet use that the governments of the industrialized world have begun to take notice. There have been long discussions about the best way to tackle the problem with legal solutions since about 1999. The discussions are made more difficult by the fact that few legislators in these countries were early adopters of Internet communications and even fewer are scientists or technologists by training. This lack of knowledge has made it an uphill struggle for many of them to contribute sensibly to the debate on this issue. The representations of the ISPs and user groups have made some inroads into their ignorance. Unfortunately those who use spam and those who offer spam services have also entered the lobbying and their tendency has been to try to obfuscate the issue, on the whole, rather than to provide clarity for legislators.

The difficulties in drafting laws against spam are not unusual to this subject, but they do have some particularly tricky details because of the nature of the technological systems in use. There have also been some constitutional questions raised about the authority of government to ban certain communications, in certain countries. The thorny difficulties come from trying to specify exactly what constitutes spam and who is liable when it is transmitted. In London, the problem of flyposting (illegal gluing of advertising posters on any blank piece of wall) was successfully tackled by going after the publisher of the material advertised or the venue hosting an event. The problem of flyposting had a number of similarities to e-mail spam – legitimate products were being advertised in a way that caused problems for innocent victims, in this case the owners of the buildings being used. Those actually performing the flyposting were paid cash by shady middlemen who provided their services to large corporations through commercial 'blinds'. Arresting and charging flyposters themselves or even the low-level middlemen was not sufficient: there were always those willing to fill the gap. What was needed was a way to get at the source of the problem: the view by record publishing companies and music venues that this was a cost-effective way to advertise. The publishers and venues are now being prosecuted for their illegal advertising, which seems to be having an effect.

As well as considering legal methods for attacking the spam middlemen, legislators have discussed ways to punish the beneficiaries of commercial spam. Unlike the flyposting example, however, this can be difficult because of jurisdictional boundaries. The Web has led to a globalization of individual trade in a volume impossible without it. Mail order catalogues have been available from foreign countries for decades and sometimes suppliers in one country would advertise their wares in magazines in another but the reach of such advertising was always relatively limited. With the Web, however and particularly with global search engines and web-banner advertising, it is just as easy to find a supplier in another country as it is to find one in the next county. The ubiquity of credit cards and the encouragement by both governments and finance organizations to use online shopping means that customers around the world can be served by retailers around the world. This leads to the problem that the recipient of a spam e-mail may be in the United Kingdom, although it was sent by a US spam organization for a retailer in Shanghai. Bringing a suitable legal case against either the spam organization or the retailer would require an international level of cooperation that is difficult to achieve, first in drafting appropriate laws and then in prosecuting cases. Even in the United States, individual state legislation has had difficulty in obtaining suitable jurisdiction over spammers based in other states. As with the Nigerian 419 issue, there may well be countries who find the benefits to their economy of allowing spam to be sent from there outweigh the negatives.

Much of the debate over anti-spam laws has focused on the issue of opting-in or opting-out: should recipients have to opt-out of receiving spam (either individually from each 'direct e-mail marketing' organization or by way of a central database similar to those used for telesales) or should those sending spam be required to have an opt-in (explicit or implicit) from a customer before sending them advertising e-mails. One of the big problems with an opt-out system is the meta-spam problem described above. So common has such meta-spam become that it is standard practice for users to be advised never to follow up on offers to unsubscribe from lists.

In 2003, the US Congress passed the Controlling the Assault of Non-Solicited Pornography and Marketing Act (CAN-SPAM Act), which came into force on 1 January 2004 (`www.ftc.gov/bcp/conline/pubs/buspubs/canspam.htm`). This act provided for a national 'do not e-mail' register, similar to the national 'do not call' register. One of the problems of this, of course, is the 'national' nature of it. Spam is international in both its reach and its sources. Recent estimates have concluded that significant proportions of the worldwide spam epidemic is sourced in the United States, with fewer than ten US-based individuals or organizations being responsible, directly or indirectly, for up to 50% of the spam received worldwide, despite the CAN-SPAM Act. Although the terms of the act would be supported by most people – requiring accurate origination details, accurate subject lines and valid opt-out procedures – the CAN-SPAM act has been criticized by many commentators as insufficiently draconian in its punishments and has sometimes been labelled as the 'You Can Spam' Act. However, as with all such legislation, it will take time to see whether it actually makes a difference. Should it really begin to bite against US-based spam organizations, the international nature of the Internet will probably mean that the problem moves out of the United States and into countries with sufficient infrastructure to support the origination of spam but without sufficient law-enforcement resources to police such activity – emerging Asian economies, such as India, seem prime candidates.

The necessary international cooperation may be developing, however. In July 2004, the International Telecommunications Union organized a spam conference including delegates from regulators in 60 countries and various industry groups (primarily ISPs and security consultation groups). The event followed the landmark signing of a Memorandum of Understanding (often the precursor to a full international treaty) between the United States, the United Kingdom and Australia on coordinating their legislative efforts against spam.

'This is great news, but legislation cannot solve the problem on its own', said Carole Theriault, security consultant at IT security firm Sophos. 'Spam is mushrooming to incomprehensible levels. International legislation will help, but only in conjunction with sophisticated anti-spam software and education will the situation be rectified' (www.sophos.com/pressoffice/news/articles/2004/07/sa_unaims.html). Although the pronouncements of those with a vested interest in selling anti-spam tools might be regarded with suspicion (much as pronouncements about computer vulnerability might be seen as advertising hype by anti-virus firms), most other analysts (government, academic, ISP and user groups) agree that legislation alone is not the answer.

Better Filters and Smarter Users

As we have mentioned above, the reason commercial spam is sent is that the senders believe it will work. It is possible that some would continue to believe it works, even if every single user in the world stopped responding. Given that the basic reason for spam is economic (meta-spam feeds upon the demand for spam and without it would wither away), the entire chain must be seen as uneconomic for it to stop. As well as legislation which raises the risk of being prosecuted (and fined or jailed) for sending spam, it must become well known to those considering sending it that spam is likely to be blocked at various stages in its transmission, from the sender's ISP to the receiving mail server to the user's own machine. Such filtering must of course be done in such a way as to avoid false positives: having legitimate e-mails deleted as spam can be as much, or more of, a problem as having an inbox overflowing with spam. Both reduce the utility of the communication medium.

Spam filtering is indeed getting better both in terms of proprietary solutions and in terms of downloadable free or open source software. The difficulty is that the spam market is not static and it is not only good filtering mechanisms that are required, but good information on which those filtering mechanisms work. As new formats and types of spam emerge and as new patterns of valid e-mail use develop (some of which may lead to false positives), the data on which filtering methods are applied must be kept updated. Small organizations do not have the manpower or resources to deal with constantly updating such systems and it is therefore up to the ISPs to improve their level of service in this regard. For home users, many ISPs are recognizing that high-quality spam filtering is a sales differentiator, particularly where price structures are converging. The same must become true for business provision for small- and medium-sized businesses – large organizations may or may not want to outsource their spam filtering.

Blocking of spam 'in the large', that is at major distribution points, has become a standard practice, involving real-time black-hole lists. These are primarily aimed at organizations that, although not sending spam themselves, are having their systems used to relay spam. Such services usually try to get relays to tighten up their act before placing them on the black lists, since legitimate users also send messages from such organizations. In some cases, the nature of such blocking can catch unrelated organizations in their net; for example groups which share portions of the IP address space with spammers or those who allow spam through their system through laziness or incompetence. There have even been law suits brought by companies alleging interference with legitimate business, both by spammers whose gateways have been blocked and by legitimate organizations who may or may not have been responsible for relaying spam. For example a recent court case in the United States involved a bulk e-mail company suing the Spamhaus project (`www.spamhaus.org`), an anti-spam organization based in the United Kingdom, for interference with its business by referring to it as a spammer. Since Spamhaus is based in the United Kingdom, it declined to respond to the case, claiming it was not subject to that court's jurisdiction. The US court ruled in favour of the bulk e-mail company and awarded it over $11 million in damages (`News.com` by way of `shorl.com/fufidrevefristu`).

Claims that black lists involve denial of the freedom of speech are usually regarded as spurious by courts, but this is an issue that will become more difficult as time goes by and e-mail becomes a more and more common form of communication. As covered in Chapter 5, any form of censorship should be regarded with suspicion, either for its intended but hidden effects or for its unintended effects on freedom of speech, but at the same time freedom to speak does not grant the freedom to force others to hear or listen.

> Real-time black-hole list: a list of Internet addresses that are the source of spam, either through mismanagement or by being owned by spam merchants

Automatic Responses: Adding to the Problem

As mentioned in Chapter 11, a certain amount of unwanted e-mail can be automated responses from virus checkers and spam filters. Although this may once have been a useful indicator to users that their machine had been compromised, the amount of spoofing of origination information in e-mails now makes this part of the problem rather than part of the solution. Having an e-mail address chosen as the spoofed 'from' address of a spam merchant can render an e-mail account unusable because of the amount of return mail it receives (one of the authors has had to drop an address because of this problem). It is difficult to filter out automatic responses from spam filters because e-mail bounce messages are an important part of the e-mail communication medium: if a user mistypes or misremembers an e-mail address, or if it is out of date and a deleted account, they need to know that their individual message has not been received. When a spam merchant has usurped an address as a spoof origin, the number of auto responses one can receive is enormous, far outweighing the problem of ordinary spam. As legislation to stop spam becomes law, it is also a risk that law-abiding individuals might be framed for someone else's spam. In fact, automatic response mechanisms can be seen as a form of distributed denial of service (DDoS) intermediary, which can be used to attack an e-mail account, or even an e-mail server. Automatic response is probably a technology that should be consigned to history, at least until better identification mechanisms are built in to the protocols.

MALICIOUS UNWANTED ATTENTIONS

So far we have described unwanted communication which is primarily a problem because of its volume rather than its content. If everyone received one commercial e-mail a day it would not be such a big international issue. In this section, we concentrate much more on communication which is a problem because of its content.

One area which is a problem both for content and volume is that of pornographic spam. Spam advertising pornography may contain small pornographic pictures or use terminology which is offensive to some people in and of itself. This topic is covered in Chapter 5, with particular reference to the problem of children receiving pornographic advertising in e-mail, and so we do not deal with it in this chapter.

Online and Telephone Fraud

There are two main types of fraud involving online and telephone communications: phishing scams and advance fee fraud. Phishing scams are covered in detail in Chapter 11 but basically consist of ringing or e-mailing someone and getting them to reveal confidential information which can be used to access financial or other services fraudulently. The best-known examples of advance fee fraud are the Nigerian 419 and unentered lottery schemes, described above. There are some grey areas, including premium-rate telephone-claim lines for competitions.

Despite coverage by newspapers, television and radio, people are still falling victim to the Nigerian 419 and other advance fee frauds. Even highly educated people can fall victim to their own greed in such circumstances. The ubiquity of the name Nigerian 419 has led to a change of tactics of the fraudsters, many of whom are still based in Nigeria, such as changing the location of the supposed funds to other failed states and corrupt regimes. Combined with the rise of unentered international lottery scams, this has led to a new need for awareness of all forms of advance fee fraud and a change in the terminology of law-enforcement officials.

The use of premium rate phone numbers as a method of funding low-level gambling has been around for some time now. However, increases in the maximum rate allowed for such lines has also increased their use for a legal variant on the advance fee. The original form of this was to have ‘scratch cards’ distributed free with various other publications or even delivered directly. The cards included ways to win a large variety of prizes, some small in value but with a few relatively large prizes (money or objects worth thousands of pounds, dollars or euros). The difficulty was that there was no way to tell from the card itself what sort of prize might have been won. Unlike purchased scratch cards (where most are ‘losers’, a small number win slightly more than the cost of the card and a tiny number win large prizes), all or most of these cards included some form of winning combination.

To find out what had been won, recipients had to ring a premium-rate telephone line to identify the prize and obtain an individual claim number. Of course, in almost all cases the prize obtained is worth less than the cost of the call.

With higher-rate, premium call services now available, such schemes are operating on a more direct method, using an automated caller to ring up and give details that the recipient has won a prize. Typically these prizes are all apparently relatively high in value but involve both a high-rate premium number to call for details and a significant charge to make the prize worthwhile. The usual 'prize' received is a 'free' holiday, in which only the accommodation is free and it is usually of low quality. Everything else must be paid for at full rates. When added up, such holidays would usually be cheaper through an ordinary travel agent's package deals. Many callers do not even bother to claim their 'free' holiday, knowing that they do not have the freedom to take such an extra holiday at the short notice allowed (usually only a few months) having rung up to see if they've won the more desirable prizes of money, cars, or costly electrical or electronic equipment. Such prize schemes are on the increase and beginning to rival telesales calls for frequency and irritation. Because such schemes use long automated messages to entice people to ring, they also have the negative aspect of tying up the phone line of recipients who answer (the recipient of a call cannot break off a call on most phone systems until the caller rings off) or filling up their answering machine or service with long unwanted messages. Increases in the limits for premium rate numbers are under review in a number of countries in a response to such legal but unethical operations.

Such schemes still retain a financial motivation and are essentially based on large numbers of contacts, adding to the spam level as well as being specifically objectionable in themselves. Such financial scams are not the only form of abuse of online communication.

Electronic Stalking

Obscene phone calls have been a significant problem for decades. When the phone system was automated but unsophisticated it took significant time for a 'trace' to be run on an incoming call, further complicating the problem. These days CLI can solve the problem of identifying the caller although it is not infallible, as indicated above. In particular, cheap switchboard equipment may neither allow companies to identify the extension used for outgoing calls nor provide a CLI for simple tracing. With the rise in the use of computer-mediated communication, a new breed of harasser has arisen: the electronic stalker. The patterns are similar to those for other forms of stalking: the stalker selects one or more victims because of some innocuous aspect of their online appearance and targets them with ever increasing levels of communication. This may start with 'following someone around' web-based chat rooms, using IM services and e-mail. More skilled computer users may attempt (and possibly succeed) in cracking the target's computer gaining access to their other data or even gaining a measure of control over their machine. Webcams are a particularly worrying aspect of this since if a machine is switched on and connected to the network then a remote controller may be able to access the output of the webcam. Even intermittent Internet connections are not invulnerable to such control since data may be stored for transmission when an Internet connection is re-established. It should be noted, however, that those with the skills to perform such access unnoticed are rare, but they do exist.

As we cover in the discussion topic 'Freedom of Speech or Online Stalking' below, online stalking can lead to physical attacks. However, the psychological impact of purely electronic harassment should not be underestimated. Whether or not the stalker has the capability to physically locate the victim may not be the issue. Just as with telephones, where people resist having to go ex-directory with their phone number because this makes legitimate contact more difficult, so changing one's electronic activities becomes a problem as people become more and more reliant on electronic communication channels. Having to withdraw from a mailing list or a chat room, where one has many friends, simply because of the actions of a stalker is a denial of the basic freedom of speech of the victim. Having to change e-mail address, IM handle and so on, can seriously disrupt valid communications and there is no guarantee that the stalker will be avoided this way: they may well be someone with whom the victim also carries on regular conversations under a different online persona.

Jake Baker

In late 1994, Jake Baker, a student at the University of Michigan, posted a story on the usenet group alt.sex.stories. It was an extreme type of story, sometimes referred to as a 'snuff' story, which involved rape and murder. Although not a significant proportion of the fiction posted in such places, such stories are not uncommon. What made this case significant was that Baker used the name of one of his classmates at the university as the victim and specifically wrote in the first person with no framing information to separate the author from the fictional narrator. The full story (with the name of the victim changed to 'Jane Doe') and other details of this case can be found on the electronic frontier foundation (EFF) web site (`www.eff.org/legal/cases/Baker_UMich_case`). Be warned, as Jake Baker himself put in the 'header' to the story: 'the following story contains lots of sick stuff. You have been warned.'

In January 1995, a graduate of the University of Michigan reported the story to the university authorities who investigated whether Baker had indeed posted the story (Baker cooperated with the investigation unwittingly). Having confirmed that Baker was indeed the person who had posted the story to usenet, the university suspended Baker for threatening another student and reported him to the authorities. Baker was later arrested and charged with a federal offence of transmitting threats across state lines. The original charge relating to the posting of the story were dropped to be replaced by a charge relating to an e-mail exchange Baker was found to have had with an unnamed Canadian in which he stated: 'Just thinking about it any more does not do the trick. I need to do it.'

These charges were later dismissed by a federal judge on the grounds that Baker's story, however distasteful to most people, was still protected free speech in that there was no evidence of intent to follow up the crime and, in particular, no evidence that Baker tried to ensure the female student named in the story would read it or that any specific person (the girl named in the story or any other) were mentioned as targets in his e-mail conversations. The consequences to the female student named in the story were significant, but she would have been unlikely to have encountered the story or even anyone who had read the story (other than Baker himself) without the furore surrounding it. Once she knew of it she was, naturally, upset by it but also by the media attention she received.

Had Baker not (rather randomly, he claims) used the actual name of a classmate in his story, it is unlikely that this chain of events would have occurred. Baker himself has said that using a real person's name was 'stupid' although whether his opinion is based on the consequences to him or the consequences to her is unknown. The media furore was partly responsible for some of her distress, which is why media reporting of rape cases generally suppress the name of the accuser.

Online Grooming

Much has been written in the press and broadcast on television and radio about the dangers of 'online grooming' – contact between paedophiles and children online as a precursor to contact offences. This is a real threat and parents must take appropriate precautions. Of course, the problem of allowing children unsupervised access to the Internet is a more general one involving access to age-inappropriate material as well as potentially dangerous contacts. However, the number of cases that have been demonstrated so far are small and children still remain far more at risk from members of the family and people in positions of trust than from strangers – whether strangers in the street or strangers online. Some of the advice given is sensible, such as talking to children about their online activities and insisting on meeting any online friends in person with the child initially. Other advice, however, such as 'put the computer in a family room not the child's bedroom', is already becoming difficult to comply with, because of technology changes. As more and smaller devices include greater levels of Internet access, such advice will become meaningless. Laws against 'grooming' are being put in place, although the exact definitions are difficult to tie down as with many new areas of online activity and the balance between freedom and protection will have to be developed by the courts over the years as always. It is the combination of appropriate legal remedies and social norms that must provide suitable safety without either harming children by overprotection or criminalizing innocent adults. See Chapter 5 for further discussion on protecting children from inappropriate online material.

DISCUSSION TOPICS

Tackling Spam at the Transport Layer

As mentioned in the chapter, one of the problems with e-mail spam is that the main e-mail exchange protocol is grounded in the original open, trusting nature of the Internet. it also maintains features from the days of much lower bandwidth. It would seem obvious that the problem of spam dictates a revision of the mail transfer protocols but the ubiquity of e-mail on Internet-connected systems causes problems here. Wholesale changes to such a basic protocol would break many existing systems. The trouble is that e-mail is not only handled by client–server programs but is also used as an adjunct by a huge number of other programs, everything from web servers and system loggers to gateways. Many of these implement the e-mail protocol themselves rather than relying on the correct running of a different process on their host machine. To replace SMTP with something more robust to block spam, all these programs would have to be re-written.

What actually happens is that systems receiving mail impose conditions on where they will receive mail from. This is a slow evolutionary process and there are many variants of the rules that mail-receiving programs impose on sending programs. One obvious rule is to require a valid IP address from the sender, the second stage being that this IP address matches the claimed domain name of the sender. This did affect spam when it began being imposed by a majority of the world's ISPs. Unfortunately, much of the world's spam is now being sent from compromised home computers which happily reveal their origins since those origins do not link in any significant way to the sender.

Another attempt to block unwanted incoming mail is to narrow down the number of systems entitled to pass mail messages along. Apart from being vulnerable to the same compromised computers as the 'valid domain name system entry' issue, this prevents new services using the e-mail protocols unless they are run on a 'backbone' computer, requiring all SMTP protocol information to pass through servers and thus denying the 'end-to-end' nature of the Internet. Various companies such as Microsoft have proposed new e-mail protocols to try to tackle spam, but since most of these include 'patented' software technology (see Chapter 12 for more information on software patents), everyone else is suspicious of these efforts.

Are there ways the e-mail protocols can be made more robust in helping to tackle spam without stopping legitimate communication?

Opt-In, Opt-Out, Shake It All About

Various jurisdictions have passed or are developing legal responses to the problem of spam (and other unwanted electronic attentions). One of the discussions that always occurs in the development of these are the opt-in and opt-out concepts.

Opt-in requires any company sending commercial contacts to have a record of the recipient deciding to accept commercial contacts from that company. Companies with a commercial relationship with a customer are thus not prevented from contacting their customers with details of new offers (sensible companies ask their customers if they are willing to receive such offers and these are less disliked by most people since they know they have some interest in that company's products).

Opt-out requires companies sending e-mail marketing to allow recipients to opt out of their lists. Unfortunately, as discussed in the chapter, so many spammers have used opt-outs as a way of confirming that messages are sent and received that using opt-outs is regarded as a way of increasing rather than decreasing spam.

Both of these options depend on the easy identification of the sending company and the ability to take action against them. Unfortunately, because there is no common position on spam worldwide such measures seem rather pointless as much spam apparently originates in countries such as Argentina and South Korea, although the United States is still one of the biggest culprits. Given that even the United States and the European Union cannot agree on common legislative arrangements, is there any reason to believe that opt-in, opt-out or similar laws will have any real impact on spam?

Freedom of Speech or Online Stalking

Human rights are often presented as absolute ('the right to freedom of expression' or 'the right to life'). Unfortunately the rights of one person are often in conflict with the rights of others (one person's right to swing their arms about ends where the arm would impact on someone else's nose). This becomes even more complicated when the consequential infringement is only a potential infringement on some random other person's rights. This precise problem is brought up when dealing with those with significant personality disorders. Someone with a psychopathic or sociopathic disorder is diagnosed by a qualified mental-health professional as potentially dangerous to others. They have committed no crime yet a qualified person has stated that the chances of them harming someone else seriously (possibly killing them) are high. At what level of certainty (both in the diagnosis and of them harming someone) should a person with a personality disorder have their freedom curtailed?

The same issue comes up with 'online stalking'. Amy Boyer was killed in 1999 (when she was 20) by Liam Youens who had attended the same junior high school as her in Nashua, New Hampshire. They had never interacted in school but Youens had become obsessed with her, leading to shooting her dead and committing suicide. Investigators found that Youens had maintained two web sites for years including threats against her. Amy never even knew of Youens' obsession until it killed her. Did Youens have a right to freedom of expression or were his threats credible enough that he should (had anyone noticed the contents of his site) have been imprisoned or subjected to mental-health treatment? At what point should such sanctions kick in? Imagine that someone annoys you at work and you blow off steam on your blog by saying 'Sometimes I could kill so-and-so for their arrogance'. Where does freedom of expression become a threat and where does protecting the public become abuse of the power of the state over the individual? Are there global standards or is this dependent on the context of the society?

REFERENCES

Hardin, G. (1968) The Tragedy of the Commons, *Science*, **162**: 1243–68.

Wiesner, J.B. and **York, H.F.** (1964) National Security and the Nuclear-Test Ban, *Scientific American*, **211** (4): 27.

RELATED READING

Goodman, D. (2004) *Spam Wars: Our last best chance to defeat spammers, scammers and hackers*, Select Books, New York. ISBN 1-59-079063-4.

Kinnard, S. (2001) *Marketing with E-mail: A spam-free guide to increasing awareness, building loyalty and increasing sales*, Maximum Press, Gulf Breeze, FL. ISBN 1-88-506868-9.

McWilliams, B. (2005) *S*PAM KiNgS*, O'Reilly, Sebastopol, CA. ISBN 0-596-99732-9.

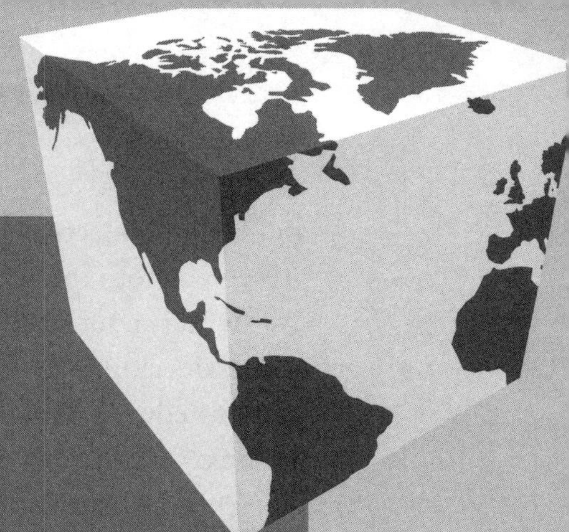

14

EDUCATION AND ONLINE LEARNING

INTRODUCTION

One of the areas of life most influenced by information technology is the teaching and learning process. Both formal education and individual study have been transformed by networked communication technologies. Recent years have seen an explosion in the amount of technology used in classrooms and distance learning systems. The learner and potential learner now have access to a far wider range of information whether from multichannel television, where documentary and factual channels consistently command a significant audience, or from access to the Internet at home, work, school, university or even just the local public library.

This chapter presents the role of IT in today's educational system. Issues such as online and multimedia course material and virtual and managed learning environments (MLEs) are discussed. It describes how these technologies have developed and some of the key issues associated with delivering education and training electronically. The impact of these technologies and applications are presented from the point of view of both the learner and the teacher.

Wider issues, such as accessibility and social inclusion, are also covered where developments in learning technologies have the potential to provide and enhance educational opportunities to those otherwise denied them for a variety of reasons.

This chapter also describes the dichotomy in the use of information technology in learning: on the one hand it can improve learning for some groups by providing anywhere, anytime learning on demand; on the other hand it can exclude learners who because of socio-economic circumstances do not have the resources, support or equipment to access the learning technology – effectively creating a 'digital divide'.

The use of ICT to support the learning experience is considered in a number of contexts; how it is used to support teaching and learning in the classroom environment, how it is delivered to individuals at home and in the work environment and interactively in managed learning environments. The delivery of learning and training experiences which utilize new technology and the Internet are often described as 'e-learning'. This chapter describes some of the key issues related to this developing technology, such as the required and necessary associated support processes and quality assurance systems in terms of content, assessment, access, security and plagiarism and the staff development needed to support and operate ICT and e-learning.

FROM THE CHALKBOARD TO THE VIRTUAL CLASSROOM

To engage the learner and impart knowledge, a number of presentational methods are adopted. Some learners work best with primarily auditory information (speech and sound), others primarily through visual information (writing and pictures) and a smaller group by kinaesthetic means (moving, doing and touching).

Generally speaking good learning takes place when a presentation combines auditory and visual elements, that is, speaking combined with the use of visual aids. In most subjects it is the visual aids (and the technology used to present them) that have most obviously changed (and continue to change). In almost all learning experiences, students can and do learn through a combination of all three modes. However, in most forms of learning delivery, one of the three modes is dominant. One of challenges in using new technology to assist in the teaching and learning process is to ensure that the important element of kinaesthetic learning is not ignored due to the limitations of the delivery method.

Technology Through the Years

Over many years, different learning styles have been supported by developing technology. The earliest historical references of organized teaching date from descriptions of Greek philosophical schools which would separately use visual (written treatises by the masters) and auditory styles (lectures by masters or discussions among masters and students). This was at the highest level of discourse, however, it is difficult to imagine any method of teaching reading and writing which does not include all three styles in at least some proportions: vocalization of letters and words by the teacher, from things written down, which are then copied by the student for practice.

The expansion and development of education and training has moved from delivery on a one-to-one basis to providing learning experiences for larger numbers in organized environments. Once teaching and learning moves from an individual to a mass basis, some form of display technology, preferably of an interactive form, becomes the obvious aid to the teacher.

Visual Aids to Learning

Chalkboard and Chalk

One of the earliest forms of interactive visual aid for multiple learners is the chalkboard. The advantages of this system are that it is highly interactive and the display is reusable, although the presentation medium is consumed. Chalkboards remain in common usage across much of the world because of the simplicity of their design and use: appropriate paint applied to any reasonably flat surface can serve and 'chalk' can be made from a wide range of materials and pigments.

The limitations of chalkboards for presentation of complicated visual material are clear: it requires artistic skill and considerable time to render a picture and the time taken for each successive picture may not be justifiable unless the process of production is a useful lesson, for example, in presenting an electric circuit diagram is the aim simply to teach the circuit or is there an additional objective of showing the learner how to draw the circuit?

Whiteboard and Marker Pen

A more modern version of the chalkboard, but sharing most of the limitations, is the whiteboard and marker pen. The principle benefits of whiteboards over chalkboards are the lower level of dust and the density of marker medium: a single pen can be used to produce many times more strokes than the same volume of chalk. The application method also allows for a somewhat higher-resolution display, in the right hands.

Projector, Screen and Photographic Slides

Slides developed from photographic negatives have been in use since not long after the development of photography. Improvements in light sources, optics and screen technology notwithstanding, the principle is still the same: a small high-resolution image printed with semi-transparent ink on a transparent substrate focused onto a matt surface gives the illusion of significant tone and colour differences because of the operation of the human visual system which interprets objects close together relatively rather than absolutely. The material of the screen remains white, but the difference in brightness between the projector lamp light falling on the screen and the ambient light level can make portions of the screen appear black. Too much ambient light 'washes out' the effect rendering the contrast too limited to be seen.

The advantages of slides include high-resolution colour images and the ability to carry large quantities of standard size slides from place to place in a pre-determined order. The major disadvantage is the non-interactive nature of the image. The image is fixed in a relatively expensive process and cannot generally be altered – changes mean that new slides must be made up. It is also a relatively expensive method of production, still, and is generally not used for simple textual material, except for occasional interjections within a mainly high-resolution graphics-based presentation. The initial cost of production also means that such materials are only produced for repeated usage, not usually for one-off presentations.

Overhead Projection

The overhead projector (OHP) is a combination of the slide projector and the whiteboard. Slides may be pre-prepared or produced 'live'. Pre-prepared slides may be interactively altered or developed. Writing on overhead slides is at 'normal size' rather than the larger format required for whiteboard systems and is therefore quicker. Pre-prepared material may be printed or copied from the same source as other printed material although, for pedagogic reasons, the amount of words on a slide is usually much smaller than the number on the same size printed sheet. Until recently, the OHP was one of the most common visual aids in use, even where more technologically advanced alternatives were available.

Computer Projection and Presentation Package

Presentation programs such as Microsoft PowerPoint were originally designed to aid in the production of slides for OHP (or sometimes slide projection) but soon became more commonly used for the production of material for 'virtual' OHP shows using computer projectors and, more recently, large, high-resolution computer screens. Various 'effects' are available for moving from one image to another, including the selective addition or subtraction of portions of a slide. However, presentation and editing are still largely separate aspects of the application programs and neither keyboard nor 'freehand' addition of material is easy with most software.

Electronic Whiteboard

Various types of electronic whiteboard are in existence, from the ordinary whiteboard with a large scanner built into the back (to allow for scanning or printing of the material) to computer projection suites with wireless 'electronic pens' which work on a similar principle to tablet PCs but on a larger scale. Until recently they were primarily used in research centres or by companies wishing to show off their up-to-date meeting rooms. However drastic price reductions have now brought them much more into mainstream education and they are becoming a common though not yet ubiquitous feature in schools, colleges and universities. A major consideration in the propagation of these devices is the issue of ensuring that staff are trained in the use of the equipment. As with any new technology, as experience levels rise the more advanced features of these devices will enhance the learning experience.

Audio Aids to Learning

The spoken word carries much more information than the words which can be written on a page: pace, tone, breathing pauses, accent, stresses and downplay of sentences, phrases or words, all add to the experience. Spoken-word recording and reproduction has as long and illustrious a history as music recording, however the technology changes in audio recording have not had a great deal of effect on most areas of education, so we will simply highlight those which have had the greatest effect.

Cassette Tapes

The primary uses of audio recording on cassette tapes has been for recording education radio broadcasts and for language teaching where the pronunciation of a foreign language can really only be taught by listening. In particular, distance learning of languages made substantial use of cassette tapes and personal cassette players, allowing people to study in all sorts of places: commuting on the train or in the car or while jogging or participating in other fitness training.

Computer-Based Audio

Unlike the music industry, where physical formats embodying digital recordings (compact disc audio, mini-disc and digital audio tape) have become the norm, the analogue cassette tape is still in operation in many learning environments. Developments in the consumer digital music environment with products such as iPods and MP3 players have increased the use of digital recording in the learning environment. Audio-only, computer-based learning aids are still relatively rare. A developing arena is in the web-casting or recording of spoken lectures where an audio file can be made available even for those with low-bandwidth Internet connections.

Audio–Visual Aids to Learning

Pre-Recorded Material

Film, video and television broadcasts have all been used for the storage and mass delivery of teaching materials. One of the largest examples of this was the broadcasting of Open University (OU) lectures on BBC television in the United Kingdom. School programming was also broadcast with suitable lengths and subjects for a variety of age groups. School teachers and college and university lecturers also record, individually or institutionally, and show general documentary or factual material as part of course delivery.

Interactive Computer-Aided or Computer-Based Learning

Educational and entertainment (sometimes called edutainment) computer programs using interactive features as well as audio–visual material have been developed to use the improvements in home and school computer capabilities. A major advantage of such systems is that they can be operated at a rate much more suited to each individual learner, in the best cases, presenting the same material in multiple ways for learners having difficulties, but also able to move swiftly on to new material for those who have grasped the necessary ideas. This contrasts with the set piece format of pre-recorded material.

Twenty-First-Century Learning

E-learning

E-learning is a generally accepted term to describe an educational process which involves the application of information communication technology in its delivery. For the learner it includes a wide spectrum of activities ranging from the earliest exposure to the learning process – the learner's application to study – through to supporting and facilitating the learner to achieve an educational objective.

E-learning can involve the use of a multitude of technologies including but not exclusively the following (`www.elearning.ac.uk/del`):

- Internet, Intranet and Web applications and tools
- Personal computers and laptops
- Mobile devices and applications, wireless, Bluetooth and infrared
- Digital and audio resources
- Interactive whiteboards
- Videoconferencing
- Virtual learning environments
- eBooks.

Managed Learning Environment

Managed learning environment (MLE) is a relatively new term in educational technology. It describes a range of computer software systems that combine and interoperate with a number of management, administration and student learning processes to improve the effectiveness and efficiency of the learner experience. An MLE typically interacts with virtual learning environments, student recruitment information, student admissions systems, student record systems, student learning materials, student learning logs, library systems, management information systems, timetabling systems, and so on.

Virtual Learning Environment

A virtual learning environments (VLE), or learning platform, is a computer software system that has been specifically designed to host learning materials, tracking the use of the materials, and to provide a range of interactive tools which allow learners and tutors to communicate online. VLEs have been designed to allow tutors to create a range of learning materials that can be accessed and used in a variety of circumstances such as online from home or work, or in face-to-face presentations with individuals or groups of learners. Access to the interactive learning material and resources can be 'tailored' to address the requirements of the individual learner such as accessibility or visual impairment. The information and learning material can be tracked and a variety of assessment systems can be incorporated including student self assessment. Access to the VLE environment is generally possible from a range of devices which can access the Web, such as computers, laptops, PDAs, mobile phones, online gaming consoles, and so on.

DEVELOPING E-LEARNING ENVIRONMENTS

The effective deployment of ICT into school, college and university environments has, in many cases, been driven by technology, building on the mistaken belief that computers would replace teachers. A more enlightened approach was that the application of new technology would enhance the student learning experience, raise educational standards and assist in the effective delivery of learning for a range of individual learning styles.

Information technology is revolutionizing schools, colleges and universities in terms of teaching and learning and as time-saving tools for administrative and support tasks. Many institutions have benefited from the considerable investment in information communications technology and related information learning software. A twenty-first-century educational institution has all or many of the following resources:

- industry-standard hardware, software and high-speed, local area network connectivity;
- high-bandwidth connection to the Internet and the Web;
- a managed learning environment;
- Internet-ready devices for all staff including access to computers, laptops, PDAs and tablets;
- fully-equipped ICT student learning resources which allow access to a range of Internet devices including computers, laptops, PDAs and tablets;
- classrooms and learning areas equipped with projector display devices, network devices and peripherals that can access the network;
- a VLE or learning platform and a range of suitable learning materials and software to support curriculum requirements of the institution;
- appropriately qualified and experienced staff to deliver and support the learning.

The use of ICT in the learning environment is no longer dependent on the learner being wholly and exclusively in the classroom location. Today's learner is encouraged to carry out research, access learning materials and complete assignments and assessments from a variety of locations. The management and support of these learner experiences is a substantial variation on the traditional role of the 'teacher'. The dynamics of this process presents both opportunities and challenges for teachers and administrators. The introduction of MLEs and VLEs presents the opportunity, if appropriately implemented, to use computerized systems to reduce a number of time-consuming and tedious tasks carried out by a teacher, thereby allowing them time to concentrate on other more important matters.

The developing use of new technology in supporting learning in the classroom provides teachers with a range of tools to complement their more traditional methods of teaching. The combination of this approach has given rise in a number of learning institutions to the term 'blended learning' (www.e-learningcentre.co.uk/eclipse/Resources/blended.htm).

ICT and e-Learning in Further Education Colleges in England

In 2006, the provision of ICT in the 388 UK Further Education Colleges was surveyed (Becta Research 2007, www.becta.org.uk) and it was determined that in the vast majority of college senior managers were committed to developing ICT and e-learning. All colleges were provided with a minimum 4 Mbps broadband access to the Internet, delivered as a part of a national initiative by the UK Education and Research Association (UKERNA). This organisation also provides access to the Internet for all UK universities.

The survey reported that 95% of the 380 000 computers located in colleges provided staff and students with access to the Internet. It was also noted that the median ratio of students to Internet-enabled computers was 4.8:1, a vast improvement on the 1999 ratio of 21:1. In addition, the target of one Internet-enabled computer per member of staff was achieved in over 58% of colleges, compared to 26% in 2003.

College intranets and networks were being extensively used for learning, with commercial and open source learning materials being used. In 2006, 82% of colleges reported using a VLE, compared to 59% in 2003, however, only 33% of the colleges using a VLE reported that it interoperated with the college management information system to provide an MLE. The colleges reported that the main commercial VLE products used were: Moodle, Blackboard, WebCT and Learnwise.

The report observed that managing the growing demand for e-learning presented colleges with constraining factors, such as demanding equipment-refresh rates, maintaining resilient, high-speed networks, the high cost of producing commercial learning materials, the lack of enthusiasm by some staff and, despite an upward trend in staff acquiring e-learning skills (62%), a lack of confidence by some staff in using ICT and e-learning.

e-Portfolio

The concept of an e-portfolio in the education world is similar to the model used in the commercial world, where there is a requirement to present work, show progress and achievement and provide a focus for discussion. For a substantial number of years, the education world has been discussing and developing an electronic portfolio system which can record and visually present a learner's educational experience from elementary through to secondary and tertiary levels of education. The essentials of an electronic portfolio include a process model that documents achievement, records what a person has learned and gained over time and records how those experiences have interacted with and influenced the learner.

With the advent of e-learning and the recognition that learning is a lifelong experience, many institutions and government bodies have encouraged the development of personalized electronic learning spaces which can support an individual's e-portfolio. In the United Kingdom, the Department for Education and Skills stated that by 2005–6 all students in higher education should have access to the functions of an electronic portfolio.

Although there are many definitions of an e-portfolio it is generally accepted that it is a personalized digital space within an integrated e-learning and assessment environment. Whatever aspects of assessment are included they should be able to be recorded in such a way that they allow interaction and comment to be added by mentors, lecturers, work-experience colleagues and so on. The key feature of an e-portfolio is its ability to allow the student to own their learning process and, through interaction, provide to external assessors and reviewers a better insight into the learner's educational journey, their capability and potential to succeed. As in any other e-learning or e-assessment tool there are considerable technical issues to be addressed particularly in terms of interoperability as students move around institutions to undertake their education and training experiences. E-portfolios must be designed to conform to technical open standards which allow a seamless integration with a wide range of e-learning platforms used by the educational sector (www.nottingham.ac.uk/e-portfolio and www.jiscinfonet.ac.uk/InfoKits/effective-use-of-VLEs/e-portfolios).

Videoconferencing

Videoconferencing is a means of connecting a number of locations using video cameras and providing a facility that enables users at each site to interact with each other. Most systems use high-speed connections with high-quality video cameras and microphones capturing sound and video images. There are many examples of education institutions across the world utilizing videoconferencing to support their distance learning programmes. By combining videoconferencing and interactive learning materials, many learning programmes have been delivered to groups and individuals in remote and distant locations from the institutions.

In 1999, a study provided evidence of demand for a £6 million integrated national video network embracing both Further and Higher Education in Wales. The study also showed that, although desktop videoconferencing was widely deployed in both of the sectors, only five institutions had dedicated videoconferencing studios. It was determined that 80 high-quality, networked video studios would be created to support the aspirations of the Welsh colleges and universities.

A Welsh Video Network Support Centre was established and studios were designed with the following equipment:

- a studio-equipment controller
- videoconferencing software suitable for use over both ISDN and IP
- two remote-control cameras and a document camera
- monitors, microphones and a VCR
- data and application-sharing facilities
- a projector and an interactive electronic whiteboard.

Initially, most videoconferencing calls used high-speed telephone lines however, as the project progressed, a transition was made toward adopting broadband Internet protocol (IP) for videoconferencing (www.wvn.ac.uk).

The videoconferencing initiative enabled universities, colleges and a number of schools to develop a wide range of learning opportunities nationally and internationally. An example of one of many programmes of collaboration and programme delivery is outlined in the 'How the world plays' case study.

How the World Plays

This project utilized primary-school children as researchers of their family, community and country or state. They connected by way of videoconferencing to a partner research team of children from another part of the world. In the virtual world classroom, the research teams of children in Wales and the United States taught one another what they discovered about how their own family plays, what traditions and rituals they observed and how their families played through the generations. One of the project aims was to encourage 'kid to kid' communication with the objective that they would find solutions to problems through understanding, rather than responding to violence with violence. Using this form of ICT provided interactive opportunities for Welsh pupils to 'meet' pupils from another area of the world rather than base their research on written or Internet material alone (www.wvn.ac.uk/casestudies/htwp/htwp.htm).

Online Encyclopedia

The Internet has created a number of online products which are easily accessible by learners. Wikipedia is essentially an online encyclopedia which has, in a relatively short time, become one of the largest reference sites on the Internet. A major feature of this resource is that the information contained in the database is written by people from all around the world and is updated to create a collaborative information resource. Ironically, this key underlying feature of the product is also its major weakness. Many observers argue that the encyclopedia is unreliable because of its reliance on anonymous entries which may be incorrect, false or misleading.

A recent article about Wikipedia (wiki-problem-pedia.blogspot.com) cites the case of Ryan 'Essjay' Jordan, who registered an account on Wikipedia in 2005, claiming he had four degrees and a professorship at a private university. Over time, he used these claimed credentials to win arguments in various discussion pages eventually becoming an administrator and member of Wikipedia's Arbitration Board. It was later revealed that he was not a professor with two PhDs, but a 24-year old college dropout from Kentucky (www.telegraph.co.uk/news/main.jhtml?xml=/news/2007/03/07/nspam207.xml).

By his actions, Jordan undermined the issues of collaboration as one of the key assets of Wikipedia. This is not to say that any anonymous user's view is without foundation, however it does bring to question that not only should all information be sourced, but that the writer and contributor of the information should have the credentials to back up the claims. There are substantial numbers of students who use Wikipedia as a resource. Because of growing concerns about credibility and accuracy of the information contained, many universities and colleges have banned its use for citations. In response to such criticisms, Citizendium has been launched; it requires contributors to use their real names and have more accountability for their contributions (en.citizendium.org/wiki/Main_Page).

Mobile Education (PDAs and Mobile Devices)

There has been a substantial growth over the last few years in 'mobile devices' which can access the Internet. These have included personal digital assistants (PDAs), mobile phones, iPods and other sophisticated integrated devices to play video and music files. More recently, advanced devices have been developed including smart phones, which are a hybrid of PDA and phone technologies. Recent research in the United Kingdom by the Learning and Skills Development Agency gave adoption rates for mobile devices of 90% for ages 15–19 and 81% for ages 20–24 (Attewell and Saville-Smith 2004). The mobile devices can now be used to access learning resources and information through connectivity methods including data synchronization with networks and Bluetooth, infrared or wireless connections. Many of these devices can capture digital and video images and many are also capable of incorporating global positioning satellite (GPS) information.

If mobile devices are to be used effectively for teaching and learning, there must be education-specific applications to support the teaching and learning process. One way in which success may be ensured is by mapping educational activities to the social practices of the students, for example, building on the communication and collaboration models they have built up with their peer groups. This work can be likened to the way in which 'chat room' systems are available in managed learning environments such as Blackboard.

Besides the use of mobile communication for the actual delivery of education they are increasingly being used for administrative purposes. Students are reminded of deadlines by text message and parents are informed of absences from school by text message or mobile phone call.

Over the next few years many more students will be attending learning institutions with an expectation that they will be able to access the institution's ICT infrastructure with these devices. These assumptions have implications for the development of revised protocols and transmission media for secure access to the institution's ICT infrastructure. As the levels of technology increase and the costs reduce, PDAs and mobile devices may become the ubiquitous access device used by learners across all learning environments.

For example, in the United Kingdom and the United States students are already accessing their information and learning portfolio anywhere, anytime and anyplace. There are many examples of the innovative uses of PDAs, for example, in such subjects as geography and environmental education where students working on field trips have used PDAs to record images, present online field maps and diagrams, and store video clips to enhance learning and assessment. In these cases, students have also been using GPS to enhance their abilities to locate and record field situations (www.ljmu.ac.uk/ECL/cetl/81403.htm).

There have however, also been cases of the serious misuse of mobile phones in educational environments. In one reported incident, seven pupils at a leading preparatory school were sent home for sending inappropriate text and mobile-phone messages to a female teacher. Bullying, 'poison pen' and malicious gossip aimed at or about other pupils and teachers and 'happy slapping' incidents are becoming far too common in schools only just beginning to get to grips with policies against physical bullying.

Electronic Books

E-books are a digital extension of the current format of text books as we know them. There are various definitions of e-books however they are generally either an electronic version of a book that already exists and is in print or a range of materials which are integrated through a database which may or may not have a printed version and importantly include a level of 'interactivity' for the reader. To date, e-books have been slow to affect education. This may be related to the fact that, for many years, copyright texts have been digitized and made available online. It may well be that a substantial number of teachers have yet to experience the developing range of web-based digital textbooks that include multimedia content and interactivity between readers and self-grading assessment facilities. There are many international research projects examining the effectiveness of e-books in education (www.jisc.ac.uk/news/stories/2007/03/news_ebooks.aspx).

Electronic Whiteboards

In terms of the presentation of information in the classroom situation, teachers have always had the opportunity to engage students by presenting textual information on a black surface with white coloured chalk. In today's educational environment, this medium has been replaced by the electronic whiteboard which provides a range of facilities that allow the teacher to project onto a surface almost any interactive learning program or information that would be available from a PC or laptop. These devices provide a multimedia technology environment where students can interact with the teacher or with other students in the group. There are many advantages in implementing interactive whiteboards, particularly as teachers become experienced in using them for delivery alongside other learning methods to create what is termed a blended learning environment. In the United Kingdom, the government has funded a substantial programme to provide interactive whiteboards in primary and secondary schools.

Following the introduction of these whiteboards, a government-funded evaluation was undertaken which indicated that in many cases pupils were reduced to 'spectators' as teachers produced faster and more complicated electronic displays. The report also noted however that the evaluation took place when many teachers would have been new to the technology and its use and that the teachers may have focussed more on the new technology than on what the students should be learning. As part of the evaluation, the minister for schools stated that he believed that whiteboard technology can be an excellent technology for helping teaching and learning, but added that 'it would never be a substitute for good teaching., only when teachers have the skills to use it properly can we expect them to use the technology to transform traditional teaching methods' (thisislondon via `tinyurl.com/2xxkga`).

Online Marketing

Schools, colleges and universities are increasingly moving to an online model of promotion of their institutions and recruitment onto the courses which they run. This has financial benefits for the institution as promotion in this way saves both the expensive printing costs of glossy and weighty colour prospectuses and the subsequent postage of these prospectuses both nationally and internationally.

There are also the benefits of the immediacy of the information to the student and the means to ensure that the content is up to date and correct. It is not unusual for printed prospectuses to be produced 18 months or more in advance, with the problem that it must contain warnings about potentially out-of-date information and avoid claims which are too specific. The move to online prospectuses means that every individual has access to the most up-to-date information.

Prospective students and their parents have embraced this means of course selection and are increasingly favouring it as it enables them to search more readily for courses meeting their needs. Not only are the course contents laid bare – so too are the league tables and results for schools, colleges and universities on a per subject and per institution basis; of course the different league tables frequently put different emphases on different aspects of the teaching and learning process - so the results are not always the best guide to the most appropriate course for an individual and this viewing on the Internet of league tables may sometimes be at the expense of personal advice from an experienced course tutor.

Electronic Application and Admission Systems

Electronic admission systems are being put in place – for example, the UK Universities and Colleges Admissions Service (UCAS) Board has changed their application procedure to a secure Web–based, online application system, `www.ucas.com/apply`, that is available to all applicants. Until recently, an online application process was only available to UK-based schools and colleges but not to individuals outside of the traditional education systems. It is now available to all applicants; in fact, it is no longer possible to make a UCAS application on a paper form unless students wish to apply in the medium of Welsh. To assist applicants without access to online computer resources, UCAS have set up centres in partnerships with local libraries and other community centres across the United Kingdom.

The new process allows more than 450 000 students to monitor the progress of their application forms and accept and decline offers online. They can access it from anywhere in the world - useful for those who spend the summer before university travelling. Other benefits include speeding up the application process (it takes three days rather than three weeks to get applications to admissions tutors after they are completed by applicants); trapping the common mistakes made on application forms; and correcting a form if a mistake is made rather than having to redo the original form completely.

Digital Library

Digital libraries and digital content are now proving successful in bringing alive concepts and issues at all levels of education and in all subject areas.

Examples include the Oxford University Bodleian Library collection of medieval manuscripts (www.bodley.ox.ac.uk/welcome.html); biomedical digital libraries (www.bio-diglib.com); the British Library, which provides access to over 13 million books, 920 000 journal and newspaper articles, and three million sound recordings (www.bl.uk); and the International Children's Digital Library, which has a mission to promote the global community by making the best in children's literature available online (www.childrenslibrary.org). Such learning resources downloaded from the Internet provide good research materials for young children and students, however there is a growing trend of unsupervised cut-and-paste and the potential for plagiarism developing at an early age.

Second Life

Second Life is a 3-D virtual world entirely built and owned by its residents. Since being made available to the public in 2003, it has grown extensively and is now inhabited by over five million people worldwide (secondlife.com/whatis). By accessing the software online, users can create a virtual person which they can personalize in whichever shape and form they wish; in effect, they create an avatar. The software also allows users to create virtual communities and worlds and, importantly, the associated social and economic structures. This online product now has millions of members who have entered for social, personal, business or educational reasons. In terms of education, many organization across the world are now conducting research into the possibilities of using these virtual environments as a method of delivering education, training and socialization.

Second Life allows students to practice skills, try out new ideas, learn from their mistakes and prepare for real-world experiences. It also allows students and educators to work together as part of a globally networked virtual classroom environment. Current examples of education in the Second Life environment includes a design economics course for real-life modelling of business practices in a business world. Would-be designers can try their designs and entrepreneurial skills on an entire market rather than a simulated market environment (www.arch.uh.edu). In the primary sector, 'Kids Connect' teaches performance, story telling and collaboration through simple (bare stage) and digital means (audio–visual creation, streaming and Second Life work and play). The Kids Connect Island is located on Teen Grid (www.teen.secondlife.com).

Early research indicates however that a level of caution is required to ensure that young learners and other people are not inadvertently interacting with 'islands' in the Second Life environment which include unsavoury and unacceptable practices of an adult nature. In response to this, the educational community has developed the ability to purchase private restricted islands which are suitable locations for learning experiences for young learners. These islands are located on the Teen Grid, which is a world strictly for students aged between 13 and 17 years old. Adult participation in this grid can only be on the private islands – adults are not allowed to set foot on the mainland.

Web 2.0

In terms of social networking and education there are a range of new technologies being developed which are worthy of interest and attention, including Web 2.0. In the education world, searching through the vast range of Internet research facilities to find appropriate sources can be cumbersome, as the user has to navigate through many pages of information and carry out cross referencing to eventually achieve the desired results. Although not yet fully defined, Web 2.0 is the Internet vision of tomorrow as a highly developed integrator of popular sites which pulls together a range of existing and new online services, user-generated content, social and business communities and collaborative and networking tools. Web 2.0 has the potential to transform the predominantly 'read-only' environment of the Internet to an environment where teachers and learners can publish, collaborate and share content with others, enabling aggregation and mixing of 'micro-content' pieces of information into new and exciting educational resources (www.oreillynet.com/go/web2).

Teachers are already experimenting and using blogs and media-sharing software to empower students and colleague staff to share and discuss innovation and new developments. Early examples of technologies which are easily accessible using

Web 2.0 would be applications such as Flickr (www.flickr.com), where e-learning applications can utilize the interactivity of the software through the Internet to annotate photographs, parts of work and digital images. If successful, Web 2.0 technologies will enable access to flexible interoperable systems for multimedia content and organize these resources in an easily accessible way that allows creators and end users to work collaboratively.

DEVELOPING AND EMBRACING E-LEARNING RESOURCES

The design and development of e-learning material is just as important as it is for traditional courses. There are a whole range of issues which must be considered if successful delivery of e-learning material is to be achieved, for example inclusion of technologically appropriate pedagogical features, development of engaging content, quality assurance of this content and adherence to agreed interoperability standards to enable shared design and delivery of learning objects such as Sharable Content Reference Model (SCORM, www.scorm.com).

Educational course materials can suffer from a lack of commitment to their sustainable production and maintenance, because of resource priorities and under-funding for education in much of the developed world in the last two decades. The concept of e-learning either in the classroom or at home has yet to be fully developed and there is limited empirical research evidence demonstrating the benefits in terms of raising levels of achievement. Consequently, there is some electronic learning material which neither meets standards nor has benefited from serious research and evaluation. There is considerable evidence to show that poorly prepared and constructed electronic learning resources become boring for the student and thus unproductive and demotivating.

The latest developments include producing bite-sized elements of learning content (sometimes referred to as 'learning objects') which can easily be integrated into a teaching experience by the teacher or by the student themselves following their particular interests.

There must be a transformation of traditional course material, intended to be taught in a classroom environment by a teacher at a set time to a group of students, into an engaging course that can be taken at any time by any student in any part of the world and often with disparate backgrounds. If substantial drop-out rates are to be avoided then the material must be engaging so that students are motivated to learn. Research indicates that simply replacing traditional courses with e-learning or online products is not the answer; specific attention must be given to the learning styles of potential groups of students and how the electronic learning content will be delivered in relation to other aspects of the course. Students who are pursuing wholly online courses do not perform well unless substantial additional support resources are employed. High drop-out rates are experienced particularly in programmes offered without support remotely and in home locations.

It is not unusual for young children to be encouraged to use computers. An example of software aimed at this market group is 'Stuart Little's Big City Adventures'. Aimed at 4-year-olds and over it is designed to teach computer basics to children through a series of simple games. There is also a range of web sites designed to encourage exploration and learning, such as `marsrovers.jpl.nasa.gov` (mars exploration), `insideout.rigb.org` (Royal Institution general science site) and `www.volcano.si.edu` (volcanoes).

Interactive computer information is being used ever more frequently by museums to help children engage with their exhibits. Printed cards within a glass cabinet do not interest children raised on multichannel television and video games. The positive value of combining interactive computer information with low-tech hands-on activities is being discovered and combined with related online material for use before and after a visit (e.g. `www.sciencemuseum.org.uk`).

The Learner Perspective

As mentioned above, e-learning can be of great benefit to learners. Learning environments in institutions allows for a combination of group teaching and individual learning to be achieved. By integrating new technology into the learning model, teachers can respond to different learner styles and devise strategies to provide the learner with expert guidance and help. Technological environments are concerned not only with individualized learning, but also intra-group communication and one-to-many communications from the teacher to the students.

Learners who operate in an e-learning environment can be accessing the system remotely from home or work, or alternatively it may be used as an integral part of the learning experience in the classroom or study centre, with or without tutors or other peer group members. In either case, the e-learning software only provides at best an integrated learning framework and a set of tools, effectively, a combined and easily accessible set of learning materials and support resources. Student learners require an enhanced set of skills and experiences to gain the full benefits from the learning experience and, possibly more important, to remain engaged in this form of learning.

E-learning in many cases is most effective when it is viewed by the learner as one of the key elements of a learning journey within a blended learning experience, which includes other forms of pedagogic stimulus. E-learning environments can accommodate a range of student learner styles, however this model of learning is demanding in terms of learner motivation, particularly if the learning is from home or at a distance where there may be little peer group support. On a more positive note e-learning can improve learner engagement because of its ability to facilitate communication and provide access to resources and communities around the world.

Increasingly, learners who are entering education and training are now more technologically aware, suitably equipped and confident in the use of new technology. Learners expect that the developments and applications that they use in everyday life will be available in an educational context. Many students engaging in a learning experience are already familiar with the Web, the Internet and its applications, high-technology multimedia edutainment and many other accessible new technologies. As a consequence, many learners find that the interactivity of their e-learning experience falls short of their expectations.

Nevertheless in a casual visit to a technologically enabled educational establishment, today's students can be observed attending lectures, recording individual lecture notes directly onto wireless laptops, iPods and PDAs. During the 'lecture', students can also search the Internet for relevant reference material. Other students who have not been able to attend the lecture have the opportunity to review it alongside the programme notes and interactive material by logging in to the institution's VLE, anywhere, any place, any time!

The Teacher Perspective

Apart from teachers and lecturers in technology subjects and those for whom their work has gradually brought them into the world of advanced computer usage, teaching staff have a combination of expertise in their subject and an expertise in the theory and practice of teaching. Those staff who now deliver education and training are expected to have the ability and energy to constantly update their presentation skills and teaching styles to take advantage of the rapidly changing technological environment. Substantial investment is required to ensure that appropriate training and retraining programmes are in place to allow e-learning to be used effectively and efficiently.

One of the key elements in all e-learning environments is creation of learning content. Before the advent of online materials, lecturers and teachers would produce course notes and learning materials and, when required, collaborate with others to improve and expand the material. If they had a particular grasp of a specific topic, they might even write a textbook or academic paper and in many cases the author would own the copyright for the material. As more and more learning materials are required for online presentation, e-learning educational institutions face the challenge of competing in the world market against commercial organizations for this material. Learning materials can be commercially commissioned, purchased and sold to institutions under licence agreements. For material being created, developed and used within the education sector, the issues become more complex, particularly with regard to copyright and royalties.

These issues are yet to be resolved. It is unclear what the outcome will be, or even if there will be any general solution or whether each university, college and school authority will have their own deals, possibly even different deals for different individuals depending on the strength of their negotiating position when taking a post. The academic habit (enshrined in copyright law) of allowing use of copyright material for educational purposes in ways which might otherwise infringe the originator's rights is a mode of working which may be under threat with such changes. To prevent other institutions or lecturers copying their content material without paying, lecturers or institutions may well make it more difficult for students to access and copy material.

There has already been a case in the United States where a private company was paying students for access to their notes from lectures. Some of the lecturers concerned attempted to stop this practice by legal action, others by requiring students to sign an agreement that notes taken from verbal lectures and OHP slides would be used for 'personal educational purposes only', in agreements similar to those sometimes on offer for software licenses (see the Borland Academic License for Delphi or the Microsoft Academic Network license, for examples). In other cases, institutions, such as MIT, have developed open-access policies where all material is published on the Web and made available for anyone else to use for educational purposes. Such efforts may well undermine attempts to commercialize education content by providing high-quality material for free (in both the monetary and free speech senses of the word) in an analogue of the clash of cultures between proprietary software and free software. (See `Boston.com` by way of `shorl.com/bamedilasiro` for details of one case of legal action to stop the re-selling of lecture notes.)

The Open University Success Story

One of the earliest and biggest successes of open and distance learning is the Open University (OU) which is increasingly using information technology to deliver courses direct to a student's desktop. The OU is the largest UK university, having over 150 000 undergraduate and 30 000 postgraduate students, most of whom are part-time and 70% of whom are in full-time employment. The university has no age limits, requires no previous qualifications and enables students to build a programme of study that reflects their individualized personal and professional needs, thereby making it the original flexible and lifelong-learning education model. The testament to this is that over two million people have studied with the OU since its inception. 100 000 OU students are networked from their homes and at work – 80% of students have access to a computer and the OU spends £1 million a year lending computers to students who need them (www3.open.ac.uk/about).

The UKeU Failure Story

The Higher Education Funding Council for England funded a pilot initiative, the UKeU, to coordinate and develop e-learning content for FE and HE students. The UKeU was set up in Spring 2003, as a joint venture between the government, which put in £62 million, 12 universities and a technology company, which was to provide the software, to act as a broker for marketing online degrees from UK universities and providing a technological platform to deliver them. It was branded a failure after only 900 students signed up for its services in the first year and individual universities proved reluctant to join the venture. It has now been dismantled and an inquiry is under way (www.publications.parliament.uk/pa/cm200405/cmselect/cmeduski/205/20502.htm). Given the expertise of the OU in distance-learning in the United Kingdom, it is surprising that the UKeU was such a failure – whether the OU could have done better with the millions of pounds spent on the UKeU is a valid question.

The Open University and Other Distance-Learning Ventures

The largest and one of the oldest distance-learning institutions of higher education in the world is the UK Open University (generally called the

OU, www.open.ac.uk). Based in Milton Keynes, the OU was founded in the late 1960s and recruited its first students in 1970. It used the 'dead time' of late-night broadcasting on BBC television (without the publicly-funded nature of the BBC, the OU probably could not have been viable). The unchanging nature of the 'core material' in some subjects such as mathematics and history led to the long reuse of televised lecture courses from the early days. When combined with the sartorial inelegance of many academics, the clothes of the presenters became something of a standing joke, but the quality of the material has rarely been challenged. By 1980, the OU was the largest single institution of higher education (though still smaller than the federal universities in London and Wales) in the United Kingdom and the viewing figures for some of its programmes showed a distinct interest by people in their presentations, outside of those taking their courses. Some material was even presented in peak viewing time slots and attracted millions of viewers.

The distance-learning nature of the OU encourages the innovative use of new audio–visual and telecommunications channels and the OU was an early user of home computers and networked access to learning material and communication between teachers and learners, and between learners. Because of the lack of individual personal student contact, the OU pioneered the use of online discussion frameworks. Early in the twenty-first century, the OU finally abandoned the broadcast of programmes on television and moved entirely to computer-based delivery, using both physically shipped CDs (and more recently DVDs) and downloaded material, moving increasingly to more interactive delivery and downloads as broadband access becomes more widespread.

The model of the OU is not the only one in distance-learning, but it has shown itself to be a vibrant and flexible institution for more than a quarter of a century and is obviously a good place to start when considering new ventures. The UHI Millennium Institute (hoping to become a new university in the United Kingdom) is a related but different concept (www.uhi.ac.uk) designed to offer undergraduate and postgraduate degrees and research opportunities throughout the Highlands and Islands of Scotland. The UHI supports 100 learning centres (some large colleges, some smaller institutions) split between the island communities and the mainland but with most communication between staff and students being by way of the Internet, e-mail, videoconferencing and virtual learning environments. Similar concepts are in development in other areas with low-population densities such as parts of Canada and Australia.

ACCESSIBILITY OF EDUCATION IN A WIRED WORLD

Accessibility is a key issue for all learners; good learning content and systems should be designed with accessibility in mind. Standards have been developed to ensure consistency across platforms and software, and these standards also include accessibility criteria. Research indicates that there is substantial scope to assist students with learning difficulties and disabilities through the use of interactive blended learning materials. This is particularly pertinent in VLEs, where students can work at their own pace and can be provided with a range of feedback appropriate to their needs.

Considerable work has been undertaken by a number of bodies to test and evaluate accessibility features on interactive Internet products. These bodies not only assess the suitability of the software but also provide environments in which the developers can improve performance in accessibility terms and gain approval. Examples of these initiatives are the UK Special Educational Needs Disabilities Act (`www.opsi.gov.uk/acts/acts2001/20010010.htm`) which requires educational establishments to offer appropriate support for students with any disability where it is feasible to do so and where the student has the basic abilities to learn the material but is prevented from accessing some or all the course because of their disability. This results in requirements, for example, to provide note takers for physically disabled students and special equipment for those with sensory impairments.

Accessibility does not simply refer to the design and usability of software, but also involves the design of specialist devices to allow those with physical disabilities to access the software products. Development programmes are under way in areas such as inclusive design of interfaces that can be used by anyone regardless of their age, disability, computer experience or native language.

There are both social and commercial pressures in the design and delivery of online service and products for adults and students who have learning difficulties or disabilities. This particular societal grouping is relatively small in commercial terms and there is little incentive for multinational software developers to seriously address these issues from a commercial perspective. Many existing products on the Internet are completely unsuitable in terms of accessibility and therefore restrict the number and range of users. Growing social awareness and responsibility has raised the level of involvement of many of companies so that new products are designed at the earliest point to address accessibility issues.

In social terms, accessibility issues can also include the inability of certain social groups to purchase the key ingredients of an e-learning experience: Internet access, computer hardware and learning software. This is further exacerbated in international terms where students in some countries cannot even access electrical power to drive the computer technology. As this situation continues and developing-world countries continue to be starved of resources then the digital divide between rich and poor nations will continue to grow. Electronic assessment and online admissions procedures may also bar students from poor countries from funded scholarship places in the universities of industrialized nations; inside the industrialized nations, the digital divide between rich and poor individuals will also grow. Already students from wealthy backgrounds gain, on average, substantially better grades in examination than do students from the poorest families. Some of this is because of familial pressure and the poor education level of the parents, but much of it is because of the extra tuition and facilities available to those from more affluent families. As the importance of access to the Internet grows, those with a personal computer and broadband connection, or handheld Internet access may gain a growing advantage over those for whom access is restricted to school and free or cheap public access points.

CHEATING THE SYSTEM

As we move toward a ubiquitously connected world with wired and wireless Internet connectivity available everywhere, the temptation to cheat the educational system becomes stronger and the means by which this can be done more abundant. Educators are now beginning to realize the extent of this growing problem and in response are starting to develop tools which can detect plagiarism and systems which are less susceptible to abuse. Even so, the problems are likely to become both more complex and more widespread.

Where essay-based coursework forms the basis of ongoing summative assessments, as it does in many school, college and university courses, students have two significant opportunities for plagiarism using the Internet. First, the Internet is a vast resource of freely published and easily copied information. In much academic work quoting from a variety of sources (with acknowledgment of those sources) is not only allowed but encouraged. However, some students copy large chunks of online material with little or no effort to rephrase the material in their own words and without attribution. Information technology also makes copying another student's work much easier and quicker and particularly tempting for those who have left starting their work until the last moment and then realize that they lack the time to complete any reasonable attempt – hand copying thousands of words of someone else's work requires much more planning and foresight than changing the name and maybe a few formatting aspects of a word-processed document. Students frequently fail to realize that staff marking the assignments will remember combinations of misunderstandings or mistakes or will recognize the constant shifts in style indicative of un-attributed quoting, the slightly off-topic nature of some or all of a copied piece or even the fact that the writing is beyond the competence of an individual student.

Increasingly automated plagiarism detectors are being used, such as OrCheck (cise.sbu.ac.uk/orcheck/), which makes use of the Google search engine, or Turnitin (`turnitin.com/static/home.html`), to report the level of commonality between a submitted piece of work and known documents on the Web. One study of 650 first-year students at London South Bank University revealed that more than

90% of essays submitted contained some degree of plagiarism with 20% of students submitting work that was more than 50% the same as other material (www.dailymail.co.uk/pages/live/articles/news/news.html?in_article_id=391516&in_page_id=1770).

More difficult for assessors to spot is the growing trend for bespoke, individualized essays available for purchase from Internet sites. Despite the protestations of those running such sites that they offer a 'legitimate service' of 'examples and guidance' to students, it is clear that in many cases this is a thin veneer they place on organized remote plagiarism. Where material has been copied from 'open' sites on the Internet, plagiarism checkers can be used, however, such checkers find it much more difficult to return results when the student uses pay-to-view sites with full essays available on various standard topics.

The use of bespoke essay-writing services by a student is difficult to spot, unless the marker has an understanding of the student's other work, abilities and knowledge. Claims of excellence on behalf of such sites were tested by a UK academic who found that although the provided essays would gain a pass mark they rarely lived up to the standards claimed, however, as with other commercial products, this situation can be improved to provide higher quality essays. While essays from an essay bank may have been repeatedly sold and hence carry an increased risk of detection, 'contract cheating' or bespoke essay providers guarantee a unique product written to a specific title or question. Essays may cost as little as £10, frequently with a bidding war taking place for the work from writers, or 'coders' as they are known, from sites around the world (www.dailymail.co.uk/pages/live/articles/news/news.html?in_article_id=391085&in_page_id=1770). It is reported that ukessays.com, a business set up three years ago, turns over £1.6 million a year and employs 3500 specialist writers. The starting price for each of its 15 000 essays per year is £120 for a 1000-word undergraduate essay guaranteed to gain a 2.1 mark rising to £720 for a 3000-word first-class essay and £24 000 for a 50 000-word PhD thesis (www.ukessays.com/quote.html).

It seems that plagiarism can occur even before the students start their university career. A survey of 50 000 applications for university places revealed that 5%

of applications included material that had been cut and pasted from model personal statements found on the Internet. This included 233 applications from would-be medical students who started their personal statements with ‘Ever since I accidentally burnt holes in my pyjamas after experimenting with a chemistry set on my 8th birthday, I have always had a passion for science’; 370 applicants who wrote ‘From an early age I have been fascinated by the workings of life. The human body is a remarkable machine’; and a further 175 who noted that ‘Living with my 100-year-old grandfather has allowed me to appreciate the frailties of the human body’ (www.timesonline.co.uk/tol/news/uk/education/article1485294.ece).

One student at a UK university in 2004 was barred from taking final exams when it was discovered that a piece of work was plagiarized and subsequent checking of prior work discovered that almost the entire academic career had been based on plagiarized work. In a bizarre twist to the tale, the student is suing the university for not informing him of the limits of copying allowed in the academic environment, for the wasted time, tuition fees and living costs involved in cheating almost but not quite to the extent of being awarded a degree. (news.bbc.co.uk/1/hi/education/3753065.stm).

Appealing to the poor financial circumstances of many students, some online plagiarism sites are offering to pay students submission fees for their own essays and even a royalty whenever their work is downloaded by someone else.

Some education experts are advocating a return to the use of coursework for purely formative assessment and reliance on examinations for summative grading. However even now it is possible to carry a mobile Internet PDA or mobile phone (education.guardian.co.uk/schools/story/0,,1740396,00.html) which can be accessed during a toilet break in an exam. Invigilators at universities are now being advised to check carefully that students with long hair covering their ears are not also covering up a wired or wireless mobile phone earpiece, allowing text or pictures to be messaged surreptitiously to the student by an accomplice outside the exam room. Examinations using a more ‘open book’ style would mean that while access to external information is not a problem, unless a biometric measure was used, it would not prevent another person doing the exam by proxy.

Honour-System Breakdown: University of Virginia

Some US universities rely almost entirely on an 'honor code' for students rather than heavy supervision of exams and attempts to detect joint or copied work in assignments. Some research has shown that institutions with 'honor codes' have lower rates of self-reported cheating than those reliant on the more 'policed' approach. Such self-report may be suspect, however, as different systems may encourage a different attitude to what constitutes 'cheating' as well as differences in willingness to confess, even in an entirely anonymous survey. Institutions with 'honor codes' tend to have much harsher punishments in place should cheating be discovered and this is the case with the University of Virginia where the punishment for violation of the code is expulsion or revocation of degree. Such harsh discipline is reported as being a possible reason for students not reporting each other for violations of the code. A physics professor at the University of Virginia, informed by a student that they felt poorly treated since their work had achieved lower marks than other students who had worked together or simply copied another's work, ran 1800 papers from the last five years of his class through a plagiarism detector designed to pick up phrases of six to 12 words which occurred in two or more papers. The work of 122 students came under close scrutiny; in many cases submitted work was found to be almost identical (see `archives.cnn.com/2002/EDUCATION/11/26/uva.plagiarism.ap`).

Bogus Degrees

Another emerging practice is the online offering of bogus or forged degree certificates from 'degree mills' (`www.geteducated.com/articles/degreemills.asp`). In a recent case a UK-based web site was found to be offering forged degree and A-level certificates for just £165 (`politics.guardian.co.uk/publicservices/`

story/0,11032,1254193,00.html). The certificates included degrees from prestigious universities and a complete set of GCSEs also incorporate forged signatures, stamps and watermarks making them difficult to distinguish from the real thing. The originator of the site was questioned by police but prosecutions have not been successful – it is not against the law to make fake school exam certificates and it has proved too difficult and expensive to prosecute for forging university certificates.

For only a few hundred dollars, at various sites offering 'diploma' and 'degree' certificates for sale, people are afforded the opportunity to create their own degree certificates. The site includes a 'certificate creator' and a search engine to enable the purchaser to find the appropriate degree certificate for courses from universities around the world, with custom crests, seals and logos. Billed as for 'novelty purposes only' and with copious disclaimers, the site is also in the process of offering 'novelty' transcripts, 'novelty' reference letters and 'novelty' letters of recommendation. These sites in the United Kingdom and United States include various caveats to keep themselves within the law as well as stating that they will not supply any fake diplomas or transcripts from a medical or dental school or that deal with flying an aircraft, driving a train or bus, securing the public interest or anything military-related.

DISCUSSION TOPICS

One Person's Plagiarism Is Another's Research

One of the great difficulties in policing plagiarism at any level of education is that of identifying the boundaries between plagiarism and research. There is an old joke in academia that 'copying from one source is plagiarism, but copying from many sources is research'. As with many other areas of life, the digitization of information and the accessibility of that digital information by way of the Internet is a change with which education must deal. Since learning is concerned with understanding information and using it appropriately, the Internet has rightly been regarded as a substantial asset. Like all great innovations, however, it comes at a price and that price is a change in the way education is conducted and, most importantly, how educational achievement is measured. Mass education used to be about learning facts and information by rote, for example, by learning to quote long passages from the Bible. As literacy became more widespread, the ability to use books as reference texts became more of a focus. Electronic calculators changed the face of arithmetic education and even had an impact on education in mathematics as calculators developed some symbolic computational capabilities.

Throughout these changes the methods of measuring achievement have slowly developed. The advent of the Internet and digital information, however, threatens to require a huge change in these methods of measurement and in the attitude and public perception of the academic results. Educational achievement is seen, rightly or wrongly, as a pathway to success. In particular, higher education is now held up as a prerequisite for most high-paying jobs. Methods of measuring achievement in education – coursework and examinations – are now much easier to overstate than previously and the difference in effort between doing the work oneself and having someone else do it or help with it is on the increase. As the benefits of being seen to be a high achiever increase, the temptation to bend or break the rules becomes harder to resist.

In a culture where the remixing of music, art and video is becoming commonplace, is it any wonder that taking a well-turned phrase from an Internet site appears appropriate? Only when the boundaries are clear, can students be expected and required, to act in accordance with the expectations of their assessors.

Overseas Education vs Distance Education

The elite of the developing world have long been educated in the industrialized world. Partly as a long-term consequence of colonialism, but also driven by the lack of higher education in their own countries, the richer portions of the developing world have long sought access to the higher education systems of countries such as United States and the United Kingdom. Many of these universities have expanded provision to attract overseas students producing in some cases substantial increases in income as well as the benefit of a more cross-cultural student environment. There are some major shifts in worldwide higher education that may change the situation dramatically over the next decade or two.

The first of these is the pressure to include higher education as a sector in the World Trade Organization (WTO) General Agreement on Trade in Services (GATS) negotiations (`www.wto.org`). So far the European Union has held back from wholehearted support for a liberalization of higher education in GATS, worried by the prospect of commercialization of what is, in most European countries, primarily a government-run sector. In this respect, changes would be less drastic for the United Kingdom than many other European countries, given the current diversity of the UK Higher Education sector. Pressure for this inclusion is primarily coming from the United States, which has an even more diverse sector including a number of commercial (i.e. for-profit) higher education institutions who already run satellite institutions in a number of countries worldwide.

The second shift that may destabilize the current arrangements is the development of more distance education initiatives aimed at educating citizens in their own countries from a foreign base. There are some halfway-house arrangements already in place, with lower-level university studies occurring in a home country such as China being 'topped up' by one or two 'finishing years' in an industrialized nation. Despite the failure of the UKeU, distance learning for higher education is a growing trend of these initiatives, both private and government funded, from many countries with highly developed education systems. To what extent differences of educational culture can be overcome with modern communications technologies is one of the major challenges to such developments.

Finally, over-reaction to a potential terrorist threat from foreign students has caused a significant tightening of visa conditions for students in many industrialized nations, most notably the United States, which may be a destabilizing factor in the worldwide recruitment of students to foreign universities.

The Net of a Million Lies

Science fiction author and computer science professor Vernor Vinge once called usenet 'the net of a million lies'. The ease of publishing information on the Internet, particularly in the world of blogs, decreases the overall level of accuracy of information to be found online. Related developments in multichannel television have fragmented information provision in the modern world (see Chapter 2 for more context on this). In the world of education, this presents opportunities and difficulties. No longer can educators assume a commonality of experience of their students.

Increasingly, there are calls for the development of 'media literacy' to run alongside basic reading literacy in early years education. Teaching students how to recognise the underlying agenda of the writer, producer or director of a piece of work, whether that work is a television programme, a motion picture or an opinion or comment on a blog, means that educators need to ensure that learners can differentiate between fact and media spin in multimedia information communications. Otherwise an increasingly polarized world will be formed, where people choose to experience only the narrow views which agree with their own personal views, while not even realizing what they are doing.

The 'tools of the trade' of English and History degrees (consideration of sources, multiple sourcing, origination and so on) need teaching not only to those specializing in English and History but to engineers, scientists and social scientists. Just as English students need 'information technology' skills, so scientists need information-comprehension skills. No longer is the interpretation of scientific results restricted to the pages of peer-reviewed scientific journals; it now occurs on television and in the pages of daily newspapers. Almost daily, controversy is created through widespread publicity in both traditional and new media outlets which create reverberations and repercussions for many years to come.

RELATED READING

Allen, I.E. and **Seaman, J.** (2006), "Making the Grade: Online Education in the United States", Sloan Consortium, Needham, MA, www.sloan-c.org/publications/survey/pdf/making_the_grade.pdf.

Attewell, J. and **Saville-Smith, C.** (2004) "Mobile learning and Social Inclusion: Focussing on learners and learning", in **J. Attewell** and **C. Saville-Smith** (eds), *Learning with Mobile Devices: Research and development*, Learning and Skills Agency, London. ISBN 1-85338-833-5.

Blake, R., **Harvey, S.**, **Heppell, S.**, **Sargant, N.** and **Thumin, N.** (2002) *Media Literacy for Adults: Why it matters*, Voice of the Listener & Viewer Ltd., Gravesend. ISBN 0-95-28151-06.

Davies, S. (2005) "ICT and e-Learning in Further Education: The challenge of change", BECTA, ferl.becta.org.uk/display.cfm?resID=12776.

Newhouse, C.P. (2002) "The Impact of ICT on Learning and Teaching: Literature review for the Western Australian Department of Education", www.det.wa.edu.au/education/cmis/eval/downloads/pd/impactreview.pdf.

Ultralab, www.ultralab.net (last accessed 25 July 2007).

Wells, J. and **Lewis, L.** (2006) *Internet Access in US Public School and Classrooms: 1994-2005*, NCES: 2007020, IES National centre for Education Statistics, nces.ed.gov/surveys/frss/publications/.

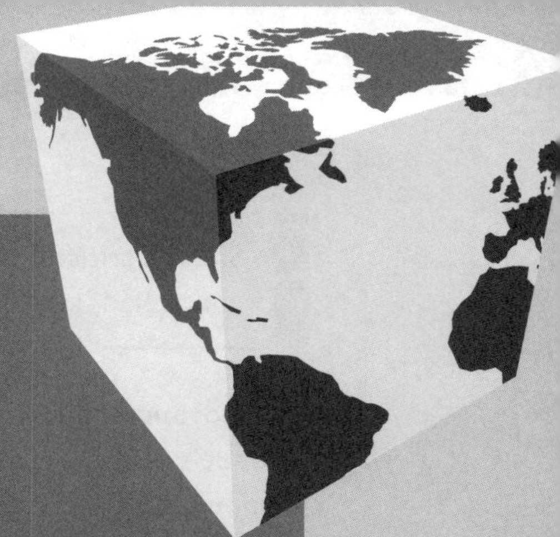

15

LIVING AND WORKING IN A WIRED WORLD

INTRODUCTION

Information and communication technologies are having a far-reaching impact on nearly all aspects of our daily lives and on the ways in which we interact with different people both at home and on a more general basis. We rely on technological advances for the most menial tasks in our day-to-day lives, from withdrawing money from the cash machine, to the safety-critical systems that control our railways or keep us alive during surgical procedures.

> Safety critical system: a computer-controlled (or partially computer-controlled) system that could cause serious injury or death if it goes wrong

Advances in technology are changing many aspects of our societal infrastructure such as corporate and community structures both nationally and globally, our shopping and lifestyle patterns and the ways in which we conduct relationships with our friends and families. Technology also affects working practices and this alters the synergy between our work and home practices and the role played by the office environment.

Technological advances not only affect the individual but also commercial organizations who may find themselves having to change their business models and react to the demands of the technological era with resultant changes in the way they interact with their customers, distribute their goods and advertise their services. Through e-commerce and the dot com boom, new businesses have emerged with mixed fortunes both on a business to business (B2B) and a business to consumer (B2 C) basis. What cannot be disputed however is that the genie has been let out of the bottle and business must move on to embrace these changes.

> Business to business (B2B) economic activity: the supply of raw materials or administrative material to another business rather than direct to the public
>
> Business to customer (B2 C) economic activity: the supply of finished products or services to the general public

Communication patterns have also changed across the whole range of the commercial and social infrastructure ranging from company to company, company to staff, company to customer and person to person within the company. This has affected the ways in which businesses operate and has at times switched the balance and set up opportunities or conflicts between the technologically enabled and the technologically naive as well as between the old and the young. Previously, the balance of power in most societies typically lay with the older generations, at least partly because of their greater experience of life's issues. The rise in the impact of technology and the fact that most younger people are now more experienced with new technologies than their elders, has introduced a new dynamic. The most obvious element of this is the old joke about parents needing their young children to programme the video recorder for them. When expanded to encompass use of the Internet, multichannel television and the workplace, this imbalance changes the entire dynamic of modern society, at least until 'older' workers have grown up in, or even helped develop, a technologically knowledgeable culture.

In essence, technology has brought about a whole range of lifestyle changes affecting the way in which people work, view their home, spend their leisure time and participate in activities such as sport. This chapter highlights and discusses a number of ways in which new technology is affecting commerce, society and the individual.

THE DIGITAL LIFESTYLE

Work, Skills and Roles

The employment world and job market now has a tendency to favour workers with ICT skills. In fact, it is beginning to expect them, even in roles where their use is limited. This is penetrating even traditional job markets. Some workers may feel threatened if they have not been brought up on the new technology and are in competition with those who have honed their computer skills from an early age. The balance may indeed swing in favour of the younger worker, manager or teacher who grew up with technology rather than the older, more experienced but less technologically skilled worker. A growing tide of unemployed workers in their late 40s and older is showing up in unemployment figures. These workers have typically been laid off from traditional manufacturing jobs and are finding their lack of ICT skills are a significant bar to finding new jobs. Few employers are willing to provide them with the level of training available to younger workers who are generally more adept with ICT and therefore cost less to train.

The introduction of electronic communications such as e-mail tends to flatten a company structure so that everyone can effectively communicate directly with everyone else; in a traditionally hierarchical and structured regime, where communication has only tended to be with immediate managers, this newly accessible structure requires some adjustment.

Teleworking

One way in which ICT has changed the working lives of individuals is through enabling them to build more flexibility into where and when they work. Many more people tend to work from home. This shift has been fuelled by the greater availability and reducing costs of broadband Internet services making it possible for a wide range of work-related activities in the 'knowledge economy' to become independent of location. Working from home used to be confined to low paid piece-workers and to the self-employed.

> Teleworking: working from home or a shared office near to home rather than at a central company building

Teleworking can be defined as work undertaken at a distance from the employer's main office and which uses ICT to overcome that distance. Telework may be undertaken in a number of different models: working at home for an agreed fixed number of days per week; working totally from home and attending the office only for occasional meetings; working in a variety of locations depending on what best fits the schedule for that week. In order for teleworking to be successful a number of criteria must be satisfied, namely that there is enough space to work at home, that there is an absence of distractions during the working part of the day and that home has the right equipment to allow the employee to work and remain in contact.

Teleworking has been shown to offer a number of potential benefits, including reducing the time spent commuting to work; providing new employment opportunities for individuals unable to travel a long distance to work; enabling flexibility between work and non-work activities, helping workers to define a better work–life balance; reducing the number of interruptions that frequently result from being in a busy office, thus increasing productivity.

An in-depth survey of nearly 2000 teleworkers at BT (conducted in 2002, see www.vnunet.com/vnunet/news/2120639/teleworking-pays-bt) found that, despite working longer hours, they felt teleworking was giving them a better quality of life and improving their work–life balance. Conversely, a small minority of respondents felt that teleworking was having negative effects on their life, mainly because of increased working hours or the isolation caused by working away from team members. Other reported benefits were:

- 33% of respondents stated that their contribution to domestic activity had increased.
- 14% reported that it had made it easier to become involved in community activities.
- 10% believed that they could not do their present job if unable to telework.

Besides impacting on the organization and on the employees, teleworking can also have a positive impact on the environment as a work-related journey is avoided. A further study of 5000 workers at BT was undertaken in 2006 (James and Hopkinson). Additionally, a report on the future of teleworking until 2020 in the United Kingdom, France and Germany can be found at www.futurefoundation.net/publications.php?disp=155.

On the downside, a significant initial investment in teleworking technology may be necessary along with significant maintenance costs and workers may feel isolated and less secure in their position. To resolve the isolation issue, 'telecottages' or 'e-work centres' may be the answer (www.peterboroughtoday.co.uk/ViewArticle.aspx?SectionID=847&ArticleID=940202&ArticlePage=2). By a number of different organizations sharing these facilities, the centres complement existing provision and opens up remote working opportunities to those who are unable to work from home.

Telecottage: a shared office in a suburb or rural location with teleworkers from more than one organization

If a majority of people were to telework, even for only one day per week, pressures on the transport network would be reduced (provided it was on different days of the week, of course); commuting time and pollution would be reduced; and less energy would be used – together all these contribute to the 'greening' of the community and environment.

UK Employers not Entitled to Secretly Monitor E-Mail

In April 2005, the UK Information Commissioner (responsible for data protection and freedom of information in the United Kingdom, www.ico.gov.uk) was asked to investigate allegations into the reading of private e-mail of workers at the National Association of Head Teachers (NAHT) (the union of school principals) by managers. These workers are the members of another union called Amicus who made the complaint on their behalf (www.theregister.co.uk/2005/04/29/amicus_email_snooping). See Chapter 7 for more details on such issues.

One member of the NAHT staff was suspended and others face disciplinary action based on the contents of e-mail sent between them at work. The NAHT did not have any policies in place which informed staff that the contents of their e-mail might be read by their employer. Misuse of electronic communications media are now one of the most common causes of disciplinary action at work, including one of the most common reasons for being fired. However, monitoring of staff use of equipment and facilities must always be done in an open and transparent way. Amicus allege that the NAHT 'without warning and in secret . . . monitor[ed] or intercept[ed] e-mail traffic'.

Amicus even threatened to ballot staff at the NAHT for industrial action if the dispute was not resolved quickly. Since no further publicity (and no industrial dispute) followed the initial flurry of interest, it is assumed that the matter was dealt with between Amicus and the NAHT with the assistance of the Information Commissioner.

The Mobile Office: the 'Non-Office' Office Job

People are working on the move more frequently than before. The number of senior-level 'portfolio' workers, handling several high-profile projects at once and constantly moving between them, is growing. Frequently, they handle their own travel arrangements, enabled by the new online travel agencies. Airports and planes become their temporary offices and senior staff travel to clinch the deals although their subordinates remain in the office, carry out the work and deliver the results remotely (electronically in the case of reports or software; by courier in the case of physical items). For such people, living close to an airport becomes more important than living close to the office. They effectively take a portable office with them – laptops, smart phones, personal digital assistants (PDAs), mini-printers and so on – and make use of wireless networks in airports and WiFi hotspots. They conduct face-to-face meetings away from the office – at a golf course, in a hotel lobby or airport business lounge. Not all recent developments have improved things for such high fliers however. The demise of the Concorde commercial service has increased the time taken for some standard long-distance flights and continued threat of terrorism introduces boarding delays and restrictions on hand-baggage contents.

The New Role of the Office

With more staff teleworking for at least part of their time, the social aspects of the workplace become more important than the productivity aspects. Centralized facilities and meeting rooms become more important, although individual offices are less important. The practice of hot desking may become the norm even for those who do attend the office daily. The office effectively becomes a 'club' and a location for team building, brainstorming, and so on, rather than the central place where productive work happens.

> Hot desking: instead of having a dedicated desk, workers pick whichever desk is available from identical options with power and Internet connectivity for a laptop (or maybe with a networked computer)

Smarter Travel

New technologies are changing the travel experience whether by plane, train or automobile. ICT has improved travel information through the delivery of online information and real-time travel data. Such services can be delivered to a PC by way of the Internet or to mobile devices, such as mobile phones and PDAs, using SMS, GPRS or 3G services.

Cars, trains, planes, boats and so on, are all becoming digitally enabled – and we are coming to expect this. More digital consumer electronics are gradually being included in the basic specification – for instance the switch from cassette to CD/DVD in cars and even the move to higher-capacity, removable hard drives or solid-state memory cards. Cars often now have satellite navigation systems, DVD players for the back-seat passengers and hands-free mobile phone connections. Satellite navigation systems are being tied in to traffic reports allowing for changes of route planning to be made not just on the basis of the general quickest route but knowledge of congestion up ahead.

Trains now have laptop and mobile-phone charging points – and a recent study concluded that trains were a good place for productive work, enabling workers to concentrate away from the office for the whole of a relatively long journey time (`http://www.shef.ac.uk/mediacentre/2007/720.html`).

However, it is in the area of flight where the most significant changes are now being proposed. There were 1.8 billion individual journeys by plane in 2004. Multichannel television has decreased passengers' tolerance for a limited choice of entertainment. Virgin flights already offer up to 300 hours of video on demand delivered by way of their V:port system, as well as multiuser games. The travel experience will also be significantly changed when Internet access and mobile phone usage become commonplace at least on some routes. The common shout of 'I'm on the train' will be replicated by 'I'm on the plane' across the world. Whether this will increase the occurrences of 'Air Rage' as the businessman next to you on an eight-hour flight makes his sixth near-identical call remains to be seen. For Internet access, Boeing's Connexion service uses a satellite broadband connection to create a WiFi hotspot inside the plane's cabin. Lufthansa were the first airline to deploy the service followed by Japan Airlines and All Nippon Airways. That was in 2004 and all the major worldwide airlines are now at least trialling such services (`www.webinflight.com/`).

It has been reported that on a typical long haul flight up to 20 mobiles are accidentally left on. The main problem this causes is not in them affecting the aircraft's avionics systems but in them disrupting mobile networks on the ground. This is because phones hop from one base-station to the next as the plane flies over them. Airlines are looking to solve this problem by including a 'picocell' (a low-power, mobile phone cell) with just enough strength to cover the interior of the aircraft. The aircraft itself is also fitted with shielding to prevent mobile phones inside from contacting other cells (www.ipaccess.com/news/press_coverage/press_cover_phones_planes.htm).

> Avionics: the embedded electronic systems that control an aircraft's operations

Also proposed are changes in the way in which we purchase tickets for air travel with a view to eliminating paper tickets. In the United States, 80% of tickets issued are e-tickets but globally this number falls to 40%. There is a great cost-saving advantage in issuing e-tickets rather than paper; it costs only $1 to process an e-ticket compared to $10 for a paper ticket, so eliminating paper tickets will save airlines billions of dollars per year. A cost benefit model for e-ticketing can be found at www.iata.org/iata/sites/whatwedo/stb/eticket/file/ET_Cost_Benefit_Model.pdf. However, for the system to become truly global there is a need to solve the problems of how to get all the different airline databases talking to each other – straightforward to implement for one airline, but it is much harder across airlines. Even now, the global airline alliances cannot access each other's frequent flier programme data.

> e-ticket: an airline ticket which is not physically held by the passenger but is held in the airline's computer system and accessed by showing suitable ID

Scandinavian Airlines is introducing new products and services that use advanced mobile technology to provide their business customers with a refined check-in notification and boarding card system and Internet and telephone facilities in business-class lounges (www.eyefortravel.com/index.asp?news=55176). To achieve a mobile phone, check-in system, software is downloaded onto the phone in a similar process to a ring-tone download; the software establishes a wireless connection with a reservation system; offers the passenger a choice of seats; and retrieves a boarding pass code which is stored on the handset. To complete the process, a reminder text message is sent to the passenger two hours before the flight. There are even moves to make the mobile phone act as the boarding card. By replacing magnetic strip readers with barcode readers, the barcode could be sent as a multimedia message to the customer's mobile phone and could be scanned by the barcode reader at the gate.

Self-service check-in kiosks are also a cost-saving mechanism, costing on average $0.16 for a transaction compared to the $3.68 cost of using a human agent. Such kiosks are normally dedicated to a particular airline but moves are under way to enable different airlines to share these kiosks and to perhaps put them in areas outside the airport, for example in the lobbies of airport hotels. Already one can check in to a flight over the Internet provided one has access to a printer to produce the boarding card.

The feasibility of switching baggage tags from barcodes to radio frequency identification (RFID) tags is also being investigated. This would increase accuracy to 95% compared with only 88% for barcodes and there is much less likelihood of them becoming damaged in the transit process. Although improving this procedure would save significant costs in compensation for lost luggage, the technology is still too costly for widespread implementation, although costs have recently fallen from US$0.37 to US$0.16 per tag in recent years.

The obvious cost savings in many of these ideas mean that airlines are pushing for their adoption. However, security concerns often prevent the swift adoption of new mechanisms. A comprehensive report of technology and the airlines can be found at `www.iata.org/iata/Sites/agm/file/2006/file/annual_report_06.pdf`.

Smarter Homes

The home may be re-emerging as the centre of human life for work and leisure, rather than a place for sleep and weekends (returning to how it was before the Industrial Revolution)! We are already living in 'the home of the future' almost as envisaged in the 1950s, with more advances in progress than ever. The home may become 'intelligent', controlling itself to meet our needs or controlled from a distance using wireless and Internet technology.

It is interesting to note that, as the number of electronic gadgets and entertainment systems we have increases, so too does the potential of these systems being integrated into single pieces of equipment. For example, we can integrate PC, television, DVD, radio and Internet functions all into one piece of equipment – the device we require being selected at a single click of an icon – a far cry from the 'hifi separates' era (www.jrf.org.uk/housingandcare/smarthomes/).

Other home-based services on offer may be the automated monitoring, diagnosis and repair of 'white goods' instigated by the goods themselves using sensors to detect faults and an Internet connection to call the maintenance engineer. Some smart machines may scan the washing as it is being loaded to detect and coins, tissues, tickets or bank notes left in the pockets of clothing while others can read garment information stored on RFID tags to recommend the most appropriate washing programme.

Systems may be installed to assist older and disabled residents to improve their security systems including entry mechanisms to homes based on iris recognition or thumbprints – no need to fumble at the door with a key any more. Alternatively the 'keyless opening' system recently introduced into cars, where an encrypted radio signal from the 'key' tells the door not only to unlock but to open may be installed. Increasingly, houses are being built and marketed ready wired with CCTV-monitoring security cameras, broadband connectivity and home-office suites to cater for the number of people now working at a least a proportion of the week at home.

Our lifestyles have also changed the way in which we access our services, keep informed and buy our goods. For example, it is now perfectly possible for us to be educated, receive legal advice, take part in polls and debates, bid in auctions and receive medical advice, all from the comfort of our living room.

Shopping

Buying goods and services in the information age is radically changing. Almost every commodity can be viewed and ordered online. According to US market-research firm Neilsen, one-tenth of the world's population has purchased goods or services online (www2.acnielsen.com/news/20051019.shtml). Cyber-businesses are having to cater for new and developing user groups, particularly the younger generation entering the marketplace who are becoming experienced 'surfers' from an early age and have no fears of using the available technologies.

Shopping Patterns and Trends

In the United Kingdom, research indicates that Internet shopping is growing 15 times faster than general retail sales. For example, in 2002 Tesco, the major food retailer in the United Kingdom, reported that its online sales were more than £10 million but by 2006 this had increased to £1 billion per year (news.zdnet.co.uk/internet/0,1000000097,39265317,00.htm). It is not only happening in the Western world: in China, where Internet use is growing steadily, there is a growing interest in Internet services and online shopping.

People are now shopping online for special-occasion and hard-to-find, unusual gifts as well as for their everyday supermarket shopping. Online technology offers us the option to buy customized products, such as Nike trainers, designed to our exact specification and complete with our name as designer. Levi jeans also may be made as a custom fit. And just to be sure we will like the product on us before we buy, virtual-reality applications with our own special avatar can model that new look for us (www.myvirtualmodel.com/en/news.htm).

It is not only the fact that we shop online that has changed. The shops on the high street are making changes to the way we physically shop, besides having to compete with the online bargains. For example, there has been a move to self-service tills in supermarkets (where large numbers of low-value goods mean the scanning by a checkout operator is a significant cost).

The barcode may also be on its way out as we move to RFID tags – they can remove the hassle of unpacking the supermarket trolley at the cash till, by recognizing the products and debiting our accounts as we walk through the check-out zone. Like many new technologies there were worries at first by civil rights groups concerned about the implications for privacy. Could people be tracked by the RFID tags in their clothing? In the main, such tags are gaining acceptance after initial reluctance by the consumer (informationweek.com/story/showArticle.jhtml?articleID=60402257 and www.trenstar.com/pdfs/RFIDJournal_Prada.pdf). For a company, RFID tags make stock control easier – and make it harder for people to steal goods from shelves or to switch labels. There are also other applications, for example if clothes are tagged then our washing machines could recognize what they are and choose the most appropriate washing cycle. Tags on everyday objects are also being used to monitor everyday behaviour of the elderly in an attempt to keep them independent in their own homes for as long as possible rather than moving them into expensive and restrictive nursing homes.

Television shopping channels are also on the increase, offering push-button purchasing for those with digital television as well as phone-in services. For some people, these shopping channels provide a means of social interaction, 'believing' the person selling the goods is selling 'just to them'. Social interaction is an increasingly important commodity as we move to an era with less direct, face-to-face contact.

The eBay Phenomenon

A huge proportion of the Internet-enabled population has now used eBay or its competitor online auction sites (see Chapter 2 for more discussion). The rise in popularity of these sites mirrors the general e-tailing trend: a few early adopters are willing to take a chance; as it becomes obvious that the risks are relatively low, more and more people are willing to buy online or at auction. The few horror stories of fraud and deception are outweighed by the general value people feel they receive. There is a noticeable rush onto auction sites just after Christmas as people dispose of unwanted Christmas gifts.

> e-tailing: electronic retail by way of Internet, mobile phone, digital television and so on

Almost anything can be found for sale on these sites including some that are rather unusual: an 18-year-old student was offered £8400 in an auction for her virginity (news.bbc.co.uk/1/hi/england/bristol/3473817.stm); a Briton sold his soul for a mere £11.61 (news.bbc.co.uk/1/hi/england/2051061.stm); other Monty Python-esque offerings have included 'the meaning of life' (blogs.theage.com.au/entertainment/archives/2006/06/last_laugh_mean.html) and a time machine (Gear Live by way of shorl.com/hogrisenagryso)!

Social Shopping

It can be also argued that these new forms of Internet shopping can become socially divergent and economically divisive. Some research has said that growing numbers of social groups use public venues such as shops and shopping malls to meet and interact with others, forming communities of shoppers. The growth in Internet shopping and e-commerce will inevitably affect the number of small business that can operate in these traditional community environments. The inability to provide 'face to face' retailing for some parts of the older community may well be detrimental to their well being, however it may also be argued that the development of cyber-shopping may encourage more online communities which could possibly provide new opportunities for wider social contact and interaction.

Customer Attraction

Internet and mobile phone shopping has now become an acceptable and in many cases preferred method of buying goods and services. E-tailers have responded to the market opportunities in a variety of innovative ways to attract customers. There has been a massive explosion in e-commerce activity, creating a marketplace and competitive environment for most companies, large and small. These new markets mirror in many ways the traditional issues faced by small business trying to survive in conventional markets and competing with the larger operators. However one major difference is related to physical environments: no longer is business activity constrained by local markets and physical buildings, shoppers can now view and buy goods and services in an anytime, anywhere world.

Automated Banking

Banks traditionally were a labour-intensive operation. The main 'clearing banks' (i.e. the high street banks that most of us have day-to-day accounts with) have long been involved in deploying new technology to simultaneously reduce their costs and improve customer experience. From the development of the ATM, which allowed customers access to their money much more cheaply and quickly (and on a 24-hour basis) than going into branches, to phone banking, the sector has changed unrecognizably in the last 30 years and change is not stopping. Many banks now offer online banking, as a replacement for traditional methods or as an additional service, and mobile services such as receiving regular account updates and statements by text message to a mobile phone. Security, though, is a constant concern, between online fraud (phishing or pharming are described in Chapter 11) and fake or altered ATMs.

The move to electronic service is all very well for many people, but not for all and older people in particular have a great desire to deal with people rather than machines. Some banks are now making a virtue of their personal face-to-face service availability, though still backed up by the convenient electronic methods.

Having reduced their costs significantly by moving to ATMs the banks are now under pressure not to introduce charges for accessing money by way of these machines. Those in rural areas are particularly hard hit by charges when there are no sensible alternatives. In early 2005, however, the United Kingdom became the first G8 country where card-based transactions outstripped physical money, so perhaps ATMs are becoming a relic of the physical-money past, too.

Shopping Crime

With increased use of the Internet for shopping, there has been a corresponding increase in cyber-crime, such as online credit card fraud and identity theft. Many online companies maintain that the level of online fraud is little different from that found in other more traditional types of commercial transactions, however there is growing evidence that this may not be the case (see Chapter 11).

The accessibility of the Internet means that a wider audience of potential criminals have access to the cyber-marketplace. Estimates of Internet and credit card fraud are difficult to obtain, as online banking and trading companies always wish to maintain the integrity of there systems to the general public. However, as early as 2001, US research company Gartner Group, estimated that online fraud losses were 19 times as high, dollar for dollar, as for offline sales.

Recent reports said that, in 2005, US consumers filed almost half a million online fraud reports totalling almost $700 million (US Consumer Protection Agency by way of shorl.com/dymonystovafa). Typical examples of reported crimes were: obtaining credit card information; spam encouraging 'get rich quick scandals'; accessing bank accounts; and identity cloning.

With the growth in Internet shopping and the associated credit-card transactions, identity theft has become a growing issue. With the transient nature of data and the ever-increasing numbers of organized and inventive criminals who now operate on the Internet, new measures are being introduced to combat these attacks. The UK government launched a new web site, in 2004, to offer advice on how to protect yourself in these circumstances (www.identity-theft.org.uk/) and, in the United States, President Bush signed the Identity Theft Penalty Enhancement Act, which adds two years to prison sentences for those convicted of using stolen personal and credit card data (www.whitehouse.gov/news/releases/2004/07/20040715-3.html).

Financial losses are not the only potential problem caused by identity theft, as one UK citizen found in 2004 when he was arrested by the South African police on an international warrant issued by US authorities. A criminal in the United States had been using this UK citizen's identity for a number of years and the UK man was held for weeks by South African authorities before his identity was confirmed (news.bbc.co.uk/1/hi/england/2799791.stm).

Buying Entertainment

There have been significant changes in the way in which we source and select goods. Customers can select their cars, holidays, insurance and so on, online, activities that were all in the past undertaken by a middleman. Consequently, the off-line middleman needs to offer us a value-added service – what can the middleman add that warrants the additional price?

The Internet can offer each individual a much more personalized store. Consider for example, the `Amazon.com` personal store and personal recommendations. No real-world shop can match that level of individuality. The successful e-tailers are those who manage to tap into this rich vein of personalized experience, not only providing better value for money but a richer experience for their customers.

The video rental store is now under threat from centralized, mail-order distribution of rental DVDs and once video on demand becomes widespread (cable television companies are rolling out significant services) that will almost certainly be the end of the high street, video-rental store.

The Sporting Life

ICT is continuing to transform how we view and participate in sport in the information age. Today's sportsperson has at their disposal an enormous range of IT-based products and systems designed to enhance and improve performance. Training techniques now use real-time, data-monitoring biometrics and interactively compare this with profiles and online training programmes. Even the recreational runner or athlete can now purchase electronic communication and monitoring equipment which can be worn during activity and from which information can be relayed by wireless technology or downloaded later for analysis and comparison.

For the consumer, advances in information technology ensure that almost all public sports are accessible, though sometimes at a cost. The Internet and BT allows the connected user to watch sports events on a range of devices in an almost limitless number of locations. Online sports coverage is no longer restricted to the television and satellite media: interactive broadcasting and on-demand Internet facilities now offer products which enable the user to select and interact with sporting events across the world. Photo finishes in races or goal scoring in soccer matches can now also be viewed live by way of a mobile telephone anywhere in the world. It is commonplace for individuals to subscribe to texting services, which update them through the mobile phone, giving the latest scores and news in their chosen sport. Through digital television, one can also have the facility to switch viewing to different matches at Wimbledon or different events at the Olympics. The advance in communication technology has fuelled many new e-business activities including online gambling, where the immediacy of the information aids and encourages the potential gambler to participate and spend more.

TECHNOLOGY AND THE INDIVIDUAL

Education

As discussed in Chapter 14, ICT has had an enormous impact on how we learn, both as children and adults, from the opportunities for lifelong learning by way of distance learning and e-learning, to the huge range of factual material now available on the Internet and multichannel television. Opinion is divided, however, as to how much we should rely on digital technologies within education. While some studies promote the benefits of an online education, other recent studies show that children encouraged to use computers and the Internet too much at too young an age have lower levels of achievement in certain standard tests such as arithmetic, than those with less ICT involvement.

Health

As discussed in Chapter 9, ICT has also had a huge impact on the practice of medicine in the last few decades. New computer technologies have offered the prospect of better and faster diagnosis, automated and home-based monitoring and diagnosis and the opportunity for more advanced surgical procedures to be carried out.

However, technology in itself may be responsible for causing a number of previous unrecognized injuries and conditions. Our increased use of computer and communications technology has been blamed for causing or contributing to a number of health-related conditions such as repetitive strain injury (RSI, an umbrella term for various muscle and joint conditions) from too much typing or repeated use of a mouse for too long.

There is still controversy about the link between poor posture and RSI. Some reports and surveys (e.g. news.bbc.co.uk/1/hi/health/2698119.stm) say that many computer users experience problems such as back, shoulder, or wrist pain along with other joint problems, muscular pain, headaches and eyestrain (www.hazards.org/strainpain.htm). In the past, advice was focused around the ergonomics of the workstation and various assistive devices to alleviate the complaints – today, alternative therapies such as Pilates, the Alexander Technique and yoga may also be promoted.

Mental health professionals are still divided about the potentially addictive nature of too much use of Internet communication technologies such as massively multiplayer online role-playing games and chat rooms, with Internet Addiction Disorder (IAD) being proposed but not yet accepted as a syndrome.

Crime

There is a developing crime problem of people being robbed for technology such as iPods and mobile phones – even leading to death in a number of mugging incidents for mobile phone. The distinctive white headphones of the iPod have been blamed by some police forces for 'advertising' the expensive nature of the equipment tucked into a pocket or purse. Despite many warnings, it appears the 'coolness' factor of being seen to have an iPod still outweighs the increased risk of being mugged for most people. New forms of unacceptable behaviour are also being fuelled by new technology such as cyber-bullying by way of text, e-mails or social community sites and happy slapping incidents.

Religion

There has reportedly been a recent trend for mobile phones to be used within a religious context. Catholics can sign up for daily inspirational text message from the Pope simply by texting 'Pope On' to a sign-up service. Irish Jesuits have the Sacred Space service accessible over a smart phone which encourages them to spend 10 minutes reflecting on a chosen script for the day. Taiwan has limited edition phones made by local handset maker, Okwap that offer Matsu wallpaper and religious ringtones – each specially blessed at a temple of Matsu, a Chinese Goddess of the Sea (see www.engadget.com/entry/1905679588167556). Muslims can use the F7100 handset from LG to remind them of prayer times (with an alarm system that works in 500 cities) and to find the direction of Mecca.

Catholic bishops in the Philippines banned people from attending confession and receiving absolution by way of text messages, although the non-denominational Ship-of-Fools organization in the United Kingdom (news.bbc.co.uk/1/hi/magazine/3623525.stm) have a 3-D virtual church where you can attend services around the clock without leaving your computer. The original highly open design of the system had to be altered when sacrilegious activity by some of the visitors profaned the virtual altar (the New York Times by way of shorl.com/jetidopufruki).

COMMUNICATION

The one thing that really embodies the information age is communication. From text messaging to multichannel television, from instant messaging (IM) to satellite phones, they're all about communicating with each other.

The Changing Face of Communication

The digital age has also influenced what we buy and how the Government measures our economy. In this age of e-mail, IM and texting, writing letters for personal and more frequently even formal communication is becoming an activity of the past. This is evidenced by writing paper being dropped, in March 2005, from the UK government's official shopping list, of which the purpose is to assess the rate of inflation. Items added recently are laptop computers, mobile phone handsets and DVDs. Also reflecting our new reliance on digital technologies are the inclusion of charges to use cash machines and the cost of supermarket home delivery for Internet-ordered grocery shopping. The 20 items included for the first time in

2007 were mainly high-technology gadgets, demonstrating the big technological shift in Britain. New additions include printers, mobile phone downloads for ringtones, games and music, and digital photo processing. Videocassette players and VHS tapes have been dropped as have the old-style deeper, widescreen TVs (www.guardian.co.uk/britain/article/0,,2038128,00.html).

Spoken language is an emotive issue. It can even be the spark that causes a war or a revolution. Speakers of a 'minority language' can feel overwhelmed by the majority. In the twentieth century, English eclipsed French as the language of international diplomacy and business. The growth of the Internet has entrenched this even further. The influence is not all one way however, as English itself is being changed by technology in many ways, not least by gaining with astonishing frequency new words to describe new technologies. Just as media literacy is a necessary skill for coping with the modern world, so too is spoken communication literacy. Conversing with another person face-to-face in the same location is one approach, but whether writing or speaking, there are many more ways to communicate now, each with their own differences from an 'ordinary conversation':

- telephone – conversation with unseen person
- answering machine or service – an asynchronous message.
- radio – monologue to unknown, heterogeneous mass audience
- letter – written conversation with a slow reply
- e-mail and instant message – written conversation with a rapid reply
- texting – rapid and informal
- video communication – timing delays and limited bandwidth

The ability of a huge number of people, not just media celebrities, to communicate worldwide with strangers brings other pressures on communication. For example, is one talking to a friend or a stranger or a mix of the two? Is the communication time-limited or will there be a record of it, perhaps passed on to other people by way of e-mail or 'broadcast' to the masses on YouTube.

Internet Chat Rooms

It is argued by some that Internet chat rooms may well encourage shy or introverted individuals to communicate more easily. However it is also possible for users to hide their true identities and masquerade as another individual. This feature is used to 'groom' children and vulnerable adults, finding common interests with their contact, creating friendly and supportive online discussions with the aim of eventually meeting the person face to face at a secret rendezvous.

Government agencies, ISPs, parents and guardians of children and vulnerable adults are now combining resources to combat these threats. Software controls are available to block or filter certain chat rooms. Children are being educated on the dangers, parents are being encouraged to ensure computers are used in visible places in the home and that a culture of openness is observed by families regarding checking 'the history of sites visited' on the computer.

Mobile Phones

Given that mobile phone ownership is now close to ubiquitous among those over 12 years old in Europe (`www.yougov.com/archives/pdf/CPW060101004_2.pdf`), it has become increasingly difficult to determine from where calls are originating. In the past it would be possible to return calls to landline numbers with a fair degree of certainty that you would know the location, but today the caller can be anywhere in the world. With the latest developments in technology it is now possible to overcome theses difficulties with products such as FollowUs (`www.followus.co.uk`), Map-A-Mobile (`www.mapamobile.com`) and VeriLocation (`www.verilocation.com`) which, although designed to help parents keep track of children, could also be used by others such as employers or husbands and wives for tracking purposes!

Unlike the PC and even the laptop, mobile phones have become an extremely personal piece of equipment: they come everywhere with us – key, money, phone; and they can show something of us – ringtone, wallpaper, and so on. They can make a fashion statement; there can be photos inside the battery compartment; one can even be buried in a giant mobile-phone-shaped coffin. In parts of

China it has become customary to take a new mobile phone to a local Buddhist monk for blessing. In Beijing, a man paid $215,000 for a lucky phone number (www.techdirt.com/articles/20041108/1525206.shtml).

Community Gatherings

A flash mob is a spontaneous gathering of strangers, organized secretively by e-mail or text message and subject to meticulous timing. Some early flash mobs are given below:

- 19 June 2003: World's first flash mob at 7:27 p.m. in Macy's rug department, New York
- 24 July 2003: First European flash mob in a bookshop in Rome
- 24 July 2004: Flash mob at 6:31 p.m. in a sofa shop in central London
- 8 July 2004: 'flash mob' added to English Oxford Dictionary (along with 'speed dating' and 'va-va-voom')
- 07 Oct 2004: Flash Mob The Opera at Paddington station.

> Flash mob: an organized gathering of strangers to perform a short, often surrealistic task to make an artistic or political statement

Another popular type of flash mob is that of the public personal dance party. Organized by advertising on the Web a particular place and time, people bring along their personal CD or MP3 players with whatever music they want and start dancing to it. Such an event in 2004 at London's Waterloo station drew hundreds of people (some who travel by way of Waterloo every day anyway) dancing to everything from jazz to swing, ballroom to hip-hop. Bemused British Transport Police allowed the event to go ahead since there was no danger of overcrowding and the dancers were careful to avoid injuring ordinary travellers. A flash mob was planned for Wednesday 4 April 2007 at 18.53 at London Victoria Station with the following rules (www.flashmob.co.uk/):

ARRIVE AT THE STATION AROUND 18.40

WALK AROUND AND GET IN TO YOUR GROOVE
SPREAD OUT THROUGH THE WHOLE STATION
NO DANCING BEFORE 18.53
AT THE INSTANT THE CLOCK STRIKES 18.53
DANCE LIKE YOU'VE NEVER DANCED BEFORE
TRY NOT TO DANCE IN ONE PLACE
AND DANCE FOR AS LONG AS YOU CAN

Flash Mobs: a New Technology-Driven Social Event

On Thursday 8 July 2004, the word 'flash mob', defined as 'a public gathering of complete strangers, organized by way of the Internet or mobile phone, who perform a pointless act and then disperse again', officially entered the English language as it became part of the 11th edition of the Oxford Concise English Dictionary.

Flash mobs began their existence in New York on 19 June 2003 at 7:27 p.m. when 150 individuals met in Macy's rug department and surrounded a $10 000 carpet. Ten minutes later, they had all gone their separate ways leaving behind bemused shop staff.

The phenomenon spread quickly in the United States and across to Europe and the United Kingdom with a whole host of web sites quickly springing up eager to discuss old flash mobs and to speculate on future ones.

After the success of the first UK flash mob, held at a central London sofa, a second flash mob was organized. In this instance at exactly 6:36 p.m. on Thursday 21 August 2003 some 60 people stood up and started circling a banana clockwise in the air, before opening their umbrellas and eating the fruit. Then they turned to the London Eye and chanted 'Beauty is in the eye of the beholder. O Wheel of fortune, turn for me' over and over before leaving as quickly as they had come.

Organizers (in the case of the London Eye flash mob, a UK national newspaper) who contact flash mobbers by text and e-mail once they have signed up to `www.flashmob.co.uk`, stipulate that watches must be synchronized with the speaking clock so that movements will be exact. Flash mobs are still continuing, the challenge now being to come up with original ideas that entice a bunch of strangers to come together to flash mob your scene.

New Communities?

Does the Internet enhance or reduce community spirit and human contact? There are arguments to be made on both sides. People travel more and hence may be frequently apart from their families, however the effects of this absence may be lessened by modern communication technologies which help to bridge the geographic divide. New ways to socialize have also undoubtedly been created by modern communications. Everything from usenet, to chat rooms, to blogs to virtual worlds such as Second Life and social networking sites such as MySpace and FaceBook, have created communities which can be strong cohesive groups, even when few of the individuals have ever met. Such sites provide a communication medium for a whole spectrum of real-life personalities – from outgoing individuals keen to promote and share their lives and exploits with others, to a way for shy and introverted individuals with interests not shared by the masses to find like-minded individuals to build a community. It should also be mentioned however that this focus on finding and developing virtual friendships and communities might, for some people, come at the expense of them not developing real relationships with neighbours and within their local communities.

Virtual Relationships

In his science-fiction detective novel The Naked Sun, Isaac Asimov posited a world in which each individual is isolated in their own geographical space with only robots for physical company but has electronic contact with the rest of the world. There are people in Japan who are suffering from acute agoraphobia who remain in one room or who creep out of that room into the kitchen and bathroom avoiding even their own families. Many of these (usually young males) are heavily involved in online communities but are psychologically unable to interact physically with people (www.hartford-hwp.com/archives/55a/547.html).

> Agoraphobia: fear of open spaces or crowds of people

Commercial products are being developed such as e-blaster, to manage and record multiple information sources such as e-mails, chat information and instant messages and forward this to your e-mail address for retrieval. Many everyday contacts, romantic or otherwise, are now conducted online or in mobile format; even the private conversations of members of Britain's royal family could not remain secure and the content of messages has been made public. Internet products have been developed to exploit the human desire to contact old friends, university or school classmates or make new friends and acquaintances. Example include Friends Reunited (www.friendsreunited.co.uk), a web site developed in the United Kingdom to help individuals find old friends and make contact with them and Craig's List (craigslist.com), developed by Craig Newmark, to help others communicate across the world.

However not all these initiatives produce the desired results. Counselling experts have suggested that electronically retrieving memories and friends from the past can have a potentially de-stabilizing effect on some current relationships, resulting in some cases of separation and divorce. Many users of these services can also become obsessively connected to the Internet, devoting more and more time to searching and engaging with previous friends and partners, again endangering current friendships and relationships.

In another social context, the Internet is being used for 'technology-assisted dating', a possible reflection of the apparently busy and hectic lifestyle enjoyed by many of the population. Evidence of the popularity of these developments is apparent with a web search for 'computer dating' giving more than 72.8 million hits, substantially up from 400 000 hits in 2005. A clear indication of the commercial potential, not only to provide a genuine service but also to dupe and exploit individuals across the world.

Today's interconnected individual operates in a social environment where many of their electronic communications can be retrieved, inadvertently or not, by others. Examples of how this can happen include mobile phone call registers and web mail history facilities, receiving misdirected copies of e-mails, viewing of satellite navigation previous destination data and lack of appropriate security measures that allow entry to address books and e-mail systems (see Chapter 7 for more discussion.)

The technology has created a new dimension in personal and professional relationships which are focused around individual privacy issues. Before the introduction of such sophisticated levels of the technology, many individuals would rely on 'trust' and would be unable to verify this by any other means. Today the technology presents the individual with the means to verify and on occasions doubt the 'trust model', possibly creating another unnecessary social pressure.

In modern society many have observed the break up of the nuclear family to a more dispersed model where family support becomes eroded. Many parenting web sites have been set up in response to this development, producing the twenty-first century equivalent of the extended family. These sites are designed to provide online support and advice and encourage the development of virtual communities. There is a growing demand for these sites.

`Mumsnet.com` was set up in the United Kingdom in 2000 by Justine Roberts and Carrie Longton and now has thousands of members. The site is designed by parents for parents and has developed a virtual supportive community based on sharing parenting experiences. The usenet newsgroup soc.support.* hierarchy has, for many years, provided help and advice for those suffering from a variety of physical and mental problems (including gender confusion, coping with having been abused as a child and many others).

Not all online 'communities' are healthy places to be. There have been a number of high profile examples of suicide pacts made online or of cannibals and potential suicides linking up through the Internet. In 2004, a German case horrified people around the world (news.bbc.co.uk/1/hi/world/europe/3443803.stm). Religious cults can also see the Internet as a fertile recruitment site and, as is discussed in Chapter 13, there are people online who can turn into cyber-stalkers or who pick their victims for physical abuse from those they meet online.

The Global Village

In The Hitchhiker's Guide to the Galaxy, Douglas Adams wrote of the Babel Fish which 'by effectively removing all barriers to communication between different races and cultures, has caused more and bloodier wars than anything else in the history of creation'. It is claimed that no two democracies have ever declared war on each other, although this claim may be limited by your definition of democracy. Techno-utopians claim that better communications will foster greater understanding between the peoples of the world and that horizontal communication between ordinary people and vertical communication between citizens and their leaders will foster greater understanding and therefore lead to a more peaceful world.

> Techno-utopians: people who believe that technology can, will or does solve all the problems of the world

But simple knowledge of how other people live does not necessarily imply acceptance of differences in culture and indeed knowledge can lead to resentment, based either upon envy or because of a dislike of how they live. For example, the dominance of English-language entertainment can lead to a strong resentment of the undermining of cultural values in other parts of the world.

It is not only in the recipients of cultural colonialism that resentment can be fostered. The globalization of trade and the increased physical and information communications structure have led to the offshoring of production (everything from textiles and consumer electronics to pharmaceutical drugs) and of knowledge worker jobs (e.g. call centres) and resultant resentment over the loss of local jobs.

> Offshoring: moving all or part of the operation of a business to a country where labour or other infrastructure costs are cheaper

The publication by a small Danish newspaper of cartoons satirizing Islam and Mohammad would probably have been ignored in 1985. In 2005, however, it caused an international diplomatic incident, riots in which people died and a boycott of Danish goods and services in Arab countries (`news.bbc.co.uk/1/hi/world/europe/4361260.stm`). Thus it is shown that knowledge of other people and countries can cause as much unrest as harmony.

THE DIGITAL DIVIDE

As is mentioned in various other chapters, many policy makers are concerned about the concept of the digital divide. There are two manifestations of this: within a country and between countries. The industrialized world has seen a mad dash to make broadband Internet connectivity 'available' to their whole population. What 'available' actually means is an interesting question, which we discuss below. In the meantime there are still significant portions of the world's population who have never even made a telephone call. Free market economies tend to converge to the most economically efficient forms of trade. Where most of a population have access to a wide range of electronic communications, including the Internet, multichannel digital television and mobile phones, the other channels for commerce may face a lack of economies of scale. This leads to greater expense, often for those least able to afford it, in obtaining basic necessities and can even lead to significant social exclusion.

These problems can exist within a country, where a digital underclass without access to many of the benefits of the information age could develop and it can exist between countries where the lack of information infrastructure can cause countries to fall further and further behind the necessary state to engage profitably in world trade.

Hewlett Packard Closes the Digital Divide

Through its e-inclusion initiative Hewlett Packard (HP) is committed to increasing access to ICT worldwide. In doing so it empowers individuals and communities and enables them to apply technology to accelerate their economic development in areas such as medicine, entrepreneurship, agriculture, banking, distance learning, commerce and cultural preservation. As a business, HP also gains from these initiatives, enhancing their own competitiveness through creating new innovations, discovering new talent and devising new solutions and business models to serve emerging markets. HP funds two types of e-inclusion project: digital villages and i-communities.

HP digital villages

These are designed to help underserved US communities use technology for learning, working and community building. One such project is the Southern California Tribal Digital Village (SCTDV). Here, more than 1000 computers in over 50 sites and 20 computer labs enable thousands of Native Americans to be connected across Southern California. Tribal members create multimedia materials for projects related to education, history, language and culture and use Internet-based video conferencing for distance learning. HP's contributions have enabled the diverse tribal communities to connect and communicate with each other and to preserve their culture through the use of this technology. They have also provided opportunities for economic growth with the establishment of a for-profit digital printing business, Hi Rez Digital Solutions.

HP i-communities

These are development initiatives in emerging markets undertaken in partnership with local government and non-governmental and community organizations. HP i-communities use ICT to promote sustainable social and economic development by increasing literacy, promoting entrepreneurship and job creation and providing access to government, healthcare and education services. This is a mutually beneficial partnership with the targeted communities benefiting and developing economically although HP learns to compete in these markets. For example, The Kuppam HP i-community in Andhra Pradesh, India, has enabled more than 15 000 citizens to access e-government, education, healthcare, agriculture and small-business information and services with an online community portal installed at 13 Community Information Centers. The use of two Mobile Solution Centers has enabled a further 12 000 people in 150 outlying villages to access health and information services each month. HP's Mobile Photo Studio project has also enabled local women to establish small businesses taking government ID photos, capturing social events, such as weddings and community celebrations, and using photos of finished saris as a marketing tool for a door-to-door clothing business. These women, known as Village Photographers, rent lightweight solar-powered digital cameras and printers from HP and in many cases have doubled their family's monthly income.

The Digital Divide in the Industrialized World

As mentioned above, governments in the industrialized world have recently been engaged in contests to see who can make Internet connectivity and particularly broadband Internet connectivity, available to the largest proportion of their populations. The challenges that must be overcome are different for each country, depending on existing infrastructure in telecommunications, population densities and geographic peculiarities. There is also a considerable difference between 'availability' and 'take-up'. Many governments are now moving from pure 'availability' measures – defined as 'you can get it if you want it and can pay for it' – to 'take-up' measures – defined as the proportion of the population who actually have and use a broadband connection.

One of the significant barriers to encouraging take-up can be entrenched commercial suppliers of connectivity. Companies who have made a significant investment in offering broadband are loath to reduce their prices to improve the take-up rate. Companies are interested in the greatest profit margins available rather than in the greatest real take-up rate. If half the population are willing to pay $100 per month for broadband connectivity but a $20 rate would persuade 90% to sign up then companies would go for the $100 option. Sometimes commercial competition will drive the price far enough down, but the infrastructure costs may militate against the development of competition, as has happened in the UK cable television market where there is effectively no competition among cable suppliers in any specific area – the first to cable an area wins as the pickings once in competition are not worth the investment. Luckily for consumers, competition between satellite and cable provision has prevented a complete monopoly in cabled areas, though this competition is far from perfect, as discussed in Chapter 3.

Persuaded that free, or cheap, broadband wireless Internet access would be a general public good and would possibly boost the local economy, city governments in some metropolitan areas in the United States have proposed municipal provision of this 'vital infrastructure'. Existing commercial providers of both wired and wireless Internet connectivity are understandably opposed to this idea and have lobbied hard against it, even bringing legal actions claiming protection against government undercutting their business model. Besides the supposed economic benefits of universal connectivity, many city councils are arguing that to ensure that everyone can have access, a municipal infrastructure is needed. Whether the cost and availability of the connection is the problem in take-up by the 'digital underclass' is rather debatable. Far more problematic are:

- lack of equipment: free WiFi is not much good if you do not have a computer or if the computer you use does not have a wireless network card;
- lack of ability to use computers and the Internet;
- lack of desire to use computers and the Internet;
- concern over where the next meal is coming from and how to pay the rent rather than how to access the Internet.

Such initiatives are coming to other countries as well, with the UK city of Norwich providing free WiFi coverage across the city (`news.bbc.co.uk/1/hi/technology/5303092.stm`).

E-Government

Perhaps more worrying in many ways than the increased cost of commercial transactions for the digital underclass is the concept that government services themselves will move online to the extent that some sectors of the population will find themselves denied their democratic rights. The UK government has a commitment to increasing the information available online about government activity and increasing the amount of interaction with government that can be done electronically.

For example, electronic filing of tax returns has been a great success in recent years, although infrastructure issues raise their head on deadline days if the Inland Revenue's servers cannot cope with the number of people trying to file at the last minute (encouraged by the government's helpful advertising campaign pointing out to people that the online system allows them to do this). Filing online is so much more efficient for the government than processing paper forms that it is conceivable that online filing could become compulsory in the not too distant future. Already the deadlines for physical return and online filing are months apart.

In the 2005 General Election, the main UK political parties did not bother printing and distributing copies of their manifestos as they had done in the past, putting them through almost every letterbox in the country. Instead they placed much more substantial documents online. Despite free or cheap Internet access available through municipal libraries this was seen by some as denying the democratic rights of those without the means to access the Internet – how can someone be expected to vote for the party they believe represents their views when they cannot find out what the parties stand for? Of course the reduction in wasted paper was a cause for environmental celebration.

The Digital Divide Between the Nations

The digital divide between rich and poor individuals in the industrialized world pales into insignificance when compared to the digital divide between rich and poor nations. On 14 March 2005, the United Nations launched the 'Digital Solidarity Fund' (`www.dsf-fsn.org`) to finance projects that will address 'the uneven distribution and use of new information and communication technologies' and 'enable excluded people and countries to enter the new era of the information society'. But it must be remembered that giving poor countries IT equipment will not instantly make them rich. Bridging the digital divide is more than just having computers – what use are these if the people in the country do not have food to eat, electricity to make the computers work and education to know how to use them?

As well as the advent of the One Laptop Per Child scheme (OLPC: `laptop.org`), another suggestion to overcoming the digital divide is to address the problem by way of mobile phone rather than computer technology. Research has shown that the impact of mobile phones on growth is twice as big in developing countries as in developed ones – an extra ten phones per 100 people in a developing country increases gross domestic product (GDP) by 0.6% according to the magazine (Economist 2005). Even the poorest African countries are rushing to embrace mobile phones: lower cost, no permanent electricity supply required and no need for the user to be able to read and write letters, just numbers on a keypad. Sunlight in equatorial regions is much stronger than in the temperate Northern regions and so solar electric cells are more productive, allowing both mobile phone handsets and cell stations to run purely on solar power. The lack of a cabled telephone network in much of Africa also helps drive the update of mobile technology. The challenge is for telephone handset manufacturers to produce cheap enough and robust enough handsets to satisfy demand in these markets and to produce sufficient economies of scale for infrastructure provision to be economical.

Even though the UN's target of 50% of the world's population to live within the coverage of mobile telephony has already been exceeded (latest World Bank figures show almost 80% coverage), there is still a long way to go before we live in a fully connected world. The number of phones per 100 people is still a telling statistic:

- Ethiopia: 0.13
- Democratic Republic of Congo: 2
- United Kingdom: 110

DISCUSSION TOPICS

The Language of the Digital Age

Communication is definitely enhanced by a common language, providing everyone in the conversation understands the language well enough. There remain cultural differences, of course and this can impact on the utility of a common language. The advent of technologies such as the Internet, digital television and the mobile phone have been influencing greatly our language and the ways in which we communicate with each other. Discuss current communication within the context of the following questions:

- Is it necessary to have a common language for the Web? If so, is it right that English is this language? What implications does this have for countries whose first language is not English?
- Should SMS texting and the language that has evolved around this be treated as a new language and accepted with the same status as other languages? Should it be taught as a written language?
- Have technologies such as e-mail and SMS destroyed our ability to write good prose? In what ways, for example, does an SMS approach to communicating information differ from writing a lengthy piece of prose. Are e-mail and text messaging making us much more casual in our approach to language and is this acceptable in some or all circumstances?

Digital Relationships

Massively multiplayer online role-playing games, Internet chat rooms, e-mail and instant messaging mean that we can talk and form relationships easily with like-minded people who we may or may not ever physically meet. Discuss whether relationships formed online and which remain virtual, can be as rewarding as meeting a person or group of friends physically.

Friends Reunited and Internet chat sites have been accused by some of causing the breakdown of marriages because of rekindling past relationships or forming new relationships. Discuss to what extent you believe this is true. Is it possible to 'be unfaithful' with someone you have never met in person?

Digital Divides

Since the beginning of civilization there has always been a disparity between what one person or one country has and what another has. Discuss whether the digital divide is different from any other divide and whether or not this gap can ever be completely bridged.

There are still a number of indigenous and technologically isolated populations in the world. Discuss whether bringing technology to these populations is a benefit or a curse.

REFERENCES

Economist (2005) Calling an End to Poverty, *The Economist*, 7 July 2005.

James, P. and **Hopkinson, P.** (2006) "E-Working at BT: The economic, environmental and social impacts", SustainIT, available at www.sustainit.org/publications/category.php?category=ework+e.g+telework.

RELATED READING

Hargittai, E. (2003) "The Digital Divide and What To Do About It", in **D.C. Jones** (ed.) *New Economy Handbook*, Academic Press, San Diego, CA, available at www.eszter.com/research/c04-digitaldivide.html.

Joinson, A.N. (2003) *Understanding the Psychology of Internet Behaviour*, Palgrave, Basingstoke. ISBN 0-333-98468-4.

Meyrowitz, J. (1985) *No Sense of Place*, Oxford University Press, Oxford. ISBN 0-19-504231-X.

Rheingold, H. (2003) *Smart Mobs*, Perseus Publishing, Cambridge, MA. ISBN 0-7382-0608-3.

Appendix

ETHICAL ANALYSIS

INTRODUCTION

Some people believe that ethics can be taught in a procedural way, much like mathematics and programming. Others follow a philosophical approach and present the thinking of great minds of the past such as Kant and their approaches to philosophy in general. Others use more modern general introductions to moral philosophy and ethics such as Thompson (2005) or texts specific to computer ethics such as Bynum and Rogerson (2003). Whichever approach is used, the goal is to provide students with experience in thinking about the professional and ethical issues they will encounter after they graduate (they will all encounter issues although they will each encounter a diverse set of them and none will encounter them all directly).

Because of the wide variety of approaches to teaching computer ethics, in this book we have not, as many others do, attempted to include a main chapter or four putting forward our approach. However, an overview of the approaches and pointers to more detailed materials, may be useful to lecturers and those studying individually. Hence, this appendix is principally aimed at providing a starting point for lecturers intending to adopt this book as a principle course text and give them pointers to suitable materials to use in developing their approach to teaching ethical analyses of the dilemmas raised in the chapters. It can also be used by the general reader, who may wish to pursue their own further studies in developing their professional attitude to ethical issues.

TRADITIONAL WESTERN MORAL PHILOSOPHY

In one sense, the search for a definition of morality is the principle question of philosophy. How can one act in a correct manner if one does not know what the correct action is? Some strands of philosophical thought equally stress correct action and correct mental attitudes. Is a positive action carried out for purely selfish (enlightened self-interest) reasons a moral act or does morality require selflessness to attract approbation? Such considerations are not confined to Western moral philosophy, but also appear in Eastern religious and philosophical thought, such as Patanjali's tenet of ahimsa which teaches the avoidance of harm to others in thought or deed (`www.yogamovement.com/resources/patanjali.html`). In this appendix, we focus mainly on Western moral philosophers through familiarity rather than any claim of their superiority to other philosophical schools. It is entirely possible to trace traditional Western philosophical thought back to ancient Greek texts and writers. However, in the interests of brevity, we cover aspects of traditional Western moral philosophy from the late seventeenth century onwards.

Philosophical writing can be difficult to understand for the beginner but accessible introductions do exist. One such accessible set of texts is the Stanford Encyclopedia of Philosophy, available online at `plato.stanford.edu`.

Rationalism

Rationality, as opposed to its opposite, irrationality, requires that all actions be thought through and their driving forces and possible consequences considered. Critiques of rationalism abound, some based upon the impossibility of knowing everything and therefore of ever making a truly moral decision, others based on the psychological fact that we are emotional creatures whose thought processes are shaded by chemical variations of chaotic subtlety and still others on the basis that many decisions are time-critical and that the time to adequately consider issues is often not available. Each of these has some merit, but it is still believed by many that rationalism is a solid basis on which to consider morality. As we shall see, the rational and emotional schools of moral philosophy have been in dialogue for millennia and particularly in the Enlightenment (www.philosophypages.com/dy/e5.htm#enl).

Locke vs Hobbes

One of the most politically influential philosophers of the Enlightenment, the English philosopher John Locke (plato.stanford.edu/entries/locke-political) was one of the main inspirations for the framers of the US constitution. His conceptions of 'natural law' and 'natural rights' (which existed before him, but of which he is a powerful proponent – see below for a discussion of natural law versus positive law) still retains significant influence on legislators and judges in the Western democracies. Locke's philosophy lies significantly in opposition to that of Thomas Hobbes (plato.stanford.edu/entries/hobbes-moral) who regarded the chaos of the English Civil War as the inevitable consequence of anything other than absolute obedience to the government and the rule of law.

Locke might be regarded as an optimist in his view of humanity as capable of rising above the 'might makes right' and oppression of the feudal systems of Europe and aspiring to the equality and respect for life (as he saw it) of groups such as some of the Native American tribes. Hobbes, on the other hand, saw the state of nature as a state of war and pessimistically regarded humanity's savagery as only capable of devolving into 'war of all against all'. Hobbes remains a significant influence and the claims of a 'clash of civilizations' between the West and Islam echo and derive from his viewpoint.

Locke's philosophy of 'self-evident truths' of natural rights, as the framers of the US constitution put it, also remains a strong influence on modern philosophical and legal thought. In the book's chapters, we have quoted from the UN's Universal

Declaration of Human Rights, the US constitution and the Charter of Fundamental Rights of the European Union. These documents draw heavily on the work of Locke and his ideological peers and successors.

Hume and Human Passion

Similarly to Hobbes, though perhaps not as pessimistic in outlook, is the work of Scottish philosopher David Hume (plato.stanford.edu/entries/hume-moral/). His position is that reason is 'a slave to the passions' and that virtue and vice are the result of emotional influences. As a reasoning being, humans are capable of considering the future consequences of their actions, based on their personal memory of previous consequences to prior actions. Whether we choose to act virtuously or not, according to Hume, depends on the emotional benefits we gain from the praise or censure of our peers as well as the direct benefits of the actions themselves. As such, Hume is another principle proponent of the positive law tradition. Modern philosophical writings such as those of Foucault (plato.stanford.edu/entries/foucault) draw heavily on the line of philosophers including Hume, John Stuart Mill and Jeremy Bentham.

Kant and the Categorical Imperative

Any discussion of Western moral philosophy almost certainly includes mention of Immanuel Kant (plato.stanford.edu/entries/kant-moral/). Probably the most significant contribution of Kant to the debate about the source of moral behaviour was the concept of the 'categorical imperative'. Kant, like many others before and since, regarded moral behaviour as the ultimate expression of rationality, the ideal goal of thinking beings. 'Categorical' means that the principle is to be applied unconditionally, without consideration of specific conditions or short-term goals. 'Imperative' simply means that this is a command rather than simply advice or guidance. The moral duty of the categorical imperative is distinguished from hypothetical imperatives which are dependent upon circumstances and goals. But what is this categorical imperative which, according to Kant, provides the sole basis for moral actions?

The categorical imperative states that maxims (general rules) should be derived which express themselves in duties toward oneself and others. These duties must be based upon rational and complete expressions of the reasons for such actions, be consistent with natural laws (for instance the laws of physics) and be subscribable to by all rational entities following the categorical imperative. Finally, you must be capable of following their dictates. Failure of the will to act (e.g. in failing to keep to a diet to improve your fitness) robs the maxim of dieting of its categorical imperative. The universal applicability of the categorical imperative to all rational actors introduces the reciprocity necessary in a social setting. This universality and reciprocity is present in most of the rationalist approaches to morality, including such concepts as the 'veil of ignorance' put forth by Rawls (plato.stanford.edu/entries/impartiality).

Although Kant's writings are deep and subtle and include significant considerations of the implications of ideas such as the categorical imperative, the world is a different place from the one which Kant was writing about and thus it seems sensible to move on to other ideas and conceptions of correct action.

Legality and Morality

What is the difference between a group of people living in a geographical area and a society or nation? Various commentators have attempted to define such distinctions and it remains a significant question today, in particular in light of substantial migrations of people, such as those experienced by the United Kingdom in the twentieth and early twenty-first centuries (of West Indians, Indians and Pakistanis and Eastern Europeans to name but a few). When some action is regarded by all as immoral then it is inconceivable that any but the mentally unstable will commit that action. Committing the action is in itself regarded as proof of mental instability (and the actor treated or punished accordingly). Where some in society have no such sense of moral obligation, or where different moralities clash, the Western democratic society reverts to the rule of law. Building upon the moral certainties of Kant's categorical imperative, legal systems impose duties upon those within their purview (plato.stanford.edu/entries/legal-obligation/).

The two main schools of legal philosophy are those of natural law and positive law. Natural law is based upon the position that there are universal rules of action and behaviour (based perhaps upon Kant's categorical imperative or upon other sources such as holy scripture or constitutional documents) and that actions must be judged in light of these natural laws. Judgement of criminality of action (and consequent punitive, restitutive or rehabilitative recourse by the community) and of resolution of disputes between citizens is done by experts or ordinary citizens with respect to the principles of natural law. Positive law is based upon the concept of clearly laid-down regulations in which judgement is restricted first to the facts of a case, which may be disputed and then to which section of the law is applicable. Once the facts and relevant elements of law have been established, the result is 'simply' a matter of formulaic application of the regulations.

Both philosophies require an acceptance by the governed, and those who are involved in their application, of the legitimacy of the laws. The limits of the obligations imposed by law are a matter for debate. One such debate is current in the United Kingdom at the time of writing. A law preventing discrimination against individuals on the basis of their sexuality was passed a number of years ago. More detailed regulations deriving from this law are under debate at the time of writing. One of the debates is taking place between the Christian church (particularly the catholic church though backed up by the Church of England) and the government. The government is claiming that the church must comply with the regulations in its 'public activities' such as providing adoption placement services. The church claims that this contravenes doctrine and that it will be forced to stop providing such services (generally acknowledged as a public benefit) unless there is a way it can be partially exempt from the regulations. The church claims that since other agencies exist which may place the same children, that there is no detriment to the children or the potential homosexual adoptive parents in allowing catholic agencies to only act as intermediaries for heterosexual couples. The government claims that it has sovereign power and that church doctrine cannot be allowed to form an exemption to non-discrimination regulations in any but the church's own internal affairs (news.bbc.co.uk/1/hi/uk_politics/6289301.stm).

The concept of legal obligations is not limited solely to laws emanating from nation states. In the realm of professional ethics, the regulations of a professional body such as the BCS (British Computer Society) or the ACM (Association of Computing Machinery), not currently backed by the state in the same way as the professional obligations of medical personnel, may be thought of as imposing similar duties.

MODERN ETHICAL THEORY

Just as moral philosophy did not begin with the Enlightenment, it did not stop developing at the end of the eighteenth century. Some of the same debates continue today as were started (or continued) then. Some issues appear to have been mostly resolved, whereas others have arisen, or gained greater prominence, because of social and technological developments.

Utilitarian Ethics

Much modern ethics in practice appears to be based on a highly utilitarian approach. Outcomes are the measure of morality and the pleasure principle rules much of this strand of thought. However, the understanding of positive useful values has been expanded beyond the directly pleasurable and concepts of quality of life have been introduced to improve computations of the moral course for individuals as well as societies. In previous centuries, the sanctity of life and the ultimate moral good deriving from its continuance, have been at least somewhat displaced by considerations of circumstances where life may be intolerable. The practical debates these considerations generate range from euthanasia or assisted suicide of the terminally ill or permanently vegetative, to the morality of late-term abortions for foetuses with significant 'abnormalities'. Each of these debates includes many 'hard cases' and 'slippery slope' arguments.

> Hard case: a legal aphorism is that hard cases make bad law. A hard case is one which raises many complex interacting issues and on which judgement is difficult. General principles should not be based on hard cases, but on the clear-cut cases, with shaded boundaries allowing hard cases to be decided on consideration of the competing clear but opposing principles
>
> Slippery slope: the argument that allowing a single (often hard case) exception to a rule will lead to the general rule being overturned

Although attractive to many people, utilitarian approaches to moral (and legal) judgements are frequently criticized because of their dependence on a required set of values. Western philosophers are often accused of assuming the superiority or universality of their value set (based on individualistic concepts embodied in declarations such as the US constitution) over others which produce equally stable societies. As modern technology 'shrinks' the world in both physical and informational terms, these culture clashes become more and more difficult to reconcile within a purely utilitarian approach.

Relativistic vs Universal Utiliarianism

Universal utilitarianism is the claim that there is a single set of moral rules for everyone in all situations. The opposition pole to this is that of relativistic utilitarianism, which represents the view that everything is situational (in the most extreme case even in which rules to apply let alone how they are to be applied). Most moral philosophers do not lie at one end or the other of the universal-relative line, but include some elements of both. However, most will lie more toward one pole or the other. Relativism comes in many forms. The non-judgemental relativism of the standard modern anthropology approach, which seeks to understand cultures on their own terms and (knowing this is largely impossible) to prevent value judgements from one's own culture from creeping into evaluation of the studied culture, can, if carried over into moral philosophy, quickly lead to apologism for practices few would regard as justifiable (female genital mutilation is still practised in some areas, for instance).

At its best, relativism takes into account the possibility of many approaches to achieve a 'good' outcome and allows for honest disagreement on the rules to be applied and how to measure the utility of outcome.

New Utilitarianism: Singer

An example of an extreme (including extreme universalist) approach to utilitarianism is taken by Singer (1996). Singer's approach (`www.utilitarian.net/singer`) is characterized by some as a talented exploration of the consequences of utilitarianist moral philosophy, but by others as the reductio ad absurdam. One's viewpoint may well depend on how one views his conclusions as much as by analysis of his methods. Singer claims that the pleasure principle should rule all moral decisions. This leads him, among other conclusions, to the idea that parents should have the right to decide if their offspring should live up to 28 days after birth, because of the lack of self-awareness shown by newborn infants and the allowance of induced abortion in many western democracies. Philip K. Dick wrote a science-fiction short story in 1974 The Pre-Persons in which 'post-partum abortion' could take place at up to seven years of age, that being the age of ensoulment. Dick's story was a reductio ad absurdam attack on the famous Roe vs Wade US Supreme Court decision upholding the right to an abortion.

COMPUTER ETHICS

Although he did not coin the term, Norbert Wiener is usually credited with inventing the field of computer ethics (`plato.stanford.edu/entries/ethics-computer`). Computer ethics comprises a narrower approach than the general field and a narrower subject of study than is in this book as a whole. Computer ethics is one of the central components of computer professionalism that requires the professional to act as a privileged member of society, just as doctors and lawyers do. IT professionals' knowledge of one of the basic building blocks of modern society, the computer and communication network, require them to have a practical ethical framework in which to set their work.

Computer and communication technologies re-frame old ethical dilemmas and create new ones. Attempts have been made to provide computing students and professionals with familiar analytical methods to apply to ethical issues, similar to the approaches used in requirements engineering, project management and program design, all core technical topics within a computing degree. The analytic method of Liffick (2004) uses the familiar top-down planning approach combined with scenario refinement to identify the pertinent elements of the ethical problem and plan not just an initial response, but a branching, hypothetical map to guide decision-making. Besides the familiarity of such approaches to computer students and professionals, the decision-making process contains appropriate break points where decisions can be re-evaluated in the light of failed attempts at resolution or changing circumstances. One of the significant differences between computer ethics and general moral philosophy is that computer ethics takes change for granted and expects circumstances to move swiftly. Many, though not all, schools of moral philosophy are predicated upon unchanging or slow-moving social circumstances allowing discussion and forethought to be brought to bear on problems. The ever-increasing pace of computer technology development requires a more flexible approach if ethical decisions are not to be overtaken by events.

Researchers and lecturers are still strongly debating what computer ethics is and in some cases even if it is a separate field at all, or if it should be regarded as consumed by (or even, in one framework, consuming) general ethics. Is it something that can be taught in the same way that one teaches programming? Is it something that can be practised only at work or does professionalism require a virtuous life in general? Can it be faked or is the result the only measure ('by their fruit shall ye know them')?

At one of the recent regular international conferences for lecturers and researchers in computer ethics (Ethicomp 2007, held in Tokyo) there were a number of papers regarding the place of computer ethics in the curriculum and the profession.

Metaphysical Foundations for Computer Ethics

Bynum (2007) bases his approach on Wiener's conceptions, but includes recent physics and cosmology results and an alternative foundation by Floridi of Oxford University which he claims also supports his conclusion. Wiener's approach was based on the idea that the universe had two elements: matter or energy (which Einsteinian physics had shown as interchangeable) and 'Shannon information'. Shannon information is the physical embodiment of information, not the higher level abstract concept that computer scientists usually refer to. Shannon information is involved in the structure and change of structure in matter or energy. Hofstadter (1999) makes a similar distinction between layers of structure and information. In justifying computer ethics as a separate field, as first defined by Wiener but continuing to the present, Bynum refers to the concepts of the industrial revolution (leading to the industrial age) and the information revolution (leading to the information age). The industrial revolution was the product of a step change in mankind's ability to control matter or energy by use of the 'heat engines' (typified by steam engines initially, but leading in an unbroken line to nuclear power stations and photo-voltaic (solar power) energy cells).

The development of programmable computers in the mid twentieth century, according to Wiener and Bynum, gave mankind the same step change in its ability to control shannon information. As control over shannon information is a significant step change, it leads to a 'policy vacuum' and requires a new approach to answering the questions it raises: information ethics. Taking Wiener's argument forward, in a manner reminiscent of some of the trans-humanist thinkers, Bynum proposes that information ethics, of which computer ethics is merely a subset, will become the dominant theme in human ethical considerations.

The broad sweep of this book, including considerations of war, health, entertainment and others, can be seen as evidence of movement in that direction.

Informed Consent Theory in Information Technology

Flick (2007) describes how a concept well-understood and applied in medical and legal ethics (informed consent) can be applied to issues in IT. This concept, grounded in ideas of moral philosophy, brings together conceptions of voluntariness, comprehension of agreement, disclosure and competence. Widespread human rights abuses have not been apparent so far because of ICT, but the idea of informed consent to prevent such issues is being raised in specific studies, such as those on privacy agreements online, click-wrap and shrink-wrap software licensing agreements and so on. Structural aspects of informed consent such as contractual expression languages and personal settings, are being suggested as methods of avoiding substantial overhead in obtaining agreement in common online transactions. Just as in medical and legal settings, where the abstruse nature of the situation requires a significant level of both intelligence and education to truly comprehend, the lack of knowledge of computer operation and information theory, presents significant difficulties in judging comprehension by the user to what is proposed. Long and poorly presented agreements produce user fatigue in reading agreements and legal conceptions of true contract negotiation are undermined by take-it-or-leave-it and obfuscatory 'small print' approaches by corporations. Flick concludes that further research on informed consent is required in the information age.

Ethical Decisions: Using the Back of the Envelope

Gotterbarn (2007) presents an overview of formal ethical approaches including:

- The 'heuristic method' of Bynum, which considers the whole situation and uses consideration by analogy to find suitable responses based on previous human responses to ethical problems;
- The 'paramedic approach' of Collins and Miller (1992), an algorithmic approach to making ethical decisions, involving gathering data, identifying obligations, considering consequences and applying utilitarian judgements to potential outcomes.

Gotterbarn then presents the concept of the 'line drawing' method, which involves placing identified responses to elements of an ethical decision in opposition to each other, for example, 'obtaining consent to an invasion of privacy' versus 'not obtaining consent'. These line drawings (which of course need not actually be on the back of an envelope) are merely an aid to understanding the situation and not a full method of answering the questions. However, such rough guides clearly have their place in aiding understanding of any complex situation and removing irrelevant notions from the consideration.

Information Ethics: ICT Professional Responsibility in the Information Environment

Mather (2007) draws parallels between the environmental ethics debate and the information ethics debate. Working within the Floridian concept, which defines the infosphere as the information environment, Mather draws conclusions that environmental ethics, where the human being no longer has a clear division between themselves and the world but a sphere of influence which disperses according to mathematical decay functions away from the central being, is highly applicable to information ethics. These concepts clearly point the way to considerations of possible sentient information beings other than humans (either technologically enhanced animals, or emergent or symbolical artificial intelligences, with or without physical form).

The broad range of ecology and environment ethics (from anthropocentric notions to Lovelock's Gaia hypothesis) taking in disaster avoidance and utilitarian notions (avoid pollution now to avoid potential disaster later) as well as intrinsic benefit notions (biodiversity is a good in itself) lends itself well to the complex range of issues raised in the information age and potentially provides a significant source of analogous argument in defining ethical and professional actions. Already biological concepts such as infection have been used to describe the action of certain types of information (viruses). The idea of spam as pollution of the infosphere is equally compelling.

The Good Computer Professional Does not Cheat at Cards

Volkman (2007) argues traditionally that ethical behaviour derives from an inner desire to lead a virtuous life. In doing so, he claims, the attitudes and actions of the professional at work are indistinguishable from the attitudes and actions of the professional in other spheres. It is generally accepted that avoiding all harm is impossible when developing ICT systems. A combination of unintended consequences of complex systems and the negative costs of almost any change (hopefully outweighed by the positive benefits) mean that judging professional behaviour purely on outcomes is difficult. In teaching ethical behaviour, therefore, argues Volkman, one must start from the person and work out to the activity, rather than starting with the activity and either ignoring the person or expecting a reflection of action in thought. The basic nature of ICT, the 'logical malleability' of Moor (1985), contributes an important element to Volkman's argument. The unconstrained nature of the potential of ICT requires a virtuous approach to its application, rather than simply a method of 'acting ethically'.

Following on from this abstract conception, a practical approach to teaching computer ethics is offered. Appealing to the geek culture in which many computing students are embedded and presenting ethical conundrums as complex questions requiring imaginative and complex solutions provides a useful method of motivation in class. Contrasting the value of a virtuous life with the mediocrity of rule-following or the evil of bureaucratic indulgences provides a spur to dealing with the computer professional as a whole person and the impact of ICT as a global concern.

CONCLUSION

This appendix merely scratches the surface of relevant ethical thought and theories. As mentioned in the introduction, this book seeks to form a starting point for students and professionals to consider the potential impact of the choices they make and to engage them in thinking about the personal and public consequences of their actions. This book does not seek to provide answers to questions. It provides relevant background information about where computers have a decisively different impact on society and where they are simply the latest in a long (centuries, sometimes millennia, long) sequence of disruptions to life as an older generation knew it.

There is no single agreed approach to teaching students how to react to the issues presented in these pages. This appendix itself is simply a starting point to many ways of approaching it. Although the authors have their own opinions and practices, the intent in writing this book has been to provide a useful resource for everyone teaching the subject, learning about it or working within it.

DISCUSSION TOPICS

These discussion topics consider general ethical issues as well as IT-related questions. Below are ten topics, in linked pairs. Each pair contains first a general ethical dilemma, then a related ethical dilemma where IT raises an interesting new twist or adds complexity to the question. The IT-related topics include pointers to the chapters which present deeper considerations of the questions raised.

General: The Death Penalty

Kant called the death penalty a categorical imperative. Bentham claimed that utilitarian calculations led inescapably away from it. One of the foremost rights enshrined in most declarations is the right to life (or, as the US Declaration of Independence puts it, 'life, liberty and the pursuit of happiness'). Yet, the United States still has a federal death penalty and although some states have repealed it or declared an aptly named 'moratorium' on execution, others practise it routinely. George W. Bush was elected to the US presidency in 2000 having presided over 152 executions as governor of Texas (www.nybooks.com/articles/17670). The

European Union requires countries which are candidates for membership to abolish capital punishment (ec.europa.eu/comm/external_relations/human_rights/adp) and lobbies around the world for its abolition.

Can the taking of a human life be justified? Those who argue for the death penalty claim that it is a just punishment for certain crimes, that it acts as a deterrent against the commission of those crimes (and without its application there is no deterrent) and that it is more merciful than imprisonment without hope of parole. Those who argue against the death penalty point out that the criminal justice system in all countries is flawed and that the potential for execution of an innocent person (an act impossible to recover from, unlike freeing a wrongly imprisoned person) is far too high. They also claim that other flaws in criminal justice systems make death penalties inherently or institutionally racist and that there is no evidence of a deterrent effect. It is even argued that ten or more years on 'death row' although appeal after appeal is heard and although execution is sometimes 'stayed' at short notice, is itself 'cruel and unusual punishment'.

ICT: Artificial Sentience Rights and Wrongs

Can a computer or a robot commit a 'crime'? At what point (if ever) would a computer program be sufficiently intelligent to qualify for human rights? Computer ethicists have been considering such questions almost since the birth of the field. Although few would claim that artificial sentience has yet been created, such questions are beginning to concern lawyers and philosophers generally as well as computer ethics researchers. When a program intended to be benign inadvertently causes significant damage, is the program at fault, or the author, or the person who ran the program, or those who programmed the environment making it liable to be damaged?

Industrial robots have injured, maimed and killed for decades, just as industrial machinery has done for centuries. Now, responsibility for such 'industrial accidents' rests with the programmers, safety coordinators of the plants and safety inspectors of the government. Sometimes a machine with a hardware or software fault will be dismantled, its logical parts patched, its physical parts changed, or even the entire line discontinued. This is done with no conception of a 'right to exist' for the machine, nor a right to liberty for the redundant machine.

(See Chapter 8 for autonomous killing machines; Chapter 12 for more information on liability for programmers; and Chapter 11 on self-replicating programs.)

General: Is Religion an Excuse for Discrimination?

Judaism, Christianity and Islam all contain significant schools of thought in which homosexuality is regarded as a serious sin, although there also exist schools of thought within each religion with different views. Where should the line be drawn between 'freedom of conscience and religion' and 'freedom from discrimination'. If a religion claimed that only one race was truly human and that all others should be regarded as less than human (e.g. not having 'souls'), would their discrimination be allowed?

A strong debate on the limits of religious conscience in the United Kingdom (`news.bbc.co.uk/1/hi/uk_politics/6478191.stm`) was sparked by anti-discrimination legislation which outlawed discrimination on the basis of sexuality in 'the provision of goods and services'. The most controversial aspects of this included requiring Christian hoteliers to provide all couples equally with access to shared bed accommodation and the requirement (delayed but to come into force after time for negotiation or alternative arrangements) that Catholic adoption agencies accept applications from gay and lesbian couples. Part of this discussion centres on the question of whether homosexuality is innate or developed (discrimination on the grounds of someone's life choices is usually regarded as more acceptable than discrimination on the grounds of how they were born or other circumstances beyond their control).

In an interesting flipside to this coin, many religious leaders have been lobbying hard for protection from discrimination on the grounds of religion in the United Kingdom (`news.bbc.co.uk/1/hi/programmes/law_in_action/4319663.stm`). Some claim that discrimination on the grounds of religion is often used as a cover for discrimination on the grounds of race, others that the race discrimination protection accorded to Jews blurs the line and that equity demands that Muslims, Christians, Sikhs and so on, should be given the same protection.

Is religion truly a choice or partly or wholly dependent on uncontrollable circumstances? Is sexuality a choice or an innate element of our make-up? Should it matter? Are exemptions from discrimination laws ever possible? If not, should discrimination against entry to religious premises and inclusion in religious rites be allowed any more than discrimination in adoption processes, educational provision or other service provision. If other agencies offer 'separate but equal' (`americanhistory.si.edu/brown/history/1-segregated/separate-but-equal.html`) access to services is that sufficient?

ICT: Search Ethics

When creating the domain name system (DNS), Postel said that the DNS was a technical naming system, not a directory service. Despite all the fuss over domain names containing trade marks and other well-known names, most information location is now done by way of search engines. This obviously gives search engines potentially a great deal of power. When search companies began taking payment not for obviously separate advertisements but for apparently 'standard' search results, this became obvious to all. Interference by search companies, whose algorithms are often closely guarded trade secrets, in the results of searching can be hard to spot. Consider a search for 'Coke' on Google. Besides the standard hits, Google suggests 'related searches' which include 'Pepsi', Coca-cola's arch rival in the drinks world. In some countries the trade name Coke has become 'commoditized' such that all colas are referred to as 'Coke'. Should a search for Coke on Google's Portuguese site therefore access a 'synonym database' and do a search for cola or not?

As with many areas where a dominant or monopoly position exists, there are calls for public regulation and openness of process. Of course, although Google is the dominant English language search engine, this is not the case for all languages and countries. Despite an agreement with the Chinese government which allows `google.cn` to operate, it remains a lesser player in the Chinese search market, with a home-grown engine remaining the most popular.

(See Chapter 4 for details of Google China; Chapter 6 for details of DNS restrictions; and Chapter 7 for the interest of law-enforcement agencies in people's search logs.)

General: Lying to Tell the Truth?

Everyone 'filters' their perceptions. At the low level, neuro-scientists tell us, we are not aware that we are doing it. Even apparently higher-level awareness is dependent on multiple low-level filters operating properly. Filtering occurs both consciously and sub-consciously. Two different people can come out of a political speech with diametrically opposed views of what the speaker actually said. When information is relayed by a third party, a journalist for example, yet another set of filters come into play, both deliberate attempts to 'clarify' and 'distort' and their subconscious filters.

Since we know other people filter what we tell them and if we think we know what their filters are, is it lying to say something other than 'the truth, the whole truth and nothing but the truth' as we understand it, to try to impart true information past a distorting filter?

We all do this to some extent. If the intent and outcome is benign, they are generally called 'white lies', which category also includes being economical with the truth or even outright lying, where telling the unvarnished truth would do significant harm.

'Spin doctors', media consultants used by politicians to avoid their message being misrepresented (deliberately or through mistaken filters) by journalists, claim that this is their job. Of course journalists and many members of the public, disagree and regard them as some of the most untrustworthy of political players.

ICT: Gender Presentation Online

It is common for people to present themselves online as a different gender to their physical status. Asai (2007) reported on the prevalence of gender mis-representation in online games in Japan. In one example, although the gender of 91% of registered players was male, the presented gender of characters was close to an even split.

Simple mathematical analysis reveals that between 45% and 55% of males on this system are misrepresenting themselves as female. There are a wide range of reasons people report when asked why they misrepresent their gender online. It should be noted that such self-reporting is not always accurate or honest (inaccurate in that people do not always realize why they do things; dishonest in that they may lie about their known reasons). These include:

- allowing their masculine or feminine personality traits to be expressed, whereas in everyday offline activity they must be suppressed;
- access to a solely or principally single-gender online group;
- avoidance of sexual harassment (usually by males aimed at those appearing female online);
- to trick others into making revelations or advances then embarrassing them;
- to explore the reactions of others (positive and negative) to the other gender.

Is misrepresentation of gender a special case or just part of the general freedoms online? Is the only unethical behaviour deliberately doing harm to others or is any element of lying unethical?

(See Chapter 3 for details of online role-playing games; Chapter 4 regarding the illusion of anonymity online; and Chapter 5 for more details of sexual activity online.)

General: Fair Fines

Punishment for crimes committed vary a great deal between societies. Fines, 'community service', imprisonment, corporal punishment (infliction of pain and discomfort) and capital punishment (termination of the offender's life) are among the most common forms. Is it possible to set monetary fines which are fair?

Even two people with identical incomes may have significantly different commitments to pay – previous debts, children or other dependents to support, and so on. In addition, people with high incomes or substantial assets (usually, though not always, sustained high income leads to accumulation of substantial assets) may live 'beyond money' in that at no point can lack of monetary assets be considered a serious inconvenience. For those at the other end of the wealth spectrum, even a small fine might cause substantial hardship or even tip them over the edge into a debt spiral. Given such disparity of effect, can fines be regarded as a suitable element of a valid justice system?

How do such ideals transfer to the other forms of punishment listed above? Is it even necessary to attempt to pursue parity of punishment between two offenders who commit similar crimes (or even collude in the same crime) from radically different circumstances? Does regarding judicial sentencing as containing different balances of punishment, deterrent, compensation and restoration change the outcome of your deliberations?

ICT: Should Internet Access be a Human Right?

The UN's declaration of universal human rights includes the right to an education. Of course this right is heavily constrained by economics. It is also undefined to what level this applies. Even where free primary and secondary education is available, tertiary education is often subject to significant monetary cost. Given the educational benefits, as well as freedom of speech (and its concomitant right to freedom of access to information), of access to the Internet, should Internet access be regarded as a derivative human right?

Even if this was recognized, would it have any impact? There are two possible impacts that it could have. First, in those countries where Internet access is highly restricted, it would provide an extra, though probably small, lever promoting freedom of speech. It might have more impact in countries with generally good human rights records, in borderline cases. Internet access is one of those things denied to those serving custodial sentences in prison. An acknowledgment of a right to access the Internet could change this situation. Though under supervision and surveillance, prisoners might gain the right to access the Internet. In the United States, arguments in court about free public municipal WiFi might be swayed by referring to a right of access.

(See Chapter 4 for discussion of freedom of access to information under freedom of speech; and Chapter 14 on the digital divide in education resources.)

General: Prediction of Harm

'Innocent until proven guilty' is claimed as one of the cornerstones of modern justice. Two distinct types of case are challenging this principle in the modern world: 'personality disorders' and terrorism.

In many jurisdictions, it is considered unreasonable to hold to account for actions which have been harmful to others individuals suffering from certain mental disorders, including some types of personality disorder. Once such a person has committed a serious assault or murder, they will typically be remanded to a psychiatric institution until they are deemed cured or they die. For some types of personality disorder, for which no current psychological or psychiatric treatments are deemed effective, this represents a life sentence with no possibility of parole, unless treatment advances occur. This is in line with imprisonment without possibility of parole for those deemed 'sane' but too much of a danger to society to ever be considered for release. The difficulty comes, however, when severe personality disorders which are deemed highly likely to lead the sufferer to commit violent acts, but where no such acts have been committed, are diagnosed. The medical evaluation is that the person suffers from a condition and statistics lead society to believe that 85% of such people will commit serious violence against others at some point. If society does not restrict the movements of people with such conditions, many innocent individuals will suffer (because it is impossible to tell which 85% will commit the crimes, although it is possible to be certain that crimes will be committed by some of them). Many medical ethicists believe that incarceration of sufferers from personality disorders in mental institutions is unethical because no treatment can be offered. Imprisonment alongside those who have already committed crimes also appears unreasonable.

A similar dilemma arises when dealing with possible terrorist actions. When the consequences of not acting against those plotting bombings, or the release of poison gas, are likely to involve the deaths of a significant number of innocent people, how can law-enforcement and criminal-justice systems not be right in imprisoning them? On the other hand, it is known that some people become involved with 'radical' groups and depart before committing any harm. So, at what point, and with what level of evidence of intent, is it just to regard someone as a criminal? Must society wait until they have set out on their journey to commit an offence (even at this stage, it has been known for people to be unable to 'pull the trigger'), or created a device, or bought the 'ingredients', or accessed the knowledge necessary to create a device. Besides the possible failure to finalize the act, there are also claims of innocent activity which merely appears to be that of someone plotting to commit an atrocity. When an act is only planned and not committed, there is always the possibility of misinterpretation by society.

Over-zealous interpretation of innocent activity and partial radicalization can lead to social pressures which legitimize the actions of terrorists in the eyes of potential radicals. 'Innocent until proven guilty' can be an inconvenient principle at times, but when it is abandoned for some circumstances, then will it be abandoned for others?

ICT: Programmer Responsibility

Are the programmers of BitTorrent clients guilty of contributing to copyright infringement? What about the programmers of BitTorrent trackers? How about those who specified the BitTorrent protocol? Are mathematicians who create strong encryption protocols and the programmers who implement them in easy-to-use services, guilty of aiding and abetting fraud, terrorism and a whole host of other criminality by providing the means for private communication.

If an automatic drug-infusor machine has a poor user interface, such that patients die because nurses have mis-set the dosage by a factor of ten (either for an overdose or a lack of medication – either can be fatal), is the interface designer at fault? Should the interface programmer be liable?

Strict product liability has long been an established fact in the production of automobiles and the provision of food and drink. What is the difference that sets computer programmers, software designers and testers apart? Should software engineers be held to the same standards as civil engineers, nuclear engineers and aviation engineers? Should software architects be held to the same standards as building architects? If they assume the name, should the profession also assume the risk?

(See Chapter 10 for concepts of due diligence and responsibility; and Chapter 12 for issues of contributory infringement.)

REFERENCES

Bynum, T.W. (2007) "Metaphysical Foundations for Information Ethics", in **T.W. Bynum, S. Rogerson** and **K. Murata** (eds), *Proceedings of Ethicomp 2007*, 81–87, Global eSCM Research Centre of Meiji University, Tokyo. ISBN 4-9903558-0-7 (Vol 1) and 4-9903558-1-4 (Vol 2).

Bynum, T.W. and **Rogerson S.** (2003) *Computer Ethics and Professional Responsibility*, Blackwell, Oxford. ISBN 1-8555-4845-3.

Collins, W.R. and **Miller, K.W.** (1992) Paramedic Ethics for Computer Professionals, in *Journal of Systems and Software*, **17**(1), ACM. ISSN 0164-1212.

Flick, C. (2007) "Informed Consent Theory in Information Technology", in **T.W. Bynum, S. Rogerson** and **K. Murata** (eds), *Proceedings of Ethicomp 2007*, 171–179, Global eSCM Research Centre of Meiji University, Tokyo. ISBN 4-9903558-0-7 (Vol 1) and 4-9903558-1-4 (Vol 2).

Gotterbarn, D. (2007) "Ethical Decisions: Using the back of the envelope", in **T.W. Bynum, S. Rogerson** and **K. Murata** (eds), *Proceedings of Ethicomp 2007*, 226–235, Global eSCM Research Centre of Meiji University, Tokyo. ISBN 4-9903558-0-7 (Vol 1) and 4-9903558-1-4 (Vol 2).

Hofstadter, D.R. (1999) *Godel, Escher, Bach: An Eternal Golden Braid*, Basic Books, New York, NY. ISBN 0-4650-2656-7.

Mather, K. (2007) "Information Ethics: ICT professional responsibility in the information environment", in **T.W. Bynum, S. Rogerson** and **K. Murata** (eds), *Proceedings of Ethicomp 2007*, 356–367, Global eSCM Research Centre of Meiji University, Tokyo. ISBN 4-9903558-0-7 (Vol 1) and 4-9903558-1-4 (Vol 2).

Singer, P. (1996) *Rethinking Life and Death*, St. Martins, New York. ISBN 0-3121-4401-6.

Thompson, M. (2005) *Ethical Theory*, Hodder Murray, London. ISBN 0-3408-83 44-8.

Volkman, R. (2007) "The Good Computer Professional Does not Cheat at Cards", in **T.W. Bynum, S. Rogerson** and **K. Murata** (eds), *Proceedings of Ethicomp 2007*, 608–620, Global eSCM Research Centre of Meiji University, Tokyo. ISBN 4-9903558-0-7 (Vol 1) and 4-9903558-1-4 (Vol 2).

RELATED READING

Asai, R. (2007) "Living with another gender on the Net", in **T.W. Bynum, S. Rogerson** and **K. Murata** (eds), *Proceedings of Ethicomp 2007*, 44–49, Global eSCM Research Centre of Meiji University, Tokyo. ISBN 4-9903558-0-7 (Vol 1) and 4-9903558-1-4 (Vol 2).

Dick, P.K. (1974) The Pre-Persons, in *Fantasy and Science Fiction*, October. ISSN 0024-984X.

Liffick, B.W. (2004) Analyzing Ethical Scenarios, in *The Ethicomp Journal*, **1** (1), www.ccsr.cse.dmu.ac.uk/journal. ISSN 1743-3010.

Moor, J. (1985) What Is Computer Ethics?, *Metaphilosophy*, **16**: 266–275. ISSN 0026-1068/1467-9973.

Wiener, N. (1965) *Cybernetics or control and communication in the animal and the machine*, 2nd Edition, The MIT Press, Cambridge, MA. ISBN 0-2627-3009-X.

Wiener, N. (1954) *The Human Use of Human Beings*, 2nd Edition, Hodder Stoughton, London. ISBN-10: 0-3068-0320-8.

Zalta, E., The Stanford Encyclopedia of Philosophy, plato.stanford.edu (last accessed 25 July 2007).

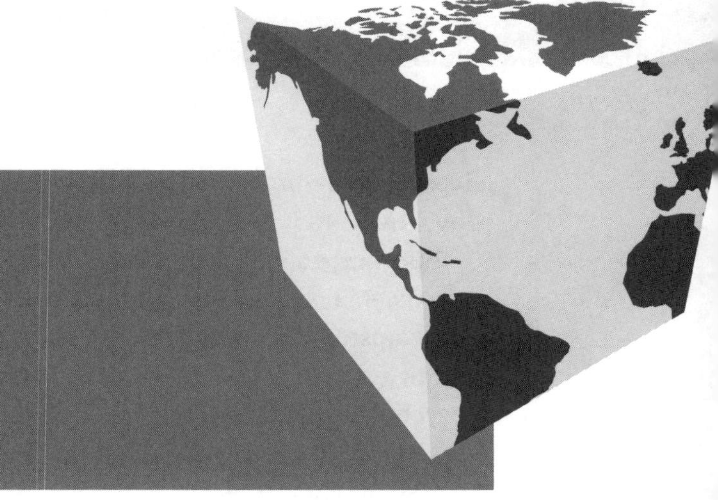

INDEX

$100 laptop scheme 579
2003 Statutory Instrument on Copyright 394
24-hour 28
  banking 560
  news 28
3Com 8
3G 27, 46–7, 51, 136, 552
  sex 137
414 crackers 246
9–11 or 9/11, *see* September 11th Attacks

A

Accenture 304
accessibility 33, 379
  of education 513, 533–4
  of health information 281
  and security 379
ACLU 101, 154, 155, 434
ACM 151, 324–5, 337, 340, 589
  Code of Ethics and Professional Conduct 327–8
  membership 334
Acxiom 252
Adams, Douglas 573
ADD, *see* attention deficit disorder
Adleman, Leonard 361
Adobe 121–2, 425–7
  e-book 415–6, 455
  photoshop 358
Adoption Act 291
Advanced Control Research 313
Advanced Research Projects Agency, *see* ARPA
advertising 36, 46, 457
  and banknote scans 122
  of books 36
  of broadband 124
  cinema 461
  and deep linking 385–6
  e-mail (*see* spam)
  fax 465, 473, 474–5
  flyposting 489–90
  junk mail 471

advertising (*cont.*)
by MMS 465
motion in 460–1
music 451
on Napster 432
nudity 459
psychology 220–1, 459
revenue 30
sex spam 139, 494–5
by telephone 463–4, 472, 473
on television 34, 135, 461
by text message 464, 473
tobacco 459
of unhealthy foods on television 70, 286–7
on usenet 466
of video games 68
in virtual worlds 91
on the Web 460, 469, 490
Afghanistan 234, 258, 261, 264
ahimsa 584
AIDS 18, 273, 274, 292, 414
air rage 553
air traffic control 244, 251–2, 336
airline ticket 32, 36
e-ticket 37, 554
Al-Jazeera 52, 267
Al Qaeda 220
Alexander Technique 564
All Nippon Airways 553
AltaVista 122
alternative root servers 188–9, 205
Alzheimer's disease 289, 303
amateur 323
reporters 250
sex photos 138
Amazon 6, 35, 58, 176, 220, 412, 452, 562
1-click shopping patent 413, 414
American Civil Liberties Union, ***see*** **ACLU**
Amicus 550–1
Amnesty International 101
Anarchist's Cookbook, The 247
Andrews, Chris 414
Annan, Kofi 123
anonymity
anon servers 146–7, 235–6
antisocial behaviour online 481
blog 265
difficulty 237–8
and freedom of speech 114, 123–4, 235–6, 237
FTP 139, 382
and grooming by paedophiles 159
illusion 144–5
and peer-to-peer 435, 451
regarding distribution of child pornography 167
regarding purchase of sexual material 136, 144–7
telephone calls 482
uploading to ftp servers 139
Wikipedia 518
ANPR 232–3, 238
Anti-Ballistic Missile Treaty 255
AOL 193
phishing 349–50

TimeWarner merger 40–41
Apache (web server) 365, 377
API 376
Apple Corp. 190, 200, 403, 438
Apple II computer 437
Apple Inc. 190, 200, 403. *See also* iTunes, iPod
architecture
code as 6–7, 110, 116–7, 147, 149–50, 153, 449
peer-to-peer 124, 143
of the Web 449, 477
Ardman, Stan D. 296
ARPA 178, 182, 246
ARPANET 178, 246
art
and child pornography 163–4
nudity in 132 (*see also* Sex-Sexual Material, Definition of)
artificial eyes 312
artificial intelligence 17, 256, 258, 259, 261
Asai, Ryoko 601–2
ASCII-porn 138
ASDIC 260
Asimov, Isaac 570
AT&T 408, 437
attention deficit disorder 84–5
audio cassette 8, 54, 453, 511
Australia 58, 137, 144, 163, 166, 262, 365, 491, 533
authorisation to access system 382
automated decision making 15–16, 225
automatic number plate recognition 232–3, 238
avionics 553–4

B

B2B 546
B2C 546
Babbage, Charles 245, 246
Baker, Jake 498–9
Bank of England 121–2
Bank of Ireland 117, 146
Barlow, Jon Perry 436, 451
Barnes and Noble 413
Bayros virus creation kit 360–1
BBC 9, 28, 29–30, 52, 75, 164, 511, 532
BBS 347
distributing sexual material 133, 137–8
BCS 151, 324–5, 337, 340, 589
Code of Conduct 327–8
Code of Practice 333–4
membership 334
beer 325, 459
Ben Hur copyright case 429
Bentham, Jeremy 586, 597
Berkeley Software Development license 438, 442–3
Berkeley, University of California at 442
Berne convention 421–2
Berners-Lee, Tim 186
Bertlesmann 433

Betamax 430, 431, 432
Bhopal 328
Bible, The 540
Bichard Inquiry 221–2
Big Brother (1984) 231
Big Brother (TV show) 76
bioMEMS 310
biometrics 562
BitTorrent 605
blue movies 141–2
Boeing 553
BOFH 328–32
Bono, Sonny 406
Borland 530
  Academic License 530
  Delphi 530
Bosnia 268
Boyer, Amy 502–3
BPI 434, 435
brain
  death 320
  implant 275, 310, 313, 314–5, 316–7
  scan 85, 282
BrainGate Neural Interface 316–7
Branson, Richard 46
Bricklin, Dan 409
Bristol, University of 282
British Board of Film Censors 99. *See also* British Board of Film Classification
British Board of Film Classification 99. *See also* British Board of Film Censors
British Transport Police 568
British Sky Broadcasting 46, 48, 52. *See also* News Corporation
Brown University 317
BSD 438, 442–3
BT 47, 112–3, 129–30, 206, 549, 562
bulletin board system, ***see*** **BBS**
Burma (aka Myanmar) 103
Bush, George W. (US President) 265, 266, 370, 486, 561, 597
Bush, Lauren 370
business to business 546
business to customer 546
Bynum, Terry 593

C

California at Berkeley, University of 442
Cambodia 292
Cambridge, University of 310
Camp Delta 395
CAN-SPAM Act 489, 491
Canada 4, 47, 58, 144, 166, 262, 293, 388, 421, 533
cannibal 572–3
Canter, Laurence 466
Capone, Al 349
Carnegie Mellon University 134
Carr, Paul 118–21
Categorical Imperative 586–7, 588, 597
Catholic Church 24, 102, 565, 599

ccTLD, ***see*** TLD, ccTLD
CCTV 231–3, 238, 266–7, 556
CD 8, 41, 53–4, 61, 63, 431, 451, 452, 568
  in car 552
  Health Information 286
  writable 453
CDA, ***see*** **Communications Decency Act**
CDC, ***see*** **Center for Disease Control**
cell phone, ***see*** **Mobile Phone**
censorship 9, 97
  by employers 112
  of listeners by 'private actors' 113
  of listeners by states 109
  physical 99
  of speakers by 'private actors' 111
  of speakers by states 107
  reasons for 100–1
  self-censorship 99, 112
  of sexual material online 150
  the Great Firewall of China 104–6, 150
  V-Chip 154
Center for Disease Control 305, 307
Cerf, Vint 178, 182
CERT, ***see*** **US-CERT**
Champagne, Antoine 12
CEOP, ***see*** **Child Exploitation and Online Protection centre**
chalkboard 508
Chartered Engineer 334
Chernobyl 328
  virus 358
Chicago, University of 296
child abuse 118–19
  images–*see* Child Pornography
Child Exploitation and Online Protection centre 160
Child Online Protection Act 155, 156
child pornography 129, 160, 161
  altered images 163
  age of consent 161–2
  art 164
  created images 163
  Japan 161–2
  naturism 164
  non-sexual images 163–4
  Operation Ore 165–6
  prohibition economy 166–8
  sexual images 165
  textual depictions 162
  trojan defence against possession charges 169
Children's Internet Protection Act 155
chilling effect 105, 112, 435
China, ***see*** **People's Republic of China**
CHIPA, ***see*** **Children's Internet Protection Act**
chocolate 286, 372
Christianity 599
CIA 234
CIH virus 358
CIPA, ***see*** **Children's Internet Protection Act**
Clemens, Samuel 421
CLI, ***see*** **telephone, caller line ID**
clickwrap software license 446, 594

client-server 124, 500
closed source software
security of 374
CMA, *see* Computer Misuse Act
CNN 52, 122
CNNIC 180–1
cochlear implant 311
Cohen, Fred 361
Coke 600
Collins, W Robert 594
Columbia 292
Communications Decency Act 154–5
Compact Disc, *see* CD
computer dating 571
computer emergency response team, *see* US-CERT
computer literacy 18, 32. *See also* media literacy
computer misuse
Act 388–91, 396
Act, scope of 390
definition of 345–6
extradition regarding 394–5
fraud 348
by insiders 348, 366–7
legislation 366, 374, 387
by outsiders 367–8
phone phreaking 347
trojan (*see* Trojan)
virus (see virus)
worm (see worm)
zombie (see zombie)
see also Omnibus Crime Control and Safe Streets Act
Conan Doyle, Arthur 421
conduct 327
confidentiality 281, 333, 339, 341, 393
convention on cybercrime 388, 391, 393
convergence 39
COPA, *see* Child Online Protection Act
Coppola, Francis Ford 34
copyright 449
and advertising 462
Ben Hur case 429–30
Betamax 430, 432
on books 419
BPI 434, 435
on computer code 419
Creative Commons 449–50
definition of 404
Diamond MP3 player 431
Digital MIllennium Copyright Act 42, 394, 422, 425, 431–2
digital rights management 425, 434, 447–8
EFF 434
European Union Copyright Directive 422, 425
on films 419
IFPI 434, 435
main provisions 424–5
moral rights 423
and MP3 430
MP3.com 431, 451
MPAA 433–4, 436
on music 419

Napster 432–3, 436
Open Rights Group 434
parody 428
peer-to-peer 432, 451
player piano case 429, 432
quoting 428
RIAA 431, 433, 434, 435, 436, 451
technological protection measures 42, 425
Term Extension Act 406
Universal (and Disney) v Sony copyright case 430, 432
user rights 428
WIPO Copyright Treaty 424
CORE 186
Council of Europe 388, 391, 393
Council of Registrars, *see* **CORE**
country code Top Level Domain, *see* **TLD, ccTLD**
cracker
employed as security expert 386
cracking 246, 347, 359, 382
black hat 367–9, 374, 387, 397
brute force 380
grey hat 367–8, 387, 396–7
identity of perpetrators 366–7
motivation for 363–364
historical roots of 364
white hat 367–8
see also hacking
Craig's List 571
Creative Commons 449–50
crime
definition of 346
and punishment 602
Criminal Justice and Public Order Act 170
Crocker, Steve 178, 182
CSS 109, 433–4
Cuba 395
cryptography, *see* **enrcyption**
cyber-bullying 564
cyber-terrorism 244, 268–9
cyber-warfare 249, 250–253
cyberchondria 285
cybersex 148–9
cyborg 3, 315–18

D

da Vinci Surgical Systems 298–9
DAB, *see* **Radio, digital**
DARPA 182
data protection 222, 381
Act 1984 224
Act 1998 224, 231, 483
calling list 482–3
credit history 226
Directive (EUDPD) 223, 227
EU approach 223
principles 225, 333
safe harbour scheme 229
sensitive data 226
US approach 227
data retention 239–40
DDoS 169, 341–3, 356–7, 387, 396, 494

De Forest, Lee 8
DEC 8
DeCSS 109, 433–4, 451
deep linking 383–5
Defence Advanced Research Projects Agency, ***see*** **DARPA**
degree mill 538–9
Democratic Republic of Congo 580
denial of service attack, ***see*** **DoS**
DENIC 204
Deutsche Telecom 206
Diamond MP3 player 431
Dick, Philip 591
Dickens, Charles 421
digital divide 13, 18, 574–8, 581–2
  in e-learning 506, 534
  toy-town divide 64–6
digital evidence 357, 389, 393
Digital Millennium Copyright Act, ***see*** **copyright, Digital Millennium Copyright Act**
Digital Solidarity Fund 579
digitization 48
direct action 368
discrimination 328
Disney
  Universal and Disney v Sony copyright case 430, 432
distributed denial of service attack, ***see*** **DDoS**
DMCA, ***see*** **copyright, Digital Millennium Copyright Act**
DNA 274, 306–7
  databases 282
  paternity test 291
DNS 179, 182
  root server 183–4
  see also IP number assignment
domain name hijacking 192
domain name server, ***see*** **DNS**
Donoghue, John 317
DoS 335, 356–7, 387, 488
dot bomb, ***see*** **dot com bubble**
dot com boom, ***see*** **dot com bubble**
dot com bubble 8, 35, 41, 47–8, 58, 186, 417, 469, 546
dot com crash, ***see*** **dot com bubble**
doubleclick 460
Dracula 34
due diligence 325, 327, 336, 338–9, 355, 381
Duke University 315
Duracell 206
DVD 45, 54, 57, 58, 61, 452, 556, 562
  in car 552–3
  health information 286
  price in inflation 565
  sex 141
DVT 71, 304
Dyson, James 407, 415

E

e-booking (of health appointments) 278, 283
e-commerce 370
e-government 578

e-learning 563
electronic assessment 513–4, 516, 520, 521, 534
digital divide 506, 534
e-mail 217, 333, 457, 566
monitoring by employers 550–1
open relay 485
spam (see spam, e-mail)
e-prescribing 279–80
e-tailing 558
e-ticket 37, 554
Earthlink 46
Easter 372
easyAnything 202
easyArt 202
easyEverything 202
easyJet 202
easy Group 202
eBay 38–9, 107, 112, 124, 558
sale of meaning of life 559
sale of soul 559
virginity auction 558–9
education
cheating 535–7
overseas vs distance 540–1
plagiarism (see plagiarism)
EFF 155, 417, 434
Elcomsoft 425–7
Eldred v Ashcroft 406
Electronic Frontier Foundation, *see* EFF
electronic patient records 276–8
Electronic Privacy Information Center, *see* EPIC
electronic whiteboard, *see* whiteboard, electronic
elevating privileges 354, 371
Elizabeth I (English Queen) 406
Ellison, Harlan 128
encryption 10, 212, 333, 605
back door 3
Caesar cipher 213
cryptography 212, 238
password 379
End User License Agreement 438
Energizer 206
English literature 325
EPIC 155
EPSRC 233
eResolution 200–1
Ericksen, Sir John Eric 7
erotica 132. *See also* sex-sexual material, definition of
escrow 38
essay-writing services 536
ethics
computer 591–4
dilemma 386
environmental 595
information 595
metaphysical foundations of computer ethics 593
relativistic utilitarian 590
search 600
of security vulnerability disclosure 373
teaching of 583
unethical behaviour 339

ethics (*cont.*)
- universal utilitarian 590
- utilitarian 589–91
- *see also* ACM code

Ethiopia 580
EUCD, *see* **copyright, European Union Copyright Directive**
eugenics 275
EULA 438
European Union Copyright Directive, *see* **copyright, European Union Copyright Directive**
EverQuest 67, 81
exoskeleton 259
expert system
- in medicine 294

F

face transplant 314
FaceBook 570
Fanning, Shawn 432–3, 435
Fanning, John 432–3
Fantastic Voyage 310
fax
- advertising 465, 473, 474–5
- preference service 483

FBI 220, 234, 252, 369, 425–7
FCC 29
FCS 255
Federal Communications Commission 29
Federal Copyright Act 421
Federal Trade Commission, *see* **FTC**
Financial Services Authority 226
firmware 358
First Amendment (to the US Constitution), The, *see* **freedom of speech - The First Amendment**
FIST 255
flame war 115, 419–20, 466
flash mob 568–70
Flick, Catherine
Floridi, Luciano 593
Foucault, Michel 586
four modalities 6, 115–16
Fourth Amendment (to the US Constitution) 215
France 11, 122, 126, 257, 423, 549
frankenfoods 3. *See also* Genetic Engineering
free culture 449–50
freedom of speech 17, 97, 125, 234
- vs censorhip of sexual material 171
- and child pornography 161, 164
- and commercialisation of higher education 530
- and domain names 201
- The First Amendment (to the US Constitution) 108, 154, 337
- human right to 98
- and online stalking 502

Freenet 123–4
Friends Reunited 571
FSA 226
FTC 227–8, 229, 230, 417, 484

Fuji 42
Funny Thing Happened on the Way to the Forum, A (film) 364

G

Gadd, Paul, *see* Glitter, Gary
Gaia hypothesis 595
gambling 80–3, 93–4
games console, *see* video game
Gartner Group 561
Gates, Bill 8
GATS 541
GCHQ 337
Geist, Michael 200
General Agreement on Trade in Services 541
General Motors 191
General Public License 438–41
generic Top Level Domain, *see* TLD, gTLD
genetic
  engineering 2, 17, 309
  modification (see genetic engineering)
  samples 282
  selection 309
  testing 289
George Washington University 297
Germany 191, 234, 251, 423, 460, 549, 572
GIF 150, 363
GIS 305
Glitter, Gary 169
globalization 12, 573
  anti-globalization demonstrators 122
  see also digital divide
GNU
  GPL 438–41
good times virus hoax 362
Google 46, 101, 122–3, 183, 207, 284, 397–8, 535, 600
  Earth 253
  noblog 479–80
googlebombing 479–80
googlewashing 122
Gorbachev, Mikhail 110
Gotterbarn, Donald 594–5
Government Communications HQ 337
Grand Theft Auto 79
Grateful Dead 433, 436
Green Card Lottery 466
GreenNet Educational Trust 102
GPL 438–41
GPRS 552
GPS 253–4, 262
GTA 79
Guantanamo Bay 395
Guatemala 292
Gun, Katharine 337

H

H5N1 274, 306
hacker, *see* hacking

Hackers (film) 364
hacking 10, 347. *See also* cracking
hacktivism 369
harassment 457
 freedom of speech 502
 online stalking 458, 495–7
hard case 589–90
Hardin, Garrett 486–7
Harper Brothers 429
Hart, James V. 34
hate speech 122
Head, Eric 480
health
 information systems 275–82
 and safety 328, 328–32
Health Canada 284
Health Education Authority 284
Health Insurance Portability and Accountability Act 282
Heckenkamp, Jerome 107–8
hectograph 114
HelpMate 299
Henry VI (English King) 406
Hewlett Packard (HP) 146, 575–6
Hezbollah 253
HIPAA 282
Hitchhiker's Guide to the Galaxy, The 573
Hobbes, Thomas 585–6, 586
honor code 538
Host Europe (ISP) 118
hosts.txt 178
HP 146, 575–6
human rights 97, 100
 Universal Declaration of 98, 215, 585–6, 603
 European Convention on 98
 European Union Charter of Fundamental Rights 215, 586
 conflicts of rights 98
Hume, David 586
Huntley, Ian 221–2
Hussein, Saddam 263, 268
Hyundai 45

I

IAB 182
IAD, *see* **Internet addiction disorder**
IANA 182, 185
Ian, Janis 436, 451
IBM 31, 412
 PC 437
 restroom queueing patent 413–4
ICANN 184, 186–8, 193, 197–8, 200, 203, 204, 207–8
ID cards 267
identity theft 561
Identity Theft Penalty Enhancement Act 561
IETF 182–3, 185
IFPI 434, 435
illiteracy 18
IM 22, 457, 462, 486, 496, 565
India 14, 112, 254, 491, 576
Indonesia 13, 165
industrial age 2, 15, 593

Industrial Revolution 2, 18, 21, 100, 248, 407, 420, 454, 555, 593
information age 2, 15, 211, 243, 244, 248, 265, 267, 345, 458, 556, 562, 565, 575, 593, 594, 595
Information Commissioner 224, 226, 231, 550–1
Information Revolution 2, 14, 18, 21–2, 593
Initiative for Software Choice 438
instant messaging, ***see*** **IM**
intellectual property 402
Interception of Communications Act 219
International Telecommunications Union, ***see*** **ITU**
Internet
Activities Board (see IAB)
addiction disorder 5, 81, 147, 564
adoption 291
Assigned Numbers Authority (see IANA)
Corporation for Assigned Names and Numbers (see ICANN)
for dissemination of sexual material 133
end-to-end 11, 150, 158, 177
Engineering Task Force (see IETF)
in hospitals 280
Movie Database 144
'no one knows you're a dog' 159
open architecture 11
origins 178
protocol 176
relay chat (see IRC)
Society 182, 185–7
Watch Foundation 119, 129–30
IP, ***see*** **internet protocol**
IP number assignment 178, 182
iPod 65, 190, 564
Iraq 9, 250, 253, 257, 258, 263–5, 265, 268, 298, 337
IRC 354
iris scan 267, 381, 556
Islam 574, 599
ISO-3166 179
ISOC 182, 185–7
Israel 60, 161, 253, 269
Italy 122
ITU 179, 181–2, 205, 207, 491
iTunes 63, 190, 433
ITV Digital 29–31
IWF 119, 129–30

J

JANET 157, 179
Japan 15, 35, 41, 62, 81, 110, 161–2, 302, 308, 312, 365, 388, 570, 601
Japan Airlines 553
Jefferson, Thomas 405, 407
Johansen, Jon 434
Jordan, Ryan 'Essjay' 518
JPEG 138, 150
Judaism 599
Jun, Yan 107

jurisdiction 13
  and censorship 107, 111–2, 115, 126
  and computer crime 346, 388, 391, 394
  of copyright 408, 424, 428
  and gambling 94
  and media regulation 53, 153
  of patents 319, 404
  and professional responsibility 328, 333, 334, 342
  and sexual material 151, 153, 163, 164–5, 168–9, 170
  and spam 473, 490, 493, 501
  and taxation 57–8

K

Kalem company 429
Kant, Immanuel 583, 586–7, 588, 597
Katalov, Alexander 426–7
KaZaA 432, 433
Kazahkstan 292
Kennedy, John F. (US President) 28
killer app(lication) 26, 27, 32, 409–10, 464–5
Kitetoa.com 12, 368
knowledge economy 548
Kodak 42, 409
Ku Klux Klan 127
Kuwait 263
Kyberd, Peter 313

L

Lady Chatterly's Lover 134
Landslide Promotions 165–6
law
  natural 587–9
  positive 587–9
Learning Styles
  auditory 507, 510–11
  kinaesthetic 507, 511
  visual 507, 508–10
Lebanon 253
Leisure Suit Larry 142–3
LeMeneger, Stephen 369–70
Lessig, Lawrence 6, 115–6, 415, 419, 449–50, 451
Levi 91, 557
Levy, Steven 43, 212–3, 235, 364, 370
libertarianism 99
licensing of software, *see* software, licensing
Limerick, University of 117–8
Lindqvist, Bodil 227
Lineage (II) 81
line swtiched 177, 178, 219
Linux 45, 365, 375, 376
literacy 23–4, 56, 74, 87, 420, 540, 542, 576
Litman, Jessica 419, 451, 453–4
Liverpool, University of 70
Locke, John 585–6
London South Bank University 535
Longton, Carrie 572
Lovelock, James 595

Lufthansa 553
Luxton, Trevor 213–4

M

mainframe 32, 370, 437
Madonna 451
Mailing Preference Service 483
Malaysia 157, 206, 422
malware 376, 380
  authors 359–62
  causing DDoS 357
  creative programmers 359
  payload phase 354
  primary effects of 352–3, 358
  propagation phase 354
  secondary effects of 356, 359
  script kiddies 359
  tertiary effects of 353
  Trojan 251, 352, 353
  virus 352, 353, 376
  worm 251, 352, 361, 399
  zombie 341–2, 352, 353–6, 363
Mann, Steve 4, 18, 164
Maoism 405
Marquis de Sade 134
Marxism 405
Mary Tudor (English Queen) 420
massively multiplayer online role-playing game, ***see*** MMORPG
Mather, K 595
Matsushita Electronics 302
McDanel, Bret 335, 337
McDonalds 200
McDowell, Andrew 179
McKinnon, Gary 394–5
McPherson, Isaac 405
media literacy 542. *See also* computer literacy
Medical Research Council 86, 282
Metallica 436, 451
Metcalf, Bob 8
Metropolitan Police (UK) 119–20
MGM 43
Michael, George 451
Michigan, University of 498–9
Microsoft 8, 44, 160, 191, 362, 376, 437
  Academic Network 530
  Excel 375
  IIS 377
  Internet Explorer 362
  Outlook 375
  Outlook Express 362, 375
  Powerpoint 509
  Windows 251, 365, 375
  Windows 2000 EULA 438, 443–5
  Windows Media Player 447
  Word 375
MIDAS 306
middleware 547
Mikler, Armin 307
MIll, John Stuart 586
Miller, Keith 594
Mine Ban Treaty 257
minicomputer 32
MIT 364, 437, 530

Mitnick, Kevin 371
MMORPG 43, 44, 67–8, 81, 581
MMS
advertising 465
boarding card 555
sex 136
mobile phone 26, 49
advertising 464
on aircraft 553–4
blessed 565, 567–8
cameras 136
cloning 217
shaped coffin 567
disturbing sleep 27
flash mob 568–70
games 44, 68
interception of calls 217
picocell 553
price in inflation 565
tracking 567
as weapons 261
monoculture (software) 375–6
monopoly
on everyday necessities 406
Statute of Monopolies 407
on weaving wool 406
Monty Python 102, 114, 465–6, 559
Morpheus 432
Motion Picture Association of America 433–4, 436
Motion Picture Patent Company 436
movable type 420
MP3 54, 61, 431, 435, 568
MP3.com 431–2, 451, 452
MPAA 433–4, 436
MPPC 436
MRI 274, 276, 309
MSN 160–1
Muhammad
satirical cartoons of 13, 574
Multimedia Messaging Service 27. *See also* Text Message
mumsnet 572
MYCIN 294
MySpace 570

N

NAF 200–1
Nagle, Matthew 316–7
NAHT 550–1
nanotechnology 311
Napster 123, 428, 432–3, 435, 436, 452
NASA 254, 293
nastygram 116, 117
National High Tech Crime Unit 170
National Institute for Health and Clinical Excellence 284
National Library of Medicine 295
National Science Foundation, ***see*** NSF
nazi 11, 53, 126–7, 235, 423
Neilsen 477, 557
Network Associates 446–7
Network Solutions Inc., ***see*** NSI
New York Attorney General 229, 447
New York Times 7, 16, 565

New Zealand 262
Newmark, Craig 571
News Corporation 48
newspaper 110
NHS 274
Connecting for Health 279
Direct 274, 276, 280, 287
electronic patient records 277
national electronic booking system 279
NHSnet 281
Newborn Hearing Screening Project 277
Numbers for Babies Project 277, 282
NHTCU 170
Nike 91, 286, 557
Nintendo 70, 72, 88. *See also* Video Game, nintendonitis
Nixon, Richard (US President) 28
Nominet 198, 204
North Texas, University of 307
Norway 434
NSA 234, 240, 265–6
NSF 181, 185–6, 205, 233
NSFNet 181
NSI 185–6, 192, 196, 208
NTT 206

O

O'Grady, Michael 15
obesity 18, 69–71, 92–3, 286–7
Obscene Publications Act 120
Obscene Publications Unit (UK Police) 120
obscenity 132. *See also* sex-sexual material, definition of
OFCOM 29
Office of the Consumer Credit Commissioner (Texas) 226
Office of the Surveillance Commssioners 233
OHP 509, 530
Okwap 565
Olson, Ken 8
Omnibus Crime Control and Safe Streets Act 219, 391
On Digital 29–31
online
body trafficking 291–2
banking 350, 370
pharmacy 290
open proxy 383–4
open relay 485
Open Rights Group 434
Open Society Institute 102
Open Source Initiative 438
open source software
and patents 410
security of 374
Open University 511, 530–531, 531–3
Operation Ore 165–6
Oppong, Joseph 307
OPU 120
OrCheck 535
Orlowski, Andrew 122
Orwell, George 231

OSI 181
Outer Space Treaty 255
outsourcing 14, 574
Oxford, University of 593

P

P2P, *see* **Peer-to-Peer**
PacBell 206
packet switched 177, 219
paedophile 118
  Unit of the NHTCU 170
pager 26
Palm 45
Paramount 43
Parkinson's disease 275, 320
password 370–1, 379
  dictionary attack 371
Patanjali 584
patent 449
  1-click shopping 413, 414
  on backups 412
  on business methods 411–2
  on coloured glass 406
  criticisms of 414–17
  defensive 418
  definition of 403–4
  on genes 319–20
  letters patent 406–7
  licensing companies 417–19
  Motion Picture Patent Company 436
  on movie making 409, 429, 436
  MPPC 436
  Office 407, 413–4, 417
  period 407
  restroom queuing algorithm 413–14
  on software 10, 411–2, 437
  on sound recording 408
  on spreadsheet 409
  on telegraph 408
  on telephone 408
PATRIOT Act 234, 266, 392
Pax, Salaam 264
PayPal 94, 124
PDA 45, 279, 551
People's Republic of China 17, 103, 116, 150, 254, 257, 422, 541, 557, 568, 600
peer-to-peer 124, 143, 180–1, 432, 451
Pennington, Shevaun 172–3
Pentagon 178
Pepsi 600
personal responsibility 323, 324, 340
pharming 351
Philips 304
philosophy
  schools in Ancient Greece 507
phishing 349–51, 495
phreaker 347. *See also* telephone, phone phreaking
Photoshop 121
PICS 156, 157
Pilates 564
pillcam 311
PIN 381
pirate 409, 421, 422

plagiarism 506, 535
essay-writing services 536
honor code 538
and research 539
in university application forms 536
plastic surgery 286
Platform for Internet Content Selection 156, 157
Playboy 140, 149
player piano 429
Plexus Digital Solutions 121–2
Polaroid 42
pop-under 457–8, 470
pop-up 457–8, 469
Pope On 564
pornography 133
child (see child pornography)
harm to the viewer 166
harm to the model 166–7
Time (magazine) 3
see also sex
Postel, Jon 178–80, 182, 185, 191, 600
PRC, ***see*** **People's Republic of China**
Princeton University 369–70
printer cartridge 42
printing press 114, 133
privacy 25
of medical information 281–2
right to be let alone 98
Privacy International 101
professional 2, 151
behaviour 336
code 325
code of conduct 325
code of practice 325, 333–4
competence 333
definition of 323, 325
ethics, violation of 334
foul 323
judgement 327
membership 325
projector
in classrooms 514
computer 509–10, 517
overhead 509, 530
slide 508–9
Protection of Children Act 1978 170
prosthetics 311, 313
public disclosure legislation 112, 334–5
Public Interest Disclosure Act 334, 337
Psion 45
public disclosure, ***see*** **whistleblowing**

Q

QinetiQ 304

R

radio 59, 110, 153, 566
advertising 461
analogue 28
digital 28–9
in hospital 280
internet

radiotherapy 16
rationalism 584
Recording Industry Association of America, *see* **copyright, RiAA**
Register, The 121
Regulation of Investigatory Powers Act 219, 238
relativism 590–1
Request for Comments, *see* **RFC**
reverse domain name hijacking 192
RFC 178
  790 178
  791 178
  799 179
  814 179
  1083 182
RFID 304, 555, 556–8
RIAA, *see* **copyright, RIAA**
Rimm, Martin 134
RIP Act 219, 238
RIPE 182
Roberts, Justine 572
Robocart 299
robot
  and crime 598
  denial files 397
  in healthcare 274, 292, 298–301
  laboratory 301
  nurse 299–300, 302–3
  surgery 298–9, 310
Roe vs Wade 591
Rolls-Royce 206
RSI 563–4. *See also* video game, nintendonitis
Russia 165, 254, 257, 266, 364, 426–7

S

Saberhagen, Fred 34
Sadowski, Luke 160
safe harbor scheme 229
safety critical systems 16, 336–7, 545–6
SARS 274, 306, 307
Sasser virus 251
Saudi Arabia 102, 150
scams
  advance fee fraud 495
  lottery 468–9, 495
  get rich quick 561
  Nigerian '419' 468, 486, 490, 495
  online auction 347
  pharming (see pharming)
  phishing (see phishing)
  premium rate phone 495
  pump and dump 495–6
  wire fraud (see wire, fraud)
Scandinavia 293
Scandinavian Airlines 554
Schiavo, Terry 320
SEC 15
Second Life 570
second superpower 122
security 379
  by obscurity 377
  vulnerability disclosure 360, 373–4

September 11th Attacks 103, 234, 252, 262, 297
Security and Exchange Commission, *see* SEC
self-diagnosis kits 288
self-incrimination 340–1
self-interest 324
sex
accessing sexual material at work 145–6
breakdown of relationships 148
call girls 134
censoring of sexual material online 150
children accessing sexual material online 152
child pornography (see child pornography)
children receiving sex spam 140, 157, 495
sex.com 194–5
cybersex 148–9
driving technology development 134
DVD 141
email 139
FTP 139
health information 156
MMS 136
mobile phone cameras 136
Offenders Register 169, 222
online grooming of children by paedophiles 159, 499–500, 567
regulating online sex 149–50
sexual material, definition of 132–3
Sexual Offences Act 2003 168, 476
spam 139–40, 494
SMS 135, 136
techno-sex 134
teledildonics 148–9
telephone 134
television 135, 141
usenet 139
video games 142
web 140
Severe Acute Respiratory Syndrome, *see* SARS
Sexual Offences Act 2003 168
Shannon information 593
Shetland
News 385–6
Times 385–6
Ship-of-Fools 565
shrinkwrap software license 446, 594
Siegel, Martha 466
Simantha 296
Sincere Kourien 302
Singer, Peter 591
Sklyarov, Dmitry 425–7
Sky, *see* **British Sky Broadcasting**
Slashdot 398
slippery slope 589–90
smoking
and cancer 328
SMS, *see* **text message**
social engineering 371–3
Soden, Michael 146
software
engineering 16, 324

software (*cont.*)
monoculture 375–6
software licensing
BSD 438, 442–3
clickwrap 446, 594
for educational purposes 530
EULA 438
GPL 438–41
Microsoft 438, 443–5, 447
no reviews 446
shrinkwrap 446, 594
warranty disclaimer 446
SONAR 260
Sony 43, 44, 66, 91
Universal and Disney v Sony copyright case 431
Sophos 491
South Africa 561
South Korea 262
Southern California Tribal Digital Village 576
Southern California, University of 298
Soviet Union (USSR) 110, 114, 245
spam 132, 459
blocking 484, 492–3
in blogs 479–80
CAN-SPAM Act 489, 491
chain letter 467–8
children receiving sex spam 140, 157, 405
e-mail 466–9
filter 159, 475, 492–3
get rich quick 561
junk mail 471, 487
lottery (see scams, lottery)
meta-spam 487–9
in meta-tags 478
Nigerian '419' (see scam, Nigerian '419')
opt-in 501–2
opt-out 501–2
and organised crime 362
origin of term 465–6
as pollution 595
real-time black hole list 493
receiver economics 474
referral economics 477
sender economics 470
sex 139–40
on usenet 466
Special Educational Needs Disabilities Act 533
Spider-Man 34
Spitzer, Eliot 229, 230, 447
sport 562–3
Sputnik 1, 245
spyware 229
SRI 180, 182
ssh 365
Stallman, Richard 370, 437
Stanford Center for Internet and Society 335
Stanford Encyclopedia of Philosophy 584
Stationer's Guild 33
Statute of Anne 420, 450
steganography 212, 238
Stoker, Bram 34

Studabaker, Toby 172–3
sucks domains 194
sunrise period 199, 202
Swires, Claire 213–4
Symantec 158
Symbian 45

T

Tati 12
tax 326
  fraud 327
  jurisdiction 57–8
  return online 578–9
TCP, ***see*** **trusted computing platform, or**
  transfer control protocol
technophile 378
technological protection measure 42, 425
techno-utopians 123, 573
Telecommunications Data Protection Directive 219
teledildonics 148–9
telegraph 216
  patents 408
Telekom Malaysia 206
telemedicine 293–7
telephone 22, 24–7, 133, 177, 566
  caller line ID 475, 481–2, 497
  cell (see mobile telephone)
  interception of calls 216
  mobile (see mobile telephone)
  over Internet (see VoIP)
  patents 408
  phone phreaking 347
  preference service 483
  sales calls 463–4, 472–3, 487
  sex 135
television 61, 73, 153
  access to Internet 52
  access via Internet 22, 53
  access via mobile phone
  advertising 30, 34, 51, 59, 70, 461
  analogue cable 50
  analogue satellite 29, 50
  analogue terrestrial 50
  for Army/Navy recruitment 88–9
  competition between formats 577
  control via Internet 2
  control via mobile phone 2
  digital cable 50, 462
  digital satellite 29, 50, 462
  digital terrestrial 29, 50, 462
  disturbing sleep 71, 75
  in hospitals 280
  in medical treatment/research 87, 295, 315
  providing medical information 286, 287
  shopping 558
  subscription 30
  video-on-demand 22, 53, 553, 562
telework 548–50
terrorism 247
Terrorism, Crime and Security Act 234, 390–1

Tesco 557
text message 22, 26, 27, 552, 566
advertising 464, 473
about flight 555
bullying 564
Thefreeworld.net 108–9
Theiault, Carole 491
Thinkofthechildren(.co.uk) 117, 118–21, 128
Tiananmen Square 99, 107
TIFF 150
Time Warner 40
TLD 179–80, 189, 208
ccTLD 179, 188, 191, 197, 198, 202, 204, 207–9
gTLD 179, 187, 189, 191, 196, 197, 203, 208–9
Tokyo Rose 110
Tonga 188
Top Level Domain, *see* TLD
Toronto, University of 4
Townsend, Pete 169
TPM, *see* technological protection measure
trade mark 122, 193–196, 206, 402–3, 449
trade secret 403
tragedy of the commons 486–7
transfer control protocol 176
Trojan 251, 352, 353
defence in criminal trial 169
trust 38
trusting protocols 484
trusted computing platform 122
Tsukuba University 308
TUG 299
Turing, Alan 245, 246
Turnitin 535
Tuvalu 188
Twain, Mark 421, 436
Ty Inc. 192

U

UAV 259
UBE, *see* spam, e-mail
UCE, *see* spam, e-mail
UCL 179
UDRP, *see* uniform dispute resolution process
UHI MIllennium Institute 532–3
UKe-U 531, 541
Ultima Online 43, 63, 84, 90
unauthorized access
to data 388
with intent to commit or allow further offences 389
unauthorized modification of data 390
uniform dispute resolution process 196–7, 199, 204, 207
uniform resource locator, *see* URL
United Artists 43
United Nations 337, 579–80
Universal Declaration of Human Rights 98, 215, 585–6, 603
Universal 430

and Disney v Sony copyright case 430, 432
v MP3.com 431

University College London 179

Unix 376, 382, 437

unsolicited business e-mail, ***see*** **spam, e-mail**

unsolicited commercial e-mail, ***see*** **spam, e-mail**

URL 175, 203, 207, 349, 369, 478, 487

US-CERT 362–3, 373, 380

usability 379

USPTO 413, 414, 417

USSR, ***see*** **Soviet Union**

US Treasury 121

V

V-Chip 154

Vaidhyanathan, Siva 419, 422

VeriSign 176
SiteFinder 192–4

Victoria's Secret 228–9

video game 41, 44–5, 61–3
advertising in 462
causing death 72
epilepsy 72
female players 66
Game Boy (Advance) 68
gamecube 88
gender presentation 602
nintendonitis 72
older players (see silver gamers)
PlayStation (2, 3, Portable) 41, 66, 90
price in inflation 566
silver gamers 88
strip poker 143
to test driving impairment 90
violence 76–80
war 261
Wii 70
Xbox (360) 44–5

Vietnam 250, 297

Vinge, Vernor 542

Virgin 46, 553

Virginia, University of 538

virtual items 38, 91

virtual learning environment 505, 507, 533

virtual reality
in medicine 274, 296, 297

virus
biological 275
Chernobyl 358
CIH 358
computer 352, 353, 376
good times hoax 362–3
original description 361
Sasser 251

Visible Human Project 295

VisiCalc 409–10, 437

Vivendi Universal 48

VLE, ***see*** **virtual learning environment**

voice over Internet protocol, ***see*** **VoIP**

voicemail 25

VoIP 8, 177
Volkman, Richard 596

W

Wallace, General Lew 429
Wanadoo 206
war
  Afghanistan 234, 264
  Arab-Israeli (2000) 253
  Boer 249
  Cold 178, 235, 246, 265
  dialling 377
  driving 378
  First World 9, 245, 246, 250
  Iraq 9, 250, 253, 257, 258, 263–5, 265, 268, 298, 337
  games 261
  Gulf 250
  Napoleonic 249
  news reporting 249–50
  psychological 264–5
  Second World 109–10, 231, 245, 246, 250, 311
  US Civil 249
  Vietnam 250, 297
  walking 378
Warwick, Kevin 318
Watson, Thomas 31
Watt, James 407
Web, The 175, 292, 382, 484
  advertising 469–70
  architecture of 477
  deep linking 384–6
  meta-tags 478
  pop-under (see pop-under)
  pop-up (see pop-up)
  scrapers 397–9
  sex sites 140–1
WebFusion 118. *See also* Host Europe
WebMD 274
Wellcome Trust 282
West Wing, The (TV Show) 100
Western Union 7
whistleblowing 325, 334–5, 337, 343
whiteboard 508, 509
  electronic 510, 512, 521–2
Whitehouse, Mary 134
WHO 305
Wiener, Norbert 316, 591, 593
WiFi 46, 551
  on airplanes 553
  landmines 256–7
  municipal WiFi 46, 578
Wikipedia 59, 480
  accuracy 60, 518–19
WIPO 197, 200–1, 203–4, 207, 422
  Copyright Treaty 422, 424
wire
  fraud 347
  money transfer 25
  tapping 218
Witness Protection programme 387
woodcuts 114
WordPerfect 437
work
  need for ICT skills 547–8

telework 549–50
World Health Organisation 305
World Intellectual Property Organisation, *see* WIPO
World Trade Organisation 205, 541
World Wide Web, The, *see* **Web, The**
worm 251, 352, 361, 399
worst boyfriend in the world, the 213–4
WTO 205, 541

X

X.25 179
XML 386

Y

Yahoo! 53, 122, 126–7, 207, 450
Yale University 369–70
Yeltsin, Boris 110
yoga 564
Youens, Liam 502
YouTube 566

Z

zombie 341–2, 352, 353–6, 363